RECONSTRUCTING CHRISTIANITY IN CHINA

The American Society of Missiology Series, published in collaboration with Orbis Books, seeks to publish scholarly work of high merit and wide interest on numerous aspects of missiology—the study of Christian mission in its historical, social, and theological dimensions. Able proposals on new and creative approaches to the practice and understanding of mission will receive close attention from the ASM Series Committee.

American Society of Missiology Series, No. 41

RECONSTRUCTING CHRISTIANITY IN CHINA

K. H. Ting and the Chinese Church

Philip L. Wickeri

ORBIS BOOKS

Maryknoll, New York 10545

Founded in 1970, Orbis Books endeavors to publish works that enlighten the mind, nourish the spirit, and challenge the conscience. The publishing arm of the Maryknoll Fathers and Brothers, Orbis seeks to explore the global dimensions of the Christian faith and mission, to invite dialogue with diverse cultures and religious traditions, and to serve the cause of reconciliation and peace. The books published reflect the opinions of their authors and are not meant to represent the official position of the Maryknoll Society. To obtain more information about Maryknoll and Orbis Books, please visit our website at www.maryknoll.org.

Library of Congress Cataloging in Publication Data

Wickeri, Philip L.
    Reconstructing Christianity in China : K.H. Ting and the Chinese church / Philip L. Wickeri.
        p. cm. — (American society of missiology series ; No. 41)
    Includes bibliographical references and index.
    ISBN 978-1-57075-751-8
    1. China—Church history—20th century. 2. Ting, K. H. I. Title.
    BR1288.W527 2007
    275.1'082—dc22

                              2007013322

Contents

PART 1
FORMATION IN CHINA, THE CHURCH
AND THE WORLD, 1915-1951

Preface to the American Society of Missiology Series

The purpose of the American Society of Missiology Series is to publish—without regard for disciplinary, national, or denominational boundaries—scholarly works of high quality and wide interest on missiological themes from the entire spectrum of scholarly pursuits relevant to Christian mission, which is always the focus of books in the Series.

By *mission* is meant the effort to effect passage over the boundary between faith in Jesus Christ and its absence. In this understanding of mission, the basic functions of Christian proclamation, dialogue, witness, service, worship, liberation, and nurture are of special concern. And in that context questions arise, including, How does the transition from one cultural context to another influence the shape and interaction between these dynamic functions, especially in regard to the cultural and religious plurality that comprises the global context of Christian life and mission.

The promotion of scholarly dialogue among missiologists, and among missiologists and scholars in other fields of inquiry, may involve the publication of views that some missiologists cannot accept, and with which members of the Editorial Committee themselves do not agree. Manuscripts published in the Series, accordingly, reflect the opinions of their authors and are not understood to represent the position of the American Society of Missiology or of the Editorial Committee. Selection is guided by such criteria as intrinsic worth, readability, coherence, and accessibility to a range of interested persons and not merely to experts or specialists.

The ASM Series, in collaboration with Orbis Books, seeks to publish scholarly works of high merit and wide interest on numerous aspects of missiology—the scholarly study of mission. Able presentations on new and creative approaches to the practice and understanding of mission will receive close attention.

The ASM Series Committee
Jonathan J. Bonk
Angelyn Dries, O.S.F.
Scott W. Sunquist

Acknowledgments

This book has been more than a decade in the making, and in course of that time, I have presumed upon a great many people and institutions for their help and support.

First and foremost, I would like to express my deep appreciation to Bishop K. H. Ting, from whom I have learned so very much. During our years of working together, and in the course of writing of this book, he has consistently urged me to "seek truth from facts" in my judgments and opinions. Without his cooperation the volume now in your hands would not have been possible.

I also want to thank his wife, the late Siu-may Kuo, as well as his son, Ting Yenren, and his wife, Shi Wen, for the many hours of conversation and hospitality I have enjoyed in their home. Other than one interview with Siu-may (in 1991), we never discussed the contents of this book. Nevertheless, conversations with family members have helped to shape and inform my perspective. The writing of a biographical study is always intrusive, and I realize that the final product can never be wholly acceptable to the subject, or to the family members who know him best. Despite the risk of misinterpretation, I persisted in my writing in the hope that this book would contribute to a better understanding of the church in China and the life of the man who presided over its growth and development in the last quarter of the twentieth century.

I also want to acknowledge all of those who granted interviews to me, formal and informal, during the course of my work on this book. Sometimes just a phrase or a snatch of a conversation helped to illuminate a particular incident or interpretation. Colleagues at the Amity Foundation, in Nanjing and Hong Kong, helped to facilitate my work on this study, particularly in its early stages. I am also grateful to the many friends in China, only some of whose names appear below, who helped me locate difficult-to-find resources.

I worked on this book during two semester-long sabbaticals granted to me by the faculty and trustees of San Francisco Theological Seminary, and I am most thankful for their support and encouragement. The Henry Luce III Foundation and the Association of Theological Schools awarded me a fellowship in theology, which allowed me to extend my last sabbatical and spend an entire year (2005) doing writing and research. I am most grateful for their support, and for the fellowship and intellectual stimulation at the yearly meetings of the Luce Fellows.

Part of this book was written while I was still a mission co-worker attached to the Worldwide Ministries Division of the Presbyterian Church (U.S.A.), and I am grateful for the support of friends and colleagues there, particularly Dr. Insik Kim. Dr. Kyung-seo Park, formerly Asia secretary of the World Council of Churches, provided housing and generous support for my visit to the Archives of the WCC and the World Students' Christian Federation in Geneva. Bob and Alice Evans of the Plowshares Institute gave me a travel grant that enabled me to visit Toronto in order to visit archives and meet with Canadian friends of K. H. Ting and Siu-may Kuo.

I am grateful to Ruth Wilson of the Canadian SCM Archives at the University of Toronto; Terri Thompson of the General Synod Archives of the Anglican Church of Canada; librarians and archivists at the China Christian Council and Chinese Christian Three-Self Patriotic Movement Committee in Shanghai, the World Council of Churches in Geneva, Union Theological Seminary in New York, the Anglican Province of Hong Kong and Macao, and the Archives of the Episcopal Church in Austin. I am also grateful to the many librarians who facilitated my work and repeated requests for assistance at the Graduate Theological Union, in San Anselmo and Berkeley, the University of California at Berkeley, the University of San Francisco's Ricci Institute, Nanjing Union Theological Seminary, and the Universities Service Centre of the Chinese University of Hong Kong.

Many people have read parts of this manuscript or have discussed with me some of the ideas and interpretations presented here. Among these, I would particularly like to thank Judith Berling, John and the late Mary-Jeanne Coleman, Theresa and the late Feliciano Carino, Rick Fabian, Kim Yong-bock, Kim Jonggu, Li Pingye, Ma Jia, Cynthia McLean, Sarah Miles, Claudia and Gotthard Oblau, Milan Opočenský, Philip Potter, Marina True, Wang Meixiu,Wang Weifan, Lynn T. White III, Ray and Rhea Whitehead, Elisabeth Wickeri, Wu Xiaoxin, Edward Xu Yihua, and Zhuo Xinping. I also want to thank my colleagues at San Francisco Seminary: Jana Childers, Greg Love, Lewis Mudge, James Noel, and Christopher Ocker, who graciously responded to my persistent questions and requests for comment; and my doctoral students at the Graduate Theological Union, many of whom have written on aspects of K. H. Ting's theology. I have also discussed aspects of my interpretation with a number of other scholars and friends in China, and I am grateful for their advice and encouragement.

For granting permission to use the photographs that appear in this book, I wish to thank the Canadian SCM Archives, Toronto; the Episcopal Church Archives, Austin; the library of the World Council of Churches, Geneva; Martha L. Smalley and the Yale Divinity School Library, New Haven; Keren and Kezia née Johnson, the daughters of Hewlett Johnson;

Sue Crabtree and Sandra Power, of the University of Kent Archives; Gail V. Coulson; and Jack Edelman.

I was fortunate to have Hyung Shin Park and Trisha Williams of the Graduate Theological Union as research assistants, who helped with everything from indexing names and terms to tracking down hard-to-find sources. I am also grateful to Shelley Calkins for her good-natured assistance and able secretarial support.

Wong Siu-ling helped me with the translation of Zhao Puchu's poetry, and he has shared with me his vast knowledge of all things Chinese over the course of three decades. I am also grateful that his calligraphy graces the cover of this book. Ryan Dunch read through the entire manuscript and offered many important comments and corrections, as did two anonymous readers solicited by Orbis Books.

I am deeply indebted to Catherine Costello and the editorial department at Orbis Books for careful and patient work in the preparation of this volume. Bill Burrows, my editor at Orbis, has been enthusiastic in his support, generous in his encouragement, and judicious in his comments and suggestions. His keen wit and good humor have helped to sustain me.

St. Gregory of Nyssa Episcopal Church in San Francisco has been my spiritual home since Janice and I moved to the Bay Area in 1998. At St. Gregory's, we pray for K. H. Ting (and the bishops of China in Hong Kong and Taiwan) every week. I want to thank all the members of St. Gregory's for their support and nurture in the course of my writing and speaking about this book.

Lastly, I wish to express my deep gratitude to Janice K. Wickeri, without whose continuing support and expertise this book would never have been completed. Janice has read through the entire manuscript, many sections more than once, and she has suggested many important clarifications and additions. She has also been a persistent critic, my translator of choice and my closest colleague.

Despite all the support, assistance and advice I have been given, the interpretation presented here is mine alone, and I am responsible for whatever mistaken interpretations and errors that remain.

Abbreviations

ANS	*Amity News Service*
BCC	British Council of Churches
CASS	Chinese Academy of Social Sciences
CB	*The China Bulletin*
CCA	Christian Conference of Asia
CCC	The China Christian Council
CLS	Christian Literature Society
CPC	Communist Party of China
CPPCC	Chinese People's Political Consultative Conference
CSCA	Chinese Christian Students' Association
CSPD	*China Study Project Documentation* (also known as *The China Study Journal* and the *China Study Documentation*)
CTR	*Chinese Theological Review*
ECSLG	Ecumenical China Study Liaison Group
FCC	Friends of the Church in China
GMD	Guomindang
HKCC	Hong Kong Christian Council
IMC	International Missionary Council
IRM	*International Review of Mission*
IRS	Institute for Religious Studies
IWR	Institute of World Religions
JL	*Jinling shenxuezhi* (also known as *Nanjing Theological Review*)
NCC	National Christian Conference (in China); National Council of Churches
NCCCUSA	National Council of Churches of Christ in the U.S.A.
NCNA	New China News Agency
NPC	National People's Congress
NUTS	Nanjing Union Theological Seminary
PLA	People's Liberation Army
PSB	Public Security Bureau
RAB	Religious Affairs Bureau of the State Council (later known as SARA)
SARA	State Administration of Religious Affairs (formerly known as RAB)

SCM	Student Christian Movement
SCMP	*South China Morning Post*
TSPM	The Chinese Christian Three-Self Patriotic Movement of the Protestant Churches of China
TSPM/CCC	The Chinese Christian Three-Self Movement of the Protestant Churches of China and the China Christian Council, the two national organizations of Protestant Christians in China (in Chinese, the *lianghui*)
UBS	United Bible Societies
UFWD	United Front Work Department
WCC	World Council of Churches
WCRP	World Conference on Religion and Peace
Wenji	*Ding Guangxun wenji (Collected Works of K. H. Ting)*
WSCF	World Students' Christian Federation

A NOTE ON THE ROMANIZATION
OF CHINESE NAMES AND PLACES

In this book, Chinese names and places are spelled using *pinyin* Romanization, the official system in the People's Republic of China, based on the pronunciation of standard Mandarin Chinese. The exceptions are the names of individuals who prefer a different spelling, or short citations from books and essays that use the older Wade-Giles system. In the case of proper names, the *pinyin* spelling will be indicated in parentheses. For example Y. T. Wu (Wu Yaozong), Siu-may Kuo (Guo Xiumei) and K. H. Ting (Ding Guangxun).

Chinese names that appear in *pinyin* are given with the surname first, as is customary in China. For example, the surname of Zhou Enlai, the former premier of China, is Zhou, and his given name is Enlai.

Pinyin Romanization also appears in parentheses for the translation of important terms, a listing of which appears in the glossary on page 447. For example, "unfinished products" (*ban chengpin*) and "running the church well" (*ban hao jiaohui*) are two terms that appear frequently in K. H. Ting's writings, and so their Chinese equivalent is listed. The terms for governance (*zheng*), religion or ethics (*dao*) and scholarship (*xue*) are used as categories for the analysis of leadership in part 3.

RUSSIA

MONGOLIA

Heilongjiang

Harbin

Changchun

Jilin

Shenyang

Inner Mongolia

Liaoning

NORTH
KOREA

SOUTH
KOREA

Hohhot

Beijing
Beijing

Tianjin
Tianjin

Hebei

Taiyuan

Shijiazhuang

Jinan

Qingdao

Yinchuan

Ningxia

Shanxi

Shandong

Xining

Lanzhou

Lianyungang

Gansu

Zhengzhou

Jiangsu

Xi'an

Henan

Shanghai

Shaanxi

Hefei

Nanjing

Shanghai

Anhui

Hangzhou

Ningbo

Hubei

Wuhan

Zhejiang

Chengdu

Chongqing

Nanchang

Wenzhou

Sichuan

Chongqing

Changsha

Jiangxi

Hunan

Fuzhou

Guizhou

Fujian

Taipei

Guiyang

Xiamen

Taiwan

Kunming

Guangdong

Yunnan

Guangxi

Guangzhou

Nanning

Hong Kong
Macau

VIETNAM

LAOS

Haikou

Hainan

PHILIPPINES

List of Photographs

A Portrait of K. H. Ting

He seems to be musing, his hair now flecked silver-gray.
I recall it silky black from my student days.
He shoulders heavy burdens, unflinching
Yet his is still a loving mother's smile.
His eyes, bright with perception,
search for signs of spring.[1]

K. H. Ting was the most important Chinese Christian leader of the twentieth century. Now in his tenth decade, he has the bearing and manner of an elder statesman and church patriarch. His charisma is more an expression of who he is than of what he represents. He speaks deliberately and to the point, choosing words carefully. He moves slowly and is beset by many of the problems of old age, but his mind is still active, and he enjoys meeting friends and colleagues.

He is a large-boned man of better than average height, with a high forehead and searching eyes. His thick gray hair is combed straight back. Both at home and on formal occasions, he dresses conservatively in well-tailored clothes. He wears eyeglasses for reading, and he has a hearing aid. He now needs help getting about.

As a young man, he was imposing and handsome, with a cosmopolitan air that matured with age. He maintained a commanding presence, yet his gestures could be described as almost feminine. At home, he was used to meeting visitors in an unforgiving series of sofas in his living room, sitting back against the cushions in a corner or on the matching chair, often with one leg crossed over the other, his chin supported on his hand, attentive to all around him. He would sometimes pause to consider carefully what had been said, making sure that he heard correctly. He did not reveal feelings or emotions easily. His demeanor was striking because it was very different from his physical presence. There was a reserve about him that was not cold, but diffident and at times hesitant. Careful in his responses, he kept his own counsel. His reserve was underscored by a softness in his speaking voice. The warmth of his personality invited others in,

---

1. A poem written in 1987 in Chinese by former Nanjing Seminary professor Wang Weifan. The translation is by Janice Wickeri and Philip Wickeri.

but only so far. He had a generous smile that could be playful when he was at ease.

His late wife, Siu-may, was as outgoing as he was introverted; they worked as a team and were deeply devoted to each other. His eldest son and daughter-in-law live with him in the simply furnished home on Mo Chou Road where they have been for most of the last fifty years. The family always had a steady stream of visitors and guests, and they were thoughtful and gracious hosts. K. H. was impeccably well mannered. His courtesy, a much neglected Christian virtue, was related to upbringing, his Anglican sensibility and his diplomatic role. He carried himself with dignity.

Meticulous in his writing, he was particular about wording and translation as a working leader. He carried what used to be called a commonplace book to record his thoughts and to note ideas from his reading. He read widely and carefully in English and Chinese, and remembered what he read. His scrupulous attention to detail could be seen in his personal habits and interests: he enjoyed pens and stationery products, household gadgets of all kinds; he did crossword puzzles, played solitaire and liked mathematical games. He used to smoke cigarettes, and he drank in moderation. He enjoyed good food, and had a particular fondness for sweets served with coffee.

In his use of power, he was steely and resolved. There were occasional flashes of irritation that could irrupt into unbridled anger. He expected his close associates to share his approach and express their support publicly. He had deep feelings for friends, and he took them into his confidence. But he was also capable of cutting off those who were once close if he believed that they had chosen the wrong path. Some people imagined him to be an imposing, kindly, and deeply religious person, others an impersonal, unapproachable, and rigid political presence. He was all of these.

K. H. Ting is a man with an abiding belief in justice and social ethics who lived by time-tested principles informed by Christian faith and socialist commitment. He shunned religious and political enthusiasm of any kind. He has been a controversial figure, criticized for his support of Chinese Communists and praised for his leadership and faithful Christian witness. He sought to understand the tide of history in order to influence its direction. Drawing generously on the views and opinions of others, he could sometimes be persuaded to change course. But the final imprint in his actions was his alone. He was always aware of his limitations in the shaping of events, and so his approach was necessarily pragmatic. Politically, he was willing to settle for what was good enough for the times, but he believed that more would be possible in the future: people change history.

He was a poor administrator, and in this sense he resembled the scholar-officials of old. He had the orientation of an intellectual, not a cadre. He was a generalist, not a specialist; a humanist, not a technocrat. He was benevolent, but not necessarily democratic. Careful in considering all sides of every issue, he could also make important decisions with alarming dispatch. He was always attentive to the cultivation of personal relationships, with those above and those below. In China, leaders have served as shields and protectors for those around them. "As long as there is a green mountain, we won't lack for firewood." K. H. Ting has been a strong mountain for the Chinese church, and although bishops have not usually been seen as sources of firewood, this could be a fitting description of a shepherd who provided for his flock.

His role in the Chinese church cannot be duplicated. He was a churchman from an age that no longer exists, a bishop in a transformed Anglican mold, in some ways more like a Chinese William Temple or a V. S. Azariah, than like his predecessor, Y. T. Wu. In retirement, K. H. Ting became an institution, unshakable in his loyalty to church and country. He casts a long shadow.

Introduction

In 1998, K. H. Ting persuaded the Protestant leadership in China to approve a resolution on strengthening "theological reconstruction" in the Chinese church. He argued that greater attention needed to be given to theology in order to facilitate the adaptation of Christianity to socialist society. Theological reconstruction provoked a wide-ranging debate on the future of Christianity in China, which continues to this day. In seminaries and provincial church gatherings, in universities and social science academies, in international conferences and in private conversations, questions about the importance of theology for the church and its mission, and whether or not there was a need for the reconstruction of theological thought, were analyzed and debated. Some evangelical critics charged that Ting wanted to force his own liberalism on Chinese Christians, changing historic Protestant beliefs so that the church would accommodate itself to the government. Supporters countered that the churches were dominated by an outdated fundamentalism inherited from Western missionaries, expressed in theologies that prevented the churches from keeping up with the times. The debate continues, and its outcome will help shape the legacy of Bishop K. H. Ting (Ding Guangxun), the patriarch of the Chinese church and the most influential Protestant leader in China of the last half century.

Born in 1915, K. H. Ting has lived through the history of modern China. The church has been the center of his life and work and political involvement. Over the last century, Christianity has been constructed, deconstructed and reconstructed in times of civil turmoil, war and revolutionary change. Protestant missionaries from Europe and North America came to China in the early nineteenth century, and over the next 150 years, they built churches, hospitals and educational institutions all over the country. After the establishment of the People's Republic in 1949, the missionaries came under attack for being agents of imperialism; and within a few years, they were all gone. The churches and institutions they had established entered a period of decline. Chinese Christians were criticized for being "semiforeign." In the early 1950s, church leaders associated with the Chinese Christian Three-Self Patriotic Movement (TSPM) sought to reconstruct a *Chinese* Christianity free from foreign control, but their efforts were overtaken by the political movements of the times. Churches all but ceased to exist during the Cultural Revolution era (1966-1976), and many observers concluded that Christianity in China would eventually disappear.

1

In the late 1970s, however, religious life slowly reemerged, and churches began to be reopened. Since then, there has been a resurgence of religious life in China. To almost everyone's surprise, it was discovered that many Christians had been meeting in informal home-worship gatherings, even during the most difficult years of the Cultural Revolution. Over the last three decades, Chinese Christianity has enjoyed an unprecedented period of growth and development, so much so that the Chinese church is now among the fastest growing religious communities in the world. But it is a fragile community, beset by problems on all sides: continuing pressures from local government officials; an inadequate number of trained leaders; underdeveloped and insecure institutions; problems with sectarianism and heterodoxy, particularly in rural areas. K. H. Ting presided over the church in China during two decades of growth and development as he attempted to address the problems the church faced from within and without.

This study of the life and times of K. H. Ting is an attempt to tell the story of his role in the renewal and reconstruction of the church in China, and assess his importance for the future of the Christian community. He was without a doubt China's most important church leader and Christian thinker in the last decades of the twentieth century. But already in the late 1940s, he was a significant Chinese voice in world Christianity as well. Ting has been compared to Protestant leaders who supported accommodation with the governments of Eastern Europe during the Cold War era, but he may be better understood as a Chinese religious leader who has tried to create space for a Christian minority as he worked for the development of China.

Raised in a middle-class family in cosmopolitan Shanghai, K. H. Ting grew up in the Anglican church and studied for the priesthood. Part 1 of this book is concerned with Ting's early life and youth, his religious and intellectual formation, and his response to the constructions of Christianity he inherited. His experience as a YMCA student worker and priest in a city under Japanese occupation (1937-1945) convinced him of the need to be involved in the struggle for national salvation and freedom from foreign domination. But he was also committed to the ecumenical movement, and after the war he went with his wife, Siu-may, to Canada, where he had been appointed mission secretary for the Student Christian Movement. He later moved to New York, for study at Union Theological Seminary and Columbia University, and from there to Geneva, where he worked for the World Students' Christian Federation (WSCF). In this capacity, he traveled widely and came to know many men and women who were involved in the formation of the World Council of Churches.

In 1951, against the advice of many friends and colleagues in Geneva, the Tings returned to China with their young son. They were committed to work for change in the People's Republic of China, and K. H. became associated with the newly established TSPM. This study will argue that there were different views on theology and the church in the leadership of the TSPM despite their unity in support for the new government. The movement came into being at the time of the Korean War, when foreign missionaries were being criticized and expelled and Chinese churches were severing connections with Christians overseas; and this period has had a formative influence on TSPM leaders. Ting served for a brief time as general secretary of the Christian Literature Society before moving to Nanjing, where he became principal of the newly established Nanjing Union Theological Seminary. In the late 1950s and early 1960s, he was active in the TSPM, and became a well-known interpreter of the Chinese Revolution in the West. His writings from this time continued to reflect his abiding conviction that Christians could work together with socialists for the reconstruction of China. With the intensification of radical movements in the late 1950s, Ting was increasingly drawn to the "ultra-leftist" political line. Even so, he was removed from all his church and political posts at the start of the Cultural Revolution. He came back into public view in the early 1970s. The period from his return to China to the end of the Cultural Revolution (1966-1976) was a time of deconstructing Christianity in China, and this is the subject of part 2 of this book.

In the late 1970s, K. H. Ting became China's preeminent Protestant Christian leader, heading both the newly organized China Christian Council (CCC) and the reestablished TSPM. He also rose in the ranks of national government bodies. Ting worked for the reopening of churches, seminaries and other religious institutions, the printing of the Bible and religious literature, and increasing contacts with churches in other parts of the world. As the church's best-known Protestant theologian, his intellectual focus has been love as God's primary attribute and the importance for Christians to practice love in their ethical witness in society. By the time of his retirement in 1996, Ting had become the most significant voice in China for the interests of the church, making use of his important government positions and personal prestige to enhance religious freedom and give attention to reforming church structures. His interest in "theological reconstruction" will be interpreted as the culmination of a life-long effort to promote reconstruction and renewal in Chinese Christianity. The period that begins with K. H. Ting's assumption of the leadership of the TSPM/CCC is developed in the four chapters of part 3, and represents about half of the book.

K. H. Ting's life and thought has been an ongoing dialogue with the church and the politics of modern and contemporary China. Even in retirement, Ting has continued to be a prominent political figure in China and an internationally respected ecumenical leader. He led the Chinese church for two decades, during a crucial time in its rebuilding. Ting has also been a controversial figure at home and abroad, criticized by some for his support of Chinese Communists and praised by others for his leadership of the church and his courageous Christian witness. This biographical study seeks to put such evaluations in historical context, as we explore Ting's place in the history of Christianity in China, from his early years in Shanghai to the present.

More broadly, this study will consider the significance of the recent history of Christianity in China for the worldwide mission of the church. Ting has been a critic of the missionary movement from the West, but in his years at the WSCF, he helped to articulate a new approach to mission (see chap. 3). He did not participate in the antimissionary "Denunciation Movement" in the early 1950s (chap. 4), and decades later he apologized for its excesses to American missionaries (chap. 9). In his role as a church leader, Ting's approach to mission has been contextual, from his advocacy of Three-Self, to his leading role in the formation of the Amity Foundation, to his encouragement of greater social involvement for the churches, to his desire to make Christianity Chinese. This has implications far beyond China and provides an approach to understanding the tension between context and globalization in world Christianity.

I first met K. H. Ting in the late summer of 1979, when I served as an interpreter for the Chinese interreligious delegation at the Third World Conference on Religion and Peace (WCRP). The Chinese came to the meeting at Princeton Theological Seminary, where I was then a doctoral student. This was the first religious delegation from China to visit the United States in a great many years, and the first Chinese interreligious group ever.[1] The visit exemplified China's new policy of openness to the world, and, for many observers, this became their first exposure to religious life in the People's Republic of China.

On the basis of my experience with the delegation, K. H., as he insisted that we call him, invited my wife Janice and me to teach in the Department of Foreign Languages and Literatures at Nanjing University, where he had recently been named vice-president. We went to Nanjing in the summer of 1981 with our three-year-old daughter, Elisabeth. During our two years in the city, I met with K. H. Ting on an almost weekly basis. He wanted to speak about international developments in theology, the church and the ecumenical movement over the past twenty years, and I was interested in everything that was happening in China. I learned a great deal about the re-emergence of church life in China through these visits and in conversations with many other people. I also read a great deal about Christianity in China at the library of Nanjing Union Theological Seminary. The research I did in those years became my doctoral dissertation, which was published as *Seeking the Common Ground: Protestant Christianity, the Three-Self Movement and China's United Front* (Maryknoll, N.Y.: Orbis Books, 1988).

In 1984, we returned to Hong Kong, where we had worked before moving to Nanjing, and the next year I was asked to serve as the overseas coordinator of the Amity Foundation in Nanjing, which was founded by K. H. Ting and other Christian leaders as a social service and development organization. I was seconded to this position by the Presbyterian Church (U.S.A.), where I was a mission co-worker. Over the next twelve years, I traveled extensively in China and spoke regularly with Ting when I was in Nanjing. In addition to my responsibilities with Amity, I became an informal consultant on international ecumenical relationships with the church in China.

In 1991, K. H. Ting officiated at my ordination to the Christian ministry at St. Paul's Church in Nanjing. Five Chinese pastors were ordained at the same time. I continued to work for Amity until 1998, when we moved to San Anselmo and I began teaching at San Francisco Theological Seminary and the Graduate Theological Union. I have regularly traveled to China since then, and my relationship with Amity and the Christian community in China has continued to inform my perspective on mission. My life and work in China has helped to shape this book, especially the material in part 3.

Over the last twenty years, China has become more open to scholars, and access to documentary materials has increased. A great deal of new research has also drawn on unconventional material, including oral histories, unpublished popular literature and case studies of rural villages. Official archives for the period after 1949 are not generally open to foreign researchers, and public figures are often hesitant to speak for the record on their interpretation of events during that time. Despite these restrictions, an enormous amount of new material on the recent history of China has been published, as Chinese scholars have led the way in providing new interpretations of controversial subjects.

A wide variety of published biographies and biographical studies of prominent individuals have added to our understanding of modern and contemporary China. Perhaps the most widely discussed in recent years has been *Mao: The Unknown Story,* by Jung Chang and Jon Halliday.[2] They present a comprehensive indictment of Mao Zedong and draw on interviews with household members and personal acquaintances, hitherto unused Soviet archives, and a great number of unofficial sources. The book documents Mao's struggle for power and brutal totalitarian rule, arguing that he was responsible for the deaths of well over seventy million people in peacetime. However, the authors' use and misuse of evidence and sources has been criticized by many scholars.[3] In casting Mao in such a thoroughly negative light and interpreting his every action as motivated by the worst of intentions, Chang and Halliday exaggerate his faults unnecessarily and in the process undermine the case they are trying to make.

At the other end of the spectrum is Robert Kuhn's *The Man Who Changed China: The Life and Legacy of Jiang Zemin.*[4] This is a court biography with fulsome praise for China's former president, a book that reveals a great deal about how Jiang Zemin wants himself to be remembered, written by an American investment banker who was granted unusual access. The book portrays Jiang as a moderate pragmatist who stood above the fray, a patriot who led China to a position of world leadership, consistently motivated by patriotic altruism. Although the interpretation does not always match the reality, the book is a useful contribution to contemporary China studies insofar as it has much hitherto-unknown information on Jiang Zemin and documents the way in which the Chinese Communist Party wants to portray itself to the world. Kuhn's biography has helped to humanize Jiang Zemin in a way that other recent studies have not.

There have also been a number of exposé-style biographies on Chinese political figures published in Hong Kong and Taiwan over the last twenty years. Some of these are fanciful interpretations that play to a popular Chinese readership, but others are serious studies based on access to records and documentary materials unavailable in the West. Among these, Gao Wenqian's *Wannian Zhou Enlai* (*The Latter Years of Zhou Enlai*) stands out as an important work on China's late premier which depicts Zhou as a tragic figure whose noble legacy was sullied by his unwavering loyalty to Mao Zedong.[5] Because of K. H. Ting's own admiration of Zhou Enlai, this book provides a perspective that has helped to clarify their relationship. However, most Chinese intellectuals of Ting's generation would not accept Gao Wenqian's conclusions.

An increasing number of academic studies of prominent historical personages have also been published in English. Among these, Vera Schwarcz's *The Time for Telling Truth Is Running Out: Conversations with Zhang Shenfu* stands out as an elegantly written reconstruction of the life of a founding member of the Chinese Communist Party who was largely forgotten after 1949.[6] Schwarcz became interested in Zhang when they met almost by accident, and her book combines public history, personal remembrance and detailed observation and analysis. Her methodological approach is both creative and controversial, but it certainly helps to illuminate Zhang Shenfu's place in the history of which he was a part. It is a model of how a biographer who knows her subject can write a critical, engaging and sympathetic study.

This biographical study of K. H. Ting draws on perspectives introduced by all of the books mentioned above. The difference is that my focus is on a religious leader and Christian theologian whose story is of interest beyond whatever light it may shed on the church in modern and contemporary China. Ting was more oriented to the church and more comprehensive in his approach to theological issues of church and society than Y. T. Wu (Wu Yaozong, 1893-1979), his predecessor as head of the TSPM.[7] Yet, he did not have the breadth of theological or cultural interests of T. C. Chao (Zhao Zichen, 1888-1979), arguably China's most important modern theologian.[8] K. H. Ting presided over the church in a period of remarkable openness in China, and, I will argue, he was among a very few religious leaders who helped to shape government religious policy. Among his contemporaries, Protestant as well as Catholic, no one else has been as concerned with the development of a Chinese contextual theology. His life and thought is of interest to supporters and critics alike, especially those interested in the mission of the church in the world and the future of Christianity in China.

A great deal has been written about K. H. Ting's life in the last thirty years. Ma Jia, who now teaches in Canada, has written a biography of Ting in Chinese entitled *Ai shi zhenli (Discerning Truth through Love)*. It is based on nine interviews conducted with Ting in Nanjing between 2000 and 2005 and makes use of many of Ting's more recent writings.[9] In addition, Ting has given hundreds of interviews to religious and secular journalists, and a Google search in Chinese or English will turn up hundreds of pages of relevant hits. These range from the popular to the polemical, and they contain both misinformation and relevant opinion. Most of the interviews and articles about him go over the same material, and journalists keep asking familiar questions about his life and his views on the religious situation in China. Even in his early nineties, Ting could be incisive and quick witted in response to journalists' questions, and he impressed his admirers and detractors alike.[10] Like any public figure, Ting was sometimes evasive in interviews, but he also ventured forthright opinions and occasionally revealed fresh information and important insights.

Despite the extensive journalistic coverage since the late 1970s, there have been no scholarly treatments of K. H. Ting that have attempted to consider his life as a whole. A vast amount of documentary material is available on K. H. Ting's life over the last thirty years, but comparatively little for other periods, and nothing at all from the early years of the Cultural Revolution. There is substantial archival material on his life and work overseas between 1945 and 1951, but relatively little on the period after that. This study is a preliminary attempt to consider the life and work of K. H. Ting in relationship to the church in China, drawing on archival resources, published and unpublished materials, and a series of formal and informal interviews with Ting himself.

For this purpose, I have made use of libraries and archives on three continents. In China, I consulted the archives of the TSPM/CCC and the YM/YWCA archives in Shanghai, as well as the archives of the Anglican Church (Sheng Kung Hui) in Hong Kong. The Shanghai collections were only partially open for review, but they contained some important material on the 1930s and 1940s in particular. I have not had access to government archives in China, and most materials from the period after 1949 continue to be off-limits for overseas scholars and researchers.

Archives in Europe and North America contain important material on Ting's work overseas, publications and papers from the Anglican Episcopal Church (Zhonghua Sheng Gong Hui) in China, and ecumenical relationships with Chinese Christians after 1949. I have made use of the Student Christian Movement archives at the University of Toronto; the archives of the General Synod of the Anglican Church of Canada, also in Toronto; the archives of the World Students' Christian Federation (WSCF) and the World Council of Churches in Geneva; the archives of the Episcopal Church of the U.S.A. in Austin, Texas; and the archives of Union Theological Seminary in New York. I have also made use of library collections at the Graduate Theological Union, the University of California at Berkeley, Nanjing Union Theological Seminary, Princeton Theological Seminary, the University of San Francisco's Ricci Institute and the Chinese University of Hong Kong. The library of the Universities Service Centre of the Chinese University of Hong Kong was particularly important for locating Chinese newspapers and hard-to-find journals.

A great many government and informal publications in China are classified for various levels of "internal circulation" (*neibu jiaoliu*). China has a very restrictive state-secrets law, and a great deal of the material for internal circulation deals with matters that are well known to the reading public but have not been approved for publication.[11] This includes historical documentation as well as material of contemporary interest. Over the last twenty-five years, publications for internal circulation have become increasingly available to foreign scholars, and many studies that have been published in Hong Kong, Taiwan and overseas have made extensive use of these materials. I have made limited use of some of these publications in the present study, particularly as they relate to the discussions of religious policy since the early 1980s.

K. H. Ting has put together a book of his collected writings in both Chinese and English, which I cite extensively.[12] Much of what he has written, particularly in the period before 1979, is not contained in his collected works but was published in *Tian Feng*, the official publication of the TSPM and the CCC; *Jinling shenxuezhi* (*The Nanjing Theological Review*); *Student World*, published in Geneva by the WSCF; and various other religious and secular publications in Chinese and English. In addition, there are a large number of Ting's unpublished writings. It has sometimes been helpful to compare the published or translated forms of his essays to unpublished or earlier versions of the same text in order to understand the development of his thought or how he wanted to present his ideas to particular audiences. I have also made selective use of his correspondence, including circular letters he sent from time to time. However, no attempt has been made to collect his letters. I am now at work on a full cross-referenced bibliography of Ting's work in English and Chinese, and when complete, it will be made available online.

An important resource for this book are the formal interviews I conducted with K. H. Ting in 1990 and 1991. These interviews were intended to allow him to say what he wanted to present about his life and work and to clarify some of the facts and details about his life that are not available in any other source. They were particularly important for Parts 1 and 2 of this study, as they relate to his family and youth, as well as to his experiences and perspective on the 1950s and the Cultural Revolution. The interviews were taped and transcribed, and the Chinese terms translated into English. Transcripts cited in this study have not been edited, except for a few minor corrections in usage. I have also conducted a number of informal interviews with K. H. Ting, mainly to clarify certain facts or elicit his views of recent events, and these are also cited in the footnotes. I have conducted a limited number of formal interviews with others in China who have been close to him, and these are cited in the text.

A key consideration in using interviews as a research technique is to determine if the respondent is offering a "correct" answer rather than a frank opinion. In a collection of essays on popular culture published some years ago, the authors ask, "How does one gauge the biases that can arise because an interview might be audited by others, or because of its formal context, or because the interviewer is a foreigner?" They conclude that one never really knows, but they also point out that extreme skepticism is not the only possible response. "When one knows an informant long and well enough to observe him or her in various moods and contexts, systematic doubt about sincerity becomes unsustainable."[13] Although interviews can never be taken at face value, they do reveal a perspective on the truth that the subject is trying to convey.

An additional note of caution is in order when the subject is a well-known public figure. In the formal interviews I conducted, K. H. Ting responded to the questions I asked slowly and deliberately, weighing every word before he spoke. He was hesitant to speak in detail about his own life, but he was quite ready to offer his interpretation, from the vantage of the early 1990s, on people he knew or on events that he had been part of. He also spoke freely about his theological views and political opinions. Supplemented by his writings and the many diverse interpretations of Christianity in China, the interviews provide an important perspective on Ting's life and thought.

Any interpretation of K. H. Ting's life and legacy will be controversial, especially among Christians who are divided over the political and theological views he has so forcefully advanced. My close working relationship with K. H. Ting over two decades has shaped my perspective, but I have attempted to analyze his life and work by drawing on a wide variety of scholarly interpretations. My interpretation is sympathetic, but not without critical assessment, particularly with regard to his role in the "Anti-Rightist" movement and the early years of the Cultural Revolution (chaps. 5 and 6), and in "theological reconstruction" (chap. 10). We shall see that Ting has himself been critical of his own role in the movements of the 1950s and 1960s. Much of the controversy about Ting concerns his relationship to the Communist Party of China (CPC), and although my discussion (beginning in chap. 2) will not be the final word on the matter, it does offer additional material for consideration.

This is not an approved or authorized biography, although K. H. Ting has cooperated with me at different stages of the process of writing and research. He has not read or commented on any part of this volume, although I have discussed some aspects of interpretation with him. I worked closely with K. H. Ting in my years with the Amity Foundation (chaps. 8 and 9) and kept careful notes on our conversations. I am also writing about the earlier period in his life (chaps. 1-7), much of which appears in this book for the first time. I am grateful for all the help K. H. Ting has offered as I worked on this volume, but the interpretation presented here is mine alone. Like the portrait painter who completes a painting he feels captures his subject, I am fully prepared for the subject, or those who are close to him, to say that it is not a very good likeness. There will be other biographical studies.

My emphasis is on the intellectual and theological contribution of K. H. Ting to religious and political discourse in modern China. More than most church leaders, in China or anywhere else, he has written a large number of theological, social-scientific and policy-oriented essays and reviews, and he has explored religious and political themes from a variety of angles in his speeches and sermons. For most of his life, he carried on an extensive correspondence with a large circle of friends and acquaintances. He did not usually keep a diary or journal, but he at times set down his ideas in a form that he never intended for publication. He had neither the time nor inclination to write a systematic or historical theology, and his preference was to write and to speak in dialogue with the events and ideas of his times. This was especially so from the 1980s onward.

If, as Barbara Tuchman has observed, biography is a "prism of history," then the form changes—the prism reflects light differently—in different periods and situations.[14] This study is set in the historical context of modern and contemporary China. In part 3 especially, I draw on the interrelated categories of governance (*zheng*), religion or ethics (*dao*) and scholarship (*xue*), which Tu Wei-ming and others have introduced in their discussions of traditional Chinese leadership, to help illuminate how K. H. Ting has functioned in his context.[15] It is important to see Ting as first and foremost a *Chinese* intellectual and church leader in order to understand the role he has attempted to play in church and society. This is taken for granted in Chinese writings, but it is a significant corrective to many European and North American interpretations. K. H. Ting has met hundreds if not thousands of Christians from overseas over the last three decades, and many more have heard him speak or have read his essays. His accessibility combined with his skill in interpersonal relationships and facility in English have led some to overlook or ignore his role as a Chinese intellectual and political figure.

In his work for the church and commitment to Christian faith, I will argue that Ting has always been a Chinese patriot and supporter of the Communist Party. Yet this has not made him uncritical. He has pressed for change and reform as a loyalist who wants his country to be better. Ting is not a political "liberal" in the Western sense, but more a scholar-official in modern dress. His political position in some respects resembles that of Josef Hromádka (1889-1970) or Milan Opočenský, both of whom he knew and respected. But Ting is not a Reformed theologian, like Hromádka and Opočenský and many who were advocates of Christian-Marxist dialogue in the former Eastern Europe. His context is different, and his liberal Anglicanism and Chinese sensibility have been more amenable to a Christian acceptance of Communist governance.

One distinctly Chinese feature of Ting's political approach has been his critique of "leftism" or "ultra-leftism," both inside and outside the church, since the late 1970s. He has at times described ultra-leftism as a "stubborn illness" of the revolutionary who wants for today what he or she cannot have until tomorrow.[16] "Liberal" or "progressive" Christians committed to radical social change are particularly susceptible to this disease. K. H. Ting and many others of his generation were at one time drawn to the extremist policies of Mao Zedong, which seemed to represent an idealism consistent with Christian faith. Their experiences during the Cultural Revolution era taught them about the danger of revolutionaries who want immediate change and are prepared to use a political ideology to justify all manner of violence and struggle against others.

Within the TSPM, I will argue, there has been a tendency toward ultra-leftism since its founding. One of the contributions of this study will be to analyze Ting's involvement in and criticism of the radical policies of the movement that he came to lead. In part 2 of this book (chaps. 4-6), I discuss Ting's differences with some of the Shanghai-based TSPM "activists," particularly Li Chuwen. In part 3 (chaps. 7-10), I also discuss ultra-leftism within the TSPM, at the national and provincial levels, but I do not focus on particular individuals. This is partly because I am describing an evolving situation in which viewpoints have changed over the past years and decades. Moreover, such terms as ultra-leftist, TSPM activist and *lao sanzi* ("Old Three-Self") may be better understood as tendencies that run through people and institutions rather than hard-and-fast positions. Although leftism or ultra-leftism are not terms that can be applied to the generation of Christians who came of age after the end of the Cultural Revolution era, younger TSPM/CCC leaders will in time have to address the legacy of the mass movements of 1950s and 1960s, insofar as they continue to influence churches in China.

In writing a book about a contemporary religious figure such as K. H. Ting, the recent past continues to have an impact on the present. Some of Ting's friends and former colleagues will disagree with aspects of what I have written here. I may have overlooked some key events and misinterpreted others. This underscores the importance of historical responsibility in the act of interpretation and calls for the careful sifting of fact and opinion on the part of the writer. The subject of any biography has an "instinct for self protection," and so the writer is forced to draw conclusions that are inferential in order to look behind what is explicitly expressed.[17] This is both necessary and risky, especially in the case of a church leader and political figure of Ting's stature. It takes interpretation far beyond what the subject may have intended, beyond what he may have imagined, and beyond what he might even have been aware of.

This is inevitable in a study that seeks to view the reconstruction of Protestant Christianity in China through the life and thought of a single person. The renewal of the church in any context is much broader. Any biographical study is inherently limited. But the limitation is also an opportunity to explore in considerable depth one perspective on the life and witness of the church that may help illuminate the wider picture. Ting's story is part of a larger story, but he remains the most important public theologian and church leader in China in the last century. He has lived through a fascinating century of turbulent change.

It is for the reader to judge whether his story as it has been interpreted here can help us better understand the ways in which Christianity in China has been reconstructed in the course of this history, and what this means for the future of the church in the wider *oikoumene*.

Part 1

FORMATION IN CHINA,
THE CHURCH AND THE WORLD,
1915-1951

1

The Early Years, 1915-1937

All things without exception mesh and interweave into a fabric, ever lively, ever changing.

Lu Xun[1]

K. H. Ting grew up in Shanghai at a time when that city was becoming an important focal point for China's intellectual and social ferment. It was already the center of Protestant mission efforts in China, and well known for its Western influences. For the first half of the twentieth century, Shanghai would witness everything from growing prosperity and labor unrest to Japanese occupation and civil war. The emerging social consciousness and growing nationalism among intellectuals during this period had a profound impact on the church and student life, two areas of work in which Ting would pursue his lifelong concerns. But it is with the intricate and ever-changing fabric of life in Shanghai that our story begins.

SHANGHAI, 1915 AND BEYOND

By the second decade of the twentieth century, Shanghai was emerging as one of the great cities of the world. It was already the industrial and financial center of China and East Asia, and it had become the base for a growing international community involved in trade and diplomacy. By the 1930s, Shanghai would be the world's sixth largest city, more than double the size of Peking, and overshadowing nearby Nanjing, which was then the nation's capital.

In 1915, Shanghai was a city in transition, remarkable for the contrast between tradition and modernity which existed side by side: old-fashioned Chinese shop fronts around the corner from modern banks along the Bund; streets crowded with rickshaws and wheelbarrows, as well as streetcars and new automobiles; westernized mansions on Bubbling Well Road and Avenue Joffre and the remnants of traditional Chinese architecture in the old city; the glitz and glamour of Shanghai's "Great World" not far from the

15

working-class shanty towns and settlements for refugees from neighboring provinces. The city was the home base for the largest number of Western missionaries in China. It also had more prostitutes per capita than any place in the world.

Shanghai was a municipality composed of three distinct areas: the International Settlement, the French Concession and the Old City. The Old City had been a growing Chinese settlement before the foreigners came in the mid-nineteenth century. Both the French Concession and the International Settlement were established through the "unequal" treaties as foreign administrated enclaves within the broader municipality. Since 1863, the International Settlement had been dominated by the British (with help from the Americans) who continued to maintain foreign privilege as well as a relative degree of law and order.

The vast majority of the population even in the foreign settlements was Chinese. In 1915, the International Settlement, where K. H. Ting grew up, had 638,920 inhabitants of whom 18,519 were foreigners. The French Concession had only 2,405 foreign residents, but 146,595 Chinese. The population for greater Shanghai was perhaps 2 million at that time, which grew to 2.5 million by 1927, and 3.35 million by 1934. Within the International Settlement, the Japanese had the largest foreign community (18,796 in the 1930 census). They were followed by the British (8,449), the Russians (7,366), and the Americans (3,149).[2]

For many foreigners, Shanghai's International Settlement *was* China, or at least the only China that they saw. Missionaries, adventurers, bankers and diplomats all came to China through Shanghai, and many went no further. Foreign banks, factories, businesses and shipping concerns dominated the economy up until the end of World War I, and continued to exercise control over the nation's international trade until the Japanese invasion in 1937. Foreigners were legally protected by extraterritoriality clauses in the nineteenth-century "unequal" treaties dictated by the foreign powers. Their rights were enforced by their embassies and by the Mixed Court that they had established. Westerners created a semicolonial cosmopolitan culture in Shanghai, from their schools and churches to their shops and clubs. They were, in the words of one observer, the "spoilt children of empire."[3]

The church inherited the privileges of other Western institutions in Shanghai. Writing in the 1925 *China Mission Yearbook*, Presbyterian missionary E. C. Lobenstein observed, "Next to London and New York, Shanghai is the most important center of missions in the world."[4] (Had he been a Jesuit or Dominican writing from the French Concession, he would no doubt have included Paris and Rome.) Shanghai was home to more than two hundred Protestant mission societies, publishers, associations, schools and colleges. Most were American, some were British, and there were a few from Canada, Continental Europe, Australia and New Zealand. A National Christian Conference was held in Shanghai in 1922, and it led to the formation of the National Christian Council, which was based here. The "Anti-Christian

Movement" had begun around the same time, as much a reaction to the foreign incursion into China as it was to Christianity per se.

In the first decades of the twentieth century, Shanghai's Chinese population viewed the foreign presence with a mixture of admiration, anger and shame. Cosmopolitan Chinese with acquired European and American tastes were the mainstay of the International Settlement, and they profited from their association with the foreigners. But the 1911 Revolution had sown the seeds for a growing nationalism in the country. This was to find much sharper expression in the May Fourth Movement eight years later, especially among students and intellectuals. Throughout the next three decades, there was a growing resistance to the foreign domination of Shanghai, even though many Chinese—among them revolutionaries and other "undesirable elements"—continued to enjoy the protection and sometimes the prosperity that the International Settlement offered.

Chinese ambivalence about a semicolonial Shanghai was also evident in the business community. Shipping, docks and the cotton mills fueled Shanghai's growth after the end of World War I and led to increasing prosperity for the municipality. The need to finance these new industries helped to promote the development of modern Chinese banks, which stood alongside foreign financial institutions on the Bund. China's economy was still dependent on international banking and business interests, but new economic forces led to the emergence of a Chinese merchant class. Chinese not only managed many foreign firms but also started businesses of their own. They helped create the culture of the modern and cosmopolitan Shanghai, and stirred consumer interest through newly opened department stores such as Sincere and Wing On. The 1920s has been termed the "golden age" of the Chinese bourgeoisie.[5] In this decade, the Chinese business community took up the challenge of economic modernization, and in time they also pressed for more say over how things were run.

Prosperity in Shanghai was not equally distributed. In addition to the bankers, managers and entrepreneurs, there were also increasing numbers of workers, day laborers and poor people. By 1929, there were 2.85 million industrial workers in Shanghai, more than 60 percent of whom were women.[6] They represented about 10 percent of the population and were involved in a growing number of strikes and walkouts.

The Communist Party of China (CPC) was founded in Shanghai in 1920 and had considerable success in organizing trade unions. By 1927, it had almost 500 unions in the city representing more than 800,000 workers. But there was growing tension between the CPC and Chiang Kai-shek's Nationalist Party, the Guomindang (GMD). That spring, after a short-lived insurgency, Communists were purged from the GMD, and many party activists were arrested and executed. The unions they led were declared illegal and the strikes came to an end. The Communist Party in Shanghai was decimated. It assumed a clandestine existence underground, where its forces would slowly be reorganized over the next decade.

Peasants and refugees from other parts of China were drawn to Shanghai, attracted by the prospect of making a living as much as by the peace and security that they thought they would find. Shanghai attracted wave after wave of refugees during the recurring periods of famine and unrest, and the city was fought over by warlords in neighboring provinces. If the refugees were lucky, they became rickshaw drivers and maids. If not, they lived on the streets or in the shanty towns as long as they could survive. It was common, especially in the winter months, to see corpses along the streets, even in the best parts of the city.

The contrast between China's poverty and wealth attracted the interest and concern of reform-oriented students and intellectuals, especially after the May Fourth Movement in 1919. The National Students' Association was started in Shanghai, drawing support from the city's many schools and universities. Shanghai was already the center of China's growing publishing industry, and books on a variety of social and political concerns found an avid readership in the municipality. Students joined with workers in a demonstration in 1925 resulting in the now famous May Thirtieth Movement. This protest against the killing of a worker by a Japanese factory manager left eleven demonstrators dead and twenty wounded. There were subsequent strikes and demonstrations in twenty-eight other Chinese cities, which helped to fuel a growing nationalism.

For the next twenty-five years, Shanghai would contribute to the movement and forces that were shaping modern China. Throughout the 1930s, the Japanese were continuing to exert pressure on China. Shanghai students and intellectuals were at the forefront of the National Salvation Movement to resist Japanese aggression and promote a greater sense of patriotism among the Chinese people. The city was occupied by the Japanese in 1937, but it emerged after the end of World War II as a center of political and social struggle in the Civil War between Nationalists and Communists. When Communist armies finally "liberated" Shanghai in May 1949, they gained access to China's most important industrial and international city, a city that had survived many years of deprivation, occupation and war, and a people who hoped that their suffering was now behind them.

All of this was in the future. In 1915, the Shanghai-Hangzhou Railroad had just been completed, and people from all over the city witnessed their first airplane show. Japan had issued its "Twenty-one Demands" for economic rights and other concessions in China. And a war to end all wars was being fought on the other side of the world.

FAMILY AND CHILDHOOD

Ting Kuang-hsun (Ding Guangxun)[7] was born in Shanghai's International Settlement on 20 September 1915, the Year of the Rabbit in the Chinese calendar.

His father, Ding Chufan (1884-1963, also romanized as Chu Van Ting), had come to Shanghai at the end of the nineteenth century. The Ding family was from Zhoushan in the district of Cezi, which is on the coast of Zhejiang Province, near the commercial city of Ningbo.[8] They were small landholders. Ding Chufan's father was a first-level degree holder in the old imperial system of the Qing dynasty.

Ningbo people had been coming to Shanghai since the late eighteenth century. Entrepreneurs from that city were known to be fiercely loyal to their native place, and they looked after newly arrived immigrants who had been recommended through local connections. In Shanghai, they maintained their own guild, their own cemetery and other local organizations. It was said that up through the early 1920s, Shanghai finance was controlled by the "Zhejiang clique," which meant the traditional bankers of Ningbo. They played a formative role in building up Shanghai before the arrival of the foreigners, and they maintained considerable influence in the community well into the 1930s.

Traditional guilds, banks and businesses were put under increasing strain in the late nineteenth century by new and powerful foreign institutions. By that time, many of the Ningbo people who came to Shanghai were menial laborers, although they were still looked after in the Ningbo network. According to Susan Mann Jones, "Ningbo people moved from positions of leadership in traditional organizations into prominent roles in modern institutions," and this provided a "thread of human as well as institutional continuity" in Shanghai finance.[9] They also continued to hire people from their native place to work in the banks and businesses they managed.

It is not known exactly how and when Ding Chufan actually came to Shanghai, but he would certainly have been part of the Ningbo network once he got to the city. He eventually became a middle-level manager in the Netherlands Trading Society, which had offices in Sassoon House on the Bund. Although he occasionally visited Ningbo with his wife and children, there was relatively little contact in later years between the family in Shanghai and Ding Chufan's Ningbo relatives.

K. H. Ting's mother, Li Jinglan (1886-1986), had been raised in Shanghai. Her father, Li Jiaqing (K. C. Li), was one of the first clergymen in the (Episcopal) Zhonghua Sheng Gong Hui (Chunghua Sheng Kung Hui), ordained a deacon in 1884 and a priest in 1907. He died on 26 January 1915, nine months before K. H. Ting was born.[10] Li Jinglan had two brothers, both of whom graduated from St. John's University and studied overseas. One brother taught physics at St. John's and other universities in Shanghai, and the other was a businessman who eventually moved to Hong Kong. In the 1920s and 1930s, the Li brothers maintained a large house in a prosperous and secure neighborhood in the International Settlement, where they lived with their widowed mother.

Ding Chufan and Li Jinglan were married in Shanghai and had four children. The eldest son, Ding Baoxun (born 1908), became an architect. Their daughter, Ding Baoli (1912-1990), became a middle-school teacher, taught for a time at St. Mary's Hall and lived in Shanghai all of her life. K. H. was the third child. The youngest son, Ding Shixun (born 1917), worked for the service corps of the YMCA during the war years, and then became an accountant. When K. H. was growing up, the family lived on Cunningham Road in the Hong Kew (Hong Qiao) area of the International Settlement, not far from the old railroad station. This was a predominantly Japanese neighborhood but also an entry point to Shanghai from the provinces. In periods of famine and civil war, refugees from northern Jiangsu would pour into Shanghai and gather around the station. The family would then move in with the Li's, the two uncles and grandmother of the Ding children, where it was safer.

K. H. Ting's earliest childhood memories recall what it was like to live in Hong Kew during this period.

When I was a little child, I remember I often went to stand in front of our house on the street, on Cunningham Road, because there were always many people arriving in Shanghai at the station, people from the countryside. What I can remember now most vividly is that at the time of famine, many people would go to Shanghai from Yangzhou. In Shanghai, the Yangzhou people were considered to be the least educated, and the poorest. House maids, very many of them were from Yangzhou, and barbers also. Barbers would probably be considered the best job that people from Yangzhou could take. Also many beggars. What I remember is that there would be hordes of people from Yangzhou, from north Jiangsu really, but in Shanghai they are all called Yangzhou. And many girls would pass by, and they were seeking jobs. They would be very happy if they could just be fed. If they would go to work in some family, some household, their work could be free, they wouldn't ask for any wage, if they could just be given food. So I had pity on them as a child.

Rickshaw pullers were mostly from northern Jiangsu too, and most of them would be barefoot, even in rain or snow. And then policemen, many of them from India, Sikh policemen in those days, went after these rickshaws, because so many of them went to the station to seek customers. The rickshaw pullers would run away, because the policemen would try to tear off their license, which had their number on it, and to get it back, the rickshaw pullers would have to pay a big sum.

And then of course, in the wintertime when I walked to my primary school, and then to my middle school, we would see dead people on the street. Many of them were probably beggars who didn't have anywhere to live. They would spend their night at some gateway, or any place where it was not windy. They would tear off sheets of paper, layers of paper on the wall advertisements. They wrapped themselves up with this paper. It was very cold, and we would come across dead people on the street just like that.

Another thing I can remember was when there was civil war. Our house was too close to the station. The station was located within Chinese territory, not the International Settlement. But where we lived was very close to the station, so when there was war, there would be fighting on the other side of the street, not Cunningham Road, but another street very nearby. So our whole family would go to live with my uncles, that is, my mother's brothers. They lived in a place near the center of the International Settlement, and it was much safer. St. Peter's Church would be full of refugees. In those days I rather enjoyed moving to a new place to live.[11]

The Ding family had a close connection with St. Peter's Church. K. H. was baptized there along with four other infants on St. Stephen's Day 1915, the day after Christmas. His brothers and sister had been baptized there as well. This was the same church that K. C. Li, their maternal grandfather, had served as deacon and priest. K. H. was baptized not as Ting Kuang-hsun but as Ting Pao-shu (Ding Baoshu). It was common practice in traditional China to identify sons in each generation by the first or second character of their given name. Apparently there had been some confusion over which character it was for this generation, *pao (bao)* or *hsun (xun)*. A mistake was made at his baptism but was then corrected, perhaps by the grandfather in Ningbo, who, with his classical education, would be more concerned about such things. Pao-shu became Kuang-hsun, the name by which he has been known all his life. All three brothers therefore had a common final character in their given names.

K. H. attended primary and middle school in the International Settlement, graduating from the Number Two Junior Middle School attached to Soochow University in 1930, and the Senior Middle School of St. John's University in 1933. By his own recollection, his primary academic interests in middle school were mathematics and physics.

The major influence on his life during his earliest years was his mother, a strong and warm-hearted woman with a deep and simple Christian faith. She was active in St. Peter's Church and for a time headed the women's fellowship there. K. H. was said to have been his mother's favorite, which was unusual because he was neither the oldest nor the youngest child. She had given him as a child the nickname Bao Bao (precious), the first character of the name he had been baptized with and a common pet name for a child. She called him Bao Bao even when he was a grown man. He remained very close to her throughout his life, and he is said to take after her in many respects. In the 1980s, K. H. made a point of visiting his mother regularly in Shanghai, where she lived with his sister. Li Jinglan looked forward to these visits, and she would excitedly announce that Bao Bao was coming to see her.[12]

Although she was delicate and somewhat sickly much of her life, Li Jinglan lived to be 101 and died in Shanghai in 1986.

This strong attachment between mother and son is not difficult to understand. Ting himself has frequently spoken of God's love in relationship to the love of a mother for a son.

> For centuries and to this day, in China anyway, what is taken for granted in the father is his severity and in the mother, her loving kindness. In fact, the proper Chinese way to refer to one's father in conversation is "the severe one in my family," while "the loving one in my family" is reserved for the mother.[13]

One cannot help but imagine that in these words, written in 1991, Ting was speaking of his own mother and father.

Li Jinglan was a devout Christian and very attached to the church. Late in her life, she even changed her name to Li Lizi, which meant to urge oneself forward in faith. She had always hoped that one of her sons would follow in her father's footsteps and become a priest. It was K. H. who fulfilled his mother's wishes. Li Jinglan's piety was of an orderly and embracing Anglican character, neither high church nor evangelical, never given to extremes of enthusiasm but still satisfying on both emotional and intellectual levels. She was responsible for the religious side of her children's upbringing, and she shaped Ting's own religious faith and character.

Her husband had been active in one of the Chinese independent churches for a time, but he subsequently lost interest. However, he apparently did not object to the regular Bible studies and evening devotions that his wife conducted in their home. The children reluctantly joined in on these services to please their mother, even though they were not very interested. Each child was supposed to read a verse of the Bible in turn, then they would all sing a hymn, and finally their mother would conclude the service with a reflection and prayer. If the children continued to be distracted during the Bible readings, she would calm them down by having them read with her all twenty-six verses of Psalm 136. She would read the first part of each verse, and the four children would join in the refrain: "for his steadfast love endures forever." They would begin by shouting out this verse as if it were a game, but eventually they would respond to their mother's rhythm. By the end of the reading of the Psalm, the children would have settled down, and their mother would continue to lead them in worship.[14]

Their regular attendance at church rounded out this solid religious upbringing and family devotion. But St. Peter's Church was a great deal more important for the Dings than simply shaping their approach to personal piety and Christian faith.[15]

ST. PETER'S CHURCH

Protestant missionary work began in Shanghai in the 1840s, shortly after the end of the first Opium War. American and British Anglican-Episcopal missionaries were among the first to arrive in the city, and in 1845, Shanghai became their base, under the direction of William J. Boone who was named China's first Missionary Bishop by the Archbishop of Canterbury. For much of the nineteenth century, missionaries focused on evangelism, translation, education and the training of clergy.[16] Four Anglican-Episcopal missions were active in China, primarily in populous cities on the coast or along the Yangtse river: the Church Mission Society, the Society for the Propagation of the Gospel in Foreign Parts, the Protestant Episcopal Church (American) and the Canadian Anglican Church. Anglican efforts to establish an indigenous church culminated in the First Synod of the Zhonghua Sheng Gong Hui, the Holy Catholic Church of China, held in Shanghai in 1912. In that year, this new church had 30,000 baptized members in eleven dioceses.[17] By 1915, the total Episcopal constituency had reached over 46,000, and by 1936, 78,000.[18]

Shanghai's Holy Trinity Pro-Cathedral was the seat of the English bishop of the Diocese of Jiangsu, but Shanghai itself was under the jurisdiction of the missionary bishop who was appointed by the American Protestant Episcopal Church. This was one of the many anomalies in the missionary system that developed in China. The headquarters of the Protestant Episcopal Church Mission was the largest of any in the city. It was located at Jessfield Park near St. John's University and St. Mary's Hall, a girls' school, which the Episcopalians had also established.

Frederick Rogers Graves (1858-1940) was consecrated missionary bishop of Shanghai at St. Thomas's Church in New York City on 14 June 1893. He was a powerful figure who influenced every aspect of church life until his retirement in 1937. It was Bishop Graves who confirmed K. H. at St. Peter's in 1930, and who later gave preliminary approval for his theological studies and candidacy for the priesthood. Graves was succeeded as bishop by William Payne Roberts (1888-1971) in November 1937, but the consecration this time was at the Holy Trinity Pro-Cathedral in Shanghai.

St. Peter's was about a mile west of the Bund on the outskirts of the International Settlement, a short tram or rickshaw ride away from the Dings home on Cunningham Road. It had been started as a mission station in 1857, and the cornerstone was laid in 1898. St. Peter's was consecrated on 28 October 1899, just a few months before the outbreak of the Boxer Rebellion in the north. The church was well constructed. Although no longer used as a church, the building was still standing in the mid-1990s on what is now Beijing West Road.

By the turn of the century, parish work at St. Peter's was regarded by Bishop Graves as among "the most encouraging in Shanghai." In 1899, Rev. J. L. Rees, the missionary in charge of the parish, had written:

The number of our enquirers keeps steadily increasing. We now have about sixty people under instruction . . . The majority are respectable middle class people, and as far as we can see, they come to seek for admission into the Christian Church, because they think that this in some way elevates them, though the full nature of this *elevation*, they cannot at first be expected to understand.[19]

K. C. Li, Ting's maternal grandfather, went to serve this church as assistant under J. L. Rees in 1904, and he was ordained to the priesthood three years later. An independence or self-support movement began at St. Peter's in 1906, and in 1914, the vestry resolved that the parish would henceforth be fully self-supporting. Also in that year, D. M. Koeh (Ge Pilu) was installed as the first Chinese rector. It was unusual for any church in China at that time to be entirely self-supporting and under the direction of Chinese clergy. But St. Peter's membership was drawn largely from the educated middle class of Shanghai's International Settlement, and they gave generously both to the church (which already had stained-glass windows and electric lighting) and to the support of its outreach. The latter included St. Elizabeth's Hospital (opened in 1903), which was not far from St. Peter's, as well as support for church schools and work among the refugees who came from the provinces.

The membership of the church was also growing, as can be seen from figures published in a volume commemorating twenty years of independent self-support in 1933:

	Baptized Christians	*Annual Contributions*
1905	229	$ 362
1915	344	$ 944
1925	718	$ 2,740
1932	835	$ 6,826

Because Li Jinglan was so well connected at St. Peter's, clergymen tended to become friends of the Dings and regularly visited the family at home. Most of St. Peter's clergy were also involved with social concerns, and the church was in the liberal "broad church" Anglican tradition. K. T. Chung (Zhong Ketuo) was attached to the church for some time and was a regular guest at the Ding household. He was rector of St. Peter's from 1921 to 1923 and later continued as assisting priest. Chung was especially concerned with questions of social morality, and when he left St. Peter's it was to become a secretary of the newly organized National Christian Council. He subsequently became head of a government committee to ban opium smoking.

The priest whom K. H. Ting remembers best when he was growing up was Dong Jianwu (H. C. Tung), who was rector of St. Peter's from 1925 to 1931. He was responsible for youth activities during Ting's formative years. The Dings were friends with the whole Dong family, as they were with other clergy families at the church. Dong Jianwu was a popular and outgoing priest at St. Peter's, but, unbeknownst to his parishioners, he secretly joined the Communist Party in 1928, while he was still rector. He later became well known as "Pastor Wang," who was instrumental in taking the American journalist Edgar Snow to meet the Communist leadership in Yanan in 1936. Snow was fascinated by Pastor Wang, his knowledge of the Communists and his connections with just about everyone, but he did not disclose his real name in *Red Star over China*,[20] the book that introduced the Chinese Communists to a popular audience in China and the West.

Dong was a complex and fascinating figure, flamboyant and secretive, Christian priest and Communist cadre all in one. Stories are told about how he would raise a red flag on top of one of the buildings of St. Peter's Church when the Communists met there. This was not a very good idea in those days, when Communist activities were under careful government scrutiny. Zhou Enlai is reported to have called a number of meetings at St. Peter's Church in the 1920s, and he may have hidden at the church when he escaped from the Nationalists during the purge of 1927. Dong Jianwu later worked in the party's security department, in which capacity he helped get hundreds of Communists safely out of Shanghai to Jiangxi.[21] After he left Shanghai in the mid-1930s, Dong served as an informal Communist ambassador and go-between with the Nationalists. He returned to the city during the Japanese occupation when he worked undercover in the army of Wang Jingwei's "puppet government."

Dong Jianwu was not the only priest from St. Peter's who was associated with the Communist Party. Pu Huaren (Paul H. J. Poo), who assisted at the church when D. M. Koeh was rector, had become a Christian in 1910. Like D. M. Koeh, Pu studied theology at St. John's University and wrote a number of influential essays on Christianity in these early years. In 1916, Pu and Koeh left the relative comforts of Shanghai to become self-supporting missionaries in Xi'an on behalf of the newly formed Sheng Gong Hui. Pu later worked with Feng Yuxiang, the "Christian General," and he visited the Soviet Union. In 1927, Pu Huaren joined the Communist Party. In the 1930s and 1940s, Pu was involved in the party's United-Front work, and in the 1950s he assumed a number of prominent positions in the government of the People's Republic.[22] Pu Huaren was an influential supporter of Christian involvement in the united front and later of the Chinese Christian Three-Self Patriotic Movement.

Much of what K. H. Ting first learned at St. Peter's Church is reflected in what were to become his lifelong concerns. The political commitments of St. Peter's priests foreshadowed his own political involvement. His approach to piety and churchmanship took shape in the church where he was baptized and confirmed. The liberal social outlook and outreach to the poor at St. Peter's reflected expressions of faith that K. H. Ting embraced. Finally, St. Peter's commitment to self-government, self-support and self-propagation forty years before the start of the Chinese Christian Three-Self Patriotic Movement were very unusual for a church at this time. The Three-Self idea, and a belief that the church should be Chinese, were ideas that K. H. Ting grew up with, and which he assumed to be the normal and proper approach to Christian life.[23] There were no foreign missionaries attached to St. Peter's when K. H. was growing up, and so he took it for granted that Chinese should be in charge of their own churches. This may help explain why he bristled under the continuing missionary leadership of St. John's University and the Sheng Gong Hui.

St. Peter's was a wealthy church growing in influence and trying to realize its Chinese identity in Shanghai's semicolonial setting. Almost in spite of itself, St. Peter's stood over against the foreign and missionary orientation of the status quo. Most important in this respect was the role of the church's socially and theologically progressive priests, and especially Dong Jianwu. His social outlook and political commitment could not but have a profound influence on the young people in the church, including K. H. Ting. All that Ting learned at St. Peter's was to be reinforced by his experiences at St. John's University, where the priests he knew from St. Peter's had all been educated.

UNDERGRADUATE STUDIES AT ST. JOHN'S UNIVERSITY

By the 1930s, St. John's University was one of the best private Christian colleges in China, attracting students from wealthy Chinese families all over the country as well as from Southeast Asia. Founded by the American Protestant Episcopal Church in 1879, its purpose was "the development of men of Christian character and of sound intelligence."[24] The moving spirit behind St. John's was the indefatigable F. L. Hawks Pott, who served as president for fifty-three years, beginning in 1888. He had a charismatic and domineering presence and became the personal embodiment of St. John's both at home and abroad. Using ideas that were then popular in American education, he had helped the university grow from a small missionary college into a comprehensive institution of higher learning. In his insistence on the use of English as a medium of instruction, he had also made St. John's into what seemed like a very "Western" place, more so than the other Christian colleges. Nevertheless, the university grew and developed. Its enrollment in 1933 was 801, and about one quarter of the students at the university and the middle school were Christians.[25] Many of the latter were young men (St. John's did not become coed until 1936) from middle- and upper-class families who lived in the International Settlement, who had attended St. John's Middle School and who were from churches in the Jiangsu Diocese.

The Ding family had moved to a larger house in Fu Tian Cun (Luckfield Village) near Bubbling Well Road, and later to Brennan Road near Jessfield Park. This was not far from the St. John's campus. When Ting entered the university as a freshman in September 1933, it had an undergraduate enrollment of 440 students. K. H. was to study civil engineering, in part because

K. H. Ting in the 1937
Johannean. Reproduced with
the permission of the Archives
of the Episcopal Church,
Austin, Texas.

of his early interest in physics and mathematics. This was a practical choice and his father approved, for he would be assured a well-paying job after graduation. Ting's father had wanted him to enter Jiaotong University, a government institution that had a better program in this field. But his mother insisted on St. John's, both because it was where her two brothers had gone and because of its church affiliation, and so his father acquiesced.

As it turned out, Ting studied engineering only for one year, and then he decided to switch to theology. There were no doubt a variety of motives that caused him to make this change, but it is worth quoting his own recollection on this subject at some length.

> I think the circumstances of this change had a lot to do with some pessimism that I experienced. I began to be in touch with the students' YMCA, with the national student department of the YMCA. I began to attend certain student conferences, against the wish of my church friends. I became concerned with national destiny. At that time I felt that engineering could not make me useful to national salvation. And I felt that the church had a role to play, or maybe the most important role to play, at that time.
>
> I also felt, quite groundlessly, that the church was a place where the morals were high. I can remember one time when the Jiangsu Diocese was having its diocesan synod. As the group of clergymen came out of the pro-cathedral, I watched them and thought, "These clergymen are not rich, but their lives are meaningful."

During those years, I think I had a period of my life when I spent a lot of time every day in private devotional practice. This was after my first year, after leaving engineering. Very often, I wouldn't have any breakfast and would spend a long time early in the morning on the bridge. There is a very small bridge, with trees overhead. That was the spot where I went to have my private prayer and Bible reading, alone . . .

I think I came into contact with the darker aspect of our society and its problems, which made me think that engineering was of no help. Maybe engineering was a way for me to earn a good income, that was what my father thought, but I felt that I would be doing something much more meaningful if I served in the church. And then my interest in religious devotion of those years, which began when I was still in my freshman year, also made me want to go into the service of the church.[26]

The bridge that he speaks of was a well-known and much-loved site on the campus of St. John's University. The image of K. H. Ting spending idyllic mornings on the bridge in prayer and devotion is not one that we would expect, but it seems to reflect his religious life for a time in his late adolescence. The bridge is the subject of a poem that appeared in the St. John's University yearbook the year that Ting graduated. It presents a quiet and idyllic picture, and reads in part:

> The old vine covered Chinese bridge,
> Outlined against the sky;
> Reflected on the placid stream;
> Peacefully running by;
> Has stood for many ages past
> Serving humanity.
> Stretching out with faultless span,
> Symbol of constancy.[27]

K. H. Ting's decision to study theology pleased his mother as much as it angered his father. Ding Chufan saw no point in his son's studying theology, and said that if he must change from engineering, why not go into medicine. Job prospects would certainly be better in this field than in theology. His father remained adamant in his opposition, but K. H. was by now quite certain that he wished to study theology. That being the case, Ding Chufan made the decision to cut his son off financially. If K. H. wanted to study for the Christian ministry, then there would be no funds available for tuition from the family. This decision resulted in an irrevocable break between father and son, one that appears never to have been fully healed. In his later years, K. H. Ting rarely spoke of his father, and when he did, it was gener-

Soochow Creek Bridge at St. John's University. Reproduced with the permission of the Yale Divinity School Library.

ally in a critical or negative way. At the end of the passage about the severe father and loving mother quoted above, where Ting compares God's love to that of a mother, he adds, "I assume that we all know of fathers of whom love was hardly an attribute."[28]

Because tuition and other fees at St. John's were quite high, Ting went to President Hawks Pott to ask for assistance. Pott has been described as one with a "genius in handling young men, in giving them freedom and yet so winning their respect, that a word from him turns the whole course of their lives."[29] This describes both his charisma and his overbearing presence. He was by all accounts opinionated, patriarchal and domineering. He was also delighted to have a new candidate for the priesthood, because it was difficult to attract young men of talent to the ministry. There were less than ten students in the theology department at this time. Pott agreed to give K. H. a full scholarship so that he could complete his degree.

The B.A. degree in theology at St. John's was not very specialized, and so Ting could take courses in a variety of areas that were of interest to him. These included the natural sciences, English and Chinese literature, psychology and education, as well as theology. Except for the Chinese department, the courses at St. John's were taught in English, and it was here that Ting developed his impeccable skills in this language. St. John's has been sometimes criticized for neglecting Chinese culture and literature; students were not well trained in the literary subtleties of classical or *wenli* Chinese, essential for educated Chinese even in the 1930s. Although K. H. Ting has a strong interest in modern Chinese literature, especially the writings of Lu Xun and other May Fourth writers, his foundation in literary Chinese fell short of his facility in the use of English. This was also part of the St. John's legacy, and that of other Christian colleges in China.

K. H. was active in many areas of university life. He was manager of the school basketball team for a time, and he took part in the foreign dramatic club. In his senior year, Ting played a leading role in a one-act Christmas play, *The Loveliest Thing,* by Roland Pertwee. His acting no doubt helped to perfect his mastery of English.

More important was his participation in the University Christian Fellowship, of which he was elected president in his senior year. The purpose of the fellowship was "to show Christian spirit through fellowship as well as to develop cooperation among students."[30] This was not a group for Christians alone; its activities were designed to reach out to all students in a spirit of service. Ting's leadership in the University Christian Fellowship became known all over Shanghai. He was appointed St. John's representative to the first meeting of the Union of Shanghai Christian Student Organizations (*Shanghai xuelian*), a citywide organization,[31] and became familiar with student work all over the city. This attracted the attention of people in the student department of the YMCA, and of Zhu Pei'en who was then general secretary.[32] Zhu helped to get K. H. interested in the work of the YMCA, and this led to his appointment at the YMCA after his graduation.

Ting joined a lay organization of Episcopal Christians called the Brotherhood of St. Andrew during his university years. This group had been founded in Chicago in the late nineteenth century with the purpose of developing a rule of prayer and service among younger people. It flourished, for a time, in Episcopal missionary areas in East Asia. One reason for its popularity was its emphasis on Christian witness among one's equals. As one of the Brotherhood's English supporters commented, "There is many a man who, especially in his youth, fails to confess Christ in his own society, and then, if I may so express it, sneaks round the corner to do something to raise the degraded or takes orders and preaches the gospel."[33] In China, the ideals of the Brotherhood of St. Andrew may have functioned to promote the indigenization of mission work, and this would have exerted a special appeal for Ting and other Christian university students at the time.

Along with these activities, much of Ting's Christian involvement continued to be centered on St. Peter's Church. Rev. Yu Enci had been named rector in 1941, and K. H. was one of the leaders of the St. Peter's youth fellowship. (Yu Enci was to become assistant bishop of Shanghai in May 1942, but died suddenly two years later.) Ting organized summer youth gatherings and discussion groups on subjects of interest to young people, especially emerging questions about their responsibility for society and the nation.

Pu Huaren, now an underground Communist activist, was back in Shanghai in the early 1930s, and he was urging young people at St. Peter's, where he still had enormous influence, to become more involved in the movement for national salvation. We will have more to say about this movement in the next chapter, but it is important to realize that a growing number of Chinese Christians were becoming involved in activities focused on resistance against imperialism and aggression. Other speakers invited to the St. Peter's Youth Fellowship also addressed questions of national salvation, and so the church continued to be a forum for progressive social thinking. More broadly, students all over Shanghai were becoming conscious of the Japanese incursion against China and the need for resistance.

As he was about to begin his senior year, K. H. Ting became aware of the fact that the church did not really take national salvation or young people very seriously. In what was probably his first published essay, Ting challenged the church to take up the questions that young people were raising. The importance of religion, he wrote, lay not in memorizing the Bible or attending church but in "its effect on our lives, for religion is a way of living which is related to every action we take." Young people have many questions about nation and society, and they are asking the church, "What must we do?" They would be put off if the church disregarded them, but they would develop an interest in and enthusiasm for the church if it can address their questions and provide concrete guidance. This is the role of the church for young people living in "a complex society with progressive thinking and advanced ideas."[34] As was true for many Christians of the time, K. H. Ting was coming to see Christian faith as inseparable from national salvation.

At the end of May 1936, sixty National Salvation Unions from around the country established the All China Federation of National Salvation Unions during a meeting at the Shanghai YMCA.[35] That August, also in Shanghai, the Union of Shanghai Christian Student Organizations was formally established. As president of St. John's University Christian Fellowship and its representative to the Union, Ting was present at both of these meetings.

Students and intellectuals were growing impatient with their government's seeming unwillingness to do anything about the Japanese, who had already occupied northeast China. In Shanghai, there had been a serious clash between Japanese and Chinese troops in 1932. This ended in a humiliating armistice that met all the demands contained in the Japanese ultimatum. The people of Shanghai were infuriated. On the eve of all-out war between China and Japan, Shanghai students were poised to assume an important role in the resistance effort.

K. H. Ting's growing political and social consciousness resulted in his increasing dissatisfaction with institutionalized Christianity and the church. He recalls the strong sense of injustice he began to feel about American and Chinese colleagues receiving different treatment and having different pay scales from the same church. This was a familiar critique of the missionary movement in the "younger churches" in the 1930s and in the decades since. As we shall see in the next chapter, K. H. Ting also believed that the church was not strong enough in its commitment to national salvation and resistance against Japanese aggression. He became increasingly critical of the social conservatism of the church and its silent acquiescence to injustice. Such criticisms would be familiar to those who have been involved in the Student Christian Movements (SCMs) in many other times and places.

More personally, Ting increasingly came to resent the presumptuousness of St. John's president F. Hawks Pott precisely because his word could and did change the whole course of a student's life. Pott was a man of strong opinions who had a conservative Western political outlook. He was something of a father figure who assumed that he knew what was best for his students. Sometime in 1936, Pott had decided, without any consultation, that K. H. Ting would become the chaplain of St. John's Middle School after his graduation and that he would continue his theological studies at the university. This was a good appointment, and Pott no doubt assumed the suggestion would be well received. When he presented the idea to K. H. Ting, however, Ting balked and refused to go along. This led to a major rift between the aging university president and the prospective priest. Ting's personal encounter with Pott may have helped shape his view of the domineering missionary, and it certainly reinforced his belief in the need for a Chinese church that was free of missionary control. In his senior year, reversing the decision he had made three years earlier, Ting began to think that he would not enter the ministry, a decision in which he was no doubt supported by many of his friends in the student movement.

His professors tried to dissuade him, but they could not. The controversy continued, and K. H. was again called in to speak with the president. Ting relates what happened then:

> So finally, Dr. Pott said to me: First, that I must return to the university all the money that I owed; and second, I was to return to the university the theological books that were given to theological students free, and there were many of them. I promised that I would do these two things. Now I found it very difficult to separate myself from these books, because I loved these books, and I had studied them very carefully. So I wept a lot for a while in a room all by myself, and then I sent back all the books. As to what I owed the university financially, I said that I would pay back gradually, and Dr. Pott was kind enough to agree to that. But after paying back small sums of money a few times, my father decided that he should pay the rest of the debt.[36]

The decision not to seek ordination had been made, and Ting prepared for a new and uncertain future, somehow related to the YMCA and the student movement.

He graduated from St. John's with a B.A. from the Department of Theology. His name is listed in the 1937 *Johannean* as Ting Kwang Hyuin, the last character following a Shanghai romanization. Besides the St. Andrew's Fellowship and the University Christian Fellowship, which he chaired, his activities included membership in the Communications League, which he also chaired, the Foreign Dramatic Club and the choir.[37] Near the front of the 1937 *Johannean*, there appears a poem "To the Graduate." The first stanza reads:

> Lamp lit buildings in the blue dusk shine
> Through fir trees stately boughs;
> O'ershadowing boat forms, line on line,
>   As their dreamy oarsmen drowse.
> St. John's, emblem of light and truth,
>   Beneath the all blessing sun
> Stands to aid aspiring youth,
>   To make all peoples one.

The sentiments in the poem show how far St. John's was from the reality of China on the eve of war and revolution. It was a world apart. Students concerned with social justice and China's social problems would find the ideals expressed in this poem almost incomprehensible.

K. H. Ting received his degree on 26 June 1937. The weather was beautiful that day, and unseasonably cool. Faculty, the graduating class, families, friends and guests gathered on the south lawn or for tea in the social hall before the ceremony. Commencement exercises began promptly at five with the singing of the national anthem, to the accompaniment of the Royal Regiment Band of the British Defense Force. K. H. Ting was among the 104 graduates who heard Dr. Zhang Boling, President of Nankai University, speak an address entitled "New Duties of Youth to the State in China's Upward Move."

By graduation day, there had already been a number of strikes and demonstrations calling for resistance against Japanese aggression. Eleven days later, a Japanese military unit near Beijing provoked the Marco Polo Bridge incident. This began a war that was to last for the next eight years. In the months after Ting's graduation, there would be fierce battles in and around Shanghai, and when they were over, the city would be an isolated island in enemy-occupied territory.

2

Life and Work in Occupied Shanghai, 1937-1945

Burn up the people's dreams,
Bring their blood to a boil,
And save their souls,
While breaking open their prison gates!

Wen Yiduo[1]

When the Japanese attacked Shanghai, people all over China came to the realization that the War of Resistance had finally begun. The Marco Polo Bridge Incident was not just another local provocation but the beginning of a prolonged conflict. Fighting broke out in Shanghai on 13 August 1937 and continued for the next three months. Chinese troops put up a courageous defense, supported by a people united to protect their homes, their city and their nation. But the outcome of the Battle of Shanghai was never really in doubt, for Chinese troops were no match for the Japanese forces. The resistance efforts did, however, frustrate Japan's hope for a quick victory and minimal use of force.

The occupation affected all areas of society, including the churches. Because it was in the International Settlement, the buildings of St. Peter's Church were not damaged during the fighting, but 30 percent of the parishioners (not including the Ting family) had to relocate themselves. In addition, St. Peter's sheltered more than five hundred refugees during and after the Japanese attack and raised an incredible US$8,000 for their support. The church itself continued to grow, and by the end of 1938 St. Peter's had a membership of 1,472.[2] Like many other Protestant churches in Shanghai, St. Peter's remained a center of community activity and Chinese patriotism throughout the years of Japanese rule.

The occupation meant increasing restrictions and deprivation for the people of Shanghai. A collaborationist regime was later set up under Wang Jingwei, but it had little popular support. Many Chinese chose to leave the city for the safety of Hong Kong or for "Free China" in the western provinces.

The people who stayed lived an uncertain and ambiguous existence which became more and more onerous as the war dragged on. For those involved in the National Salvation Movement against the Japanese, there was also the question of whether it was morally right for them to remain in occupied territory rather than go elsewhere to join in active armed struggle against the invading army.

During the early years of the occupation, the International Settlement and the French Concession continued to be administered by foreigners. These areas became safe havens for intellectuals and others involved in resistance efforts, and remained free from direct Japanese rule until the attack on Pearl Harbor, which brought the United States into the war in the Pacific. The freedom even before that was only relative, for Western authorities were under pressure to maintain order and punish "terrorists" who resisted Japanese control. What freedom there was could also be used by both Nationalist and Japanese agents to dispense their own forms of justice to those who sought refuge in the areas of the city under foreign rule.

The years following university graduation are a formative time in a young person's life. The fact that for K. H. Ting these were also the years of the Japanese occupation made this period doubly significant. It left a distinctive imprint on his approach to nation, church and society, one that has informed his understanding ever since.

INTELLECTUAL AND MORAL CHOICES
IN WARTIME SHANGHAI

When the Japanese attacked, those involved in the National Salvation Movement became exuberant over what the novelist Ba Jin termed the "holy roar of the cannon." They were no longer just talking about national salvation as a movement, but would now be actively engaged in the work of national salvation. When the city fell on November 12, however, they realized that the heady and heroic times were over. Now they would have to settle down and see what they could do in this changed and more repressive environment.

In his compelling study of Shanghai intellectuals in wartime Shanghai, Poshek Fu describes three different ways in which intellectuals responded to the complex and ambiguous situation in which they now found themselves: passivity, resistance or collaboration. These choices correspond to the archetypal response of traditional Chinese literati during times of upheaval—eremitism, loyalism and cooption. Fu avoids a rigid or moralistic approach to the decisions that intellectuals made by stressing the ambiguities involved in any choice. Drawing on the insight of Primo Levi, he argues that moral choices in situations of oppression and terror are seldom clear-cut; they are always shaped by individual weakness, inconsistency and compromise, as well as by moral courage and human dignity. In situations such as the Shanghai occupation, intellectuals entered a morally "gray zone" of existence where there are no idealized polarities of right and wrong. They had to survive, but they also attempted to remain true to their beliefs and convictions.[3]

The choices that Shanghai intellectuals made after the occupation were important for themselves personally, but they had an impact on their families and the people with whom they associated as well. Fu describes the situation facing Shanghai intellectuals as the "dilemma of choosing between private and public morality, a choice of (individual) survival or patriotic commitment." The dilemma tended to leave people with troubled consciences in either case, for the choices they made were rarely unequivocal.[4]

This was especially so for those who lived and worked as isolated individuals and who were in varying degrees alienated from the society around them. For those associated with a broader movement of resistance, the situation was different. They saw themselves as part of a community or an organization that extended far beyond the world of occupied Shanghai, a world that gave them historical perspective and a sense of purpose. The choice between a private and a public morality could be provisionally resolved. Despite inconsistency and compromise, the choice of those involved in the National Salvation Movement was clear: they would resist in whatever way they could, for they were a part of the anti-Japanese effort in occupied territory.

The Shanghai YMCAs and YWCAs drew together many young men and women who wished to identify themselves with such a movement. This was especially so in the student department, where work focused on the situation of displaced students and refugees, and was informed by a rigorous social analysis. Student workers were interested in questions of politics and national salvation, which the occupation only made more urgent. They did not take part in YMCA and YWCA activities designed for a particular evangelistic purpose, but organized meetings and activities that addressed questions about social involvement. YMCA and YWCA programs attracted progressive students and intellectuals with diverse political and religious affiliations, including both Communists and Christian activists who were committed to resistance against the Japanese.

Among the Christian social activists, Y. T. Wu (Wu Yaozong, 1893-1979), head of the publications department of the YMCA, had by far the greatest influence on K. H. Ting and his generation of students working for change in church and society.[5] Wu was a dynamic and inspiring figure, whose own intellectual journey focused on the relevance of Christianity for social change in China. He had been converted by an American missionary and had studied at Union Theological Seminary in New York, but he was not part of the Protestant missionary establishment. In the 1930s, he moved from pacifism to the "social gospel" to an increasing identification between Christian faith and Communist ideals.

Wu's theological journey was very far from that of the indigenous church leaders who also emerged in the 1920s and 1930s, and who, in their own way, were also critical of the missionaries and the mainline churches. Evangelists such as John Sung, who had also studied at Union Seminary in New York, Watchman Nee and Wang Mingdao had an enormous influence among Christians at the grassroots.[6] The division between Wu and Chinese Christian evangelicals became a prominent feature of Chinese Protestantism, and, as we shall see, it contributed to many of the struggles that Protestants continue to face in China today.

In the mainline Christian community, Y. T. Wu was the most outspoken leader calling for a united front against Japanese aggression. By the time of the occupation of Shanghai, Wu was already moving toward identification with the position of the CPC, and by the late 1940s, he would stand firmly on the Communist side in their struggle against the Nationalists.

Ting first heard Wu speak at a student conference when he was still an undergraduate at St. John's University. Although Wu was at the time still a pacifist and opposed to taking up arms under all circumstances, he challenged students with the question of national salvation and their own political accountability. As K. H. Ting tells the story, he listened respectfully to Y. T. Wu while carrying "in one pocket my lexicon on New Testament Greek and in another my textbook on the Thirty-Nine Articles of the Church of England." The image is telling. Wu's interpretation of Christianity stood in sharp contrast to the theological approach that was being taught at St. John's University, and this came as something of a revelation to the young K. H. Ting.

> He opened up before me a whole area which I had not known to exist, and hence had never entered, but (which) was now summoning me. At that time, I felt myself to be above politics, and indeed above the world, but, on the other hand, I was quite dissatisfied with Chiang Kai-shek's non-resistance policy vis-à-vis Japanese aggression which resulted in the loss of the entire Northeast, and was disgusted with many of my school mates leading a life given to wine and nonsense, and so imbued with the compradore mentality and un-patriotism as to be discussing which was the best world power for China to become a colony of! When I saw how closely Y. T.'s love for Christ and his concern for the well-being of the people were harmonized and how his loyalty to Christ generated in him a great passion for truth, for life's ideals and for the people, I as a young man seeking something meaningful in life felt inspired and sensed that a direction for my seeking had been pointed out to me.[7]

Y. T. Wu had a lasting influence on K. H. Ting. Wu followed Ting's career in the ecumenical movement and welcomed him back to China after the establishment of the People's Republic. Ting looked up to Wu as a mentor, and he was a strong supporter of Wu's leadership of the Chinese Christian Three-Self Patriotic Movement. Intellectually, what Ting learned from Wu was not a theological perspective but an interpretation of politics and society that could be related to a liberating Christian message. In a certain sense, Wu anticipated Latin American liberation theology by drawing on Marxist social analysis to understand the world around him and work for change. He introduced Marxism to Ting's generation of Christian students, and they discovered in Wu's interpretation a Marxism that accurately described the problems facing Chinese society.

Y. T. Wu was not alone in the Christian movement in advocating the Communists' approach to social change. Cora Deng (Deng Yuzhi), Liu Liangmo, and others in the YMCA and YWCA had similar political positions. However, the discussion of Marxism and Marxist ideas of social change was a taboo in Shanghai universities and in the churches under the influence of the Nationalist government. Interest in the subject among liberal Christian intellectuals was never widespread, but the CPC was able to revive some discussion of Marxist ideas in the National Salvation Movement. Because the Ys and other student organizations were also part of this movement and shared an interest in radical social change, they became instrumental in the spread of revolutionary thinking in Shanghai. Students avidly read Edgar Snow's *Red Star over China*, published by the YMCA, when it came out in Chinese translation, and this was for many their first introduction to the ideas of the CPC. In later years, other pamphlets and books on Marxism and the Chinese Revolution would also be published by the YMCA. The work of Wu and his colleagues in the Ys enabled Marxism to become one of the moral choices available to Christian students in wartime Shanghai.

University campuses were important arenas for intellectual struggle between the Nationalists and the Communists. Part of the general strategy of the CPC was to win over students and intellectuals by working with individuals who had "leftist" leanings in groups like the YMCAs and YWCAs. The Communists welcomed the intellectuals' moral support for their cause, and some Christians admired the Communists' commitment. The CPC was more skillful than the Nationalists in attracting progressive students and intellectuals to their cause. The CPC had been legalized in China with the establishment of the Anti-Japanese United Front, and it established party branches on university campuses in western China. Whenever possible, there would be both public and secret party members.[8] The former would carry out recruitment and propaganda work, while the latter would be involved in direct action against the Japanese. For security reasons, different branches of the CPC would not usually communicate with one another, or even know who the other party members were.

Public party affiliation with the CPC was out of the question in wartime Shanghai. There, the CPC remained a highly secretive and underground organization that worked both in and through sympathetic groups in the

National Salvation Movement.[9] The Communists could not control all the organizations they worked with, but they cooperated in different ways with a variety of people, including Christians, businessmen, students and workers in order to promote nationalism and resistance against Japanese aggression.[10] CPC influence was considerable in some organizations, but Communists and their supporters were also known to exaggerate their contribution to the resistance efforts in Shanghai after the end of the war. It is therefore difficult to assess how much influence the CPC underground actually had.

By 1938, underground party branches had been established in a number of educational institutions in Shanghai, including St. John's University. Already, while an undergraduate at St. John's, Ting had heard about the activities of the Communist Party from classmates and teachers, as well as from speakers such as Y. T. Wu. St. John's was important for the CPC both because of its prestige and because it was one of the only universities that remained open in the city during the war years. The size of the student body at St. John's swelled to more than three thousand, and many of the new students were impoverished refugees. Because of the growth in the number of students from poor families, and the fact that progressive intellectuals were sympathetic to the CPC program, St. John's University became a fertile ground for recruiting CPC members and supporters. According to one estimate, there were more than sixty party members at St. John's by the end of the war, some of whom had been recruited from among the Christian students.[11]

Many of these students were involved in one way or another with programs of the YMCA and YWCA, where the CPC was also active. There they could find Christians who shared their commitment. A number of student workers in the YMCA and YWCA joined the Chinese Communist Party around this time, including Gong Pusheng, Julia Chen and Yu Pei-wen, all of whom became friends and colleagues of K. H. Ting in the student department. All three assumed prominent positions in China's foreign ministry after 1949, and they continued to value the relationships they had with Christian friends even after 1949. During wartime, working within the YMCA and YWCA was a good cover for their other activities, and they were helped and protected by staff members who were not Communists.

Many people in China and overseas have speculated or assumed that K. H. Ting also joined the Communist Party in the late 1930s or early 1940s. No substantial evidence for Ting's supposed party membership has ever been put forward, but rumors to the contrary have persisted, and the same stories have been repeated again and again.[12] The assumption is that one could not support the Communists without being a party member, and because membership is usually denied to religious believers, Christians in the CPC must have compromised their faith. The assumption is questionable, given the relationship between Christians and Communists in other times and places and the stance of many intellectuals in Ting's generation. There is no doubt that K. H. Ting supported the efforts of the CPC underground in wartime Shanghai, but it cannot be assumed, on the basis of sources that are now available to us, that he himself became a party member.

It is true that some Christians became party members, including Pu Huaren and Dong Jianwu, who had served as pastors of the church in which K. H. Ting was raised. It is also true that some TSPM leaders in the 1950s were underground CPC members, including Li Chuwen, the first general secretary, and probably a number of other early TSPM leaders. Because CPC membership records from the 1930s are not open, it is not possible to come to a conclusion that all would accept. However, one can put the question in historical perspective and assess Ting's own response to the question that has been put to him again and again.

Not everyone who sided with the Communists in the 1930s and 1940s was prepared to join the party, and support for the CPC political program did not mean identification with its strategy or worldview. Like many other intellectuals in the 1930s, K. H. Ting was becoming interested in Marxism as a means for understanding and changing society. He was identified with the progressive wing of the student movement and was part of the National Salvation Movement. Many of his friends in both movements were underground CPC members. They did not make their identities known at the time, because that would have been a breach of party discipline. By 1938, one can say that K. H. Ting was in broad agreement with the CPC approach, close to underground party members, and supportive of some their work. None of this necessarily implies that he himself joined the Communist Party.

Patricia Stranahan has argued that because the class background of most students was suspicious, student groups were never fully integrated into the CPC underground.[13] For this reason, new recruits had to be introduced by a trusted member to apply for party membership. To be so recommended for party membership was considered to be an honor. Given his own family background, Ting would not have been a likely candidate to be so honored, but this did not rule out the possibility that he may have been invited to join, given the fact that he was close to many people who were or who became underground CPC members. These included people from his own church, the YMCA and YWCA workers in the student department, and underground organizers such as Zhang Zhiyi, Xiao Zhitian, and Feng Wenbin. Zhao Puchu, then a lay Buddhist leader, was also a covert CPC organizer in the Shanghai of the 1930s and 1940s.[14] Ting became lifelong friends with many CPC members, and he worked closely with Zhao Puchu in the 1980s and 1990s. But one cannot conclude that an individual was or was not a party member by reason of association.

Because party membership in Shanghai was secret, one may not have known that close friends and colleagues were part of the CPC. K. H. Ting has recalled that he did not have any direct or conscious relationship with anyone in the Communist Party.

In those days, I didn't even know that certain people around me were Communist Party members, but we did have certain people who were sympathetic with the political platform of the CPC, and we met quite often in study groups around Y. T. Wu. My assumption was that everyone of us was not a Communist. In those days, it was a very, very secret thing for a person to be a Communist Party member. Even party members would not know who were (other) Communists. So, I just assumed that we were intellectuals who were progressive and sympathetic to the political platform of the Communist Party . . . I think . . . the underground Communist Party probably considered me as a good friend, because what I did was to protect the students, and the left-wing students.[15]

In retrospect, this may sound naïve, but, as we shall see, it is consistent with Ting's reasoning when he decided to return to China in 1951. Many committed intellectuals in the Shanghai of the 1930s, active in the resistance movement, could argue in the same way. In the 1980s and 1990s, K. H. Ting repeatedly denied that he was ever a member of the CPC or any other political party.[16] Those who continue to argue to the contrary have wanted to cast doubt on his integrity and his leadership of the Chinese church. Ting has never made any secret of his support for the CPC, but this is quite a different matter. It is never possible to prove a negative, but it is just as reasonable to take Ting at his word as it is to pursue a line of questioning that cannot be finally resolved given the sources that are currently available.

In the passage just quoted, Ting again speaks of the importance of Y. T. Wu for his understanding of the relationship between Christians and Communists. Ting developed a social and political analysis similar to that of Wu, but they differed in their approach to theology and the church. Unlike K. H. Ting, Y. T. Wu was not interested in a broad range of theological and ecclesiological questions. In one interview, Ting spoke of the difference between them:

Somehow I never felt that his interest in theology was quite complete. That has always been my feeling about Y. T. Wu. He showed no interest in many theological problems (other than those having to do with society). I have never mentioned that to anybody until now, actually. But there is this little distance between us.

And then some of the difficulties since Liberation in winning certain groups of Christians to Three-Self, I think, has been due to this lack of attention to certain theological issues. Today, in our Three-Self Movement, we still have people who got used to thinking that the YMCA and the YWCA are the only good form of Christian movement. They tend to be unsympathetic to issues that certain (Christian) groups consider to be terribly important, and they are usually neglected. That makes people feel that the Three-Self Movement is intransigent on these problems. But in those days, I (myself) never thought that was very important.[17]

The "little distance" he speaks of may also help to explain why Ting would *not* choose to join the Communist Party in the 1930s. It was a question of churchmanship. His own faith and theological interests were never limited to the concern to relate theology to social and political issues. This difference will also help to interpret the contrast between Y. T. Wu's approach to Three-Self in the 1950s and 1960s and Ting's leadership in the 1980s and 1990s.

STUDENT WORK AND THE YMCA

K. H. Ting did not immediately begin work at the YMCA in the months following his graduation. This was in part because of his change in career plans, but also because of the confusion and unsettledness of the times. The battle for Shanghai meant that the entire municipality had become a war zone. All over the city, people were preoccupied with questions of survival and just getting by. Refugees were flooding in, but many families and even whole institutions were trying to get out. St. Peter's and other churches again became havens for refugees from the countryside, and the hospitals were filled with the dying and the wounded. The Japanese air raids caused extensive damage throughout the city. As the battle wore on, everyone saw that it was only a matter of time before the city would fall.

All through the late summer and fall, K. H. was meeting with friends and fellow students about their response to the situation of war and dislocation. Even before the beginning of the occupation, he had helped organize the Christian Service League, whose membership was drawn from students associated with St. John's University and Middle School, St. Mary's Hall and Jinling (Ginling) College, which had moved to Shanghai from Nanjing. In December, Ting was elected chairman of the league. Under his leadership, the Christian Service League became quite successful in raising funds, collecting clothing for soldiers, and working with refugees and needy students.[18] Still, there were those who felt that the league did not bring students into close enough contact with the church, and so a St. John's faculty member was appointed director of its religious activities.[19]

It was clear that Ting's main interest in working with students was not to relate them more closely to the church but to relate Christian faith more closely to the movement for national salvation. As an undergraduate, he had been active in the "Shanghai Christian Student Union" (*Shanghai jidujiao xuesheng tuanti lianhehui*), known by the abbreviated name of *Shanghai Lian*. This was an umbrella organization that brought together student YM and YWCAs and student Christian fellowships from the thirty-five univer-

K. H. Ting, Siu-may, and YMCA colleague Yu Pei-wen, circa 1945. Reproduced from the collection of Jack Edelman.

sities, colleges and middle schools in the city. Student workers were mostly volunteers drawn from the schools and universities, and they were deeply committed to their cause. *Shanghai Lian* was divided into separate departments concerned with organization, religion, recreation, study and international relationships. There were also separate areas for work concerned with Christian and non-Christian universities and Christian and non-Christian middle schools.

In September 1937, *Shanghai Lian* had decided to actively support resistance efforts against Japan. It would do this through fundraising, work with refugees, care for injured soldiers, summer retreats and other student meetings, mobilizing community support, and the publication of the student magazine *Lian Sheng*.[20] *Shanghai Lian* also organized student appeals for international support in China's war effort. Student Christian Movements (SCMs) had special access to Christians in the West by virtue of their participation in international ecumenical organizations such as the World Students' Christian Federation (WSCF) and the International YMCA and

YWCA. *Shanghai Lian* became an important force in the resistance effort and informally linked the students to the underground work of the Communist Party. Because the schools and colleges were all in the International Settlement or the French Concession, the student movement enjoyed a certain amount of freedom of action until the attack on Pearl Harbor. And because its work was Christian in origin, the SCMs were more likely to be tolerated by the authorities. Both factors made *Shanghai Lian* a protective umbrella for progressive and left-wing students.

Early the next year, K. H. Ting was appointed secretary of the student department of the Shanghai YMCA. In this capacity he also became executive secretary of *Shanghai Lian*. Although this latter appointment was *ex officio*, it soon became a major part of his work and interest. Ting was accountable to the National Committee of the YM and YWCAs and to the National Student Division, headed by Kiang Wen-han (Jiang Wenhan, 1908-1984), who was already internationally known in the ecumenical movement for his work with students. He worked with a number of colleagues during this time who would become lifelong friends. In addition to those mentioned above, they would include Zheng Jianye, Luo Guanzong, Yang Shouning, Yin Xiang, Chen Zhonghao and Huang Peiyong.[21]

Kiang, Y. T. Wu and most of the senior leadership of the YMCA and YWCA were based in West China during most of the occupation. They visited Shanghai infrequently in the late 1930s, and not at all after December 1941. Their absence gave the young YMCA and YWCA secretaries a great deal more freedom and responsibility than they otherwise would have had. It meant that they had to make decisions about routine work on their own, because communication with "Free China" was irregular. It also gave them the opportunity to work out their own strategies in the broader student movement, and this was invaluable in the development of their leadership skills.

In his first yearly work report, Ting listed the following five areas of responsibility:

(1) To promote the Student Christian Movement, organizing and guiding Christian fellowships among students in all of Shanghai's colleges and middle schools;
(2) To develop service opportunities and activities for students;
(3) To train student leaders;
(4) To encourage opportunities for student reflection;
(5) To assist and provide relief for students in straightened circumstances.[22]

These five areas encompassed a broad range of responsibilities. Ting's time was organized according to the work he did among Christian students, students in general and students in need of relief and assistance. Much of this work centered on what today would be termed consciousness-raising activity. For example, Ting organized charity bazaars and book sales not only to raise funds but also to increase students' awareness of the war and social conditions.[23] Students appealed to the business community to support the war effort, which gave them experience in approaching the rich and powerful and learning about the class differences in Chinese society. Bible studies and lectures on subjects such as "students and democracy" and "understanding the times" attracted a great many students, and they became opportunities to develop a new perspective on China's social problems. Exposure tours were organized to help middle-class students better understand the contradictions of the society in which they were living. They would visit factories, housing areas and refugee camps, and meet with the poor. Then they would tour the famous pleasure center known as the Great World, where anything could be bought by the wealthy for the right price. Finally, they would reflect on what they had seen and heard with a student leader. This exposure process, organized by K. H. Ting and other colleagues, would inevitably lead them to a more sympathetic understanding of the progressive cause.[24]

Relief and assistance for impoverished students was a very practical aspect of the work of the YMCA Student Department, and separate from the activities of *Shanghai Lian*. K. H. Ting also became executive secretary of the Shanghai Student Relief Committee, which provided scholarship support and ran a dining hall and youth hostel for students in need. A National Student Relief Committee was set up in 1938 to coordinate relief efforts all over China. It was itself an outgrowth of the Shanghai Student Relief Committee, which had been started the previous year. Funds for the committee came largely from international sources, including the WSCF, World Student Relief and International Student Service, and they were administered by the National Committee of the YMCA and YWCA through twenty-five local committees. Such funds also supported indirectly the kind of work Ting was doing in *Shanghai Lian* by directing support to students in need and maintaining contact with them.

In addition to coordinating relief efforts, student relief committees were also involved in work-study projects, mass education, rural development and direct social service. In order to understand the social situation, the student secretaries organized research projects on price trends, inflation, housing and working conditions.[25] This provided student secretaries with concrete experience in relating their religious and political commitment to the conditions of the poor. It also brought them into closer contact with students from poor families, which made them more conscious of the need for social justice and fundamental change.

The National Student Christian Conference met for the last two weeks of August 1939. The conference was held in Guandu, near the southwestern city of Kunming, where a number of eastern universities had been relocated following the Japanese invasion. It was difficult to hold a national conference of any kind during the war years, for funds were scarce and travel arrangements difficult. Still, more than twenty representatives came from eight SCMs in both occupied and "Free China" to attend the Guandu conference. K. H. Ting and Julia Chen represented the Shanghai YMCA and YWCA at Guandu. They sailed from Shanghai to Hong Kong and then to Hanoi, from where they traveled overland to Kunming. The journey to and from Kunming took more than two months.

One of the speakers at the Guandu conference was Professor T. C. Chao (Zhao Zichen, 1888-1979), who was then in Kunming for a sabbatical year. He was dean of the Yenching (Yanjing) School of Religion, and China's most creative theological voice. Deeply immersed in traditional Chinese culture, Chao combined a philosophical theology with a careful reading of the Bible and a gentle mysticism. He was well known internationally as an influential interpreter of developments in China. During the war years, Chao became an Anglican priest, ordained by Bishop R. O. Hall in Hong Kong. In 1948, he was elected to be one of the first presidents of the World Council of Churches, but he resigned after the outbreak of the Korean War, and shortly thereafter fell into political disfavor in China.[26] Ting met Chao for the first time in Guandu, and he saw him again in Amsterdam in 1948. He respected T. C. Chao, but there is little evidence that he was influenced by his theology. Speaking in 1988 on the centennial of Chao's birth, Ting described him as a "patriot" who had been unfairly rejected by overzealous revolutionaries in the early 1950s.[27]

The Guandu Conference helped student organizations in different parts of China understand that they were facing similar problems and fighting for the same things. This was significant because it put the SCMs, and by extension the YMCAs and YWCAs which sponsored them, firmly on the side of the progressives in the Anti-Japanese United Front. The delegates sent open letters to both the WSCF and the Japanese SCM, reiterating their stance against Japanese aggression, but also expressing their hope for strengthening international Christian fellowship. The conference issued a manifesto which spoke in no uncertain terms about the war and students' determination to work for a free and democratic "New China." It declared that Christian students would have to match their faith with their actions as they responded to the "needs of the times." This implied support for both the united front against Japan and democratic change in the Nationalist government.[28] K. H. Ting had helped to draft this manifesto, and he was also named as one of three secretaries of a National Association of Student Christian Unions which was formed in Guandu.[29] After the conference, he and Julia Chen returned to Shanghai, accompanied by Kiang Wenhan.

The following year, *Shanghai Lian* held its own representative assembly, where Y. T. Wu delivered the keynote address. This meeting endorsed the promotion of four movements or emphases among students: a "movement of commitment" to give students self-confidence so that they could reform their lifestyle and build strong characters; an "understanding Christianity movement" to help students learn about the biblical implications for society and for their own lives; a "movement to understand the times," especially the social and political realities of China; and an "international friendship movement" to develop overseas contact and promote the students' message.[30] In this and other actions, the Shanghai assembly went further than Guandu in endorsing a progressive social program for the churches and the nation, and once again K. H. Ting was one of the principal organizers.

Because of the wartime conditions, *Shanghai Lian* was unable to act on most of these proposals. The students' rhetoric went far beyond what was practical for the times, and the situation became much more restrictive after the outbreak of the Pacific war. By this time, there was little information of any kind about the activities of *Shanghai Lian,* and sometime in 1942, the organization effectively ceased to exist. With the occupation of the International Settlement and the French Concession by the Japanese, all resistance work of an open and public nature came to a halt. Nevertheless, the direction in which *Shanghai Lian* and the students associated with it were moving was clear. Reports, reflections and reminiscences about *Shanghai Lian* confirm that it was more closely identified with the left in wartime China than the Protestant denominations, the national YM and YWCAs or the SCMs in other cities. This was largely due to the influence of underground CPC members associated with the student movement, but in no small measure, it may also be attributed to the consciousness-raising efforts of K. H. Ting and other student leaders.

Emily Honig has argued that the first organization to provide political education for Shanghai's women textile workers was not the Communist Party but the YWCA. It taught them how to read, how to speak in public and how to analyze social structures.[31] Although not as well documented, *Shanghai Lian* played a similar role in transforming the political and social awareness of Shanghai students in the late 1930s and early 1940s.

RETURN TO THEOLOGICAL STUDIES
AND THE PRIESTHOOD

Although K. H. Ting had decided not to enter the priesthood, he never lost his interest in theology. He read theological books when he worked for the YMCA during the war years, which was unusual for those in the student movement, many of whom thought that such study had no relevance for the issues of the day. Ting also continued his association with St. Peter's Church and the Sheng Gong Hui. William P. ("Billy") Roberts became bishop of Shanghai in November 1937, following the resignation of Bishop Graves in January of that year.[32] He was much more open to the work of the SCM than his predecessor. Roberts encouraged Ting in his position as secretary of the student department of the YMCA, and he wrote to say that the YMCA offered "wonderful opportunities for Christian service."[33]

Ting began to reconsider his decision about the priesthood shortly after he began his work at the YMCA. He credits Luther Tucker, an American

Episcopalian working with the WSCF with playing an important role in this regard. Ellis Norris Tucker had been a professor of mathematics at St. John's when Ting was a student there, and perhaps Luther learned about Ting through this relative.[34] Luther Tucker arrived in Shanghai in late 1938 as a traveling student secretary attempting to create understanding between SCMs in China and Japan. He got to know K.H., supported his work in the YMCA and student movement, and thought he should be ordained in this capacity, even though he would not necessarily be attached to a particular parish church. Tucker spoke with newly elected Bishop Roberts, a personal friend, about the possibility, and Roberts concurred. Arrangements were now in place for Ting to once again become a candidate for holy orders.

In 1940, K. H. wrote Dr. Hawks Pott at St. John's to inform him of his change of heart. He said that he now saw the value of a closer relationship between the SCM and the churches. "At least in China," he wrote, "the SCM is not existing as a very close component part of the Church and is not sufficiently educating its membership in a deeper appropriation of the Church, even though I think the latter is not entirely without responsibility for the situation."[35] His decision to enter the ministry, as explained in this letter, again illustrates the importance that K. H. Ting attached to the church. Like many in the student movement, he continued to be critical of its conservatism and political stance, but he also believed that the church played an essential role in the work of the SCM. Also in 1940, he applied to ordination for the diaconate in the Sheng Gong Hui, and his application was accepted by the Standing Committee of the Kiangsu (Jiangsu) Diocese.

Ting resumed his theological studies while working for the YMCA and *Shanghai Lian*. The year he returned to St. John's School of Theology there were only nine students, four in the upper class and five in the lower, including one Baptist and the wife of a candidate for holy orders.[36] Ting was a full-time B.D. student for only about a year, and much of the work he did on his own. Amidst all his other responsibilities, he attended the required classes and worked on his thesis until his graduation in June 1942.

The theology that was taught at St. John's was liberal and Anglican. The Sheng Gong Hui in Shanghai was part of the American Protestant Episcopal mission. At St. John's, all of the professors were either American or Chinese who had studied in the United States. Besides Hawks Pott, who taught Christian ethics, the faculty included William Sung, who was acting president; Montgomery Hunt Thropp, who served as dean and professor of Old Testament and church polity; John Williams Nichols, who taught in theology and church history; Y. Y. Tsu, professor of pastoral theology, who later became a bishop; Chen Li, who taught church history; Millidge Penderell Walker, who lectured on church finance and bookkeeping; and Tang Zhongmo, who taught New Testament. Bishop Roberts taught homiletics, and other Shanghai clergy served as adjuncts.

The late 1930s came toward the end of an era in Anglican theology that extended from Charles Gore, who edited the influential *Lux Mundi* in 1889, to William Temple and the onset of the Second World War. According to Archbishop Michael Ramsey, theology in this half century was characterized by an "emphasis on the Incarnation, the striving after synthesis between theology and contemporary culture which the term 'liberal' broadly denotes, (and) the frequent shift of interest from dogma to apologetics." Contemporary trends in secular thought, including evolution and socialism, were regarded not as "enemies to be fought but as friends who can provide new illuminations of the truth that is in Christ." The best theology written during this time was ready "to risk untidiness and rough edges and apparently insecure fences" for it is "in and through the intellectual turmoil of the time—and not aloofness from it—that the Church teaches the catholic faith."[37]

Anglican and Episcopal thinking in the first half of the twentieth century remained largely isolated from continental and American theology. This was to a large extent true of the Protestant Episcopal Church in the United States and its mission in China. In contrast to the christocentric turn in Protestant theology, associated with Karl Barth, Emil Brunner, Rudolf Bultmann, Paul Tillich and other German theologians, Anglican theology was not concerned with the recovery of Reformation themes and confessions. There was no interest in the creation of either a church dogmatics or a new systematic theology. Steering a pragmatic course between the entrenched positions of both the evangelicals and the Anglo-Catholics—and between Geneva and Rome—it was attempting to follow a tolerant and encompassing *via media*. Anglican theology pursued a dialogue with the various "isms," but it accepted the authority of scripture and the church fathers. Attentive to the centrality of worship, spirituality and the life of prayer, Anglican theology was both liberal (or modern) and catholic (or traditional). It was responsive to the concerns of society and attentive to the religious quest of individuals as it maintained a high sense of churchmanship rooted in the Bible and the Christian tradition.

In later years, Ting criticized theological education at St. John's as of "the Thirty-nine-Articles" type, meaning that it was not very relevant for the situation of the church in China. This may say more about the way theology was being taught at St. John's than the influence it had on his own theological formation. Many of the ideas that Ting developed in his writings are derived from the Anglican theology of this era: the centrality of the Incarnation and the Trinity; the connection between creation and redemption; a historical and critical approach to the Bible; love as God's major attribute; dialogue between Christianity and contemporary culture; the catholicity of the church. His theology over the last seventy years has been remarkably consistent. His interest has been to relate enduring theological themes to the social situation in which Christians lived, while, at the same time, preserving the authentic faith of the church. This reflects the words of Michael Ramsey, quoted above, that theology must discover its vocation "in and through the intellectual turmoil of the time—and not aloofness from it."

Ting made use of his theological studies in the work he did at the YMCA. There he had responsibility for religious activities and would regularly lead Bible studies and worship services for students. He frequently wrote for the student magazine *Lian Sheng*, but unfortunately, his writings from this publication have not been preserved in the archives or libraries I have visited. Yet at least one of his biblical reflections from this time survives. It was published in the YMCA student magazine, and it affords a glimpse of Ting's emerging theological and biblical perspective. The reflection is actually a series of short Christmas meditations on what it means for Jesus to come into our world, each of which illustrates the relationship between the Incarnation and daily life in wartime Shanghai. The third meditation is based on the passage in which the angel of the Lord meets the shepherds tending their flocks and says, "Do not be afraid; for see—I am bringing you good news of great joy for all the people" (Luke 2:10). It is short enough to be quoted here in full.

> Fear is the most common phenomenon on this earth. Millions of people live in fear all the time because of some event or another. Fear is like the giant hand of the devil hovering above us, ready to seize hold of our lives.
>
> What people basically fear is insecurity. People need to have a sense of security, for if a person feels insecure, if he or she feels that there is nothing to "depend on," that "food, clothing or shelter" are threatened, then that person is afraid. Millions of people today fear that tomorrow they will be jobless and their wives and children will starve to death.
>
> Fear and anxiety cause people to shrink back and become passive. Only active struggle can root out fear.
>
> "Do not be afraid . . ." This is the gospel the shepherds heard. "Therefore I tell you, do not worry about your life, what you will eat . . . what you will wear." Yes! What is the use of being anxious? "And can any of you by worrying add a single hour to your span of life? But strive first for the kingdom of God and his righteousness, and all these things will be given to you as well."
>
> Only by participating in the great work of "building of the kingdom of God on earth" can we overcome fear. Great love drives out fear. Haven't we seen mother love expressed in a life of never flinching from difficulties or dangers? Only when we begin to see the people through the eyes of fervent love, only when we deliberately sacrifice our own interests for their sakes (which is also for our own sakes) in order to establish the kingdom of heaven on earth, only then will we be truly able to overcome fear and hold back the devil's hand. In that kingdom, the people will no longer fear insecurity of any kind.
>
> This is the good news of great joy for all the people.[38]

This approach to Bible study has always been popular in the SCM, but here it is cast in K. H. Ting's personal style and reveals his own wrestling with the biblical message. He interprets the gospel in light of contemporary experiences of suffering and struggle and then suggests a way forward. Many Anglican themes that Ting was learning at St. John's can be seen in this meditation. His interest in struggling to change the social situation is illustrated here as well. The interpretation is disarmingly simple and straightforward, but it would have challenged and encouraged the students in occupied Shanghai for whom it was intended.

His relationships in the international ecumenical movement contributed to Ting's emerging theological and social perspective. Luther Tucker has been mentioned as a person who encouraged K. H. Ting in discerning his priestly vocation. Michael Bruce, who had been sent to China from the British SCM, was also in Shanghai in the late 1930s, and he too became a close friend of Ting. Both Tucker and Bruce were, like K. H. himself, ecumenical Anglicans who began their careers in student work. Robert Mackie and Paul Moritz of the WSCF also visited K. H. in Shanghai during this time, and Mackie would play an important role in Ting's future work in the ecumenical movement.

But the most important and lasting international friendship from these years was the one that he developed with the English missionary David M. Paton. Paton arrived in Shanghai on 12 December 1940 and stayed for only a month before he left for Beijing (then called Peiping) to do language work. During that month, he and K. H. Ting had several long conversations, and these left a lasting impression on both men. Their meeting marked the beginning of a relationship that continued, through correspondence and infrequent meetings, until Paton's death fifty years later. David Paton was working on a "liberal catholic" approach to church and society inspired by the work of F. D. Maurice and Roland Allen. Like K. H., he was often critical of the church and supportive of progressive social causes. Paton's writings, especially *Christian Missions and the Judgment of God*, were widely respected among those with whom he worked in the SCM and in the ecumenical movement as a whole.[39] They were also well received in China.

It was also through his international ecumenical contacts that Ting was introduced to the Oxford Group Movement. This movement was started in Oxford in 1921 by Frank N. D. Buchman, an American Lutheran pastor, to promote "a program of life issuing in personal, social, racial, national and supranational change." Within a decade, it had spread to many other parts of the world, including China. The Oxford Group Movement concentrated on small group experience as a means of Christian renewal, emphasizing sharing, guidance, inner conversion and the moral strength of the individual within the small fellowship group.[40] Oxford "Groupism" presented an uncompromising version of Christian faith and fellowship that appealed to those who saw the church as utterly compromised and its adherents as lukewarm. In 1939, it became known as Moral Re-armament in many parts of the world.

The movement attracted a certain following in the Chinese student movement of the late 1930s, and Oxford Group fellowships were set up on a number of Shanghai campuses.[41] K. H. Ting would have been connected with these groups as part of his work with the YMCA, but he was for a time genuinely sympathetic to this movement. Oxford Group fellowships may have appealed to his sense of religious devotion. He was seen by some contemporaries in the SCM as "too religious," which implied that he was not "political" enough, and participation in Oxford Group fellowships would have been indicative of this. But his relationship with the Oxford Groups was consistent with the picture we have of him from this time, for Ting took his religious and political involvement to be complementary aspects of his life and work.

The Oxford Group Movement and Moral Re-armament are not to be confused with the Oxford Movement, a nineteenth-century movement of catholic restoration and renewal within the Church of England. K. H. Ting wrote his B.D. thesis—which does not survive—on this earlier nineteenth-century Oxford Movement. The two movements associated with Oxford were not at all alike, and it is interesting that Ting should be drawn to both of them. He recalls presenting a favorable view of the Oxford Movement in this thesis, even though it was written under time constraints so that his Bachelor of Divinity degree could be awarded in June 1942.[42] The subject of the thesis is far removed from the concerns of the student movement and his emerging social and political consciousness, but it again reflects K. H. Ting's abiding interest in the catholicity of the church.

Ting became a deacon in early 1942, and he was ordained to the priesthood at Holy Trinity Pro-Cathedral by Bishop Roberts on 1 June. He was not attached to a particular parish, for he continued his work at the YMCA. Much later he recalled that his mother encouraged him to be a priest when he continued to have doubts about his calling. She quoted the words of St. Paul in 1 Corinthians 4 that he should not judge himself too harshly, but that he should above all be trustworthy.[43] Despite personal concerns about his ability to preach and his suitability for the priesthood, K. H. took his mother's words from St. Paul to heart. Upon his ordination, she presented her son with the clerical vestments that had belonged to her father and which she had carefully preserved since his death some twenty-five years earlier.

After ordination, Ting lectured part time on religion and the Bible as literature at St. John's University.[44] He also became attached to the historic Church of Our Savior, where he served every Sunday and preached once a month. He remembers bringing quite a number of student activists from *Shanghai Lian* to the church in the French Concession and taking part in its youth fellowship.[45] There was not much happening in the student movement after the start of the Pacific war, and this kind of youth fellowship became a way of rechanneling the energies of progressive students. It also introduced them to the church, thus strengthening the link between the church and the SCM.

MARRIAGE, THE STUDENT CHURCH
AND THE END OF THE WAR

The Student Christian Movement brought like-minded individuals together, inside and outside the church. A close camaraderie developed among co-workers in the movement, and it often led to close friendships and more long-lasting attachments. One of the students whom K. H. Ting met in *Shanghai Lian* was Siu-may Kuo (Guo Xiumei, 1916-1995), who was head of the organization department that worked to strengthen student groups on the various campuses. Siu-may Kuo was born on 5 May 1916 in the central city of Wuhan, where her father, who was originally from Guangdong, was employed as chief engineer for the Wuhan Iron Works. Her mother died when she was not yet one year old, and her father subsequently remarried and took the family to Shanghai. By this time, the family had grown to include two younger brothers and a sister, in addition to Siu-may and two older brothers. Siu-may began her studies at Yenjing University in Peiping (Beijing) in 1936, but because of poor health, she had to withdraw and return home to Shanghai for a period of rest and recuperation.

By then, St. John's had become coeducational, and once she was strong enough, Kuo resumed her studies there. She learned about Christianity through her activity in the student movement and was baptized in 1940. Siu-may received her degree in education from St. John's in 1942. At Yenjing, Siu-may Kuo had come to know Gong Pusheng (Kung Pu-sheng), K. H.'s counterpart in the student department of the YWCA, and her sister Gong Peng (Kung Peng), who would become Premier Zhou Enlai's personal secretary in the late 1940s. Kuo and the Gong sisters had also been schoolmates at St. Mary's Hall. Ting recalls that it was Gong Pusheng who brought him and Siu-may together.[46] After a short courtship, they were married at the Church of Our Savior on 12 June 1942, just after both had received their degrees and after K. H. had been ordained to the priesthood.

Siu-may used to tell a story about her marriage to K. H. that was apparently quite popular in the Ting family. On the day of the ceremony, K. H. was standing outside the church waiting for the service to begin. A group of his friends walked by and seeing that the church was all decorated and how he was dressed they asked if there was to be a wedding. "Yes," he replied. "Whose wedding is it?" they asked. "Mine," he said, without a hint of irony. She would always laugh at the end of the story which so obviously reflects K.H.'s diffidence and sense of self-deprecation in matters that concern his private life. After their marriage, the couple lived with Ting's parents, who now lived in a large house at 31A Brennan Road.

Siu-may stayed on to teach at St. John's and St. Mary's Hall. She even became the headmistress of St. Mary's for a time, before it merged with the Mateer School. Some years later, she worked for the *United Daily*, the Central News Agency, and, after the end of the war, she was connected to the United Nations' Relief and Rehabilitation Agency (UNRRA). She and K. H.

worked closely together for the next five decades, and they shared a common commitment to the Chinese Revolution. Their home was open to friends and colleagues wherever they lived, and it was Siu-may who made sure that their guests were well taken care of. Her outgoing and effusive personality matched Ting's shyness and introversion. Siu-may had her own career, but she was also there to advise K. H. in his work and responsibilities.

By mid-1942, Shanghai was not only an "isolated island" but also a "dark world" in which there was increasing repression and little communication with the rest of China. After Pearl Harbor, the British, the Americans and other citizens from allied countries were put into internment camps, where they would remain until the end of the war in 1945.[47] K. H. was still working with the YMCA, but there was less and less to do after the outbreak of the Pacific war, and there was increasing danger for those who were involved in resistance efforts.

T. Z. Koo (Gu Ziren, 1887 - 1971), a senior YMCA leader, was in Shanghai during the occupation, and in 1942 he was approached by Community Church (the present International Church) to become its acting pastor. Koo was active in the ecumenical movement and was a popular interpreter of Chinese Christianity in the West, so it was natural that the congregation of this English-speaking nondenominational church would turn to him. Up until then, the Community Church had always had an American pastor. All missionaries and foreign clergy were now in internment camps, and so no one was left to serve the English-speaking residents in Shanghai. Koo was an Anglican layman, and he declined the church's offer, but he did agree to chair the church's Committee on Pulpit Supply in which capacity he arranged for people to preach and conduct services. Koo later approached K. H. Ting and asked him to assist on a regular basis at Community Church, and Ting agreed. The next year, T. Z. Koo decided to leave Shanghai, and Ting was appointed acting pastor of Community Church. This was an unusual appointment for a young Chinese Anglican priest, and it was also Ting's first and only pastorate. He and Siu-may moved from his parents' home to the small house adjoining the church.

The congregation of Community Church was drawn from many countries, but it was commonly referred to as the "American Church." There was only one worship service during the week, on Sunday morning at eleven o'clock. The order of worship was Protestant and ecumenical, an early example of the type of union church services that one finds today in many cities all over the world. The service was supposed to last for exactly one hour, with fifteen minutes for the sermon and careful attention given to the ministry of music. Worship at the Community Church was conducted "decently and in good order" in a form and manner that was appropriate for the business and diplomatic community who formed the majority of the congregation.

The church board members were either Europeans from neutral countries or English-speaking Chinese. The board had appointed Ting as pastor, and the members took their work and responsibilities very seriously. They met regularly to discuss and decide on church business with the pastor. One board member worked in the church office every morning, and two secretaries from the congregation were kept busy throughout the week. The church was a center for the international community in wartime Shanghai just as it had been earlier, and the Tings had many social obligations. There were teas and lunches they had to arrange, and Sunday dinner was a time for entertaining board members. The Community Church had good facilities for such social functions, as one can see when visiting the church today. The Tings also received regular invitations to visit church members in their homes. In addition, there were many weddings, for the church was one of the few places in Shanghai that conducted marriage services for foreigners. Ting remembers writing a little booklet in English for the prospective bride and bridegroom concerning marriage and family life; it included an appropriate selection of prayers.[48] Wedding receptions were held after the ceremony, and the pastor and his wife were always in attendance.

Many Community Church members were in the Shanghai internment camps, and Ting also had the responsibility to minister to them. He visited the camps when allowed to do so and was called in to conduct funeral services when someone died. The contrast between the social whirl of Community Church and the deprivation in the internment camps must have been striking, but Ting was able to serve Shanghai's international community effectively in both situations. Ting's ability to work naturally and unselfconsciously in the ecumenical world in later years must in part be attributed to this early pastoral experience.

Shortly after he went to the Community Church, and while T. Z. Koo was still in Shanghai, Ting proposed starting a nondenominational Student Church, which would meet for worship, fellowship and discussion when the facilities of the Community Church were not in use by the congregation. Koo, who himself had been active in the SCM, was supportive of the idea, and upon his recommendation, it was approved by the board. Because there was little work in the YMCA and other student organizations, K. H. Ting was able to recruit colleagues and other clergy to help with the Student Church. His lifelong friend and fellow Anglican Zheng Jianye (also known as C. Y. Tsen) became a key person in the Student Church Organizing Committee, which was chaired by Lanier Yang (Yang Liyi). They recruited others to help with Student Church services, including Peter W. H. Tsai (Cai Wenhao), who later joined the staff of the Church of Christ in China.

Community Church was prepared to host this new fellowship, but it was unlikely that the congregation knew very much about its activities. The Student Church met for worship on Sunday afternoons so as not to conflict with either Community Church worship or services at other churches. Nevertheless, the idea of beginning an ecumenical student fellowship was met with resistance by some local churches. To tell the story in K. H. Ting's own words,

When we started the student service we encountered a lot of obstacles from the churches in Shanghai. The pastors of many of the churches . . . were against us; they said we were drawing away young people from their churches. But actually this was not true. We wanted students to come, not young people in general, especially not young people in the churches. Many of the participants in student services came from Jiaotong University, because there were very enthusiastic Christian professors there, and they brought their students to the student services. And I think (they) liked the student services because they were more lively than services in churches.

At that time, Bishop Roberts was either in concentration camp or in the United States. We had a new bishop, Bishop Yu Enci, a Chinese.* He was a very good friend of our family; again, he was rector of St. Peter's Church . . . Because of his friendliness towards our whole family, he was sympathetic to our student services. He was the preacher of the first student service. At that time he became very important in Shanghai among the churches, because it was already after Pearl Harbor, and the Japanese had already occupied the International Settlement and the French Concession. Bishop Yu was (regarded as) the leader of the Protestant churches, so with his support, we were able to carry on. And before very long, the pastors in Shanghai realized that we weren't drawing people away from their churches, because the participants were mainly non-Christians from various universities. The student YMCA secretaries at that time didn't have very much to do because student activities were not allowed. So the student service became important.[49]

Services at the Student Church began in August 1942.[50] More important than the worship services were the discussion groups and resistance activities of the students who came together. These activities illustrate the work supportive of resistance activities that K. H. Ting continued to be involved in during the 1940s. The discussion groups focused on social and political issues and involved both Christian and non-Christian students, including many activists who had been part of *Shanghai Lian*. Sometimes the discussions would involve visiting speakers who brought reports on the war effort and news from other parts of China. The Tings were now living in the Scout House on the grounds of Community Church, and their home was often filled with friends and visitors from the Student Church, some of whom would come and talk into the night, and even sleep in their sitting room. The students could meet safely in their home and at Community Church, for although it was under Japanese surveillance, as a church it did not attract undue attention.

Many students learned about socialism and the CPC through their participation in the Student Church. This was clearly part of its purpose. The

---

* Bishop Roberts was in the United States, and he returned to Shanghai in December 1945. Bishop Yu was consecrated as assistant bishop on 31 May 1942, but he died two years later.

Student Church was an ecumenical fellowship that also became a cover for student activities organized by the CPC underground. In extraordinary times, the church has always had a role to play as a sanctuary, a forum for social and political discussion, and a center of resistance. Many years later, Peter Tsai spoke critically about the discussion groups and other Student Church activities because of their political content. Referring to the political discussion conducted under church auspices, he said the discussion groups organized by K. H. Ting were "very lively, perhaps too lively" for a Christian fellowship.[51] This criticism notwithstanding, Shanghai's Student Church may also be seen as an appropriate response of Christians living under foreign occupation. It has been termed by a contemporary Chinese church historian to be an important source for the development of a contextualized Christianity in China.[52]

Across the street from the Community Church stood the Shanghai American School. It had been taken over as the headquarters of the Japanese Army in early 1942. In 1943 or 1944, a Japanese pastor named Sakamoto was assigned to the Community Church and asked the Tings to cooperate with him. He said he could intercede on their behalf if they had any trouble with the authorities. They treated him with courtesy, but they did not know if he knew what was going on at the Student Church. Their relationship was strained because the Tings never knew if he was there to help them or to spy on them.[53] In any case, the work of the Student Church continued up until the last months of the war.

On another occasion, a Japanese soldier knocked on the door of their home. Siu-may Kuo remembers that they had "subversive" literature in the kitchen which they thought had been discovered. But the soldier was not interested in these materials. He was only nineteen or twenty years old and lonely, and he asked if he could be treated as the Tings' adopted son. They told him that they were too young to be his parents but that he was welcome in their home. He returned often, sometimes to talk, sometimes for a meal and sometimes just to stand outside the gate and sing Japanese songs.[54] The Tings' Christian hospitality was extended to people in every sector of society in Shanghai: Chinese, European and even Japanese.

As the war turned against them, the Japanese became worried about the rumors that the Communist controlled New Fourth Army, which had been fighting around the city for the past year, would enter Shanghai. There were increasing guerrilla attacks against the military and the government, and more Japanese soldiers could be seen patrolling the streets. By the early summer of 1945, Germany had already surrendered, but the Japanese army in Shanghai refused to believe that the end of the Pacific war was just a matter of time. They tightened their control over the city and occupied many larger buildings around the American School, including Community Church. The church could now only be used on Sundays. The Tings were forced to move out of their home and stayed in a nearby apartment, at the invitation of a single European woman from the congregation.

The Japanese formally surrendered on 15 August 1945. Nationalist troops came to Shanghai by plane to take over from the Japanese, and they began to reestablish control. It was important for the Nationalists to take over important cities such as Shanghai because of the looming prospects of civil war with the Communists. The Tings and their friends in the Student Church were disappointed that the New Fourth Army had not marched into the city, but at least the war was over. Although there were severe food shortages all over the city, the municipal government was finally back in Chinese hands.

Shortly after the surrender, American, British and other prisoners were freed from the internment camps, and they began to return to their homes. Community Church had a special service to welcome back the members of their congregation and to celebrate the end of the war. After this service, church members took the people from the camps home for a bath and a meal as part of their reintroduction to peacetime life. The British Baptist couple who went home with the Tings had been missionaries in Shandong before the war. They soon left China, but became good friends of the Tings, and kept in touch into the 1980s.

In the Fall of 1945, K. H. Ting was named director of the "Chinese Christian Democracy Research Society," which was organized by Y. T. Wu and other progressive Protestant leaders after their return to Shanghai.[55] In this position, he was able to maintain contact with Christians committed to social change, including many who had been part of the Student Church. He also continued to work at Community Church for the next ten months, but he was now assisted by C. C. Boynton, an elderly American Presbyterian missionary who had been imprisoned during the war. In early 1946, K. H. and Siu-may announced their decision to leave Shanghai. Community Church eventually appointed a former U.S. navy chaplain as Ting's successor.

Shanghai was once again approaching a turning point. By the time K. H. Ting left, the Community Church was even more popular within the international community than it had been before, especially among new arrivals from overseas. These included American servicemen, UNRRA workers, business people and missionaries returning to China. The American military was working with the Nationalists to consolidate their rule. UNRRA, where Siu-may worked for a time, was helping to keep Shanghai afloat through the provision of desperately needed food and resources. The missionaries were returning to China or beginning their work in stations that had remained unoccupied for the past eight years, and the business people were picking up where they left off.

Great changes were on the horizon, but, in 1946, it was still not clear what shape they would take. K. H. Ting had accepted a rather unusual appointment from the SCM of Canada to serve as their missionary secretary. As the Tings made their way to Hong Kong in May, they were beginning a new form of ecumenical involvement that would be closely linked to the changes taking place in both China and the churches overseas.

3

Service and Studies Overseas, 1946-1951

I roamed till peace be to my mind restored.
The pillar of the earth I stayed beside;
The way was long, and winding far and wide.
Qu Yuan[1]

The Chinese people have stood up.
Mao Zedong[2]

K. H. Ting was appointed missionary secretary of the Canadian SCM in 1946. This was a unique assignment, designed to expose Canadian students to the realities of postwar China, as seen through the eyes of a young student worker. It meant that K. H. and Siu-may would leave their work in Shanghai for what they anticipated to be a few years overseas.

International travel was still difficult, and so K. H. and Siu-may flew from Shanghai to Hong Kong in May, where they hoped to get a plane to Geneva, and from there they would go on to Toronto. They had been asked by the Chinese SCM to attend the General Committee meeting of the World Students' Christian Federation (WSCF) before beginning their new assignment in Canada. In Hong Kong, they tried for three weeks to get plane tickets, but the demand for the few flights to Europe was very high. Finally, they had to give up their plans to go to Europe and instead booked passage on an American cargo ship that was sailing to Vancouver by way of Seattle.

The voyage across the Pacific took twenty-eight days. Siu-may was pregnant, and she was seasick much of the time. When they arrived in Vancouver, no one was there to meet them because their telegram had apparently been mislaid.[3] They finally made contact with a local church, however, and eventually the Tings boarded a train for the two-and-a-half-day journey across the Canadian Rockies to Toronto.

Most of the summer was spent getting settled in Toronto and becoming acquainted with the work of the Student Christian Movement of Canada. As it turned out, the Tings spent only one year in Canada, but they established relationships that were to be important for them and for their Canadian friends for the rest of their lives.

SCM SECRETARY IN CANADA

The SCM of Canada's decision to appoint a young Chinese as missionary secretary to Canadian young people was both unusual and farsighted. It was seen as a way to stimulate interest in missionary work among university students. A representative from one of the "younger churches" was invited to interpret his faith and experience to North American students, contributing to their reevangelization and their understanding of the missionary task in North America and the world as a whole. This was also a very early example of "mission in reverse" or "two-way mission," which did not become popular in churches in North America until the 1970s.

A vacancy was created in the Canadian SCM in 1945 when Malcolm Ransom announced his decision to resign in order to pursue missionary work in China. The Missionary Committee subsequently recommended that a missionary secretary and associate secretary be appointed in 1946, and that one of them be "a non-Anglo-Saxon" from overseas. With this mandate, the Personnel Committee wrote to people in different parts of the world to get their suggestions for a suitable person. These included Kiang Wen-han in China.[4]

Canadians had a great interest in China in the mid-1940s, in the work of the church, in the experience of the Chinese people in wartime, and in the rebuilding of their country. This interest was largely based on earlier reports from Canadian missionaries. There were a few socially progressive missionaries, including Jim and Mary Endicott, Earl and Katherine Wilmot, and Kay Hockin, who were already stressing the economic and political implications of Christian faith in China.[5] In contrast to most of their American and European counterparts, they increasingly identified with the Communist cause in China, laying the groundwork for a sympathetic understanding of the Chinese Revolution, at least in some quarters of the Canadian churches.

In the fall of 1945, T. Z. Koo, Ting's senior colleague at the Community Church and a well-known speaker in the West, had been invited to Canada to speak to students. Koo cut a singular if somewhat exotic figure, with his Chinese flute and his blue silk gown, and he was a popular speaker on university campuses. He had a long-standing relationship with the WSCF and the SCM, and his speaking tour of Canada contributed to the more general interest in China. Koo's visit also contributed to the SCM's interest in hiring a missionary secretary from China.

A number of people in international ecumenical circles and in the Canadian SCM already knew Ting as a promising young student secretary based on his work in Shanghai and his relationships in the WSCF. Ted Johnson, a Presbyterian who had been a missionary in northeast China in the 1930s, was chair of the personnel committee of the Canadian SCM, and he knew about K. H. Ting's work in Shanghai. Kiang Wen-han enthusiastically recommended Ting for the Canadian position, and supporting letters were also received from T.Z. Koo and Roland Elliot of the WSCF. On this basis, the executive committee voted to extend an invitation to K. H. Ting as of 1 September 1946. K. H. suggested that he be allowed to bring his wife, and the missionary committee agreed. Siu-may was invited to do "special types of work" with the SCM and accompany her husband. The committee reiterated its belief that the appointment of a missionary secretary from China (there was to be no associate secretary) would be "a demonstration of the solidarity of the World Church and the reality of its fellowship."[6]

The solidarity of the world church in the ecumenical movement was increasingly important, but so too were the tensions within the ecumenical movement as a whole, and within the SCM in particular. These tensions were based on contrasting approaches to theology and social action. By the mid-1940s, the neo-orthodox theology of Karl Barth had replaced other theological viewpoints as the dominant stream in many SCMs in North America and Europe. The Canadians did not share this enthusiasm for neo-orthodoxy, but they were influenced by the recovery of biblical theology. This meant that they tended to prefer the theological discussion of political concerns to the adoption of a particular political stance that would involve them in concrete action for change. The more radical wing of the SCM of Canada stressed social action and political involvement based on a critical view of capitalist society. One group of SCM radicals based at McGill University in Montreal combined Anglo-Catholic sensibility with Marxist social analysis.[7] Although their influence was marginal in the movement as a whole, they kept questions about the SCM's political standpoint to the fore, and they were important for what K. H. Ting was attempting to do.

Tensions within the SCM also influenced the relationship between the movement and the churches. Students in the SCM were often critical of the churches, which they saw as too conservative. For their part, the churches expected the SCM, acting through the missionary committee, to be a recruiting ground for missionaries and supportive of the churches' mission efforts.[8] These assumptions were not necessarily shared by the students.

Nor were they shared by the committee's new missionary secretary. Although K. H. Ting was in effect, a missionary from China to Canada—one Montreal newspaper even announced that he had come to "Christianize" the Canadians[9]—he did not bring a strong message of missionary recruitment for foreign fields. Like many Asian, African and Latin American SCM leaders, Ting had a critical perspective on the missionary enterprise, and the relationship between the missionary movement and colonialism. His experience with Y. T. Wu and the Shanghai student movement had deepened this critical consciousness, and this helped him develop a clear position on where he stood with respect to the political tensions in the SCM.

In the course of his work over the next year, K. H. Ting visited almost all of the universities in Canada. He spoke to student groups, preached in churches, met with church youth fellowships, attended YM and YWCA meetings, and participated in the life of the Student Christian Movement at the national level. He offered Bible studies at SCM gatherings, planned con-

K. H. Ting as SCM secretary
in Canada, 1946. Reproduced
with the permission of the
Canadian SCM Archives at
the University of Toronto.

ferences, lectured on China and international relations, and led worship services. He particularly enjoyed meeting with students informally, when they spent long hours in conversation, often joining in fellowship around a common meal.

One strong message that K. H. Ting delivered to Canadian students was the importance of the changes taking place in China for the future of the church and the world. His approach was not that of a Christian ambassador of goodwill, for he was firmly rooted in the politics and analysis of what were termed the progressive and democratic forces in China. These included all groups opposed to Chiang Kai-shek and in favor of a coalition government, but the Communists were the most important force opposed to the Nationalists. Ting criticized North American support for Chiang Kai-shek and the Nationalists in the Civil War. In his earliest published essay in English, he questioned the link between missionary good works and American government policy:

The churches of the West continue their missionary work in China. But in China, people are asking how so many missionaries can honestly preach the gospel of peace and reconciliation, supposedly representing the goodwill of the West towards China, while at the same time giving unquestioned support to the hostile policy of the American government.[10]

In subsequent articles and talks at universities, he continued to criticize the errors of American policy and the need for a coalition government in China. In an unsigned article published in 1948, Ting presented an overall socioeconomic interpretation of the Chinese Civil War. He analyzed the peasant problem in terms of the traditional land-tenure system in China and described the Civil War as "a war of liberation" involving the class interests of the privileged few versus the peasants and democratic forces. His assessment of the Civil War was not very different from that of other leftist interpretations of the late 1940s, but it certainly was a departure from mainstream thinking in the churches. Writing anonymously, he was able to use the same language that characterized most of the pro-Communist writing of the times. "Washington war-mongers and American finance-imperialist adventurers," he wrote, "are still stubbornly credulous of the possibility of successful intervention on the side of the reactionary forces of China." Who were these reactionaries? They were the "fascist-minded class of landlords and wealthy industrialists, in union with their sycophant hangers-on among army officers and government bureaucrats."[11] This was strong meat for North American Christians, but an accurate reflection of the thinking of many in the Chinese SCM.

It is unlikely that Ting would have used the same kind of language in his talks at churches or at most student Christian gatherings. For one thing, he respected the fact that the language of the church was different from the language of politics. This was consistent with the theological and political approach he had already developed in Shanghai, an approach that is reflected in all his subsequent writings. In addition, K. H. has always been extremely cautious in the way in which he reveals himself to people, especially foreigners. Vince Goring, who in 1946 was one of the radical leaders of the McGill SCM, saw K. H. "as a person who really didn't let his right hand know what his left hand was doing." According to Goring, Ting supported the political position of the Anglo-Catholic Marxists, but not openly. And when a split later developed in the SCM, both sides claimed K. H. would have been on their side. Cyril Powles, another friend from those days, has described K. H. as being a man of "tempered steel, but well covered."[12] This is a perceptive comment. The tempered but well-covered aspect of Ting's character is a function of his personal reserve as well as his political judgment, and it has helped make him an unusually effective communicator to many different audiences.

Goring and Powles were involved with the Anglican Fellowship for Social Action, and later in the Society of the Catholic Commonwealth (S.C.C.). The S.C.C. was an Anglican society of priests and laypeople based at the Oratory of St. Mary and St. Michael in Cambridge, Massachusetts. It worked through local revolutionary "cells" in the 1940s and the 1950s, a number of which were established in the United States, Canada, England, Korea and Japan.[13] Founded by F. Hastings Smyth, the S.C.C. combined a high-church liturgical theology with Marxism, a position that Hastings Smyth characterized as "dialectical sacramentalism" or, to use the word he invented, "metacosmesis." This approach enjoyed a certain influence in the Canadian SCM in the late 1940s and 1950s, and it informed the McGill SCM's understanding of social justice and world events.

Ting was intrigued by the views of the S.C.C., although he never became a member. He visited Hastings Smyth in Cambridge in 1946 and 1947, and they had a correspondence that reveals a sense of graciousness and shared commitment. K. H. , who was ever attentive to matters of form in personal relationships, addressed his host as Father Smyth, as did everyone else who understood the Oratory's Anglo-Catholic sentiments. Ting's article on the Chinese Civil War quoted above was one of two he published in the S.C.C. bulletin. He could reveal a different side of himself in this publication, because he shared its overall political perspective. The S.C.C. was pro-Communist, but not adventurist or ultra-leftist. Ting and Smyth were both critical of the (Canadian) Fellowship for Social Action, whose members Ting dismissed as being "politically naïve and careless." This stood in contrast to his own inherent political cautiousness. Smyth criticized the Fellowship for Social Action as lacking "objective knowledge of the social process."[14]

One letter that Ting wrote to Smyth provides an early reference to Ting's understanding of the relationship between culture and politics. He had loaned Smyth a book of woodcuts made by young artists in the Communist areas of China, and in this handwritten letter, he comments on the new influences visible their work.

> They show how art and the toil of man are synthesized and break up the traditional detachment of art and the life and struggle of the masses.
>
> You will notice that those woodcuts produced before 1942 still contain in themselves certain defects—the emptiness and narrowness of content (due to the poverty in the life experience of the artists who produced them), and extreme western technique and style (due to uncritical imitation of western pieces). But in 1942, Mao Zedong started a movement among the artists and cultural workers for self-criticism and for identifying themselves much more clearly with the life and struggle and aspiration of the people. The result is the emergence of a new art—which expresses in a rich, varied, vivid and simple way the Chinese national characteristics and reality.
>
> The new culture is the outcome of social reconstruction and personal reconstruction. Our artists are no longer standing aloof in human struggle but are a part of the total struggle. Art comes from the masses and goes back to them as a weapon leading people to truth, i.e. for education.[15]

In this letter, Ting is describing the socialist realism that Mao Zedong had been promoting in his "Yanan Talks on Art and Literature" (1942). Mao's position was that art and literature should be put to the service of peasant and proletarian politics, as these were defined by the CPC. This meant that there could be no "art for art's sake," and it severely restricted any independent or creative approach to literature. Ting more or less identified himself with this position at that time. Behind this position lay Ting's persistent suspicion of "high culture" and elitist tastes disconnected from progressive politics. His own cultural preference was for a simpler and more popular approach not only to art and literature but to religion, theology and missionary work as well.

In his report to the missionary committee at the end of his stay in Canada, Ting also stressed a grassroots approach to student work. For missionaries and all church workers, he wrote, it is more important to understand the people of the land, "their aspirations and struggles and their spiritual and ideological movements" than it is to study their language, culture and history. This will help them to understand a country like China, "not always as a static, old nation, but also in the setting of the struggle of her common people." It will also help the church to identify with "those very young people who are the most important section of the population for the church to win."[16] The missionary, therefore, should base his or her message on the life and struggles of the common people, not the priorities of the foreign mission boards or the abstract representation of a theology and a culture which were developed elsewhere.

We can understand why in this light, K. H. Ting would distance himself from Hasting Smyth's high-church "dialectical sacramentalism." Ting was an Anglican—he was attached to the Cathedral Church of St. James during his time in Toronto—but he was never high church. The Christianity that he understood was all there in the Bible, the sacraments and the creeds, and it was not something one had to be anxious or defensive about, or which required elaboration into theological dogmatics and philosophical systems. He took his Anglican faith very seriously, treasured it in his personal life, but he certainly did not wish to impose it on others as a way of being Christian that was better than all the rest. Ting's broad-church approach helps to explain why he could work so well in relating to a diverse and divided group of students in the Canadian SCM.

This should not imply that Ting's understanding of the missionary and ecumenical task among students was based on pure tolerance. It had a cutting edge to it, for he believed it was important to push students to ask questions about their faith and the purpose of their lives. Canadian students, in his understanding, were in a dilemma. They were receiving excellent university educations that would enable them to become accomplished scientists, social workers and teachers. But unless they asked what this was all for, unless they saw a broader purpose for their lives, then their education counted for very little. "We must define the ends for which we live and concern ourselves," he wrote in one article, "so that we will dedicate our knowledge and skill only to the right cause."[17] It was the purpose of the SCM to push this kind of questioning and challenge the students, and it was the job of the missionary secretary to see that this happened.

Challenging the students to represent "the right cause" meant taking sides in the struggles and debates within the SCM. In August 1947, Ting attended the Dixie Student-in-Agriculture Camp, which was meeting near Toronto. Work camps, combining work and worship, had developed in the SCM to lead Christian students to ask questions about their comfortable middle-class lives. That August, Philippe Maury, who was on the staff of the WSCF in Geneva, was also at the Dixie Camp. Maury was a courageous Barthian and seasoned SCM leader who had fought in the French underground during World War II. But many students found his theology difficult to understand, for he seemed unable to offer a coherent Christian rationale for political action. One evening, a "gentlemanly debate" was arranged between Ting and Maury on the subject of Christian participation in society. They represented very different approaches to the subject. No record of the talk exists, although the McGill radicals all remember K. H. as presenting a clear analysis of current world events based on his Christian and Marxist analysis of social forces, and Maury as developing an abstract theological analysis. It was Ting's contribution that was recorded in the camp log: "His statement to the effect that God might disown the Church and work through other organizations if such were more effective in doing his will reverberated far into the night."[18] The "other organization" in the case of China is an unmistakable reference to the CPC. Such words would have been challenging indeed for Canadian students.

He enjoyed his visit to the Dixie Camp and had grown very close to many of the students. They worked together as friends and equals, not as leader and students. One evening, the students organized several light-hearted performances and skits, and they saw that K. H. was unhappy with the whole affair. Vince Goring remembers him as being "disgusted by the fact that in this series of skits there was no political analysis at all." This kind of organized fellowship without any religious or political purpose was not part of Ting's idea of SCM work.

Ting pushed students to ask questions about their own personal lives, and not only about their political and social views. Cyril and Marjorie Powles remember him visiting them in Boston on one of his trips to see Hastings Smyth. They were at Harvard doing language work in preparation for going to Japan as missionaries, and K. H. tried to get them to reconsider the idea by stressing the many contradictions he saw in the missionary movement. "By the end of the weekend, he had really put us through the mill," Marjorie Powles said. "Why were we going?" he asked. "What did we expect to do? And what were our motivations? And all the rest of it. Afterwards, when he saw we had made up our minds, he gave us his blessing."[19] K. H. did not try to force his beliefs on the Powles. He took them seriously as friends and colleagues, and this meant that he had to speak his mind.

Both K. H. and Siu-may made many lifelong friendships during their year in Canada. In addition to the people who have already been mentioned, their friends included Ted Scott, Jean Ross (Wordsworth), Jack Bishop, Margaret Prang and Gerald Hutchinson, who was SCM general secretary in the late 1940s.

There were also friends outside the church. Ting remembers Gregory Vlastos, who was then teaching at Queens University in Kingston.[20] Vlastos was a philosopher specializing in Plato; he had written *Christian Faith and Democracy*, a book that was quite influential in the Canadian student movement because of its Christian interpretation of Marxism.[21] He had been active in the Fellowship for a Christian Social Order in the 1930s, which was based on a Christian understanding of Marxism and social change. Vlastos and his wife, who was a member of Canada's Labor Progressive Party (a Communist Party), frequently met with the Tings during their time in Canada.

One student who was profoundly influenced by K. H. Ting was Lois Wilson. She was later to become the moderator of the United Church of Canada and the first woman president of the Canadian Council of Churches. Wilson also served as president of the World Council of Churches. She and K. H. met in the fall of 1946 at a meeting of the Winnipeg SCM, where he had been asked to lead the Bible studies. She was very impressed by his approach to the Bible and went up to speak to him after the session ended. He asked her at one point what she was going to do with her life. "Get married," she said. "That's not good enough," he responded, with uncharacteristic directness.[22] He went on to urge her to think of doing something more, and she credits him with having had a major impact on her career decision.

Already in the 1940s, Ting took seriously the contribution that women could make to church and society. He saw the contribution they were making in China, the most obvious example being his wife Siu-may. From the beginning of their time in Canada, both of them were involved in the work of the SCM, although this was not explicit in his contract. Shortly after their arrival she wrote, "To change this world of ours into a Christian world requires the effort of every Christian—you and me included—however insignificant we may be. What are we going to do about it?"[23] Siu-may always seemed to know that she was going to change the world, and she put all her energy into this task.

Siu-may did not have the same travel schedule as K. H., but she also was invited to church and SCM gatherings, and she could be quite outspoken. She once spoke to a church group on the "Liberated Areas" of China where the Communists were in control, and a small report was carried in the local Canadian newspaper. The Chinese embassy, still in the hands of the Nationalists, phoned K. H. to express its displeasure and to tell him that he should keep better control of his wife, "especially her tongue."[24] Ting, of course, ignored the request. But the incident illustrates Siu-may's enthusiasm for the cause. Her lively directness was in sharp contrast to K. H.'s prudence and reticence.

Siu-may was pregnant when she went to Canada, but the baby died only three days after he was born later that year. This left a lasting impact on both parents. Siu-may wrote a moving circular letter to the friends who had supported them during this time of sadness, and she related the death of their child to the broader struggle for social change.

> So I think the sight of the little face grasping for life is just a signal from God calling me to work more earnestly and more vigorously for a better China, a better society where there will be no unreasonable reasons for mothers to suffer and babies to die . . .
>
> Personally there will be an emptiness in my heart and thus in my life left by that thing buried, unmarked in Mount Pleasant cemetery . . . an emptiness which nothing can fill up again. But as God wills it, it is only through pain that you can really know pain; it is only through suffering you can really understand suffering; and it is only through tears you can really see tears. Through this, God has made me to feel for certain things and certain people with an intensity I did not have before.[25]

Toward the end of their year in Canada, K. H. presented his final report to the SCM, which summarizes the Tings' time in Canada.[26] Unlike their Canadian student counterparts, Ting wrote, women in China saw themselves as part of a broader social struggle. He was speaking here of women involved in the movement of revolutionary change, not women in traditional China. The home was for Chinese women "too distantly related to the struggle to spend all their time in." Women, and here he could have been speaking about Siu-may, believed in working for political democracy and peace, and they were insulted by the idea that their place should be in the home. In Canada, most women students he met hoped to marry after graduation and have nice homes. "How can you have a good society without good homes," they asked?

This difference, Ting continued, was part of a more general contrast between Canadian and Chinese students. Students in Canada had a privileged, prosperous and peaceful life in comparison to their counterparts in China, and this is reflected in their approach to politics in society. "While students in China have always played a pioneering role in cultural, social and political movements of their country, students here [in Canada] are more concerned over their own careers and the establishment of happy homes and social positions," he observed. This was not an option for students in China and other Asian countries because their own personal plans could not be realized under existing conditions. Asian students had therefore become convinced that their only hope was to change the status quo. Although Cana-

dian students understood that all was not well in the world, the large majority of them accepted things as they were. Politically, they lacked a sense of
direction, Ting concluded.

In this situation, the SCM had a definite contribution to make. Ting went
on to speak of several things that inspired him about what the various chapters were doing. Despite the tensions we have alluded to above, the SCMs
maintained generally good relationships with the churches. They also
encouraged students to develop a world consciousness that pushed them
into asking new questions. But Ting also posed questions to the SCM and
offered suggestions for the future. The SCMs should do more to encourage
"two-way traffic" between the church and the students, especially in reflecting the students' criticisms of the churches.

> In this way, the SCM perhaps will be playing an unpopular role of
> being "too critical of the Church." Its relation to the churches perhaps
> will not be one of pure "fellowship," but, possibly, will be mixed with
> some "tension." But the churches do not really need to get excited and
> become defensive, but should rather thank God, that, in the SCM, the
> Church becomes self-critical, remembering that self-criticism is the
> course to real progress.

Ting wrote that the religious emphasis and theological discussion in the
SCM was often too vague and abstract, an "armchair or parlor" theology
that had no practical effect. The students needed to focus more on their
experiences and on the concrete implications of what their religious beliefs
stood for. "Christianity can mean much more to us if we only have five ideas
or convictions from the New Testament that we can really claim to be our
own than merely tossing back and forth ten thousand tremendous theological terminologies which are empty words only." The SCM was not about
purposeless "fellowshipping" with friends but about how students could
discover their commonality in suffering and struggle.

In the closing pages of the report, Ting observed that Canadian students
no longer had a very optimistic view of going out to Christianize the world.
This was "not a bad sign at all," he wrote, because "many students feel that
their efforts to evangelize the world are constantly driving them back to re-
evangelize themselves because they sometimes feel that they have been pretty
well de-evangelized." Christians still had a message to share, but they would
have to rediscover the meaning of Christianity as an intrinsically missionary
faith, whether in the far corners of the globe or in Canada.

For twelve months, K. H. Ting and Siu-may had been part of this reevangelization and rediscovery within the SCM. Their work in Canada was
drawing to a close because they were going to New York to pursue further
studies. In his closing report to the National Missionary Conference in 1947,
the Canadian SCM chairman spoke very warmly about the Tings and their
work in Canada.

The most significant things which the missionary committee has done in the past year has been to bring the Rev. and Mrs. K. H. Ting from China to Canada. Their very presence among us has served to give a new vision of the meaning of the World Church. Here are two talented and consecrated Christians from one of the younger churches who have, during their stay in Canada, done what no Canadian could do. First, they have given us a new and greater picture of China than we had before, and henceforth, as we think of our sister churches in that great land, we shall think of them in terms of K. H. and Siu May [Siu-may] Ting and of what they have told us. But second, and perhaps even more important, they have helped us to see ourselves objectively. With clear insight and vigorous expression, they have examined the strengths and weaknesses of our own Movement.[27]

K. H. was replaced in his position by Hilda Benson, a Canadian. Despite the obvious success of Ting's appointment, the decision to invite a "non-Anglo-Saxon" to serve as SCM missionary secretary was not immediately repeated. This may have been because of the need to address some of the immediate and practical concerns for the SCM and their relationship to the churches, some of which are raised in Ting's closing report. Such work would have best been dealt with by a Canadian.

The Tings maintained an informal relationship with the SCM of Canada for the next several years. K. H. made several visits to Canada from New York and Geneva in connection with his work in the WSCF, and he continued to be in regular correspondence with friends and colleagues even after he had returned to China.

STUDIES IN NEW YORK

The invitation to work for the Canadian SCM had been open-ended, but K. H. wanted to pursue further studies. He applied for and received a Hazen Foundation Fellowship for the year 1947-1948, which enabled him to study in any institution of his choice. The Tings chose to go to New York, where K. H. could pursue a joint degree at Union Theological Seminary and Teachers College of Columbia University. A number of Ting's teachers at St. John's School of Theology including F. Hawks Pott, Y. Y. Tsu (Zhu You-yu), and William Sung had graduated from Teachers College. So had Alice Gregg, who taught both K. H. and Siu-may as undergraduates. Siu-may also received a scholarship from Teachers College to do graduate work in education, and so in September, both Tings became full-time students.

Union had attracted a large number of Chinese theology students since the 1920s. Many seminary professors had visited China in the early years of the republic, and they helped to promote the image of Union as a progressive and forward-looking institution. Before 1949, twenty-eight Chinese had received advanced degrees from Union.[28] These included prominent theologians and church leaders such as Y. Y. Tsu, Cheng Jingyi, Liu Tingfang, Hsü Pao-Chien (Xu Baoqian), and Ting's mentor in the YMCA, Y. T. Wu. John Sung (Song Shangjie), the prominent Chinese evangelist, also attended Union, but, following a personal crisis, he later rejected its liberal theology and embraced fundamentalism. There were seven other Chinese students at Union in 1947-1948, including Yu Pei-wen, who had been a colleague of K. H. in the YMCA, and Kiang Wen-han, who received a Ph.D. in religious education the same year that Ting graduated. Both were also enrolled in the joint degree program with Teachers College. Because of his interest in education, the prominence of Chinese students at Columbia and Union, some of whom had been his teachers, and the progressive atmosphere of both institutions, Ting's decision to pursue further studies in New York is easy to understand.

His theological thinking around this time is reflected in two short articles he wrote for *The Canadian Student*, entitled "The Simplicity of the Gospel."[29] In Western countries, he observed, the vague "cultural atmosphere" of Christianity had robbed the gospel of its dynamic force and original intent. He had seen this in his work with Canadian students. In contrast, he continued, Christianity speaks with a disarming directness to people from Asia, Africa and Latin America because they were able to identify with the suffering and struggle of the early Christians. "Entering into the life which Jesus offered, they (the people of his day) immediately experienced the simplicity and freedom from fear and from the sense of frustration and sin that were oppressing them under the old regime." This was also the experience of the Indian or Chinese Christian, he noted.

Ting believed that commitment and conversion are what Christian faith requires, not theological reflection detached from life in society. Here as elsewhere, one detects Ting's impatience with both academic theology and Christian complacency.

> Try to lay aside your biblical criticism and exegesis and even your theological assumptions and enter into the New Testament, particularly the four Gospels to start with, for the first time, as it were . . . It is only this experience constantly maintained and enriched, that gives content to your theological pursuits. And to make this possible, you have to realize that the environment of Christianity here cannot be considered to be Christian, that there is a long distance between the environment as it is and the ethic of the New Testament.[30]

The impact of Christian faith on an individual's life and on the church's involvement in society are what concerned Ting, not theology per se. His was an applied Christianity that developed in the course of his work with students in China and Canada. It was this perspective that he would now bring to his graduate studies.

Union Seminary was one of the leading seminary faculties in the world in the late 1940s, and it was at the forefront of progressive and liberal theological thinking. Henry Pitney van Dusen was president, and he had an expansive vision for Union Seminary and the church in the world. According to Robert Handy, one could also detect in this vision "a longing for a new version of the nineteenth century dream of an American Protestant Christendom in ecumenical guise."[31] This would also have been noticed by the Chinese students at Union. Faculty members in the late 1940s included Reinhold Niebuhr, Paul Tillich, and John Bennett—all of whom K. H. Ting took courses from. He was interested in what his teachers had to say, but there is no evidence that he was particularly attracted to the thinking of Union's leading Protestant theologians, or to van Dusen's ecumenical vision. His Anglican formation, his experience of the SCM and his direct approach to Christian faith as it applied to social issues mitigated against the theological outlook that Union had to offer.

Ting may have been unenthusiastic about the theology that was taught at Union, but he did have other academic interests he was excited about. The educational environment at both Union and Columbia was open and flexible, and it was directly concerned with contemporary social issues. In the joint M.A. program, a student could read books and attend lectures in whatever subjects he or she wished. Besides his three courses in theology and ethics, all of the remaining courses Ting took were in education, three at Union and five at Teachers College. He had developed an interest in psychology and education during his undergraduate days at St. John's, and at one time he had even considered pursuing graduate studies in one of these fields. Instead, he focused on religious education as it applied to his own interest in social change.

Many Chinese students at Union and Columbia were interested in education as it was applied to social concerns. Ting remembers a course on psychology and social change taught by Professor Goodwin Watson,[32] probably because it brought together two areas of study that interested him. At Union, the leading Christian educator was Harrison Sackett Elliot (1882-1951), who had been in China as an advisor to the International YMCA Committee. Ting took two courses from Elliott, who also served as the liaison between the seminary and Teachers College. The approach to education at both institutions was shaped by the perspective of John Dewey, emphasizing education for democracy and an experimental approach to learning in service to society. Elliot related Christian education to political and economic issues of the day in order to "open the way for action by individuals and groups in line with their convictions and commitments."[33] Such ideas about education would have resonated with Ting's view of the role of the church in society in the late 1940s and over the rest of his life.

K. H. and Siu-may also spent a good deal of his time at Union in activities outside the classroom, especially in the Chinese Christian Students' Association (CSCA). Their friend Paul Lin was then general secretary. The CSCA had begun in 1909 as a "grafted branch" of the Chinese SCM on American campuses. Its membership was drawn from the three thousand or more Chinese graduate students studying in the United States, most of whom were from non-Christian backgrounds. The CSCA was a fellowship of mature Chinese students "in search of faith," rather than one of convinced Christians.[34] What brought the students together was an interest in Christianity, a desire for fellowship with other Chinese students and a commitment to social change in China.

The CSCA leadership was very outspoken on Chinese issues and advocated the "progressive and democratic" line with which K. H. and his friends were identified. It had good contacts with China, maintained by the Chinese students who were always coming and going and receiving letters. By 1947, the Communists were enjoying increasing successes in the Civil War, and the CSCA was an important voice supporting their cause in North America. This brought the organization into tension with the YMCA and YWCA, which were the CSCA's sponsoring organizations, as well as with other church bodies in the United States—a conflict that was not very different from that between the SCM and the Ys in China. Siu-may contended that the CSCA was "the most effective link between the American churches and the future leaders of China,"[35] but the YM and YWCAs were concerned that the organization was "too political."

The Tings were living in a student apartment at Union Seminary, and their home again became a place where many students and other friends would gather. In 1949, Siu-may succeeded Paul Lin and became the first woman general secretary of the CSCA. By this time, the Tings had moved to a larger apartment. With K. H. traveling so much of the time, their home became almost a dormitory for Chinese students visiting New York and living on small stipends. They would go there to have a meal or take a bath or meet to discuss the latest news from China. Siu-may remembers their time in New York as "a very happy life," with the constant stream of visitors and hectic pace of meetings.[36] This offset the tensions generated by her work with the CSCA.

Maude Russell was a special friend and frequent visitor to the Ting home. She had been a YWCA worker in Changsha and Shanghai and now edited the *Far Eastern Newsletter* from New York, a publication she continued for the next three decades. Russell was an indefatigable supporter of the Chinese revolutionary movement and a tireless worker for radical social change in her own country. She introduced the Tings to other left-wing progressives in New York. This provided them with a picture of American society which, although very different from what they heard in the churches, was increasingly consistent with their own appraisal of the world situation.

In New York City, K. H. Ting was attached to the Cathedral of St. John the Divine, which was just a short walk from Union, Columbia and the Ting home. He went regularly to the Eucharistic service on Wednesday mornings, and he remembers occasionally preaching or conducting services there. His long experience at St. Peter's Church in Shanghai and his ordination in the Sheng Gong Hui taught him that it was important to report to the bishop and be attached to a local church during his time overseas. He continued his relationship with the SCM, and attended the "North American Conference on Christian Frontiers" which met in Lawrence, Kansas, between Christmas and New Year, after which he went to another student conference in Maryland. Participation in these winter conferences gave him an experience of student life south of the Canadian border and kept him in touch with the international ecumenical movement.

K. H. Ting received his M.A. in Religious Education on 1 June 1948. He had a very distinguished academic record, receiving A's in all of his eleven courses except one course in Christian ethics in which he received a B+. That spring, he accepted a position with the WSCF in Geneva, and he needed to take up his duties as soon as possible. Siu-may, who was again pregnant, received her M.A. from Teachers College at the same time. She stayed on in New York to continue her work with the CSCA and to await the birth of their child. Two weeks after his graduation, K. H. sailed for Plymouth, England, on the S.S. Marine Jumper to begin another assignment in the ecumenical movement.

WSCF SECRETARY IN GENEVA

The WSCF had begun recruiting Ting for its staff in Geneva the previous year. Robert Mackie, who was general secretary, had met Ting in Shanghai before the war, and he was very impressed. He asked K. H. to represent the Federation at the Whitby Meeting of the International Missionary Council in July 1947.[37] Ting was still in Canada at the time, and the theme of the conference, "Christian Witness in a Revolutionary World," was related to his earlier involvement in student work. This was the first international mission conference after the end of World War II and the last before the formation of the World Council of Churches. It became known for its advocacy of the *missio dei* and the slogan "partnership in obedience." Whitby focused on the new relationship envisaged between European and North American churches and those from Asia, Africa and Latin America.

That same summer, Siu-may attended the World Conference on Christian Youth in Oslo as part of the Chinese delegation. For both Tings, these ecumenical gatherings were times to catch up on events in China as well as to make their respective contributions to a very creative and exciting period in the life of the ecumenical movement. In Norway, Siu-may also met with Robert Mackie and others from the WSCF, and they explored with her the possibility of K. H. joining the staff of the Federation after his year at

Union.[38] Another person was needed in Geneva to focus on Bible study, mission and evangelism, and K. H. was seen as the ideal candidate for the position.

Ting was quite interested in going to Geneva, and the only problem was that the Chinese YMCA wanted him back in Shanghai. Kiang Wen-han was vice-chairman of the WSCF, but he had not been consulted about the possible appointment and wrote to Mackie that K. H. should return to China. Mackie responded saying that the Federation dealt with individuals, and although he realized that individuals had organizational responsibilities in their home countries, he did not want to lose someone who, quite apart from China, seemed "quite the man we need to have on many other grounds."[39]

Kiang sent back an angry reply. "K. H. has been away for two years and there is a big job for him in China. I hope you won't create another T. Z.(Koo) on the WSCF staff. The support of the China movement on such a thing is important."[40] Kiang was referring to T. Z. Koo, who had been a traveling secretary for the WSCF since the 1920s. Although Koo was for many in the West the embodiment of Chinese ecumenism, he had become alienated from China and cut off from church life there. This was the dilemma of more than a few Christians in the ecumenical movement: they developed an expansive vision of a world church but were unable to relate or readjust to their own context, and the situation resulted in tensions between international ecumenical bodies and the national church.

There was never a question of K. H.'s desire to return to China. His involvement with the student movement, his outlook and his relationships were very different from those of T. Z. Koo. The problem of his appointment was eventually resolved in correspondence between Geneva and Shanghai,[41] and probably also in the personal correspondence between K. H. Ting and colleagues in China. He therefore accepted what was initially a two-year appointment to the WSCF, beginning in June 1948.

He arrived in England in time to attend his first executive committee meeting, which was held in St. Catherine's, Cumberland Lodge, in Windsor. It was chaired by W. A. Visser 't Hooft, who would be elected the first general secretary of the World Council of Churches at Amsterdam in two months' time. Robert Mackie, who would become Visser 't Hooft's deputy in the WCC and his successor as chairman of the WSCF, was also there, as was Philippe Maury, whom K. H. had met in Canada and who replaced Robert Mackie as WSCF general secretary. Other colleagues at Windsor included John Coleman (Canada), Marie-Jeanne de Haller (Switzerland), and Harry Daniel (India). Daniel became Ting's successor as mission secretary in Geneva in 1951. Among the colleagues K. H. also worked with during his years at the Federation were Keith Briston (U.S.A.), Kyaw Than (Burma), M. M. Thomas (India), Bill Nicholls (England), and Wynburn Thomas (U.S.A.).

In the late 1940s, the WSCF was a growing ecumenical fellowship on the cutting edge of issues and concerns facing the churches in almost every corner of the globe. The strong Asian presence in the Federation during these postwar years meant that decision making was not entirely in the hands of white Europeans and North Americans, as it was in many other ecumenical organizations. The young and diverse staff was brought together by Robert Mackie, who, in the words of one colleague, had a genius for drawing "out of us abilities we did not know we possessed."[42] The staff worked together as a team, often without clear-cut divisions of responsibility. Their sense of hope for the future and expectation about the church and the world were contagious, but they would be continually tested in the years ahead. The relationships the staff maintained with one another held them together as a family, even when they were severely strained.

Ting's first assignment for the WSCF was to assume responsibility for the conference on "the growing church," which met in July 1948 at Woudschoten in Holland. This was a youth conference held in cooperation with the International Missionary Council (IMC) just prior to the inaugural assembly of the World Council of Churches (WCC). It was designed to awaken the understanding that the church in each place was part of a growing movement of the world church, through its faith in Jesus Christ (Ephesians 4:15-16). The conference brought together 140 students and student leaders from 36 countries for twelve days of study, in order to see what was to be done for the mission of the church.

The IMC hoped that Woudschoten would stir interest in the missionary vocation among students. The primary concern of the conference was to give special attention to the missionary concerns of the "younger churches," which meant that K. H. Ting was the perfect choice as secretary. There was a small but significant representation from younger churches at the conference, including Philip Potter, who had started a position with the British SCM similar to the one K. H. had held in Canada. Potter was one of the outstanding ecumenical leaders of his generation, and he served in future years as president of the WSCF and general secretary of the World Council of Churches. Potter and Ting began their lifelong friendship by working together at Woudschoten to promote the involvement of Christians from Asia, Africa and Latin America in the life of the ecumenical movement. In a letter written to national SCMs after the conference, Ting pointed out that any future dialogue must now include contributions of those churches at the "receiving end" of missions insofar as "the missionary outreach of the church is to be a total effort of the total church."[43] Students discovered at Woudschoten the reality of a "growing church" whose missionary life was enhanced by the participation of all parts of the body of Christ.

The inaugural assembly of the World Council of Churches opened in Amsterdam a week after Woudschoten, and Ting was on hand to address the youth rally.[44] There were six official delegates from China at the assembly, and several other Chinese Christians were there in other capacities.[45] More than forty years later, and just a month after the China Christian Council had joined the WCC at its Seventh Assembly in Canberra, K. H. Ting reflected on his own role at Amsterdam.

> My aim during those days—in fact this aim has continued in the fol-
> lowing years—was to understand what it (the WCC) was all about.
> The assembly was something very gigantic, I could not size it up so
> easily. But, I spent some time with my Chinese colleagues, and I spent
> a lot of time with friends from Czechoslovakia and Hungary. They
> were very helpful to me at that stage to understand WCC. I spoke with
> Hromádka from Czechoslovakia, and from Hungary there was a
> bishop whose name was Bereczky. He showed special interest in China.
> And T. C. Chao (Zhao Zichen) was a bit worried about what was
> going to happen in China, and I remember that Bishop Bereczky had
> quite a bit of influence on T. C. Chao's way of looking at Liberation.
> I found it very difficult to make up my mind as to what (the Amster-
> dam Assembly) really represented. But I did feel that in some ways it
> was a Cold War tool . . . A lot of anti-Soviet things were said at the
> assembly.[46]

The Cold War was in its infancy, but it was already creating political tensions in the ecumenical movement. Josef Hromádka and John Foster Dulles
spoke in Amsterdam, providing equal representation for both sides in the
struggle between East and West. But churches from North America and
Western Europe still dominated the assembly in terms of their theological,
organizational and personal leadership. Although a sincere effort had been
made to include representation from the younger churches, only 30 of the
147 founding members were from Asia, Africa and Latin America, including 5 from China.

It is not surprising that K. H. Ting, like many other Asians in Amsterdam, found it difficult to understand what the WCC was all about. During
his years at the Federation, he was able to learn a great deal, not only about
the missionary and theological concerns of the churches, but also about their
political understanding and involvement. Ting was generally sympathetic to
the ecumenical movement, but he was also concerned about its international
political impact. One of the contributions he would make after his return to
China was to interpret the ecumenical movement and the churches in the
West in a political environment that was increasingly hostile to both. In this
way he would continue in the role he assumed in Toronto as a bridge
between China and the international Christian community.

Not all Chinese who were in Amsterdam would play such a bridge role.
Li Chuwen (C.W. Lee) was also at Amsterdam as a youth delegate for the
American Baptists. He had worked in the World Alliance of YMCAs in
Geneva and served as chairman of the World Christian Youth Commission
until his own return to China in 1950. Li assessed the Western churches
from a more political vantage point than K. H. Ting, and he was much less
sympathetic to the ecumenical movement as a whole. As we shall see, Li

Chuwen played a prominent role in the Chinese Christian Three-Self Patriotic Movement in the 1950s and early 1960s and also served for a time as pastor of Shanghai's Community Church. He was reportedly a member of the Chinese Communist Party even then. He repudiated his church affiliation during the Cultural Revolution, and in the 1980s he became a high-ranking government official, serving in both Shanghai and Hong Kong.[47]

A great deal of travel was involved in the work of the Federation staff, more so for K. H. Ting than most. This had partly to do with his family situation. At the end of October, he returned to New York, where he arrived one week before the birth of his son, Stephen Yenren Ting, on 7 November 1948. Siu-may was on maternity leave but was still active in the CSCA. K. H. stayed with them in New York City for about a month but then set off on a two-week visit to universities and SCMs in the American South. An informal travel diary survives from this trip, which was Ting's first real contact with American student life. Many of the observations he records there are quite perceptive.

In Atlanta, he was entertained by Murray Branch, and this was his first contact with a black American family.

> I would feel sorry to meet a negro who has no awareness of the situation of racial injustice and who does not harbor a sense of protest against that situation. But, at the same time, I would feel sorry also for the negro who can only express his indignation in violent manners which cannot help the situation at all. In the Branch family, I somehow sensed a very harmonious balance. They have a sense of urgency, but no bitterness. They are disappointed at the long persistence of the illogical situation but are not cynical . . . They are very sorry for the situation not merely for the good of the negro people who are hated but also for the good of the white people who hate others.

In Baton Rouge, Ting was asked to give a talk on "the needs of the world" at an interdenominational prayer breakfast. He observed,

> It is certainly very magnanimous of Americans to think of other people's needs. But I cannot but fear the danger of this mentality to the Americans themselves. Should they not realize that it is really beyond their ability to meet the needs of the world? Should they not realize that there are needs on the part of Americans which they ought not overlook and which other peoples perhaps can help to meet? Should they not realize that, in thinking of the Marshall Plan as the great humanitarian expression of American abundance, their greatest temptation is spiritual pride? Should they not know that there are people in the world today who, in spite of their hunger and want, have turned back the American material relief because of what they consider to be a very insulting way in which that relief is "thrown at them"?

He also addressed a number of Southern Baptist worship meetings, although Southern Baptists were not members of the United Student Christian Council, which related to the WSCF. There, he found it difficult to adjust to the Baptist way of worship.

It is something that is a mixture of revivalistic hymn-singing, spontaneous jokes, prayers, voluntary (and, therefore, often ingenuously funny) announcements of all sorts of activities that are going on, suggestions for topics or persons for the group to pray for and address,— a completely free combination of the serious and the light-hearted which reminds me of the American "Breakfast Club" over the radio every morning which also inserts devotion into a hodgepodge of advertisements, jokes, jazz music and what not.[48]

Following his trip to the American South, K. H. spent Christmas with his family in New York. He then went to Lawrence, Kansas, for the Quadrennial of the USCC, and in late January, he returned to Europe by himself.

Over the next six months, Ting traveled to different parts of Europe visiting SCMs and participating in ecumenical meetings in preparation for the General Committee of the WSCF that would meet in Whitby, Canada, in August. K. H. was secretary for the Whitby Commission on "The Growing Church," which his friend Philip Potter chaired. Together they drafted the commission report, which is discussed in the next section of this chapter.

An especially important visit for K. H. was his trip to Czechoslovakia and Hungary in April and May of 1949. Both countries had recently come under Communist rule, and there was a concern in the WSCF to maintain contact with student movements in Eastern Europe. The opportunity to travel in Eastern Europe also enabled K. H. to see first hand the experience of Christians living and working under socialism and to spend time in conversation with some of the people whom he had met in Amsterdam. It was on this trip that he got to know the young Milan Opočenský who was already part of the Czech Student Christian Movement. Opočenský became another lifelong friend, and he would in future decades play a prominent role in the ecumenical movement

Ting went to Prague to see Y. T. Wu, who was there for a meeting of the World Peace Council, and they spent many hours together in conversation. Wu brought enthusiastic reports of the new life of people in the Liberated Areas of China, and, referring to Matthew 25, he said that the Communists were putting love into practice. He criticized stories about religious persecution that were appearing in the Western press, but added, "Even in the eventuality that religion will be harassed, I will still love this motherland."[49] Wu was Ting's friend and mentor, and he had a great deal of influence on how K. H. understood socialism and life in China on the eve of the establishment of the People's Republic.

Ting shared Wu's political understanding, but he was by nature more cautious and reserved, and, in matters he did not fully understand, he was more attuned to the wisdom of Gamaliel (Acts 5:33-39). His perspective was to see how things would develop in a changing situation. Ting met Christians in Eastern Europe who were strongly opposed to the Communists' new order and also those who were strongly supportive of it. He was aware of the ways in which anti-Communism was being used in Western churches to justify the status quo, and he rejected this approach.[50] He came to believe that the church could remain obedient to God in a socialist society, which meant that it was better for Christians to be open to new possibilities for cooperation with Communists rather than be dismissive of them.

> Upon entering the new situation of Communist control, if we must err, I would prefer to err on the side of naivety rather than cynicism. The cynic bangs the door of opportunity himself and lands himself in nothing but spiritual frustration and greater cynicism. But the naïve Christian worker sticks to his job. Doors banged against him will eventually give him the needed corrective to make him a true realist. There seem to be some redeeming possibilities in naivety which cynicism lacks.[51]

Ting had not been in China for three years, but the WSCF had had some contact with the CPC. In 1946, Dong Biwu and Li Fuqun, both high-ranking officials, had written a letter thanking the WSCF for supporting student relief efforts in the Liberated Areas under CPC control.[52] Roland Elliot, the WSCF treasurer, had visited Yanan, where he met Mao Zedong and Zhou Enlai.[53] Nothing immediately followed from this visit, but it did indicate that there were people in the Federation who were open to further conversation and cooperation with the Communists.

In light of this openness, Ting and his colleague John Coleman wrote a confidential memorandum for the consideration of Asian Christian leaders proposing the opening of Christian work in universities in Communist China.[54] "We must hurry to make ourselves instrumental for the evangelization of students there," they argued. "Even if we should fail to help them owing to our shortcomings . . . we cannot fail to understand our faith better through the 'confrontation' and 'dialogue' we shall have with Communism in China." A WSCF initiative in China would begin with the visit of a small team to assess the situation, meet with the Communist leadership and bring greetings from the Federation. Coleman and Ting had hoped that the proposal would be taken up at the Asian Leaders Conference in Ceylon, but it was not given serious consideration. They wrote a second proposal to WSCF officers in early 1949, but still no action was taken.[55]

In hindsight, this was unfortunate. Although it is unclear what the WSCF could have accomplished in China, the initiative would have opened up the possibility for dialogue between the Chinese Communists and an international ecumenical organization that did not side with their opponents in the

Y. T. Wu and Mao Zedong at CPPCC, 1949.

Cold War. A visit to the Liberated Areas would not mean that the WSCF was identifying itself with the position of the CPC. As K. H. Ting wrote in the travel diary cited above, the Communists "will hate a violently anticommunistic Christian as much as he will fear a Christian who is completely and unconditionally sympathetic with Communism." But he also observed that an overture from the WSCF would "to a considerable extent affect the future opening or closing of Church work in China."[56] That the visit did not take place meant that this was a missed opportunity.

Ting's work in the WSCF was not focused on China. Probably his most significant trip from the viewpoint of the Federation was the nine weeks he spent in South America in 1950. This was the first postwar visit from the WSCF to that continent, and Ting was asked to look into future initiatives in cooperation with national SCMs. He left New York on January 13 and traveled through Uruguay, Argentina, Chile, Brazil and Puerto Rico during the hot summer months of the Southern Hemisphere. He spoke at summer student conferences and met with the representatives from the SCMs, the churches and the missionary community in each place he visited.

Ting concluded from this visit that Latin America "provides the most difficult environment for the SCM to exist in the university" of any place he had experienced.[57] As isolated and minority communities within the university setting, the SCMs faced religious indifference, Roman Catholic intolerance, and opposition from conservative evangelicals. The SCMs in most places were small and weak, and the difficult environment was compounded by the fact that "too few students were Protestants and too few Protestants were students." Yet the SCMs in Latin America had a courageous, gifted and able leadership, which Ting felt deserved much stronger support from the WSCF.

This was Ting's first visit as a representative of one of the "younger churches" to another land of younger churches, and the experience invited comparison. There had been much less emphasis on the evangelization of intellectuals in Latin America as compared to China, Ting observed. As a result, there were three times the number of SCM secretaries and a much higher proportion of (Protestant) Christian intellectuals in China than in the whole of South America.[58] This also meant that Protestant Christianity had a higher intellectual standing in China and that more had been done in terms of indigenization and dialogue on contemporary and cultural concern.

Part of the problem in Latin America was the harm done by many conservative and fundamentalist missionaries from the North. One of these was Carl McIntyre, who had visited Brazil the previous year and whose message was one of division of the churches and judgment on those who disagreed with him. Ting was told that "in the churches as a whole sanity is gradually being restored and people have recovered from the damage he has done." It was worrisome that more such visits were projected for the future.[59] Even in the mainline churches in Brazil, earlier missionaries had preached a narrow and exclusivist theology. A new generation of missionaries would have to begin by undoing what their predecessors had done. Prior to evangelization, there would have to be an "un-evangelizing" of people from the "false, pagan Christianity" they had received from North American missionaries, Ting wrote. "Evangelism is not only witness *for* the gospel," he continued, "but also witness *against* many things which have claimed to be that gospel."[60]

Ting was not entirely opposed to foreign missionaries, in Latin America or anywhere else. Yes, they should work under national leadership, but they should be allowed to make their own contribution. "Partnership in obedience" (a theme that was popularized at Whitby in 1947) implies the discipline and humility of all parties, and it demands the best from each. "And the missionary," Ting wrote, "is neither a boss nor a guest, but a co-worker who seeks only the long range good of the Church with all his heart and soul and mind, without any reservation and inhibition."[61]

The churches in Latin America had to give greater attention to indigenization, in Ting's view. Roman Catholics criticized Protestantism as being "foreign, imported and unnatural," which made it all the more urgent to stress what today we would call the inculturation or contextualization of the gospel message. The alternative was for Christian intellectuals to become "a detached group of culturally rootless cosmopolitans saved away from their earth and existing in semi-foreign forms," Ting wrote. Using almost the same words he would repeat again and again in talks to visitors to China forty years later, Ting observed:

> The undeniable fact is that there does exist in the gospel something hopelessly "foreign" and hardly "natural" to man everywhere so we must not allow any extra burden of foreignness through our own faults in communication to make it even more unacceptable.[62]

The Latin American visit was of great value for the WSCF, but it also helped Ting better understand who he was and where he had come from. He saw promise in the South American church and the SCM, despite the enormous difficulties it was facing. The SCM had to discover for itself the full implications of what evangelism would mean in the new situation. Extended visits such as his could accomplish very little. Ting concluded that the church of South America had to discover itself and become itself, for in so doing, it would be "offering the best it can offer to the Whole Church in the world."[63]

The People's Republic of China was established on 1 October 1949. The Tings had intended to return to China in the summer of 1950. K. H. flew back to New York in mid-March in order to spend time with his family and work on his reports before beginning another series of meetings. He left for Canada in mid-April to attend the National Council of the SCMs in Guelph, where he led the Bible studies and took part in related meetings. He had planned to rejoin his family in late July, when they would proceed to San Francisco to board a ship for China in August.

As it turned out, K. H. was never able to return to New York. The Korean War broke out on June 25, and this threw all travel to and from East Asia into chaos. The ship on which they wanted to travel was cancelled. In addition, K. H. was prevented from reentering the United States from Canada because of the uncertain status of his passport and residency. For similar reasons, Siu-may and Yenren were unable to enter Canada. Hundreds of Chinese students and intellectuals were similarly stranded in North America. As the war continued, and tension between the United States and China increased, the prospects of their returning to China became increasingly remote.

Ting was in Whitby from July 7 to 23 for the Third Meeting of the World Christian Youth Commission, which was chaired by Li Chuwen. At about the same time, the Central Committee of the WCC was meeting in Toronto, less than forty miles away. It was at this meeting that the WCC passed its statement on "The Korean Situation and the World Order," which backed the American-sponsored UN resolution on Korea.[64] This action of the WCC Central Committee resulted in T. C. Chao's resignation as WCC president and a rupture between China and the World Council that would last for more than forty years.

World events continued to impinge on the Tings' personal situation, and for two months Siu-may in New York and K. H. in Toronto were wondering when they would get to see each other again. In early August, the Canadian government finally granted Siu-may and Yenren visas. K. H. went to the border to meet their train, and from there they continued on to Toronto for a short holiday and visits with Canadian friends. By now they understood that they would not be able to return to China in the near future.

Two days after Siu-may and Yenren arrived in Toronto, K. H. received a telegram saying that the WSCF had extended his appointment for one year and that the family should move to Geneva as soon as possible. This was confirmed in a letter from Philippe Maury sent the same day. He made it very clear that this appointment was not done out of sympathy for the Tings' personal situation, but because the Federation wished to have him take up its missionary concern in a more systematic and integrated way. Maury urged K. H. to put off thoughts of returning to China for at least one year.[65]

K. H. booked passage on a ship sailing from Quebec to Le Havre, France, on August 29. The family arrived in Geneva in mid-September, and they settled into a new apartment. Although K. H. had worked out of New York for much of the previous year, a great deal of his time had been spent traveling. Now the family would be settled, at least temporarily, in one place.

TOWARD A NEW UNDERSTANDING OF MISSION

Throughout the five years he spent in North America and Europe, K. H. Ting was primarily trying to understand and interpret the mission of the church. He was present at all of the important postwar mission conferences, during which time he developed an abiding commitment to what was being called the "new missiology," especially as it was being interpreted by people such as Max Warren and Stephen Neill.[66] He got to know the leading figures in the IMC and the WCC and counted among his personal friends many of his own generation who were helping the churches develop a more creative and ecumenical approach to mission in the modern world. Yet little attention has been paid to K. H. Ting's role in helping to reformulate an understanding of mission for the ecumenical movement.

His primary responsibility at the WSCF was to bring the concerns of ecumenism, mission and evangelism before the Federation as a whole. In his first two years, Ting spent most of his time traveling and interpreting mission and evangelism in a general way. This enabled him to see what was really happening in the ecumenical movement. In the year before he returned to China, he spent more time in Geneva with his family. It was during this period that he could give sustained and systematic attention to the missionary concern. His writing and reflection over this time culminated with the WSCF Consultation in Rolle on the theme "The Witness of the SCMs."[67]

Much of his thinking about mission was derived from the new missiology, which was being developed more fully by others. His special concern was how this thinking could be made relevant for students and the younger churches, and his reflection has its distinctive emphases. It is important to review K. H. Ting's thinking about mission prior to his return to China for two reasons. First, it represents the summation of his understanding of theology and mission in the WSCF and, therefore, brings to a close one stage in his own theological development. Second, it foreshadows his thinking about the church in China and his future theological writing. Intellectually, Ting's view of theology and mission made it imperative that he return to China to continue his ministry there.

K. H. Ting's starting point was the need to recover the idea that Christianity is essentially a missionary faith. The older churches of the West had become complacent, while the younger churches had been too passive, as if their only responsibility in mission were to "wait and grow old." But the church could remain strong and alive only insofar as it reached out to the world in mission. This was the basis of the faith of the church.

> Is there a missionary call? . . . Let us not be too sure that we have any right to say that we and our Church are "too weak" to be missionary . . . Let us rather say that we and our Church are not missionary enough to be strong.[68]

Ting believed that the decline in a vital understanding of mission and the missionary vocation in both East and West was rooted in a confusion over the nature of Christian faith and its relationship to the world. The report that he and Philip Potter drafted for the Commission on the Growing Church at the WSCF General Committee in Whitby (1949) identified both the cause of this malaise and the way forward:

> The present student situation comes from a vagueness in the minds of many about the reality of the sovereign God in history and in the world today and the obligation to share in it however dangerous and difficult the task may be . . . Students who have not the assurance that God is the Lord of history and of the world cannot be expected to commit themselves passionately to the service of the world-wide church either in their own community or in any other part of the world . . . The primary task, therefore, is not in the realm of educational methods but in rediscovering under the guidance of the Holy Spirit the nature of the gospel for our day.[69]

Mission requires faith in the God who acts in history, and it can be understood only eschatologically, in light of the coming of God's Kingdom into our world. This began with Jesus Christ, but God continues to act in the present day. The totality of human life must therefore be considered as important for mission. It is the human task to discover and discern how and where the living God is active, and what we are to do about it. This is the vocation of mission, and mission is the vocation of the church and of every Christian.

Evangelism is the starting point for mission, announcing the coming of God's Kingdom as it builds up the Body of Christ through the witness of men and women everywhere. This implies a forward-looking orientation, one that allows people to face the future without fear. There is a hopefulness and optimism about evangelism that should encourage others to be drawn into the Christian vision. There is also a direct relationship between evangelism and the Kingdom. Evangelism actually hastens the coming of God's Kingdom (2 Peter 3:12), according to Ting, because it encourages a sense of urgency and expectancy about the future and helps move things forward.

The phrase "expectant evangelism" had come from Whitby (1947), and it conveys the hope and future orientation of the evangelical task. Ting gives the term a new emphasis by concentrating on the human response to God and what men and women should expect from their relationship with God. The human response is a necessary corollary to God's action in history, and it gives human beings an important historical role to play. This is dramatized in the story of the Annunciation. There we find that Mary's positive response—"let it be with me according to your word" (Luke 1: 38)—was necessary for God's purpose to be fulfilled. "The Angels themselves," Ting writes, "together with the rest of the Creation looking for God's grace, must have waited with bated breath upon St. Mary's choice."[70] And she did not disappoint them.

Evangelism, therefore, should not be seen as the duty of fervent Christians, nor as a subjective feeling to go out and convert the nations, but as a human response to an objective and divine fact that is important for God's continuing work of creation and redemption. Evangelism is grounded in our understanding of the church, and it becomes the duty of each and every Christian.

> If Christ has become anything to you, He must be everything to you. And if He is indeed everything to you, how anxious you must be that He should mean everything to all people everywhere. That anxiety in you corresponds in a small way to the eternal hunger in the heart of God Himself, His longing for the whole of mankind to return to Him.[71]

However, evangelism must not be undercut by feelings of spiritual superiority in relationships with non-Christians. Christians should work cooperatively with those outside the church, even though they believe and know that their cooperation must be seen in light of the coming of Christ's Kingdom.

> We Christians ought to be absolutely sure of our gospel and yet utterly humble. We are to win the regard and confidence of our fellow citizens

by our personal friendship. We can also extend our full co-operation
to non-Christians in all efforts that make for national reconstruction,
social betterment and economic justice.[72]

The ultimate fulfillment of mission and evangelism depends on God
alone. But human cooperation with God is necessary for mission. "Yes,"
Ting observes, "God depends on us, not that the Almighty Creator has to,
but that the Loving Father must."[73] God has permitted human beings to dis-
rupt his creation through sin, and now God calls people to redeem and fulfill his creation in mission. Mary at the Annunciation represents the kind of
human cooperation with God that is needed to restore creation to its proper
order.

Mission involves extending the "New Humanity" in which the human
vocation will be fulfilled and within which the church will take root. For
this to make sense, it means that human activity must in some way be con-
tinuous with God's action in history. Grace is the fulfillment and not the
negation of nature, and so the continuity is established. It is at this point
that Ting departs from Barthian and neo-orthodox theologies which were
then popular in some quarters of the ecumenical movement. He was never
attracted to the theology of Karl Barth, and he never strayed very far from
his Anglican roots and Chinese humanism.

Ting liked to emphasize the continuity rather than discontinuity between
God and creation. He criticized the emphasis on discontinuity between God's
action and the human response that was implied even in the theme of the
inaugural assembly of the WCC:

> For us to stress the chasm between "God's design" and "man's dis-
> order" so absolutely as to deny that continuity is to cut the nerve of
> any Christian doctrine of history, work and vocation, and is to sanc-
> tion moral irresponsibility and cynicism.[74]

He believed that this chasm would inevitably result in a sense of pes-
simism about all human efforts to change the world. The evangelistic and
missionary vocation had been undercut "in certain fashionable theologies of
today," and this was what caused the confusion and complacency among
students and the churches in the West. What use was there in trying to
change the world if Christians did not believe that in some imperfect way
they were responding to God's call? K. H. had been involved in such efforts
since his student days in Shanghai, and he saw them as directly related to the
imperative of Christian faith.

Ting was pointing out the failure in some contemporary theologies to live
up to their missionary calling. This criticism would have been difficult for
colleagues such as Philippe Maury and others in the WSCF, the WCC and
the IMC to accept. (In the official version of the paper just cited, "God's
design" and "man's disorder" have been replaced by "God's glory" and

"man's corruption," thus muting the implied criticism of the WCC.[75]) They would have criticized Ting's perspective as being "too optimistic" about human possibilities for change and too casual in its rejection of neo-orthodoxy. In future years, there would be other voices in the WSCF calling for a better theological basis with which to understand the possibilities of human cooperation with God to change the world.[76] In the 1960s, this same emphasis on human cooperation with God to change the world enabled a new generation of students to push for radical change in the ecumenical movement.

He may have been critical of certain kinds of ecumenical theology, but Ting was absolutely committed to the church, which he saw as a divine society focused on mission. He saw the church as both a "church militant," which witnesses to God's reign, and a "church expectant," which prepares for God's coming. But there continues to be a discrepancy between the church as it now exists and the church that God intends it to be. The church often says the same thing as everyone else, but in a pious way. What was needed was a rediscovery of the mission of the church in each place in relationship to the international ecumenical community.

Missionary work is always concrete, and so it depends on the witness and wisdom of the church wherever it is found. Missions should never "denationalize" people and take them out of their context for this would not allow the church to fulfill its true vocation. The need for indigenization follows from this. For K. H. Ting, indigenization was based on an understanding of the Incarnation that owes more to his reading of the Jesus of the Gospels than the interpretation of Christ in St. Paul. The meaning of "partnership in obedience" is to affirm and support the witness of each particular church as an extension of the Incarnation and as a constituent part of the ecumenical family.

> In asserting that the immediate responsibility for evangelism in any area should normally lie with those churches which, by virtue of their cultural affinity, geographical nearness and other advantages, can most naturally and economically fulfil it, we are actually rediscovering missions—because they work on behalf of the whole church and, of course, the backing of the whole Church ought to be made available to them in all forms feasible.[77]

Every Christian has a vocation for evangelism, not just "professional" missionaries. Mission is not a "specialized ministry" of a few individuals sent overseas. Ting wanted to downplay the idea that mission depended on the sending of foreign missionaries. Instead, he viewed the meaning of the missionary vocation for each individual in light "of the whole on-going, creative and redemptive struggle of God for humanity."[78] This vocation begins not in foreign fields, but wherever the church exists.

Because mission involves human efforts to change the world, the church must be concerned about the social and political movements of every age. Unlike our faith in God, these movements are passing historical phenomena. They may work for good or for ill, but in either case, they vie for human souls. To the extent that they work for the good of humanity, social and political movements represent the moving of the Holy Spirit in the world and thus reveal the ongoing purpose of God in human history. The Christian is therefore called to discern what is redeemable within the social political ical movements of the time.

The church should neither uncritically embrace contemporary social movements nor should it stand aloof from them. It must continue to be involved with them, regardless of the consequences.

> The Church cannot rest at peace when the world seems to treat it well; it does not grumble (but rather calls itself blessed) when people find it necessary to persecute it. And persecution cannot make the Church hate its enemy or cease to pray for him any more than supposed freedom can give the Church any illusion or complacency in it.[79]

Ecumenism and mission come together at this point. They are not opposed to each other but continually interact and are mutually interdependent. Ecumenism involves concern for the world as well as for the church in every place. The witness of ecumenism, which grew out of the missionary movement, helps to recover this unity.

The WSCF is a good example of what this relationship can mean. But the WSCF had not been seriously concerned about articulating its own view of mission in the postwar years. As K. H. Ting wrote in 1950, "in the area of missions our role has been merely the passive one of transmitting to the students the current missionary presentations and apologetics."[80] He believed that the WSCF and the SCMs maintained their vigor and effectiveness through their sensitivity to the ideological conflicts and changes of the contemporary world. Students were always interested in new ideas and questioning basic assumptions. Therefore, the WSCF was in the best position to take the leadership in both developing and promoting a new missiology.

In his last year at the WSCF, K. H. was trying to take the initiative in thinking about mission away from the IMC and over to the WSCF.[81] SCMs and the WSCF were better prepared to respond to the line he was advocating. Students were more interested in social and political concerns, and they did not see mission as primarily involving the sending of missionaries. The Rolle Consultation helped to articulate the Federation's view of mission, and K. H. should have been pleased that it endorsed much of what he had been saying. Although Rolle did not seriously challenge the IMC, the missionary concern of the WSCF would be taken up by others in the years ahead. This is part of K. H. Ting's legacy to rethinking mission in the postwar years.

Ting always wanted mission to involve "two-way traffic"—between older and younger churches, between the SCMs and the denominations, between God and the world. The church would in this way promote the cross-fertilization of the gospel, as churches and individual Christians shared their gifts with one another for the mutual enrichment of all. In his final report to the WSCF, Ting spoke of how the gifts and fruits of the Holy Spirit would be distributed to the whole of humankind:

> The Communion of Saints is the way in which individuals and communities within the Church, glorifying God for the gifts which have been bestowed upon them severally, use and multiply them and strengthen each other in them.[82]

Ting adds that this was what St. Paul had in mind as he anticipated his journey to Rome (Romans 1:11, 12). The ecumenical movement to which he had been called was one expression of the communion of saints, and K. H. had used his gifts to strengthen its work and witness. In their five years away from China, K. H. and Siu-may Ting had developed a deep affection for the ecumenical community, and they had made lasting friendships with many men and women within it. Now they looked forward to their return to China.

The WSCF discussed Ting's final report when the executive committee met in Berlin in late August. Participants also sent their greetings and good wishes to the Ting family, who were already on their way back to China. Even as this community gathered in Berlin, the Tings were anticipating their own journey home, where their gifts would be used in new and different ways.

Part 2

DECONSTRUCTING CHRISTIANITY
IN CHINA, 1951-1976

4

Returning to a "New China," 1951-1956

Ruffle the perfect manners of the frozen heart,
And once again compel it to be awkward and alive,
To all it suffered once, a weeping witness.

W. H. Auden[1]

Religion will continue to exist for a long time, and its future develop-
ment will depend upon future conditions. But as long as there are ques-
tions which people are not able to explain and resolve on an
ideological level, the phenomenon of religion will be unavoidable.

Zhou Enlai[2]

In the late 1940s and early 1950s, reports about China that were reaching the West painted an increasingly grim picture of life under the Communists. The Chinese Revolution had become a new arena for the Cold War,
and a propaganda campaign was being conducted by both sides. Western
journalists tended to focus on the violent and coercive nature of the new
regime, and their stories, combined with the war reporting coming out of
Korea, reinforced the image of "Red China" as a hostile and aggressive
power that had to be opposed, lest other dominoes fall in Asia.

This same picture was reflected in the churches. China, which had been
the world's largest "mission field," had been lost. Western missionaries
began their exodus from China in 1950, and by late 1951 almost all foreign
personnel had left, with the exception of those who had been arrested or
jailed. The Christians with whom they had worked were encouraged by the
Communists to distance themselves from the missionaries, especially after
the start of the Korean War. Stories about the persecution of Chinese Christians added to the general picture of doom and gloom that was emerging in
Europe and North America. All of this had an enormous influence among
those who were trying to understand China from afar.

In Geneva, London and New York, the leaders of the churches and mission boards held countless meetings trying to assess the new situation and determine what they should do next. The end of the missionary era in China reverberated around the world. Although the ecumenical community was not completely averse to cooperation with churches in socialist countries, the Chinese Revolution had raised many new questions. What did it mean for the missionary movement as a whole? Was Christianity now part of the East-West struggle? [3] Could there be real religious freedom under a Communist government? What was the future of Chinese churches suddenly cut off from missionary tutelage? How could ecumenical relationships be maintained?

In this situation, many friends and colleagues began to advise K. H. and Siu-may not to return to China. Even such a long-time friend and sympathetic observer of the Chinese Revolution as David Paton cautioned him against going back, at least for a few years. W. A. Visser 't Hooft, general secretary of the World Council of Churches, made the strongest case against the Tings' decision to return. His advice, although motivated by a genuine pastoral concern, presupposed the anti-Communist bias of most Europeans and North Americans in the ecumenical movement. At one point, Visser 't Hooft even suggested to K. H. that his presence in China might be neither needed nor welcomed by the Chinese church. He offered suggestions about job possibilities elsewhere. Four weeks before he and Siu-may left for Hong Kong, K. H. sent Visser 't Hooft a handwritten letter, typically diffident and indirect, but also expressing his clear intention to return to China.

> Under the present circumstances, so far, I have not felt clearly that my colleagues in China wish me not to go back. While the situation will be difficult, I do not think I want to take the initiative myself to decide to stay abroad and then look for something to do. So we are proceeding, though inevitably slowly, with our plans of returning to China.[4]

In this letter and in his conversations with friends in the West, K. H. was always polite and discreet, but he had always said he would return to China, and he would not change his mind for personal reasons. We may assume that he was also relying on the advice of his friends in China, but no correspondence survives.

Marie-Jeanne de Haller, who had worked very closely with K. H. in the WSCF, seems to have understood him better than most other colleagues. In her response to a letter from a missionary in Hong Kong asking why K. H. had returned, she was able to interpret his decision in a positive light.

> I am quite sure from our conversations that he felt that his duty was to go back to his country and bear his Christian witness there. He has had a very difficult time over here in the West, meeting exclusively people who found it difficult to understand why he intended to go back and who did not seem to have the imagination to realize what may be

going on in China from a positive angle. This I think has motivated still more the feeling of urgency that K. H. has had to go back.[5]

Like many Chinese who were preparing to return to their country, the Tings did not accept the bleak picture of life in "New China" that was projected in the West. Overseas Chinese intellectuals from all over the world were returning to China in large numbers in the early 1950s, responding to the call to "serve the motherland." The Tings were part of this movement. They had their own sources of information about what was happening in China, and they had been following the progress of the CPC for years. China was their home; it was where they belonged, and they believed that the Communist Revolution would bring needed social changes.

K. H. and Siu-may Ting had been frustrated in their attempt to return in 1950 and early 1951, but they persevered. Long before the start of the Chinese Civil War, they were committed to the progressive and democratic cause in China, and they were ready and willing to devote their lives to a "New China." They had worked with the Communists in Shanghai, they had a number of friends who were working for the new government, and they were part of the progressive and social action oriented wing of the church. Most importantly, they believed they were needed in China for this was their Christian calling.

By the summer of 1951, the Tings' travel documents were in order, and they had their visas for Hong Kong. Having said their goodbyes, the family left Geneva on August 18 and flew to Hong Kong, with overnight stops in Karachi, Calcutta and Bangkok.

In Hong Kong they stayed at the Anglican Church Guest House, courtesy of Bishop R. O. Hall, whom K. H. had first met in Shanghai after the war. K. H. had served as Bishop Hall's interpreter at a meeting of the House of Bishops in Shanghai in 1945. Hall was a powerful personality who served as Anglican bishop of Hong Kong from 1932 to 1966, and he was a well-known supporter of progressive social causes. He viewed the changes taking place in China much more optimistically than most, and when they met in Hong Kong, he was one of the very few who encouraged the Tings in their decision to return. [6] Hall also expressed his hope that the Anglicans in Hong Kong might continue to relate to the church in China in positive and helpful ways.

Braving the sultry summer heat with their three-year-old son, the Tings were busy during the week they spent in the British colony. Hong Kong was already the destination for the many refugees, émigrés and missionaries coming across the border from the mainland, and K. H. met with quite a number of them. Some people wondered why anyone would want to return to China when they saw themselves as lucky to get out. The Tings met relatives and friends in Hong Kong who presented conflicting stories of China and the church. K. H. and Siu-may listened thoughtfully, but they were undeterred in their resolve.[7]

At ten o'clock on the morning of 29 August 1951, they boarded the through train to Guangzhou at the Kowloon-Canton railway station. After a brief stop in Guangzhou, they continued on by rail to Shanghai. They had come home.

REORIENTATION

The Shanghai to which the Tings returned had changed dramatically in the five years they had been away. After the end of the war, the city began rebuilding, and the businesses and banks resumed their commercial activities. The missionaries and Chinese church leaders returned, and the universities and other institutions that had been in western China moved back. Within months after the end of the war, civil war broke out between the Nationalists and the Communists. The city became an important area of contestation in the political struggle between the two sides, and a growing number of intellectuals sided with the CPC because they had witnessed firsthand the corruption of the Nationalist government. [8] In the meantime, Shanghai once again began receiving large numbers of refugees from neighboring provinces, which contributed to the growing unsettledness and disorder of the times. The inflation rate was skyrocketing, and the government seemed unable to cope.

The People's Liberation Army entered Shanghai on 27 May 1948, and the troops created a good first impression. Order was soon restored, prices for basic necessities were stabilized and the new government began to tackle the problems of crime, prostitution and opium addiction. The CPC quickly established a public security system to deal with saboteurs, dissident elements and other opponents. Popular support for the new order was encouraged through propaganda campaigns in the mass media and a new street committee network. Intellectuals were assured that their experience and skills were needed to help rebuild the country, and businesses were encouraged to reopen and increase production. Most of the people with whom the Tings had worked in the late-1930s and 1940s supported the Communists and welcomed the new order.

In rural areas all over China, land reform began very soon after the Communists assumed control. But the cities were a different matter, for the CPC had to build a new base of support and establish a governing structure. This not only involved encouraging popular participation but intensifying the struggle between the "people" and the "enemies" of the new order, and this was particularly the case in Shanghai. Some newspaper reports were describing Shanghai as a "parasitic" and "nonproductive" city that had to be radically transformed. More than two thousand neighborhood committees were formed in the city. Their job was to find people believed to be supportive of the Nationalists and resistant to the Communists.[9] In early 1951 there began a series of mass movements designed to consolidate Communist control over the urban population, the most important of which were: the "Campaign to Suppress Counterrevolutionaries"; the "Three Anti's" campaign against corrupt cadres; the "Five Anti's" campaign against unlawful business practices; the campaign to "Resist America and Aid Korea" at the time of China's entry into the Korean War; and the program of ideological remolding for Chinese intellectuals. Under the supervision of Communist cadres, the various campaigns sought to undermine the existing patterns of social relations, encourage mass participation in the political process, eradicate remnants of the opposition and destroy the control of the bourgeoisie as a class. This would represent the beginning of the transition to socialism.

The CPC also saw these mass movements as a fundamentally new approach to the political process, a way of involving people in the transformation of society. However, the campaigns introduced an atmosphere of intense social and psychological pressure that encouraged mutual distrust. Forced and often fabricated confessions were elicited through accusation meetings and public trials. Business people, supporters of the former government, and those who had worked with foreigners became the targets of the various movements. The Korean War made these campaigns harsher than they otherwise would have been, but they probably would have been conducted in any case.[10] Governance through the movements helped to consolidate political power, establish a sense of national purpose and foster commitment to the new order, but this came at great personal and social cost that cannot be justified by attributing it to the revolutionary excesses of the times. The campaigns of the 1950s have been criticized in China since the early 1980s, even in official CPC government documents.[11] While the criticisms may not have gone far enough, they do begin to address the injustices done to the tens of thousands of people who were unjustly accused.

The Christians who were part of the democratic movement in the late 1940s came together around Y. T. Wu after the establishment of the People's Republic of China and actively participated in the political movements of the early 1950s. Wu had recruited a number of young activists from the YM and YWCAs, and they became his key staff people in Shanghai. They were critical of the leadership of the churches, and, like Wu himself, they were close to the CPC. A thorough study of Y. T. Wu after the founding of the People's Republic has yet to be written, and many documentary sources from the period are not open to the researcher. There continues to be a great deal of controversy about Wu's political role. His theological views are debated among Christians inside and outside of China.[12] Wu was China's most important Christian leader in the 1950s and early 1960s, and his influence was felt in all aspects of the work of the TSPM. He is revered in the TSPM and the CCC as a founding father and the leading spirit of "Three-Self patriotism," but he is also criticized in many quarters for his role in orchestrating Christian participation in the political movements of the time.

Wu was interested in the reform of the churches, but he also became a key advisor on religious policy for the new government, which had not yet developed a policy of its own. Together with eighteen other Protestant leaders, Wu met with Premier Zhou Enlai in Beijing the month before the outbreak of the Korean War to discuss the difficulties the churches were facing in the new situation.[13] Zhou spent many hours in conversation with the church leaders, urging them to separate Christianity from its foreign connections in order to get on with their own work of reform and reorientation. He was sympathetic to the concerns that the Christians were raising, and he was not opposed to religious belief per se, but Zhou Enlai was also a committed Communist who was adamant in his opposition to the foreign influence in Chinese churches.

As a result of these meetings, Y. T. Wu and others drafted the "Christian Manifesto," which expressed support for the new government and its effort "to build an independent, democratic, peaceable, unified, prosperous and powerful New China" in which Christians would be required to be independent and free from overseas support and control.[14] They began a campaign for signatures in support of the Manifesto in the churches in July, and over the next four years, more than 417,000 Christians had put their names to the document. The statement itself was subsequently published on the front page of *Renmin ribao* (*People's Daily*), the main newspaper of the Communist Party, indicating government endorsement and encouraging Christians to support the ideas of the manifesto.

After the outbreak of the Korean War, Protestant leaders were called to Beijing for a series of meetings with the State Administrative Council. The new government had already intensified its criticism of the churches' dependence on foreign funds and personnel, but more direct action was now called for. President Truman had frozen all Chinese assets in the United States in December, and the Chinese government responded in kind by cutting off overseas funding for the churches. This decision was presented to the 151 church leaders at their meeting in Beijing in April 1951. There would no longer be foreign interference in the work of the Chinese churches. By this time, most of the missionaries had already left China, and the churches were in the hands of Chinese Christian leaders themselves. The Chinese Christian Three-Self Patriotic Movement (TSPM) Preparatory Committee was organized at this same meeting, led by Y. T. Wu and twenty-five other Christian leaders. It was based in Shanghai and staffed by former YM and YWCA workers. This committee was the key structure for the political involvement of Chinese Protestants until the First National Christian Conference in 1954.

One of the first tasks of the preparatory committee was to oversee the "Denunciation Movement," which was launched in the spring of 1951 to sever the connection between Christianity and imperialism.[15] Unlike the other mass movements of the early 1950s, the campaign to denounce or accuse missionaries, Chinese church leaders and other Christian institutions was conducted by Christians, although in many places it was initiated or directed by government officials. The course of the movement was similar to other mass movements, but it was designed to sever the personal link and sense of attachment that Christians had for the missionaries. For fifteen months, denunciation meetings were held in churches and public places all across China. These were particularly intense in Shanghai, where the TSPM Committee was based. There, dozens of meetings were organized over many months, the largest of which drew a crowd of more than 12,000 people.

Like other campaigns of the 1950s, the Denunciation Movement went to extremes. In this movement, a number of young Three-Self activists came to the fore, many of whom were key leaders or staff persons in the TSPM Preparatory Committee. Some activists, including Li Chuwen, the first TSPM general secretary, were underground CPC members. They encouraged popular participation and manipulated a crowd psychology consistent with the tenor of the times. In contrast to the activists, church leaders who spoke up at the denunciations probably felt that they were being forced to do so. People attending the mass meetings made exaggerated charges against missionaries and fellow church members. For the churches, this became the means through which the TSPM consolidated control of the churches, identified "friends" and "enemies" and generated support for the new order. The Denunciation Movement was a Christian counterpart to other mass movements of the 1950s and was a formative experience for the TSPM.

Unlike the political movements of the 1950s that have been criticized in China, the TSPM has never officially made a statement critical of the Denunciation Movement. It is true that this movement helped to sever the link between Christianity and imperialism, but the human cost was enormous. Many respected and revered Protestant leaders and missionary colleagues who had been denounced were deeply hurt, and the churches were left with wounds and broken relationships. Some of these wounds would take many decades to heal, and others were never really healed. The Denunciation Movement became formative for the TSPM in the eyes of both its supporters and its opponents, yet there remain very different assessments of its significance. We shall see that the Denunciation Movement and the history of the TSPM in the 1950s continued to be controversial in the TSPM and the China Christian Council after the end of the Cultural Revolution.

In early September, when the Denunciation Movement and the campaign to suppress counterrevolutionaries was in full swing, K. H. and Siu-may arrived in Shanghai. They had been away for five years. With their young son, they moved in with Ting's parents and began their readjustment to the new order. The churches, the YMCA and YWCAs were still open as they had been before, but funds were scarce and huge changes were taking place. Most of the Tings' friends were still at work in Shanghai. K. H. and Siu-may spent hours in conversation with them, catching up on all that had taken place in the last few years, and trying to get a sense of what was going on.

Siu-may was appointed headmistress at her old high school, St. Mary's Hall, which later became the Second Girls' Middle School. But for the next six months, K. H. did not have a regular job. He had not been involved in the struggles in Shanghai in the late 1940s; he had not been there for the formation of the TSPM Preparatory Committee; and he did not participate in the Denunciation Movement. Although Ting was sympathetic to the TSPM and supportive of Y. T. Wu, he was not at this time a Three-Self insider, and he had not yet reconnected to any Christian organization. He had a lot of time on his hands, which enabled him to read up on things, observe what was going on, think about the changes that were taking place, and decide what he would do.

In late 1951, not long after his return to China, K. H. visited Beijing, where he met Gong Pusheng, his colleague from YMCA–YWCA days, and her sister, Gong Peng (also known as Gong Weihang), who was Premier Zhou Enlai's private secretary. The two sisters were both in key positions in the CPC and confidants of Zhou Enlai. Gong Peng informed the premier that K. H. Ting had come to Beijing, and Zhou suggested that he stay on a few extra days so that they would have a chance to talk.

Zhou Enlai was many things to many people, and he has left an ambiguous legacy. A veteran revolutionary and close ally of Mao Zedong, Zhou was a brilliant thinker, a gifted strategist and a skilled diplomat. He was a man of enormous energy, and he charmed political leaders the world over with his insight and practical approach to the art of governance. Zhou has also been criticized for his seeming uncritical support of Mao's most extreme policies, despite his reputation for protecting others during political campaigns and serving as a force of moderation.[16] Cosmopolitan and urbane, Zhou combined a Confucian style with Marxist-Leninist practice. At the time of Liberation, he had spent more time abroad than all his colleagues in the Politburo combined.[17] For intellectuals of Ting's generation, Zhou was the Chinese leader they most admired. They saw him as an incorruptible leader who consistently put the interests of the Chinese people above his own. Recent scholarship has emphasized the darker side of Zhou Enlai's role in the Chinese political process, but this has not lessened the high regard in which he is held by people from all generations in China.

Zhou invited K. H. to a meal at his home in Zhongnanhai, the secluded compound for government and party leaders. One can imagine that Ting would have felt deeply honored by this invitation from the premier, whom he greatly admired. Feng Wenbin, who was then head of the Communist Youth League, was also at the dinner, and so was Gong Peng, but the purpose of the meal was for Zhou Enlai to get to know K. H. Ting.[18] This was Ting's first meeting with Zhou Enlai, but they would continue to see each other from time to time in the years and decades to come. Zhou had heard about Ting from the Gong sisters and probably from Y. T. Wu, and he was no doubt interested in bringing him into the fold and assessing his perspective as a potential Christian leader. From this time forward, Zhou Enlai became a powerful friend and promoter of K. H. Ting. They had a personal relationship that was of critical importance for Ting's public life, a relationship based on common commitment and mutual affection, not on political expediency.

K. H. Ting was especially drawn to what he saw as Zhou Enlai's humanitarianism, his patriotism and his commitment. For Ting, Zhou's political approach emphasized tolerance of different worldviews and respect for differences, rather than the fierce revolutionary struggle that was characteristic of many CPC leaders.[19] Tolerance and respect were needed to work for social change and build up the country. Ting's respect for Zhou Enlai deepened through the years. The well-known photograph of Zhou Enlai sitting in an armchair and looking off in the distance hangs in a place of honor in his home. Ting's perspective on Chinese politics, his understanding of Communism, his relationship to government officials and perhaps his own diplomatic style reflect the influence and vision of Zhou Enlai. Forty years after they met, Ting reflected on his first impressions.

> I can't remember now what we talked about, but I just remember that we talked about everything that came up. The atmosphere was very relaxed, very friendly, and very egalitarian. I didn't feel that he was someone different from me. He asked me many questions about life abroad. And I think he was a bit unhappy that I came back to China. My impression was that he probably thought that I could do a better job for China by staying abroad. Of course, he was glad that I got back to China. But somehow he felt that it would not be a bad idea if Siu-may and I stayed abroad much longer . . .
>
> A very important point that he made to me on that first occasion was that I should not think that Communists were necessarily opposed to religion. He said that there could be many motivating forces to make people do good things, to be patriots and to be revolutionaries. It is not just communism that motivates people to do good. Religion can also be one of those motivating forces. And he emphasized that he had high respect for religious people who are patriotic and progressive and revolutionary. Religion can make people progressive.[20]

To be patriotic, progressive and revolutionary did not mean for K. H. Ting that one should become uncritical of the new order. In returning to China, Ting saw that the situation was changing for the better, but he also saw many things he did not like. Foremost among these was the Denunciation Movement in the churches. He felt that many statements made in this campaign were biased, insincere and unfair, and he chose not to participate in the campaign. Subsequent conversations with Zhou Enlai and his wife, Deng Yingchao, at least one in the presence of He Chengxiang (1902-1967), who was then head of the Religious Affairs Bureau (RAB), seemed to strengthen Ting in his decision not to take part in the Denunciation Movement.[21] Zhou certainly would have been aware of the excessiveness of the movement.

TSPM activists from his own generation, such as Li Chuwen and Li Shoubao, gave the impression that Zhou Enlai supported or even initiated the Denunciation Movement, but Ting had a different view of the movement itself and Zhou's relationship to it. Forty years later, he spoke very directly about his own perspective.

> As we look back today, I think we should recognize that the Denunciation Movement was not a Chinese Christian movement. Some of its leaders were non-believers, people who did not understand religion, who did not appreciate the thoughts and feelings of Christians, or who despised religion and denied its longstanding character. They lashed out at religion and were anxious and impatient to accomplish their task, but they did not take into account their methods or results. They took control over those with power. Except for a very small minority, most Christians were passive or semi-passive about the movement. Many were forced to get up and denounce church leaders, but their hearts were full of contradictions, and after their speeches they continued to blame themselves for speaking against their convictions. The Denunciation Movement went against the principle of seeking truth from facts in facing trials and hardships. It hurt many people and damaged our international reputation.[22]

This is more than a judgment made in hindsight. Ting did not share the perspective of many of the more radical political activists in the TSPM who welcomed the Denunciation Movement and political struggle. His patriotism and commitment were never in doubt, and he became a strong advocate for the work of the TSPM. But his sense of churchmanship and fairness would temper the strong invective and bitter accusations coming from other quarters. At the time, Ting shared his reservations about the Denunciation Movement with Y. T. Wu and other close friends, but there was no way he could voice such opinions publicly. He had only recently returned to China, and he needed time to prove himself and better understand the situation. Ting had not been in China for the government meetings after the outbreak of the Korean War; he was not on the TSPM Preparatory Committee; and he was not part of the inner circle in Shanghai involved in the various political campaigns and patriotic initiatives. Because of his association with the WSCF and the ecumenical movement he may even have been regarded as an outsider, and perhaps not entirely trusted. However, there were different political and theological positions within the emerging TSPM, and there were many others in the church whose position was similar to that of K. H. Ting.

Ting did not participate in the Denunciation Movement, but even more surprising is the fact that K. H. Ting never put his signature to the Christian Manifesto. He said that this was not because he was against it but because he had no opportunity to sign it.

If I thought it was a very important thing that my signature should be there, then I would have tried to put my name somewhere there. But it just happened that I haven't signed it. It's not any indication of my attitude towards it.[23]

This disclaimer notwithstanding, it should be pointed out that more than one million Christians signed the manifesto *after* the Tings had returned to Shanghai.[24] There was a great deal of social pressure to make one's position known, and although K. H. Ting did this in many other ways, the fact that he never signed the Christian Manifesto is not without significance. He did support the position of the document, but his own approach to the issues involved as they affected the churches would have been somewhat different. The Anglican House of Bishops never endorsed the document but instead issued a pastoral letter that had more of a theological tone.[25] Almost all Anglican bishops in China subsequently became active supporters of the TSPM, as did the Sheng Gong Hui as a whole, but their alternative statement—like K. H. Ting's missing signature on the Christian Manifesto—indicates that there were different ways of situating oneself in support of the new movement, at least in those early years.

Ting's reorientation to China found expression in the early essays he wrote for *Tian Feng*, the journal that became the official publication of the TSPM Preparatory Committee. The first of these was a short interpretation of Genesis 3, the chapter where God asks Adam, "Where are you?" This was the question which Ting put to Christians in China and to himself in light of the tremendous changes taking place in the new society.

In the period when darkness ruled, there were Christians whose pure faith and moral rectitude shone like "bright lamps in a dark room." But today, when "the East is Red and the Sun is rising" we no longer have any reason to congratulate ourselves. The people's high sense of morality is so brilliant that our "bright lamps" have lost their luster. In the face of this high morality and the mighty movement that is opposed to every kind of evil, we have become like Adam, with no way of hiding from God's searching question, "Where are you?"[26]

Ting went on to say that Christians must repent and confess their sins before God and the people. They should be humble and willing to fight against corruption, waste and bureaucratism (the "Three Anti's"), so that they could once again face God and move forward with the people of the whole nation. In this essay, written just six months after he had returned to

China, Ting was adding a new theological voice to the work of the TSPM, and his own position was being reformulated in the process.

This essay is clearly influenced by the politics of the times, but Ting's distinctive approach to the Bible and theology are also evident. He used all the appropriate political rhetoric but never lost sight of the way in which the Bible spoke personally to people. The view of mission that he had developed in Geneva emphasized how God was active in history, and this could be applied to the Chinese Revolution and movements for change and liberation all over the world. God's action in the secular world implied a need for Christian humility about one's own accomplishments and human cooperation with God in making the world a better place. He was attempting to make theological sense of what was happening in the Chinese Revolution. This essay reflects Ting's belief that something new was happening in China, and so he draws on many examples of how a new morality was emerging outside the church in the People's Republic.

His second article in *Tian Feng* attacks the alleged use of bacteriological warfare by the Americans in Korea. We will have more to say about these allegations below, but here it is important to consider Ting's emerging theological perspective. He contrasts those who promote death using bacteriological weapons with those who conquer death, such as the self-giving resistance fighters and the heroine of the new revolutionary opera, *The White-Haired Girl*. Christians should side with the revolutionaries not the American aggressors for this is a way of life, not death. Jesus refused a narcotic on the cross (Matthew 27:33, 34), and so his followers must discipline themselves in the fight for a better tomorrow, fully conscious of what they are doing. Christianity must never become a narcotic to dull the senses or destroy life; Christian faith is not an "opiate for the people," in Marxist terms. Christians are engaged in a struggle for life over against death as part of the Easter experience.[27]

The two essays cited above have both a political and a theological purpose. They also reflect that Ting's identification with the new order was more than a political choice; it was grounded in the incarnational perspective on the Bible and theology that he embraced during his seminary days and that developed during his time in North America and Europe. As we reread the essays today, the language and examples are dated, but Ting's contextual approach is still relevant. If they sound too "political," then they should be read alongside many of the theological essays that were being written in other parts of the world at the time. K. H. Ting's reorientation meant coming to terms with a new social and political environment, but he did not see a basic conflict between this environment and his Christian faith.

Ting's theological approach is also evident in a series of Lenten meditations that he delivered to the Jiangsu Diocese of the Sheng Gong Hui for Good Friday in 1952.[28] In these meditations, he uses a personal and political hermeneutic as he seeks to understand what God is saying to the Chinese church in the new situation. Ting explores many familiar themes, including

God's immanence, faith and works, and God's love and concern for people. He is reinterpreting what Christian life might mean in the new order. Christians should be repentant and humble, but they should also rejoice in this new situation.

> When Christ saw Jerusalem oppressed by the enemy, he wept over the people's misery (Lk. 19:41). He rejoiced seeing the devil fall down from heaven like a flash of lightning (Lk. 10:18). Today, we in China no longer suffer under the heel of our enemies. The devil has been defeated. Would not Christ rejoice at this too?[29]

These meditations were later published as a devotional booklet by the Christian Literature Society (CLS). The previous year, the CLS had become an important target in the Denunciation Movement. Its general secretary, Hu Zuyin, delivered an emotional diatribe against the CLS, charging that it had been promoting imperialism since its inception.[30] Like all other published accusations, this one was carefully edited and gives a thoroughly distorted picture of the situation, making it appear as if the missionaries had done nothing in the CLS without an ulterior motive and suggesting that they were always conscious agents of cultural imperialism. The accusation must have been written under extreme pressure, and this was common in the Denunciation Movement. Hu Zuyin "confessed" that he himself had been implicated in cultural aggression against China, and sometime thereafter he was removed from his position in the organization.

Hu's removal was followed by a thorough reorganization of the CLS. In early 1952, K. H. Ting was appointed general secretary, a temporary and ad hoc assignment. He had not been involved with the CLS or Christian literature work previously, and he had not taken part in the denunciation meeting in which the CLS came under attack. This was his first position after his return to China, and it might also have been a kind of testing of his leadership and commitment. Coming in as a relative outsider with the support of the TSPM leadership, Ting may have been seen as an appropriate choice for the new position. But he was not able to do very much once he got there.

> The main work that I did in the Christian Literature Society during that half year was really to keep the CLS staff paid, because that organization was in a very difficult financial situation. I remember we got rid of all the accumulated old books, sent to be recycled in order to increase the income. And then I was instrumental in having the salaries of people cut in half, in order that the CLS could last longer, and meanwhile we could get some new books published. That was very hard. At that time, church people weren't sure what they should say and what they shouldn't say, so not many people dared to write. I don't know if it was a fault on my part or a merit, to have people's income cut in half, for that was difficult for the people [involved].[31]

He did not stay on as CLS general secretary for very long. In the summer of 1952, Ting was appointed secretary of a new theological education committee organized by the TSPM, a position that was more suitable for his theological interests but also important politically. Kiang Wen-han, his former superior in the YMCA, replaced Ting as general secretary of the CLS.[32] The CLS survived until the "Great Leap Forward" in 1957 when it became part of the United Chinese Christian Publishers, but this new organization was never able to do very much and ceased to exist in the early 1960s.

The Tings' second son was born in Shanghai in July 1952, and he was named Heping, which means "peace." By this time, the family had moved into the pastor's apartment at Community Church, the church that K. H. had served during the Japanese occupation. This would be the Tings' last residence in Shanghai. K. H. moved to Nanjing that fall, although the family did not join him there until 1954.

NANJING UNION THEOLOGICAL SEMINARY

In early 1952, the TSPM Preparatory Committee took up the issue of theological education, which had become an area of concern for practical and political reasons. No longer supported by funds from overseas, the seminaries and theological colleges were in financial difficulty, and they would soon be unable to continue. The denominations themselves were hard pressed financially, and they had no funds for theological education. Something had to be done to create a viable alternative to the existing situation, especially in the East China region where many seminaries and churches were concentrated.

Theological education was also a politically sensitive area because the government saw Christianity as a potentially subversive movement allied with the West. Education at all levels was supervised by the government, and although theological education was still nominally the province of the churches, it would be subject to careful scrutiny, especially for the political implications of religious training. Preparation for the ministry had never been a very attractive career option for Chinese intellectuals, even those from Christian families, but now there could be adverse political consequences for the choice of a church career. Both the government and the preparatory committee would assume that it was important to instill in those who wanted to become pastors and church workers a better understanding of the new political order and Three-Self patriotism, alongside the usual program of theological training.

The TSPM Preparatory Committee called an East China Theological Education Forum in the late summer of 1952 that brought together church leaders and educators from a wide variety of backgrounds to discuss their common problems. Luo Zhufeng, head of the Religious Affairs Bureau in

K. H. Ting preaching at the opening of Nanjing Seminary, November 1952.

East China, addressed the assembly on the responsibilities of patriotic Christians. He was to become another important friend and promoter of K. H. Ting in government circles. Other major presentations at the conference were made by Y. T. Wu, who spoke on the general position of the TSPM, and K. H. Ting, who delivered a critique of the way in which theology had been distorted and manipulated by imperialism and by theologians in capitalist societies.[33] Ting's writings were increasingly in tune with the politics of the times. The articles in *Tian Feng* describe this meeting in glowing terms, but one can imagine that it was difficult for many participants, given the political climate and pressures to unify very diverse streams of theological education.

On the basis of this meeting, a plan of "voluntary" union for theological seminaries in East China was approved. The plan may have been voluntary, but there was really no other alternative. The principles of union emphasized belief in the Bible, adherence to the government's political and educational program, acceptance of the leadership of the TSPM Preparatory Committee, and mutual respect in matters of theology, tradition and church order.[34] The new theological institution was named Nanjing Union Theological Seminary (NUTS), and it would occupy the buildings and grounds of the former Presbyterian Women's Bible Teachers' Training School. The newly elected seminary Preparatory Committee was headed by Y. T. Wu, with Cheng Zhiyi (a theological liberal) and Jia Yuming (a well-known conservative evangelical) serving as vice-chairpersons. K. H. Ting was appointed committee secretary.

The work of union proceeded very quickly. Eleven theological institutions came together to form Nanjing Union Theological Seminary on 1 November 1952.[35] The seminaries ranged from fundamentalist to conservative evangelical to liberal, representing most of the large Protestant denominations in the provinces of East China. Fifty-nine faculty members and more than one hundred students came to Nanjing from the former seminaries. The seminary Preparatory Committee was reconstituted as a twenty-six-member board of directors in December 1952, chaired by Y. T. Wu.[36] Wu recommended that the board elect K. H. Ting principal, and Cheng Zhiyi and Ding Yuzhang (a theological conservative) became vice-principals. Ting was only thirty-seven years old when he became principal, but he had the confidence of Y. T. Wu, and his education and experience would make him an appropriate candidate for the job. The fact that Ting came into the TSPM as a relative outsider meant that he could lead a new theological seminary without the baggage of having been personally involved in earlier struggles.

In many ways, Nanjing Union Theological Seminary resembled other educational institutions in the China of the early 1950s.[37] It was under the general supervision of the Communist Party, and all students were required to attend political-education classes, as stipulated in the Common Program (Article 47). Patriotic education at the seminary was directed by Xu Rulei, who also chaired the institution's Three-Self Reform Committee. Seminary students, together with all other students in Nanjing, took part in activities and demonstrations that were organized or orchestrated by the new government. This was a period when everyone was supposed to learn from the Soviet Union, and so the seminary had its own branch of the Sino-Soviet Friendship Society. The Korean War and continuing mass movements politicized the atmosphere of seminary education, and this produced a mixture of responses among seminary students ranging from revolutionary fervor to vocal or unspoken resistance.

Many intellectuals in the early 1950s were still riding the high tide of patriotism, and these included intellectuals in the Christian community beyond those in the Three-Self leadership. Contemporary accounts about how Christians were learning to "love the motherland" reflected the feelings of many students and intellectuals in those years, even though they were usually cast in a standardized political format. The atmosphere at Nanjing Union Seminary was more political than most students and faculty from more conservative Christian backgrounds were used to. A diversity of theological viewpoints was represented, but real power was in the hands of political activists identified with the Three-Self Reform Committee, and they were often impatient with conservative theology.

Ting recalls that the Three-Self activists were firmly in control when he arrived at the seminary, and he wanted to do something about it.

> When I came to be the principal of Nanjing Seminary in 1952, I found that the Three-Self Organization was considered to be what a party was to the government. That is, authority was concentrated in Three-Self.
>
> The church didn't have any authority on its own but it was Three-Self that decided everything for the church. And there was a Three-Self organization in Nanjing Seminary when I came, and Xu Rulei was the chairperson. And before I came Cheng Zhiyi was the (acting) principal, and Cheng Zhiyi didn't make any decisions. Anyway he didn't like to make decisions, and he was probably rather glad that decisions were made for him by Three-Self. I remember very clearly that once Xu Zhigang (a support staff) wanted to buy a raincoat with seminary money because he needed it when he went out. He had to get the permission from Three-Self first. That was the state of affairs in the seminary.
>
> But Luo Zhufeng at that time was Religious Affairs Bureau Director of East China, and he had very much to do with the union of the theological schools. So I discussed this matter with Luo Zhufeng in Shanghai. I somehow felt that Nanjing Seminary mustn't be controlled by Three-Self, and he supported the idea, so we organized a meeting on responsibility. We got the heads of the various theological schools which joined to serve on (it), so in this way authority was shifted away from Three-Self. I think this must have been within a year after I arrived.[38]

This was another instance of the way in which Ting saw himself, in retrospect, as distancing himself from the more activist TSPM position. Under his leadership, Nanjing Seminary became more autonomous from the local TSPM committee in the running of its affairs. The seminary was under the authority of the preparatory committee and firmly committed to its political platform, but now the faculty could give greater attention to the preparation of students for the ministry.

Writing six months after the seminary's opening, Ting declared that the institution was now free from "imperialistic control," and that students and faculty were discovering that faith and patriotism could be compatible. They were "enthusiastically plunging into activities in response to the call of the motherland."

> So that our motherland can accumulate more funds for heavy industry, our students pulled up weeds for road construction and economized on their use of water and electricity, thus expressing the attitude that they were now masters of their own country.[39]

Faculty and students at Nanjing Seminary, ca. 1952.

The seminary could promote patriotism, but its primary purpose was theological education. Nanjing Union Theological Seminary was one of the very few places in China that continued to train students for the Christian ministry. At about the same time, Yanjing Union Theological Seminary was established in Beijing, bringing together seven theological institutions from northern China. Theological seminaries in Shanghai, Guangzhou and Chongqing also continued to function for the next decade, after they had been reorganized by local TSPM committees. But NUTS soon became the most important theological institution in the country. Its faculty and student body was, at the time, more theologically diverse than any seminary in the world. It was one thing for Christian students and teachers to adjust themselves to a new political order, but it was quite something else for them to learn what it meant to live and work with one another under the same roof. Before this time, there had been very little interaction between Christians from fundamentalist, evangelical and liberal backgrounds, but now all at once they were brought together. The question was, would they be able to get along with one another?

As the one who presided over this undertaking, K. H. Ting recalls that "the most important problem and the most important achievement" was the evolution of the policy of mutual respect in matters of faith and worship.[40] Mutual respect meant that people from different traditions had to learn to accept one another as representing valid expressions of Christian understanding.[41] It was the only way possible for a union seminary to be attempted at all. The policy was developed more to encourage tolerance and peaceful coexistence among different theological traditions than to promote dialogue and church unity, for the distance between the established positions was enormous.

Biblical interpretation was especially controversial, and therefore separate courses were taught in the Pentateuch, Isaiah and the Gospels. Separate classes were also arranged for students preparing for ordination in the different denominations. But students were together in other classes and in services of worship, even though many may have wished they were not. Theology was not taught in separate classes, but professors representing different theological viewpoints lectured on alternate days. There were complaints voiced by students about what professors said in classes and how worship was conducted, but the seminary did not split apart. The unity which emerged at Nanjing Seminary was fragile and in some ways superficial, but everyone could see that these were difficult times for the churches. Given the tenor of the times, the fact that seminary education continued at all was an accomplishment.

The policy of mutual respect was the linchpin of what Ting saw as a sincere effort to ensure that theological education would continue. It was what held the students and faculty together. K. H. Ting was instrumental in the development of the policy of mutual respect and in its implementation at NUTS. His integrity, his attention to interpersonal relationships, and his concern for other people, as well as his theological broad-mindedness and his sense of churchmanship all contributed to his understanding of mutual respect. Ting was able to hold a broadly diverse group of people together, both in the 1950s and 1960s and again in the 1980s and 1990s. Many of the original faculty and staff served the seminary during both periods, including Sun Hanshu, Chen Zemin, Han Bide, Wang Weifan (one of the first students), and Xu Rulei. Other longstanding faculty came to Nanjing from Yanjing Seminary in Beijing a few years later, including Luo Zhenfang, Xu Dingxin and Mo Ruxi.

In the 1950s, Ting regularly preached and lectured to the student body, and he sometimes taught courses to more advanced students on theology or logic.[42] His lectures to the students as a whole dealt with topics of theological and political interest, and they indicate in published form that he was wrestling with his own theological position. Through his talks and sermons, he was attempting to articulate a new vision for the church and the seminary. Although he had limited time for theological writing and reflection, Ting published several essays and sermons between 1953 and 1955 that reflect the direction in which he wanted the church and seminary to move.[43] These writings illustrate how he was recasting some of the themes he had developed in the WSCF and responding to the new situation.

Ting was not attempting a new Christian *apologia,* a Christian-Marxist dialogue or a theological approach to non-Christian intellectuals. It was far too early for any of these, and Ting was still developing his own theological position. His concern in his lectures was to engage students, pastors and ordinary Christians in a discussion of the situation in New China and what this implied for the mission of the church.

In his published essays, we can see what might be called a double movement at work. First, Ting hoped that Christians would accept the new order and adjust themselves to life in a socialist society. This was their new context and the setting for Christian ministry. Second, he stressed the continuing importance of Christian witness, by which he meant spreading the gospel and building up the church. He believed that Christian faith could be compatible with political life in New China, for church and society were complementary categories of Christian involvement. What I term a double movement in his writings suggests that Ting moved back and forth between the political and religious responsibilities expected of Christians, which he saw as two different dimensions of a common task. This approach was not inconsistent with what he had been writing in the ecumenical movement, although the context was vastly different.

As Ting has told a number of audiences in the 1980s and 1990s, he spent several months rereading the Bible after he arrived in Nanjing, and especially the Gospels and Epistles of Paul. His family was still in Shanghai, and his Bible reading became a way for him to discern what he should do in his new role as seminary principal. The essays and sermons he wrote during this time are based on careful biblical exposition, as were most of his theological writings over the previous ten or twelve years. The difference is that now he was attempting to search the Bible in order to understand the ideas of patriotism, love of the motherland, purification of the church and the struggle against injustice, all of which were important politically in New China. In some of his essays, such as those that were later published as *How to Study the Bible*, he adopted an evangelical language. For these essays, he may have worked with evangelicals at the seminary to help him develop a language and style appropriate for this audience. In other essays, he developed new ideas from his own theological tradition. In all of his essays, he writes directly of his political convictions. Ting maintained that Christians had no cause to reject China's new order on biblical grounds, for in this new situation they could discover that the Bible itself had many things to say about loving one's motherland.

> Formerly we believed that since Christians were spiritual, they need not be concerned with the affairs of their country. Consequently, the many examples in the Bible expressing the love of one's motherland became "closed gardens and forbidden wells." It is true that there are no direct references to the word patriotism in the Bible. But there are many obvious examples of the true feelings of love for one's motherland. The strange thing is that our former blindness and ignorance hid these from us.[44]

He went on to cite biblical references *inter alia* from the prophets (Isaiah 66:10-11), the Psalms of Ascent, the Gospels (Luke 19:41-45) and St. Paul to offer more biblical evidence for this position. His citations on Christian patriotism are even more extensive in other essays. As Christians become patriotic, Ting reasoned, they must also "build a temple worthy of the motherland." This meant that there should be reform of the internal life of the church (i.e., the separation of the church from imperialist influences), and the elimination of corruption and unjust practices in Christian life.

> Building up the Body of Christ includes purifying the church. If people leave the church who do not really love the Lord but only want to control the church to benefit imperialism, is this not to the church's advantage? And if they do not leave, then we should chase them out. This is precisely what Paul did in Corinth (I Cor. 5). To purge the church from corruption is in effect to love the church, to purify the church and to build up the Body of Christ.[45]

Christians reading this essay in the 1950s would think of the Denunciation Movement and the other political campaigns of the times, although there are no direct references.

In his essays from the 1950s, one area in which Ting departs from the generally accepted Protestant understanding was his critique of the doctrine of justification by faith. This had never been as prominent a theme in liberal and catholic Anglican theology as it was in the Lutheran, Reformed and Baptist traditions. Ting's warning against the exaggeration of justification "to the exclusion of every other doctrine" also has a basis in his own theological background, and, as we shall see, it foreshadows a subject he would take up again forty years later. An emphasis on justification by faith tended to neglect the moral and ethical dimension of faith, in Ting's understanding. It was also contrary to the Chinese humanist tradition and socialist ethics.

Ting's critique of justification was set within the broader context of "witness bearing through deeds," which also became a continuing theme for the TSPM. In his writing, Ting argued that "justification by faith" neglected the importance of "works" in Christianity in two important ways: it slighted the ethical achievements of those who were not Christians, and it ignored the faults and sinfulness of those who were.[46] The former could result in a false sense of Christian pride, while the latter could become an excuse for condoning sin and neglecting the need for a doctrine of sanctification and the pursuit of holiness. Justification needed to be balanced by other Christian teachings, such as the doctrine of the Incarnation.

His friends and former colleagues in the ecumenical movement overseas would have understood his perspective, even if they did not always agree with what Ting was saying. Sometimes Ting's biblical interpretation seemed forced, as when he cited God's call to decrease the numbers of Gideon's army (Judges 7) as an argument against church growth, or when he searched for proof texts to support his position on patriotism.[47] But unlike many others in the TSPM who were writing in those years, Ting always maintained an interest in theology, and his writings went far beyond the usual discussions of anti-imperialism and patriotism. Ting never claimed to be a biblical scholar, but he was willing to wrestle with the biblical text, personally as well as theologically. He had no interest in developing a theology derived from socialism or Marxism-Leninism. He was not espousing a "radical theology" in the manner of Y. T. Wu. Rather, he was making a case for supporting the new society and the TSPM on biblical grounds, in a way he thought a broad range of Christians could accept. Ting was very clear about his own political stance and his support for the CPC, but he wanted to bring hesitant and skeptical Christians along as well.

Ting took the biblical message seriously, and so he saw it was necessary to reinterpret the Bible in light of the new order. Theologically, we may say that he was engaged in the task of accommodation, which was a first step toward contextualization and inculturation. Politically, his writings were perfectly acceptable to the authorities, even though they might not accept his use of the Bible. But if accommodation and the endorsement of the new order were his entire purpose, then Ting would have had little to offer to men and women preparing for ministry. There were many people writing for *Tian Feng* in the 1950s who only wanted to show how patriotic and revolutionary they were and who seemed to think that because the church was so backward, the best that could be hoped for was to follow the Communist Party and build a New China. They almost seemed to be embarrassed by their faith, and so they sought to recreate a "progressive" version of the church in conformity with the new society.

This, however, was not the purpose of Nanjing Seminary, nor was this the vision of its principal. True to his conviction that the Christian's primary purpose was to bear witness to Christ, there was another important dimension to K. H. Ting's thinking in these years, and it was concerned with the particular role of the church. This is the other side of the double movement that was introduced above. Christianity not only had to learn from others in the new situation. Christian faith also had something to offer to others, just as it has had in every other time and place. Ting drew on the language of "missionary vocation" and "expectant evangelism," which he had learned in the WSCF when he wrote about spreading the gospel and building up the church in the early 1950s. His essay "Why Must We Still Be Preachers?" was written in response to a question raised by his friends from university days who had suggested that Christianity was no longer needed. In this essay, Ting offered a passionate and very personal defense of his vocation as a Christian. Another essay, "The Spirit of Wisdom and Revelation," was based on a Bible study that he gave to church workers in order to show how God can open new doors for the church when others are closed. Both essays clearly show the importance that Ting attached to the continuing Christian witness.

He believed that Christians needed to learn to love the Chinese people and draw close to them, not only to accommodate themselves to the new order but to bear effective witness.

> Fellow Christians, we are the Chinese people, we should love ourselves and our lovely motherland, we should draw close to and unite with our own people. There is another reason for this (besides the fact that it follows the example of the Incarnation); entrusted with the task of spreading the gospel, we need to enter deeply into the people's midst, thinking as they think, caring for what they care for, loving what they love, hating what they hate. Our Lord Jesus acted in this way and so did St. Paul.
>
> If we keep our distance from the people, and harbor feelings of opposition, then the Lord will not be able to use us to spread the gospel to them. For if we have no common ground, then how can the gospel, no matter how beautiful it is, make any sense to them?[48]

For Ting, spreading the gospel to the people is the first part of the Great Commission (Matthew 28:19). But "teaching them to obey everything that I have commanded you" follows in the very next verse (28:20), and it should not be neglected. Christians needed to build up the church and attend to pastoral work, both of which were always part of K. H. Ting's understanding of the missionary task. The church needed to be purified, and growth in numbers was never as important as the "quality" of Christian faith. Christians had to put their own house in order by attending to education and pastoral care. Ministries of friendship, prayer, worship, preaching and Christian education would strengthen the church and spread the gospel.

Spreading the gospel and building up the church were not political requirements but missionary and pastoral concerns. They were addressed to Christians in biblical terms and emphasized their life in a "religious" realm that was related to and yet distinct from political life. There is no evidence of direct political objections to what Ting was saying, at least on the part of the government, but government officials and Three-Self activists might not have approved of what he was claiming for the role of church in society.

Ting skillfully navigated the space he had been given at Nanjing Seminary to chart a way forward for the church. But this could go only so far. As the decade wore on, there was the beginning of a separation of religion from politics in the theology of K. H. Ting and the end of what I have termed a double movement. This was inevitable in the China of the late 1950s, but it made the church as a church increasingly irrelevant to domestic political life and social concerns. Chinese Christians from evangelical and fundamentalist backgrounds may have welcomed this development, provided they could accept the need for political accommodation. It implied a compartmentalization of Christian life, and in this sense it represented a major departure from the ecumenical approach Ting had developed in Geneva. As we shall see, by the late 1950s, K. H. Ting's theology was not as integrated as it once was. This was the cost of accommodation, a function of the politics of mass movements and political campaigns imposed upon the church.

K. H. Ting was struggling to come to terms with the new order theologically as well as politically. His vision contained a message that, at its best, could inspire seminary students to continue in their vocation. As preachers and pastors, they still had something to offer. There was the need to accommodate to the new order, but it was important that the church be the church. If only the first part of the message was stressed, then the church as the church would have nothing to say, and there would be no need for theological education. But if it were still possible to spread the gospel and build up the church, then there was hope for the future. Up until the mid-1950s, it *was* still possible for seminary students and teachers to draw on this hope at Nanjing Seminary, but after that time it became increasingly difficult.

THREE-SELF LEADER

K. H. Ting spent a great deal of time traveling back and forth between Nanjing and Shanghai after the opening of the seminary. Siu-may was still working at the Second Girls' Middle School in Shanghai, while looking after their two young sons. In Nanjing, K. H. lived in a small apartment near the campus. Chen Zemin and his family occupied the first floor of the same building, and he often had his meals with the Chen family. It was not until 1954 that Siu-may and the boys joined K. H. in Nanjing. They moved into the house on Mo Chou Road which, with the exception of a few years during the Cultural Revolution, has been their home ever since. The house had been a former missionary residence, built in a Western style, with an attached garden. It is just a short walk from the Mo Chou Road Church, which was still a congregation of the Church of Christ in China.

Ting also had to go to Shanghai to meet and consult with seminary board members and leaders of the TSPM Preparatory Committee. It was already clear that he had support of key leaders in both the government and the church, and he had demonstrated his leadership abilities in holding together the diverse faculty and student body of Nanjing Seminary, in his theological writings and in his political stance. Although not a member of the preparatory committee, K. H. Ting was becoming an important new voice in the TSPM, and someone who could write theologically. Because he was well known overseas, he was also important internationally.

Hewlett Johnson, the pro-Communist "Red Dean" of Canterbury Cathedral, visited China with his wife in 1952.[49] Johnson was a prominent church figure in the international pro-Communist movement, and in China he was regarded as an "old friend" who took the message of the Chinese Revolution to the world outside. At the end of this visit, Johnson was presented with an appeal signed by 410 Chinese Christians protesting the alleged use of bacteriological warfare by the American Army in Korea. When he publicized the letter, Johnson was widely criticized in the West for accepting at face value the charges that were made in this letter. The alleged American use of biological weapons in Korea has never been proved, but, as early as 1950, the United States government threatened to use "weapons of mass destruction" in the Korean War, which included atomic, chemical and biological weapons. Chinese and North Korean leaders believed at the time that they were facing germ warfare.[50] The use of bacteriological warfare by the Americans in the Korean War is still taught as fact in Chinese history textbooks, although today most Western scholars reject the Chinese allegations.[51]

We have seen that K. H. Ting had already made his own critique of the Americans' use of bacteriological weapons in an essay he wrote shortly after his return to China. His name (where he is identified as general secretary of the CLS) is also prominent in the list of signatures given to the Johnsons, in the letter itself and in the Chinese translation published in *Tian Feng*.[52] Published lists of names are an important indication of position and status in China, and the inclusion of his name among more senior and influential leaders (twenty-seventy on the list) suggests that Ting was already in 1952 a rising star in the Christian leadership. In the 1950s, Ting never became a Three-Self activist, but he would become increasingly important to both China and the TSPM in the years to come.

On 27 July 1953, a truce was signed ending the Korean War. The civilian death toll had reached more than two million. China had lost close to one million men in the conflict, as many as North and South Korean casualties combined, and the war had put a tremendous strain on China's economy.[53] By 1953, the series of urban mass movements had been brought to an end, and the first phase of rural land reform had been completed. The government could now turn its attention to social and economic reconstruction, beginning with the "First Five Year Plan" (1953-1957) that set China on a path of integrated development according to the Soviet model, which emphasized rapid industrialization.

In the churches, the Denunciation Movement had ended, but it was followed by a new movement of "ideological remolding" for younger pastors, church leaders and Christian intellectuals.[54] K. H. Ting's own reorientation and readjustment continued, although the political atmosphere was no longer as intense as it had been during the Korean War. Plans were made for the First National Christian Conference, which met for sixteen days in Beijing in July and August 1954. This was the first national gathering of Protestant Christians since the establishment of the People's Republic of China, and it marked the end of the preparatory stage of the TSPM and the formal establishment of the National Committee of the Chinese Christian Three-Self Patriotic Movement of the Protestant Churches of China.

K. H. Ting was a representative at the First National Christian Conference. Although he had not been on the TSPM Preparatory Committee, he was named as one of the forty-two members of the newly established TSPM Standing Committee. An excerpt from his speech at the conference dealing with Christian unity at Nanjing Seminary was among those published in *Tian Feng*. It is among the most theologically oriented contributions from this gathering, emphasizing that the principle of mutual respect in matters of faith and worship should be based on an attitude of Christian humility and love, and not just political considerations.[55] Mutual respect, he suggested, was applicable not only to Nanjing Seminary but to the TSPM as a whole. Much work had to be done to encourage Christians from diverse denominational backgrounds to work together, especially among the theological conservatives. In this spirit of mutual respect and in order to dispel the fear among conservatives that the TSPM might be promoting the reform of Christian doctrine, the word "reform" was dropped from the name of TSPM.[56] Y. T. Wu saw this as a concession to conservative evangelicals in order to promote and expand the unity of the TSPM. It was K. H. Ting who drafted the conference statement on why the name should be changed based on the principle of mutual respect.[57]

The unity of the TSPM in the 1950s was mainly the *political* unity of "anti-imperialist patriotism," not the *theological* or *ecumenical* unity of Christians and churches from different denominational backgrounds. This was especially stressed in relationships with evangelicals and fundamentalists so that they would not feel their faith was in any way being "watered down" or compromised through their participation in the TSPM. K. H. Ting recalls that Tang Shoulin, a conservative leader from the "Little Flock," said he was willing to cooperate on this basis. He compared the TSPM to a guild of barbers that "comes together to talk things over. They don't need to bring scissors to cut each other's hair."[58] Tang's point was that the unity of Three-Self was political, and because the TSPM was not "religious" there was not even the need to pray together when it held its meetings. There was prayer and worship at the First National Christian Conference, but the theological element was not central for the TSPM as an organization in the 1950s. Many TSPM leaders and activists from YMCA backgrounds had no interest in theology or advancing ecumenical unity or even theological discussion among Chinese Christians. They were promoting Christian support for the new government and anti-imperialist patriotism. Theologically conservative Christians and those like K. H. Ting who were more oriented to the work of the church could accept this as a way of working in the new situation without compromising their religious commitments.

Each time the TSPM met in the 1950s, the emphasis was on enlarging unity in light of the requirements of the current political situation. Although the political atmosphere was not as intense as in earlier years, it was still important for Christians to demonstrate their support for the political policies of the government. When the standing committee of the TSPM met in 1955, it passed a resolution reaffirming support for unity among Christians based on anti-imperialist patriotism.[59] Part of the mandate of the TSPM as stated in its 1954 Constitution was to work for world peace.[60] The Cold War put Christians around the world on different sides over how to pursue peace, and for the TSPM, world peace could be achieved only through identification with the international goals of the Communist movement.

Throughout the 1950s, the Chinese government was putting pressure on independent religious groups that refused to align themselves with the new order. Most of the Protestant groups were led by charismatic evangelical or fundamentalist separatist sects, including Wang Mingdao (the Christian Tabernacle), Watchman Nee (the Little Flock), Jing Tianying (the Jesus Family) and Isaac Wei (the True Jesus Church), all of whom refused to affiliate with the TSPM. The TSPM joined in the attacks against the leaders of these groups, and many of their criticisms are recorded on the pages of *Tian Feng*.[61] Some of the articles were written anonymously, but other speeches and essays were written by well-known Three-Self leaders. K. H. Ting, beginning with his speech at the 1955 meeting of the standing committee of the TSPM, was at the center of the attack against Wang Mingdao (1900-1991), a staunch fundamentalist and the most prominent opponent of the TSPM in the 1950s.

Ting's speech was on unity and cooperation among Christians, and it was cast in the anti-imperialist rhetoric of the times. He argued that unity among Chinese Christians was essential in the present international climate and criticized those who, on the grounds of their distinctive theological characteristics, would reject the TSPM. "Joining this movement does not necessitate the change of a single word of one's faith," he wrote. [62] For many evangelicals and fundamentalists, this assertion was debatable. Drawing on Pauline texts that emphasize unity in diversity (Romans 12:6; 1 Corinthians 4:5 and 12:24), Ting emphasized the importance of the principle of mutual respect, which he had developed and implemented at Nanjing Seminary. But in his speech to the TSPM Standing Committee, he went on to attack those who rejected fellowship with Christians who were not like them.

> Whenever Christians, on the train or in any other public place, meet with other Christians, their hearts rejoice. This is a natural and healthy reaction. But now there are some Christians who, although the faith of others is essentially the same as theirs, show no gratitude to God but, on the contrary, look for and exaggerate all possible divergences. They want to wipe out all the agreements in our faith or in our opposition to imperialism. Their temper is high, but I cannot find the slightest thankfulness or love or desire to glorify God. All we encounter is a cold hostility . . . A yet sadder fact is the way in which some people carelessly affix the label of unbeliever to others . . . When other people are saved by faith in Christ who died for them and yet we do not call them brothers but "unbelievers," then we are condemning them in the presence of God; we are reviling them and praying God not to save them.[63]

Ting's criticism of Christians who label brothers and sisters "unbeliev-ers" is an unmistakable allusion to Wang Mingdao. Wang was internation-ally known for his opposition to China's Communist government and the TSPM, and he enjoyed considerable popularity among conservative Protes-tants in China and the West.[64] By 1955, Wang was already under pressure from the government because of his opposition to the CPC. A few months after Ting delivered his speech, Wang Mingdao published a diatribe against the TSPM in a widely circulated pamphlet entitled "We, Because of Faith!"[65] In this tract, Wang presented the familiar fundamentalist critique of theo-logical modernism, criticizing the writings of T. C. Chao, Y. T. Wu and other Three-Self leaders, and offering a detailed rebuttal to the speech of K. H. Ting we have just cited.

Wang Mingdao's argument followed the lines of the fundamentalist-mod-ernist controversy as it had developed over the last three decades in China.[66] Wang argued that he had maintained the same views for more than twenty-five years and that they had nothing to do with imperialism or anti-imperialism. He claimed that he was not urging division within the Christian community but rather the separation of believers from a "faction of non-believers within the church," citing St. Paul (2 Corinthians 6:14) in support. To claim that Y. T. Wu and others in the TSPM were nonbelievers was not a criticism, according to Wang, but a description of a fact. Fundamentalist and modernist beliefs were not the same, and he singles out K. H. Ting in partic-ular for glossing over essential differences. Modernists were "false brothers" who did not believe in the literal truth of the Bible, the creation account in Genesis, the Virgin birth, or the bodily resurrection of Christ. They were, therefore, not Christians at all. Wang Mingdao was unwilling to unite with them or have fellowship with them in the TSPM or anywhere else.

Over the following months, a large number of essays refuting Wang Mingdao were published in *Tian Feng*, including K. H. Ting's own response.[67] Ting reiterated his consistent defense of patriotism, the TSPM and the importance of Christian unity. Citing numerous references to Wang's writings and activities, he argued that Wang Mingdao was inconsistent. He indeed had a political position, but he had not recognized it as such, and he had attacked and slandered the TSPM based on a distorted interpretation of the Bible shaped by Western fundamentalism and imperialist ideology. Chris-tians needed to separate themselves from imperialism, Ting argued, not from one another. They should emphasize what they had in common:

> On the foundation of anti-imperialism and patriotism let us be united, neither obliterating nor exaggerating our differences in belief, and thankfully accepting all that is held in common. As for where we dif-fer, we will not enforce uniformity but respect each other, so that no one feels wronged in matters of faith.[68]

Ting concluded by reasserting the need for the test of love and the principle of mutual respect in relationships between all Christians. Despite the irenic tone of the concluding paragraphs, Ting's stern warning was in fact a political and theological attack against Wang Mingdao.

Even before *Tian Feng* published K. H. Ting's response, Wang had been arrested and imprisoned for organizing a "counterrevolutionary clique" in Beijing. He eventually wrote a confession and was released from prison, but he subsequently repudiated his confession and was arrested again on unspecified charges. Wang Mingdao spent the next twenty years in prison, and even after he was released, he was kept under police supervision or house arrest. He continued to rebuff approaches from the TSPM and the China Christian Council to meet. In the 1980s, he conducted services of worship in his home and met with evangelical and fundamentalist leaders from China and around the world. He died at home in 1991, by this time almost totally blind, but he was still firm in the beliefs that had sustained him all his life.

There has not yet been a thorough study of Wang Mingdao's arrest and imprisonment, and it is unlikely that Chinese government records will be made available for this purpose at any time in the near future. There can be no question that Wang Mingdao's imprisonment represented a serious violation of universally acknowledged standards of human rights and the utter inadequacy of legal safeguards in the China of the 1950s. In a liberal society, Wang Mingdao would have been ignored by the government and left to himself, and the debate over his fundamentalist views would be seen by Christian opponents as counterproductive. But the People's Republic of China has never been a liberal society, and neither Wang Mingdao nor his critics, including K. H. Ting, were political liberals. Unlike many others who served lengthy prison sentences in the People's Republic, Wang Mingdao was never rehabilitated and his case was never reopened. Wang's life and witness, as well as the experience of Watchman Nee and many other Christians who were imprisoned in the 1950s and the years since,[69] continue to cast a shadow over the history of Christianity in that period.

What concerns us here is the conflict between Wang Mingdao and K. H. Ting in 1955 and the years since. The two men had radically different views of the church and its relationship to the political order, and they represented two poles in Chinese Christianity in the 1980s.[70] In 1955, theirs was not really a theological debate but a highly charged polemic shaped by the struggles of the times. In Wang Mingdao's viewpoint, Ting was a "modernist" allied to the government, and the debate was over essential principles of Christian belief. From K. H. Ting's point of view, Wang cared nothing for relating to Christians unlike himself and was indifferent to patriotism and the anti-imperialist struggle. This in itself represented a political position and played into the hands of the West. Wang Mingdao was rejecting Ting's theology, while K. H. Ting was criticizing Wang's politics. Wang Mingdao saw the church in sectarian terms as a gathered community of true believers. Ting had a more expansive view of the church, and he emphasized mutual respect to ensure unity in diversity. But for Ting, mutual respect did not extend to the realm of politics. Mutual respect was accepted by some prominent evangelicals in China, including Jia Yuming and Marcus Cheng (Chen Chonggui), but it would never be acceptable to a militant fundamentalist like Wang Mingdao. Ting's theology was different from Wang's insofar as it allowed other voices to be heard in the church, but his politics set the tone for his critique.

Many Christians admire Wang's stubborn resistance, but his fundamentalism could never become the basis for a creative Christian engagement in a socialist society in the 1950s or today. To make all questions revolve around those of a fundamentalist belief or nonbelief in Christ necessarily leads to antagonism with those who hold different viewpoints, both inside and outside the church. Fundamentalism is a common response to modernity in many religious traditions, but it is always a reactionary rather than a creative response.[71] Wang Mingdao's writings still appeal to some sections of the church in China, but they provide no opening for dialogue. In contrast, Ting's understanding of mutual respect has offered the possibility for Christians from different backgrounds to work together. His perspective on cooperative relationships among Christians was influential for the TSPM in the mid-1950s, and it became even more influential for the CCC under his leadership in the 1980s and 1990s.

There can be no doubt that Ting's criticism of Wang Mingdao in the mid-1950s was part of the government-initiated struggle against separatist religious groups. It cannot fully be understood as a conflict between two Christian leaders with radically different theological and political positions. Although Ting was not responsible for the arrest and imprisonment of Wang Mingdao, his criticisms have made him suspect among evangelicals ever since. At the same time, his theologically oriented critique helped to shape him as a Three-Self leader, and Ting became increasingly prominent within the TSPM.

B y 1956, the international situation had improved, and the general social and political climate in China had eased considerably. This had a positive impact on China's cultural and religious life, and foreshadowed a new (but short-lived) period of openness. In some areas, Zhejiang and Fujian provinces, for example, the church had begun to grow again. Despite the excesses of the early 1950s, the TSPM was able to attract some Christians from conservative backgrounds and was learning how to work with them.

All of this was reflected in the Second Enlarged Plenum of the TSPM, which met in Beijing in March 1956. This meeting had representatives from almost *all* churches and denominational groups in China, and it became the most significant gathering of Chinese Christians before the Cultural Revolution. More attention was given to church affairs at this meeting than in the past, as can be seen in Y. T. Wu's speech, "Three Witnesses and Ten Tasks," as well as in the many proposals brought from the floor.[72] Although major difficulties loomed on the horizon, from the vantage point of 1956, the Second Enlarged Plenum showed that the TSPM had a stronger relationship with a more diverse Christian constituency than any national Christian body ever had before.

K. H. Ting has spoken of the TSPM during this period as representing the interests of two very different groups of Chinese Christians.

> I think the early history of the Three-Self Movement was a history of a "united front" between those whose main interest was anti-imperialist patriotism and those whose main interest was to do a good job in church building. These two groups found in common Three-Self. To the first group, Three-Self was an important vehicle to promote anti-imperialist patriotism, and to the second group, Three-Self was a pre-condition for the church in China to be built-up. During that first period, these two groups didn't need to clash with each other, and so it was a united front. And in 1956, I think, the second group was very happy, and I think some people in the first group came to see the importance of church building in order for more people to be embraced into political consciousness, into the movement of anti-imperialist patriotism.
>
> I think I was in the second group, but I wasn't very self-consciously in the second group at that time, because I was also for anti-imperialist patriotism.
>
> To come back a little to these two groups. Those who were in leadership positions in the Three-Self organizations were representatives of the first group, largely; not all of them, but the more important elements, the real decision makers, belonged to the first group. But the rank-and-file pastors and ministers and Christians did support the Three-Self Movement, but their thinking was a bit different. They emphasized more that the future of the church in China depends so much on Three-Self. Their approach is one of "loving the church" (*aijiao*) and the approach of the first group was "loving the country" (*aiguo*).[73]

Ting is describing the contrasting positions of what we have been calling the Three-Self activists (the first group) and the patriotic Christians interested in building up the church (the second group). Li Chuwen, TSPM general secretary, was the leader of the first group, and the second group was composed of denominational leaders. In the 1980s and 1990s, Ting may have seen himself as part of the second group, but in the 1950s he, together with his friend Zheng Jianye, could in some ways identify with both. Ting's interpretation in these paragraphs is partly hindsight based on the church situation in the 1990s, but it reflects two different strands of thinking that have been in the TSPM from the beginning. There are different interpretations of the 1956 Enlarged Plenum in the TSPM about the extent to which it emphasized anti-imperialist patriotism and the extent to which it represented a shift toward church building. But the two emphases, one more activist and political and one more church-centered, have been present in the TSPM since the early 1950s, and they continue to be present today. The importance in 1956 was that more space was given for the church-centered approach, not only in the TSPM and the denominational structures that remained, but also in the participation of Christians in the Chinese political process.

For Christians and other non-Communist groups, the Chinese People's Political Consultative Conference (CPPCC) became the organizational embodiment of their political participation in national affairs. Founded in 1949, the CPPCC was an advisory body for the new government. Real power was in the hands of the Communist Party, but the CPPCC did represent a forum for consultation and the airing of viewpoints.[74] Chinese Protestants were well represented in the First CPPCC in 1949, setting a pattern for their participation in the political and social life of the People's Republic for most of the next decade. Involvement in the CPPCC was the means by which they could bring their concerns about national affairs and religious policy to the wider public, and where they could meet with people from other sectors of society with similar concerns. The CPPCC became a channel of communication between Christians and society in the 1950s and a means for enlisting the support of the TSPM leadership for the united front and socialist construction. In the 1950s, Christians were represented in consultative conferences as well as in people's congresses at national, provincial and local levels. TSPM leaders took justifiable pride in such participation, and they encouraged Christians to become active in local political life.

K. H. Ting began his political career within the participatory framework of the united front. He was given his first political appointment when he was named one of forty-eight delegates to the First Jiangsu People's Political Consultative Conference (JPPCC) in 1955.[75] Wu Yifang, then president of Jinling Women's College, was also appointed to the standing committee of the JPPCC, so Christians were well represented in Jiangsu. K. H. Ting was only forty years old at the time, and this made him one of the younger members of the JPPCC. His inclusion in this select group of delegates meant that he had the trust of the political establishment, which was no doubt a result of his relationship with Zhou Enlai. More than a seminary principal or TSPM leader, he was regarded as an influential member of the community.

In 1955, Ting's speech was among those published after the meeting, and it illustrates the way in which he used the JPPCC as a forum to express his views and concerns. He spoke about the importance of the consultative process, the world situation, the division between capitalist and Communist camps, reunification with Taiwan and the need for vigilance against imperialism, especially in the Christian community. Toward the end of his speech, he also spoke of the continuing relevance of the Christian faith.

I believe that Christians are for the truth, but I do not deny that there are Christians who have not yet seen the truth. With open minds, we should learn from others. Today in China, the people's material life and moral spirit has been raised and improved, and true Christians should be happy and welcome these developments. We should by no means be shaken in our Christian faith because of this, and I myself am not at all pessimistic about the future of the church. This is because the gospel of Christ provides the most perfect answer to the most pressing human questions. What we should concern ourselves with today is how to rectify the church so that it may recover its rightful purity. We don't have to worry about a tomorrow when no one will come and ask us to tell them about the gospel. With this conviction, we must strive to build up our church and make it better.[76]

This is an extraordinary confession made on the floor of a political meeting in Nanjing. He continues his remarks by underscoring the importance of training a new generation of ministers at Nanjing Seminary who would "love the country and love the church," men and women who would stand with the rest of the people with whom they shared common aspirations and a patriotic responsibility. Ting was embracing his role as a JPPCC delegate to help create space for the seminary and the church in the broader political process. He was also asking the rest of the society to accept the Christian community and to help it solve its problems. Christians could be as supportive of New China as any other citizens, and their contributions should, therefore, be of value.

BISHOP OF ZHEJIANG

Protestant denominations had begun to fall apart during the Korean War. The cut-off of funds from overseas posed serious financial difficulties to the churches, especially for the denominational headquarters, and the various political movements, especially the Denunciation Movement, diminished the institutional importance of the churches. Some church leaders left China, and many of those who remained were confused and disoriented. Tension in the churches became more relaxed in the mid-1950s, and this allowed church leaders to consider ways of reorganizing and strengthening their denominational structures. This led to a short-lived period of internal renewal for some churches, including the Methodists, the Church of Christ in China and the Anglicans.

In the Anglican-Episcopal Zhonghua Sheng Gong Hui, an ambitious program of reform was begun by Robin Chen, the presiding bishop, and Zheng Jianye who served as Sheng Gong Hui general secretary. Zheng Jianye had been made bishop in 1953 and was a member of the standing committee of the TSPM. From 1954 onward, however, his main energy was devoted to the reorganization of his own church. Because Chinese Anglicans had related to seven different foreign missionary societies—the most important of which were the Church Missionary Society (CMS), the Society for the Propagation of the Gospel (SPG) and the Protestant-Episcopal Mission from the United States—there was considerable variation in church practice from place to place. There were also great economic disparities. In general, churches and dioceses along the coast were stronger and wealthier than those farther inland. Beginning in late 1954, Robin Chen and Zheng Jianye visited dioceses all over China in order to assess the situation, reorganize individual dioceses and in some places prepare for the election of new bishops.

The Zhejiang (Chekiang) Diocese was formed by the Church Missionary Society in the late nineteenth century, and Herbert James Maloney became its first bishop in 1907. The diocese was mostly low-church evangelical. In 1918, T. S. Sing (Shen Zaisheng), son of the first Chinese Anglican cleric, was consecrated assistant bishop of Zhejiang. He was the first Chinese bishop of the Anglican Communion.[77] Anglicans were active in educational and medical work in the province, and self-support was growing in the churches up to the time of the Japanese invasion. By 1940, there were over twelve thousand baptized in the diocese, twice the number of twenty years before. John Curtis from Scotland served as bishop of Zhejiang from 1928 to 1950, when he resigned. The diocesan synod elected Kimber Den (Deng Shukun) as his successor. Den "disappeared" in 1952, and his family and friends knew nothing of his whereabouts. He was highly respected both in China and internationally, and there was much publicized concern about him. It turned out that he had been arrested by the government on unspecified charges, and he was not released until 1957.[78] A visiting delegation of Australian Anglicans was told in 1956 that Den's arrest had been a mistake and an injustice.[79] Den's imprisonment is but one of the great many violations of religious freedom in the early years of the People's Republic of China. After his release, he was said to be working as assistant bishop in the Anjing Diocese in Anhui Province.

By 1950, Zhejiang Diocese had more than seventy parishes, mostly in the northern part of the province. The provincial capital of Hangzhou had four Anglican churches. One estimate puts the number of Anglican "seekers" and communicants at around ten thousand in the mid-1950s, served by ten or twenty priests and deacons.[80] Den's disappearance had left the Diocese of Zhejiang in particular need of episcopal oversight and more church workers. When the General Synod decided that a new bishop was needed in Zhejiang, K. H. Ting was approached by his friend and colleague Zheng Jianye to take up this responsibility. Ting has said that he never wanted to be bishop of Zhejiang, for he was fully occupied with work at Nanjing Seminary. He also was concerned about what had happened to Kimber Den but could do nothing about it.[81] However, Ting supported the move to strengthen the work of the church, and since there was no suitable candidate for bishop from Zhejiang, he was persuaded to have his name put forward.

中華聖公會主教院會議留影 1956年5月13–20日秋上海

Sheng Gong Hui bishops, 1956, with the permission of Keren and Kezia Johnson. (From left to right; back: Xue Pingxi; K. H. Ting; Zheng Jianye; Lin Xianyang; Cai Fuchu; Mu Rongxian; Wang Shenyin; Liu Yucang; front: Zhang Haisong; Zhang Guangxu; Shen Zigao; Chen Jianzhen; Gu Huoling; Xu Jisong; Mao Kezhong; Liu Yaochang)

Ting was elected bishop by the clergy and laity of the Zhejiang Diocese on 9 and 10 March 1955. This was their first diocesan meeting in three years. It was reported at this meeting that the number of communicants had grown by more than 16 percent since 1952. Because there was no bishop, confirmations were performed by bishops from neighboring dioceses. In addition, giving for the support of the church had increased by more than 45 percent.[82] Zhejiang was one of the wealthier dioceses of the Sheng Gong Hui, and the church had potential for further growth and development. Although all churches had been weakened after 1949, churches in Zhejiang were stronger than those in most other provinces.

Together with Xue Pingxi and Liu Yucang, who had been elected assistant bishops of the Fujian Diocese, K. H. Ting was consecrated on 19 June 1955 (the Second Sunday after Trinity) at the Church of Our Savior in Shanghai. More than seven hundred people attended the service, at which Bishop T. K. Shen preached on the Great Commission.[83] The sermon touched on Three-Self and the political themes of the time, but its most important message was the need to give greater attention to the pastoral, evangelical, and educational work of the church and to strengthen the church organizationally.

For the next few years, Ting visited Zhejiang at least twice a year, each time for two or three weeks. Routine work was handled by Niu Zhifang, a former YMCA worker who was ordained to the priesthood by Bishop Ting, and served as the general secretary of the diocese in Hangzhou. Ting's episcopal visits were of a pastoral nature, to ordain priests and deacons, hold diocesan meetings, perform confirmations, and speak at retreats and other church conferences. On one visit, he confirmed seven hundred people between fifteen and eighty-one years of age.[84] According to Deng Fucun, Ting ordained eleven men to the priesthood between 1955 and 1958. Five of these were still working in the church in the early 1990s, including Deng himself and Sun Xipei, both of whom became important provincial and national leaders in the 1980s.[85]

During his visits to Zhejiang, K. H. Ting saw firsthand the changes that were taking place in the countryside. He wrote glowing reports about the agricultural cooperatives and positive changes he saw taking place in rural areas. Consistent with the growing optimism of his own political perspective, he also related the changes in living standards to a change in Christian spirituality.

> It is known to all how, in the past, misery drove men and women in despair to their knees. Now we can see that spirituality does not thrive on misery. On the contrary, all alleviation of suffering now draws the same men and women, in thankfulness, to the brightness of God's presence.[86]

This was just two years before the start of the Great Leap Forward (1958-1962), which resulted in famine for large numbers of Chinese peasants; but in 1956, what Ting was saying was consistent with many of the reports coming out of China.

Yu Mingyue was ordained by Bishop Ting in 1955. He remembers the pastoral visits Ting made to Zhejiang and his proposal for setting up a church conference and retreat center at a beautiful site in Fuyang, where Yu had a church. "He said this in order to protect the church when most social forces were against it," Yu commented. "He also saw that we needed such a center for the nurture of our church life." [87] The conference and retreat center were never started, but the church in Fuyang is still standing. Yu served as a pastor in Fuyang in the early 1990s, but in the interim, he had spent twenty-seven years (1958-1985) in exile in the far western province of Xinjiang. Yu and hundreds of other church workers were sent to Xinjiang after the beginning of the "Anti-Rightist movement" in 1957 (see chap. 5).

In 1956, two months after the Second Enlarged Plenum of the TSPM, the House of Bishops and General Synod of the Sheng Gong Hui met in Shanghai. Reports and speeches from this meeting reflect the revived interest in church affairs, reform and reorganization.[88] All seventeen bishops attended what turned out to be the last meeting of the House of Bishops of the Zhonghua Sheng Gong Hui. As a sign of what was seen to be their new independence and unity as a national church, the House of Bishops decided to authorize a new prayer book which would be used all over China. At that time, eight different versions of the prayer book were used in the church's fourteen dioceses.* As a further expression of unity, Holy Trinity Cathedral in Shanghai was dedicated on Pentecost Sunday as the national cathedral.

K. H. Ting preached the sermon at this service in which he made a strong defense of the integrity of the church and the importance of its ministry. The creeds, he said, testify to the fact that the activity of the Holy Spirit is intimately related to the existence of the church, and, therefore, the two are inseparable. It does not matter if the church is small and weak, for God has chosen the weak to shame the strong (1 Corinthians 1:26-28). The Chinese church is no longer dependent on foreign political power and economic privilege, for it has now chosen to identify itself with the Chinese people. Theologically, it is dependent on God alone.

> Over these last few years, the Zhonghua Sheng Gong Hui has made the Lord's power manifest in her weakness, and the glory of the church has been revealed through the way of service. We have many difficulties, but they do not destroy us. If we dwell on them all day long, then we

---

* This did not include the Diocese of Hong Kong and Macao, which had been separated from the South China Diocese in 1951, according to a report from *Ta Kung Pao* (5 August 1951), the pro-China newspaper in Hong Kong. A resolution was passed at the 1956 meeting declaring that Taiwan was part of the Diocese of Fujian. (Today, the Episcopal Church in Taiwan is still part of the Episcopal Church of the U.S.A.) It should be added here that the prayer book authorized by the Sheng Gong Hui bishops in 1956 was never published. Holy Trinity Cathedral was returned to the TSPM and CCC in 2004 (see chap. 10).

will be finished and unable to raise our heads high. But as we lift up our hearts to the Lord, we will know more clearly than ever before that God's grace is sufficient for our church.[89]

Anglicans like K. H. Ting and Zheng Jianye were deeply committed to patriotism and socialism in China. They also believed that Three-Self could strengthen the church and help it develop a more authentic witness. This was their hope in 1956. Ting and the TSPM as a whole were also becoming interested in international ecumenical relations, receiving church delegations from abroad and preparing to send delegates to church meetings in Europe.

REESTABLISHING INTERNATIONAL CONTACTS

The TSPM set up an International Affairs Committee in May 1956 which would concern itself with "protecting world peace, promoting Christian fellowship and friendly cooperation with Christians and peoples internationally."[90] Because of their experience and wide range of ecumenical relationships, both K. H. and Siu-may Ting were appointed to this new committee.

Conversations with the Tings at their home in Nanjing in the 1950s generally left a deep impression on international visitors. Both K. H. and Siu-may Ting were persuasive interpreters of the Chinese position because of their commitment and their personal integrity. Always courteous and attentive, they would ask foreign visitors about mutual friends as they entertained their guests with a simple yet gracious hospitality. K. H. Ting's theological insight reinforced the Christian perspective of his commitment, something that visitors did not always detect in conversations with other TSPM leaders.

The Tings met almost all international Christian visitors to China, beginning in the fall of 1955 when they received a delegation of British Quakers, the first Christian group to visit China since 1949.[91] The following year they saw Bishop Rajah Manikam, who had close links with the WCC and the International Missionary Council (IMC), who was traveling with Gustav Nystrom, a former Swedish missionary to China; Josef Hromádka and Bishop Janos Peter from Eastern Europe, who had been invited to lecture at Chinese seminaries; visiting delegations of Australian and Japanese Christians; and the Endicotts and the Johnsons, old friends of China from Canada and Britain respectively. Bishop and Mrs. R. O. Hall from Hong Kong also visited China in mid-1956, but they did not see the Tings, who were visiting Europe at the time.

The visit of Josef Hromádka was especially important for the Chinese, and for Ting personally. Hromádka had criticized the WCC position on the Korean War, just as he had challenged John Foster Dulles at the Amsterdam

Assembly in 1948. Throughout the 1950s and early 1960s, he was a consistent advocate of the Chinese position. In a tribute to the Czech theologian written decades later, Ting spoke of Hromádka as a reconciler and an "apostle of the ecumenical movement" who had helped to bring the Chinese churches closer to the WCC in the 1950s.[92] Chinese Christians did not participate in the WCC in the 1950s, but Hromádka's visit helped the TSPM decide to send K. H. Ting as an observer to the Central Committee meeting of the WCC in Hungary later that year.

Another significant early visit was that of Bishop Manikam. The fact that India's Prime Minister Nehru supported Zhou Enlai's proposals for peace and nonalignment no doubt added to the welcome he received. Manikam met Zhou Enlai in Beijing, and later had an extended conversation with church and TSPM leaders, including K. H. Ting. He presented the Chinese invitations from the WCC, the IMC, the WSCF and National Council of Churches (NCC) of India. The TSPM understanding of the international ecumenical situation is reflected in Manikam's notes from this meeting.[93] The Chinese were dissatisfied with the WCC for "meddling in politics" and siding with the West in the Cold War. They were also critical of the report that had been presented on China at the preassembly meeting of the WCC in Evanston. They further questioned why there should still be an IMC alongside the WCC if churches from developing countries were truly equal partners. TSPM leaders were dismayed by the hostile reports on China coming from some former missionaries, and they asserted that they would refuse to participate in any conference in which there was even implicit recognition of Taiwan or of "two Chinas." At the same time, after rejecting the invitation from the IMC, TSPM leaders said they welcomed further international contacts and invited a delegation of Indian Christians to visit China.

The NCC of India never did visit China, but the Chinese did send representatives to the General Committee of the WSCF in Tutzing and appointed K. H. Ting as an observer at the meeting of the Central Committee of the WCC in Galyateto, Hungary. The Sheng Gong Hui was also invited by the archbishop of Canterbury to send a representative to the preparatory meeting for the Lambeth Conference, which was meeting around the same time; and Bishop Robin Chen appointed K. H. Ting to attend this meeting. At the end of June 1956, K. H. and Siu-may Ting left Beijing for a two-month visit to Europe.

The Tings spent their first three weeks in England visiting with friends and attending various church meetings. K. H. was invited to celebrate at a bilingual service of communion at the Church of St. Aldermany in London, which was designed to be an expression of the Anglican Church's openness and welcome to China. At the Lambeth Preparatory Meeting, Ting assured the Anglican Communion that the Sheng Gong Hui would send delegates to the Lambeth Conference the following year. Ting met with representatives of the Conference of British Missionary Societies, which had produced an *aide memoire* outlining its position on the Chinese church and future rela-

K. H. Ting and Visser 't Hooft, Galyateto, Hungary, 1956. Reproduced with the permission of the WCC Archives.

tionships with Christians in China and Britain.[94] Although nothing concrete came from this meeting, the document was an extraordinary sign of acceptance and support for the Chinese church and the TSPM by the British, and it foreshadowed international relationships with the TSPM and the China Christian Council (CCC) twenty-five years later.

The Tings also visited with Hewlett Johnson at Canterbury Cathedral and with other old friends and former China missionaries, including Margaret Garvie, Gilbert Baker, and David and Alison Paton. On this visit, K. H. got to know Alan Ecclestone, the only Anglican priest in England ever to have joined the British Communist Party. He presented Ecclestone with a banner written in Chinese characters saying "Truth Will Triumph," which Ecclestone had adopted as his personal slogan.[95] Ecclestone hung the banner proudly in his Darnell Church. Despite infrequent contact, the two men remained friends for life. Ting sent a message that was read at Ecclestone's memorial service in Sheffield in 1993, and which read in part:

> In joining the Communist Party in England, Alan seems to me to be bearing witness against the narrow-mindedness of the Cold War years in which Christ was not truly recognized. Like some prophets in the Old Testament, Alan resorted to taking certain actions as symbols to communicate a message from God. He upheld "Truth Will Triumph" as his slogan, just like what John Milton said in his *Areopagitica*: "If truth is in the battlefield, let us not fear the issues of the conflict.[96]

From London, the Tings went to Hungary, where they visited churches and met with Bishops Bereczky and Janos Peter, whom K. H. had first met at the Amsterdam Assembly. Bishop Peter had been with the Tings in Nanjing together with Josef Hromádka earlier that year. The Hungarians had invited the WCC Central Committee to meet in Galyateto after the Evanston Assembly, and the WCC accepted this invitation to give the appearance of balance between both sides in the Cold War. Visser 't Hooft introduced K. H. Ting to members of the Central Committee, noting that present contacts would be easier because of "old ties of affection and links of friendship with leaders among the Chinese churches."[97] Manikam reported on his recent visit to China, and Ting spoke on the life of the churches there.

Ting restated the position of the TSPM regarding the WCC and relationships with churches overseas, but his message also probed the theological significance of the changes that were taking place in China. He emphasized that Chinese Christians had rediscovered the sufficiency of Christ's grace in the years since 1949, as well as the unity of the church and the need to identify with the people in a spirit of Christian love. His speech was widely circulated in ecumenical circles, for it represented one of the very few efforts to understand what was happening in China theologically. His short reflection on Christian–Communist relations in China is worth recalling.

The Communists do not believe in God or Christ and think that in one or two hundred years religion will wither away. In all these matters

K. H. Ting with ecumenical friends at Galyateto, 1956. From left to right: D. T. Niles, Eugene C. Blake, Franklin C. Fry, K. H. Ting and Ward Nichols. Reproduced with the permission of the WCC Archives.

we do not agree and have frequent arguments with them. But we do not think that this should prevent us from recognizing the many good things they have done for China.

We think we know the essence of the Communist. He is a child of God and in him there is something God regards as worth saving.

Are we really going deeply enough into the essence of the Communist? If I must err, I much prefer to err on the side of naiveté than cynicism.[98]

The last sentence is repeated from an essay he had written in 1949, and which is cited in the previous chapter.[99] It expresses an important feature of K. H. Ting's understanding of Christian–Communist relations then and in the years since. He believed it was better for Christians to be open to new possibilities for cooperation with Communists rather than dismiss them out of hand. In this brief response, he suggests the theological reasoning behind his position, as well as the practical political considerations involved. Ting has never written at length on Christian–Communist relationships, but his position has been consistent and clear. This short response, together with the essay he wrote in 1949, indicates some of the reasons for his decision to support the CPC on theological as well as political grounds. It also helps explain the tendency of many progressive intellectuals in the 1950s and 1960s, including K. H. Ting himself, to naively support Communist excesses, something to which we will turn in the next chapter.

At Galyateto, Ting was reserved in his public comments, but he met privately with a number of church leaders, and in private he was more forthcoming. During one meeting, he spoke with John MacKay, president of Princeton Theological Seminary and an important member of the WCC Central Committee. They agreed on plans for a future visit of American church leaders to China, "to join the Christians here (in China) in the fellowship of prayer and reconciliation and understanding one another."[100] This is an extraordinary statement of Christian hope coming at the very height of the Cold War. The idea for such a visit was premature, but the fact that it was discussed at all is an indication of Ting's interest in 1956 in promoting renewed international ecumenical relationships.

From Galyateto, K. H. and Siu-may Ting proceeded to Tutzing in Germany, where they were once again among friends and former colleagues in the WSCF. Siu-may, Zhao Fusan and Huang Peiyong were the official Chinese representatives at this meeting, but K. H. had been invited to speak at the student conference preceding the meeting of the General Committee of the WSCF. Ting told the students that the Chinese church had rediscovered the sufficiency of Christ in their new situation of independence from the West, emphasizing what the church had learned about its life and witness in relationship to the Communists.[101] One participant observed that Ting's criticisms were not as sharp in Tutzing as they had been in Galyateto, for here he was within the Federation family. But the Cold War intruded on this gathering as well and proved that the ecumenical family was by no means together. The South Koreans were surprised that the Chinese had been invited, and despite efforts on the part of Federation staff to bring the two sides together, the whole South Korean delegation eventually walked out of the meeting in protest.[102] Chinese and South Korean Christians had spoken with one another in Tutzing and had achieved some sense of mutual understanding, but because of the pressures they would face at home, the South Koreans felt they could not be present at a meeting in which a Chinese delegation was officially represented.

On their way back to China after Tutzing, the Tings spent a few days in Moscow to visit the Russian Orthodox Church. The Russians were not part of the WCC at the time, and so the stopover in Moscow was an effort to develop TSPM relationships with churches in the East as well as the West. K. H. reported in China that the monasteries and churches he saw in Russia were flourishing. He wrote about the friendly relations between Christians of China and the U.S.S.R., but because this was his first visit in an unfamiliar situation, his short report reads like a travel diary designed for readers at home.[103] This was perhaps the first visit to Moscow by a Chinese bishop, and it indicates an important aspect of TSPM international ecumenical relationships in the 1950s.

In 1956, K. H. Ting was involved in what seemed to be a new ecumenical beginning for the church in China, both domestically and internationally. He and Siu-may returned to Nanjing with a great deal to do, but the unfolding events over the next year would lead them in directions they had not anticipated. From the point of view of international relationships, the new beginning turned out to be an unfulfilled hope, a result of the political changes on the domestic and international political scene.

5

Turning with the Tide, 1956-1965

> *As if I were a river*
> *The harsh age changed my course,*
> *Replaced one life with another,*
> *Flowing in a different channel*
> *And I do not recognize my shores.* *
> Anna Akhmatova[1]

> *The life of dialectics is the continuous movement toward opposites.*
> *Humankind will also finally meet its doom. When the theologians talk*
> *about doomsday, they are pessimistic and terrify people. We say the*
> *end of humankind is something which will produce something more*
> *advanced than humankind. Humankind is still in its infancy.*
> Mao Zedong[2]

K. H. and Siu-may Ting returned to Beijing from Moscow in early September 1956, just before of the opening of the Eighth Congress of the CPC. This was the first party congress in eleven years and represented a significant political milestone. The CPC leadership looked back over this period with increasing confidence. The government enjoyed growing popular support, and a basic institutional transformation had been achieved.[3] The international situation was improving, the country was peaceful and stable, and the economy was developing. This allowed for some liberalization and the relaxation of social controls, changes that were welcomed by intellectuals like K. H. and Siu-may Ting.

By 1956, the standard of living in China's cities and in many rural areas showed a marked improvement. In the countryside, collectivization had been completed, and new experiments in private agricultural production were generating extra income for peasants and better diets and living conditions for the rural population. More consumer goods, fewer political campaigns and the easing of social restrictions improved the lives of workers and intellectuals in the cities. There was also somewhat more openness in journalism, calls for the strengthening of the legal system and greater toleration for the

---

* © Oxford University Press. Used by permission.

critical spirit that was once again emerging among writers and intellectuals after the campaigns of the previous years.[4] The country had entered the stage of socialism, and in the late summer of 1956, the domestic situation appeared to be heading in the direction of unity and stability.

By mid-September, when the Tings returned home to Nanjing, the fall term had begun, and K. H. immediately plunged back into his work as seminary principal. This was the work he most enjoyed. He was committed to the educational and theological aspects of seminary leadership, and he was hoping to help prepare a new generation of pastors and Three-Self leaders. With Y. T. Wu's encouragement and support, and a growing number of influential political contacts, Ting would use his personal and political skills to help create the space needed for theological education. The situation for the church seemed much better than it had been in the early 1950s.

And yet, despite all these changes, the overall situation remained ambiguous, especially for intellectuals. It was clear to some Chinese Communist leaders that educated people were needed for economic development, and so they had to be encouraged and treated well. But within the CPC, there were different positions on what this implied for social policy. The more open approach, exemplified by the urbane and cosmopolitan Zhou Enlai, represented one side of the debate. Zhou favored cooperation with intellectuals, trust in their political participation and sense of patriotism, and toleration of their criticisms. K. H. Ting was close to Zhou Enlai and supportive of this position. He also believed that his participation in the united front was part of his patriotic support for China and the leading role of the CPC.

But there was another position in the CPC more rigid in its approach to intellectuals and more suspicious of those outside the party. Many senior leaders, including Liu Shaoqi, number two in the party hierarchy, wanted stronger party control and stricter discipline in the country as a whole. They had little patience with criticism and dissent from any quarter, and they closely followed the example of the Soviet Union. The CPC went back and forth between these two positions up until 1957, and Party Chairman Mao Zedong always held the balance. Yet this remained an intraparty division, deliberately kept from the wider public and unknown to those outside the inner circle of the Central Committee.

The nationwide campaign against editor and writer Hu Feng in 1955 had shown that there were strict limits to criticism directed at the CPC. Hu Feng was a literary theorist opposed to the politicization of literature advocated by Mao Zedong.[5] The new campaign against him created a sense of fear and demoralization among liberal intellectuals. Activist leaders of the Three-Self Movement joined in the attack against Hu Feng, just before they launched their own criticism of the fundamentalist preacher Wang Mingdao. Yet within a year after the start of the campaign against Hu Feng, intellectuals were again being courted by Zhou Enlai in an effort to show that their skills were needed and their opinions valued. They were, of course, not apprised of the contending views of party leaders, and this intraparty division would shortly be resolved by a shift away from liberalization to increased repression. Patriotic intellectuals such as K. H. Ting who continued to trust the party would in time pay a high price for their loyalty because greater expression of support for CPC policies would be demanded.

Two international events in 1956 were of crucial importance for this change of course. The first was the Twentieth Party Congress in the Soviet Union in February, and Nikita Khrushchev's "secret speech" denouncing Joseph Stalin. This sent shock waves through the Communist movement all over the world. In China, it resulted in a reassessment of the relationship between the party and the people, an interpretation that was reflected in two major speeches made by Mao Zedong in the spring of 1956.[6] Both speeches emphasized an open and united-front approach to those outside the CPC. Mao seemed to be suggesting that China could avoid the mistakes of the Soviet Union and the party could change. Within the CPC, however, the policy debate continued behind closed doors. The second event was the Hungarian Uprising in October 1956 and its suppression by the Soviet army the following month. This resulted in an even more vigorous intraparty debate in China. For many CPC leaders, the Hungarian Uprising and the less dramatic efforts for reform in Poland signaled the danger that internal dissent continued to pose for socialism. They argued that opposition to the CPC would be exploited by "anti-China" forces at home and abroad to weaken the Communist bloc. Once again, attention was focused on the relationship between the party and the people, and this time, the effect was to strengthen the hand of those who wanted a stricter approach to party social control.

Zhou Enlai, Deng Xiaoping and others still believed that the party had made errors, and their views, with Mao's tacit support, prevailed. They believed that the CPC had nothing to fear from the "gentle breeze and mild rain" of criticism, and so intellectuals were encouraged to speak their minds and contribute to the process of reform. In the spring of 1957, the "One Hundred Flowers" movement was begun, unleashing a torrent of stinging criticisms directed at the CPC from intellectuals all over China. Party officials on all sides were stunned by the depth and vehemence of the criticisms that seemed to challenge all aspects of their rule. The criticisms came from many different quarters and were directed at almost every aspect of party policy.

After five weeks of "blooming and contending," the CPC decided to draw back. On 8 June 1957 *Renmin ribao* (*People's Daily*) published the editorial "What is this for?" which brought the movement to a close. This was the beginning of the Anti-Rightist movement, and a campaign against those who had criticized the party was begun. This new campaign was decisive and marked the end of the united-front approach to cooperation with intellectuals for the next twenty years. China now changed course. The "Great Leap Forward" in the following year, the Sino-Soviet split (1961) and the "socialist education" movement (1962) continued to push China further and further toward a more repressive leftist position in the years leading up to the Cultural Revolution.

The liberal social climate in 1956-1957 had a positive effect on the churches. But the continuing intraparty debates would in time lead to a new emphasis on mass movements and a politics of struggle that was disastrous for society and culture in China. K. H. Ting would be swept up in the politics of the times, and he became a willing participant in the Anti-Rightist movement. His carefully crafted position on the relationship between theology and politics came to an end. In late 1956 and early 1957, however, K. H. Ting, like almost everyone else, was anticipating a new period of intellectual liberalization and openness in the life of the church.

CONTINUING CHRISTIAN PRESENCE

Nanjing Union Theological Seminary was growing. In the fall of 1956, 107 students were enrolled, the largest number in the seminary's four-year history. They were drawn from sixteen denominations in thirteen provinces, mostly in East China, with the largest number (thirty-nine) from Zhejiang, where churches were already growing beyond where they had been in 1949. The students were all lower- and upper-middle-school graduates in their early twenties. Ninety-seven students had already graduated from the seminary, and most of them were serving in churches in the provinces and denominations from which they had come.[7] Despite the generally hostile climate for religion, Protestant churches associated with the TSPM were adapting to the new order.

K. H. Ting wanted to encourage churches, and particularly seminary graduates, in this process of adaptation to life in a socialist China. As seminary principal, he would occasionally write circular letters to recent graduates. His advice to them in the 1950s, and again in the 1980s and 1990s, was remarkably consistent. In 1955, after reviewing some of the changes that had taken place at the seminary, he urged seminary alumni/ae to work closely with colleagues and fellow Christians in a spirit of Christian unity and love. They should resist temptations to pride and cultivate a spirit of Christian humility. This would help build up the church in China, and it would improve their working relationships with local government officials.

Today, we are faced with the greatest danger when people flatter us, saying we are good in this and that, and choose us to "lead" others. If, hearing these compliments, we become complacent, pose as a leader, and even become swollen with arrogance, bossing people around, then we are falling into the trap of the Devil, who attacks us precisely at our point of our fatal weakness, pride.

On the whole, our alumni/ae are modest, but we cannot say that all of you have learnt well the lesson of modesty. We must always learn to be modest and to love others sincerely. We must learn to live in unity with other co-workers, tolerating and helping each other. We must pay all the more respect to older co-workers and maintain the sincere desire to unite with and seek advice from them. If there is a difference of opinion in work, we must try to reach an agreement before going forward, guarding against arbitrary decisions and actions. It is the virtue of modesty that is the most worthy and admirable subject in prayers for Nanjing Union Seminary students. We ask God in His compassion to grant us this most precious virtue.[8]

In many places, the church situation had improved after the end of the Korean War and the movements of the early 1950s, but it was still difficult to recruit well-qualified students for the ministry. The political environment discouraged active involvement in the church, and promising Christian young people avoided careers as pastors or church workers. Prospective seminarians had to get permission from the government or their work units to study theology, and this was never easy. Teachers, soldiers and government workers were not allowed to go to seminary at all, and leaders in other work units discouraged any interest in religion. China was now building socialism, so why would religious life or Christian faith be necessary? Seminary students tended to be poorly educated men and women from small cities and towns in the countryside. They had little preparation for theological study, and job prospects were not good. Students at Nanjing Seminary had to be either deeply committed Christians or people without other prospects. As was true in other socialist countries in the 1950s and 1960s, Chinese theological students had to be prepared to make great sacrifices to live out their Christian commitment and serve the church.

K. H. Ting knew this better than anyone. As seminary principal, he wanted his students to do well and serve the church and their country. In his writing he addressed questions of theology and biblical interpretation that young church workers and seminary students were asking. He wanted to support them in their ministry, prepare them for their future work in the church and help them deal with the difficulties he knew they would encounter.[9] Ting urged students to get along well with government officials, even when the officials looked down on them and criticized the church.

The political situation posed new theological questions to the churches. Ting has written that after Liberation in 1949, grassroots church workers had to grapple anew with questions about the relationship between Christianity and the world around them: Is the world in the hands of God or the devil? Should Christians be concerned with issues of right and wrong, or only questions of belief or nonbelief? How should Christians relate to non-Christians in society? Does grace negate or fulfill nature? There were debates on these questions published in *Tian Feng* and elsewhere in the mid-1950s, and Ting encouraged his students to take part. He has spoken of these debates as a "theological mass movement" or a "theological fermentation at the grassroots" which emerged among young pastors and lay leaders.[10]

Even though this theological mass movement was orchestrated by the TSPM, young people who became involved wrestled with the questions that the new order posed for the faith and beliefs they had grown up with.

Ting's own process of theological reorientation continued to be reflected in his sermons, Bible studies and lectures to seminary students. He did not advance a radically new approach to doing theology in the 1950s. He had the more immediate and practical concern to hold the seminary together and help students understand and reinterpret the Bible in ways that would be acceptable. Most of the booklet later published as *How to Study the Bible* was written in the mid-1950s with this idea in mind.[11] This little devotional guide found wide acceptance in Chinese churches in the early 1980s, and we can imagine that seminary students in the 1950s would also be responsive to its religious message. *How to Study the Bible* also had a clear political position on how Christians should relate to the new order, and so it is another example of what in chap. 4 I termed Ting's double movement in relating theology to politics.

How to Study the Bible is traditional in its approach, written in a popular style and in a language that in some ways resembles William Temple's *Readings in St. John's Gospel,* one of Ting's favorite devotional works. Ting wished to encourage students to put their own questions to the Bible, and to allow the Bible to question them. In the space of very few pages, he ranges from the careful exegesis of selected passages of scripture to broad generalizations about the system and theme of the Bible. There is the unmistakable influence of his own theological training and the Bible studies he did in the WSCF, for he deals with many of his favorite subjects in this pamphlet, including the love of God, the need for humility and obedience, the importance of human reason, and the nature of biblical paradox. He also presents once again his qualified approach to the doctrine of justification by faith, saying (in good Anglican fashion) that this is not the central doctrine of Christianity and arguing that it should not become an excuse for condoning unrighteousness, justifying spiritual pride or ignoring ethical action.

Patriotism and anti-imperialism are discussed in *How to Study the Bible,* and although they are not particularly prominent themes, they are there to help educate Christians on how to relate to the political order. Christian unity, which Ting saw as important for seminary students and the church as a whole, is central to Ting's understanding of the Bible. He writes,

"To unite all things in Christ, things in heaven and things on earth" (Eph. 1:10), we can say that this is the direction in which the whole Bible is pointing. "One" is the briefest, and at the same time the fullest character in Chinese. The Bible tells us that in God's eyes God and humanity should be one and in harmony. But this unity has been broken. Both the relationship between God and humanity, and that among people, lost their harmony. Afterwards, through the great sacrifice of Christ, this "oneness" of relationship has been restored (Eph. 2:14-

16) . . . This progression from unity to division, and from division to unity, is the clue to penetrating the meaning of the whole Bible.[12]

How to Study the Bible deals with issues that the church was facing in its internal life. But seminary students were confronting even more serious challenges from the outside. Karl Marx had said that religion was the opium *of* the people, and Vladimir Lenin had gone a step further saying religion was opium *for* the people, manipulated by reactionary leaders to maintain their power in a class society. In the China of the 1950s, churches were criticized as "reactionary" and "foreign," and Christian faith was dismissed as "unscientific" and "idealist." In the political understanding of the times, religious faith of any kind was an opiate by definition. This had become the way of defining the very nature and essence of Christianity, and it was reflected in almost everything that was written in textbooks and the mass media about religion in China. Religion could be tolerated, but it really had nothing to contribute.

In this situation, theological students and prospective pastors needed guidance on what to do and how to respond. Ting's own answer came in the form of a candid and well-reasoned defense of the Christian belief in God, originally delivered as a lecture to seminary students toward the end of the spring term in 1957.[13] It was published under the title "On Christian Theism," and it was the last theological essay Ting would publish for more than twenty years. At the time, the Indian theologian M. M. Thomas termed it a profound interpretation of the "theology of society" in the Asian context, and a former American missionary observed that it was "one of the most remarkable and forthright statements that have come out of Communist China."[14] The reaction to this essay among Ting's activist colleagues in the TSPM was not at all positive, as we shall see. In light of its historical significance for the church then and now, the essay deserves careful attention.

K. H. Ting had urged students at NUTS to be logical and careful in their thinking, and "On Christian Theism" is an example of his own measured and reasoned tone. He writes at the beginning: "We do not subscribe to the various atheistic theories, but we must also know wherein they are wrong and, still more, what the right view is." What follows was his response to the various ways in which Christianity was being criticized. He discusses these in terms of the question of idealism and materialism; the idea that Christianity is an opiate; the evidence for God's existence; the role of sin in Christian understanding; the reasons why many people choose not to believe; and the Christian's approach to the atheist. Throughout the essay, Ting again and again reiterates the point that simplistic characterizations of Christians or of atheists are unhelpful and misleading. Instead, one must discern how Christianity functions in particular situations. His emphasis is on the practical implications of Christian faith.

For Ting, it was illogical to divide all people into idealists and materialists and assume that the former were reactionary and the latter were progressive. Materialism and idealism have interacted with and influenced each other throughout history. Christianity is neither idealist nor materialist, but rather a transcendent reality derived from God's revelation that calls all ideologies into question and cannot itself be identified with any. Because Christianity is not simply a product of history, it is therefore not an ideological rival to communism.

> We must ever remember that what we preach is the gospel, is Christ, something in nature entirely different from an ideology, something which moves in a different orbit from any system of thought, and then we will have a clear understanding from which to perceive that all talk of a comparison of Christianity with Communism, of likenesses or differences, is beside the point and superfluous.

Ting then asks, "Is Christianity an opiate?" This is an especially important section of the essay, and Ting straightforwardly confronts the Communists' assertion that religion by its very nature has a narcotic function. Implicit is the discussion from the 1930s and 1940s about whether Christianity and Communism could ever work together. Religion, writes Ting, *may* function as an opiate in certain times and under certain conditions, but so may literature, art and even science. Even a refusal to believe in God can become an opiate, because it could mean that people "continue to sin, avoid responsibility and stifle the reproaches of their conscience." The point is to distinguish religion from its social function, to differentiate between the intrinsic character of faith in itself and the uses to which it may be put politically. Ting argued that we needed to "study religion completely, and not proceed from a priori definitions." Religion as an opiate is not basic to Christian belief nor is it essential to its social function.

He uses, at this point in the essay, one of his favorite examples to make his point, that of Jesus refusing a narcotic on the cross (Matthew 27:34).[15] This refusal shows that Christianity in its original form did not endorse the dulling of one's senses in the face of social injustice.

> What Christ gives men is forgiveness, consolation and strength, not a benumbed spirit. We pray, "Thy will be done on earth as it is in heaven." Where is there any opiate in that prayer?

His whole line of argument is important, for this was the only essay written by a Chinese Christian before the Cultural Revolution that challenged the Communist idea of religion as opiate. It foreshadows the debate that became known as the "Third Opium War" in the 1980s (discussed in chap. 7), a debate about how religion should be understood scientifically. It was only in the 1980s, and not in 1957, that the matter was resolved in favor of the position that K. H. Ting had advocated twenty-five years earlier.

"On Christian Theism" did not try to "prove" the existence of God. In good Anglican fashion, Ting suggests that there is evidence for God's existence from natural theology and from everyday life, evidence that can lead

Hewlett Johnson and K. H. Ting, 1959. Reproduced with the permission of
Keren and Kezia Johnson.

people to probe the meaning of existence and the order of the universe,
although the witness of nature is not in and of itself sufficient for Christian
faith. Yet Christians should recognize that creation is the handiwork of God,
because, following St. Thomas Aquinas, "grace does not negate nature, but
fulfills it." This is true, even though in the final analysis, "the knowledge of
God comes only through revelation." Creation and redemption need to be
considered together in Christian understanding. This is yet another theological theme to which he returns to again and again in his work.

The question of sin is fundamental to Christian faith, but Christians have
been too biased in attributing all evil to the innately sinful nature of human
beings. The fact of human sin should not become the argument used to persuade others to believe in Christianity, for this would mean starting from a
negative reality. Despite the fact of sin, it continues to be important to work
for the improvement of the social order. Moral life and ethical action are
essential for the Christian, and Christians should realize that a bad social
environment is harmful for people in general. Christians should therefore
welcome positive changes in society, even if these changes come from outside the church and even though the question of sin remains unresolved.

We should welcome a social system that is able to raise the level of
moral life. But the change of a social system can only limit the effec-

tiveness of sin, it cannot solve the problem of sin. Sin can only be healed by love, forgiveness, salvation and grace. It is not a matter of social progress.

In welcoming such a social system, Ting explicitly says that ideologies are not all equal, and that the difference between capitalism and socialism is enormous. What the gospel does is lead people to make relative choices for themselves and for a system that they believe will help to improve society and moral life.

On this basis, Ting makes the unambiguous political choice for socialism—similar to the choice made by many Latin American liberation theologians years later. Christianity continues to transcend ideology, and no system can be equated with Christian faith. But an individual's or a society's choice is based on a judgment about the creative moral forces for justice and human development that are available to a people or nation at certain points in history.[16] Church and society could not be equated with each other, but they could be compatible and complementary. This would become important in Ting's political development, and we shall return to it shortly.

"Why do some people choose not to believe in God?" K. H. Ting asked. Arrogance and sin are common to the human condition, and they lead people away from God. This is why Christian faith must begin with repentance.

K. H. Ting with the Johnsons and Zhou Enlai, 1959. Reproduced with the permission of Keren and Kezia Johnson.

Wu Yifang and K. H. Ting, 1960. Reproduced from *Tian Feng Gan Yu: Zhongguo jidujiao lingxiu Ding Guangxun (Heavenly Wind and Sweet Rain: China's Christian Leader Ding Guangxun)*.

But there is another reason for unbelief, according to Ting, one of the church's own making. Insofar as Christians themselves failed to manifest God in their own lives, they have not been credible witnesses. Here Ting lays the blame squarely on the political alliance of the churches with imperialism before 1949. He asserts that the TSPM was attempting to purify the church so that this second obstacle to belief could be removed. The church could then reflect the truth of the gospel for the entire world to see.

Despite the churches' failures and weaknesses, the question of atheism and theism should not become a political issue, for theism and atheism are matters of personal faith and worldview. Christians should be able to live alongside atheists, "learn how to profit from their criticism of religion, and learn how to present the gospel" to them. Likewise, "a state or government cannot hold to either theism or atheism," for these are beliefs that do not pertain to the political realm. Ting was making the very subtle distinction here between the state, which said that it guaranteed religious freedom, and the CPC, which was atheist. Western countries were wrong to use the difference between atheism and theism as a weapon in the Cold War, Ting continued. They had identified theism with anti-Communism, and they called their own governments "Christian"—despite the fact that Christ said his Kingdom was not of this world. As Ting had argued against Wang Mingdao, the question of atheism or theism should not be allowed to foment division and disorder, for different worldviews should not obstruct political unity.

"On Christian Theism" was a very public *apologia* for Christian faith, but it was at the same time a very personal statement. It was K. H. Ting's mother who had nurtured him in the faith, from which he never wavered, and it is worth noting that two key illustrations in this text draw on the example of his mother's love. In the first paragraph he says that we know God through spiritual insight not reasoning or persuasion, just as "we know our mother not because we have been persuaded by some argument or demonstration, but because from childhood up we have felt her love." Several pages later, he says that the evidence for God's existence that we see in nature may be compared to the evidence we see of our mother in our homes when she is not there. "You know her and love her, and as you go in and look around, everything in the house reminds you of her." Ting experienced the love of God through the love of his own mother, and we can see from these examples that he was interpreting his own faith indirectly.

Such indirect references provide clues about how to understand K. H. Ting as a person in the late 1950s. He was never one who wanted to reveal much about his personal life. Many of the things he felt most deeply about, he never expressed. He is at heart a very shy man, and he is reluctant to speak about himself, his family and his faith. In part, his reticence went with being a public figure in China, but it was also a personality trait. Many Westerners, particularly Euro-Americans, find this frustrating, but we should not project our own cultural expectations on others. There are not many places in his writings or in his public appearances when we get a sense of who the man is, and so we continually fall back on his public persona; and it is his public role, after all, that makes his life historically significant.

As a theologian, K. H. was always trying to create more space for Christianity, and in this essay he made use of the space he already had for developing a Christian apologetic with which to challenge religion's Communist critics. At the same time, he upheld the new order and argued for Christian unity. Others in the TSPM were saying that in the New China, theology, or even the church, was no longer needed. K. H. Ting would never say this. His theological perspective and method of argument provided seminary students with one way of defending their faith in the broader society and developing the work of the church. Ting's views in "On Christian Theism" are not new, and his ideas are not thoroughly developed. Yet this remains an important essay written at a critical time in Chinese Christian history. This short reflection may be seen as one of the most significant theological contributions to emerge from the China of the 1950s.

Ting's own theological position at this time was clear and consistent, and so was the way he interprets that position in light of his own political context. He drew a careful distinction between theology and politics, and he attempted to walk a fine line between the two. This is another illustration of his tendency to compartmentalize Christian life that was noted in the last

chapter. Such a distinction could never be accepted by a thoroughgoing
Marxist-Leninist, nor, for example, by a Barthian theologian committed to
a clear yes and no. But in the 1950s, Ting's position helped steer clear of the
criticism that he was advocating Christianity as an ideological rival to Communism. He was affirming both Christian faith and socialist revolution as
two separate but complementary areas of life and thought.

Yet, it was precisely on this point that difficulties would arise for him in
the years ahead. What M. M. Thomas had termed Ting's "theology of society" could only be viable if there were some measure of pluralism and tolerance in the nation as a whole. Ting's theology would have a contribution
to make in a political order that valued cooperation from those outside the
CPC. This was possible in China as long as a more open-ended interpretation of united-front politics was in force, but not under the ultra-leftism of
the late 1950s and 1960s. After 1957, all public expressions of Christian
faith would collapse into politics, and theology would be swallowed up by
its context. Christians could no longer do anything publicly but affirm socialism or patriotism. In the process, the theological complement to socialist
revolution would be lost, which is to say that Ting's theology of society
would cease to have any meaning in the society from which it emerged.

It is, therefore, all the more extraordinary that Ting chose to present and
publish this essay when he did. Perhaps it was coincidental, for in mid-1957
most people were still unclear about what was happening. Other Christians
had spoken out during the previous weeks of "blooming and contending,"
when intellectuals were encouraged to speak their minds, and many leading
Christians criticized the government. Ting had not spoken out during this
period, which was over by the time he delivered his lecture. By August, when
"On Christian Theism" was finally published, the government's counter-
attack against intellectuals was in full swing.

It is possible that his essay "On Christian Theism" was ignored by critics because the seminary was comparatively inconspicuous, and the circulation of the *JL* was extremely limited. It is also possible that because K. H.
Ting enjoyed the support and the patronage of Zhou Enlai, he would not
have been singled out for criticism in any case, or at least he would not be
criticized for a theological essay that had not been widely distributed.

But the essay did not go unnoticed by everyone in positions of power. In
1959, there was a broad political campaign against "right-wing revisionism" in the wake of the Anti-Rightist movement. Ting later recalled that
TSPM activists in Shanghai, led by Li Chuwen, proposed that there should
be a meeting to study the opposition to right-wing revisionism in Christian
circles, and they wanted Ting to take part. He went, and in that meeting he
found that he and his friend Zheng Jianye were the two targets of criticism.
K. H. Ting was specifically criticized for writing "On Christian Theism."
Such theological essays were no longer needed, he was told, for theology
was being replaced by socialism.

They [i.e., the TSPM activists] thought that I should not have written such an article, for they considered it a strong defense of Christianity. I think their assumption was that it would be quite enough if we did not attack Christianity. To put forward a strong defense, an apologetic, that would not be good, it would be in violation of the principle of liquidating religion. That's my words. But this is my real understanding of their position, even if they have not said so in so many words.[17]

Nothing came of this meeting, but it showed that even though Ting had changed with the times, he was still vulnerable to attack by others in Shanghai in the inner circle of the TSPM. We shall see in the following chapter that the controversy over this essay would again be raised during the Cultural Revolution.

THE ANTI-RIGHTIST MOVEMENT

The Anti-Rightist movement began in 1957 with an attack against intellectuals who had criticized the party and the government during the One Hundred Flowers period of the previous weeks. The movement ushered in an era of repression that foreshadowed the Cultural Revolution nine years later. Intellectuals were criticized, harassed and sometimes exiled or imprisoned. Many more intellectuals were purged during the Anti-Rightist period than in previous campaigns, as many as 700,000 according to one estimate.[18] It drove many people to suicide, ruined tens of thousands of careers, and set back intellectual and cultural life in China for the next twenty years.

The campaign has been termed "a muddled and inconclusive movement that grew out of conflicting attitudes within the CPC leadership."[19] This may have been true of the Anti-Rightist movement itself, but the increased political control established over all aspects of intellectual, cultural and religious life was by no means inconclusive. The movement marked the end of the party's more open approach to cooperation with intellectuals, and it cast a shadow over anyone who dared to criticize the CPC, the government or even particular policies.

The most prominent victims of the Anti-Rightist movement were intellectuals, writers and artists, both inside and outside the CPC. As in earlier movements, Christians—especially Christian intellectuals—also came under attack. The TSPM was instructed to identify and expose "rightists" in the churches. As was true in subsequent campaigns, work units were given quotas of the numbers of people who had to be targeted, which meant that the identification of individuals was often arbitrary or even farcical. Since a certain number of rightists had to be produced, it was natural to look for people who had exposed themselves in one way or another, or who were in other ways unpopular. In this situation, Christians who were known to be critical of the government or strong in their religious convictions became obvious targets.

K. H. Ting accepted the government's justification of the Anti-Rightist movement at the time. Like many other patriotic intellectuals, he believed that the dangers that China faced from within and without were very real. He had not voiced any criticisms during the One Hundred Flowers Movement, and he became an active participant in the campaign against rightists, particularly in Nanjing. Like others in the TSPM, he followed the lead of Y. T. Wu and government officials in the Religious Affairs Bureau (RAB) who were actively involved in the new campaign.

The Tenth (Enlarged) Plenum of the TSPM was the context for targeting rightists in the Protestant churches at the national level. The government called 130 Protestant delegates to the Tenth TSPM Plenum in Beijing for more than five weeks in late 1957 to study socialism and learn about the new campaign from the RAB and other government bodies. K. H. Ting was among them. At the meeting, seven prominent Christian leaders—all of whom were supporters of the TSPM—were singled out for attack, and others were also subject to various kinds of criticism.[20] They were questioned and criticized by colleagues and fellow Christians for days on end in small groups and in plenary sessions, and the charges leveled against them were written up as the major portion of the report from the Tenth Plenum. All of these sessions were carefully orchestrated by the government through the RAB.

In the months that followed the Tenth Plenum, meetings to expose rightists in the churches were held in cities all across China. This was initially termed a "socialist-education" movement for people in religious circles, rather than an Anti-Rightist rectification movement. Thousands of prominent Christians, pastors, students, and local TSPM leaders were criticized and lost their positions. Many of them were sent to remote parts of the country, and some were even driven to suicide when they faced yet another campaign against them. Some Christians who were sent to the far western region of Xinjiang never returned. During the movement, one could be criticized and not labeled, but once labeled a "rightist," an individual's situation would not improve until the label was removed. In the country as a whole, it was later estimated that up to 98 percent of all labels had been wrongly applied.[21] Most labels, for Christians and everyone else, were not removed until the late 1970s and early 1980s, often posthumously.

In Jiangsu Province, the socialist-education movement began in the late spring of 1958. It was organized by the provincial RAB, with the participation of people from religious circles in the Jiangsu People's Political Consultative Conference (JPPCC), which included K. H. Ting and other Christian leaders. At the initial stage, individuals were not labeled as "rightists" but were interrogated, criticized, asked to examine their faults and write self-criticisms under supervision. Dozens of Christians from Nanjing churches were brought under investigation as their "crimes" and "errors" were identified at a series of mass meetings.

As seminary principal and one of the most prominent Christian members of the JPPCC, K. H. Ting was expected to play a leading role in the socialist-education meetings to criticize Christian rightists. He had participated in the Beijing TSPM meeting, where he took part in the small group sessions that criticized Fan Aishi and Jia Yuming, prominent evangelicals from Zhejiang and Shanghai respectively. By his own account, Ting took part in the criticism sessions of his own accord—he did not have to be persuaded to do so—for he believed that criticism and self-criticism were necessary to protect the new order.[22] Ting was himself becoming more of a leftist, under the influence of the movement of the times.

Nanjing Theological Seminary was also a venue for the Anti-Rightist movement. Wang Weifan, a recent graduate, was among the first in the seminary to come under attack. Wang was a profound and moving writer and a passionate evangelical preacher. In the mid-1950s, he began editing *Sheng Guang*, an informal church magazine for evangelicals promoted by the TSPM. K. H. Ting had come to know Wang Weifan when he was a seminary student, and the two men, representing different theological positions, came to respect each other. Nevertheless, Ting presented a speech criticizing Wang Weifan in the spring of 1958. He recalls that he stood up in front of a meeting to read from a sheet of mimeographed paper that documented certain things that Wang Weifan was supposed to have said. He said that the paper had been prepared by the local RAB.[23] It made no difference that the statements were taken out of context, drawn mainly from things Wang had said during the One Hundred Flowers period when he had been encouraged to "express the things that were in his heart." Because Wang had once suggested that the Communist Party was in danger of becoming a Stalinist party, and because of his deep religious commitment, he was an obvious target. K. H. Ting read from the paper that he had been given, then analyzed Wang's remarks and delivered his own criticism. The result of this meeting was that Wang Weifan had to undergo further "supervised" criticism and was relieved of his duties at *Sheng Guang*.

In the fall of the same year, the Nanjing RAB organized a second series of citywide mass meetings, and it was at this time that Wang Weifan and several other church workers in Nanjing were actually labeled as "rightists." Wang's earlier self-criticism was found to be inadequate, and in any case there were quotas to be filled at the seminary. Mao Zedong had said that perhaps 3 percent of the population were rightists, and so this percentage had to be identified in each work unit. As a result of being labeled, Wang was sent to labor in Qixiashan on the outskirts of Nanjing, together with other "rightists" from religious circles.[24] He did not return to work at the church or seminary for the next twenty-one years.

Other seminary faculty members and students were also labeled "rightists," and all were expected to take part in the criticism meetings, which were carefully planned by the RAB. Luther Shao (Shao Jingshan), a NUTS faculty member who had voiced criticisms of the government during the One Hundred Flowers movement, committed suicide. Zang Antang and Chen Shiyi were the two other faculty members singled out to meet the seminary's quota, and they were sent with their families to Xinjiang. Neither of them ever returned to work at the seminary. A number of students were also labeled "rightists," and they too were sent away. The injustices done to patriotic students and teachers at the seminary were obvious, and in microcosm, this reflected what was happening in society as a whole.

An individual's actions during a time of political upheaval such as the Anti-Rightist movement are never consistent, and the personal struggles and political pressures called forth different responses at different times. There were situations in which K. H. Ting tried to protect or comfort students who were reported to be under suspicion. In one case, he sought out a young man in his dormitory and told him to leave Nanjing immediately. When the student hesitated, Ting ordered him off the campus and took him forcibly to the seminary gate in order to protect him. The student returned to his home in Guangdong, and some years later left for Hong Kong. Hong Guangliang, another student, from the southeastern city of Shantou, was labeled an "ultra-rightist" and he was led away from the seminary compound in handcuffs. Ting was unable to do anything to help him, but he did escort Hong to the seminary gate, an action of support that was seen as an expression of his love and concern for the student who had been arrested. On one level, then, Ting supported what he understood to be the political goals of the Anti-Rightist movement. But because he was attached to his students, at times his personal affection overcame political commitment when he saw that they were in trouble.

However, Ting believed at the time that the criticism of rightists was necessary and correct. This was why he was willing to criticize Wang Weifan and others in 1958. As he later recalled,

> All of this happened at a time when Chairman Mao enjoyed tremendous prestige and the Communist Party enjoyed tremendous prestige, and I think the assumption on the part of many people, including me, was that the party and government got hold of many other things about these persons. This is what was actually said by people like Luo Xunru, the head of the (Jiangsu) RAB. In this Anti-Rightist movement, many of us really believed that these people were rightists, enemies of the party and of the government of New China.[25]

K. H. Ting had been critical of the earlier TSPM campaigns of the 1950s, but he became a willing participant in the Anti-Rightist movement. In the course of only one year, Ting and countless other intellectuals identified themselves with the increasingly leftist line that had come to dominate all areas of political and social life. We do not know the internal struggles that brought him to this new position. It is easy to make a historical judgment on the horrors and injustices of the Anti-Rightist movement, but it is much more difficult to assess the responses of individuals who were involved at different levels and to different degrees when the movement was in process. Ting, like most others, was unclear about what was happening in the intraparty struggle, and he maintained idealistic hope in Chairman Mao and the New China. Anyone who did not live through the times will find it impossible to imagine what the Anti-Rightist movement and the Cultural Revolution era were like, what pressures people were subject to, what hopes they held on to and what motivated them to act in the ways they did. It is even more difficult to discern the threads of politics and individual responsibility for those who were not directing the political process in the complex tapestry of the times.

All through the 1940s and 1950s, Ting wanted to affirm Christian faith and the Chinese Revolution, not as coequal categories but as complementary aspects of life and thought. He had developed a theological position that allowed him to do this, a framework in which Christian faith and socialist politics could be compatible and to a certain extent compartmentalized, each with its own contribution to make in its own respective sphere. His was the Anglican theological middle way expressed with moderation combined with a clear political option for the CPC. By late 1957, however, the complementariness or compatibility of theology and politics could no longer be held together, at least publicly. Theology collapsed into politics as the "high tide of socialism" rolled over all other ways of thinking. In practical terms, theology became irrelevant. We do not know whether K. H. Ting ever questioned Christian faith and belief in this process, but he would no longer be able to write the kind of theological essays that he had up until that point. After 1957, theology was no longer tolerated in any public sense. It seemed to have nothing to offer to a society and culture in which politics was in command.

From the testimony of his published writings and his subsequent reflections, K. H. Ting identified himself with the "high tide of socialism" from 1957 onward. He did so as a patriotic Chinese and as an individual committed to socialism. The church had become less important for him as a category of social thought. We no longer hear about "mutual respect" in matters of faith until after the end of the Cultural Revolution. The harsh age had indeed changed his course. Unlike Anna Akhmatova, the great Russian poet who is quoted at the beginning of this chapter, K. H. Ting willingly joined the flow and moved in a new direction. There were others who later said that they played along and did not really believe in the Anti-Rightist movement at the time, but K. H. Ting was more honest. In the late 1950s, he did believe in the politics of mass participation and criticism–self-criticism which the Anti-Rightist movement exemplified. From here, it was a small step to extend the criticism to people he saw to be opposed to New China and the socialist system, even if they were colleagues or friends.

Forty years later, he saw things very differently. He has confessed that it was wrong for him to have taken part in the Anti-Rightist movement and to have criticized colleagues such as Wang Weifan.[26] This conviction and change of heart emerged in the early seventies, but it began to be reflected in his public critique of ultra-leftism only in the early 1980s. K. H. Ting closely followed the wider debate on the Anti-Rightist movement and the Cultural Revolution in the 1980s and 1990s, and he has done everything in his power to right the wrongs of the past. As we shall see, his critique of ultra-leftism became a cornerstone of his leadership of the TSPM and the China Christian Council, and it was important both for the internal life of the church and for church-state relations.

In 1979, K. H. Ting brought Wang Weifan back to Nanjing University's newly opened Institute for Religious Studies, and for the next twenty years, they worked closely together as friends. As is true of many who were sent down during the Anti-Rightist movement, Wang Weifan harbored no bitterness toward his accusers. He was subsequently rehabilitated; his "rightist" label was removed, and some restitution was made for what he had suffered. A number of other colleagues at Nanjing Seminary had also criticized Wang Weifan, but only K. H. Ting and one other faculty member made a formal apology. Ting not only apologized privately, but also admitted his mistakes in a sermon he preached in the Nanjing Seminary chapel.[27]

Ting saw to it that many other students and faculty members who were attacked during the Anti-Rightist movement and after were also rehabilitated. [28] Zang Antang was rehabilitated posthumously, and Chen Shiyi was able to return with his family from Xinjiang. Ting arranged for Hong Guangliang, the student mentioned above, to return to Nanjing, where the government made a formal apology and the church and seminary held a service of reconciliation. Hong became a Lutheran pastor and worked in churches in Hong Kong and Canada to promote mutual understanding with the TSPM and CCC in China.

JOURNEYS TO THE EAST

The Anti-Rightist movement was shaped in part by developments in other parts of the Communist bloc. The Hungarian Uprising and the events in Poland in October 1956 had indicated to many CPC leaders that intellectual dissent in any socialist country could weaken political control and play into the hands of the West. This was the reason why China backed the Soviet invasion of Hungary, where reformers were calling for the overhaul of the socialist system.[29] Zhou Enlai visited Eastern Europe in January 1957 in order to demonstrate CPC support for the newly installed leadership in Hungary and in Poland. In the months that followed, there were many reports in the Chinese press about the "Hungarian events" and their broader international implications. In November, Mao led a delegation to the Soviet Union and declared that "the East Wind is prevailing over the West Wind."[30]

The Cold War rivalry between East and West was intensifying, and this had a profound effect on Christian churches all over the world. Political leaders in the Soviet Union and Communist bloc believed that the churches in the West and the ecumenical movement as a whole had played an important role in supporting the Hungarian Uprising.[31] Because of their ecumenical relationships, this put Christians in China and in Eastern Europe in a difficult position. Churches in Hungary and other Eastern European countries spoke out in support of the restoration of socialism once the Hungarian Uprising had been suppressed. Chinese Christians also had to demonstrate where they stood.

The TSPM publicly echoed the Chinese government's position on Hungary, as did all other united-front organizations. In late June 1957, just weeks after the beginning of the Anti-Rightist movement, *Tian Feng* published a letter to Hungarian Christians signed by eighteen TSPM leaders, including K. H. Ting. The letter expressed support for Hungary's decision to preserve socialism and asserted that "in preaching the Gospel of God's Kingdom our own solidarity is a most important factor."[32] The same issue carried an article sharply critical of the WCC and its general secretary W.A. Visser 't Hooft for their alleged efforts to support the "reactionary forces" in Hungary.[33] It mentions the Galyateto meeting of the Central Committee the previous summer as a contributor to the events that led to the uprising. Ting had been at Galyateto as an observer, and he was critical of Visser 't Hooft's position on Christianity in Eastern Europe.[34] After the Hungarian Uprising, the WCC was seen in China as a tool of the West. The possibility that there could be reconciliation between the WCC and China, which was still hoped for in 1956, was now at an end. It would be twenty years before a serious dialogue could resume between the international ecumenical community and Chinese Christians.

A delegation of Hungarian Christians was invited to China in the fall of 1957. This was followed by a return visit from the TSPM to Hungary at the end of that year. Both delegations were intended to show solidarity between China and Hungary and to reestablish friendly people-to-people relationships between Christians from "brother socialist countries," so as to contribute to popular support for changes that had taken place in Hungary and in China in the previous months. The initiative for Chinese Christians visiting Hungary had been transmitted through the Hungarian Religious Affairs Bureau, a government body that had visited China that year. The Hungarian government wanted Chinese Christians to talk to their churches about patriotism, and the Chinese wanted to establish closer links with Eastern Europe.

The four-member TSPM delegation that went to Hungary was led by K. H. Ting.[35] The other members were Huang Peiyong, Shen Derong and Chen Jianxun, all members of the TSPM Standing Committee. They flew to

Budapest via Moscow at the end of November, leaving before the close of the Tenth TSPM Plenum, and spent five weeks visiting churches and meeting with various other groups. During this visit, Ting was granted an honorary doctorate from Debrecen Theological College, in recognition of his leadership at Nanjing Seminary. This honor was also an indication of Ting's growing importance in people-to-people diplomacy for China and of his stature as a Chinese Christian leader, as well as recognition for his theological leadership from a well-respected European institution.

The visit of Chinese Christians to Hungary was well publicized in both countries. On his return to China, Ting wrote a report on his impressions for *Tian Feng*. He had not published a similar report after his 1956 trip,[36] but from a political point of view, the Hungarian visit was much more significant. Ting was very clear about the purpose of this second visit to Europe.

> We went this time in order to represent Chinese Christians in expressing our greetings in Christ to Hungarian Christians, deepening the mutual fellowship and understanding between the Christians of our two countries, learning from all the precious witness and experience of Hungarian Christians in loving the church and loving their motherland, working for peace and walking the socialist road, and expressing the concern and support of we Chinese Christians for the many efforts of the Hungarian churches in overcoming all obstacles, and continuing in unity over the past year since the counter-revolutionary revolt. [37]

As their plane approached Budapest, Ting wrote that he was remembering "the dark days of the previous year when the imperialists instigated a counter-revolutionary revolt." At that time, he continued, the Chinese were asking themselves whether Hungary would "leave our large socialist family." Now that the uprising had been put down and socialism restored, the concerns that "troubled people's hearts" had been set to rest. Ting interpreted the restoration of socialism in light of the father's words in Luke's story of the Prodigal Son: "We . . . celebrate and rejoice, because this brother of yours was dead and has come to life; he was lost and has been found." This was theology in common cause with socialism, similar to the theology of many Christians who were working with their governments in Eastern Europe. Throughout their five-week stay, the TSPM delegation would join in the celebration of the return of Hungary to the socialist fold, as they shared their own views as patriotic Christians committed to socialism in China.

K. H. Ting had spoken of love as God's major attribute, but by the end of 1957, he had begun to speak of love as socialism's major attribute as well. This is another instance of theology in common cause with socialism. What Ting saw in China and in Hungary confirmed his belief in socialism as an organized expression of God's love, allowing him to voice his enthusiastic support for the socialist program.

Socialism is love, organized love, love which is spread to the masses. The politics of socialist countries is that of benevolent government. Even the dictatorship it exercises over its enemies arises from love. Human exploitation is the most immoral act. Socialism proclaims that exploitation is illegal and criminal, and this is the most lofty morality. For this reason, all the politics, culture and religious activities in capitalist countries are marked by their hypocrisy.[38]

These words reflect the spirit of the times in which they were written, and they indicate how much K. H. Ting had changed with the times. "Socialist love" could even be used to justify the Anti-Rightist movement. As one who has always carefully measured how he uses words, he would not have put things in the same way before the start of the Anti-Rightist movement. To do so in late 1957 was not in any way disingenuous but rather a forthright indication of his political and theological change. Socialist thought had replaced theology, or, at the very least, guided theology, and in the process, Ting had become much more closely identified with China's radically new socialist experiment, a position that he himself would later call ultra-leftism.

In 1961, K. H. Ting led another Chinese delegation to Eastern Europe, this time to Prague. This visit was in the aftermath of the Sino-Soviet split, and it came at a time when China was seeking to expand its influence in Eastern Europe and the Third World.[39] As an expression of people-to-people diplomacy, the TSPM had decided to send Ting, together with Li Shoubao and Zhao Fusan, to the All-Christian Peace Assembly. Josef Hromádka, the Czech theologian who had visited China a few years earlier, had urged Chinese Christians to come, and the Chinese government was assured by the Czech Bureau of Religious Affairs that the meeting would be conducted in accordance with accepted socialist principles.[40] The presence of the Chinese delegation in Prague came as a surprise to many in the West, and it again led some to hope that Chinese Christians would begin to play a more active role in the ecumenical movement, or at least attend future meetings in Eastern Europe.

In the opinion of a number of participants in the East and the West, K. H. Ting appeared to be under political pressure during this meeting. Hromádka said that this was a different K. H. than the man he had met in China in 1956.[41] Margaret Flory, an American Presbyterian who was close to Ting in the WSCF, remembered him as being the "hard-liner" in the Chinese delegation. He was uncharacteristically stiff and aloof all through the meeting. Zhao Fusan and Li Shoubao were seen as more accessible and open to private conversations.[42] This was another indication of how he was changing with the times, even in the eyes of his European and North American friends. The Chinese had decided that Ting would present the main speech at the assembly, probably because of his wide international recognition and his status as a bishop. The speech was an analysis of the Chinese view of the international situation, and, in published form, it is a sharp critique of the politics of the West.[43] In 1991, K. H. recalled the circumstances under which the speech was prepared and delivered:

> My speech was prepared in China. I worked on it too, but several of us worked on it together. And that speech was probably the most political speech I have ever delivered. At that time the idea was that I ought to deliver it in Chinese because being a Chinese I must respect my own language. So it was delivered in Chinese and translated by somebody into English. I think this person's English was worse than mine, but anyway a Chinese must talk Chinese. So, all these stiff things we did.[44]

This explains in part Ting's posture at the meeting, and why he was remembered by others as being so rigid and inaccessible.

But he also preached the sermon at the ecumenical service of worship at the Christian Peace Assembly, where he spoke in English. This sermon was more a reflection of Ting's own thinking on theology and politics. It too reflected the divisions between Christians in the East and the West, but it was more theological in orientation. Invoking the tradition of the great Czech patriot and religious leader Jan Hus, Ting called on Christians to take a stand in defense of justice. This sermon can still convey the moving and dynamic power of an experienced preacher committed to socialism in the cause of justice.

> Today, in this Bethlehem Chapel, we are praying where once Jan Hus prayed, and we are praising God where once Jan Hus praised Him. We cannot but recall how Hus, seeing with sorrow the corruption and degeneration of the church under the influence of foreign political power and the control of reactionary domestic autocrats, bravely unfurled the banner of the church's holiness. It was not an empty, passive holiness which sought to stand for nothing in the world of realities, but a holiness with content—a true concern for the suffering and the aspirations of the people, a search for their welfare and resolute fight against sin and evil.[45]

Ting had taken his own stand, as a Chinese Christian patriot who supported socialism. Now he had become a Christian ambassador to the East, not the West, and he modified both the tone and the content of his writing accordingly. In the process, he emerged as an increasingly important international spokesman for New China and its political and social program.

POLITICS IN COMMAND

The Anti-Rightist movement had inaugurated a new period in China's national life, one in which intraparty political struggles affected all areas of culture and society. There were periods of respite, as the concern for political relaxation (*fang*) and economic development were reasserted by different factions in the Central Committee of the CPC. But in general terms, there was a growing politicization and tightening of control (*shou*) of all areas of life. The Great Leap Forward, the People's Communes, the socialist-education movement and the Sino-Soviet split generated a sense of enthusiasm and anxiety among the people, and each movement contributed to the intensified political atmosphere.[46] The years after the Anti-Rightist movement, despite the periodic loosening up and relaxation, saw an inexorable leftward drift in the values of Chinese political culture. To use the slogan that was popularized during that era, the late 1950s and 1960s was a time of "politics in command."

The politics of the early and mid-1950s, even in the upheavals of the mass movements of the day, had been a politics of participation, associated with the united-front line. The CPC welcomed nonparty participation in the united front, and this showed some measure of tolerance and acceptance of different points of view. The politics of struggle were of an entirely different order. They were anti–united front and characterized by an ultra-leftist political line that rose to dominance at the start of the Anti-Rightist movement. Both lines were always reflected in the CPC leadership and were embraced by different party factions. Although they were never separate, a distinction needs to be made between them, for this will help clarify the shift in Chinese political life that took place after 1957, changes that were reflected in K. H. Ting's own political outlook.

The united-front-oriented politics of participation began with the founding of the People's Republic of China, when it was expected that people from all walks of life would play an active role in Chinese political life. This was what the united front was all about, and it was the reason why 1949 could be regarded as a time of "Liberation" by many Chinese. Political participation did not mean that politics was in command, but that all sectors of society would be represented in "the people's democratic dictatorship" which was envisioned at the founding of the People's Republic of China. This vision inspired K. H. Ting and his generation of intellectuals, and they saw the vision embodied in the person of Zhou Enlai.

In the years after the Anti-Rightist movement the united front was set aside in favor of a more intense political orientation. This was reflected in changes at Nanjing Union Theological Seminary. The seminary continued to function in the late 1950s, but it was no longer possible to have a full program of study after 1957. In 1959, the seminary, under government pressure, closed its doors, as did all other seminaries and religious training centers in China. This was the time of the Great Leap Forward and the creation of the People's Communes. Pastors and theological students all over China participated in the Great Leap in the countryside and in urban areas. Many students and faculty members from Nanjing Seminary were sent to Xinjiang, the remote region in the far west that became the home for intellectuals who were criticized in the 1950s. They were told that their education and skills could be of use in developing China's frontier areas. With practically no hope of ever returning to their homes in eastern China, seminary students and teachers settled down in Xinjiang. Most maintained their faith and helped found Christian churches, which met secretly for the next twenty or thirty years. Some Christians left the church, joined the Communist Party and became government officials.

In 1961, Yanjing Theological Seminary in Beijing became part of NUTS, and a large number of faculty and staff moved to Nanjing. Nanjing Union Theological Seminary was now the only Protestant training center in China.[47] That May, a new class of eighty-six students from all over the country was enrolled. K. H. Ting reported that politics was the primary consideration for recruiting and educating this new class of students.

> Nanjing Union Seminary stresses the political studies of students and staff, especially their political standpoint and the transformation of their political thinking. More than one hundred years of history has taught China that we must stress politics and intensify our political study . . . Our political standpoint means love for the motherland, standing with the people, opposition to imperialism, resolutely accepting the leadership of the Communist Party and going the socialist road.[48]

Nowhere in this report does he say that the seminary had been closed for two years (1959-1961), and no reason is given as to why it should now be reopened. According to K. H. Ting, the initiative to reopen the seminary was taken by Zhang Zhiyi, deputy director of the United Front Work Department in Beijing. Zhang, who was then a close friend of K. H. Ting, believed that China would still need religious researchers, and that Nanjing was the best place, and now the only place, to train them.[49] Most of the students in this new class remained at the seminary for less than a year, however, and then returned to their homes.

In 1962, another new class of twenty students entered the seminary in a program specifically designed to train researchers who would staff a new center for religious research. This was also the idea of Zhang Zhiyi. From this time forward, there was little to distinguish the seminary from any other educational institution in China, except for its area of study.[50] The faculty for the new program in the social-scientific study of religion included seminary staff as well as government officials. K. H. Ting offered a course in logic, as he had done before in the seminary, but there were no longer courses in theology.[51] Courses were also offered in the history of Christianity in China, religious studies and politics.

Most of those who were enrolled were church workers who had been working in local congregations and Three-Self organizations. They were seen as among those most able to take up the task of religious research. In the

1980s and the decades that followed, many people from this class became active in rebuilding the church, including Deng Fucun, from Hangzhou; Ji Jianhong, from Nanjing; Shen Cheng'en, from Shanghai; and Bao Jiayuan, from Suzhou. As it turned out, this was the last class to enter Nanjing Seminary before the start of the Cultural Revolution. In June 1966, the students were all sent home and reassigned to other work.

In the years leading up to the Cultural Revolution, K. H. Ting continued his political involvement at the provincial and national levels. He was reappointed to every Jiangsu People's Political Consultative Conference (JPPCC) up until the Cultural Revolution, and at the Second JPPCC in 1959, he was named to its standing committee. In 1959, Ting was given his first national appointment, when he was named a delegate from Jiangsu to the Third Chinese People's Political Consultative Conference (CPPCC) in Beijing. This meeting was chaired by Zhou Enlai, Ting's friend, mentor and patron, and Zhou probably had a great deal to do with his appointment. Ting now had a position of considerable importance in China's national life.

By 1959, the corner toward ultra-leftism and "politics in command" had already been turned. The CPPCC no longer served the same function as it had in the early and mid-1950s, or at least there was no longer very much space for alternative viewpoints. K. H. Ting was a patriot, a loyal supporter of the government and the CPC. Like other intellectuals from his generation, he had turned with the tide, and he believed that the new leftist line was correct for China. The church seemed to be less and less a factor in his thinking. There is no public record of the speeches he made at political consultative conferences in the late 1950s and 1960s, but we can assume that he endorsed the actions and conclusions of these meetings along with everyone else.

Today, the whole period after 1957 is seen as one in which ultra-leftism turned China away from social construction and economic development and set the country on a disastrous path that moved inexorably toward the Cultural Revolution. The Great Leap Forward and the organization of People's Communes raised wildly exaggerated hopes about rural production, but their overall effect on agriculture was catastrophic. This was a time of famine in many parts of China, but the reality was kept hidden from the world.[52] Instead, everywhere there were reports of the strides being made toward a utopian Communist society.

K. H. Ting worked in the fields during the movement to establish People's Communes, and he took part in the effort to generate production using small backyard furnaces during the Great Leap Forward. He visited northern Jiangsu Province with a JPPCC delegation during this period, and he joined in the praises of those who were celebrating a new era of wealth and power. He wrote enthusiastically about the communes he visited and reported an upsurge in agricultural production, exemplified by the size of the harvest, the enormity of the cotton plants and peaches that weighed almost two pounds![53] Such exaggerations were common reflections of a revolutionary spirit and a vision that was out of touch with reality. Ting's report shows that he was out of touch with what was happening in the rural areas, and on his trip to northern Jiangsu, he and other JPPCC delegates were shown only what the government wanted them to see.

In the late 1950s, political pressures on the churches increased dramatically. It was during the Great Leap in 1958 that the unification of worship services began.[54] The political rationale was that there was no longer the need for so many churches, and the unification of worship would be more efficient and allow more time for production. In towns and cities all over the country, churches were brought together and consolidated by administrative fiat, regardless of differences in denomination and church tradition. Thousands of churches, most of which had a small or declining membership, were closed and turned over to the government for other uses. Denominational structures ceased to exist. Protestant Christians were now worshiping together, but this was far from an experiment in ecumenical unity. There is little documentation about either the end of the denominations or the unification of worship.[55] Most information we have from this period is from reports from occasional foreign visitors, articles in *Tian Feng* and the recollections of Chinese Christians decades later.

The unification of worship was orchestrated by the government through the Religious Affairs Bureau, and with the concurrence of the TSPM leadership in Shanghai. K. H. Ting has said that the decision to do away with denominationalism went beyond the platform of Three-Self. It was done too hurriedly and roughly, without any kind of negotiation or planning.[56] He himself was not involved in the decision or its implementation, but despite his own reservations about the process, he did support the idea for the unification of worship.

> At the time I supported it. I supported it because most churches were not well attended at all. In Nanjing for instance there were over thirty Protestant churches and some of them would only have ten people worshipping on a Sunday, so I supported the idea of joint worship. However, the National Three-Self Committee never held a meeting to discuss whether we wanted to do that or not. It all started in various parts of China.
>
> Today when we look at the matter consciously we realize that this whole political atmosphere had much to do with it. Within that atmosphere the idea was that religion was of not much use and religion was being discarded by the masses of religious people. There would be very few who would believe in religion. Communism would be in China within ten years. The People's Commune was the bridge, a golden bridge to Communism. There was the general conception that history was moving very fast in China. One day was equivalent to twenty

years. That was one of the slogans. And in ten or fifteen years' time China was going to reach the level of Great Britain, all that sort of thing. And unity . . . So there was the pressure of public opinion to make Christians want to get the churches united. And in addition to that there is the teaching in the Bible and prayer of Jesus Christ of how the disciplines should be one, and so on, so all these worked together in the mind of the Christian, consciously and unconsciously. So it was rather smooth that churches began to worship together and many church buildings were put to other uses.[57]

Despite the increasing pressures, Christians continued to meet publicly for worship in the churches that were still open. This was the time in which home meetings (*jiating juhui*) began to grow in China, and they continued to meet all through the Cultural Revolution in many places. The Christian home meetings were to become a significant force in the renewal of the churches after the end of the Cultural Revolution. In October 1963, a former German missionary visited China and described vital worshiping communities and signs of church growth.[58] She was not allowed to see very much, however, and her report is based more on impressions than on facts.

Even as the political atmosphere became more restrictive, K. H. Ting and other TSPM leaders maintained contact with Christian friends around China, although their knowledge of what was going on locally, particularly in churches in rural areas, was quite limited. The Sheng Gong Hui no longer existed, and so he made no more pastoral visits to churches in Zhejiang. He was still a bishop, but there was no longer a diocesan structure. In any case, the focus of Ting's interests and activities was by this time largely political.

Ting continued to interpret what was happening in China to friends overseas, at least to those whom he thought would be willing to listen. These included friends in Canada and from his years in the WSCF, and some former missionaries who visited the Tings in Nanjing. In the fall of 1959, he accompanied Hewlett Johnson and his family on their fourth visit to China. Ting had met the Johnsons on their earlier visits, and he visited with them on his trip to England in 1956. Johnson, the "Red Dean" of Canterbury Cathedral, continued to be an enthusiastic supporter of the People's Republic, and through his books and articles, he brought the message of a romantic and revolutionary China to the West. K. H. Ting was his guide and companion in 1959, and Johnson wrote that he was not only a gracious host, but that he enabled the Johnsons to understand "the meaning of the new socialist order."[59] Even in later years, Ting valued his friendship with the Johnsons and the support they gave to China during these difficult years. K. H. has always been loyal to his friends, and he believed that Johnson and others like him kept channels of communication open between Christians in China and the West.[60] Both K. H. and Siu-may also maintained a regular correspondence with friends from their years abroad right up until the start of the Cultural Revolution.

In the early and mid-1960s, direct contact with Christians overseas became less and less possible, as all communication between China and the outside world was restricted. The All-Christian Peace Assembly in Prague turned out to be the last international visit of the TSPM prior to the Cultural Revolution.[61] Increasing isolation was not the result of Chinese political considerations alone. The Cold War and the United States policy of containment discouraged communication and exchanges of any kind with the People's Republic of China. This further inhibited ecumenical contact with Chinese Christians, especially for Americans. Many of the statements and reports coming from churches in Europe and North America during this time reflected the other side of the rhetoric of the Cold War.

On the domestic scene, the TSPM continued to serve as a channel for communication between the government and Chinese Christians. The communication was now largely one-way, however, from the government to the churches, and directed through the TSPM national offices in Shanghai. The government believed it was still important to mobilize Christians in their own mass organization, and this was behind the call for the Second National Christian Conference, which met in Shanghai for two months in 1960-1961.[62] This was both a very political meeting and an extraordinarily lengthy one. Much of the time was spent in socialist and patriotic education conducted by the government for the more than three hundred delegates. Reports and speeches focused on the political consciousness of Christians, the People's Communes, the unification of worship and the continuing dangers of imperialism. The TSPM approved a new constitution in which the article on mutual respect was dropped and a lengthy new article strengthening the patriotic and political functions of the TSPM was added.[63] There is very little emphasis in conference reports about theology or the church as a worshiping community.

At this conference, K. H. Ting was named a member of the standing committee and vice-chairperson of the TSPM, appointments that followed from his increasing importance in national political life. Although he now had much greater standing in the TSPM, his influence within the organization was still nominal. He was not part of the inner circle in Shanghai that gathered around Li Chuwen and others. They had all worked closely together since the early 1950s and were much more attuned to the ultra-leftist politics of struggle. Li was in charge of the day-to-day affairs of the TSPM. Y. T. Wu served as TSPM chairperson, but it was the office staff that handled organizational details. Ting was living in Nanjing, and although he visited Shanghai regularly, he had little to do with the running of the organization or the determination of its policies. This was also true of most other vice-chairpersons of the TSPM in the 1950s and 1960s,

The Second National Christian Conference was termed a "celestial meeting" (*shenxian hui*) by the United Front Work Department (UFWD), which suggests that it was to be a time for relaxation and reflection on developments in the country and the church. Participants were encouraged to speak their minds and have no worries that what they said might be used against them. The object of the gathering was to begin with people where they were, so that they might somehow come to a clearer sense of political purpose. K. H. Ting has explained what this was supposed to mean.

> The idea was that after a period of tension there should be a period of relaxation. I think that is a teaching of Chairman Mao, "to alternate tension with relaxation" (*yi zhang yi chi*). It is not good for people to remain in tension all the time, so the idea was to relax things and relax relationships. But unfortunately after having been in tension for so many years it was not easy to really get people into relaxation. People (were) afraid. This "celestial meeting" was a means by which the United Front Work Department would like to help people get relaxed. There was another expression, the "three don'ts": don't seize on other's faults; don't put labels on people; and don't use the big stick. It means, something you have said before will not be used to criticize you, to work against you. Three-Self was also meant to help relaxation. So this meeting in Shanghai was a "celestial meeting." It was especially arranged to help [relaxation] by meeting at the International Hotel, you know that very big building near the race course, near the present People's Park. It is a very luxurious hotel. We all met in the hotel and the food was very good. Although those were difficult years in China, we were given pretty good food. All of this was meant to make people relax. However, these factors didn't achieve much, because the substance of the meeting was still politics.[64]

Ting's own speech at the meeting was also very political. He delivered a wide-ranging analysis of the ways in which international Christianity was being manipulated by capitalism and imperialism to attack China and oppress the Third World. His tone was much sharper than in earlier speeches, as we can see from the following extract:

> We Chinese Christians are patriotic and anti-imperialist, we accept the leadership of the Communist Party and participate in socialist construction. We have cut off relationships with imperialist mission boards and "missionaries," and we expose and denounce them. We should be proud of this. No matter how imperialism opposes us, its actions will be noticed by millions upon millions of people overseas, and they will admire and welcome us . . . Our efforts have borne some fruit because in the present international situation, the East Wind is prevailing over the West Wind, and because China's international position has been raised, we Chinese Christians now have the right to speak out. Therefore, we have no reason to claim credit for ourselves or rest on our

laurels, but in all humility we must study harder, and unite with the Chinese people to press forward in the anti-imperialist struggle.[65]

Most of the speeches and articles by Chinese Christians published in the early 1960s were similar in substance and tone. During these years, there were fewer and fewer reports about the work of the TSPM. *Tian Feng* was published only irregularly. The Second National Christian Conference was the last major meeting of the TSPM before the start of the Cultural Revolution, but the organization continued to function at a reduced level until that time.

There is even less reliable information on the life of the church in China in the years leading up to the Cultural Revolution. Organized worship was in decline, although the few churches that there were remained open. The home-worship gatherings were growing, but there was very little information about them.

Government religious policy was abruptly changed in 1964. Li Weihan, head of the United Front Work Department (UFWD), was purged and his department was accused of "capitulationism" for its "conciliatory" treatment of religions and national minorities.[66] Xiao Xianfa (1914-1981), head of the RAB, took the lead in articulating a new anti–united-front religious policy and attacked Li Weihan and the UFWD. Xiao charged that class struggle was still necessary against religious groups, for there should be a radical reform of faith and belief. Another socialist-education movement was started for religious leaders in 1964, whose purpose was to encourage believers to be "more revolutionary, more enlightened and less religious."[67] Xiao Xianfa would himself be removed from his position two years later at the start of the Cultural Revolution, and the RAB, which he headed, would be dissolved. Politics was in command, and the struggles became even more intense.

Ting was among the religious leaders required to take part in the socialist-education movement in Nanjing in 1964. At the time, it seemed to many observers inside and outside of China that Christianity would somehow continue, but on a vastly reduced institutional scale. No one, and certainly not K. H. Ting, was prepared for what was to happen next.

6

The Cultural Revolution Era, 1966-1976

So many deeds cry out to be done,
And always urgently;
The world rolls on,
Time presses.
Ten thousand years are too long,
Seize the day, seize the hour!
The Four Seas are rising, clouds and waters are raging,
The Five Continents are rocking, wind and thunder roaring.
Away with all pests!
Our force is irresistible.

Mao Zedong[1]

tomorrow, no
tomorrow is not the other side of night
whoever has hopes is a criminal
let the story that took place at night
end in the night.

Bei Dao[2]

The origins of the Cultural Revolution may be traced to the struggles in the Communist Party discussed in the last chapter.[3] The debates of the mid-1960s were similar to those of the Anti-Rightist movement, but they became much more violent and extreme, as the struggle for power and control became more prominent. For this reason, the Cultural Revolution was unlike anything that had happened before. China was plunged into a period of self-consuming anarchy and near civil war that lasted for ten years.

By the mid-1960s, political lines were drawn between veteran party leaders in Beijing and anti-establishment radicals who made Shanghai their power base. The former upheld the status quo and a politics of gradual change; they were against any radical critique of culture or society. Veteran party leaders were associated with Liu Shaoqi, Zhou Enlai and Deng Xiaoping. The radicals wanted a thoroughgoing critique of traditional and bourgeois culture in order to promote a purified revolutionary society. Their cause was championed by Lin Biao, and later by Jiang Qing, Mao's wife. They have now been totally discredited in China, but the tremendous influence and appeal they exerted at the time should not be dismissed too easily. The radicals were unrelentingly critical of a party and a government that had become bureaucratized, complacent and corrupt, problems that had plagued China for centuries. Behind the power politics and intraparty struggles of the Cultural Revolution era, there were real issues about corruption and China's road to development.

Mao was the undisputed leader to whom both factions deferred. His revolutionary idealism was inspiring to many, and Mao could call upon tens of millions of loyal followers to "make revolution." He was at the same time a ruthless dictator, quixotic and unpredictable in his exercise of power and authority. Time and again, he played the different party factions off against one another. Mao's erratic inconsistency grew with advancing age, and in his last years he became suspicious of almost all those around him.[4] In the spring of 1966, he seemed to be supporting Lin Biao and party radicals who had already begun to take control of the reins of government. They soon controlled the Politburo, and in May they began the process of "criticizing and exposing" the cultural establishment, a criticism that was soon extended to the whole party and government apparatus.

The first act of the Cultural Revolution was played out in Beijing, with Mao directing from offstage.[5] In late May 1966, Beijing University students put up a poster denouncing the university leadership. On June 2, the *Renmin ribao* (*People's Daily*) expressed its editorial support for the dissidents. Liu Shaoqi, Zhou Enlai and Deng Xiaoping pondered a response, but Mao said nothing. Meanwhile, the Politburo organized a "Cultural Revolution Group," which on 8 August issued a sixteen-point "Decision Concerning the Great Proletarian Cultural Revolution." The revolution now began in earnest.

On 18 August, hundreds of thousands of students rallied in Beijing in favor of the new movement, and they had the explicit support of Chairman Mao. They formed themselves into "Red Guards," and by the end of the summer, similar student groups were active all over the country. Over the next months, the Cultural Revolution grew into a social upheaval that engulfed the nation. University students put up big character posters that criticized school officials and existing educational policies. The "Red Guards" supported Chairman Mao in a struggle against high-ranking party leaders "taking the capitalist road." Mao's target was Liu Shaoqi, and the students believed what Mao said. The spectacle of millions of young "Red Guards" in Beijing, many of whom were only junior-middle-high-school students in their early teens, chanting slogans, marching in unison and whipped into a revolutionary frenzy was either exhilarating or frightening, depending on who was watching. They traveled free of charge on trains all over the country, destroying the "Four Olds" (old ideas, culture, customs, and habits), attacking representatives of the cultural and political establishment, and "making revolution." The "Red Guards" were inspired by Mao's statement that "to rebel is justified," and they acted on their convictions.

The struggles became more violent, and the situation more confused and chaotic over the next year.[6] By 1967, neither the party nor the government seemed to be in control. Despite attempts to put a stop to the violent excesses, the disorder increased. Rival groups of "Red Guards," sporting their own faction's Mao badges and clutching *Little Red Books*, began fighting one another. Armed struggle broke out in many cities. People from all walks of life were drawn into the chaos, both on the giving and the receiving end. A great many people were killed in mob violence, the settling of old scores and group-inspired criminal activity. There was extensive and indiscriminate property damage as well, often directed against buildings and cultural artifacts representing the "four olds." The People's Liberation Army was finally called in to restore order, and by the summer of 1968, there was relative peace and stability. "Educated youth" (*zhishi qingnian*) from urban areas were sent to the countryside for "reeducation" by the peasants, and their departure from the cities contributed to the restoration of order in urban areas.

The "activist phase" of the Cultural Revolution ended a year later. But the struggle sessions, the imprisonments, the discovery of new "plots" and "conspiracies" continued for six more years. Enthusiasm gave way to disillusionment in the early 1970s as an increasing number of students and intellectuals developed a greater awareness of the destructive chaos. In 1971, Lin Biao was killed in a plane crash after the failure of an alleged coup attempt and assassination plot against Mao. Early the next year, Richard Nixon made his historic visit to China. Zhou Enlai assumed more of a role in running the government, but despite increasing attention to restoring order and a tentative opening to the outside world, the struggles and campaigns continued. In 1976, Zhou Enlai, Zhu De, and Mao Zedong all died, and China was rocked by the Tangshan earthquake. In the ensuing struggle to restore order, the radical "Gang of Four" was arrested, which marked the formal end of the Cultural Revolution era. [7]

China was deeply wounded by the turbulent decade, and the people were relieved when the Cultural Revolution was finally over. The hopefulness of Mao's poem at the head of this chapter needs to be read alongside poems expressing the negation of hope that came years later. The stanza from the "misty poet" Bei Dao (Zhao Zhenkai) is an example of this.

The turmoil of the Cultural Revolution affected tens of millions of people, physically and psychologically. The lives of many men and women were irrevocably damaged, and the spiritual and emotional costs were extraordinarily high, even by twentieth-century standards of political violence. The Cultural Revolution changed the way people felt about one another, and about where China was headed. Although the period as a whole cannot be explained by any single all-embracing theory, why it became so violent may be easier to understand. According to Lynn White, the violence was not just random, but was related to particular policy decisions that were made in the 1950s and 1960s.

> Permanent flaws of patriarchy in Chinese culture or dubious idealism in Communist ideology may indeed be related to some of the underlying causes of the Cultural Revolution; but specific coercive measures to promote group labels, personal control, and frightening campaigns channeled these cultural or ideological tendencies powerfully, so as to instigate the violent result, rather than a more peaceful one.[8]

In other words, the violence of the times was at least in part a result of systemic flaws in the Communist system. This violence is perhaps the greatest legacy of the Cultural Revolution era. Yet the contradictory movements within the Cultural Revolution working for and against one another make it difficult to understand the decade as a whole. The twists and turns of the individual campaigns are so complex; the analyses by scholars and persons involved are so different; the course it took in different provinces is so various; and the access to the evidentiary record (i.e., Chinese documents that are open to the scholar) is so limited that any interpretation needs to be carefully qualified. The study of the Cultural Revolution era continues to be politically off-limits in China, where the role of Mao has a direct bearing on the present. It may be decades before any serious and open debate will be tolerated.

Despite these difficulties, reflection on the lives and experiences of women and men who were caught up in the Cultural Revolution can help to illuminate its wider meaning. Information about K. H. Ting's life during the Cultural Revolution is extremely limited, and he himself has been reticent to talk about the period. There are many questions about his experiences during the Cultural Revolution that cannot now be answered. Like many of his generation, Ting had contradictory reactions in the early years of the Cultural Revolution. His revolutionary idealism was characteristic of many who wanted a more equitable society. He did not like what he saw happening to the church and the seminary, but at the same time, he welcomed new initiatives for social transformation. He was close to veteran government and party leaders, but he was drawn to the revolutionary movement that the radicals seemed to represent. He was unwavering in his support for Mao Zedong, but he was also deeply attached to his friends and colleagues, many of whom became casualties of the movement that Mao had initiated.

THE CULTURAL REVOLUTION IN NANJING

Nanjing was important right at the beginning of the Cultural Revolution. On 12 June 1966, "revolutionary" students, teachers and staff members rallied at Nanjing University to denounce Kuang Yaming, university president and first party secretary.[9] Kuang, a veteran revolutionary, was well known for his liberal views, his interest in Confucian philosophy and his support for intellectuals; but he was unpopular with some students and teachers because of his dictatorial style. Kuang was also a close friend and supporter of K. H. Ting, and of Siu-may Kuo, who taught in the Department of Foreign Languages and Literatures at his university. On June 12, he became the first university president deposed during the Cultural Revolution, and his removal marks the beginning of the movement in Nanjing. His fall also signaled the start of the attacks against senior party leaders and intellectuals that were to come.

Religion was one of the early targets of the "Red Guards," because it typified the problem of the "four olds." The "Red Guards" proclaimed that they were atheists who believed only in Mao Zedong, and saw traditional beliefs as out of date now that a new socialist age was on the horizon.[10] Buddhist and Daoist monasteries and temples, Catholic and Protestant churches, and Islamic mosques were desecrated all over China. Scriptures and relics were burned, and many religious leaders were paraded through the streets, put in makeshift prisons (*niu peng*) or sent to the countryside. Persecution of religious believers during the Cultural Revolution era was as extensive as it was severe: celibate clergy were forced to marry; Muslims were forced to eat pork; Christians were compelled to renounce their faith; stubborn clerics were beaten or even executed; residences of religious leaders were ransacked; recalcitrant believers were imprisoned, exiled or put to death. Some temples and religious communities in more remote regions were unaffected by the Cultural Revolution, but these were the exception. In urban and most parts of rural China, the public expression of religious belief came to an end.

In Nanjing, the attacks against religion began in the early summer of 1966. By that time, seminary students had been sent home, and the seminary compound was closed. Churches in the city and the surrounding counties were also closed, as were the city's Buddhist temples and its single mosque. Some Christians continued to meet for worship, prayer and Bible study in their homes in Nanjing, as they did in other cities in China, but they did so quietly so as not to attract attention. They had practically no contact with Christians overseas from June 1966 onward.

The Tings' home on Mo Chou Road was ransacked ten or eleven times by marauding "Red Guards," beginning in the summer of 1966. One particularly violent group destroyed almost everything of value in the house. All of K. H. Ting's books were carried away or destroyed, and the clerical vestments that had belonged to his grandfather and that had been given to him by his mother were also lost.

The Nanjing Seminary compound was taken over by "Red Guards" in the early months of the Cultural Revolution. They began burning books from the library, but the faculty reasoned with them, saying that some library books were written by Marx, Lenin and Mao, and others were valuable cultural relics. The seminary was then given twenty-four hours to select the books that could be saved, and the rest were burned in front of the main teaching building. The compound was subsequently occupied by "Red Guards," mostly university and middle-school students from Nanjing. The buildings later became the headquarters of another armed "Red Guard" faction, and faculty members remember that they placed a machine gun in one classroom overlooking the main entrance.

There have been no reports that Nanjing Seminary faculty were paraded through the streets in dunce caps, as happened to clergy in other places. But faculty members were sent away for reeducation. Faculty and staff were divided into two groups: one was sent to work in the fields on the outskirts of Nanjing, in Qing Liangshan; the other remained in Nanjing.[11] Among the senior leaders, Chen Zemin and Cheng Zhiyi were in the first group; K. H. Ting, Han Wenzao, and Sun Hanshu were among those in the second group. According to Ting, the two groups were divided arbitrarily by people who did not know the faculty. The RAB in Nanjing, headed by Luo Xunru, reportedly told the "Red Guards" that there was no "power holding group" (*dangquanpai*) in the seminary, for power was in the hands of the RAB itself.[12] This inadvertently drew attention away from the seminary and toward the RAB, which soon found itself under attack by the "Red Guards." The RAB in Beijing was closed by the end of the summer, and provincial RABs, such as the one in Jiangsu, suffered a similar fate.

"Big character posters" (*dazi bao*) were put up in many cities denouncing religions as feudal or bourgeois ideologies and singling out particular individuals for attack. The TSPM was criticized as being "a conspiracy between Liu Shaoqi and Y. T. Wu" designed to present a sympathetic picture of Christianity, and all TSPM leaders were implicated by this attack. One observer remembers seeing K. H. Ting denounced on posters in Shanghai as a petit-bourgeois intellectual who lived in a grand style and whose home boasted four bicycles. This poster may very well have come from ultra-leftists within the TSPM, according to the observer. Christian intellectuals and church leaders in some cities were beaten and put into makeshift prisons in the early months of the Cultural Revolution, but this did not happen to church leaders in Nanjing.

In these early months of the Cultural Revolution, Premier Zhou Enlai reportedly began to take action to protect certain institutions and individuals from attacks by the "Red Guards." It is believed by many older intellectuals that Zhou helped to moderate the more extreme effects of the Cultural Revolution. He has been portrayed in more recent scholarship as a dutiful servant of Mao and an opportunist who willingly followed the ultra-leftist line during the Cultural Revolution, but even so he is said to have protected a large number of individuals after first checking with Mao.[13] In the 1980s, visitors were routinely told that on Zhou Enlai's orders, many cultural treasures were protected and many prominent people were saved from imprisonment or humiliation.[14] For example, the "Buddhist Sutra Woodblock Printing Bureau" (*Jinling kejing chu*) in Nanjing was said to been have protected under Zhou's instructions, and its centuries-old treasures preserved. I was told in the early 1980s by a representative of the printing bureau that sometime in 1967 or 1968, the Buddhist relics and woodblocks were moved to the basement of Nanjing Seminary for safekeeping.

In late August 1966, it is believed that Zhou sent a message to the still-functioning provincial party headquarters in Nanjing, instructing them to guarantee the safety of three non-party people. This story is beyond verification at present, but it fits with facts that are known, and it is consistent with subsequent events.[15] Zhou Enlai was issuing orders to protect a great many intellectuals and veteran cadres in China at that time. The three he reportedly identified in Jiangsu were: Liu Guojun, a wealthy capitalist and member of the national bourgeoisie; Wu Yifang (1893-1985), a prominent Protestant intellectual and president of Jinling Women's College; and K. H. Ting. Liu and Wu were many years older than Ting, who was fifty-one at the time. All three were non-party representatives on the JPPCC. We argued in chap. 4 that Zhou Enlai became a patron and protector of Ting after his return to China in 1951. Stories about their relationship have been widely repeated, and Zhou's protection of Ting during the Cultural Revolution would help to explain his situation at that time. Zhou may have believed that Ting needed to be protected because he would one day be needed again as a church or government leader.

K. H. Ting has said that he was moved under armed guard to the northern Jiangsu city of Lianyungang on the orders of the provincial CPC. This must have been in late August or early September 1966. He stayed in Lianyungang for about three months in a provincial government guesthouse that was practically deserted. He continued to be in touch with Siu-may during these months, but he remained in the guesthouse under guard, free to move about the grounds, but kept away from the chaos in the streets.[16] Being away from Nanjing during these early months of the Cultural Revolution spared Ting from the humiliations to which he would have been subjected had he stayed home.

Soon after he left Nanjing, "Red Guards" came into the Ting home for one last time, again preparing to ransack the house and looking for evidence of the "four olds." They then instructed Siu-may that the family would have to leave the house in four hours, and they began throwing things out of the house from the second-story window.[17] Siu-may gathered what she could carry, and, with the two boys and the help of her maid, she moved first to a little house in back of the church down the road, and a short time later to a small house in the compound at Number 5 Da Jian Yin Xiang near the seminary.[18] Following this hurried exit, the family would not move back to their home until late 1972.

Along with other senior professors at Nanjing University who had been trained before 1949, Siu-may Kuo came under criticism from the "Red Guards." She never spoke of being physically abused, but at one point, together with other university teachers, she was assigned to wash the university swimming pool with a small brush. In order to accomplish this task, she stood in water above her ankles for hours on end. She wore rubber boots at first, but then the "Red Guards" decided that the boots should come off. It was at this time that her arthritis became more severe, and by the late 1960s, she needed assistance in getting about.[19] By the end of the Cultural Revolution era, she was confined to a wheelchair.

K. H. returned to Nanjing sometime in November 1966 after the initial rampaging was over. The family was together again. Despite all that had happened, Ting said many years later that at the time, he was still convinced that the Cultural Revolution was both necessary and correct. There may have been some mistake in his case, he reasoned, but, after all, he too needed to be changed and reformed. The Cultural Revolution was a campaign that had been started by Chairman Mao to carry the revolution to a higher level and to oppose revisionism.[20] Ting remained devoted to Mao's leadership, and he was inspired by the promise of a better society. He believed that China needed to avoid the type of revisionism represented by the Soviet Union and remain vigilant against the possibility of attacks and incursions from the United States and the West.

K. H. and Siu-may read all the articles, essays and books that they could find about what was going on, but there was very little to read. The ransacking of their home, the charges that had been made against them, and the personal abuse had done little to alter their views about the Cultural Revolution. This may seem almost unimaginable in retrospect, but many others in similar situations continued to believe as they did. It is not possible, from the vantage of the present, to fully understand all that was involved. Only gradually, and with the passage of time, did his skepticism grow. Ting recalls,

> I studied the *Little Red Book* very carefully, line by line. I don't know when my skepticism began, but it began gradually. More and more facts began to tell me that this is not the right sort of thing that China needs. Some of the things were very foolish. Siu-may and I had very few books to read in those days so the two of us would lie in bed, side by side, and then recite Chairman Mao's poems. So we could recite every one of his poems, although I can't do that anymore, today. So there was personality worship, definitely. But I became more and more sober because one movement after another came into being and some of my best friends became enemies of the people. I could not believe that.[21]

The madness of the Cultural Revolution and its vision of "justice" was unique, but not unprecedented in modern history. In the final paragraph of

Moral Man and Immoral Society, Reinhold Niebuhr writes about what is required for human beings to struggle for a more just and equitable society.

> In the task . . . the most effective agents will be men who have substituted some new illusions for the abandoned ones. The most important of these illusions is that the collective life of mankind can achieve perfect justice. It is a very valuable illusion for the moment; for justice cannot be approximated if the hope of its perfect realization does not generate a sublime madness in the soul. Nothing but such madness will do battle with malignant power and "spiritual wickedness in high places." The illusion is dangerous because it encourages terrible fanaticisms. It must therefore be brought under control by reason. One can only hope that reason will not destroy it before its work is done.[22]

Ting would probably not agree that Niebuhr's judgment applied to China during the Cultural Revolution, but the illusion of a perfect realization of justice and of an egalitarian society generated a certain madness in the souls of tens of millions of people. They held to an illusion that was inspiring and redeeming for many, at least at first. But it encouraged terrible fanaticisms that were not brought under the control of reason for many more years.

THE REVOLUTION CONTINUES

The violence in the streets became more intense in the early months of 1967. By the middle of the year, the "Red Guards" had lost interest in their old enemies, and different factions started fighting one another, often encouraged and supported by rival party leaders and government cadres. Facing increasing chaos and anarchy all over the country, most national leaders, and even Mao himself, came to see that something needed to be done to bring things under control. Mao's decision was to call in the People's Liberation Army (PLA), under the leadership of Lin Biao, to restore order and establish a "Proletarian dictatorship." Local government and party organizations were in disarray, and so revolutionary committees were set up to replace them, with membership drawn from the PLA, trustworthy leftist party cadres and representatives of "the masses."

In this way, a measure of stability was restored in Nanjing and other cities. Most people were tired of the violence and factional clashes. The PLA responded by shifting their emphasis from attacking "capitalist roaders" and "bourgeois intellectuals" to the intensive study of Mao Zedong's thought. The *Little Red Book* of Mao's sayings became popular, and everyone had a copy. In the fall of 1968, May 7th Cadre schools began to be set up for cadres and intellectuals, named after a directive Mao had issued on that date two years earlier. These schools, often far from one's home, combined hard manual labor, criticism and self-criticism and the line-by-line study of Mao's works and other essays.

During the previous three years, university and middle-school students spent much of their time traveling around China. They were ostensibly "making revolution" but often doing no more than seeing the sights as they traveled through the country. The PLA and the revolutionary committees reined in the "Red Guards," but something needed to be done with the students. In December 1968, Mao called on all educated youth to learn from the poor and lower-middle-class peasants. Following this directive, the high school graduates of 1966, 1967 and 1968 (who were known as the *laosanjie*) were sent "down to the countryside or up to the mountains," especially to the poor rural areas and border regions. This had an enormous impact on the first generation of young people who had been educated under socialism. Communes and farms in these areas often had a difficult time absorbing large numbers of these "educated youth," many of whom had been "Red Guards." It has been estimated that over the next decade, sixteen million young people were "rusticated," one million from Shanghai alone.[23] Some have written of their positive experience in the countryside, but many more have emphasized the disillusionment brought on by the rigors of rural life.[24]

The Tings' two sons were part of this generation. Their eldest son, Ting Yenren (Ding Yanren), was among those who traveled around China at the start of the Cultural Revolution, full of hope for the future and dedicated to the cause of revolution. After graduation from middle school, he recalled that he and his younger brother, Heping, went to the countryside together. Their father took them to the bus stop to see them off, but like most young boys of their age, they didn't want to be seen with him.[25] For the children of intellectuals who had a bad "class label" and were under criticism, rustification was to help them reform and achieve "working-class" status.[26] Ting Yenren spent a number of years in Sihong, a poor rural area in northern Jiangsu, where he taught literacy to the peasants, as did many other middle-school graduates. Several years later, Ting Yenren went to work as a mechanic in a large steel mill close to Nanjing, where he stayed until the mid-1970s.[27]

In 1967 and 1968, K. H. Ting joined the tens of thousands of volunteers who helped build the Yangzi River Bridge in Nanjing.[28] The Chinese took great pride in this project, which was completed after the departure of Russian engineers, who said it could not be done. The rail section of the bridge was opened on 1 October 1968. Ting's job was to pull nails out of wooden boards used in the construction of the bridge. He did not work there for very long, however, for he was transferred to the less strenuous job of helping peasants grow vegetables on a farm on the outskirts of Nanjing. Sometime late in 1968, he developed acute appendicitis and had to get himself to the Drum Tower Hospital in Nanjing in a pedicab. He had his appendix removed, and was then cared for by a nurse who had to look after a great number of patients. As a result of this operation, Ting was given lighter tasks on the farm. This also meant that he did not have to go to the May 7th Cadre School with other seminary faculty members who were still in Nanjing.

For many intellectuals, the later years of the Cultural Revolution meant involvement in a continuing series of meetings. K. H. Ting was enrolled in a political-study class for much of this time, and in the beginning, it met six days a week.[29] He was assigned to a group with eighty other prominent people who had to be rehabilitated—intellectuals, capitalists and former Guomindang officials. The class had a disciplinary purpose, but it also functioned as a form of protection for these people, for it prevented harassment by neighborhood organizations due to their past histories and "bad class labels." The political study was conducted by the revolutionary committee from the former United Front Work Department, and the texts were from the writings of Mao and recent policy directives.

On more than one occasion, the class allowed K. H. to visit his mother in Shanghai. This had to be a group decision, for the members were responsible for one another. As the situation in the country became more relaxed, he also was sent to Beijing at the request of the provincial authorities. They wanted him to plead for the return of seminary faculty members who were still in the countryside outside Nanjing. Their living conditions were terrible, and they were engaged in hard physical labor. Ting was in no position to plead for anyone, and so it is uncertain whether his visit to Beijing had any impact.[30] But the very fact that he was sent showed that Ting still had a certain standing in the eyes of the officials. The seminary faculty members were eventually moved back into the city, perhaps as much a result of the changing nature of the times as intervention by K. H. Ting on their behalf.

K. H. Ting and Siu-may led quiet lives during these years in their small home near the seminary, but there are few details about their experiences during this time. At one point, a European visitor was told that K. H. Ting was living quietly and working on a writing project in Beijing,[31] but there is no evidence that this was the case. Scattered reports about K. H. Ting and other prominent Christians came to the West in the early seventies, but they add little to our understanding.

Wherever the Tings have lived—in Shanghai, Toronto, New York, Geneva and Nanjing—they have received and entertained many visitors. The graciousness and warmth with which they received guests from China and from all over the world is an expression of their Chinese and Christian hospitality. After their return to China in 1951, this also became an aspect of their informal role in people-to-people diplomacy. During the Cultural Revolution, the Tings continued to receive visitors from other parts of China, but the people with whom they visited were not necessarily of their own choosing. Beginning in the early 1970s, individuals who were suspected of being counterrevolutionaries were subject to a lengthy process of investigation.

Dossiers would be compiled, and reports would be written of interviews with people who knew them. This procedure was termed "internal investigation and external inquiry" (*nei cha wai diao*). Countless days, months and even years were spent in such investigations and inquiries, and the information that was collected, much of it of dubious validity, was put on file. This became a way of ensuring political conformity and mutual responsibility for people in the same group or neighborhood.

Both K. H. and Siu-may were potentially important sources to find out about those who were or had been involved with the student movement or the church from the late 1930s onward. Anyone who had been connected with foreign missionaries or who had spent time overseas was under suspicion, including the Tings themselves. We do not know all that was involved in these investigations and inquiries, but we do know that Ting was very much aware of their real intention early on. We can also surmise that he would have been hesitant to say too much to assist the investigators in their work. As he recalled,

> In those days there were many, many "external inquiries." Some of the people who came just wanted to make a trip and visit scenic spots and play around, but some of them were very serious about their job. So much of my time was spent in "external inquiries," in meeting other people. There were many people coming to see me. Sometimes two a day, sometimes three a day! Of course, I had very little to tell them, because most of the persons were not very familiar to me. They were students mostly, and I was a YMCA student secretary, but I could not know them very much.[32]

> Usually, they would ask me to look at this person from a higher political level. "You were friends in those days, but now you must stand on the correct line of Chairman Mao and look at him again in the light of a new political perspective." They would like you to incriminate these people. And some of them went to my friends to try to incriminate me too.[33]

We have seen that activist TSPM leaders in Shanghai criticized K. H. Ting during the Anti-Rightist movement, particularly for his essay "On Christian Theism." They had argued that there would soon be no need for religion or theology in a socialist society, and so what Ting was writing was politically incorrect. Ting has termed their position extreme, for they believed that

> the 1949 Liberation and the founding of the People's Republic of China meant the realization of the Gospel of Christ in China and the coming of the Kingdom. Christ was the revolutionary proletariat and the apostolic church was communism in embryo. The aim of the

church on earth lay in moving people to live by the Sermon on the Mount and sacrificing themselves for others. In this way the Kingdom of Heaven would spread across the earth.[34]

TSPM activists were closely associated with the ultra-leftist political line, and during the Cultural Revolution they came back to the essay he had written in 1957. Whether for reasons of political opportunism or "revolutionary" conviction, the TSPM radicals in Shanghai attacked K. H. Ting again in the early 1970s.

He Chengxiang (the former RAB director from Beijing) was paying a visit to Shanghai, and I was invited to go to Shanghai to meet him. But after reaching Shanghai, I was told that the "activists," which is a very undefined term, would be having several sessions to go into the question of rightist deviation or opportunism, at that time a target of criticism, and they wanted me to join. So I joined. At those meetings, I was criticized because of that article. The strongest attack was that it was *edu* (which) means very evil in intention. It was Li Chuwen who used those two characters to describe me in writing that article. But before I could defend myself, the head of the United Front Department of the Communist Party of Jiangsu Province somehow got the notion, maybe Siu-may told him, that I was in Shanghai, and I was attending such sessions. And he said that since I belonged to Jiangsu Province, there was no point for me to be engaged in such sessions in Shanghai, so I got back to Nanjing, before there was any verdict.[35]

Ting has publicly described the Shanghai activists who wanted to attack him as a "rebel faction" or "secret group," but it is clear who he had in mind.[36] During the Cultural Revolution there were many such groups who became part of the revolutionary committees of their former work units. Ting mentions that his good friend Zheng Jianye was another object of attack at this meeting. He says explicitly that Li Chuwen, former TSPM general secretary, was the leader of the group within the TSPM that was persecuting Zheng. "I think 'persecution' is the right word to use," he commented. "Zheng Jianye was really persecuted."[37] Zheng's situation in Shanghai was much worse than that of K. H. Ting in Nanjing. Ting has never said or even hinted that he was persecuted or harshly treated during these years. He endured the day-to-day deprivations of intellectuals in disgrace, but he was not an object of direct attack after this.

In addition to the support that came from party officials in Jiangsu, Ting was also helped by Luo Zhufeng, a veteran party leader in Shanghai. The activists visited Luo to get support for their attack on Ting.

They told Luo Zhufeng that I was a suspect because I wrote an article "On Christian Theism," and Luo Zhufeng told me the way he answered. He said, "Any president of a Party school would write articles on Marxism-Leninism. What's wrong for a president of a theological school to write an article on theism?"[38]

Ting was moved by this support, coming at a time when Luo Zhufeng was himself under criticism. Luo had been thrown out of his home in Shanghai and was living alone in a cramped space under a stairwell. In supporting K. H. Ting, Luo was risking his own safety. In contrast, there were people in the TSPM who attempted to gain favor and advancement by attacking their former colleagues. People responded in different ways under the pressures of the Cultural Revolution, and there are stories about those who sacrificed themselves to save others, just as there are stories of betrayal and deceit. Luo Zhufeng was rehabilitated shortly after the end of the Cultural Revolution, and he was to become an important ally in the struggle to reform religious studies in the 1980s.

The political support from party officials in Nanjing and Shanghai was related to the orders that came from Zhou Enlai to protect K. H. Ting, so as not to expose him to public humiliation. Although this support cannot be confirmed with documentary evidence, it would help to explain why Ting was not more severely attacked during the Cultural Revolution era.

RETURN TO PUBLIC LIFE

The activist phase of the Cultural Revolution had come to an end in 1969; but the radicals were still in control, and their position seemed even stronger with Lin Biao named as Mao's second in command and chosen successor. But there were growing concerns in Beijing among party veterans still in power about the need for greater attention to economics and to international affairs. The following year, Chairman Mao issued new guidelines for rebuilding the party that deemphasized demands for the sort of revolutionary zeal that Lin Biao had been promoting. To oversee this rebuilding, Zhou Enlai was named head of state.

The tension between the need for order and rebuilding and Lin Biao's own political ambitions became increasingly pronounced over the next two years, and this was followed by a totally unexpected turn of events. After what was reported as a failed coup and assassination attempt, Lin Biao was killed in a plane crash with his wife and son on 13 September 1971. When this was announced to the Chinese public the following year, Lin was denounced as a "renegade and traitor." The death of Lin Biao brought "a silent intellectual liberation" to the Chinese people, according to the history of the Cultural Revolution written by Yan Jiaqi and Gao Gao.[39] Lin Biao had sworn undying loyalty to Chairman Mao, but he now became his ultimate betrayer. If Lin Biao was a fraud, then what could be said of the Cultural Revolution which he had done so much to promote? As reports of the "13 September incident" became more widely known, a growing number of intellectuals began to analyze what was happening for themselves. Their skepticism and doubts about the Cultural Revolution deepened.

As all of this was happening, China began cautiously to reopen its doors to the outside world. The United States was also exploring a diplomatic overture to China. China's reopening was reinforced by Mao's growing suspicions of the Soviet Union. There had been border clashes in 1969, and Lin Biao's plane had been heading toward Russian territory before it went down in Inner Mongolia. Informal diplomatic overtures to the United States had begun in April 1971, when the U.S. ping-pong team was invited to China. In July, Henry Kissinger made a secret visit to Beijing to confer with Zhou Enlai about changes in U.S. policy and the possibility of a presidential visit to China. In October, the People's Republic of China took over Taiwan's seat at the United Nations. The visit by Richard M. Nixon took place in February of the following year, concluding with the signing of the Shanghai Communique, which became the basis for a new period in Chinese-American relations.

These domestic and international developments also help to explain the subtle changes in religious policy in the early 1970s. By the time of the Nixon visit, there had been a limited restoration of RAB functions in Beijing to oversee the reorganization of services of worship for Muslims, Buddhists and Christians.[40] Some mosques in western China were also reopened, and some isolated Buddhist retreat centers quietly resumed their activities. Visitors from Asia, Africa, Europe and Canada again began to meet Chinese believers, at least in Beijing and Guangzhou. Shortly after the Nixon visit, the Rice Market Street Church in Beijing held its first Easter service in many years, mainly for foreigners. Reports on religion from overseas visitors, including Americans, increased after 1972, even though most contacts with religious believers were on official tours and in strictly controlled settings.

K. H. Ting's return to public life should be seen in the context of these developments. The first mention of his name in the national press since 1965 was in a news release dated 6 September 1972.[41] It came toward the end of a long list of names of those attending the funeral service for National People's Congress vice-chair He Xiangning, whose remains were taken to Nanjing to be buried alongside her husband Liao Zhongkai. Wu Yifang was also included in this list, as was Liu Guojun, the two others from Jiangsu Province who had been protected since 1966 on the instructions of Zhou Enlai. The seemingly unimportant inclusion of these names in an international news release was significant, for it indicated that the three had been "rehabilitated" enough to deserve mention as public figures from Jiangsu. This did not go unnoticed among Ting's friends in China and overseas. The mention of his name in a press release indicated that he might be able to meet visitors from overseas, and it raised the hopes of Christians in China.

In November, K. H. Ting and Wu Yifang met with Maude Russell, formerly a Chinese YWCA secretary in Shanghai, who now edited a pro-China newsletter from her apartment in New York City. Later that year, he met Doak Barnett, the American Sinologist who had grown up in China, who also saw Y. T. Wu and Liu Liangmo in Shanghai. Ting remembers meeting an Australian Anglican bishop and a woman from the Australian peace movement in 1972. Before he could meet with any of the foreign visitors, he had to get permission from his political study group. Before one such visit, the leader of the study group came to see him. During their conversation, he asked Ting if he still believed in God, and when he said he did, it put the leader in doubt as to whether he was ready to see overseas visitors.[42] It had already been decided at a higher political level that Ting would be allowed to meet with foreign visitors, and so it is unusual that his study group would take such an interest.

It was also around this time that the Tings moved back to their home on Mo Chou Road. K. H. had avoided returning to his old neighborhood until then, because he assumed that the neighbors would be angry with him as a "class enemy." But when he returned to supervise the renovation of his house in late 1972, he discovered his fears were unfounded, and that his neighbors actually welcomed the family's return, for it suggested that the situation would be returning to normal.[43] Once back in their home, the Tings would occasionally gather with a small number of people from the seminary for prayer and Bible study. By this time, there were many Christian home meetings in Nanjing and other parts of China, although the groups were mostly unknown to one another. K. H. Ting drew on his own experience with home meetings in his conversations with foreign visitors, and he often met visitors from abroad in the same sitting room where he gathered for fellowship with seminary and church colleagues.

In April 1973, Dr. and Mrs. E. H. (Ted) Johnson, former Canadian Presbyterian missionaries in China, visited K. H. Ting and Siu-may in Nanjing.[44] Johnson was a "friend of China," and he had been close to Ting in the past. His report, and the reports of other foreign visitors, became important sources of information for Christians overseas. They provided a Christian perspective on what was happening in China, and news of Christian leaders. The Johnsons' 1973 visit also became important for Christians in China. When K. H. and Siu-may Ting spoke to the Johnsons, Ting said that the home meetings mentioned above represented a new form of deritualized Christian worship.

> I told Ted Johnson that Christians would only meet in homes from now on and Ted Johnson reported on that somewhere in Canada. And what he wrote appeared in *Reference News* (*Cankao xiaoxi*), and mentioned my name, referring to me as saying that Christians were only to meet

in homes. [*Reference News* (*Cankao xiaoxi*) was a widely circulated compendium of news about China; it included translations from foreign publications. Although intended for restricted "internal circulation" (*neibu*), *Reference News* was widely circulated in China and considered to be a more reliable source of news than that which appeared in published newspapers.] And at that time, the "Gang of Four" in Shanghai was trying to suppress Christians meeting in homes, and those Christians meeting in homes in Shanghai quoted from *Reference News*. They said that K. H. Ting had *"said that we could meet in homes."* I supported them but that wasn't to my advantage at that time, because I said things that the "Gang of Four" wanted to suppress.[45]

This story, repeated to me in the early 1980s on a number of occasions, illustrates the importance for both church and state of having K. H. Ting as a public figure with a measure of official acceptance. For the government, it helped with propaganda work overseas by showing that Christians in China supported what was going on and could speak their minds. It also encouraged Christians in China to continue to meet for worship and fellowship in their homes, for K. H. Ting had said as much in *Reference News*. The appearance of the story in *Reference News* is known in Chinese as "the export of news for reimport" (*chukou zhuan neixiao*). In this particular case, it unintentionally strengthened the Chinese Christian community.

Zhao Puchu visited K. H. Ting in Nanjing in December 1973. Zhao was in Nanjing to look into the restoration of the "Buddhist Sutra Woodblock Printing Bureau" (*Jinling kejing chu*), which had supposedly been authorized by Zhou Enlai.[46] Zhao, who had been president of the China Buddhist Association at the start of the Cultural Revolution, was associated with Ting in the CPPCC. The two religious leaders were friends who first met in Shanghai under Japanese occupation. Both men were sidelined at the start of the Cultural Revolution, but both had now returned to public life. We do not know what they talked about during their short visit, but Zhao wrote a poem for his friend, which has hung in the Ting's sitting room ever since. An annotated translation of this poem is appended to this chapter. The poem alludes to Zhao's dissatisfaction with the course of the Cultural Revolution, and the last two lines speak of his hope that the two friends would persevere and work for change.

May we two forever work in harmony
like sturdy pines in youth and old age
brave as the new-sprouted bamboo, ever strong, yet ever humble.[47]

As K. H. Ting became better known overseas as a spokesperson for Chinese Christians, contacts with him increased. In 1974, he received an invitation from Burgess Carr to attend the Third Assembly of the All Africa Council of Churches in Nairobi. This was the first time in many years that he was invited to attend a Christian conference overseas. Ting was still not able to travel overseas because of the restrictions of the Cultural Revolution era, but he did write Carr a return letter in which he reiterated his support for China's position of solidarity with the struggles of African people. For Chinese Christians, Ting writes, "the present time offers us the best opportunity to summarize experiences and draw lessons for ourselves" about the independence and self-government of the church. He expresses his regret that he must turn down the invitation "from the point of view of a basic policy on the part of our Christian body," and he asks for Carr's understanding.[48] Ting's return to public life made it possible for him to speak for "our Christian body," even though the TSPM had not met for at least a decade, and there were no institutional expressions of the church.

Between 1973 and 1975, Ting met with Australian, North American and British visitors at his home in Nanjing, a few of whom were old friends and many others who had specifically asked to see him. Most visitors in those years were traveling to China on tightly organized tours arranged through various friendship associations, and so the visits tended to be short and carefully orchestrated.[49] In the eyes of the Chinese government, it seems that K. H. Ting had already replaced the ailing Y. T. Wu as the most visible public representative of Chinese Christianity. This would most probably have been the view of Zhou Enlai, who continued to be in charge of China's international affairs.

Reports of conversations with the Tings and fragmentary information on religion in China gathered by foreign visitors were read with great interest overseas, but they revealed very little about what was actually happening with Christianity in China. These were years in which the church was "underground"—to the extent that Christians met for worship at all. K. H. Ting's reported comments reveal his views on the prospects for Christianity in China, but at the time he had a pessimistic appraisal of the future of the institutional church. This was understandable, given the times in which he was speaking, and it was a judgment he maintained through the end of the Cultural Revolution era. In 1974, when Ting met with Don MacInnis and a group from the U.S.–China People's Friendship Association, he even spoke of the "withering away" of religion.

> Our society is not static; it is changing all the time. Our church cannot remain static either. We are changing all the time too. What we are witnessing now is the withering away of organized religion. Protestantism now is becoming more and more de-institutionalized, de-clericalized—more and more a worldview among those who call themselves Christian, and the religious fellowship among them.[50]

These are the reflections of one who had only begun to raise questions about the Cultural Revolution and its ultra-leftist line. But they are also accurate reflections of what Ting saw happening around him. His deinstitutionalized view of Christianity was reflected in his earlier comments on Christians meeting in their homes. His declericalized Protestantism was a departure from his Anglican past, but he now said he preferred to be called "Old Ting"—an informal form of address in Chinese—rather than "Bishop."[51] His ideas about the future of Christianity in China are cast in an extreme form in light of the politics of the time. They come from one who was well aware that he was speaking as a representative of China to "progressive" Christians from overseas who tended to be supportive of the Cultural Revolution.

Although he himself was increasingly disillusioned with the politics and policies of the Cultural Revolution, Ting's questions about where China was going are not at all discernible in reports from overseas visitors. This is partly due to the perspective of the visitors themselves. They were predisposed to see God at work in the unfolding of the Cultural Revolution, and they went back to their churches with glowing reports of what they had seen and heard on their official China tours. The Cultural Revolution came at a time when mainline churches in the West were embracing a "theology of secularization" and sought to discern God's work in the revolutionary movements of human history. This shaped their view of China. The ecumenical China meetings at Bastad and Louvain in 1974 reinforced a vision of "New Man and New Society" in China at a time when most Chinese intellectuals were becoming more and more doubtful about the course of the Cultural Revolution, let alone the existence of a "new man" in any kind of theological sense.[52] Ecumenical China studies laid the foundation for a more open and sympathetic view of a revived TSPM in the late 1970s, but the China programs in New York and Toronto, Geneva, London and Louvain were all politically and theologically naïve in exaggerating the achievements of the Cultural Revolution.

It is important to note at this point that Protestant evangelical groups overseas had a very different perspective. The *Love China '75* assembly in Manila and the Chinese Congress on World Evangelism in Hong Kong (1976) saw evangelism to China as a key priority. Most evangelicals, Chinese as well as Western, were skeptical about the Cultural Revolution, and in this way they were more in touch with the faith of Chinese Christians. Among Roman Catholics, Lazlo Ladany, S.J., and others also raised questions about the soundness of the judgments of the ecumenical China programs.

K. H. Ting's doubts about the Cultural Revolution were growing, partly a result of the "silent intellectual liberation" after the death of Lin Biao, but also through increasing contact with people whom he knew and trusted. Radicals of the Cultural Revolution, including some who had been part of the TSPM in Shanghai, made use of the "internal investigations and external inquiries" to concoct all sorts of conspiracy theories and link people to supposed plots against the government. Christian radicals reached back to the months before Liberation in 1949 in order to "expose" a plot that had supposedly been hatched by missionaries and Chinese church leaders to oppose the Communist Party. This "plot" became known as the "strategic measures to oppose the change in government" (*yingbian cuoshi*). The idea that American missionaries and their Chinese associates were plotting to overthrow the People's Republic of China had been first raised during the Denunciation Movement in the 1950s, but during the Cultural Revolution, it was brought up again. According to K. H. Ting,

> The whole thing was gone over once more, and some of the people who were exposed as "leaders" of the "strategic measures to oppose the change in government" received strong pressure to tell the truth. And they told the truth by lying. One of them was Cora Deng; another was George Wu. Those were the two whom I know. In 1974, probably, or early 1975, I made a visit to Shanghai, the first time in many years, supposedly to see my mother. I got the permission to leave Nanjing and I visited Li Shoubao and Shi Ruzhang. That was one couple I saw, and the other couple was Zheng Jianye and Liang Suning.
>
> Li Shoubao and Shi Ruzhang were still talking about how serious the "strategic measures to oppose the change in government" was. Shi Ruzhang gave me the impression that things were still developing, that there were more and more exposures about that conspiracy. But Zheng Jianye told me that the whole thing was not true. And later we learned that because of the false exposures of Cora Deng and George Wu, two hundred people were put under suspicion as involved in a conspiracy against the Communists.[53]

This type of accusation was common during the later years of the Cultural Revolution, and the false exposures among some Christians were not unlike the "exposures" in society as a whole. People responded differently. The nature of the "conspiracy" or "counterrevolutionary plot" varied from place to place. It left many people with deep emotional scars that in some cases were never fully healed.[54] Not everyone chose to "tell the truth by lying," but many did, even in the church. Some felt they had been forced into positions where they "had" to betray others. Others were themselves too weak to resist the political pressures imposed on them. There were also some who participated willingly. Because there were so many prominent Christians in Shanghai, including many former TSPM activists, and because the city was the base of the radicals in power, it was inevitable that Shanghai would become an important place for ferreting out the various "conspiracies" among Christians. Those implicated by the "strategic measures to oppose the change in government" conspiracy would wait until 1978 to begin the process of rehabilitation. By then, some had already died; the rehabilitation came too late.

THE FOURTH NATIONAL PEOPLE'S CONGRESS

In mid-1973, Jiang Qing and her radical allies had initiated a campaign to criticize Lin Biao and Confucius. Separated by 2,500 years, the two were linked in yet another arcane political debate to promote the radicals' cause. It became evident that the indirect object of their criticism was Zhou Enlai.[55] The campaign further eroded the little support for the Cultural Revolution that was left among Chinese intellectuals. Zhou was already dying of cancer, and by the middle of 1974, he had moved into the Capital Hospital, where he lived for the remaining eighteen months of his life. Deng Xiaoping was called back to take up the day-to-day work of government, although he would be removed once again in April 1976 because of criticisms by Jiang Qing and the radicals and loss of favor with Mao.

Zhou Enlai's final public speech was at the Fourth National People's Congress (NPC), which was held in Beijing 13-17 January 1975. It should have been held five years earlier, but it was repeatedly postponed because of the chaos of the times. To convene the NPC required a high degree of political control, and it was not certain that Zhou had the political support he needed before this. He was in charge of preparations for the Fourth NPC, often working from his hospital bed, with doctors in attendance around the clock. Zhou still had to contend with Jiang Qing and the radicals who were pushing their own agenda, and who were attacking him both publicly and behind the scenes.

The selection of delegates to the NPC was controlled by Mao, Zhou Enlai, Jiang Qing and the provincial revolutionary committees in the provinces.[56] There were 2,885 delegates in all, and from Jiangsu, these included K. H. Ting, Wu Yifang, Liu Guojun—the three who had been protected by Zhou Enlai in the early months of the Cultural Revolution. The vast majority of delegates were radicals selected by provincial revolutionary committees, but there were also a number of veteran cadres and other prominent figures who were against the excesses of the times. Although the selection process for delegates was controlled, the appearance of a democratic election process had to be maintained at the local level. The list of proposed delegates was given to the neighborhood organizations and the political study groups that just about everyone in urban areas was attached to.[57] These small groups were said to represent "the people," and they were asked to study the slate of delegates and endorse the candidates.

K. H. Ting said that he was surprised by his own selection as a delegate, and when his name was announced, he had to say something about himself in his small group.

> I said that whether I am an enemy or a part of the people is still something uncertain. How can I be a representative to the National People's Congress? And then the leader of the class, who was in the room, had to say, "Of course you are a part of the people, otherwise you would

not be nominated to be a member of the Congress." And that was the first time I was declared a part of the people.

The list of deputies from Jiangsu had to be circulated, supposedly all over Jiangsu Province, for the people to say yes. Now we have a friend who is a tailor, not far away from here, and his wife came to see us rather often. She told us that when the list was presented to the group in that neighborhood organization, the cadre said to the group: "A person like Ting—that is me—a person like Ting could be beheaded several times, but out of the kindness of the party he is now to be made a deputy." He, I think, assumed that people out of their class hatred would be opposed to my appointment so he wanted to do some work to convince them that the policy of the party was correct and they should support it and they should not object. That gives you an idea of the political atmosphere at that time.[58]

The political atmosphere was also reflected in the secretive way in which the Fourth NPC was convened. As the delegates prepared to go to Beijing, they themselves were not told where they were going or even what they were going to do.

So I went to a place in Nanjing, and we became a group, and they sent us to a big hotel in Zhong Shan Ling, and we stayed there for several days and during that time we were told that there was going to be a meeting of the National People's Congress. But because of fear of the infiltration of the enemy from outside, we must make it very secret. So one day we were sent to the Nanjing railway station. There was a curfew so that nobody would see us. When we arrived in Beijing, the train stopped in a very small station on the outskirts of the city, and we were taken to a place to stay. We were told not to go out and not to make any telephone calls.

And then one evening Jiang Qing said she would come to meet us so we had to wait. We waited and waited and waited. Of course I could wait, but Wu Yifang was already pretty old and Liu Guojun was also very old. We all waited and she came early in the morning about two o'clock to meet the Jiangsu delegation. But she didn't even shake hands with us. She was only interested in the rebel faction from Jiangsu. So we just sat there as onlookers and for probably a little over half an hour she was with the group, and then she left, and then we went to bed.

And then every session was secret. Because at that time there was a most unnecessary political alertness, concerning infiltration. So those of us who were older had a right to go to the Great Hall of the People in cars or in buses, but all the other delegates had to go by underground, and also in a very secret way. There was a curfew so that nobody would see the delegates. There was a secret passage from the underground station to the Great Hall of the People, and the delegates all went through this secret passage. The announcement about the Congress was made only after its close. Then we came back to Nanjing.[59]

The most important actions of the Fourth NPC were the endorsement of a new slate of national leaders and the approval of a new constitution. The new leaders and the wording of the constitution had already been decided beforehand. This constitution, in effect, deprived the people of their power, and it elevated the power of the party over the power of the state. It was pushed through by the radicals, moderated somewhat by Zhou Enlai and Deng Xiaoping, and approved by Mao. Zhou Enlai delivered the "Report on Government Work," during which he announced the "Four Moderniza-tions," a vast program for economic development that became the corner-stone of China's open policy after 1978. An inner-party balance was reached between Jiang Qing and her radical allies and the moderates, represented by the ailing Zhou Enlai. Mao Zedong maintained the balance between these two factions. Deng Xiaoping, Zhou's ally, was named first vice-premier.[60] The holding of the Fourth NPC was something of an achievement for Zhou Enlai, and the government work report was his final political testament. However, the meeting did not change the fundamental realities in society, and the Cultural Revolution still overshadowed everything.

K. H. Ting did not meet with Zhou Enlai during the NPC, nor did they ever see each other again. He did speak with Y. T. Wu, who was then in his early eighties and not in very good health. Wu was an NPC delegate from Shanghai, the radicals' stronghold. This was the first time the two had met in many years. They discussed the future of the church in China, and Ting has written about this final meeting.

> When we met again in Beijing in 1975, the first question we got into after the long separation was whether from now on Chinese Chris-tianity could do without church buildings and clerical professional-ism. Y. T. was still the idealist he had always been. Throughout that conversation and in our subsequent conversations we never had time or interest to go into our personal experiences [during] the years of the Cultural Revolution.[61]

Article 28 of the new constitution produced by the Fourth NPC guaran-teed the freedom of religious belief but also included a clause about the "free-dom not to believe in religion and to propagate atheism."[62] No similar propagation of theism is stated or implied. Neither Ting nor Wu was happy with this article on religious freedom in the new constitution they had voted for. They had voiced their objections, but they were unable to do anything to change it. Y. T. Wu died in 1979, shortly after the end of the Cultural Revolution era, and so he was unable to join K. H. Ting and others who continued to work for the change in this wording.

Ting became involved in editing and translation work after he returned to Nanjing at the end of the Fourth NPC. China had joined the United Nations, and the minutes of meetings and other documents had to be translated into Chinese. Universities from around the country took up this task, and because Nanjing Seminary faculty were thought to be good in English, they were recruited by the government to join in this translation work. This indicated that subtle changes were taking place in China, for religious believers were again being asked to contribute to the broader society.

Around the same time, the seminary faculty was also asked to work on a new Chinese-English dictionary, which was eventually published by Jiangsu People's Publishers. K. H. Ting was listed as an editor of the dictionary when it was finally published in 1983.[63] This kind of work drew on his experience in the wording of statements and documents in English and Chinese. The dictionary definitions and illustrations were chosen according to the Cultural Revolution criteria of "politics in command." But because it was not published until after the Cultural Revolution had ended, Ting and his colleagues were able to make the illustrations less political, a fact in which they took great pride.[64] As the political struggles became less intense in 1975 and 1976, work on the dictionary and other translation projects became meaningful occupations for Ting and the seminary faculty members.

THE END OF THE CULTURAL REVOLUTION ERA

The year 1976 was a momentous one for China. On the morning of 8 January, Zhou Enlai died after a long struggle with cancer. Although the official period of mourning was truncated by the machinations of Jiang Qing and her radical allies, there was a spontaneous outpouring of grief and respect which began a few days after Zhou Enlai's death and which started again in the period leading up to the Qingming Festival (5 April), the day for the sweeping of the graves and remembering those who had passed away in the traditional calendar. On 4 April, two million people gathered in Beijing's Tiananmen Square, leaving poems and wreaths to commemorate Zhou Enlai's death. When I first met K. H. Ting and Zhao Puchu in 1979, Ting told me that Zhao Puchu was sought out by many students and intellectuals to give advice on the poems they placed in Tiananmen Square on that day.[65] One eulogy to Premier Zhou read:

His work is not consummated:
Demons run amok
But where to seek another pillar to shoulder the skies?

Throughout the land,
Eight hundred million share
The same endless thoughts,
The same intense emotions.[66]

The next day, all the poems and wreaths were removed on the orders of the radicals then in power in the government, and a series of violent incidents resulted in hundreds of deaths and injuries, and thousands of arrests. The square was closed to the public, and the Tiananmen demonstrations were condemned as "counterrevolutionary."[67] On 7 April, Deng Xiaoping was removed yet again from all of his posts, initiating a period of criticism of his "right deviationist wind." It seemed as if the radicals had consolidated their power, even though Hua Guofeng, rather than one of their own, was named by Mao as acting premier. But it was the people's spontaneous response to the death of Zhou Enlai, their "beloved premier," that foreshadowed what was to come.

In early July, Zhu De, hero of China's war of liberation, died. At the end of that month, one of the most destructive earthquakes in Chinese history shook North China, from its epicenter in Tangshan. China refused foreign assistance in dealing with this tragedy which left at least 242,000 people dead, according to official figures; but recovery, led by the PLA, was swift.[68] On 9 September, Mao Zedong died, and this was followed by a weeklong period of mourning. The deaths of these three national leaders, combined with the tragedy of the Tangshan earthquake, suggested to many that the Mandate of Heaven had been removed, and with it the right of Mao's radical successors to hold on to the reigns of power.

On 6 October, the four radical Shanghai leaders that the world came to know as the "Gang of Four" were arrested. Although the political situation continued to be ambiguous, there was rejoicing in the streets in the days after the announcement of their arrests in mid-October. In the weeks and months that followed, the "crimes" and subversive actions of the Gang of Four were widely publicized and exposed. Their most ardent followers were also rounded up, put on trial and imprisoned. The future was still uncertain, and few people dared to voice their deepest thoughts about the Cultural Revolution in public. Yet there was a sense that the page had turned and that the darkest period of China's recent history was over.

Two weeks after the fall of the Gang of Four, a small group of American religious leaders met with K. H. and Siu-may Ting in their home.[69] The visit had been planned for some months, but it assumed added importance because of its timing. Ting spoke with the Americans about the spontaneous demonstrations in Nanjing in support of the overthrow of the "Shanghai Gang," as he called them, and he offered his interpretation of the events that had preceded it. Many of his remarks are typical of the reports found in newspapers and journals in China in late 1976. But his views in this interview are revealing for what they say about how he was seeing things and what they suggest about his understanding of Christianity and the church.

In explaining the Cultural Revolution to his American visitors, it is clear that Ting had already begun to work through his own critique of ultra-leftism. His perspective would deepen and develop over the next several years, as more and more intellectuals added their voices to the ongoing debate.[70] In Eugene L. Stockwell's detailed interview notes, Ting speaks of the evil done to people wrongfully attacked during the Cultural Revolution; he denounces the deception and power plays of the Gang of Four; he argues that the radicals preyed on people's fears and insecurities; and he criticizes the detachment of the power-holding elites who separated themselves from the masses. In all of this, K. H. Ting was speaking with conviction from his own experience. He admitted that he too had been deceived during the Cultural Revolution. Those who had attacked him and his friends were allied with those who had opposed Zhou Enlai and veteran party leaders during the Cultural Revolution.

The Tings also spoke with their visitors about the future of the church in China. K. H. said many of the same things he had been telling visitors since 1973: the church would become deinstitutionalized and declericalized; Christians would decline in number, but they would continue to meet informally in their homes; Christianity and the church should never again be associated with foreign missionaries. During this visit, Ting also began to suggest some new post–Cultural Revolution ideas. He spoke about the participation of Christians in China's united front, which had been dormant for more than twenty years. He reflected on the future of a "postdenominational" Christianity in China. And he expressed both his welcome to and wariness of churches and Christian institutions overseas that wanted to relate to China. These were all themes that would be important for the Chinese church in the years ahead.

The two-hour meeting with the Americans ended, and K. H. was asked to lead the group in prayer. He did so by reciting the Lord's Prayer in Chinese, an experience that the Americans found deeply moving. "It was a beautiful moment," Stockwell observes. "We walked out into Nanking's night rain uplifted by the warm contact with a man and a woman whose radiant faith strengthened ours."[71] Neither K. H. nor Siu-may ever spoke much about their own Christian faith with Chinese or foreign friends, but they continued to believe in God even during the most difficult years of the Cultural Revolution.[72] Over the next few years, the Tings would entertain many other Christian visitors from overseas in their home, but this first visit after the fall of the Gang of Four marked a new beginning of ecumenical relations with Chinese Christians.

There were no immediate or dramatic changes for Christians in China after the fall of the Gang of Four. It was not possible for them or anyone else to offer ready interpretations of what soon would be called the "Ten-Year Catastrophe." The rebirth and renewal of the church institutions would not begin for another two years, although preparation had commenced well before then. Only after 1978 would Christians begin to sing with conviction that "Winter is passed, the rain is o'er," in the words of the popular post–Cultural Revolution hymn.[73] In late 1976, they could express their faith somewhat more freely, but Christians were still not free to worship openly or speak about the past.

In the late 1970s, the changes in China attracted the attention of journalists and a wide variety of commentators all over the world. Overseas observers became extremely interested in the experience of the Chinese Christians during the difficult years of the Cultural Revolution. In Hong Kong and other parts of Asia, in Europe and North America, a large number of popular interpretations were published based on snatches of conversations with Chinese Christians or reports on recent visits to the mainland. In Christian publications, particularly in evangelical Protestant magazines and journals, these were sometimes followed by the author's reflection on the importance of suffering for the Chinese church, and what this meant for Christians and churches elsewhere.

In 1983, in his closing address at the Enlarged Joint Committee of the TSPM and the CCC, K. H. Ting offered a reflection of his own perspective on the Cultural Revolution era.

> A foreign Christian once asked me, "During these thirty years, what aspect of faith have you come to understand more deeply?" I replied, "It may be summed up in one point. Chinese Christians have come to know more deeply the truth of the resurrection. Our experience has confirmed the power of the resurrection and its truth." At one time we were weak, but weakness has turned into strength. During the Cultural Revolution, churches were all closed, pastors and church workers became the special target of a dictatorship. We were unable to resist. We did not organize "Red Guards" to protect ourselves or attack other people. We did not write "Big Character posters" with which to frame other people or attack them. We did not resort to violence, nor did we beat, smash and grab.
>
> People beat us, but we did not return the blow, so weak did we seem to be. But now see how strong we are. We are troubled on every side, yet not destroyed. In those days it was as though nobody knew us, as though everyone had forgotten us. But now, even though we may not be known to everyone, yet the whole country acknowledges that Christianity is one of the religions of the people. We are as dying, and behold, we live, as sorrowful, yet rejoicing. Paul's words have indeed found their fulfillment in us. Although we are poor, yet we make many rich, as having nothing, yet we have much. We have a greater recognition of the risen Lord, a clearer understanding of the

truth of the resurrection, a greater sense of the precious truth of resurrection faith.

The general run of people may not share this experience, but in their
hearts they are convinced that suffering should not last forever, that
death should not be our final destiny, that darkness should not be in
control of everything forever . . . The weakness of the Chinese church
in the period after Liberation and during the Cultural Revolution was
clearly exposed. But it is only in losing one's life that one can save
it . . . The experience of the Chinese church during these thirty years
has provided evidence of the power of the Lord's resurrection.[74]

This short reflection remains his most extended theological comment on
the Cultural Revolution era. He was speaking as a Chinese to Chinese Christians who had themselves suffered during the Cultural Revolution. Ting
never wrote a detailed theological reflection on the period, not in his other
addresses to the China Christian Council nor in his talks to students at Nanjing Theological Seminary nor in his speeches overseas.[75] It cannot be said
that he was avoiding the subject, because he was ready to answer the many
questions that were put to him in private and in public. Yet this unwillingness to deal with the theological significance of the Cultural Revolution era
more directly or extensively has led some observers to question why Ting or
other Chinese theologians have not wanted to develop a theology of suffering based on their experience in the years between 1966 and 1976.

At the first meeting of the TSPM after the end of the Cultural Revolution
in 1980, the organizers had set aside three days to allow people to discuss
their experiences during those years. According to K. H. Ting, no one
wanted to go into their past, at least not in this way, but instead they wanted
to discuss what the church would do in the years ahead.[76] One can imagine
that there would be different emotions and feelings, even about one another,
among those who gathered at this meeting. In one sense, it was easier to
move on and discuss the future and leave the Cultural Revolution behind.
This may seem surprising to Christians in the West, who believe it is important to "process" all the difficulties of the past. Chinese Christians have not
chosen to dwell on their own suffering during the Cultural Revolution era
or to isolate their experience from the more general suffering of the times.[77]
It is true that a great many stories from the Cultural Revolution came up in
sermons and informal settings in the early 1980s, and that Christian suffering is still an important subject in Chinese sermons. But no "theology of the
wounded" (*shangheng wenxue*) emerged in the Chinese church to correspond with the Chinese "literature of the wounded" in the 1970s.

There are political reasons for this; writing about the Cultural Revolution
era was discouraged by the government after the early 1980s. Even the short-
lived "literature of the wounded" was later discouraged by government officials. It may also be the case that in the late 1970s and early 1980s, the
wounds and the suffering were too fresh. Prominent intellectuals, including

the late Ba Jin (1894-2005), urged that a Cultural Revolution museum or memorial be established, but this was rejected out of hand by the Chinese Communist leadership. There would be no "Truth and Reconciliation Commission" in post–Cultural Revolution China, although in the 1980s, the government did begin to make amends for the past. Many accounts of the Cultural Revolution era have been published by Chinese who have gone overseas, and in time, and with increasing freedom of expression, the Cultural Revolution era may become more fully documented and interpreted by scholars in China.

But even when they could have spoken or written more directly about the period, as in the 1980 meeting, Chinese Christians were reluctant to do so. This was a time in which the government was seeking to redress the wrongs of the Cultural Revolution and try in some way to compensate people who had suffered. It may be argued that the delegates were fearful of speaking of their suffering, in light of their past experience. It may also be argued that Christians were being told not to air their grievances in religious terms. But another explanation is possible. By 1980, it was already clear that the churches were beginning to experience something of a revival. This was, as K. H. Ting said, an experience of resurrection. Rather than dwell on the suffering of the past, many church leaders may have felt it was time for the church to move on. There were many new things crying out to be done, and urgently. Dwelling on past experiences might be a luxury that the church could not afford. Coming out of a cultural tradition in which feelings are not easily shared, Christian leaders may have preferred to bury the past in their collective memory, leaving the uncertain historical legacy to future generations. Asians from a variety of cultural and religious traditions have addressed questions of suffering in more muted and indirect ways than Europeans, Africans, Latin Americans or North Americans. Something may have been lost in the process—the church may have become more reconciled had grievances been fully aired—but this we shall never know.

In the China of the late 1970s, one of the most serious challenges for the society as a whole was reconciliation. For Christians, reconciliation between God and humankind was the starting point of faith. Reconciliation was also needed to bring people together in community. There were many in the church who had betrayed one another or who had been enemies during the Cultural Revolution. Reconciliation does not necessarily mean righting the wrongs of the past but learning how to live with one another again, in the power of the resurrection. The context, in this sense, is relational not juridical. A relational understanding takes the suffering of the past into consideration, but it sees the past in light of present realities and future hope. This seems to be reflected in the open letter to all Chinese Christians from the TSPM leadership following their first meeting in 1980.[78] The letter gives thanks to God who accompanied Christians through the valley of the shadow of death during the Cultural Revolution, but then immediately goes into the "common concerns" of all Christians and the tasks for the future.

K. H. Ting's theological starting point has been that "reconciliation between God and humanity is the eternal theme of Christian theology."[79] As we shall see in the following chapters, he developed this theme through his focus on love as God's major attribute and in his writings on "the cosmic Christ." But his concern for reconciliation may be seen more clearly in his post–Cultural Revolution actions (his practice) than in anything he has written or said (his theology or theory). It is entirely consistent with Ting's theological approach, and appropriate for his role as church leader, that his ideas find their major expression in what he has tried to do.

If reconciliation is an eternal theme of Christian theology, then its political counterpart in post–Cultural Revolution China was the critique of leftism or ultra-leftism, which K. H. Ting discussed with his American visitors shortly after the fall of the Gang of Four. (I am using the terms "leftism" and "ultra-leftism" interchangeably. When Ting spoke in English he generally used "ultra-leftism" as a translation of *ji zuo sixiang* to distinguish the term from distinctions between "left" and "right" in non-Chinese political contexts.) Or, to put it another way, if a theology of reconciliation was important for the pastoral ministry of the church, then the critique of "ultra-leftism" was essential for its prophetic ministry. More than anyone else in the TSPM, K. H. Ting consistently opposed the influence of ultra-leftism in church and society in the years after the end of the Cultural Revolution. We have seen throughout this chapter that his critique emerged from his own mistaken ideas and his own experiences during the Cultural Revolution. His critique of ultra-leftism represents Ting's personal attempt to work through his own past, and, more importantly, to ensure that the things that happened during the Cultural Revolution could never happen again.

K. H. Ting has admitted on a great number of occasions that he was overly influenced by ultra-leftism after the start of the Anti-Rightist movement and in the early years of the Cultural Revolution, and he has taken this message to heart. Speaking to students at Nanjing Seminary in 1988, he observed,

> On the basis of what I know today, I am doing what I can to oppose "leftism." In the seminary, in the church, in society, I use whatever strength I have to keep "leftism" from continuing to harm people. I ask God to accept this way of showing my repentance. "Leftism" attacks people politically, extending the scope of attack and shrinking the scope of unity. From a faith point of view, "leftism" tramples love underfoot; it is a negation of the gospel. We oppose "leftism" today and raise up love, spreading the spirit of mutual love in the world, to let love, the love of Christ, awaken many frozen hearts.[80]

Repentance, in the form of a personal commitment to oppose "all that tramples love underfoot" and negates the gospel, was a powerful message for people recovering from the traumas of the Cultural Revolution. Ultra-leftism, as we have seen, could be found inside the church as well as outside; it was contrary to the gospel because it refused to recognize the human heart-edness which holds people together, and which is of infinite worth to God.

The critique of ultra-leftism was a political and, at its deepest level, a theological response that said move on, but maintain a critical perspective. Repentance allows people to live again, without forgetting the past, but without letting the past set the terms for the future. The critique of ultra-leftism as an expression of repentance and as a prophetic critique is an essential counterpart to the theology of reconciliation. Both repentance and reconciliation are derived from faith in a loving and incarnate God, a faith that finds its expression in words as well as deeds. This faith became extremely important for rebuilding the church in the era of reform and reopening after 1977 when new life was in the offing.

APPENDIX TO CHAPTER 6

Ode to the Plum Blossom
A *Ci* by Zhao Puchu, written for K. H. Ting*
26 December 1973

Standing before the mountains in thickly falling snow
I lift my gaze to the plum blossoms,
Their branches towering iron-like in the cold air, I sigh—
They sway the human heart,
Their color resplendent as the morning clouds.
Ah, plum blossom, though your frozen branches hang high upon the
    precipice,
Your smiling countenance warms a myriad of homes,
Announcing the coming of Spring throughout the world.

---

* Mao Zedong also wrote a poem entitled "Ode to the Plum Blossom." Many words and allusions used by Zhao Puchu reflect those used by Mao in his poem, but with a different purpose.

The "three friends"—the "plum blossom" (*mei*), the "pine" (*song*) and the "bamboo" (*zhu*)—are traditional references for strength, loyalty and steadfastness. All three are mentioned in this *ci*. The bamboo represents uprightness (for it is straight) and flexibility (for it is connected joint by joint). The bamboo is hollow, and hence the idea of humility comes from its empty center.

This *ci* was written as the poet faced the calamity of the Cultural Revolution, as suggested in the line about "the frozen branches (that) hang high upon the precipice." He writes to encourage people to persevere like the "iron-like" plum blossom that does not fear the wintry cold but announces the coming of spring. The poem alludes to the death of Lin Biao in a plane crash—"the flames that rage in the distant forest and the sands drifting in the vast desert"—and the popular cheers over the news of Lin's demise. In writing to his friend K. H. Ting, Zhao Puchu urges that they continue to work together in youth and in old age (the pine), in strength and in humility (the bamboo).

Let us climb the highest mountain,
to view the flames that rage in the distant forest
and the sands drifting in the vast desert, telling us—
The dark clouds of winter have already lifted
the remnants of tyranny have been obliterated.
Now unfurls the red flag that fills the whole sky
From all directions resound the cheers of joy.
May we two forever work in harmony
like sturdy pines in youth and old age
brave as the new-sprouted bamboo, ever strong, yet ever humble.

Part 3

RECONSTRUCTION AND RENEWAL OF CHURCH AND SOCIETY, 1977-2006

7

Restoration and Renewal, 1977-1983

China is like a great ship bearing a heavy load on a turbulent sea. To make a great about-face on the rolling sea requires calm and care and it will be a fairly long process. But to be careful does not mean we needn't be bold and resolute, nor does to be calm mean we should be slow and lax. It is difficult to run such a big country as China, and it is all the more difficult to govern it after ten years of turmoil.

Cao Yu[1]

Through democratic reform and socialist transformation, all nation-alities in China one after another have long since taken the socialist road, and they have formed a new, socialist type of relationship among themselves—a relationship of unity, fraternity, mutual assistance and co-operation. China's patriots, whatever their nationality and religion, have made considerable progress along this road.

Deng Xiaoping[2]

The exhilaration after the fall of the Gang of Four was followed by a period of uncertainty. Hope for the future was tempered by doubts about whether a new day would really come to pass. People who had fought with one another were now back in their old neighborhoods and work units, and forced to be together. Former "Red Guards" were again working with those whom they had attacked. There was cautiousness over how much one could really say and to whom. Intellectuals spoke about their "lingering fears" (*xin you yu ji*) that it could happen all over again, and so it was better to stay silent and wait and see. This was the Hua Guofeng interregnum.

In July 1977, after nine months of coalition building and political maneuvering, Deng Xiaoping returned to power. Although still deputy to Hua Guofeng, Deng's rehabilitation meant that there would be a quicken-ing of the pace of change, and it brought reassurance for intellectuals. "Every speech by Deng was a blast of fresh air," wrote Jung Chang in *Wild Swans*.[3] There was more open discussion as Deng Xiaoping mobilized elite opinion through the press. By the end of the next year, he had turned the tables on

Hua and was firmly in charge of the party and government.[4] Deng then began setting new policy directions with his own people in key positions.

The most extreme effects of the Cultural Revolution began to be reversed. There was some settling of old scores, but the government was attempting to make the restoration a juridical process, not a new political campaign. On 15 November 1978, it was announced that all those who had been wrongly labeled and criticized over the past twenty years would be rehabilitated. On the same day, those who took part in the demonstrations to memorialize Zhou Enlai in 1976 were cleared of all wrongdoing. Other actions, from the public trial and sentencing of the Gang of Four to the return of property that had been confiscated and occupied made further restitution for the injustices of the Cultural Revolution.

The return of properties was often a long and time-consuming process that proceeded unevenly in different parts of the country. Church buildings, for example, continued to be occupied well into the 1990s, and not all were returned even then. There would never be a righting of all wrongs. Former enemies would have to learn to work together again. Many who had come into positions of power during the Cultural Revolution kept their posts. A start had been made in redressing the wrongs of the past, but there was only so much that could be done. There would be no "Truth and Reconciliation Commission" in China, for too many people would be implicated in the injustices of the previous twenty years.

This whole process was termed "bringing order out of the chaos" (*ba luan fan zheng*). Politics was no longer in command, and the emphasis was shifted to social and economic development. Policy decisions were based on the slogan "seeking truth from facts." The "Four Modernizations" in agriculture, industry, science and technology and national defense, originally outlined by Zhou Enlai in 1976, became the order of the day. The slogan "Practice is the only criterion of truth," popularized by Deng Xiaoping during this time, captures his approach to governance and stands in contrast to the revolutionary sayings of Mao Zedong.[5] Ultra-leftist ideology had failed, and so "facts," modernization and practice became the new means for liberation.

Deng's program of *aggiornamento* would be a fairly long process requiring calm and care. In steering the ship of state, to use Cao Yu's imagery, Deng's experienced hand at the tiller was preferable to the bravado of the "Great Helmsman." The images used to describe the Cultural Revolution had been vivid and predictable: red and not black; light opposed to darkness. Excess and thoroughness were praised; golden means and limitations were bad.[6] Post–Cultural Revolution images tended toward a greater variety of colors, against a backdrop of different shades of gray. Nuance in meaning was preferable to clear definition. Reform might be a less "exciting" process than making revolution, but it was also more realistic and accommodating, and, given time, more effective and embracing, perhaps even humanistic.

The early reforms culminated in the Third Plenum of the Eleventh CPC

Central Committee that met 12-22 December 1978. A watershed event, the Third Plenum marks the start of internal structural reform and openness to the world.[7] Decentralized decision making was to be encouraged, beginning with private enterprises in rural areas. Peasants would be allowed to sell their products on the free market, even if this meant that some would become richer than others. Other reforms included initiatives for electoral reform, the introduction of a retirement system for senior cadres, and an examination system for people wanting to enter universities. The political culture began to move, slowly and deliberately, in the direction of greater openness and social mobility.

But not democratization. Deng Xiaoping's reforms did not mean that the party would relinquish control or make any movement in the direction of liberal democracy. Just prior to the opening of the Third Plenum, Wei Jingsheng put up a poster calling for greater democracy as a "Fifth Modernization." But Wei was arrested, tried, and sentenced to a lengthy prison term the next year, and other dissidents were dispersed. The political framework for the Four Modernizations would not be democracy but the "four cardinal principles": the leadership of the CPC; the socialist road; the dictatorship of the proletariat; and Marxism-Leninism-Mao Zedong thought. If the public trial of the Gang of Four marked the end of the Cultural Revolution era, then the public trial of Wei Jingsheng symbolized the limitations of openness and reform.

Intellectuals who had supported the Communist Party in the years before 1949, or who had come of age in the 1950s, understood both the possibilities and limitations of this new context. Timothy Cheek has written of an "unwritten social contract" between intellectuals and the state in China, based upon *patriotism*; *patronage*, in relationships with superiors, peers and subordinates; and the *paternalism* of respected elites in a neotraditional political order. Like the scholar officials of old, cadres and intellectuals supportive of the CPC have been willing to surrender individual claims to wealth and power to serve a government they see as fostering a just society and a strong nation.

Their service (here, Cheek draws on the perspective of the philosopher Tu Weiming of Harvard University) is rendered in three overlapping spheres of activity: in "politics and governance" (*zheng*); in "study and learning" (*xue*); and in practicing "the way" (*dao*) of humanistic values and ethical life, including religion.[8] These three areas provide a means for analyzing the effectiveness and quality of leadership in both traditional and modern China. After the end of the Cultural Revolution era, intellectuals needed to publicly reaffirm the social contract. Those who did so could expect to have a degree of influence on the formulation of government policy (*zheng*), and the right to exercise independent initiative in their own particular sphere of activity (*dao* and *xue*). This may be interpreted as the way in which "patriotic" intellectuals came to express responsible participation in a society under the leadership of the CPC.

It was in this period and on these terms that K. H. Ting became undisputed leader of the TSPM and the recognized spokesperson for the Christian movement in China. He began to urge change and reform in church and society without the hesitation and "lingering fears" that beset many others. In his own overlapping spheres of activity, from the restoration of government religious policy to the promotion of religious studies; from the renewal of church structures to the reform of theological education; from attention to social development to the reestablishment of relationships with the international community, Ting became the most important Christian voice for openness and reform. How he came to exercise this leadership in governance (*zheng*), learning (*xue*) and the promotion of humanistic values (*dao*) is what concerns us in this chapter. These terms will appear in parentheses at different points in this and subsequent chapters to indicate the areas in which Ting was exercising leadership.

The emergence of K. H. Ting as China's preeminent Christian leader is not difficult to understand. In a sense, he had been preparing for this role all of his life. Y. T. Wu died after a long illness at the age of eighty-six in September 1979. The other first-generation TSPM leaders who were still living and who had achieved national prominence—Liu Liangmo, Cora Deng, Wu Yifang and Jiang Wenhan—were all in their seventies or eighties. Because of their advanced years and declining health, they would not have been able to lead a revived TSPM or to help form the China Christian Council. New leadership would have to come from the second generation of Three-Self leaders, and there were not many to choose from.

Ting was the obvious candidate for several reasons. He had proven experience in church and society, and he was well connected politically on the national level. Ting was the only TSPM vice-chair from his generation at the Second National Christian Conference in 1961. He returned to public life in 1972, relatively early, and was a recognized spokesperson for the Christian community. He was well known internationally as both an ecumenist and a churchman. Zhou Enlai had seen Ting's potential early on, and he had been impressed by Ting's cosmopolitanism and his knowledge of the situation overseas.

But K. H. Ting was not the only Christian leader with these qualifications. Two others with similar backgrounds were Zhao Fusan and Li Chuwen. Both had also been important Christian spokespersons in the early 1960s, and they were also well connected politically.[9] But Li was not popular with many Christians because of his activism during the Cultural Revolution, when he was also said to have admitted that he was a member of the Communist Party.[10] Li had been at both the First and Second National Christian Conferences, and had been TSPM general secretary, but he was not even listed as a delegate to the Third National Christian Conference in 1980. In 1981, Li Chuwen became the deputy director of the Xin Hua News Agency in Hong Kong, a position he could not have had were he not a member of the CPC and a position in which he wielded considerable political influence.

Zhao Fusan was also involved in government work after the Cultural Revolution, but he continued to be part of the TSPM in Beijing and at the national level.[11] In 1978, Zhao was appointed deputy director of the Chinese Academy of Social Sciences (CASS) and its Institute of World Religions (IWR), and he played an important role in promoting religious studies and international academic exchanges in the 1980s. Zhao Fusan is a brilliant thinker who has taken contradictory positions at different points in his life. According to some sources, he became a CPC member while a student at St. John's University in the 1940s.[12] Given his position at CASS, he must have been a party member, but he has said on more than one occasion that he continued to see himself as an Anglican priest. In the 1960s, Zhao penned crude attacks against Christianity under the pseudonym of Yang Zhen, but in the 1980s, he played a crucial role in promoting a more open view of religious studies. In 1987, he took a stand in favor of the government against "bourgeois liberalization," but in 1989, he opposed the Tiananmen crackdown and now lives in self-imposed exile in the United States.

K. H. Ting had never been as politically active as either Zhao Fusan or Li Chuwen, and he was more closely identified with the church than either one. He was not in the inner circle of TSPM decision making in the 1950s. He came into his positions of leadership as a patriotic intellectual, a perceptive theologian and a cosmopolitan thinker who understood that reform was needed in the church as well as in politics. In the 1980s and 1990s, Ting would rely on friends in the government and the church who had the ability to get things done, and who were committed to work for openness, reform and change. Other voices would be accommodated, and adjustments would need to be made in light of the changing situation. But the order of the day would be reform and renewal, beginning with the restoration of the government's religious policy.

THE RESTORATION OF RELIGIOUS POLICY

Religious life in China had been devastated during the Cultural Revolution era, and even in the late 1970s, there were very few public expressions of faith or sites for worship in most Chinese cities. From a political point of view, before there could be public worship and a reopening of churches, temples and mosques, there would have to be a restoration of the policy of the freedom of religious belief at least to the level of the mid-1950s.

In China, the freedom of religious belief has been seen as the freedom of an individual to believe what he or she wants to believe and to take part in "normal" religious activities as part of a recognized religious community. But belief is circumscribed by social and political considerations. An individual has the right to believe or not believe in religion, to change religious affiliation, and to express his or her faith openly. Religious communities have the right to organize services for worship, train clergy and perform other religious functions without interference from the state. There are vast areas of ambiguity in this understanding, for, unlike the West, the freedom of religious belief has not been undergirded by a strong legal system. This means that there is always a process of dialogue and negotiation in the implementation of religious policy.

Most scholars agree that in the late 1970s the Chinese government began to liberalize religious policy, a conclusion that is supported by available documentary evidence.[13] Chinese sources do not speak of "liberalization," but of a return to the "correct" policy that had been rejected by the Gang of Four, which amounts to more or less the same thing. I use the term "restoration" to describe the phenomenon and cover both meanings. A full discussion of the restoration of religious policy is beyond the scope of this study.[14] Instead, my discussion will be limited to an exploration of K. H. Ting's role in the process of restoration. He was by no means the only religious person who was promoting a more open religious policy, but Ting and his friend Zhao Puchu (1907-2000) were the most influential religious leaders involved in the process.[15] They were never as influential as senior government officials working on religious affairs, but Ting and Zhao Puchu had the power and prestige to exert considerable influence on the formulation of religious policy.

The restoration and reimplementation of religious policy reflected the new openness and reform in society as a whole. Religious policy was not as important to Chinese leaders as political reform or economic development, but to the extent that it was related to questions about intellectual freedom, cultural policy, public order and international relations, it was a significant consideration. The development of religious policy after 1978 was inconsistent, for there was a "tightening up" (*shou*) and a "letting go" (*fang*) at different times. Moreover, there would be continuing problems with policy implementation at the local level, as well as intermittent persecution in different parts of the country, as local officials, particularly those in the Public Security Bureau, took matters into their own hands. Bearing all of this in mind, the restoration of religious policy after 1978 created the conditions for an unprecedented revival of religious life all over China.

The first real hint that there might be a change in the offing came with the convening of the Fifth Chinese People's Political Consultative Conference (CPPCC) in February 1978. The last meeting of this body had been in 1964, and the fact that it began functioning again signaled a subtle shift in the official attitude toward the united front and non-party leaders, including those from religious circles. The previous month, Ting had been elected a vice-chairperson of the Jiangsu People's Political Consultative Conference (JPPCC). He was now among sixteen representatives from religious circles in the CPPCC, including Luo Guanzong, Liu Liangmo and Wu Yifang from the Christian community, and he was elected to the standing committee. At a second meeting of the CPPCC a few months later, a religion group was set up to solicit the opinions of religious leaders and help "bring order out of chaos."

Chinese delegation at WCRP III, Washington, D.C., 1979. From left to right: Chen Zemin, K. H. Ting, Yang Pinsan, Zhao Puchu, Li Shoubao, Li Rongxi, Ming Yang, Ma Xian and Han Wenzao. Photograph taken by the author.

K. H. Ting was also one of the thirty-four religious delegates to the Fifth National People's Congress, which also met in February and March 1978. This meeting approved another new constitution, one more oriented to economic development, but the clause on religious freedom was identical to the 1975 version. The inclusion of the clause "the freedom not to believe in religion and to propagate atheism" in both the 1975 and 1978 constitutions was discriminatory and unacceptable to religious delegates. No other constitutional freedom was qualified by its opposite. Why guarantee the freedom to propagate atheism when the state would do this anyway? The religious delegates could do no more than express their dissatisfaction, but they were already working to change the offensive wording, and within a year, K. H. Ting was voicing his criticisms publicly and in government meetings.[16]

He did this in part through the official organizational channels open to him, and in part through the publication of his remarks, which helped shape opinion, particularly in the Christian community. The CPPCC and the NPC generally meet one after the other, the former as a consultative body and the latter as theoretically "the highest organ of state power."[17] Although real power was in the hands of the Communist Party, the CPPCC and the NPC

have served as important indices of public opinion after the Cultural Revolution era, and the NPC does help shape policy decisions. The participation
of leaders from religious circles in these two bodies became a way in which
they expressed their views, exercised political leadership (*zheng*), and cau-
cused with other religious leaders and government officials.

The state and party offices concerned with religious affairs, notably the
RAB and the United Front Work Department (UFWD), had to be reorganized before there could be a restoration of national religious organizations
and religious institutions.[18] The UFWD held a meeting in October 1978 to
discuss religious work. It proposed at this meeting a "thorough implementation" of the constitutional provision for the freedom of religious belief in
order to gain the active participation of religious believers in support of the
Four Modernizations and put an end to underground religious activity.[19] In
December, just before the Third CPC Plenum, the Eighth National Conference on Religious Work was held in Beijing, the first such meeting since
1962.[20] It proposed overturning all the decisions made on religious work in
1964 and 1965, the restoration of the RAB and patriotic religious organizations at all levels, and the reimplementation of the policy of religious freedom.[21] Xiao Xianfa, who had become RAB director before the start of the
Cultural Revolution and who was viewed by many religious leaders as ultra-
leftist, presided at this meeting.

Even though there were no major references to religious issues in its
report, the Third Plenum made possible the more sweeping changes in religious policy that were to come. K. H. Ting referred to the significance of the
Third Plenum again and again in his speeches and writings at the time. It
became a convenient marker for speaking about the real beginning of the
new period of reform. In February 1979, the RAB was revived by the State
Council. In time, it would assume functions consistent with the new political direction, including the rehabilitation of religious leaders, the restoration of national religious organizations and continuing oversight of religious
organizations. The RAB had been operating at a reduced level since 1972,
mainly in connection with looking after the few churches, temples and
mosques that were opened for foreigners. Now, it would oversee the resumption of religious activities that were designed to unite people in religious circles, promote the Four Modernizations and encourage friendly relations with
religious groups overseas. The UFWD was also revived in 1979, and the
"revisionist" and "capitulationist" labels that had been attached to it were
removed. The united front would again set the terms for Chinese religious
policy, and the RAB and UFWD were supposed to ensure that this would be
consistent with government policy and not disturb the social order.

Religious life had already begun to be revived in many major cities, especially along the east coast. In some rural areas, folk religious practices and
Christian home worship gatherings that had never entirely disappeared
became more public. Churches and other places of worship were returned
and renovated; clergy were rehabilitated, and religious institutions tenta-

tively resumed some former activities. Young people especially were curious about religion. Their interest in religion was discouraged, but nonetheless tolerated, by the government. In interpreting religious freedom to the reading public, many of the early policy statements drew the distinction between organized religion, which was acceptable, and "feudal superstition," which was not.[22] This was given a theoretical foundation using the arcane language of the Marxist understanding of religion that was of no interest to most people drawn to religious practices in the first place.

There were more direct ways of reassuring religious leaders that times had changed. At national meetings of the CPPCC and NPC in June 1978, both Hua Guofeng and Deng Xiaoping made brief references to the policy of religious freedom and the contribution of religious leaders in their speeches. K. H. Ting was among those whom the press cited as being delighted with Deng's statement to the CPPCC that "religious persons had made considerable progress." The reconstituted RAB invited K. H. Ting and other religious delegates attending the meetings of the CPPCC and NPC for a discussion in a further attempt to assure them that the freedom of religious belief was a "long-term and fundamental policy" of the government and the CPC. The Communist Party was not the Gang of Four, they were told, and the errors of the past would be corrected.[23] In return, religious leaders were asked to support the policies of reform and openness, which were in their interests in any case.

Over the next months, the government attempted to make good on its promises, and publicized policies on religious freedom at home and abroad. On 17 October, *Renmin ribao (People's Daily)*, the official CPC newspaper, published a lengthy editorial, "Fully Implement the Policy of Religious Freedom."[24] This was the most complete statement on religious freedom thus far, and it was widely cited by Chinese Christians as evidence of how far things had come since the time of the Gang of Four. Certainly the tone of policy discourse had changed, and this, they believed, would continue to help improve the situation for religious believers.

In concrete terms, the "reimplementation of religious policy" meant several things: the rehabilitation of those wrongly accused since 1957; the return of buildings and properties; the resumption of worship activities; the reorganization of patriotic religious bodies; the training of new leaders; the publication of religious materials; and exchanges with religious groups overseas. The pace of change in religious policy was slower than in other areas of Chinese life that were deemed more important for political and economic reconstruction.[25] For example, the RAB did not issue its report on the return of properties until July 1980, well after the process had begun.[26] It was always easier and safer for local officials involved with religious work to "hasten slowly," delay action and postpone decisions, practices that Chinese bureaucrats had relied on for centuries. Policy implementation was often heavy-handed. Especially in remote rural areas, local officials were used to giving orders that they expected to be obeyed. When they were not obeyed, they took matters into their own hands or called in the Public Security Bureau.

A major problem with religious policy implementation was the artificial distinction between "normal" and "abnormal" religious practices. This was more than a problem of semantics, for it had to do with the government concern for maintaining social order. The government was concerned that the "underground" religious activity that had developed during the Cultural Revolution could become disruptive or subject to the manipulation of "anti-China" forces.[27] Part of the rationale for the new openness in religious policy was to bring groups that had been driven underground out into the open. But many religious believers still had "lingering fears" and did not trust government assurances. For Protestant Christians, this was related to the acceptability of informal "home-worship gatherings" by both the state and the TSPM.

Both the slow pace of policy implementation and the heavy-handedness of officials concerned K. H. Ting, but in these years, he was even more interested in defending the rights of Christians who worshiped in their homes. In his understanding, this was normal religious activity. His words in their defense even appeared on the front page of *Renmin ribao* (*People's Daily*) in September 1980:

> There are great obstructions to implementing religious policy. During the "Cultural Revolution" all Christian churches were closed down, and few are now open. The great majority of believers now hold worship services in their homes. We cannot let Christians who take part in home gatherings be labeled as a group apart. As one of the leaders of the TSPM, I cannot bring myself to say that they are illegal. In interpreting the constitution, we cannot say that there is religious freedom in church buildings but not in homes.[28]

The publication of these words on page one of *People's Daily* came just at the time that Protestant Christians were preparing for their Third National Christian Conference, their first national gathering since the end of the Cultural Revolution. Ting wanted to expand the limits of "acceptable" religious activity. His defense of home-worship gatherings was a demonstration of "mutual respect" for the sake of unity. In negotiation and dialogue with government officials at the highest levels (*zheng*), K. H. Ting was not only creating more space for religious freedom but also contributing to the renewal of the church (*dao*).

Xiao Xianfa was head of the RAB and an important official with whom Ting had to negotiate. Xiao had denounced UFWD head Li Weihan for his "capitulationist" views on religion in the early 1960s, and he did not have a particularly open view of religious policy. In 1980, he authored a long editorial clarifying the policy of religious freedom, in which he said that it was the state's responsibility to "manage (or supervise) religious activities."[29] That the state had a role in the supervision of religious affairs was understood all along, but the relationship between the RAB's "management" and the religious organizations' own role had been a continuing source of tension.

Ting believed it was necessary to challenge Xiao's interpretation. "If it is the state's responsibility to manage religious activities, then what is there for the religious bodies themselves to manage?" he asked rhetorically. Ting said he would not assume leadership of the two national Christian bodies under such conditions, but Xiao would not retract what he had written. Joined by Zhao Fusan and other Christian leaders, Ting went to Beijing, where he saw Peng Chong, the former Jiangsu party secretary and now the member of the CPC Central Committee who was responsible for religious affairs. Peng had been Ting's friend when they were both working in Nanjing, and he supported Ting's position that religious organizations should manage their own affairs. This trumped Xiao Xianfa. With the matter decided in his favor, Ting agreed to become head of the TSPM and the CCC.[30] This story provides an illustration of how Ting used his position to stretch the limits of religious policy through dialogue. The CPC and the state still had the power to control religious policy. But Ting was not willing to accept whatever the government said. Although he did not change Xiao's mind, in this case, he had achieved a symbolic victory.

Many statements and articles on the restoration of religious freedom were published after the Third Plenum, but the most significant of these by far was the 1982 directive entitled "The Basic Viewpoint and Policy on the Religious Question during Our Country's Socialist Period," issued by the CPC Central Committee on 31 March 1982.[31] This lengthy statement, known as Document 19 (because it was the nineteenth document issued by the Central Committee in 1982), was the most thorough exposition of government religious policy that had ever been published. Document 19 takes its point of departure from the resolution on CPC history that had been adopted the previous year.[32] That resolution was written in order to explain the Cultural Revolution and the ultra-leftist mistakes of the past, and a statement on religion was now needed to provide a realistic reassessment of the current situation with guidelines for policy makers. Document 19 presents a united-front approach to religious matters appropriate to the era of reform and openness. While adhering to a moderate interpretation of the Marxist-Leninist theory of religion and insisting on the need to maintain control, the document provides a generally tolerant and flexible understanding of religious belief. Significantly, it has no mention of religion as "opium"; it rejects the forced suppression of religion, and it explicitly states that religious belief will continue to exist under socialism for a very long time.

All of this was unprecedented for an official statement on religion by the CPC. Its significance was not lost on K. H. Ting. By virtue of his standing in the NPC and CPPCC, he would have been asked to comment on earlier drafts of the document. Once it was issued, Ting became enthusiastic in his response and used its publication to urge further work on problems that remained. He promoted the study of the document within the church and the seminary, and he spoke of its significance for religious policy with foreign visitors and on trips abroad. He even lectured government officials about the importance of Document 19. His remarks to them were published under the name Ru Wen so that those who saw him only as a church leader would not be confused or put off by the fact that he was speaking in a social-scientific language to government cadres.[33]

In contrast to previous statements and ultra-leftist theories of religion, Document 19 does not begin with concepts and definitions, but with "facts" and "practice," two key words in the reformist lexicon. Religion is not something to be feared or rejected as an opiate, nor is it a reactionary remnant of the past. Rather, religious belief should be accepted as a fact of history and culture. It is recognized that religion has a mass base, that it is related to the culture of ethnic minorities, that it has international connections, and that it will exist over the long term as a complex reality.[34] Religious policy must therefore be flexible and adaptable enough to accommodate the needs of believers. This was Ting's understanding of Document 19, and the reason why he was enthusiastic in his support.

For the next twenty years, Document 19 functioned almost as a *textus receptus* for religious policy formulation in China. It was not without internal contradictions, but it was far better than what had come before. Ting called attention to the need for improvement in the relationship between the government and religious bodies, and he gave specific examples of areas where improvement was needed. For Christians, the most serious problem was the distinction made between "normal" and unacceptable worship activities, and this is again related to the legitimacy of Protestant home-worship gatherings. In the very same paragraph of Document 19, religious activities in believers' homes were both sanctioned and "disallowed in principle."[35]

In the original version of his remarks to government officials, K. H. Ting levels his strongest criticisms at this point. It is interesting to note that a half page of text is omitted from the versions published later, perhaps because of their specific and timely nature, or perhaps because these remarks were deemed too controversial.[36] For the TSPM and the CCC in the early 1980s, the relationship between home-worship gatherings and newly opened churches was an especially divisive issue. Home-worship gatherings—sometimes called house churches—were seen by many government officials as beyond their institutional control and potentially disruptive. Ting supported the Christian home meetings, even though he may have shared some of the officials' concerns.

By providing a political and theoretical basis for greater tolerance and flexibility in religious policy, Document 19 paved the way for the revision of the clause on religion in the constitution a year later. The 1982 Constitution was different from earlier versions in many ways, and it reflects the new emphases in Deng Xiaoping's reforms. Article 36 eliminated the offensive phrase on the freedom to propagate atheism but added several new clauses to qualify what the freedom of religion does and does not mean.[37] K. H. Ting and other religious leaders had worked long and hard in drafting the constitution. They contributed to a two-year process of "democratic consultation," much of which involved the tedious writing and reading of letters and reports. In the end, K. H. Ting felt that they had done the best they could.[38]

The adoption of the 1982 Constitution was a significant breakthrough that marks the end of the first phase of the reform era and the completion of the restoration of the policy of religious freedom. Ting would continue to be involved in efforts for advocacy and reform after this, and, as we shall see in the next chapter, the pace of change would both wax and wane with developments in the rest of society. Over the next twenty years, he would be consulted about or involved in the drafting of dozens of laws, regulations and policy decisions.[39] He was not always successful in pressing for more religious freedom, but his participation in the political process (*zheng*) gave Christians an important voice on religious policy, reflecting and reinforcing his standing as the leader of the two national Christian bodies (*dao*).

K. H. Ting never saw his support for CPC religious policy as a way of establishing a *modus vivendi* for Christians in a totalitarian society, as some earlier studies claimed.[40] Like other intellectuals of his generation, he welcomed the changes after the fall of the Gang of Four, and he helped to promote them. His participation in national life was an expression of his patriotism. This gave him a standing in society, but it also helped him work the system. He would make use of the freedom he already had in order to push it further, realizing all the time there were limits to what could be accomplished. His was a refined "politicized loyalty,"[41] one that could be creatively reinterpreted, again and again. Ting was part of Deng Xiaoping's political establishment when speaking about Chinese policy to foreign visitors, but a member of the loyal opposition when criticizing the 1978 Constitution or pressuring the RAB. It all depended on a realistic assessment of what was required in the situation. Principles were important, but principles always needed to be flexibly applied.

Ting was not a liberal democrat in his views on governance. He is better understood as a responsible participant in the united front as it was reconstituted after the Cultural Revolution era, a loyalist with a deeply rooted sense of integrity who had rejected ultra-leftism, including his own leftist past. He was committed to a more open social process and thus a more open religious policy, but he supported the leading role of the CPC. He was neither a liberal, as that term is usually understood, nor a supporter of dissidents. I remember very clearly the time he presented me with a copy of Zhou Enlai's writings on the united front, with all the passages on religion clearly marked in red. "You might be interested in reading this," K. H. Ting said, "because it has helped me understand how to work as a Christian in China."[42] This meant that his position would be close to those in power who were working for a faster pace of political change, such as Hu Yaobang, Zhao Ziyang and their allies, all of whom favored a more open religious policy.[43]

The reformist position, on religion or any other policy, necessitated a continuing and deepening critique of ultra-leftism.[44] The ideological debates of the early 1980s pitted party reformers advocating "humanism" against the old-fashioned ideologues and entrenched bureaucrats. The humanists rejected the cruel struggles that had been part of Chinese politics since the late 1950s in favor of policies encouraging human initiative and individual creativity. Humanist values were promoted by writers, artists and intellectuals against the dogmatism of unreconstructed theory. For them, practice and the problems of real existing society were to take priority over an abstract theory of religion that emphasized the stages of historical development under socialism.

> The major question of today is not that people have expectations of socialism which are too high and not in accord with reality; it is rather that bureaucrats have given inadequate thought to many questions which are timely, resolvable and related to the personal well-being of the masses . . . They have overlooked questions of human value.[45]

In this debate, K. H. Ting's sympathies were firmly on the side of the humanists, many of whom were personal friends. Ting's critique of ultra-leftism was in part a self-critique, based on his remembrance of the Anti-Rightist movement and his support for the Cultural Revolution in its early years. Now the critique was very concretely related to the reform process and the restoration of religious policy. He criticized ultra-leftists for proceeding on the basis of definitions, not practice. They were impatient for change. Ting was fond of saying that "the leftist wants for today what he or she cannot have until tomorrow." Their cause could also be opportunistic, for in the China of the 1960s and 1970s, it was always better to be "left" than "right" in the furtherance of one's career. Ultra-leftism translated into a simplistic or even crude approach to politics and religion. The ultra-leftist lacked mutual respect, good manners and concern for human values, and so was prone to error, arrogance and the use of force.

In contrast to the ossified scientific theories of the party dogmatists, K. H. Ting began looking at an approach to Marxism that was ethicized and "daoified" (*dao*) in its encounter with Chinese culture.

> Daoism as a religion is now pretty weak but it has been formative of the Chinese culture and is the marrow of many a Chinese practical philosophy. *Wu Wei,* to do nothing, can be an attitude of resignation to fate, but *wu wei er zhi,* to achieve good governance by not doing unnecessary or untimely things is aimed at positive results. It is in the best Maoist tradition to let many things take their own courses and not to interfere unless really necessary. The united front which survives on

stressing common points and preserving differences is a good example of the Taoist *wu wei* spirit. Totalitarianism is certainly not Maoist. It is ultra-leftism in action.[46]

Ting is drawing on the humanist tradition of Communists whom he admired, people such as Zhou Enlai, Chen Yi, Kuang Yaming, Luo Zhufeng and others who have been mentioned in this study. His viewpoint may be faulted for its idealist interpretation of Chinese Communism, but it reflected an important aspect of the debate of the times.[47] There were many in China who believed that a humanized or ethicized interpretation of Marxism could guide the reforms, and there are some who still believe that this is needed.[48] Although the prospects for a reform-oriented Marxist humanism faded after 1989, the critique of ultra-leftism continued, especially in the economic realm. In the early 1980s, an interest in Marxist humanism and ethics spurred developments in other areas, including a new approach to religious studies, an area in which K. H. Ting made a very important and direct contribution.

THE REBIRTH OF RELIGIOUS STUDIES

Religious studies emerged in China in the late 1970s, not as an area of disinterested academic inquiry but because it was relevant to reform and openness in general, and to religious policy questions in particular. K. H. Ting's interest in religious studies was based on the same considerations. It was only later that he came to see that the social-scientific study of religion might also contribute to theological education, but in early years after the fall of the Gang of Four, there was not yet the possibility of reopening Nanjing Seminary.

In 1978, the Institute of World Religions (IWR) of the Chinese Academy of Social Sciences reopened in Beijing and accepted twenty-two postgraduate students in a variety of areas of specialization, including the study of religion in contemporary society, theoretical studies of religion and the historical study of Chinese religious traditions.[49] The director of the IWR was Ren Jiyu, an authority on Chinese Buddhism and Daoism who had started the IWR in the early 1960s at the explicit request of Chairman Mao. In 1978, Ren's deputy director was Zhao Fusan. Their working relationship was by all accounts not a happy one, for they represented different, or even contradictory, approaches to the study of religion. Ren was a Marxist-Leninist traditionalist who studied religion in order to criticize it. Zhao Fusan, who was closely connected to the church, was to become the leading exponent of a reformist view of religion and religious studies in the early and mid-1980s.

Shortly after the establishment of the IWR, Zhao and several colleagues went to Nanjing to meet with K. H. Ting about the possibility of establishing a second religious research institution at Nanjing University. Ting took them to see his friend Kuang Yaming, who was known to have a long-standing interest in religious and philosophical questions. Kuang had developed an appreciation for Christian ideas and the work of the YMCA in the 1940s. Kuang was a broad-minded humanitarian and a high-ranking cadre in Jiangsu Province, who had only recently reassumed the presidency of Nanjing University, having been disgraced at the start of the Cultural Revolution. He was immediately enthusiastic about the project to start a religious studies center at Nanjing University, and he spoke about the possibility of establishing a very large institute with a hundred or more researchers.[50] Kuang was firmly in the reformist camp, and he saw a new religious studies center as contributing to the changes China needed.

Within a few months, Kuang Yaming authorized the establishment of the Institute for Religious Studies (IRS) at Nanjing University, and he appointed K. H. Ting as its director and a university vice-president. Members of the former seminary faculty became the teachers, researchers and writers of the IRS, and it was located in the compound of Nanjing Union Theological Seminary. The IRS formally opened on 1 January 1979, which, coincidentally, was the same day that China and the United States resumed normal diplomatic relations.

The seminary compound had still not been returned, and the new institute was able to use only one of its buildings, the old house to the west of the main teaching building. The seminary had been the headquarters of a group of "Red Guards" during the Cultural Revolution, and when they left, the buildings were used as a hostel to accommodate the many people who were conducting traveling investigations during those years. It was subsequently occupied by the Bureau of Agriculture and Forestry, which still had control of the seminary buildings in 1979. As part of the restoration of religious policy, and pressure from Ting and others in the Jiangsu People's Political Consultative Conference, the buildings were finally returned to the seminary. Ting had given a speech in the JPPCC on the urgency of the need to return the seminary compound, and some had joked that he was preaching a sermon. But he also relied on his friendship with Xu Jiatun, who was then the Jiangsu party secretary, to help make his case.[51] Close personal friendships with people like Kuang and Xu and Peng Chong helped Ting a great deal in getting things done in these years. Such relationships were part of the dialogue he maintained with senior government officials, as a way of fulfilling his responsibilities for governance (*zheng*).

In March, Kuang Yaming visited the newly opened IRS with other university leaders. He had become well known in Christian circles for his view that a "true" Christian and a "true" Communist both seek to "serve the people" in their own ways. This showed that he had a sympathetic view of Christian faith. Kuang later wrote that a thoroughgoing Marxist materialist (like himself) should have nothing to fear from religious believers, for although they maintained different worldviews, they should be able to discuss them openly and work for the same political goals.[52] In Beijing, Ren Jiyu was saying that religious believers could not have an "objective" view of religion and religious studies. In contrast, Kuang Yaming had appointed K. H. Ting, a religious believer, to be the head of an institute to study religion at his university.[53] It was unusual, particularly in those days, for a high-ranking Communist to be so outspoken in his support for religion and religious studies. Although Kuang's vision of a very large center for religious studies at Nanjing University was never realized, his support contributed to the reforms then underway.

The reinterpretation of religion was related to the implementation of religious policy, to all areas of study in the social sciences and the humanities, and to China's policy of openness to the outside world. By virtue of his leadership of a university institute for the study of religion, Ting and his faculty came to be recognized as religious scholars as well as Christian believers in the academic world. K. H. Ting's first published essay after the end of the Cultural Revolution may have been the text of the short talk he gave to tour guides who were being trained to better understand the culture and beliefs of the tour groups coming from Western countries.[54] In it, he offers a "fact"-oriented exposition of Christian faith, history and contemporary realities for people with practically no background in religion. This was a very different viewpoint than what the guides would have received from Ren Jiyu.

But there were much deeper levels of interpretation as well. A new Association for Religious Studies was founded at a conference in Kunming in February 1979. The IWR had convened a national planning meeting on religious studies the year before, and the Kunming conference was a step toward developing a more systematic approach to religious research in the country as a whole. Ren Jiyu was named honorary president of the Association for Religious Studies, but Zhao Puchu was made president and K. H. Ting became vice-chair of the executive committee.[55] At the Kunming conference, Ting presented a lecture on liberation theology in order to demonstrate to a mostly scholarly audience that religion and theology did not have to function as an opiate in society.[56] The whole subject of religion as opium was to be an important point in the debate on religious studies that was just beginning.

The atmosphere for religious studies was still quite restrictive, and the official line was articulated by Ren Jiyu. He saw religion as different from "feudal superstition" (the popular beliefs of uneducated masses), but it was still a backward and unscientific approach to reality. He had written that religion was opposed to civilization, culture and science, and was an obstacle to modernization. The Gang of Four had turned Marxism into a quasi religion, and like all religions, this resulted in the construction of "lifeless dogmas."[57] For Ren Jiyu, a liberation of thinking was needed that only Marxism could provide; religion was, in essence, an opiate, and therefore reactionary in function. More research was needed—this was the purpose of the IWR—in order to advance the religious critique and in time eliminate the need for religion altogether.

K. H. Ting rejected Ren Jiyu's understanding of religion, and particularly his view that the Gang of Four had made Marxism into a quasi religion. If this were the case, he argued, if religious belief and Cultural Revolution dogmatism represented the same social phenomenon, then there could be no basis for real religious freedom in China. Religion, according to Ting, was not necessarily opposed to civilization and culture, because it functioned differently under different social conditions. Religious studies could not have its a priori purpose in the critique of theology and religion. No study could begin with abstract definitions; on the contrary, concrete research and hard "facts" are needed to understand religious phenomena and religious practice. Ethics may provide a meeting point between religion and culture, both in traditional Chinese civilization and in Ting's view of Marxism.[58] A humanistic or ethical approach to religious studies—something that Ren rejected as impossible—would begin with China's socialist context and could become a new basis for understanding the compatibility between religion and reform. Religious studies in Ting's understanding could contribute to civilization, and religion should be seen as a legitimate part of culture.

Ting and his Nanjing colleagues expressed their ideas in the public forum and in a series of meetings and conferences, where a lively debate was emerging. Other allies included Luo Zhufeng, the senior government cadre from Shanghai who had defended Ting during the Cultural Revolution and whom Ting regarded as "the leading spirit" behind the new approach to religion.[59] Zhao Puchu and Xiao Zhitian, a friend of K. H. Ting since the 1940s and now affiliated with the Shanghai Academy of Social Sciences, and many other scholars and religious leaders were also involved in the reform efforts. This was a Christian-Marxist dialogue, with Christians and Marxists on both sides. The debate was not about being for or against religion, but was part of the larger struggle for reform against ultra-leftism in the particular area of religious studies. Similar debates were underway in almost all sectors of the academic world in the early 1980s.

Religion (*Zongjiao*), the journal of the IRS, which Ting directed, became a key forum in the debate representing the reformist view.[60] The journal was read by cadres involved in religious work as well as by academics and theologians. Zhao Puchu provided the calligraphy for the masthead, and essays by the scholars mentioned in the previous paragraph, plus the faculty and staff of Nanjing Seminary, were prominently featured. They advocated change and reform within the Chinese socialist context, not the exploration of issues or ideas from alternative theological or religious viewpoints. Ting's approach to the reform of religious studies in China was separate from his work on theology. We shall see that China's churches and seminaries were not open, at least at first, to an academic approach to religion because of their conservative theological views. There has been little interaction between theology and religious studies in China until quite recently.

The debate over the nature of religion was a civil war, a struggle conducted in a civil manner. It was debate over "mixed accents" (*nanqiang bei-*

diao), pitting the north (Beijing's IWR) against the south (Nanjing and Shanghai). It was also known as the "Third Opium War" because Ting and those in his camp were pressing for a rejection of the idea of religion as opium. Religion, Ting argued, may play the role of an opiate in society, but it had other possible functions as well. Religion had served as the ideology for peasant rebellions and as an inspiration for bourgeois democratic revolutions. "It is a sign of theoretical immaturity," he continued, "and political naivety to equate religious theism to political reaction, or to equate materialism and atheism to political progressiveness."[61] Opium was an insufficient definition of religion, the reformists argued. In an early issue of *Religion*, there is a compilation of statements by Marx, Engels, Lenin, Stalin, Mao Zedong and Zhou Enlai on religion that nuance the ways that Communist leaders understood the subject and puts their understandings of religion into a broader context.[62] Another early essay cites ten instances in which religion was described as an opiate before 1843-1844, when Marx first used the phrase "religion as the opiate of the people."[63] This simple listing showed that "opium" could not be the essence of the Marxist definition of religion, because it was not even original to Marx.

By 1985, Zhao Fusan was able to make the case for a more open approach to religious studies from the floor of the CPPCC. Religion is an integral part of every civilization, he argued, and should be studied in an open-minded way. "The view that religion is entirely a spiritual opium is unscientific and incomplete," he said.[64] Zhao received a standing ovation for his speech, and the members of the CPPCC religion subgroup were elated. The reformists had won the Third Opium War. By this time, Ren Jiyu had already retired as director of the IWR, although he continued to write and express his views, and new avenues for religious research were being explored in social-scientific institutes and the universities.

The successful conclusion of the Third Opium War was a breakthrough for religious studies, which together with the restoration of religious policy contributed to the renewal of the church and theological education. There would be other struggles for religious studies, but a new beginning had been made. K. H. Ting had expended an enormous amount of time and energy on political (*zheng*) and academic (*xue*) matters, but, except for this early work, his efforts for the renewal of the church (*dao*) would not have been possible.

THE RENEWAL OF CHURCH LIFE

The renewal of Christianity in China had begun during the Cultural Revolution era when Christians began meeting quietly for prayer or worship in their homes. After 1972, the year that K. H. Ting returned to public life, the relaxation of the political climate resulted in the growth of these home-worship gatherings, especially in the coastal provinces.[65] By the late 1970s, even before the restoration of religious policy, the number of Christian home

meetings had increased dramatically. These new or revived Christian communities were unplanned lay initiatives, in which women played a major
role. They represented a movement of renewal *from below* among mostly
uneducated people with little pastoral leadership or even access to the
Bible.[66] Many reports from foreign visitors and Chinese Christians were testimonies to the faith of Christians who believed in a religion of pure grace,
often unencumbered by formal teachings, theologies and doctrines.[67] They
were also prone to heresies or sectarian beliefs. K. H. Ting had been right
when he spoke about the deinstitutionalization of the church in China after
the fall of the Gang of Four, although the Christian revival was not at all as
he imagined it would be.

The restoration of religious policy and the reorganization of the TSPM in
the late 1970s was a response to Deng Xiaoping's call "to bring order out
of chaos" on the part of a Christian leadership committed to the reform and
reconstruction of church institutions. This was a movement of renewal *from
above* that sought to relate the Christian revival at the grassroots to the
structures of governance and the authority of the church in society. Through
the TSPM, Christians could press for the improved implementation of religious policy, the rehabilitation of pastors and other Christians, the return of
church properties, the printing of Bibles, the training of new leaders, and
the reopening of theological seminaries.

The reestablishment of the TSPM was also a means of social control, and
there were many who saw this as its primary function. But the TSPM in the
early 1980s was not the same as it had been in the 1950s and early 1960s.
The top leadership was different, and there would be established alongside
the TSPM an institution that would be devoted to church affairs. The government wanted to curb underground religious activity and to put a stop to
foreign infiltration, and the best way to do this was to allow for legal and
above-ground religious activity run by Christians themselves. The hope was
that this might encourage the active participation of the Christian community in the new modernization program and create the conditions for unity
and stability. This was not a Machiavellian scheme designed to suppress
authentic evangelical faith, as some TSPM critics maintained.[68] K. H. Ting
and other TSPM leaders indeed supported government efforts aimed at
ensuring political stability and modernization, but, in addition, they hoped
to encourage the reconstruction and renewal of a church that was well
grounded in Christian doctrine, nonsectarian, active in society and unified.
For Ting and other leaders, rural Christianity was too much a reflection of
the millenarian traditions of Chinese folk religion and the fundamentalist
Christian sects that had begun earlier in the twentieth century.

The TSPM was an urban-based movement, but it sought to include rural
Christian communities as part of its constituency. Urban churches began to
reopen in the spring of 1979, beginning with the Centenary Church (*Bainian
Tang*) in the coastal city of Ningbo, and followed by churches in Guangzhou,
Shanghai and other cities. Some provincial and local TSPM committees

began to be reorganized early that summer, largely drawing on people who had led these organizations in the past. By Christmas, newly reopened churches and TSPM committees could be found in almost a dozen cities. On 25 January 1980, the CPC Central Committee authorized the reorganization of national religious organizations.[69] Protestants, Catholics, Muslims, Daoists and Buddhists all held their first national meetings since the 1960s, beginning with the Protestants who met in an Enlarged TSPM Committee just one month later.[70] This was a hastily called ad hoc meeting of those who had been elected TSPM committee members at the Second National Christian Conference in 1961 and who could be contacted at short notice. K. H. Ting delivered the opening address at the meeting, and in the first issue of the revived *Tian Feng* magazine, he is referred to as "acting chairperson."[71] He was the only vice-chair of his generation from the Second National Christian Conference, and by this time it was already assumed that he would become head of the TSPM, despite the fact that he had not yet sorted out all his difficulties with Xiao Xianfa, as mentioned above.

The discussion in the six-day meeting focused on what the TSPM should do in this new period. Ting was primarily concerned with building up the church, expanding its unity and maintaining the Three-Self principle, as he explained in essay after essay written during this time.[72] He realized that many Christians saw the TSPM as an organization interested in control. For this and other reasons, he believed that another national Christian organization was needed. The TSPM had taken over many of the functions of the church since the closing down of the denominations in the late 1950s, often by default, because no other structure existed. Some "activist" Three-Self leaders had alienated a great number of Christians, not only after the Anti-Rightist movement, but since the early 1950s. Merely to revive the TSPM Committee would do little to win them back. Ting had been speaking out on the right of Christians to worship in their homes, and he wanted to find a way to include them in the broader Christian movement.

It is unlikely that all of the Shanghai leaders saw things the same way. Li Chuwen was no longer part of the TSPM, but Ting still had to contend with some of those who had been activists since the 1950s. There were problems on other fronts as well. Not all government and party leaders concerned with religious affairs were committed to reform. There were also fundamentalist Christians, including Wang Mingdao, released from prison in January 1979, who would have nothing to do with K. H. Ting or the TSPM, no matter what they were promised. Christians dissatisfied with the TSPM were in touch with overseas groups involved in "Bible smuggling" and "underground" missionary work in China. Ting had to navigate his way around the different parties in the church as well as the government, and to better understand what was happening overseas. It was a new day in China, but the test of his leadership was just beginning.

At the Shanghai meeting, Ting introduced his idea for a new national church-affairs organization alongside the TSPM. It would strengthen the pastoral work of local Christian communities and practice the principle of mutual respect in matters of faith, but it would not be a "super church" or a council of churches. Although there were problems with the TSPM as an organization, Ting was unwavering in his support for the Three-Self principle and the patriotic stance of Christians. The new church-affairs organization would complement the work of the TSPM, not replace it. In contrast to the TSPM, it would concern itself with how the church should be run, be financially supported and do the work of evangelism.[73] Here we already see the beginnings of what Ting termed a movement from Three-Self to "Three Wells" in the life of the church that he would further develop at the Third National Christian Conference (NCC) seven months later.[74]

Ting drafted the open letter that was sent to Christians all over China in early March, which announced the Third NCC and emphasized the need for a church-affairs organization.[75] The Shanghai preparatory meeting made two other important decisions. One was to reprint the Bible and hymnals and resume publication of the church magazine *Tian Feng*. The other was to reopen Nanjing Union Theological Seminary and start a training program for pastoral workers. There was also discussion of plans to begin another translation of the 1919 Union version of the Bible, although nothing was decided. Ting and other church leaders believed that this would make the Bible more accessible to Christians and other potential readers.[76] Everyone at the Shanghai meeting was given a Bible from among the several hundred that had been stored at the TSPM headquarters for safekeeping at the start of the Cultural Revolution. This was the first Bible that many had handled since the Cultural Revolution, and they were deeply moved.

The only government official present in Shanghai was Zhang Zhiyi, Ting's old friend from the UFWD and the deputy director who looked after relationships with religions. Xiao Xianfa did not attend, but, according to Ting, he said that Christians needed to decide what to do on their own.[77] Xiao apparently said this, although he wrote just a few months later that it was primarily the government that should manage religious affairs. Zhang Zhiyi did not give a formal talk in Shanghai, but he did speak informally, using an image for leadership that Ting referred to on a number of occasions in the 1980s.[78]

> He said that this group in Shanghai ought to consider themselves as a locomotive, not any locomotive but one which pulls many carriages. Just to be a locomotive is of no use no matter how fast it can move; but locomotives which are pulling many carriages go more slowly, yet the carriages are all moving forward. The meaning is that Three-Self leaders should not forget that when they move forward, they are bringing the masses along with them, and this is why they may have to travel more slowly.[79]

To "go slowly" meant responding to the needs and wishes of the Christian community at the grassroots. Zhang Zhiyi had also told Ting that the

TSPM should never do things that the "masses" did not want. The implication was the same: go slowly so that others could be brought along; don't impose heavy political burdens on them. This reinforced Ting's own idea that Three-Self had to be more like a church than a political movement. To race forward as some Christian activists had done in the past would be impetuous, and it would separate the TSPM from the masses of believers. To lead as a locomotive pulling many carriages meant taking into account the opinions and beliefs of others.

Between the Shanghai Meeting and the National Christian Conference, there was a great deal to do. Ting used this time to reach out to conservative church leaders who had not been connected with the TSPM in the past, soliciting their opinions and inviting them to take part in the forthcoming Christian conference.[80] Some conservative evangelicals, including Bi Yongqin and Wang Zhen, joined the revived TSPM, even though they had been opposed to it in the past. Evangelicals were welcomed at Nanjing Seminary, where there were well-known conservatives on the faculty, and they were free to purchase the Bibles that the TSPM had begun publishing.

In order to introduce K. H. Ting to a new generation of Christians, the series of essays originally written for seminary students in the mid-1950s was published in the first issue of *Tian Feng*. Rewritten for lay readers in nineteen short chapters, it was subsequently issued as a separate pamphlet entitled *How to Study the Bible*.[81] In light of his intended audience, Ting makes no mention of the historical-critical approach to biblical studies in this pamphlet, but he speaks instead of the unity of the Bible as a devotional text.

> Let us be clear right from the beginning: the Bible is not a riddle; it is a letter written by the Father in heaven to his children. He wants us to understand it. He does not want us to grope blindly in the dark, nor to depend on this or that authoritative interpretation. He certainly does not want us to blindly accept any person's deliberately mystifying explanation of the Bible. Our heavenly Father has given us his word as a lamp for our feet and light on the road, to illumine our paths in the world. (p.1)

Although he introduces the Bible devotionally, Ting presents an interpretation that was consistent with his own theology. In the passage just quoted, he is implicitly criticizing the "authoritative interpretations" and "mystifying explanations" that were popular among fundamentalists in China.[82] He argues that the Bible intends the Christian community to be unified (pp. 2-3); that God wants our cooperation in the work of creation, salvation and justification; that justification by faith should not become an excuse to dispense with ethics, become spiritually arrogant or separate from non-Christians (pp. 32-35). Theological thinking is important, writes Ting, and God's revelation is not opposed to human reason (pp. 35, 41). The Bible, therefore, needs to be interpreted in light of the new situation in which Chinese Christians now find themselves (p. 38).

How to Study the Bible helped some evangelical Christians in China better appreciate Ting's commitment to the Bible and the historic tenets of Christian faith. Some Christians overseas were, in contrast, surprised that Ting sounded so theologically conservative in this pamphlet.[83] But he had reissued *How to Study the Bible* to show that he could be a leader for the whole church, one who stood for unity rather than division, a churchman who concentrated on more than just the political role of the TSPM. Ting was a church-based theologian in a way that Y. T. Wu could never be. There was a proposal sometime around this time that the TSPM should republish Wu's major theological work, *Meiyouren kanjianguo shangdi (No Man Hath Seen God)*, but Ting put a stop to it even though the text for a new edition had already been typeset.[84] To publish this book as one of the first theological initiatives of the newly revived TSPM would have alienated the very people Ting was trying to win over. This was a new day, and Ting was attempting make Three-Self unity as broad as possible.

The Third National Christian Conference met in Nanjing 6-13 October 1980. There were 176 delegates from 25 provinces, mostly older men and women who had been at the first and the second national conferences.[85] They met in K. H. Ting's city, not in Beijing where all the other national religious organizations held their meetings, and not in Shanghai; they gathered in the church on Mo Chou Road down the street from his home. The delegates visited the campus of the soon-to-be-reopened Nanjing Union Theological Seminary (NUTS). The TSPM headquarters was still in Shanghai, but a "Nanjing office" (*ning ban*) was set up and was to become of almost equal importance in the 1980s and early 1990s.

The Third NCC established the China Christian Council (CCC), the church-affairs organization Ting had proposed. According to its constitution,

> The objective of the Council is: to unite all (Protestant) Christians who believe in the one Heavenly Father and confess Jesus Christ as Lord, and who, under the guidance of the one Holy Spirit and abiding by the common Bible, with one mind and in co-operative efforts, seek to further the cause of a self-governing, self-supporting and self-propagating church in our country. (Article 2)[86]

The CCC would be a service organization, attending to the pastoral needs of Chinese Christians, based on the principle of "mutual respect in matters of belief" (Article 3). There would be a division of labor between the TSPM and the CCC, working in cooperation "like two arms of one body." Ting's close friend Zheng Jianye was named general secretary of the CCC. Zheng did a great deal to help articulate the vision of the CCC, for like Ting, he was responsive to the needs of grassroots Christians and committed to reform of the TSPM.[87]

In his keynote address Ting reaffirmed the continuing relevance of the TSPM, but he put much more emphasis on the CCC.[88] The purpose of the TSPM was to encourage patriotism, and it would continue to play an important role in this area. "But how could an organization with such a purpose regularly and permanently take on the duty of developing the work that is the church's own?" he asked.[89] His answer was that it could not, and so a new church-affairs organization was needed. "Running the church well" became Ting's way of referring to the work of the CCC. In response to a question I asked in one interview as to whether this was his special contribution and emphasis, he said,

> You may say so. Because if we didn't point out that we wanted to *run the church well* then we could not get the support of rank-and-file church members. And before that many people in the Three-Self Movement didn't dare say *run the church well*, because in their mind, the Communist Party wanted to liquidate the church, so it would be reactionary to speak of *running the church* well. You see, during the Cultural Revolution there was a debate on: where is politics to be implemented or *put* itself *into effect*? They emphasized politics and political studies. What's the implication? How is politics to be implemented? There were people who said, "Politics is to *be put into effect in* actual work, and the completion of our tasks." That was considered a reactionary idea because it emphasized *actual affairs* too much; you are putting too much emphasis on *actual affairs* and not enough on politics. So the result of the debate was that politics is to *be put into effect* in politics. Through political study, your politics will be improved. *Likewise, Three-Self is also to be implemented in Three-Self*. There is no need for any running the church well.[90]

By emphasizing "the work that was the church's own" and "running the church well," Ting was making a shift away from politics and Three-Self patriotism (*zheng*) toward the pastoral concerns of the church (*dao*). In order to gain support among veteran TSPM leaders, he argued that this was similar to what Y. T. Wu had tried in 1956. But the formation of the CCC was at the same time an expression of Ting's dissatisfaction with the history of ultra-leftism in the TSPM. Those who have seen the creation of the CCC only as a strategy to bring in the evangelicals and strengthen TSPM control have missed the point entirely.[91] As part of the dialectics of political reform and church renewal in a changing situation, Ting was fending off Three-Self "activists" on the left, and the fundamentalists on the right, all the time attending to "the work that was the church's own," as only he could do.

The government officials who attended the Third NCC were Xiao Xianfa from the RAB and Zhang Zhiyi from the UFWD. Their published remarks should be read with an eye for the different ways they interpreted the role of their respective organizations, their expectations of the conference, and their views of reform.[92] Not included in the published excerpts of Zhang Zhiyi's speech is the apology and self-criticism he made for his errors from the 1960s onward, when he said all Christians were members of the exploiting class. This confession encouraged the NCC delegates, for it revealed an openness on the part of at least some government officials.[93] In his closing remarks at the conference, Ting went out of his way to thank Zhang Zhiyi, but he pointedly made no reference to Xiao Xianfa.[94]

It came as no surprise that Ting was elected chairperson of the TSPM and president of the newly formed CCC. He became, in effect, China's paramount Christian leader. The vice-chairs and standing committees of the two organizations were made up of older church leaders who had been involved with the TSPM since the early 1950s. The two national organizations, abbreviated in Chinese as the *lianghui*, were intended to work together and meet at the same time. But there was no overlapping membership in the two committees except for K. H. Ting and Han Wenzao, who was elected deputy general secretary of the CCC and deputy general secretary of the TSPM.

Throughout the 1980s and the 1990s, Han Wenzao (1923-2006) was K. H. Ting's major associate and collaborator. They spoke with each other almost every day, and they traveled together on most of the important visits overseas. The two came to know each other in the 1940s when Han was at the university and attended the Shanghai Student Church which Ting had organized (see chap. 2). After the war, Han worked as a YMCA secretary, first in Shanghai and later in Nanjing. He and Zhao Fusan were the youngest members of the national TSPM Preparatory Committee in 1954, when Han was already one of the leaders of the Nanjing TSPM. The working relationship between Ting and Han dates from the early 1960s, when Han became associated with Nanjing Union Seminary.[95]

The two men complemented each other, in their strengths and weaknesses, in their working style and in their approach to the TSPM. Ting was the visionary leader concerned with the formulation of ideas, principles and policies; Han was a man of action, concerned with practicalities, negotiation and the flexible implementation of policy. Ting was disorganized and a poor administrator; Han was very well organized with a fine grasp of administrative details. Ting had a commanding presence, but was diffident and often shy in public. Han was an extroverted networker with a wide circle of friends and acquaintances. They were a good team and accomplished a great deal in the TSPM and the CCC from the early 1980s through Ting's retirement in 1997, when Han succeeded him as CCC president.

With the TSPM and the CCC in place, "the work that was the church's own" could proceed, and K. H. Ting wanted to move quickly. Bible production had already begun, but Ting and Han had already begun looking for ways in which this work could be done more effectively with assistance from overseas. They believed this would not contradict the principle of self-support, since the TSPM and the CCC would not become dependent on financial contributions from overseas. Nanjing Seminary would open in just a few months' time. A new hymnal was published in 1983; a catechism was approved in 1984; and other pastoral and devotional materials began to be published.

It was reported at the Third NCC that fifty or sixty Protestant churches had already been reopened.[96] Over the next few years, one or two churches and Christian meeting points would be reopened or newly built every day. The rate would increase to four or five per day by the end of the decade, and in the 1990s, to almost seven a day, according to the TSPM and CCC leadership.[97] This was an unprecedented rate of growth, which led the TSPM and the CCC to make leadership training its most urgent priority. In addition to NUTS, the only national theological institution, more than a dozen Bible colleges and seminaries were started in different parts of the country over the next several years, and hundreds of short-term lay training courses were organized for lay church workers. Between 1980 and 1984, K. H. Ting presided over an ambitious program of rebuilding that contributed to the renewal of the church in almost every part of China.

Most new initiatives in church development were taken at the local level. Provincial-, municipal- and county-level Christian councils and Three-Self committees were set up, but there were no direct lines of authority between local and national organizations. As in the reform process as a whole, reconstruction efforts proceeded most quickly in the coastal provinces. Inland provinces lagged behind, and reports of problems with the implementation of religious policy came most frequently from poorer provinces such as Henan and Anhui, which had growing Christian populations but inadequate leadership. Even within a given province, there were often vast differences in policy implementation. Local Three-Self committees and Christian councils were accountable to the provincial government and party authorities, not the TSPM and the CCC. Local churches, however, often contacted church offices in Shanghai and Nanjing when they had grievances. They had problems with everything from the closing down of meeting points to the confiscation of Bibles to the detention of church workers by the Public Security Bureau. The TSPM/CCC had no authority to deal with provincial governments, but they could report problems to the RAB or to other government bodies in Beijing. Sometimes the CCC and TSPM would send out a team to investigate local grievances, but this was not always possible. The investigation of local church problems was extremely time consuming, and because religious policy implementation was not always an official priority, complaints often went unanswered.

In the early 1980s, K. H. Ting became increasingly aware of the problems local churches faced. He received letters, phone calls and personal visits from Christians in many parts of the country. He wanted the CCC and the TSPM to address local problems, but not all provincial and national leaders were in agreement with him. Some were still under the influence of ultra-leftism, while others felt that it was safer not to challenge the status quo. Ting personally spent a great deal of time dealing with problems that were brought

to his attention; he wrote letters and made phone calls to government officials to communicate his findings, and called on them when he was in
Beijing. He did not have the time to visit all of the places where problems
were reported because of his own busy schedule. But he did make use of his
position in the NPC, the CPPCC, and his connections with friends in high
places to try to resolve at least some of the problems for local Christian communities. In a country as vast as China, however, there were limitations in
what he could do.

Not all of the local problems were of the government's making. Ting
knew that some were caused by sectarians and fundamentalists, and others
were the result of people who used the church for their own ends. He spoke
about people who took advantage of the credulity of new believers to "cheat
honest people in the name of Christ." There were also areas in the church
where pastoral work had been neglected.

> Today, the reality of the Chinese Church is still far from the Church in
> the mind of Christ. In some places, there is a lack of content in wor-
> ship services and Christian meetings about which our members have
> their complaints . . . In other places emphasis is put only on church
> growth, without knowing that nurture should be more important in
> the present situation, for otherwise our faith would become one-sided
> and even heretical.[98]

In their new experience of freedom, the churches were growing. There
were many new Christians who often had little understanding of what Christianity was about. The heretical beliefs Ting alludes to were very real, particularly in rural churches. Heterodox groups, often led by charismatic
personalities, sometimes rejected orthodox church teaching. Fissiparous sectarian groups as well as belligerent fundamentalists rejected Ting's call for
unity. Despite repeated attempts at reconciliation, Wang Mingdao refused to
relate to the TSPM or the CCC. Wang and Ting never met, and neither man
was ready to compromise or make peace with the other. Neither Wang
Mingdao nor Watchman Nee (who died in 1972) was ever rehabilitated.
Their cases predated the Anti-Rightist movement, and the files on both men
remain closed to the public. There were other fundamentalist leaders—
including Yuan Xiangcheng (Allen Yuan) in Beijing and Lin Xiangao
(Samuel Lamb) in Guangzhou, both of whom were imprisoned before the
start of the Cultural Revolution—who never came to terms with the CCC
and the TSPM.[99] Ting opposed the fundamentalists not only because he disagreed with their theology but because they encouraged separatism, opposed
the reforms, and seemed to welcome "underground" Christian activity from
abroad.

Ting also spoke out against the "Yellers," an unorthodox sect that had
been inspired by the teachings of Witness Lee (Li Changshou), a former fol-

lower of Watchman Nee based in California.[100] The Yellers were seen as a heretical group, not only by the TSPM and the CCC, but by many evangelical Christians as well. They were later proscribed by the government. Ting has also rejected the activities of other sectarian groups, including the "Children of God," and, more recently, the non-Christian Falun Gong.[101] Ting was not a liberal democrat, and he did not believe in religious toleration as an end in itself. He rejected sectarian groups that could neither be won over nor included within the unity that he sought for the Chinese church.

Ting could be unyielding in attacks against opponents or those whom he perceived to be "enemies" of China. Love, according to Ting, does not mean overlooking wrongdoing because truth and justice must oppose falsehood and injustice whatever the consequences.[102] Ting was not adverse to conflict, and he did not avoid vigorous debate when matters of principle were at stake. There was sometimes a sting in his verbal attacks. "His surname is a homonym for nail," observed one colleague, and "we sometimes use that as a nickname." Ting could be tough when he thought he had to be, a quality that is absolutely essential for a Chinese leader, even a religious one. This toughness is a side of his character that is not often seen in public, especially when he is abroad, but it is one that can help us understand K. H. Ting as a church leader working with all the contradictory dynamics and pressures of the reform process in China. As with any leader, Ting could be wrong in his assessments and overly sensitive politically, but he could also be courageous and outspoken in his defense of the church.

The Shanghai preparatory meeting of the TSPM had authorized the reopening of Nanjing Seminary, and efforts for recruiting students began shortly thereafter. In the first issue of *Tian Feng,* a notice appeared that the seminary would reopen, but by then the news had also spread by word of mouth. Hundreds of requests for admission came in from all around the country.

Most of the faculty who taught at the seminary before the Cultural Revolution had returned to Nanjing by the late 1970s, and they were also part of Nanjing University's new Institute of Religious Studies, discussed earlier in this chapter. The senior faculty members included Luo Zhenfang, Zhao Zhi'en, and Xu Dingxin in biblical studies; Chen Zemin and Sun Hanshu in theology; Xu Rulei and Wang Yuming in church history; and Mo Ruxi and Situ Tong in English. Jiang Peifen and Han Bide combined biblical studies with the practical life of the church. Wang Weifan taught biblical studies as well as theology and church history. Many of the seminary administrators who had been there in the 1950s returned to their old positions. The faculty and administrators who returned in 1981 had for the most part been in Nanjing or the nearby countryside during the Cultural Revolution era.

The seminary faculty was extremely diverse theologically. Wang Weifan

K. H. Ting with seminary students, 1982.

and Chen Zemin, for example, represented almost opposite approaches to theology. Wang was an evangelical, rooted in the church, and had a passionate and almost poetic approach to theology and culture. He was extremely creative, and at times erratic, impatient with those whose viewpoints were at variance with his own. Chen was a liberal systematician, at ease in English, cosmopolitan in outlook, and perhaps better suited to conversation with academics than with Christians at the grassroots. Chen had been Wang's teacher in the 1950s, as had Sun Hanshu, who was from a fundamentalist background, and K. H. Ting. Chen became dean of the seminary in 1981. K. H. Ting's own theology was closer to Chen's, but Wang Weifan became his close collaborator in the 1980s and early 1990s. Ting relied on Wang's writing and literary skills and his understanding of the evangelicals, but he needed Chen to oversee the academic work of the seminary.

The seminary formally reopened on 20 February 1981 with an entering class of forty-seven students. This first class—eighteen women and twenty-nine men—came from twenty-two provinces, and ranged in age from seventeen to thirty-five.[103] The students were all middle-school graduates, and a few had graduated from university or had attended postsecondary institutions. They were chosen through an entrance examination and the recommendation of their local churches and local government authorities. Most, but not all, were from Christian families. That young people could come out of the Cultural Revolution with a desire to risk an uncertain future and serve the church was inspiring for Chinese Christians, and, indeed, for Christians from around the world. K. H. Ting was extremely pleased with the reopening of the seminary, and he was proud of his faculty and students for their commitment and dedication.[104] The seminary received a second class of students in the fall of 1981, and in a few years time, advanced programs of study were begun.[105] In addition, the seminary began a correspondence course for lay leaders through a simple journal called *Jiaocai* (*Curriculum*), which contained outlines and guides for biblical study, theology and the practical work of the church.[106]

When the IRS started, it was still not clear that there could even be a seminary, but now that theological education had begun, the faculty had a heavy burden of responsibility. It was clear for K. H. Ting that the priority was theological education. The work of the IRS continued, but on a reduced scale and with fewer students in religious studies. The journal *Religion* continued to play an important role in the ongoing debate on religious studies, but the seminary began publishing *JL* in 1984, and this became the primary publication for the seminary faculty.

In the 1980s, K. H. Ting used to say that of all his church and government positions, the one he most enjoyed was being principal of Nanjing Seminary. It was a position that he had assumed in 1952 and from which he never retired, which probably makes him the longest serving seminary principal of all time! Students from the early 1980s remember the time he spent with them. He offered lectures or preached almost weekly, and regularly presided at services of Holy Communion. He liked to be with the new students, joining in on their activities and inviting them to his home for informal conversation. He made himself available to all students, for he wanted to get to know the likely church leaders of the future. Ting saw Nanjing Seminary as a microcosm of the Chinese church, and he described his vision of the seminary to new students in the summer of 1983:

A seminary is not some lovely garden, a haven set apart from the world, like the poet's hermitage in Tao Yuanming's "Peace Blossom Spring." I cannot guarantee that all your experiences here will be good ones. But I think you should view the seminary as a community in the Lord, a big family, a learning community where we are all learning how to accept the Lord's love, and how to love each other. Our goal is to train up on behalf of our Chinese church, a church that is now practicing self-government, self-support and self-propagation, able servants who have their own special gifts, who never cease to grow, who can witness to Christ's gospel, who have something to offer believers spiritually, and who can lead many to become patriotic and church-loving Christians. This common goal unites us, but we are still learning the lesson of love.[107]

Beginning in the mid-1980s, seminary graduates began assuming key positions in local churches, TSPMs, Christian councils and newly opened theological seminaries all over China. Many students from these early years remember Ting telling them that they should not model themselves after government cadres or feudal lords in control of their own ecclesial kingdoms, but after the model of Jesus, who was a servant-leader. Ting hoped that seminary students would see themselves as intellectuals, theologians (*xue*) who identified with the people of China in their patriotism (*zheng*), and who identified with the Christians of China in their desire for a well-run church (*dao*).[108] The goal of theological education in China was to produce servant-leaders who were also Christian intellectuals, in Ting's understanding.

Some who had been influenced by ultra-leftism in the TSPM saw no real need for theology, because the main thing was for Christians to better ground themselves politically. But the "right" in the church—fundamentalists and sectarians—saw no need for theology either, because all that was needed for them was faith in Jesus and knowledge of the Bible. For both groups, Ting's emphasis on the reorientation and reconstruction of theology and theological education came as a challenge. Ting wanted to see the liberation of thought in both politics and the church.

> Today, we must proceed on the basis of a theological reorientation movement; we must not retreat. We should encourage that spirit of daring to think, daring to blaze new trails, daring to enable theological thinking to open its doors to the reality of the world. In this way we not only usher Chinese Christianity into the possibility of dialogue with others, but also strengthen its theological foundation, develop its own characteristics and substantially enrich the catholicity of the church.[109]

By 1982, when Ting spoke these words, Document 19 had already been approved, and the new constitution, with revised wording in the clause having to do with religious freedom, was being discussed in draft form. Just prior to this meeting, Ting had attended the Twelfth CPC Party Congress as one of a small number of specially invited guests, a recognition of his growing standing in society. The Twelfth Party Congress called for deepening the pace of reforms, and Ting's presence underscored the fact that Christians were not only part of this, but involved in a reform process of their own.

Ting was leading the church in a movement of reconstruction and renewal that went far beyond what the TSPM had been in the 1950s. The problems of the church could not all be solved, and the more he became aware of them, the greater they seemed to be. But the important thing was that the church had not been overcome by its problems; it stood shaken, but erect. The church was still very weak and fragile, and Ting could say that it lived quite literally in the power of the resurrection. "Life does not depend upon power and riches, it relies upon the risen Lord. This is our experience and the light which we can clearly perceive, and we must bear this unique witness before the whole world."[110] And the world was most interested in the unique witness of the reemerging church in China.

REESTABLISHING INTERNATIONAL RELATIONSHIPS

To demonstrate his commitment of openness to the world, Deng Xiaoping became the first Chinese Communist leader to visit the United States. He went in February 1979, just a few weeks after the establishment of formal diplomatic relations, and less than two months after the close of the Third Plenum. In a private meeting the American president Jimmy Carter raised the subject of religious freedom in China. He reportedly asked Deng to do three things: permit the return of Western missionaries to China, make possible the distribution of Bibles, and promote religious freedom. Deng's answer was that he would do the second two, but that China could not allow the return of missionaries because it carried the connotation of Western domination. Carter later said he believed Deng was sincere in his commitment to religious freedom.[111] It is an irony of history that Deng Xiaoping, who wrote almost nothing about religion or religious policy, was a pragmatist who did more for religious freedom than any other Chinese Communist leader before or since.

Religious freedom and the international relationships of religious organizations were a function of China's policies of reform and openness. Government and party documents clearly stated that "friendly relationships" based on equality and mutual respect could be established with religious organizations overseas, but that foreign "infiltration" under the guise of religion sought to destabilize China and remained an ever-present danger.[112] This was the essence of government religious policy regarding international relationships in the late 1970s and early 1980s.

K. H. Ting's most important international visitor after the fall of the Gang of Four was William Tolbert, the president of Liberia and an active Baptist layman who was honorary president of the Baptist World Alliance. Tolbert was on a state visit to China in 1978, and he expressed his wish to meet Chinese Christians. In Nanjing, it was arranged that Ting and eight colleagues would meet Tolbert for conversation and prayers. He was in Nanjing on a Sunday, and, because no churches were open, they further arranged for twenty-five people to meet for a worship service at T. V. Soong's old residence in the eastern suburbs.[113] This was the first time that a service of worship had been organized for a visiting head of state.

By this time, Ting was already developing a correspondence with friends in many parts of the world. In his letters, he would interpret recent events in China, inquire about developments in the church overseas, and ask about old friends. His letters, typed or written by hand, always had a personal

touch and were written with a particular person in mind. He was also seeing many overseas visitors and church leaders during these years.[114] They
met with church leaders in other parts of China as well, but in the view of
most visitors, the time they spent with Ting seemed to carry more authority. He gradually began to use the title of "Bishop," and overseas visitors
assumed that this was how he should be addressed. Some visitors reported
on their conversations with Ting as if they were receiving official church
pronouncements in an audience with a high-ranking prelate. He himself did
not necessarily see things in this way, but he enjoyed opportunities to meet
with old friends and learn about different perspectives from overseas.

The Tings were always dignified and gracious hosts who opened their
home to foreign visitors. It was Siu-may, in particular, who made sure that
all preparations were in order and that their guests would feel welcome.
Vera Schwarcz, who was among the first American scholars to do research
in China, was introduced to the Tings by a friend back home. She remembers how she was struck by "the informed, analytical, reasoned morality"
of the Tings.

> Something familiar yet new as well here. K. H. and his wife are sophis-
> ticated but not Western bourgeois in their ways. They have simple, his-
> torically tested political concerns. I don't know how China can tolerate
> or use such people. But I sense that they are necessary to what China
> is trying to accomplish. They seem to foreshadow a broad kind of
> humanism. Perhaps in the distant future, when other Chinese people
> also have more leisure, more living space, better news of the world,
> this humanism will flourish. I don't think the Chinese government
> wants to, can, or should keep the masses from becoming more like the
> Tings.[115]

After a few short hours of conversation, Schwarcz, who came with no pre-
conceptions or agenda other than a historian's desire to understand and a
natural human empathy, got it right in a way that many overseas church
"insiders" did not.

In August 1979, K. H. Ting went to North America as part of a religious
delegation attending the Third World Conference on Religion and Peace
(WCRP III) at Princeton Theological Seminary. This was his first visit to the
United States in almost thirty years, and his first overseas trip since before
the Cultural Revolution. The participation of the Chinese delegation at
WCRP III became another signal to the outside world that the situation in
China was changing. Zhao Puchu was the leader of the delegation, and Ting
was the deputy leader. (Zhao Puchu became a WCRP president in the 1980s,
and Ting became a president in the 1990s.) There were eight others, Bud-
dhists, Muslims and Protestant Christians (Li Shoubao, Chen Zemin and
Han Wenzao), but no Catholics or Daoists. The invitation to attend WCRP
III had been extended to Zhao Puchu by Nikkiyo Niwano, president of

Japan's Rissho Kosei-Kai, and an honorary WCRP president. Ting had suggested the names of the Protestants, but the actual composition of the delegation as a whole was made by Zhao Puchu and Xiao Xianfa. Xiao wanted a member of the RAB to accompany the group, but when both Zhao and Ting objected, he withdrew the proposal.[116] Because this was the first multireligious Chinese group ever to visit North America, the Chinese became the toast of the conference.[117] They were prepared to meet as many people as they could and spoke about the new freedom for religious believers in China after the fall of the Gang of Four and the changing situation overall. Ting and Zhao Puchu also emphasized the efforts that were then underway to change the clause on religious freedom in the constitution.

The WCRP was an important occasion, but neither Ting nor Zhao believed that an interreligious movement for world peace was politically viable.[118] They saw the conference as an opportunity to make friends, learn more about religious developments overseas, and meet church and other religious leaders. Ting also wanted to catch up on his theological reading and writing, for he needed to prepare the lectures and sermons he would be delivering in Canada after the conference.

The four Protestant delegates visited the National Council of Churches of Christ in the U.S.A. (NCCCUSA) at their headquarters in New York City after the end of the WCRP conference, and from there they went to churches in six other American cities. Eugene Stockwell, who had been with the Tings in Nanjing shortly after the fall of the Gang of Four, helped make arrangements for this visit, and Ting and his colleagues accepted an invitation to send an official Protestant delegation to the United States at an opportune time. There had been some concern on the part of the Chinese about going to the Interchurch Center, because the Dalai Lama was visiting New York at the same time. This was eventually sorted out when the NCCCUSA agreed not to invite the Dalai Lama to the Interchurch Center. During his time in New York, Ting visited Union Seminary, his alma mater, and preached a sermon entitled "Human Collectives as Vehicles of God's Grace" at Riverside Church across the street.[119] The delegation discovered that the mainline American churches were eager to learn about Christianity in China and were open to their message.

The three other Protestants returned to China in late September, but Ting left for a private seven-week stay in Canada, an unprecedented sabbatical for a Chinese public figure of Ting's stature. His visit to Canada had been arranged by the Canada China Program, and was his longest time away from China since 1951. Ting's international perspective was needed in a nation that was suspicious of things foreign, especially in the aftermath of the Cultural Revolution. He therefore needed time to develop a better understanding of the international church situation in a place where he could feel he was relaxed and among friends.

The Tings had spent only a year in Canada (see chap. 3), but their presence there had left a lasting impression on them and on those whom they came to know. The difference between Canada and the United States for the Chinese needs to be underscored. Canada had established formal diplomatic relations with the People's Republic of China in 1970, nine years before the United States. In contrast to the United States, a number of respected Canadian missionaries had been sympathetic observers of the Chinese Revolution.[120] K. H. and Siu-may's year in Canada had helped Canadians appreciate what the Communists were trying to do, and it is doubtful that their message would have been as well received in churches in the United States. Canadian churches had developed an openness to the People's Republic in the early 1950s.[121] Canada's first three ambassadors to China were children of missionaries, and there were cultural exchanges between China and Canada even during the years of the Cultural Revolution.

In his speeches, interviews and published essays in Canada, Ting spoke about what was happening in post–Cultural Revolution China and the future of the Chinese church. He explored his theological understanding of recent events and engaged in deep and extensive conversations with old friends. At a reunion with people from SCM days, everyone was surprised that K. H. could remember all their names, including those he had not seen since 1947.[122] He preached at the church that sent Jim Endicott as a missionary to China.[123] Endicott was a staunch supporter of the Communists, but he had been defrocked by the United Church of Canada because of his unorthodox views. A few years after Ting's visit, Endicott was reinstated by the United Church, in part because of K. H. Ting's support.

Ting's advice on the renewal of international Christian relationships was to go slowly. The church in China was small and weak and unable to do many things internationally. At the same time, he spoke in no uncertain terms about his opposition to those who persisted in their imperialistic approach to China. He was particularly angered by an essay that had recently been published by Joseph Spae, a European Catholic China-watcher.[124] In response to Spae, Ting wrote "Facing the Future or Restoring the Past?" in which he argued that there were "two opposed lines of approach to China" in the West, one that was open to a new future and one, represented by Spae, that wanted a return to the past.

> Let me call the reader's attention to an alarming and dangerous matter: For thirty years now, anti-New China groups abroad have never ceased in their efforts to foster separatism within Chinese Christianity. They talk ecumenism and oneness but do the work of undermining our unity. They send in money and secret messages and instructions and beam radio programs, all designed for nurturing opposition and carrying out smearing and splitting moves.[125]

The words are jarring, but Ting's tone and message were deliberate. This was his first attempt in print to criticize the practice and methods of Christian groups who could not accept the new religious order in China, and he wanted to be perfectly clear. In the late 1970s, there were Christians, both Catholics and Protestants, who were using all kinds of methods to get into China. They claimed they were responding to Chinese Christians who could not accept the post–Cultural Revolution order, and perhaps they were. The Chinese government termed the secretive activity of overseas religious groups as foreign "infiltration." In "Facing the Future or Restoring the Past?" Ting spoke out as a Chinese Christian leader in support of government policy and on behalf of a church that had many difficulties of its own.

All through this period, and in the years since, Ting has remained resolute in opposing Christian initiatives from overseas that show no regard for China's national sovereignty or the jurisdiction of the Chinese church.[126] Because of his prominence, there have been numerous personal attacks against him from conservative Christian groups overseas. In contrast, Zhao Puchu never had to face such criticism from Buddhists overseas. Ting's position reflects his political standpoint as a Chinese leader and his theological understanding as a Christian. He opposes activities that the government terms "infiltration" that have long been rejected by mainline churches and the ecumenical movement. Ting's principled stance against the neo-colonialism of overseas mission groups has won the admiration of many church leaders from overseas, especially in the Third World.

Ting returned to China in late November 1979, three months before the Enlarged Shanghai TSPM meeting. Over the next twelve months, he would be occupied with church affairs closer to home, but he continued to meet frequently with overseas visitors. After the Third NCC, he gave increasing attention to international relationships. Ting's perspective on the two opposing lines of Christians in the West—and in other parts of the Christian world as well—was refined during this time, and he chose the opportunity of a visit from two Lutheran pastors in Hong Kong to clarify his position. His prepared remarks to Andrew Chiu and Arthur Wu systematically presented the international position of the TSPM/CCC in the early 1980s. It was widely reprinted with the title "Fourteen Points from Christians in the People's Republic of China to Christians Abroad."[127] It begins with the principles and organizational relationships of the TSPM and the CCC, highlighting the importance of the need for Christian unity. The Chinese church cannot and should not be divided into a "house church" and an "official church," as some overseas reports had maintained. (This was one reason why Ting preferred to use the term "home-worship gatherings.") It would not return to denominationalism, for its unity was based on the Three-Self principles of self-government, self-support, and self-propagation. Evangelism is the responsibility of Chinese Christians, so there should be no sending of foreign missionaries to China, and Christian radio broadcasts should also stop. Chinese Christians welcome "friendly" relationships with Christians overseas, but because the priority is rebuilding at home, international commitments would be limited. The Chinese church would consider accepting contributions from friendly overseas church groups, but the principle of self-support would be maintained. Finally, the TSPM and the CCC would practice a policy of "differentiation" in relationships with churches overseas. Differentiation between friends and enemies was a united-front concept, and Ting saw Christians as part of China's united front and as contributors to it. The Fourteen Points was issued just three years after the fall of the Gang of Four, and was Ting's elaboration of a position based on a realistic understanding of what he saw as possible.

The principle of differentiation may be seen in the invitations the CCC extended to churches overseas and in the delegations they sent abroad.* Bishop and Mrs. Gilbert Baker of the Anglican Diocese of Hong Kong and Macao were the first official visitors invited to China by the TSPM and the CCC in January 1981.[128] WCRP general secretary Homer Jack and Christian Conference of Asia (CCA) general secretary Yap Kim Hao had made official visits to China in 1980, but their invitations had been extended by K. H. Ting as an individual.[129] All three of these visits were extended to people seen to be friendly to China and sympathetic to the CCC. Baker's visit is reminiscent of that of his predecessor, Bishop R. O. Hall, in 1956. Both were Englishmen with extensive China experience, both were long-standing friends of K. H. Ting, and both were generally supportive of China after 1949. Also in 1981, Bishop Peter K. K. Kwong, Baker's successor and the first Chinese bishop of China's only Anglican diocese, made a private visit to Nanjing to see Bishop Ting, his first trip anywhere after his consecration.

In March and April, an eight-member delegation from the TSPM and the CCC visited Hong Kong at the invitation of the Hong Kong Christian Council (HKCC).[130] This was an opportunity to reconnect after years of separation and mutual mistrust; to meet friends, family members and former colleagues; and to begin thinking about future possibilities and cooperation with churches in the territory. After meetings with the HKCC and visits to Hong Kong churches, the delegation participated in a consultation organized by the CCA and arranged by Yap Kim Hao.[131] Although China had no plans to join the CCA, this was an opportunity for Chinese Christians to learn more about Asia and the ecumenical movement. In both sets of meetings, Ting reiterated what he had already said about overseas relations in the Fourteen Points and indicated that this applied to Hong Kong and Asian churches as well. Also in Hong Kong, Ting attended the consecration service of Bishop Peter Kwong, but out of concern that he not be considered "too Anglican" in a postdenominational church, he did not take part in the service.

The Canadian Council of Churches was the first Western delegation invited to China (in June and July 1981), and this came as the Canadians

---

* The TSPM and the CCC are in China referred to as the two national organizations (*lianghui*). For the sake of simplicity, I will speak of the CCC in referring to international relationships, but the TSPM presence should be assumed, for there is a functional equality between the two organizations. International invitations were sometimes extended by the CCC, and sometimes by the TSPM and the CCC. It was the CCC alone that became part of the WCC at its Seventh Assembly in Canberra in 1991.

were planning a historic conference in Montreal. The idea for such a China conference had emerged in conversations between the Canadians and K. H. Ting during his visit two years earlier. The 1981 Montreal conference, was entitled "God's Call to a New Beginning: An International Dialogue with the Chinese Church." It drew 158 people from around the world, including seven Protestants and three Catholics from China.[132] It was intended to launch a new beginning in relationships and understanding, allowing Chinese Christians to speak for themselves in an atmosphere of mutual respect. The reports from the conference indicate that it was successful in this regard. Two people whose views Ting had criticized (Jonathan Chao and Joseph Spae) were excluded from Montreal '81, an example of the policy of differentiation in action.

Montreal '81 was the first time that Protestants and Roman Catholics from China had prayed together in a public setting. Protestants and Roman Catholics in China were almost two different religions, a reflection of the separation between the two communions, neither of which had been part of the World Council of Churches or Vatican II. Ting worked with Chinese Catholics for the better implementation of religious freedom. He also provided the first books for Catholic Bishop Jin Luxian's library at Sheshan Seminary in Shanghai. But he did not push ecumenical dialogue in China, because neither church was ready for it and because he had doubts about Rome's intentions for China. Just before the Montreal conference, Ting issued a statement highly critical of the Manila message on China issued by Pope John Paul II.[133] Because of this statement and his earlier criticism of Joseph Spae, Catholic detractors began to refer to Ting as "the Protestant Pope." Ting quipped that this showed they did not have much respect for the Holy See. The Chinese Catholics were developing in their own way, but they also relied on K. H. Ting's advice in the early 1980s.

Ting was also uneasy about the network of Protestant and Roman Catholic China study projects that had emerged in Europe and North America in the 1970s. He said on a number of occasions that he did not think China constituted any new theological problem for Christians. The overseas China study projects met informally as the "Ecumenical China Study Liaison Group" (ECSLG) and were coordinated by Pro Mundi Vita on the Catholic side and the Lutheran World Federation for the Protestants. Some ECSLG members believed that this group, and not the Canadians, should have organized the Montreal conference. After the conference was over, Ting and his Chinese colleagues felt that Montreal was a new beginning, and so there would be no need for the continuance of the ECSLG. In any event, Chinese Christians would not join such a gathering. Some ECSLG representatives were unhappy with Ting's position, but he had made his point. The final ECSLG meeting was held in 1982, and this marked the end of overseas Catholic-Protestant coordination on China.

After the Montreal conference, the Chinese Protestants made an official visit to the NCCCUSA. Over the next four years, there were visits to and from churches in Europe, Asia and Africa. K. H. Ting led all of the delegations going abroad, and he received all of the visitors coming to China. These exchanges were the "new beginning" hoped for in Montreal. Han Wenzao became the CCC's expert on international relations, but Ting's charisma and presence elevated the importance of the visits for the foreign delegations. M. M. Thomas, an Indian theologian who was Ting's contemporary, once termed the ecumenical movement a journey among friends. The many friendships that K. H. Ting maintained with Christians in the ecumenical movement, some since the 1930s and the 1940s, added an invaluable personal dimension to the outreach of the CCC in the 1980s.

Among the many visiting church groups, the two visits of Archbishop Robert Runcie were particularly important. He was the first archbishop of Canterbury to visit China. On his planned visit to Hong Kong in 1982, rather than ask Bishop Ting to come see him in Hong Kong, Runcie made a forty-hour visit to Nanjing. Ting and his colleagues were deeply moved by this act of humility on the part of the archbishop, and the visit was the beginning of a lasting friendship between the two churchmen.[134] Ting was invited to the next Lambeth Conference as a bishop who was still part of the Anglican communion. The CCC was "postdenominational," but for Runcie, this meant that Ting's bishopric had been enhanced, not taken away. He was "an Anglican plus something," Runcie said. In China, Runcie's visits attracted more media attention than all the other early church visits combined.[135] He spoke firmly and with authority about his personal support for the TSPM and the need for Christians to be patriotic Chinese, comparing Three-Self independence in China to the experience of the Church of England in the sixteenth and seventeenth centuries.

Robert Runcie had an understanding and a perspective that the Chinese government leadership could understand, even when he asked difficult questions. On his second visit in 1983, this time as head of a delegation from the British Council of Churches, he and BCC general secretary Philip Morgan met with Li Xiannian, the president of China. The archbishop asked the president if the campaign against "spiritual pollution" and Western cultural influences would affect the churches.[136] Li replied that it would not, and added that "normal" religious activities were protected by the new constitution. In a humorous aside, he said that if religion were a spiritual pollutant, "we would not have invited you here to pollute us, Archbishop."[137]

In reestablishing international relationships, the CCC chose to relate to Christian councils and ecumenical organizations overseas. This was natural, as the CCC saw itself as a postdenominational body. Only later did the Chinese Christians begin to develop bilateral church-to-church relationships, initially with the mainline denominations, and after 1985, with evangelical groups. This progression illustrates the evolution of the China Christian Council's understanding of the international church situation.

K. H. Ting had himself been part of the ecumenical movement, and it was with friends there that he was most at home internationally. At the same time, he had misgivings about the World Council of Churches. It was Ting who had asked in the 1950s whether the "W" in the WCC should be "Western" not "World." In the early 1980s, he was concerned over the WCC position on China and its stance on the Taiwan issue.[138] There were also different attitudes within the WCC over how to relate to China. The WCC had been part of the ECSLG, and some remained wary of the Chinese because of the experience that ended in its demise. The WCC's development office had started a mariculture project in southern China which some saw as a new venture in ecumenical cooperation, while others saw it as a new missionary or developmental rush into China.[139] The WCC's international affairs office, led by Ninan Koshy, had a favorable view of China's reform and openness, but Raymond Fung in the office for evangelism was suspicious of K. H. Ting and the CCC leadership. Taiwanese Presbyterians had questions about what a new WCC relationship with China would mean for them. This was a complicated picture for Chinese Christians to sort out, especially right at the beginning of the period of reform and openness.

WCC general secretary Philip Potter's major concern was the Chinese church, for he never regarded the Chinese churches as having left the WCC. Potter had a personal interest in China and was an old friend and colleague of K. H. Ting. He had quietly invited Ting to attend the Nairobi Assembly of the WCC in 1975, but Ting said that the time was not yet ripe.[140] The relationship between Ting and Potter was renewed through correspondence and messages carried back and forth through visitors beginning in the late 1970s. Potter kept Ting informed about all developments related to China within the WCC, and he always accepted Ting's advice on what was best for China. Ting shared his questions and concerns with Potter about the WCC, including why he could not formally endorse the mariculture project. Potter and Ting met privately at the Vancouver Assembly of the WCC in 1983, which a small CCC delegation attended as observers only. This laid the groundwork for future exchanges.

The CCC visited the WCC in Geneva in November 1983. K. H. Ting saw many other friends from his WSCF days, but one encounter in particular is worth noting. The first WCC general secretary W. A. Visser 't Hooft still lived in retirement in Geneva, and he had been among those who had urged Ting not to return to China in 1951. On the way to a reception for the visiting guests, Paul Albrecht, director of the WCC unit on Church and Society, said he was going to fetch "Vim." K. H. asked if he could go along to have a few minutes alone with Visser 't Hooft at his home. There, the two men spent a short time together, a private reconciliation before they went on to the formal gathering.[141] Visser 't Hooft later told friends that he had been wrong to urge K. H. and Siu-may not to return to their country in 1951.

In the short sermon he preached at the Ecumenical Centre, Ting spoke of the need for the Chinese church to be part of the church universal. As he said on other occasions, Three-Self does not include self-isolation. But just as the Chinese needed the ecumenical movement, he suggested that churches in other parts of the world might have something to learn from China. Three-Self, reasoned Ting, was a process

> through which the church in China ceases to be a dot on the missionary map of some other churches but comes to be itself. The Church Universal needs us to be true to our identity as Chinese Christians in order to add to the richness and breadth of its understanding and worship of Christ. So might not Three-Self really be a child born in the household of God and destined to be a sign for something beyond itself? Could it be really one of the important breakthroughs in history that has a significant breakthrough for Christians elsewhere too? We hope our visit here can mark the beginning of a process of give and take within the family of God that will bring about a better and deeper understanding.[142]

Philip Potter visited China a year later to underscore his commitment on behalf of the WCC that churches elsewhere were indeed interested in developing a better and deeper understanding of China. Potter's letter of thanks to K. H. Ting, written after his return to Geneva, contains a paragraph that almost seems as if it were written in response to Ting's words at the Ecumenical Centre.

> I am aware that you are only at the beginning of the building of the Church in China with its own integrity and yet as a part of the one, holy, catholic and apostolic Church. There is also the question of how to relate to churches around the world without in any way losing your own identity. China is a vast country with a vast population, and you have the big problem of communication and of how to maintain community in diversity. But these are normal crises of churches, remembering that "crisis" in Chinese means both danger and opportunity.[143]

The two friends had come to a common understanding of the ecumenical movement and the church in China. Potter never tried to press K. H. Ting to have the CCC formally become a member of the WCC, and it would be seven more years before the CCC actually did so. Because of their common faith, their mutual understanding and their long-standing relationship with each other, the corner had been turned. Even as Potter was writing his letter to K. H. Ting, Chinese Christians were exploring new ways of relating to the church ecumenical. These were related to changes taking place all over China in the mid-1980s, as the process of openness and reform deepened and faced new crises.

8

The Vicissitudes of Openness and Reform, 1984-1989

Long, long is the road, and far, far the journey,
Up and down I would go, always searching.
Qu Yuan (340-278 B.C.E.)

Have you found, my soul, what you were seeking?
You were seeking God, and you found him to be that
Which was highest of all, than which a better cannot
Be thought; you found him to be life itself, light, wisdom,
Goodness, eternal blessedness and blessed eternity,
and to exist everywhere and always.
St. Anselm (ca. 1033-1109)[1]

By the early 1980s, a sense of order had been restored to society under the steady hand and iron fist of Deng Xiaoping. The critique of ultra-leftism continued, but reform and openness had become accepted policies, and discussion and debate centered on the extent and pace of change. By the time of the Twelfth Communist Party Congress in September 1982, the reform policies had a momentum of their own, generating new opportunities, a focus on economic development and new problems.

The early initiatives in "market socialism" brought significant improvement to people's lives. Farmers earned money by selling their goods in free markets, and urban dwellers enjoyed a greater availability and variety of fresh produce. With the economic reform came improved housing, better salaries and an increase in consumer demand. Students and intellectuals began to enjoy more intellectual freedom and educational opportunities, as well as a better standard of living. Religious groups of all kinds were growing. But the pace of change varied from place to place, with coastal provinces developing much more quickly than those farther inland. The social safety net began to be weakened, and the gap between rich and poor was increasing. Crime, inflation and personal insecurity—all of which were practically

243

unknown in the past—were on the rise, the inevitable by-products of a society in transition.

The government spoke of the importance of maintaining "unity and stability" and adhering to "the four cardinal principles," but reform and openness were inherently destabilizing. Even without the "Fifth Modernization"—the democracy that human-rights advocates called for—the reform process was unpredictable. It encouraged individual initiative, generated new ideas and led to popular participation in a socialist country moving away from a command economy and centralized political control toward market-oriented reforms and a more open society. The tension between "unity and stability" on the one hand, largely a political concern, and "reform and openness" on the other, viewed primarily in economic terms, shaped the development of Chinese society in the 1980s.

Many journalists, scholars and analysts viewed this tension in terms of a cycle of relaxation, or "letting go" (*fang*), followed by a period of "tightening up" (*shou*), or the strengthening of control. According to Richard Baum, this ambivalent cycle of relaxation and control produced a recurrent and periodic pattern in the 1980s.

> The result was a distinctive *fang-shou cycle*, characterized by an initial increase in the scope of economic or political reform (in the form, e.g., of price deregulation or intellectual liberalization), followed by a rapid release of pent-up social demand (e.g., panic buying or student demonstrations); the resulting "disorder" would set off a backlash among party traditionalists, who would then move to reassert control. A conservative retrenchment would follow, marked by an ideological assault on "liberal" tendencies and an attempt to halt (or even to reverse) the initial reform. The ensuing freeze would serve, in turn, to exacerbate internal contradictions and stresses, leading to the generation of renewed pressures for relaxation and reform—and so on.[2]

Baum describes three intensifying cycles of relaxation and control in the 1980s.[3] The first began with the reforms of the Twelfth Party Congress in 1982 and efforts to construct a "socialist spiritual civilization" as the ideological basis for the new policies. The vigorous campaign against "spiritual pollution" and the criticism of Western influences in literature and the arts extended through the end of 1983.

The second cycle began with a renewed critique of ultra-leftism. Hu Yaobang affirmed, and Deng Xiaoping agreed, that the major danger to reform continued to be ultra-leftism and not Western influences, and so there should be a speeding up of the pace of economic reform, especially in coastal areas. Deng Xiaoping asserted that some people would get richer earlier than others, but he left it to his protégés in the "third echelon" to develop the specific policies. Increased economic reform and intellectual freedom were followed by stirrings of worker and student unrest, increasing crime and rural disorder, and the outspoken criticism of party policies by prominent intellectuals. Student demonstrations at the end of 1986 convinced Deng Xiaoping and party elders that they had to pull back. In January, they forced the resignation of party general secretary Hu Yaobang and began a campaign to criticize "bourgeois liberalization." Many intellectuals and people from religious circles believed that cold water had been poured on the reforms.

The new campaign was even more short-lived than the one against spiritual pollution. Zhao Ziyang succeeded Hu in 1987, and after perfunctorily denouncing "bourgeois liberalization," he pressed forward with an ambitious agenda for reform. Zhao outlined his program in his report to the Thirteenth Party Congress in October of that year. China was still in the "primary stage of socialism," he said, and building up the material base had to be the priority. He called for the separation of party and government functions; devolution of power to the provinces; the development of a professional civil service to replace the cadre system; enhancing the supervisory role of the CPPCC, the NPC and mass organizations; and strengthening of the socialist legal system.[4] Most importantly, Zhao stressed quickening the pace of economic reform. Many saw Zhao's report as "revolutionary," and it encouraged leaders in all sectors of society to pursue their own agenda for reform.

But in less than a year, new problems arose in an overheated economy with an inflation rate as high as 20 percent in urban areas. Many people who had supported the reform program of the previous decade began to voice their concerns, and there was renewed social unrest, protests over official corruption and "bureaucratic racketeering" (*guandao*), and a new crime wave.[5] In the summer of 1988, the series *River Elegy* (*Heshang*), reported to have the largest audience in the history of television, criticized the unrelenting backwardness and conservatism of Chinese civilization and gave voice to those who were dissatisfied by the current state of reform.[6] The protests later that year and the following spring pressed for an even faster pace of reform. These were further indications of popular dissatisfaction, not only among students and intellectuals but among factory workers and the urban populace as a whole. The violent government suppression of the nascent "democracy movement" and the popular protests that culminated in the events of June 1989 signaled the end of the third and final *fang-shou cycle* of the 1980s.

The *fang-shou cycle* has its uses in coming to terms with the complex political and social forces at work in the China of the 1980s. But we also need to recognize the limitations of any all-embracing interpretation. These rely on vast generalizations and are inevitably selective in their choice of facts. In Baum's view, the cycle makes "the road to Tiananmen" seem almost inevitable and takes inadequate account of other interests and ideas that were shaping society and that might have produced different outcomes.

For the church and other religious communities, the entire 1980s were a time of tremendous growth and development. The religions in China were affected by the cycles of relaxation and control in society as a whole, but not always in the same ways. There were times when the churches seemed to be out in front of society, as in the reopening of churches or the organization of home-worship gatherings in the early 1980s. At other times, churches tended to lag behind, as in their approach to intellectual life or their involvement in social service. The reforms created new space for the churches, but they would have to struggle with how they would make use of that space in light of continuing political restrictions. As China's foremost Christian leader, K. H. Ting presided over the development of the Protestant community and responded to the changes that were taking place in the political arena. To use one of his favorite metaphors, he was listening to what the Spirit was saying to the churches.

Ting's reputation and influence at home and abroad continued to grow. He became much more of a force for change in Chinese political and religious life. In 1987, he was named to the prestigious Foreign Relations Committee of the NPC, and the following year to its Standing Committee. In 1989 Ting was elected to be one of the thirty plus vice-chairpersons of the CPPCC, a position he holds to this day and one that gives him the authority of a national leader. All of these government posts enhanced the ways he was able to work for the church.

Ting continued to lead church delegations to different parts of the world, and he hosted an unrelenting stream of overseas visitors in Nanjing. In the 1980s, he received four honorary doctorates,[7] in addition to the many other honors and awards he was given by churches and theological seminaries worldwide. As his reputation as an international Christian statesman grew, so too did the criticisms and attacks from fundamentalist and conservative church groups in China, as well as in Hong Kong and North America.[8] They continued to criticize his closeness to the government and his theological liberalism. But some evangelicals were changing, and they were thankful for what Ting was doing for the church in China. In the 1980s, these were still the minority.

K. H. Ting had taken on the work of governance (*zheng*), which carried its own duties, burdens and responsibilities. But he remained a church leader (*dao*) and an intellectual (*xue*), and both his political standing and international reputation were in some sense a function of these. In the 1980s, Ting emerged as a theologian for the Chinese church and the wider *oikoumene* with a perspective consistent with his long-held Christian beliefs and political convictions.

THEOLOGICAL RETHINKING

K. H. Ting's theology has always been written in dialogue with his times, but his basic approach has not changed a great deal since the 1940s. From his training at St. John's in Shanghai and Union in New York to his work with the YMCA and the WSCF; from his return to China in the early 1950s to his theological rethinking in the 1980s, his categories of understanding have remained remarkably consistent. He wrote in response to issues of church and society, and his thinking developed around a few central themes: the love of God in Christ, the work of the Holy Spirit both inside and outside the church, the interrelatedness of creation and redemption, the importance of ethics, and human cooperation with God in historical movements for change.[9] Ting's theological rethinking in the 1980s was a summing up of these themes in a new situation.

The 1980s was the time of his greatest theological output. More than 60 percent of the Chinese edition of his selected works was written between 1979 and 1989, and the great majority of these were theological essays, sermons and speeches to church audiences. He wrote and published more than any other theologian or church leader in China.[10] There has been a further outpouring of his theological writing since his retirement, and we will come to that in our discussion of "theological reconstruction" (chap. 10). But it was in the 1980s that Ting identified what he believed was needed for theological reorientation and church reconstruction in the era of reform.

Ting is a theological essayist, and he had neither the time nor the inclination to produce a systematic theology. He wrote and preached in response to the challenges he was facing as a church leader. Much of his work was done on the run, as it were, and under the pressure of time. But he read widely, in Chinese and English, and carefully prepared his sermons, speeches and essays, no matter what the deadline. His speeches sometimes went through many revisions before they were delivered, as he took into account comments on earlier versions from colleagues.

Many of his essays were presented as lectures at Nanjing Seminary or speeches at church meetings in China. In his writing and speaking, Ting was always very conscious of his audience. He wanted to broaden the theological horizon of Chinese Christians, especially seminary students, as well as provide a convincing rationale for the work of the Three-Self Movement. He also wanted to develop an apologetic for intellectuals and even government officials to show that Christian theology could be "patriotic," progressive and a worthy area of learning. For overseas audiences, he introduced and defended the changes taking place in church and society in China.

His theological rethinking was generally (but not always) first presented in Chinese, for Chinese Christians were always his primary constituency. Many of the presentations to Western audiences were summaries of his Chinese work or of a more introductory nature. As is the case with many theologians who are church leaders, he often used the same thoughts and ideas on different occasions, and one can detect a good deal of repetition in his speeches and writings, including those in his collected works. The presentation of his theological views differed depending on his intended audience. For example, the Chinese version of *How to Study the Bible* uses an evangelical language popular in Chinese churches. Ting worried that an English translation using the same language might make him appear "too pious" for Western audiences, and so there were subtle changes in the use of words in translation. In some speeches, the political language was moderated somewhat in translation to make them accessible to Western readers.

In the early 1980s, K. H. Ting believed that he had to catch up on his theological study and reading so that he would better understand developments in theology and the church since the 1960s, and discover their possible contribution to the life of the church in China. Three-self did not mean "self-sufficiency" or "self-isolation," he had said on many occasions, and he certainly demonstrated a creative use of non-Chinese sources in his eclectic reading of theology.[11] In the 1980s, Ting became interested in liberation theology, Teilhard de Chardin and process thought, as well as in the newer currents in ecumenical, contextual and feminist theologies.[12] He showed little interest in relating his theology to the Chinese cultural tradition, and it may be said that his own orientation was to address the immediate challenges facing the Chinese church. He regularly shared his thinking and reflections on what he was reading in the lectures he gave to seminary students. He also spoke to students about his visits abroad and invited theologians from overseas to speak at the seminary. This came at a time when there was tremendous interest among young people about life beyond China. One of Ting's hopes was to encourage students to become interested in theology so that they would become a force for reform and renewal in the Chinese church.[13]

For Ting, "theological reorientation" (*shenxue zaisi*) meant "daring to think, daring to blaze new trails, daring to enable theological thinking to open its doors to the reality of the world . . ." Ting was advocating a reorientation for the church in the 1980s, drawing on the example of the movement of theological fermentation that the TSPM had encouraged among grassroots Christians in the 1950s.[14] At issue was the way in which Chinese Christians would relate to Three-Self, to China's reforms, to social and ethical questions, and to "goodness, truth and beauty" outside the Christian community.

Since his early days as a theological student in the 1930s, Ting wanted to move the church beyond the narrow evangelical conservatism and otherworldly orientation of most of its members. Ting believed that the church in China was largely fundamentalist, and captive to a nineteenth-century missionary mentality. Only by moving beyond this could the church become genuinely self-governing, self-supporting and self-propagating, and thus make possible an authentic contextualization of Christianity. Chinese Christians were no longer subject to foreign domination, but this did not necessarily make their theology Chinese.[15] In daring to think anew and "blaze new trails," Ting was calling the church to respond to the promptings of the Holy Spirit in new ways.

The Holy Spirit both sustains people in the Christian community and leads them into "the world of which the church is but a part."[16] The Holy Spirit leads Christians into greater enlightenment and is the means by which they relate themselves theologically to the wider society.

> I like to emphasize this, that the Holy Spirit is not only the Comforter of believers, and the Guardian of the church, but also the Enlightener of the whole human race. The work of the Holy Spirit is not limited to those who believe in God in the Christian way.[17]

Goodness, truth and beauty outside the church were all related to the work of the Spirit. This implied that Christians and nonbelievers should be able to work together for the betterment of society, and that the difference between belief and nonbelief should not be an obstacle for cooperation in society. The Holy Spirit enables Christians to respond to history in new ways, provided they are able to listen to what the Spirit is saying to the churches in their particular times and places.

If the Holy Spirit is the Enlightener, then God the Creator is the Cosmic Lover. Love is God's major attribute. Ting repeats this single thought again and again, on page after page in his sermons and essays.

> What is the most important and most fundamental attribute of God? It is God's love, the love shown in Christ, the love which does not hesitate before suffering or the cross, the love which made him give up his life for his friends. The justice of God is also God's love. If love spreads throughout humankind, it becomes justice. This is love entering into the world. Love does not come to destroy, but to sustain, heal, teach, redeem and give life.[18]

God's love is the basic point of departure for Ting's theology. It is derived from his Anglican upbringing and theological training, and from his social-ethical orientation, informed by both Marxism and the Chinese philosophical tradition. The theme was not very prominent in Ting's writing in the 1940s and 1950s, but in the 1980s, the gospel of love appealed to him personally, coming after a time when those who "took class struggle as the key link" were in control.[19] God's abiding love and a theology of reconciliation also struck a chord among men and women recovering from the "ten years of chaos." Those who were becoming Christians "were first touched by love . . . by the kind of love with which Christ loves us" and not by particular points of Christian doctrine.[20]

It is in our encounter with the historical Jesus that we see and experience God's love. Ting was fond of saying that "Jesus is God-like, but through Christ, we first learn that God is Jesus-like." His is both a low Christology, emphasizing the humanity and the ethical teachings of Jesus, and a high Christology that speaks of the cosmic Christ, the Christ of the Johannine writings, of Ephesians and Colossians, who embraces the whole world.[21]

The New Testament texts for the majority of Ting's sermons are taken from the four Gospels and are related to the person and work of Jesus Christ. He was never interested in the christological controversies of the early centuries, or the christocentric theologies of the Reformation traditions, but his writing does reveal the attraction he feels to the Jesus of the Gospels, with an accent on God's immanence and presence in the world.

In Ting's trinitarian perspective, Father, Son and Holy Spirit work together in the continuing process of creation, redemption and sanctification. Our human task is to join in and contribute what we can. His understanding of the Incarnation becomes central in this regard. In a sermon based on the story of the Annunciation, Ting develops an idea he used when he was WSCF secretary. Mary, in saying "let it be with me according to your word," becomes a co-creator with God in God's work in the world.[22] She makes this decision on behalf of all of humanity and becomes the first missionary. Human cooperation with God is a key New Testament message and an essential part of the mission of the church.

Christians must, therefore, take historical movements for social change very seriously. The Christian's role in such movements is to take an active part and to relate their participation in history to the eternal work of God. This helps people outside the church understand the deeper and broader significance of God's action in the world, and so it has evangelistic significance.

> There are situations in which the Church has to tell the Inquirer, 'Go and sin no more.' But quite often the Church's message is to encourage the people to carry on their valuable work, to see it from a higher point of reference and to relate it to the loving purpose of God in all his work of creation, redemption and sanctification, thus to gain a newer and fuller sense of its value. Then the undertakings acquire a deeper grounding and are in tune with the love which is the reality at its deepest level, thereby giving the Christian a peace, a confidence, a calm, a faith, a lack of fear that is the result of his or her consciousness being at one with the ultimate.[23]

For Ting, the participation of human beings in God's work in the world requires a positive assessment of human potential and the possibilities for change. Like countless other Chinese Christian intellectuals, Ting does not take Adam's fall or the traditional Christian doctrine of sin very seriously. He has less than a dozen pages on the subject scattered throughout his collected works. One former colleague in the WSCF quipped that Ting's approach is "semi-Pelagian," which is true insofar as he emphasizes the possibilities rather than the limitations of human beings created in the image of God. The doctrine of original sin is not the gospel, and not even a precondition for Christian faith.

Ting argues instead that God's free gift of grace in Jesus Christ surpasses the sin of Adam. To be sure, human beings are still sinners, and it is in recognition of this that people may come to accept salvation in Jesus Christ. But the grace of Christ abounds even more than the sin of Adam (Romans 5:15), and the awareness of sin should encourage its own transcendence.[24] Ting urges a balanced view of the human condition and the potential for human life. This puts him closer to the Orthodox position of the East than to the Augustinianism of the West, although he does not make this connection in his work.

Human beings remain "unfinished products" (*ban chengpin*) of God's creation, with their own weaknesses and shortcomings, but also with the possibility of improving themselves.[25] In cooperating in the work of creation, redemption and sanctification, they are called beyond themselves, and they thereby help to contribute to their own salvation. Human action in history also involves an openness to society and the world beyond the church. It allows people to learn from their mistakes as they grow in the knowledge and love of God and the world. At the very least, Christians should practice the wisdom of Gamaliel (Acts 5:38-9) with respect to movements for change in history and society,[26] for this makes possible an openness to further learning.

This all-too-brief summary of K. H. Ting's theological position in the 1980s was very far from where the Chinese church actually was, and he knew this. His theology was a creative reinterpretation of the liberal, ecumenical and Anglican theology that he had learned in the 1930s and 1940s, but it certainly could not be termed "radical," at least by contemporary standards. Ting wanted a theological reorientation, but he knew that he could not impose his own thinking on the church. As a church leader conscious of Zhang Zhiyi's metaphor of a "locomotive pulling many carriages" (chap. 7), he wanted to unify the church and bring Christians together, not alienate them. The need for change and the importance of unity remained in constant tension throughout these years.

Because unity was so important, K. H. Ting believed that a church leader or a theologian needed to be in touch with the church in his or her own context, even if this meant proceeding more slowly than he or she would have liked:

> With all the importance given these days to contextualization, it may not be in fashion to say that in our view theology must be in conversation not only with the social and cultural context within which the church finds its being, but also with the minds and hearts of the masses of the Christians within the fold of the church. A "contextualized theology" appreciated only by socially conscientized intellectuals abroad but foreign to its own church constituency right at home is an anomaly . . . We write first of all for domestic consumption, that is, for Chinese Christians' nourishment and edification. We meet them where they are in ways they can accept. We do not impose on them anything they are not ready for. Theological changes are definitely taking place,

but these changes, instead of attuning themselves to elitist tastes elsewhere, must reflect and push forward changes—slow as these may seem—in the spirituality and intellectuality of the masses of Chinese Christians.[27]

These lines were written shortly after a delegation from the Urban Rural Mission of the WCC and the CCA had visited Nanjing and expressed their disappointment over not finding in China any kind of "liberation theology." Other theologians from the West were also making this criticism. Ting reacted sharply to such observations, for they offended his sense of pride in his country and his church. He did not want Chinese theology to be attuned "to elitist tastes elsewhere," however progressive they might seem, because he believed theology should be "mass based," drawing on a dialogue between the theologian and rank-and-file Christians, and grounded in the Chinese reality.

A liberation theology did not make sense in a "post-liberation" China. Whether one speaks of the 1950s or the 1980s, a government with its own language of liberation would not have allowed it, and a conservative church with a nineteenth-century theology could not have accepted it. Even when Ting voiced his own appreciation and support for liberation theology, he was not prepared to endorse it in its entirety.

Reconciliation between God and humanity is the eternal theme in Christian theology. Under this theme there will certainly be discussion of social and political liberation. The latter cannot easily be denied, but they are not the same theme. China has experienced political liberation, but the question of reconciliation between God and humanity still exists. Some liberation theologians give a broad meaning to "liberation," and this is fine in our view, but some do not. One professor puts it thus in one of his essays: "I still contend that the gospel is identical with the liberation of poor people from socio-political oppression." He says it is "identical," he does not say "supports." If he said he "supports," we could agree; if he had said "includes," that would also be good; "requires," would also be fine. But he says "identical," identifying the gospel with social and political liberation. We have reservations about this.[28]

As with any theologian or church leader, Ting's theology was also reflected in his personal understanding of prayer. He led a very public life, but by nature he was shy and reserved, and remained guarded and reticent, seldom speaking about his spiritual life or about a personal communion with God, even with those who were closest to him. Yet behind his public persona and theological rethinking lay a life deeply rooted in prayer and Bible reading. This was something he grew up with and never left behind. It would be out of character for him to speak openly about such matters and might even appear to be a form of self-indulgence, as if he were displaying his piety for the public benefit. But this in itself provides a clue to his spirituality: a lack of self-centeredness. For Ting, prayer was not asking for something, but the exposure of the self "to the light of God, to see if what we want is in line with the will of God, and to affirm or to strengthen our desire that God's will be done, in all cases."[29] Prayer means listening, waiting and developing an awareness of the truth that God wants for us. What K. H. Ting wrote about Y. T. Wu's view of prayer may more appropriately describe his own understanding.

> Through prayer, we readjust our relationship with God, abandoning our own selfishness and seeking harmony with God's truth. In this way, we consecrate to God the potentiality within our own being so that it may flourish and be brought to a higher level and that, invigorated, we may be partakers in God's work of creation, redemption and sanctification.[30]

The one time Ting was uncharacteristically revealing about himself and his life of prayer was when his mother died in the summer of 1986 at the age of 101. For the next several months, he spoke of his mother often, in public and in private, always with deep affection, but also with an understandable sense of sadness and loss. His mother was the one who prayed for him most deeply and most often, he said. He related his experience of his mother's love to the love that God has for us all. As he said on a visit to Hungary a few months after her death,

> My mother loved me so much. Her love for Christ, for the Church and for me was the same love; it could not be separated. Of course I was somewhat prepared for her death, but it was the most momentous event of my life. During these several months, I have often thought of her and I have often thought of death. Sometimes I feel she is very close to me, but at other times, I am overcome by the feeling that she has already turned into nothingness, that only her ashes remain.

In the same speech, after developing his view of God's love more fully, Ting returns to his mother, offering a reassuring perspective on the communion of saints.

> She died, but then again she is not dead. She is still progressing, still praying for me. I can still say as before that she is the one person in the world who prays most fervently for me. There where she is there are also many other saints who love us and who even now sustain us with their prayers. All this because God is love, because Jesus Christ died for us, because Christ conquered death, because he is the Risen Christ, who sustains creation with his power.[31]

This is as personal as he gets in relating theology to his own life and relationships. But it is enough to show that the faith that went into his theological rethinking was based on a personal communion with God and his own life of prayer. Ting's theology would be put to the test again and again in his efforts for reform, but he would continue to draw on a deeply rooted faith and spirituality as he worked for the reordering of relationships in church and society.

REORDERING RELATIONSHIPS I: CHURCH AND STATE

K. H. Ting was one of several dozen specially invited non-party dignitaries to the Thirteenth Party Congress in 1987. He listened carefully to Zhao Ziyang's sweeping agenda for change. China was still in the "primary stage of socialism," and so there would have to be a deepening and expanding of the reforms.[32] Zhao proposed that the party's role in local government and in economics be restricted, so that more control could be put into the hands of experts and elected officials. This would require the strengthening of the socialist legal system and enhancing the united-front idea of "democratic consultation and mutual supervision" through the people's congresses and consultative committees at all levels. It would also mean more debate over national policies.

Zhao used the March and April (1988) meetings of the CPPCC and NPC as forums to develop his reform program even further. The majority of delegates to both bodies was newly elected, and the new representatives were generally more outspoken than the ones they replaced. For the first time, the main sessions were open to foreign journalists, encouraging greater transparency and public discussion of the proceedings. Voting was no longer unanimous, and lively debates among members were shown for the first time on national television.[33] The increasing momentum of the reform program spilled over into the broader society and led to new proposals for change.

With Deng Xiaoping's apparent support, Zhao Ziyang pressed for more reform and openness because he believed that this would lift China out of its backwardness and liberate the productive forces for economic development. This would also mean reform in the realm of religion. An editorial in the official *Guangming Daily* made this point very clearly, arguing that the criticism of religion as opium and other theoretical issues were now secondary to economic considerations.

In order to develop productive forces, the enthusiasm of people (the most important factor of the productive forces) should be motivated to the greatest extent. That is to unite the masses of people, which include religious believers, and to feed their energies into the four modernizations. Theoretical study workers and people in religious circles should emphasize this point, but should not emphasize the differences of opinion of whether there is a god or not, and the "mistakes" of religion. Of course, it is also unnecessary to explain Marxism from a religious standpoint, and to bridge the fundamental differences between Marxism and religion. Does this propose that we find a harmonious compromise between Marxism and religion? No. In world outlook, materialism cannot compromise with idealism. However, in politics, atheists and religious followers can completely join a united front. The most important political issue at present is to focus on economic development, uphold the four basic principles, uphold the policy of reform and opening up, and build China into a strong socialist country with four modernizations as soon as possible.[34]

The emphasis on economic development in the late 1980s reduced the influence of politics in Chinese life and created more space for communities beyond the direct reach of the state, including religious institutions. China was moving from a situation of having a big state and a little society, to a smaller state and an enlarged society that would allow more independent social and cultural initiatives. A great deal has been written about "civil society" in China in recent years, centering on whether or not a public sphere began to emerge in 1988 and 1989.[35] Without entering into that discussion in full, we can say that religion was becoming an important expression of civil society in the mid-1980s. Ting and other religious leaders welcomed Zhao Ziyang's reform proposals because they created more space for the types of changes they had been urging on behalf of their own communities since the end of the Cultural Revolution era.

K. H. Ting served in both the CPPCC and the NPC. In 1988, he was named to the standing committees of each, and the following year he became one of the vice-chairs of the CPPCC. This put him at the center of the discussions of political reforms that were just beginning, and he experienced in the highest levels of government the new openness that appeared to be coming to Chinese political culture. He believed that the general call for reform could open the way for needed changes in church-state relations and that this would make possible changes within the church itself, and in the two national Christian bodies, so that the CCC could more effectively do "the work that is the church's own."[36] Change in church structures was dependent on change in church-state relations; both involved what Zhao Ziyang was calling the separation of political from administrative functions in the government and in nonstate enterprises.

On the government's part, this meant more attention to "democratic consultation" and "mutual supervision" with non-party individuals and groups. For religious bodies, it meant pressing for the better implementation of religious policy in order to create more space for churches, temples and mosques. Urging improved policy implementation and criticizing government officials was new for religious bodies in China. Religious leaders had not been able to play this role in the 1950s, at least not publicly, and the fact that they became more critical in the 1980s showed how much the times had changed. In the course of this decade, Zhao Puchu and K. H. Ting both became increasingly critical of the restrictions placed on the full exercise of religious freedom, but the issues were somewhat different for their constituencies. For Christians, these included: refusal to allow home-worship gatherings in some places; repeated delays in the return of church properties; control over religious life by government officials with little understanding of religion; and the manipulation of personnel in TSPM organizations. There were countless ways in which local cadres could use their power to make things difficult for religious believers. In the country as a whole, religious-policy implementation was uneven, with the inland provinces lagging far behind most coastal areas. On top of this was the lingering ultra-leftism among government cadres, based on their time-honored experience that it was always safer to delay making changes rather than act too quickly.

Some scholars have interpreted the period between 1984 and 1986 as a time of liberalization of religious policy (*fang*), and the period between 1987 and 1989, in the aftermath of the campaign against "spiritual pollution," as a time of increasing restrictions (*shou*).[37] They argue that this was the result of the state's growing concern over the growth in grassroots religion and "infiltration" from "hostile overseas forces." This was partly true, but it suggests that all decisions about *fang* and *shou* were being dictated by the government at the national level and that all officials were in agreement about what should be done. It does not take into account the dynamics of openness and reform, the give-and-take involved in the understanding, formulation and implementation of religious policy, and the role of religious leaders who were pressing for reform. An alternative explanation is that as the situation for religious groups improved through the 1980s, strengthened by the spirit of the Thirteenth Party Congress, new tensions arose in different provinces and locales, and new issues emerged.

With increasing openness, there was more information about the difficulties that religious groups were facing, as well as greater awareness of the disjunction between stated policy and the public statements of K. H. Ting and other leaders, on the one hand, and the actions of government cadres and religious communities in the provinces and at the grassroots on the other. In their efforts to deal with new problems, local authorities often placed new restrictions on religious groups; churches reported these to the CCC, and sometimes to news agencies overseas; and religious leaders responded by calling the problems to the attention of national bodies concerned with religious affairs. The effectiveness of religious leaders in resolving local problems is debatable, but throughout the 1980s, they increasingly exercised their right to call the government to account.

When K. H. Ting became head of the TSPM and the CCC, he began to receive a steady stream of oral and written reports about what was happening in churches all over China. He also met with church leaders and individual Christians who came to Nanjing to see him. As telecommunications improved, he began to get phone calls and faxes about urgent problems. Occasionally, he went to the provinces to see what was happening for himself.[38] But more often he sent representatives, including seminary students, to go and see what was happening and report back to him. This enabled him to be better informed about the situation of the churches in the provinces and develop an overview of religion in the nation as a whole.

Local Christians sought the support of Ting and other church leaders in dealing with particular problems in their own situations. This form of direct entreaty reflected the needs of growing Christian communities with insufficient resources as well as problems with the implementation of religious policy. Requests ranged from help with securing more Bibles and trained church leaders to support for the renovation or building of churches, to assistance with the return of properties and the easing of government restrictions. The latter required putting pressure on local officials by taking problems to a higher level. The sheer volume of requests was overwhelming, and dealing with local problems was always a time-consuming process. It involved getting more information, contacting government officials and following up to see whether any action was taken. Although Ting was able to handle some requests directly, in most cases he had to refer the problems to the TSPM and the CCC, or to an appropriate government body. Some requests were ignored altogether, which led to anger and frustration at the local level.

Ting also learned about the situation of churches at the grassroots from students at Nanjing Seminary. They became his eyes and ears and provided him with a sense of what was happening in different provinces. For example, Li Yading, from Liaoning Province in the northeast, was in the first class of Nanjing Seminary after its reopening in 1981, and he became an elected leader of the student body. Churches in the northeast had had a particularly difficult time during the Cultural Revolution, and Li's own father, a "Little Flock" leader, had been persecuted since the 1950s. Li was interested in Chinese church history, and in 1984, he visited churches in Shandong to collect materials on the churches in the province. There he discovered that Shandong churches were in continuing difficulties, at the mercy of both government officials and local TSPM leaders. Li coined the term *lao sanzi* ("Old Three-Selfer") to describe TSPM leaders who were so attached to the political orientation and working style of the 1950s that they could not address the problems of the church in the 1980s. He wrote an eight-page report to K. H. Ting on his visit to Shandong, and Ting used the report to press for changes in the situation.[39] Nanjing Seminary students came from all over the country, and Li Yading is but one example of those who spoke with Ting about the problems they encountered in the provinces.

Documented reports on the abuses of religious policy enabled Ting to press for change more effectively at the national level. He criticized cadres whose actions did not conform to the more open religious policies set down in Document 19 and the new constitution.[40] As he received more and more reports about problems in religious-policy implementation, his advocacy for the churches became more direct and outspoken. In the 1988 session of the CPPCC, Ting made a strongly worded speech criticizing RAB cadres who were interfering with local religious practice.

Cadres in many localities are stressing that "in those areas where policy has already been implemented, oversight of religion should be strengthened." They further say that "administrative leadership of religion should be strengthened." These two vague ideas have functioned to encourage government cadres to meddle into the matters which belong to religions themselves. These cadres neither believe in religion nor understand it, and they have no sympathy for the feelings of religious believers. They are disgusted by religion and their inclination is to reduce the scope of religious activity in order to hasten its demise. They exceed their authority, act arbitrarily and dictatorially, designate their trusted supporters whom religious believers despise to be in charge of patriotic religious organizations and venues for religious activities. They see leading persons in religious circles as objects of supervision and do not permit them to be in contact with the masses of believers which naturally leads to negative feelings on the part of their constituencies.[41]

During the same CPPCC session, Ting received a letter from Zhang Shengcai, a house-church leader in Xiamen.[42] The letter complained of newly drafted regulations in some provinces that were aimed at restricting home-worship gatherings. Zhang also sent an open letter to the CPPCC, detailing his charges, and he enclosed a copy of one set of regulations from Shanxi. In his reply to the letter, Ting commended Zhang Shengcai for his criticisms but urged him to get all his facts right and report accurately. He said that he would "never agree to the government imposing things on the church which would be harmful to it," and that the Shanxi regulations were problematic. Ting also expressed the hope that as fellow Christians, he and Zhang could cooperate in the future. The house churches and their supporters overseas welcomed Ting's letter as an indication that Ting was willing to argue their cause and stand up for the church in his dealings with the government.[43]

At the time, there were regulations similar to those in Shanxi being prepared in Guangdong. Ting was not opposed to legislation on religion as a matter of principle. Strengthening the legal system was part of Zhao Ziyang's reform program, and Ting believed that an openly promulgated religious law would serve to reinforce the legal standing of the churches. However, he objected to arbitrary rules and ad hoc regulations imposed by local cadres and provincial authorities. The regulations in Guangdong were provincial documents that seemed to contradict national religious policy.[44] In a widely reprinted interview, Ting had told Ewing W. Carroll, a United Methodist Church executive with close ties to the Chinese church, that "the structure and style of Chinese government and society neither requires nor provides any process whereby Christian groups must be registered."[45] When it was reported a few months later that new national regulations mandating registration were in process, Ting was caught off guard. His credibility with churches was undercut, and he therefore had to speak up.

In private, Ting was angered about the new regulations, but they now appeared to be a *fait accompli*. In a second interview published the next year, Carroll asked about the regulations in Guangdong. (The Guangdong regulations had been formally issued on 1 May, and just as Zhang Shengcai had warned, they called for registration in a manner that was designed to restrict home-worship gatherings. Although they were not issued publicly, they were widely available in Hong Kong within a matter of weeks.) Ting, aware that he was speaking for both an international and a domestic readership, offered a measured response.

> Some time ago, government agencies in Guangdong Province asked that places for religious activity apply for registration. If this is a measure aimed at eliminating meetings of Christians in their homes without first providing more suitable places for them, it is an infringement on religious freedom. At least for the sake of openness and public supervision, the appropriate government agencies should make public the grounds for permission to be granted or denied. We are watching developments in Guangdong carefully and have already written to the Religious Affairs Bureau of the State Council and other related bodies about our concern and views.[46]

This was his published response. However, in the letter he wrote to the RAB two months earlier, and which was made public at about the same time as the interview, Ting spoke much more strongly. He is explicit about his displeasure with the new regulations, and he asks that steps be taken to rectify the situation. In addition, Ting criticized the heavy-handedness of Guangdong authorities in their relationship with religious believers.

> Insistence upon the use of administrative measures in dealing with the beliefs of the masses or with human relationships has never brought good results. This is an important experience finally gleaned at bitter cost after thirty-odd years of religious work. Why should we want to repeat it today? Such measures will certainly not cause the home gatherings to disappear, but will inevitably result in their turning underground, fan the flames of fanatical religion and mission activity and contribute to a mood of opposition to the party and the government.[47]

In this letter, Ting goes even further and defends Lin Xiangao (Samuel Lamb), the internationally prominent house-church leader in Guangzhou. Ting supported Lin's right to continue his activities, despite the fact that he refused to register, was opposed to the TSPM, and was the subject of repeated government harassment.[48] It was not the house churches, but the new regulations that were at fault, Ting wrote, for they went against the constitution, Document 19 and united-front efforts in religious work. Ting repeated his request for government redress in the letter's final paragraph, but ended on an acerbic note in the expectation that his words would fall on deaf ears.

> I hope that the Religious Affairs Bureau of the State Council will move quickly to make its attitude concerning the steps adopted in Guang-dong clear, in order to facilitate religious work throughout the nation. If my views are felt to be biased, I would appreciate having this pointed out as soon as possible. This is preferable to having my correspon-dence regarding crucial issues ignored, as happened in the past.[49]

Ting's prediction that his criticisms would be ignored proved correct, and the Guangdong regulations, as well as similar ordinances from other provinces, remained in place. The very next month, the RAB and the Pub-lic Security Bureau (PSB) issued a "Circular on the Control and Handling of Those Who Use Christianity to Undertake Illegal Activities."[50] It is ostensi-bly about the maintenance of public order, but it provides further indica-tion that many government departments harbored deep suspicions about Christian practice. The bureaucracies that had direct responsibility for reli-gious affairs and public order at the national level were concerned that Christianity could become a base for anti-government activity, and that the house churches were particularly susceptible to "infiltration" from hostile "anti-China" forces overseas.

Judging from this circular and the new provincial and national regula-tions, the RAB's efforts to strengthen control over religion appeared to be gaining ground. Zhao Ziyang had called for quickening the pace of openness and reform, but RAB and PSB officials seemed more intent on "tightening up" (*shou*) rather than "relaxing" (*fang*) control over religious institutions and local churches, even in the reformist era of the late eighties. They justi-fied this on the basis of a neo-authoritarian adherence to the "four cardinal principles" as applied to religious groups, but the regulations also suggest that there was a greater ultra-leftist influence in religious work than in other areas of society and culture. Whether from a sense of self-protection, polit-ical expediency or bureaucratic inertia, officials in the RAB, the UFWD, the PSB and other government organizations seemed to be resistant to address-ing the need for the reform of religious work.

This was not true of all officials, however, and it was not consistent with the spirit of the times. Even as he was criticizing RAB officials, Ting was also seeking out others in the national government who might be more sympa-thetic. One of these was Yan Mingfu, an ally of Zhao Ziyang, a member of the Central Committee and the director of the UFWD in the late 1980s, a role that put him in a good position to work for change in religious policy. Yan was a rising star in the national leadership who was popular with intel-lectuals and religious leaders. His father had at one time been a YMCA secretary in Chongqing, and this may help explain why Yan had a sympathetic understanding of the church. Ting met Yan Mingfu in the fall of 1986, when they had extensive conversations and became allies. Yan also saw the need for reform in the administration of religious affairs, and Ting saw him as representing the changing attitude of many national leaders. For Ting, a friendly official in such a prominent position was reason for hope. This was despite the fact that the regulations had been a disappointment and a step backward.

In late 1988 and the first part of 1989, Ting and Zhao Puchu proposed a thorough overhaul of the system of administration and leadership of religious affairs. In this, they had the tacit or explicit support of Yan Mingfu and other well-connected senior party officials. At the end of 1988, Ting co-authored an influential report addressed to scholars and government administrators, which represented a radical restatement of his ideas on religion and religious policy.[51] He spoke of the need for "seeking truth from facts" and a practice-oriented approach to religious studies, and of the positive role that religion could play in socialist society and Chinese culture. The most radical section (part 7) calls for reform in the leadership of religious affairs.

> There has long been an over concentration of power in China's system of religious affairs leadership and administration, resulting in serious abuses in the system taking on for itself things which should be left to religious groups.[52]

Ting goes on to argue that there should be the separation of religion and the state, for religious organizations should be left to govern themselves. Ting was writing only a month after he had written his letter on the Guangdong regulations. The RAB had always been resistant to calls for reform, especially when these came from religions leaders, but Ting continued to object to the RAB's continual refrain of their need to "strengthen administrative leadership" over religious bodies. He was now asking why there could not be a simpler formula such as "leadership [by the RAB] in politics; self-government in religion"[53] This was the same criticism he had been making since 1980, but now there was support from some high-level government officials. Ting's words reflected the spirit of Zhao Ziyang's report to the Thirteenth Party Congress. If the RAB were reformed, it would mean the beginning of a separation of politics from religion, which would enhance the independence of religious bodies.* Religious groups and government

---

* The Chinese phrase *zheng jiao yao fen kai* means the separation of religion from politics, not the separation of church and state. It should be interpreted within the context of China's reforms rather than the context of liberal democracy. The Chinese state, traditional or Communist, would never tolerate a bifurcation of political and religious authority. The separation of religion from politics meant that there should be less government control over the internal affairs of religious communities, greater independence for religious institutions and "mutual supervision" between the two.

departments had different functions, and their functions and roles should be "reordered" (*lishun*). This kind of reform was appropriate for a country seeking to liberate the productive forces of society in the "primary stage of socialism." It was also consistent with changes taking place in other sectors of society.

At about the same time, Ting told a gathering of TSPM and CCC leaders that government and party leaders were aware of the fact that relationships with the church had to be reordered.

> The essence of the Thirteenth Party Congress includes a readjustment (or reordering) of the function of government Religious Affairs Bureaus. It is considering seriously rectification of its relationship with various religious groups. I believe that we can anticipate the principle of church-state separation being put into greater effect.[54]

In the NPC and CPPCC sessions in the spring of 1989, K. H. Ting and Zhao Puchu continued to press for the reform of the RAB. They also called for the creation of a law on religion so that religious communities would not be subject to the arbitrary actions of individual officials.[55] Zhao Puchu argued that relationships between the RAB and religious groups needed to be rationalized and "reordered" and that greater effort had to be made for the full implementation of religious freedom.[56] It was at this same session, in March 1989, that Ting was elected a vice-chair of the CPPCC, so it appeared that his influence was on the rise. The prospects for change in early 1989 seemed very good, and, despite the setbacks he had witnessed, Ting was optimistic and upbeat in his assessment of the political situation.

REORDERING RELATIONSHIPS II:
BUILDING UP THE BODY IN LOVE

The reform or reordering of the government's system of religious administration would make possible reform in the church. But Ting knew that the TSPM and the CCC had serious problems of their own that would have to be resolved by Christian leaders themselves regardless of what the government did.

Naturally enough, Ting praised the TSPM on its thirtieth anniversary, giving credit to the generation of Christian leaders and government officials who had helped to make the movement possible, and summing up the accomplishments of Three-Self in the present.

> The number of Christians in China has grown, not diminished. Though there have been many twists and turns in the Three-Self path, though its work has not always been what it might or should be, it

has improved. Many people who had all sorts of reservations about Three-Self now praise it, and so Three-Self has grown strong and not weakened.[57]

In the four years since the Third NCC in 1980, the TSPM and the CCC had done a great deal to reestablish an institutional-church presence in China. Provincial TSPM committees and Christian Councils had been started in most provinces. More than 4,000 churches had been newly built or were reopened, and almost 17,000 meeting points (or home-worship gatherings) had been organized. Using its own resources, the CCC and the TSPM had printed more than 2.7 million bibles; 700,000 hymnals and 800,000 catechisms, as well as church magazines and other Christian literature. In addition to Nanjing Theological Seminary, 9 regional and provincial theological training centers had been established. Lay leadership programs were conducted all over China to meet the needs of a burgeoning church with an officially estimated 3.4 million Christians in 1986.[58] The churches in China were experiencing a revival, despite the continuing problems with the implementation of religious policy discussed above.

In recognizing these accomplishments, however, the tremendous problems that the churches were facing could not be overlooked. Their leadership was aging, and not enough young people were interested in becoming pastors. The resulting leadership vacuum meant that there was inadequate pastoral and theological guidance for churches and Christian meeting points. A great number of sectarian and heretical communities had emerged, especially in the rural areas where most Christians lived. Most seminary teachers were poorly trained local pastors, who were not only out of touch with recent theological and educational developments but also insufficiently aware of the challenges that society posed to the church. The CCC and the TSPM promoted church unity, but that unity was extremely fragile. There were serious tensions, not only among different denominational traditions but even among Christian leaders within the same tradition. A great many Christians still distrusted the TSPM or local Three-Self leaders, and they were wary of any connection with the government. As the Chinese economy developed, the churches' self-support became increasingly difficult. The maintenance of churches and church institutions required increasing resources, but Christians had little access to funds beyond those that the local community could raise and, in the cities, the money that came from the rental of church properties.

No one was clearer about the difficulties the church was facing than K. H. Ting. In the 1980s, he was never one to paint a rosy view of the church situation, whether speaking of its political context or its internal problems. He did defend the church against the negative reporting that was coming from Hong Kong and the West, but in public and private, he urged Chinese and foreign Christians to look at the serious difficulties in the churches. There were problems with each of the three selves (self-administration, self-support and self-propagation) in the TSPM. To address this situation, Ting emphasized the need for well-administered, well-supported churches in which the work of propagation is also done well, the so-called "three wells" (*san hao*). The TSPM could not respond to new challenges by falling back on familiar slogans about patriotism and Three-Self independence. Ting's insistence on "running the church well," first articulated at the Third NCC, was a persistent theme in the 1980s and 1990s. [59] More than a pious call to do better, it was his way of addressing the need for the TSPM and the CCC to attend to "the work that is the church's own," a deliberate shift toward building up the church and away from "Old Three-Self" (*lao sanzi*) patriotism.

The direction in which he wanted to lead the TSPM and the CCC had immediate and practical implications for the Protestant community. He had spoken with reformers in the government about reordering relationships, not only in church-state relations but in the church itself, and in the relationship between the TSPM and the CCC. Government officials associated with the policies of Zhao Ziyang clearly supported this move. In the case of the Catholic Church, there is even a government document urging clarification and the reordering of relationships among the three national patriotic organizations: the Catholic Patriotic Association (the equivalent of the TSPM), the Church Administrative Committee, and the Catholic Bishops' Conference (in some ways equivalent to the CCC).[60] No similar government document relating to the Protestants was published, but it can be assumed that the government had similar concerns on the relationships among the churches, the TSPM and the CCC.

At the Fourth NCC in 1986, Ting clearly articulated the priority for strengthening the churches and church structures. More than in 1980, he was able to shape the agenda of the Fourth NCC, despite considerable opposition from some Shanghai and provincial leaders. This was the first time that concerns for strengthening the church as the church featured so prominently in a national conference. The 1980 conference had to focus on rebuilding after the Cultural Revolution, and the NCCs in 1954 and 1960 were more concerned with political matters. In contrast to any previous conference, the Fourth NCC proclaimed that the church needed "to be built upon truth and faith" and grounded "in the sacred love of Christ."[61] The patriotic work of the TSPM would be continued, but ecclesial concerns and theological training would become the main priorities in the years ahead. This new emphasis was due to the vision and efforts of K. H. Ting, who, as expected, was reconfirmed as leader of the TSPM and the CCC.

Ting preached at the closing service of worship of the conference, and, more than in any other sermon before or since, he elaborated both his vision for the church and the obstacles in the way. Entitled "Building Up the Body in Love," his sermon texts were Ephesians 4:15-16 and Revelation 2:1-7. Ting had preached on the chapters in Revelation on a number of occasions in the past, each time urging Christians to read the signs of the times and listen to what the Spirit was saying to the churches. This time, Ting spoke to a movement that "had abandoned the love [it] had at first" and reminded those who had gathered of the need to "remember from what [it] had fallen." His reference to the TSPM was clear. To achieve its original goals, the TSPM had, in the past, devoted much time and attention to struggle, but this had led to bitterness and misunderstandings. Now, "the Holy Spirit wants the church to repent," and "struggle must give way to reconciliation" in order to build up the body of the church in love.

He spoke of particular struggles and difficulties in the Christian community by implication only. Yet Ting's message throughout would be understood by the assembled delegates: the church is founded on adherence to faith in the lordship of Christ and on Christ alone. Guided by the Holy Spirit, it must be built up from the grassroots, allow for a wide diversity of Christian beliefs and work toward reconciliation among its members. For the sake of reconciliation and the acceptance of diversity, the relationship between the churches and the TSPM would have to be changed.

> We need a correct understanding of the relation between Three-Self and the church. The church is not subordinate to Three-Self. The church is the body of Christ, the dwelling of the risen Christ, the fellowship of saints through the ages. The Church is our subject while Three-Self and Christian Councils are products which have emerged under certain concrete historical conditions. They are servants of the church.[62]

Neither the TSPM nor the CCC is the church. Nor is the church a sectarian or purified "gathered community" of the "saved" who set themselves apart from other Christians. The church is inevitably a mixed community, a field in which there are both good seeds and bad. "A church with weeds is still a church," Ting said. He continued,

> Jesus does not ask us to spend all of our time in trying to pull up the weeds, nor does he want us to move the wheat or have it transplanted to some other field. Jesus says, "Let both grow together until harvest." In other words, he will separate them. Today, in our church, our task is to grow, to enable the wheat to grow faster than the weeds and not allow the weeds to grow so fast as to crowd out the wheat. Those who are good seeds are not to remain outside of the field, accusing this one and that one of being bad seeds or weeds. Our job is not to blame or pull out, but to enter, to grow, so that our church grows in size and quality.[63]

Ting's sermon is a stirring defense of the church, and, as we read it today, it does not seem very controversial. But it was certainly controversial at the time, and following consultation and debate with other leaders, the sermon went through many revisions. The sermon had been scheduled for the second day of the conference, but it was rescheduled for the final day because of the behind-the-scenes negotiations. Despite the qualifications he made about the importance of continuing with the work of the TSPM, work that Ting thoroughly supported, some Shanghai leaders continued to object to his message and suggested further changes. For example, the original version said, "In the overall work of the CCC and the TSPM, where there is brokenness, we must yield to others; where there is struggle, we must yield to tolerance; where there is tearing down, we must yield to building up." This was omitted from the published sermon, but there were those who continued to be against any statement on repentance, arguing that struggle "was also a kind of love." According to one close colleague, Ting rejected this kind of argument and became angry.

> How could someone call the struggles of the past a kind of love? The atmosphere in the room froze and he said in a steely voice, "Allow me to really be president of the China Christian Council for just one day, and then no one will keep me from speaking out!" [64]

Ting was directly challenging the ultra-leftist line among some leaders in the TSPM. But the tradition of collective decision making in the CCC and the TSPM meant that Ting would have to accept some of the suggested changes for the sake of unity in the leadership, even though he was reluctant to soften his message. The controversy over this sermon illustrates the tensions in the Christian leadership over the extent to which TSPM and church relationships should be reordered.

Ting believed that a reordering of relationships was necessary if there was to be genuine mutual respect in matters of faith, a respect that would allow for diversity. "In matters of faith and worship," Ting said in his sermon, "we must not force the minority to follow the majority." All through the 1980s, Ting continued to reach out in this spirit to conservative sectarian groups and expand the unity of the TSPM and the CCC. He made it clear that as president of the China Christian Council, he wished to serve all the church. Bibles were provided for Christians whether or not they were related to the TSPM and the CCC, and students from all church backgrounds were welcomed at the seminaries set up by the TSPM and the CCC. Ting made special efforts to meet with conservative and evangelical leaders in order to share with them his efforts in reordering relationships and improving the implementation of religious policy.

His efforts bore some fruit. Before the Fourth NCC, Ting had arranged for the publication of a small book which consisted mainly of affirmations of the TSPM by many well-known evangelical leaders, and this volume was well received.[65] Chinese Christians were encouraged when they read reports about K. H. Ting in the newspapers, or when they saw him on television, whether or not they accepted his theological views. His public presence showed that Christianity was becoming more widely accepted. When he was elected vice-chair of the CPPCC in March 1989, Ting's photograph appeared for the first time in the major national newspaper, *Renmin ribao (People's Daily)*.[66] It was reported to me that on hearing that the vote in the CPPCC was 1,666 for and 66 against, some evangelical groups saw a sign of divine favor. In their view, the 666 was the beast from the Book of Revelation (Revelation 13:18), yet the beast was subdued by the "1" God, thus 1,666. The 66 against were the small devil, also easily defeated. This simple, and perhaps apocryphal story, was widely retold, which indicates that some of the fundamentalist groups had warmed to Ting's leadership. More importantly, it was also reported in churches all over China that many such groups and home-worship gatherings were now praying for his leadership.

Ting understood that he could not treat Christians with the heavy-handed tactics that the TSPM had used in the past. Nor could there be a top–down approach to church unity, for evangelicals had a more congregational approach to ecclesiology. But at the same time, Ting and many others in the CCC and the TSPM felt it was time to begin to move toward the formation of a unified church. This too would be an effort in church building, and an ecclesial structure would further promote reordering relationships.

The China Christian Council was not a council of churches, for it was not made up of member churches or denominations, and it was not a unified church either. Ting liked to describe the CCC as somewhere in-between, but also on the way to becoming a national church structure. In the words of some in the CCC, its mandate was to remove the character *xie* ("council") in the Chinese term for the China Christian Council (*zhongguo jidujiao xiehui*), thus transforming it into the Christian Church of China. Ting said that a new church would have congregational, presbyterian and episcopal elements of church order, and it would strive to unite all Protestants into a single structure. But in informal conversations after the Fourth NCC, he also hinted that there might even be room for a small number of "free churches" to remain outside. The possibility of working toward a Christian Church of China was discussed at the Fourth NCC, and an informal committee was set up to consider the possibility. As it turned out, little progress was made, except that a "Church Order for Trial Use in Chinese Churches" was formally approved at the Fifth NCC five years later.[67] But the very fact that there was serious discussion of the proposal shows that Ting was having some success in promoting the importance of strengthening the church in the CCC and TSPM.

Another expression of church building during these years was the consecration of two new "postdenominational" bishops in June 1988. This was the first consecration in thirty-three years—K. H. Ting had been one of three Anglican bishops consecrated at the previous service—and it attracted a great deal of attention both in China and overseas. The new bishops were not Anglican and they had no administrative responsibilities or power. They were chosen to be pastors for pastors, "shepherds among shepherds." The two who were consecrated were Shen Yifan (a former Anglican) and Sun Yanli (a former Methodist). Four of the six remaining Anglican bishops in China participated in the laying on of hands, but so did other senior pastors in Shanghai from non-Anglican backgrounds. No bishops from overseas participated, although church representatives from overseas were welcomed at the service. Significantly, the consecrations were done under the authority of the Shanghai Christian Council, not the CCC, which meant that this was a local action rather than something for the country as a whole.[68]

The consecration of new bishops was something that Ting had wanted for some time, but there was not a great deal of support in the churches. He realized that the office of bishop was not accepted by evangelicals or by most other Chinese Protestants. Nor did it have a strong basis in Chinese Protestant tradition. Before 1949, only the Anglicans, the Methodists and the True Jesus Church had bishops, but a different Chinese term was used for "bishop" in the other denominations. There have been no consecrations of non-Roman Protestant bishops in any part of China since 1988, although the subject was discussed within the TSPM and the CCC in 2004 and 2005. This suggests the opposition may have won the day. But the episcopacy represented an important aspect of Ting's understanding of the church, and his views on the subject are important in this respect.

He did not see bishops as representing a return to denominationalism, for there would be no dioceses and no episcopal system of church governance. But the office of bishops and the threefold order of ministry meant for Ting that the church could be more fully the church. "By having bishops, the ministry of our church becomes complete, or more complete," he said in the sermon he preached at the consecrations.[69] Archbishop Runcie had said in 1983 that Ting was an Anglican bishop "plus something," and Ting now referred to the new bishops in the same way. The bishops would have no dioceses but would be theological, moral, spiritual and pastoral exemplars. Like all Chinese clergy, the bishops would depend "on the power of love and of example, and not on the power of position," Ting said in his sermon. The bishops would symbolically represent the church in society, and so they would have to be above reproach in their personal and public lives.

What was true for bishops should also be true for the church as a whole. Between 1986 and 1989, there was a great deal of discussion about church leadership and church order in the TSPM/CCC. For Ting, the key issue was a correct understanding of the theological nature of the church, and over these years, he made use of every opportunity he had to make his point clear. He was attempting to reorder relationships between the TSPM and the churches so as to facilitate "building up the body in love." In so doing, he had to negotiate a way for the church to be the church between the so-called "old Three-Selfers (*lao sanzi*)," TSPM traditionalists who wanted to keep things just as they were, and those who called for abolishing the TSPM or who did not see a need for any national structure at all.

K. H. Ting and Archbishop Robert Runcie at Canterbury, 1988. Reproduced with the permission of the late Robert Runcie, 102nd archbishop of Canterbury.

Ting believed that in its essence, the church was a divinely constituted society, but historically churches were a mixture of saints and sinners. This was the classical Anglican teaching that Ting grew up with and learned as a theological student in the 1930s and 1940s. But this came to have particular relevance for him as a church leader in the 1980s. At the consecration service, he said

The church is not to be made into a bureaucracy, an office, a recreational center, an economic enterprise, a mouthpiece of anything not the church. First of all, the church has to be the church.[70]

The church is a social body, but it is different from other social organizations such as the All-China Women's Federation or the Red Cross.

It has its sacred dimension. The church is not only a spiritual fellowship of believers, it is the temple of the Holy Spirit. It is the Body of Christ with Christ as its head. In the words of the familiar hymn, "She is his new creation, by water and the word." The church is a "golden lamp stand." The Apostle's and Nicene Creed, after expressing our faith in God the Father, Son and Holy Spirit, goes on to say that we believe in the Church. We can see that Christians throughout the ages have accepted the church as part of the Christian mystery and as part of the Christian faith.

It is precisely for this reason that Christians found it "uncomfortable and out of order" to have any other organization set above the church, for "it would be as if the foundation of Christ as head of the Church were taken away."

Therefore, the idea that "Three-Self leads the Church" or that "the church is a religious organization under the administration of the Religious Affairs Bureau" is grating to Christian ears. This is not because Christians do not love their country or support their government, nor is it caused by anti-China feelings abroad. It is a matter of faith. [71]

Ting was now criticizing the TSPM in the same way that he criticized the RAB and its meddling in the work of the churches. In many places, the TSPM had become "a management department, like a church, yet not really like a church; like a government, yet not really like a government."[72] The TSPM was also caught up in the ultra-leftism that had dominated Chinese political life since the late 1950s, and it had taken over many of the functions of the church in the process. In many places, local TSPM leaders, most of them laymen and laywomen, were more powerful than church leaders, and they made decisions for the churches. Ting believed that the TSPM needed to be reordered and that its function needed to be changed.

In the fall of 1988, Ting was proposing that the TSPM should limit itself to three major tasks: *education* in "patriotism" and the Three-Self principle, *monitoring* religious-policy implementation, and *developing* social-welfare projects in order to strengthen self-support in the churches. This would represent a severe curtailment of power for the TSPM at all levels. At the December 1988 meeting of the TSPM/CCC, where he had introduced the idea of "reordering relationships," no drastic decisions were made, but it was decided that the TSPM and the CCC would act according to their constitutions, and this in itself was a kind of reordering. He continued to press for strengthening the church as the church, and this was a step in that direction.

In criticizing the TSPM and arguing for a "change in function" (*gaibian zhineng*) of Three-Self organizations, Ting was responding to the widespread dissatisfaction that he was hearing from Christians at the grassroots. The criticism of the TSPM by overseas groups reflected, at least in part, the criticisms of many Christians in China. They were not necessarily opposed to the Three-Self principle, but they were opposed to leaders who lorded it over the church in collaboration with patrons in the RAB or other government bodies. Ting stood against many other TSPM/CCC leaders in his wish to wrest power from the TSPM and give it back to the churches. He liked to say that the TSPM was the "scaffolding" of a building, not the foundation.[73]

Once the building of the church was complete, the scaffolding would no longer be necessary.

By late 1988, Ting was even suggesting in private conversations that the TSPM had outlived its usefulness and could be dissolved in a few years time. Clearly, he was encouraged by developments in society as a whole and by people close to Yan Mingfu and other reformers. In an interview in early 1989, Ting was reported as telling *News Network International* that the TSPM would be dissolved by the end of 1991.[74] This report led to great controversy and debate within the TSPM/CCC leadership, because no decision had yet been made by either body. In response to this publicity, Ting denied what he was quoted as saying in the report. He continued to say that changes were forthcoming, but that no decision had been reached about the future of the TSPM.[75]

Despite this denial about what he had said in public, Ting himself seemed to believe that the TSPM had outlived its usefulness and that it obstructed rather than promoted church unity. He could not say this publicly, because there was no agreement on the point within the Christian leadership. But he did make his views clear in private. He had said privately the previous November,

> Theologically, it is impossible to account for such an organization [i.e., the TSPM] on top of the church. No one in China opposes the Three-Self principle, but many people oppose Three-Self organizations . . . When we have changed the function of the TSPM, then I will go to see Wang Mingdao and Lin Xiangao. Today, it would not be useful to do so because Three-Self is holding too much power. The China Christian Council was intended to correct the situation I have just described, but it was not able to do so . . . Therefore, we need either the demise of the TSPM organizations, or a change in their function.[76]

This is a startling statement, but it reveals how closely reordering relationships was tied up with church building and reconciliation with evangelicals in his mind. Ting understood the forces that were at work in the government and in the church, and he had good grounds for optimism that the reordering of relationships would eventually prevail. This was not only because he was caught up in the political changes of the late 1980s. It had to do with his basic theological perspective and his vision for the church.

THE AMITY FOUNDATION AND
INTERNATIONAL CHRISTIAN COOPERATION

Ting's theology and vision shaped the way that he believed the church should relate to society and the wider world. He wanted Christians to play a more constructive role in society, but this was not possible within the existing organizational framework of the RAB, or the CCC and the TSPM in the mid-1980s. Something more had to be done.

Ting was becoming more open to the wider *oikoumene* and more relaxed in relating to churches overseas. He was increasingly confident that Three-Self was not only right for China but accepted and even advocated by some churches and Christian groups overseas. For example, he was deeply moved by his conversations with African American Christians attending an international conference in Nanjing who voiced their support for Three-Self.[77] Although he still believed it necessary to maintain vigilance about hostile "anti-China" forces overseas, Ting also saw that there could be greater flexibility in the application of Three-Self in the eighties than there had been in the fifties, sixties and seventies. Three-Self, as he had said on many occasions, did not mean "self-isolation."

The reforms themselves created new possibilities for openness to the world and to Christian-initiated involvement in society. The critique of ultra-leftism continued in the mid-1980s, but this now found expression in concrete humanitarian initiatives. The Chinese Welfare Fund for the Handicapped was set up in Beijing in April 1984, and among the initiators were several of Ting's colleagues and friends, including Zhao Puchu, who was made an honorary board member.[78] Deng Xiaoping's son Deng Pufang, who had been paralyzed below the waist when he was thrown out of a window during the Cultural Revolution, became deputy director. He became a leading voice in reformist efforts to promote greater awareness of humanitarianism and the need for social-welfare programs. In one of his speeches published in *Renmin ribao* (*People's Daily*), he said that the China Welfare Fund for the Handicapped was socialist, humanitarian, patriotic and reformist, serving the people according to the new demands of the times. "Our work is one of humanism," Deng said, "that is to say we wish to raise the material and spiritual level of the people, so that everyone may feel useful, especially the physically handicapped, who are especially unfortunate."[79] He invited Mother Teresa to visit Beijing and commended her for her spirit of sacrifice on behalf of the poor in India.[80] The younger Deng then went to Hong Kong, where he praised the activities of Christian voluntary organizations working with the poor, the elderly and the disabled.

Shortly after the establishment of the China Welfare Fund for the Handicapped, Hu Qiaomu, a conservative and member of the Central Committee of the CPC, began to encourage religious groups to undertake activities for social welfare. Specifically mentioning Buddhists and Christians, he said that "in the old society, religious believers did social work, and we should advocate this even more strongly today." Working for the betterment of society would bring religious believers and nonbelievers closer together and, according to Hu, undercut "wasteful superstitious activities." This would represent a new stage in the party's relationship with religious groups and enhance their standing in society.[81] Social and political changes in China

Press conference announcing the formation of the Amity Foundation, Hong Kong, 1985. From left to right: the author, K. H. Ting, Han Wenzao. Photograph taken by Janice Wickeri.

were creating a framework that would make possible the increasing Christian activity in society that Ting hoped for. "The Decision on the Reform of the Economic Structure," approved by the CPC in October 1984, called for the expansion of enterprise autonomy, which would include new initiatives coming from different sectors of society.[82] Taken together with the example of the China Welfare Fund for the Handicapped and Hu Qiaomu's proposal on religious involvement in social welfare, there was now both the political possibility and structural framework for the emergence of nongovernmental voluntary organizations, including Christian-initiated ones.

The churches themselves had few resources of their own for this kind of initiative, but Chinese Christians could draw on the support of churches in other parts of the world. In December, K. H. Ting and Han Wenzao spoke about this possibility, and their views are reflected in the informal statement "On Contributions to China from Churches and Christians Overseas." [83] They now said more clearly than they had before that overseas contributions to nonreligious programs and enterprises in China were welcomed, when given with due regard to Chinese national sovereignty and out of a sense of Christian love in an open and above-board manner without any strings attached. They did not want to ask churches overseas for such support, for there were rumors in Hong Kong that they were being pressured by the government to encourage foreign investment in China. Ting was concerned that they not give the appearance of undercutting the principle of self-support in the church. Ting and Han elaborated these views over the ensuing months in conversations they had with Christians from abroad.

Yet even at this early date, Ting and Han were already thinking of setting up a social-welfare organization initiated by Christians.

> We expect that in time there will be more and different kinds of opportunities for making contributions to social service projects in China. In addition to existing non-Christian enterprises which are likely to increase in number, there may be other projects or welfare foundations in which Christians play a leading role. We are considering projects of the latter kind because, aside from making contributions to social modernization, they make way for more Christian presence and involvement in the people's common tasks and thereby change the image of Christianity among the Chinese people.[84]

Three weeks later, Ting sent a circular letter to twenty-nine friends in church institutions overseas, to solicit their opinion about the creation of such an organization.

> The waning of ultra-leftism in China has now reached a stage when local and individual initiatives are encouraged so long as they work towards socialist modernization. We think this is a good environment within which Chinese Christians can not only do our share as citizens in nation building, but also make the fact of Christian presence and participation better known to our people, without in any way weakening the work of the church proper.[85]

As he expected, the initial response from friends overseas was almost universally favorable. Four months later almost to the day, on 19 April 1985, the Amity Foundation was established in Nanjing.[86] The idea for Amity had come from both Ting and Han. Ting had the vision and the reputation in China and overseas; Han was able to develop the connections and get things done. As overseas coordinator, I was very much involved in Amity programs and relationships during its early years, and worked closely with both Han and Ting. For this reason, the narrative in the pages that follow will have a different tone than in other parts of this book. The full story of Amity's early history is beyond the scope of this book, but here it is important to set down the essential role that K. H. Ting played in its formation and early development.

It was Ting himself who came up with the word *Aide*, the Chinese name for Amity; the two characters mean love (*ai*) and virtue, or moral power (*de*). He had briefly considered the name *Enlai*, which could be translated as "the grace which comes" and which also recalled the memory of Zhou Enlai, but he rejected it because he knew there would be opposition in China and inevitable misunderstandings overseas. The characters *ai* and *de* convey the sense of love and the power of love, as they do in Arthur Waley's translation of the *Dao De Jing,* which was entitled *The Way and Its Power.*[87] *Ai* and *de* also express Ting's sense of love as God's primary attribute and the dimension of Christian practice in society. The translation "Amity" was suggested by Janice Wickeri, and this became the official English name.

Ting received encouragement for the idea of Amity from friends in the CPPCC and in the government in Jiangsu and Beijing, but questions about the new foundation were coming from other quarters. These centered on the possible involvement of overseas churches in China, and whether Amity would inadvertently subvert the Three-Self principle. In Beijing, Ting discussed Amity with senior officials from the RAB and the UFWD, who approved of the idea but continued to raise questions throughout the 1980s. At one point in 1986, Xi Zhongxun, the CPC Central Committee member who was concerned with religious and cultural affairs, asked to see Ting about Nanjing '86 (see below), the conference on international ecumenical sharing which was then in the planning stages. Xi wanted Ting's "clarification" on Amity's position on project funding and his assurance that the conference was not a fundraising event for the church.[88]

Voluntary, nongovernmental organizations were new in China, and Amity was breaking new ground as a nongovernmental organization.[89] In the Chinese social structure, Amity had to have a government or party department to relate to. In Chinese this is termed a "leading body" (*guikou* or *zhuguan bumen*). Amity was located in Jiangsu, and so its "leading body" became the Jiangsu UFWD. This worked to Amity's advantage, because it meant that Ting and Han could draw on their provincial connections to get things done rather than having to channel everything through Beijing. Because they both held prestigious positions in Jiangsu, it also meant that their decisions about Amity would be more readily accepted by the provincial government.

In order to demonstrate that Amity was a Christian-initiated, but not a church-sponsored, organization, Ting and Han recruited both Christian and non-Christian board members. Three of the original seventeen board members were not from church circles, including Ting's friend, Kuang Yaming, who had recently retired as president of Nanjing University. The Christians were senior TSPM/CCC leaders from Nanjing, Shanghai and Beijing. There were no Chinese Catholics on the board. Bishop Jin Luxian of Shanghai had declined Ting's invitation to serve. Although an international board of advisors had been anticipated, Ting thought it unwise to proceed with this because of internal sensitivities about overseas involvement. Ting was named president of Amity, and Han Wenzao became the general secretary and the main person behind early programs and project initiatives.

Han Wenzao liked to say that Amity was "the result of the implementation of the consistent principles of Chinese Christians in a new stage."[90] By this he meant that Amity emerged out of the continuing commitment of the TSPM to contribute to Chinese society, a commitment that assumed a new organizational expression in the era of reform and modernization, one that drew on historic connections with Christian churches overseas. Through Amity, Ting and Han also hoped to make Christian presence more widely known in China, thus indirectly strengthening the witness of the Chinese church. Ting reasoned that Amity was a *praeparatio evangelica* that would help make Christian participation in nation building better appreciated and more widely accepted.[91]

In order to do this, Ting believed that Amity had to make an impact on society and the church by serving as a channel of funding and personnel "for existing but inadequately-supported institutions."[92] With the idea of the China Welfare Fund for the Handicapped in mind, he assumed that these would include centers for the disabled and the mentally handicapped. In the early months after Amity was founded, Ting took foreign visitors to a number of hospitals and social-welfare institutions in Nanjing. He wanted to support their work, but he did not enjoy these "promotional" visits, for they put him in the awkward position of being perceived as a benefactor. Some Amity board members, including Kuang Yaming, wanted Amity to initiate its own social-welfare institutions, but Ting had to persuade them that this would not be possible or desirable in the present context. The teachers' project probably had the greatest impact overseas of any early Amity initiative, and Ting approved the initial plan in February 1985. The following fall, twenty-two teachers supported by churches with historic links to China came to teach at tertiary institutions, mostly in and around Nanjing. Ting said that they were to be language teachers, not missionaries, and they rendered outstanding service in this capacity. Ting Yenren, who had just returned from studies in the United States, served as coordinator of the teachers' program. He was an inspiration to the teachers and staff and worked tirelessly to make Amity a success.

Bible printing was the third major area of initial Amity involvement. The TSPM and the CCC had been printing Bibles on commercial presses in China since 1981, and Ting often spoke of how proud he was that this could be done with the limited resources that Chinese Christians had at their disposal. By 1985, 2.7 million Bibles had been printed, but this was nowhere near enough. The lack of Bibles in Chinese churches was the subject of continuing attacks from critics and was used to justify the "smuggling" of Bibles by evangelical and fundamentalist groups overseas. Such groups had no interest in relating to the CCC or the TSPM, but the United Bible Societies (UBS) and many of its national members did. There had been contact between Chinese church leaders and Bible societies overseas since 1979 when Ting, Han and others visited the American Bible Society in New York. Heyward Wong from the Hong Kong Bible Society and Moses Hsu, a translator for the UBS, visited China in 1979 and 1980 respectively.[93] On both of these visits, Ting and other leaders indicated that they had reservations about what the UBS had been doing in China, and Ting reiterated his position that the CCC did not want to import Bibles printed overseas. He knew that this would not be allowed by the government, and that the importation of Bibles would mean the continuing identification of Christianity with overseas financial support.

This may be illustrated by a simple story. In the early 1980s, a wealthy Christian businessman from the United States (not affiliated with the UBS) approached K. H. Ting and said that the Holy Spirit had moved him to offer to import one million Bibles for distribution by the TSPM and the CCC in China. Ting thanked him for his concern and said he would discuss the matter with other church leaders. The next day he told the businessman, "The Holy Spirit has not moved us to accept your offer. We want to print Bibles in China." This was only one of many such offers coming to Chinese churches in the early 1980s. But the principle of self-support was essential for the CCC, and Bible printing would have to be done in China.

The UBS got the message. In late 1984, representatives of the Hong Kong UBS office came to an agreement with the CCC to supply paper for the printing of Bibles in China. As the Amity Foundation was being formed, the UBS also began to explore the possibility of establishing a printing press in association with Amity for Bible production. Following several months of negotiation and consultation, K. H. Ting as president of Amity and chairman of the CCC, signed a memorandum of understanding with John Erickson of the UBS for the construction of the Amity Printing Press, which "would give priority to the printing of the Bible" but would also print other literature for education and social welfare insofar as they were also part of Amity's work. This was in March 1985, before Amity was formally founded. The Amity Printing Press was opened in December 1987, and by 1990 it was printing millions of Bibles every year. At the twentieth anniversary of the Amity Foundation in November 2005, it was reported that almost forty million Bibles had been printed and distributed in China thus far.[94]

Amity was not without its critics overseas. Those in the evangelical community who were opposed to the TSPM/CCC saw Amity as yet another government-sponsored initiative to undercut "true" Christian faith. Curiously, Raymond Fung, then evangelism secretary of the WCC, voiced a similar concern. He too suggested that Amity was a government initiative and "an attempt to control, if not the churches, at least the channels for ecumenical relationships with churches outside."[95] Ting was furious that this kind of response would come from the WCC, and he sent a sharply worded letter to Eugene Stockwell at the WCC.[96] Philip Potter, who had recently retired as general secretary, sent assurances that Raymond Fung did not speak for the WCC. Other voices in the WCC, especially Ninan Koshy and Kyung-seo Park, spoke up for Amity and the Chinese church, and the WCC would become one of the strongest supporters of Amity in its formative years. The CCC was not ready to join the WCC, but after this, relationships continued to improve.

A very different kind of critical response was coming from the left-leaning wing of the church, which included many of Ting's closest Canadian friends. They were not only unsure about Amity, but also skeptical about the whole direction China was moving under Deng Xiaoping. Ting sensed their alienation and sought to win them back. In a circular letter to those whom Ting called "time-tested friends of China," he praised them for their loyalty and commitment to justice, but also told them that times had changed.

> In recent years, to a great extent thanks to the foundation work our old friends have done, more of those in leading positions of the churches have come to show their friendliness towards China and their under-standing and support of our Three-Self stance, including a growing number of evangelicals. Some of our old friends may regard their understanding of things as questionable theologically and politically. But we have no reason to reject their change and approach. What we are witnessing is a polarization phenomenon very much to our liking. Our policy of differentiation draws the line between those who take a hostile line and those who don't, not on other grounds. "All those who are not against us are for us,"—that may be our motto.[97]

Ting was using the language of the united front in speaking to people whose friendship and support he deeply valued. He was also saying that changes in the international Christian situation held new promise and opportunities for China.

The Amity Foundation did not replace the CCC in developing interna-tional ecumenical relationships, but because it involved concrete projects, funding and personnel from church bodies overseas, it became a major focus of international Christian attention. Still, Amity was not the church, and the exchanges between the CCC and churches and ecumenical organizations overseas continued to develop in the 1980s. These included visits to China from churches in East and West Germany, North Korea, Hungary, and the Philippines as well as delegations from the World Alliance of Reformed Churches, the Baptist World Alliance, the Lutheran World Federation, the Ecumenical Association of Third World Theologians and the World Students' Christian Federation. K. H. Ting met with all the visiting groups. CCC del-egations also traveled to many countries in Asia, Europe and North Amer-ica in the mid- and late-1980s, sometimes led by Ting and sometimes not. Ting traveled overseas on his own on several occasions, to speak at church conferences, to meet with church leaders and to receive honorary degrees. In September 1985, he became with Robert Runcie a patron of the Friends of the Church in China (FCC), a British-based fellowship of churches and indi-viduals that promotes ecumenical exchanges with churches in China.[98] This is the only organization of its kind in the world, and the only church-related organization overseas for which K. H. Ting has agreed to serve as patron.

There was a growing sense of hope and excitement among churches in Europe, North America and Asia over what was taking place in the churches of China. Much of this hopefulness was due to the role that K. H. Ting played in relating on a personal level to overseas visitors. He met with a great number of people in his home, often with Siu-may or other family members. [99] He also spoke to overseas groups who were visiting the seminary, and he seemed energized when meeting with overseas church leaders. Ting gave all his visitors the impression that they had his full attention. He patiently listened to the proposals and suggestions they made; shared his own views on the current situation in the church, often in confidence; and gained the understanding and trust of most of the people with whom he spoke.

In 1986, two international conferences were held in Nanjing to explore new ways in which churches overseas might relate to China. The organizers of both gatherings asked for and received Ting's blessing, and the meetings provided opportunities for the Chinese church to be more publicly visible as a community that had relationships all over the world.

In May, 150 Protestant and Catholic delegates from China and overseas gathered for a conference on the ecumenical sharing of resources. In some ways a follow-up to Montreal's "A New Beginning," Nanjing '86 addressed the subject of Christian sharing in a world of tremendous material imbalance and sought to bring China into the more general ecumenical discussion. This was the most diverse Christian meeting ever held in China, for it involved Catholics, Protestants and even some Orthodox. In his own speech at Nanjing '86, Ting summarized many things he had said previously about the church in China and welcomed the "theological criticism and self-criticism" that he heard and saw at the conference. [100] The excitement about this conference also led to the proposal that another conference would be held in Edinburgh in three years time.

A second gathering in Nanjing two months later (also convened in the Jinling Hotel) may have done even more to promote mutual respect and understanding. Entitled "Spring Has Returned . . . Listening to the Church in China," this conference met under the sponsorship of the Baptist World Alliance Friendship Tour to China, and specifically focused on the life of the Chinese church. [101] The two hundred Baptist leaders (from nineteen countries) did not come from churches that were generally sympathetic to the CCC. The Baptists met seminary students and church leaders in Nanjing who spoke personally and in their own words about their life and witness. These testimonies moved the Baptist delegates, and it helped to change their perspective. Southern Baptists close to the CCC, particularly Britt Towery, were important bridge-builders in this regard. [102] K. H. Ting was very warmly received when he spoke, and he was able to win over many of those who had distrusted him. After this conference, there was increasing contact between the CCC and evangelical churches worldwide, and Southern Baptists even began to cooperate with the Amity teachers' program.

The most widely publicized Christian visits to China in the late 1980s were those of Bishop Desmond Tutu and the Reverend Billy Graham, but they were important for different reasons and publicized overseas for different constituencies. Both visits brought prestige to the church in China in the eyes of the government, and they showed different public sides of Christianity among world-renowned church leaders. Tutu's visit was important for the ecumenical outreach of the CCC, while the Graham visit helped the CCC relate more effectively to evangelicals. Ting held Tutu in very high regard. He was a fellow Anglican, who, like Ting, had a commitment to progressive social causes. Ting also respected Graham, and although there was never a close relationship between them, Ting believed the American evangelist was sincere in his desire to build bridges of understanding with China and the CCC.

Bishop and Mrs. Tutu were invited to China by the TSPM, the CCC, and the Chinese People's Association for Disarmament and Peace in 1986.[103] The visit was widely publicized in the Chinese media. Tutu was even featured on the cover of a number of popular magazines, and he created excitement wherever he went. Tutu was given the very rare honor of speaking to government representatives at the Great Hall of the People in Beijing. He spoke as a churchman committed to social justice, specifically on the need to end apartheid and support the boycott of trade with South Africa. Chinese officials asserted that they stood in solidarity with Tutu in the struggle for freedom and justice in South Africa. Ting often appeared with Tutu in the public media, and he introduced him to government officials at the Great Hall of the People. This, together with the fact of inviting a churchman who was passionately committed to social justice, gave increased importance to K. H. Ting's diplomatic role in China.*

Billy Graham's first visit to China in April 1988 was a diplomatic event of a different sort, much more carefully orchestrated by the Billy Graham Evangelistic Association, the Chinese government and various intermediaries.[104] The Grahams were invited by the Chinese People's Association for Friendship with Foreign Countries and the China Christian Council. The invitation was originally going to bypass the CCC, but since this would have been a public slight, Ting insisted with Graham and his own government that the CCC join in the invitation. The Grahams were received by Premier Li Peng and other senior government officials in Beijing, where they also met with Zhao Fusan, K. H. Ting and other religious leaders. Ting was unable to accompany the Grahams to Nanjing—he was about to leave for North America—but they did visit with Siu-may and other friends at the Ting home. Before coming to Nanjing, the Grahams visited Ruth Graham's birthplace in Huaiyin, where her parents had served as Presbyterian missionaries. They also met privately with well-known house-church leaders in several cities, including Wang Mingdao in Shanghai and Lin Xiangao in Guangzhou. In a press conference after the visit, Billy Graham praised the witness of K. H. Ting, and he urged evangelicals to be more tolerant of the CCC.

---

*Ting and Han were invited to Tutu's enthronement service in Johannesburg in late August, but they went only as far as Hong Kong because the South African consulate refused to grant them visas. At the time, South Africa maintained diplomatic relations with Taiwan, not the People's Republic of China.

K. H. Ting and Siu-may Kuo, Nanjing, 1985. Photograph taken by
Gail V. Coulson.

Ting's involvement in these well-publicized visits underscored his growing
importance as a diplomat and Christian spokesperson. This was recognized
in China when he was elected to the Foreign Relations Committee of the
NPC in 1987, and it was recognized overseas. He could represent his church
and his country with integrity, and he could speak in ways that created understanding and trust. Yet there were always limits to what he could accomplish.

K. H. Ting had an understanding of what could and could not be done
in China, even as he pushed for change. He stood firmly for the Three-Self
principle in relationship with churches overseas, which meant that he did not
welcome all the proposals that came to him and could not accept all new initiatives, however well meaning. For example, the WCC was considering
holding its Conference on World Mission and Evangelism in China (CWME)
in 1988. There was a great deal of excitement about the proposal in Geneva,
and at the end of 1985 Eugene Stockwell went to Nanjing to confer with
Ting. Because of his respect for the WCC, Ting did not want to say no to the
WCC leaders, but because the proposal was unrealistic, he could not exactly
say yes either. In the end, following careful prodding by Ting, it was Stockwell himself who concluded that it was ill-advised and premature to hold
such a conference in China at this time.[105] The CWME conference eventually met in San Antonio, Texas, in May 1989; and for the first time, a CCC
delegation took part, thus indicating that the CCC was interested in continuing the dialogue with the WCC.

Ting was much harder on overseas Christian groups that rejected Three-
Self or whom he regarded as being "anti-China." In 1986, he issued a state-

ment denouncing the Children of God, a sectarian group founded in the United States that used promiscuous sex and other immoral methods to attract young people to Christianity. The group had been active in Hong Kong, Macao and Guangzhou, but was later banned in mainland China.[106] In 1987, he spoke out against Kairos Radio, a Norwegian project seeking support from the Lutheran World Federation and claiming to have implicit CCC and TSPM endorsement for Christian broadcasting to China. In his statement, Ting rejected any suggestion that the CCC supported the project and said that the growing Chinese church had no need to rely on outside help for evangelism.[107] As a result of Ting's objection, the proposal was dropped.

The controversy over Chinese participation in the Second Lausanne Conference on World Evangelization was more difficult to handle. At the urging of Billy Graham, the organizing committee decided to invite the CCC to send a delegation to Lausanne II, which was to be held in Manila in July 1989. But various "China Ministries" who were also active in the planning insisted that representatives of what they were calling the "house-church movement" also be invited. The planning committee decided to invite 150 delegates from each group and asked the Chinese government to agree to grant passports to all 300 before they had seen their names. Ting realized that some evangelicals overseas were trying to reach out positively to the CCC, especially after Billy Graham's visit the previous year. In February, he met with members of the Lausanne planning committee and tried to find a way to make Chinese participation possible at some level. But the two sides could not reach a satisfactory agreement. In the end, the CCC issued a strongly worded statement that criticized the organizers' proposal and rejected any Chinese participation in Lausanne II.[108] Ting's hope for better relationships with evangelicals could only go so far, and it was clear that the Lausanne planners never really understood the position of the Chinese church.

The CCC issued its statement on Lausanne as a budding democracy movement had taken to the streets in Beijing and other major cities. In the late spring of 1989, a spirit of change was in the air, and people all over the world were increasingly optimistic about China's future.

In the first part of May, K. H. and Siu-may traveled to Canada, where they were both awarded honorary doctorates from Victoria University in Toronto. This was Siu-may's first visit to Canada in almost forty years and her first trip abroad since the end of the Cultural Revolution. But even as they relaxed with colleagues and old friends, the Tings' attention remained focused on the drama being played out in Beijing. They returned to Shanghai in time for K. H. to approve the CCC statement on Lausanne II. Back home in Nanjing, they began to take stock of what was happening in the democracy movement—as the government met behind closed doors and more and more people went to Tiananmen Square.

APPENDIX TO CHAPTER EIGHT

Selected Theological Writings of K. H. Ting, 1979-1989

1. Sermons and Speeches to Church Gatherings and Theological Essays Originally Published or Delivered in China, 1979-1989

"How to Study the Bible" (1980)
"Retrospect and Prospect" (1981)
"Forerunner Y. T. Wu" (1981)
"Another Look at Three-Self" (1983)
"The Truth of the Resurrection" (1983)
"Love Never Ends" (1984)
"The Holy Spirit and Us" (1984)
"Life Needs a Mission" (1984)
"Theological Education in China" (1984)
"You Have the Words of Eternal Life" (1985)
"Inspirations from Liberation Theology, Process Theology and Teilhard de Chardin" (1985)
"It Is the Lord" (1985)
"God Is Not Male" (1985)
"Opening Address" (1986)
"Building Up the Body in Love" (1986)
"Speech at Memorial Service for Wu Yifang" (1986)
"A Reconciling Faith" (1986)
"Bishop Ting's Speech at Shanghai Symposium on Theological Education" (1987)
"Changes in Forty Years" (1987)
"Creation and Incarnation" (1988)
"An Untrodden Path" (1988)
"The Love That Loves to the End" (1988)
"Incarnation and Transcendence" (1988)
"What Can We Learn from Mr. Y. T. Wu Today?" (1989)
"The Ever Reforming Mr. Y. T. Wu" (1989)
"On Theological Education" (1989.)
"Preface to *New Thoughts on the Bible*" (1989)

2. Sermons and Speeches to Church Gatherings and Theological Essays Originally Published or Delivered Overseas, 1979-1989

"Give Ye Them to Eat" (1979)
"Human Collectives as Vehicles of God's Grace" (1979)
"A Chinese Christian's Appreciation of the Atheist" (1980)
"Theological Education in China" (1981)
"Jesus' Protest" (1983)

"A Rationale for Three-Self" (1984)
"Theological Mass Movement in China"(1984)
"A Chinese Christian Selfhood" (1984)
"Sermon in Sydney Cathedral" (1984)
"The Greater Christ" (1985)
"This Is Your Brother" (1985)
"Preface to *CTR*" (1985)
"Unity with Evangelicals: A Chinese Approach" (1985)
"God Is Love" (1986)
"Psalm 23" (1987)
"Address to the Lutheran World Federation" (1987)
"John 18: 31-32" (1988)
"Matthew 13: 31-32"(1988)
"The Theological Task in China" (1988)
"Address at the Graduation Ceremony of Victoria University" (1989)

Note: Some of the texts which are cited above appear with different titles or in different years in later publications.

9

Repression and Resurgence, 1989-1996

What of all things is most yielding,
Can overwhelm that which is most hard,
Being substanceless, it can enter in even when there is no crevice.
That there can be teaching without words,
Value in action which is actionless,
Few indeed can understand.

Laozi, *Dao De Jing*[1]

Will the future ever arrive?—Should we continue to look upwards? Is
the light we can see in the sky one of those which will presently be
extinguished? The ideal is terrifying to behold, lost as it is in the depths,
small, isolated, a pinpoint, brilliant but threatened on all sides by the
dark forces that surround it; nevertheless, no more in danger than a
star in the jaws of the clouds.

Victor Hugo[2]

The last weeks of May 1989 were times of heady exuberance for many students and young people in China. The "Goddess of Democracy" symbolized the aspirations of a generation that had come of age during the reform era, and the gathering in China's capital resembled student demonstrations in other times and places in their hopes and in their weaknesses. The movement was driven as much by emotions and traditional cultural elements as it was by a reasoned approach to social change. Growing numbers of students from the provinces joined Beijing students who were camping in Tiananmen Square, and they organized demonstrations in their own cities and towns. The workers and residents of Beijing supported the growing movement; people all over China were inspired by the students and began expressing their own feelings of dissatisfaction about government corruption, and the whole world watched live and uncensored news reports of the events that were unfolding in the Beijing Spring.[3]

But these weeks were also a time of deepening concern for a growing number of intellectuals and reformers. Many of the older generation of intellectuals were worried about the possibility of suppression, for they had lived through earlier movements of dissent and protest. Some government officials wanted to negotiate with student leaders, but as time wore on and the students did not leave the square, the time for dialogue had passed. In any case, hard-line officials were never really interested in meeting student demands, for it would have been a sign of weakness. All during these days party elders met to decide what was to be done, and intraparty debates between the reformers and the hard-line conservatives continued.[4] When the decision was made to declare martial law, Premier Zhao Ziyang continued to defend his policies. But the handwriting was on the wall, and on the early morning of May 19th, Zhao Ziyang and his close supporters visited Tiananmen Square to try one last time to persuade students to return to their campuses. As he said at the time, he had come too late. His own days as party leader were over.

Two weeks later, the government acted decisively. On the night of June 3rd and the early hours of June 4th, troops moved into Tiananmen Square to suppress the student movement on the orders of Deng Xiaoping himself. The government-induced violence dashed the hopes of students and intellectuals as the rest of the world looked on in disbelief. Over the next few weeks, there was confusion over what had happened and what else might happen, as well as an outpouring of anger and horror from the students who survived, journalists who had witnessed the events and people all around the world. The Chinese government had already declared that the student demonstrations were a "counterrevolutionary revolt," and Deng Xiaoping suggested that hostile forces in China and overseas had helped precipitate events.[5] The government had been badly shaken by the "June 4th events" which seemed to put the whole program of reform and openness in doubt. It was clear that Zhao Ziyang and his supporters were out, but what would June 4th mean for other government policies, particularly economic reform? And could a new time of relaxation (*fang*) follow such a violent end (*shou*) to a democracy movement that seemed to have so much promise?

These were the questions that would be discussed and debated over the next two years, both inside and outside the government. Within a short time, the provinces were informed that they did not have to use violence to suppress demonstrations in their own locales, but that the students had to be brought into line. Jiang Zemin was installed as the new general secretary, and Li Peng was made premier. The government began to put the case in defense of its actions before the public. Government meetings were called in Beijing, and political-study sessions were organized on university campuses in the fall. The internal debate continued over the future direction of economic policy and of international relationships, particularly with the United States, but a certain order was reestablished, and leaders were in agreement on the need for "unity and stability." Deng Xiaoping wanted to continue with economic reform, but he was not yet able to eliminate the conservative opposition, which had risen to prominence after June 4th.

The fall of the Berlin Wall in late 1989 and the dissolution of the Soviet Union were viewed very differently by CPC leaders in China than they were in most other parts of the world. Rather than being a "triumph of hope," as one American historian has termed it, it confirmed the belief of party conservatives that the government had acted correctly in suppressing the democracy movement, for in so doing, "chaos" had been averted.[6] The events in Eastern Europe figured prominently in shaping government policy decisions over the next months and years. Yet no clear direction had been established as to whether economic reform or political ideology or some middle path would take precedence.[7] Martial law was lifted in January 1990, and Zhu Rongji was brought in to manage the economy in the spring of 1991. But it was not until Deng Xiaoping's famous "Southern Tour" (18 January-21 February 1992) that the priority for reform and openness was forcefully re-established as the government's policy line. In visiting Shenzhen and the economically prosperous Pearl River Delta, Deng was demonstrating his own commitment to speeding up the pace of reform and arguing that "leftist" ideology remained the greatest danger to China.

The Fourteenth Party Congress in October of the same year consolidated Deng's victory for reform over ideology, and for the next five years, economic development in China went from strength to strength. China became an emerging world power and an important actor in the global economy. Foreign trade and all the leading economic indicators increased dramatically, spurred in part by a growth in the number of dynamic rural enterprises. Pressure was increased for most-favored-nation status with the United States and negotiations had begun for China's entry into the World Trade Organization. As Deng retired from his remaining positions of leadership, there was a smooth transition to a new generation of leaders led by Jiang Zemin. New problems were brought on by increasing privatization, economic growth and the removal of the safety net that had protected the poor. The gap between rich and poor, and between different regions, began to grow. Corruption, crime and peculation outstripped anything that had been seen in the 1980s. But by emphasizing economic development, the Chinese government avoided the fate of the Soviet Union and Eastern Europe and won back a measure of popular support.

Increasing economic freedom, especially in the cities and wealthy rural areas, brought with it a renewal of cultural and religious life. Even among university students, economic concerns gradually overshadowed political protest. Urban people made use of their growing incomes through increased consumer spending on everything from cell phones to designer clothing, and from eating out in restaurants to domestic and overseas travel. In the 1990s, commercial and popular culture developed in new and unexpected ways as China became more connected to the rest of the world and drew on both a long-suppressed traditional heritage and Western cultural influences. The government had very real concerns about the role that the churches had played in the downfall of Communism in Eastern Europe, but there continued to be popular interest in Protestant and Catholic Christianity, Buddhism, Daoism, Islam and folk religious traditions.[8] In cities and rural areas, among Han Chinese and ethnic minorities, religious life was flourishing in the cultural and social space that had been created by the growing pace of reform.

Intellectuals began to speak up once again. Having criticized the radicalism of 1989, they now debated questions about civil society, the relationship between markets and reform, the growing commercialization of culture, the new nationalism, and the need for the recovery of ethics and a humanistic spirit.[9] Some intellectuals and student leaders who had been prominent in 1989 had gone overseas, but those who stayed chose among a variety of options. Some "took the plunge" (*xiahai*), developed their own businesses, and left politics behind. Others assumed a more traditional intellectual role in universities and research institutes, producing a growing body of important scholarly literature in all fields. Still others saw themselves as social critics, and they made use of the critical space that was afforded to debate social, cultural and political questions in new ways.

June 4th had been a turning point. For K. H. Ting and religious and intellectual leaders concerned with continuing reform, it was both an end and a beginning. Their responsibility for politics and governance (*zheng*), study and learning (*xue*) and ethical and religious life (*dao*) did not come to an end.[10] Through the 1980s, Ting had been both a contributor to and a beneficiary of the reform policies. He and other leaders like him, including the Buddhist leader Zhao Puchu, had wanted to use humanism to reform the system.[11] To work for reform in the 1990s did not mean renouncing one's dissatisfaction with the repression that put the student movement down or ceasing to criticize hard-line government policies. K. H. Ting saw the events of 1989 as they were unfolding; he took a stance, and he made necessary adjustments in the years that followed. For the new beginning that was needed after June 4th, he would respond by drawing on the same values and commitments he had all along, but also by moving in ways that no one could have anticipated in the 1980s.

JUNE 4TH AND THE AFTERMATH

Immediately after his return from Canada to China in late May 1989, Ting met with colleagues in Shanghai and received reports from a variety of sources about what was happening around the country. In Beijing, seminary students and other Christians were joining the demonstrators on Tiananmen Square, and a church choir drawn from young people all over the city sang hymns for the students. In Nanjing, more than half the students at the seminary had organized themselves to march with students from the colleges and the universities. They wrote banners with verses from the Bible, including the well-known words from the prophet Amos: "Let justice roll down like waters, and righteousness like an ever-flowing stream" (Amos 5:24). Christians in every part of China were caught up in the events of the Beijing Spring, just like everyone else.

On May 18th, the same day that he approved the statement about Lausanne II, and two days before the declaration of martial law in Beijing, K. H. Ting issued a statement in support of the students:

> We wholeheartedly affirm the student demonstrations in Beijing, Shanghai and other cities in recent days. The hunger-strikes are a patriotic activity. Their demands arise from a feeling of patriotism. We sincerely hope and call upon the top level leaders of the Central Committee of the Chinese Communist Party and the State Council to carry on a dialogue with the students as soon as possible. We deeply hope that the students end their hunger strikes and take care of their health. Our motherland needs you.[12]

Back in Nanjing, he also issued a public statement affirming his personal support for seminary students and other Christians participating in the demonstrations:

> I am glad that Christians are making their presence felt in these demonstrations. I am very glad that students in the Nanjing Theological Seminary are taking an active part. They not only join the demonstrations but also try to serve their fellow students by sending them drinking water and bread. I understand that Christians in Beijing are also playing an active role. I have joined with some 40 other members of the Standing Committee of the National People's Congress to propose that there should be an emergency meeting of the Standing Committee to be called as soon as possible to discuss the whole question so that the democratic process could be facilitated and bloodshed avoided. We are grateful for the patriotic action of the people of Hong Kong in supporting our motherland, and we ask that Christians around the world continue to remember us in their prayers.[13]

The forty members of the NPC Standing Committee who called for an emergency meeting represented a very small minority of its members, and, in such an august body, they were courageous in taking the stand they did. Ting unambiguously supported moves toward greater democratization, and he took pride in the fact that seminarians were involved in the demonstrations. In Nanjing, the students were grateful for their principal's support, and they drew closer to him. Churches from around the world also responded positively to the statements K. H. Ting and other church leaders had made, and they sent their expressions of solidarity and prayerful support.

But Ting was also worried. He was telling people in late May that he hoped the students in Beijing would return to their campuses, for there could be no peaceful resolution of the standoff unless they did. In informal conversations, Ting spoke about growing government corruption and the need for more democracy and greater freedom, but change could not happen overnight. He was openly critical of Li Peng and his conservative policies, and generally supportive of Zhao Ziyang and his reforms. His friend Yan Mingfu was one of Zhao's important allies. But Ting saw the real possibility of violence if the demonstrations continued, and he believed that this would mean the government would be less inclined to support reform efforts in the future. Dialogue and negotiation were needed on all sides, but by late May, neither the students nor the government hard-liners were willing to compromise.

The government's action in sending troops and tanks into Tiananmen Square on June 4th marked a violent and decisive end not only to the democracy movement of 1989 but to the democratization efforts of those inside and outside the government which had begun in the late 1980s. The early days after the suppression were a time of disbelief, anger, grief and indecision for students and supporters of the reform agenda. All sorts of reports were coming out of Beijing and other cities, but no one was sure about what was actually going on. Students continued to demonstrate in other cities; the people of Hong Kong were taking to the streets in large numbers, and the news media was filled with stories about the "Tiananmen Massacre" and the "Bloodbath in Beijing."

A poem attributed to a Christian hunger striker captures the way in which many Christians who had welcomed Ting's support of the democracy protestors responded to the government action. It reads in part,

> People say: You fasters are only kicking against the thistles
>   You are but eggs dashing against a rock.
> Yet thistles get blunted only by being thwarted,
>   Eggs furnish nourishment only when broken.[14]

June 4th was a Sunday, and prayers for Chinese students were offered in many churches in China and all over the world. In Beijing, however, church attendance was far lower than usual, and there was still fighting in the streets. A special service of worship was conducted at Nanjing Seminary on June 5th, with prayers for all who had died in Beijing. K. H. Ting was at home with Siu-may, but he was in touch with churches in other parts of the country.[15] A few days later, a pastor from Beijing came to see Ting in Nanjing to report on what he had seen and heard. Ting himself was deeply moved by the reports he was receiving, but he was also thinking about what would come next, particularly for the church and the seminary.

One of his immediate concerns after June 4th was protecting the seminary and the students who had taken part in the demonstrations. College and university students in China were sent home in early June, including those from the seminary. Some who had been especially active in the protests were advised to stay at home, where they were safe. Ting maintained contact with many of his students, just as they regularly prayed for him and sent him letters about their situation.

On June 6th, K. H. Ting and Han Wenzao faxed a letter to me and other colleagues in the Hong Kong Amity office. Choosing their words carefully, they expressed their shock at what had happened in Beijing and observed that in this drastic turn of events, they must continue "to act responsibly—to the best interest of the church as God guides us to see."[16] The letter was intended to be an initial expression of concern and reassurance for Christians overseas, for it suggested that the work of the church would continue. In the phrase "act responsibly" we can see that the process of adjustment to the new reality for the sake of the church had begun.

In private, many Chinese continued to express anger and disappointment with the government's violent response, and in no uncertain terms they were critical of the military suppression of the students. K. H. Ting said that he would continue to serve in the CPPCC and NPC, but this did not mean he would defend all the actions that the political leadership had taken. He believed it was still possible to continue to work for change. Ting did not want to express his feelings publicly for this would be detrimental to his commitment to continue to work for change and build up the church.[17] This was not a time for "personal heroism or impulsive acts," he said. Quoting an old Chinese saying, such adventurism would be tantamount to "using eggs to break rocks." In unpublished reflections, he began to set down his thoughts about what the new situation might mean for the church.

> There are several million Protestants in China and the number is growing. It is not the right policy to quit and evacuate and leave them to be led by conscious and unconscious agents of autocratic rule. We ought to see the church as a classroom or training ground for democracy.
>
> The church with its faith in God the Father to all humanity and in Jesus Christ and the Holy Spirit as the Saviour and Enlightener of all men and women naturally values the individual person and cannot endorse any arbitrary treatment for his or her welfare. This is the Christian ground for respecting human dignity and equality.
>
> For Protestantism to govern itself well and support itself well and to do the work of evangelization itself well entails the application of the democratic principle. To experience in church circles the application of the democratic principle helps Christians see the contrast on returning to the outside world and makes them eager to work for democracy there. This is the way we are to see the political value of our church most.[18]

These were private reflections as he began to think through what was to be done in the post–June 4th situation. But they are consistent with Ting's position in the 1980s, that the church needed to approach reform through legal means and that democracy and reform should be reflected in the church's own structures. Church leaders should not sacrifice themselves, nor should they sacrifice their principles. Ting's position in this regard was the same before and after June 4th. He was loyal to socialism and the Chinese political system, but he also wanted to see reform.

By the middle of the month, some semblance of normalcy had returned to Beijing. There would be no violent suppression of students in other cities; but the students had to be brought into line, and all social organizations had to declare their support for the new order. In Chinese, this meant that they had to "declare their position" (*biaotai*) in support of what had been done. This put prominent individuals who had supported the students in a difficult position, but they had to say something, if only in a perfunctory way. The TSPM/CCC issued a brief statement from Shanghai on 27 June affirming its support for the government's actions as interpreted by the June plenum of the Communist Party.[19] Protestant Christians were the last of the religious organizations to issue such a formal declaration of support, and it was formulaic in tone. Provincial TSPM committees and Christian councils followed suit.

Also on 27 June, the same day that the TSPM/CCC issued its statement affirming its support for the government, Ting sent a circular letter to all those overseas who had sent messages of support and solidarity, expressing his own grief over the "tragic and shocking turn of events." "We pray for the faith which assures us that the visions of the young and the dreams of the aged are not lost in God's memory," he wrote, "and will in his good time come to fruition."[20]

Later that month, Ting went to Beijing for a specially called meeting of the NPC. By this time, all political representatives were expected to "declare their position" in personal statements, many of which would be made public, and there was great pressure on members of the standing committee, who in late May had called for an emergency meeting of the NPC, to speak up. Ting's friend, the Buddhist leader Zhao Puchu, had already issued a terse and vaguely worded statement. On 1 July, the New China News Agency published the following statement by K. H. Ting:

> Delegate Ding Guangxun said: Comrade Deng Xiaoping has stressed that in opposing corruption, we should not be soft hearted, but we should bring the facts to light. We should not let others raise the banner of opposing corruption. And so I hope that our news media, in addition to reporting on putting down the recent turmoil, should also report on the great efforts of the Party and the Government in opposing corruption. Only in this way, will the people be satisfied and supportive.[21]

This significant statement has not usually been cited in understanding K. H. Ting's public response to Tiananmen. In it, he makes no mention of the suppression of the student movement other than his use of the word "turmoil," the government's code word for speaking about what was euphemistically referred to as the "Tiananmen Events" or the politically correct "counterrevolutionary rebellion." By concentrating on the reasons behind the student protests, Ting was able to publicly declare his position in support for the government and at the same time maintain his principles and integrity.

There were rumors and reports that summer and fall that K. H. Ting would be removed from political office, that he would have to make a confession (*jiantao*) of errors in supporting the students, and that he was the subject of stern criticism in internal party documents.[22] There was also the report that he offered to resign. None of the reports have been substantiated. Ting continued to be a member of the Standing Committee of the Seventh National People's Congress until 1993, and he has maintained the far more important position of vice-chair of the CPPCC to this day.[23] In this position, Ting is regarded as a "national leader," with all the corresponding responsibilities, duties and privileges, a designation that is not given to members of the NPC Standing Committee. He had strong criticisms about the government's suppression of the student protests, as did many other Chinese leaders, and he has never retracted his statements of support. Hard-line government officials may have had reservations about him, and they may have written criticisms for "internal" (*neibu*) circulation, but this is not unusual in China. K. H. Ting continued to be regarded as a patriot and a loyalist in the government's eyes, and there is no hard evidence that his response to June 4th changed that.

The situation after June 4th did affect the church's international and ecumenical relationships, however, although not as much as might have been feared. In the early days of June, K. H. Ting asked that an ecumenical conference on China planned for September in Edinburgh be postponed indefinitely, but he did indicate his hope that a continuation committee might be organized to keep the possibility of a conference alive.[24] In August, Ting had planned to lead a small Chinese delegation to Seoul to take part in the assembly of the World Alliance of Reformed Churches, at the invitation of his old friend, WARC general secretary Milan Opočenský, but this had to be cancelled.[25] Most foreign teachers working for the Amity Foundation left China after June 4th, and there were fewer teachers and fewer new projects in the fall. Christian exchanges with China continued, however, and we shall see that in a very short time the situation improved dramatically. By the late summer, the government's general policy was to welcome foreign exchanges while demanding more political conformity internally (*wai song, nei jin*). This was reflected in the situation of the church as well.

The political atmosphere through the end of 1989 was quite restrictive. The CPC continued to be influenced by the events that were unfolding in Eastern Europe, including the role some churches were playing to oppose the Communist governments. In August, political-study sessions were mandated on all college and seminary campuses, and these continued through the academic year. Ting told the Nanjing Seminary students that they should cooperate in the political study, and see it as something they could get through, for the situation would not last long. Young people still had to learn to work with the government at all levels, he believed, and in the process, they needed to maintain their sense of integrity and protect themselves for the sake of their work for the church. For Ting, seminary students who would contribute to the cause of greater democracy in China were the future for the church. One of the very few essays he published in *Tian Feng* in 1989 after June 4th was entitled "On Theological Education," written to underscore the importance of young people and the study of theology for "running the church well."[26]

Many Christian young people had been supportive of Ting's stance in support of the students. So too were many Christians, including those that were not affiliated with the TSPM/CCC. However, some house-church leaders were extremely critical of what Ting said, on theological grounds. Lin Xiangao believed that people should first turn to Christ rather than engage in secular activity to work for change. When local authorities tried to close his church a few years later, Lin Xiangao (Samuel Lamb) was quoted as telling the government that "we didn't demonstrate [on 4 June 1989] even though Ding Guangxun supported the students."[27] It was not "house churches" that were under pressure in the aftermath of June 4th, but TSPM/CCC leaders such as K. H. Ting. Lin's theology did not permit him to see support for justice and democracy as connected to his view of salvation by faith alone. Ting's response to June 4th and his continuing actions in defense of Chinese house churches would play a part in his relationship with Chinese evangelicals in future years.

On September 17th, the tenth anniversary of the death of Y. T. Wu, the founder of the Chinese Christian Three-Self Patriotic Movement, meetings or memorial services were held in many cities to mark the occasion.[28] These were the first public events of the TSPM/CCC since June 4th, and Ting spoke at church meetings in Nanjing, Shanghai and Beijing, as well as at a CPPCC memorial service for Y. T. Wu in the Great Hall of the People. His two published speeches—one from the TSPM/CCC gathering in Shanghai and the other at the CPPCC—are carefully crafted reflections on the significance of Y. T. Wu for today. They are different in tone from other published speeches,[29] and they show that Ting was attempting to relate Y. T. Wu to the post–June 4th situation in China.

In all these speeches, Ting was reflecting on some of the reading he had been doing over the last months—on Dietrich Bonhoeffer, on liberation theology, and on Y. T. Wu, as well as his reading of the Bible in the present context. He stressed the importance of patriotism for Chinese Christians, and of "running the church well," the theme he had introduced in the 1980s. The new note he introduces is something he had begun thinking about that summer, that the church should be "a school for the democratic spirit."

If we wish to avoid conflict and make our church a fellowship of love, we must let the democratic spirit penetrate into all our relationships . . . The democratic spirit consists not only of majority rule in voting, but also of respect for other people's opinion and giving them due authority if they are given their office; as well, it consists of keeping in touch and keeping informed. On major issues, we must seek consensus in charity and in a spirit of fellowship, after full consultation and discussion, having taken into serious consideration the desires and aspirations of others. We must avoid coercing others and pay attention to our unity and cooperation. We must not readily believe hearsay, and we must guard against the sowing of discord, whether done wittingly or unwittingly.[30]

This was a new idea for Ting and is an indirect response to the suppression of the "democracy movement." Given the restrictive political context in which these words were written, Ting is making a bold claim for the church as a social organization that could help to promote democracy in China. One Chinese scholar has written that June 4th revealed the failure of China to develop social organizations between state and society, organizations that could mediate the inevitable tensions that developed in the course of modernization, and in this way promote democracy.[31] In his own way, and speaking publicly just a few months after June 4th, Ting was saying something very similar as he attempted to articulate his position in the ongoing dialogue between state and society.

RENEWING AND NEGOTIATING THE SOCIAL CONTRACT

Not everyone was convinced that there could again be a dialogue, whether in the government or among the students. That summer and fall, Ting spent a great deal of time trying to reassure seminary students that their efforts for reform should continue, but in different ways. He was interviewed by some seminarians just before Christmas and said that the work of building up the church in China had only just begun. He urged them to focus now on their theological studies. "For almost two thousand years," he said, "the church under God, has endured in spite of and through all of its problems and shortcomings to become what it is today."[32] Students should maintain their youthful idealism, he said, but at the same time develop a sense of humility in relationships with Christians as well as those outside the church.

There were ominous forebodings and reports about a wave of religious repression that would be part of the new campaign against "bourgeois liberalization," but K. H. Ting said publicly that there had been no new "crackdown" on any religious group, and that the work of the Christian churches went on as before.[33] In late August, a new Bible school had opened in Yunnan; in September, the Amity Printing Press produced its one millionth Bible; and new churches were opening all over China at an increased rate of growth. Although the situation was still uncertain, and although many people were angry about the government repression and the change of leadership, they began to come to terms with the new reality.

K. H. Ting and intellectuals like him were patriotic reformers who maintained an "unwritten social contract" with the government. Even though they may have felt betrayed by June 4th, they were faced with the unavoidable fact that there was no functional alternative to the Chinese Communist Party.[34] After June 4th, the contract had to be renewed, and this would entail a long-term process requiring negotiation on all sides. This had important implications for relationships between church and state, and K. H. Ting's personal role was crucial in this regard, as policies were debated and negotiated. Making full use of the limited critical space that was still open, relying on his positions of political and church leadership and personal prestige, Ting helped to make negotiation a two-way street. The one other religious leader who was in a similar position was Zhao Puchu. After June 4th, Ting and Zhao made repeated appeals on questions of religious policy, pushing for more freedom, greater autonomy for religious organizations and the reform of religious work on the part of the RAB.

They did this now with fewer government allies. High-ranking officials who supported the reform policies of Zhao Ziyang were removed from their positions, and they were replaced by conservative hard-liners. Yan Mingfu, Ting's friend in the United Front Work Department (UFWD), was dismissed from his position and from the Secretariat of the CPC Central Committee.* Yan's replacement in the UFWD was Ding Guan'gen, known for his conservative views. Ren Wuzhi, also a conservative official, remained director of the RAB of the State Council. Zhao Fusan, a TSPM leader who had headed the Chinese Academy of Social Sciences and who also was prominent politically, was no longer on the scene. Zhao had played a very important role in the 1980s in helping to develop a more open view of religious studies. He had been in Europe at a UNESCO conference in early June, and he chose not to return to China. [35] Although there were many provincial and lower-ranking officials who had supported the changes in religious policy in the 1980s, they were not very influential.

The dissolution of the Soviet Union and the changes in Eastern Europe convinced the party leadership that it had to retain a strong hold on power. But it also increased concerns among conservative officials about the role that the church had played in the downfall of Communism in Russia and Eastern Europe. They were worried about the rapid growth of religion in China and its possible use for subversive purposes or "foreign infiltration."[36]

---

* Yan did, however, avoid more serious penalties. He became vice-minister of the Civil Affairs Bureau in 1992, and after his retirement, president of the China Charity Foundation. Although these were relatively unimportant positions, he continued to work for reform.

With this in mind, the government began preparing a new document on religious policy. In contrast to the 1982 statement on religion known as Document 19 (see chap. 7), the new draft document put its main emphasis on foreign infiltration, religious disorder, illegal religious activities and the adverse influence religion exerts on youth and society in general. Because it painted such a very dark picture of religion, the statement advocated the need for a more rigid enforcement of policy and the need to "strengthen supervision" (the word in Chinese may also be translated as "control" or "oversight") over religious groups, religious personages and religious finances. Protestant home-worship meetings, for example, which had not yet been approved by the government, were to be "strictly forbidden." Unlike the 1982 statement, there was no ambiguity about whether such informal gatherings could continue.

This new statement began circulating in draft form in the summer of 1990. It was sent to religious leaders and other policy makers for what was to be a perfunctory review, but the reaction from Ting and Zhao Puchu was quite pointed. Zhao criticized the draft almost immediately that summer. In September, Ting made a widely publicized speech at a meeting of the NPC Standing Committee. Although he referred to the draft document only by implication, he alluded to the "worrying signs" that there may be a reversal of the religious policy of the 1980s, as evidenced by new language about "strengthening the supervision" over religious organizations. This would lead to greater interference by government officials in internal religious affairs, by cadres who did not understand the feelings of religious believers. Ting went on to criticize the "widespread opinion" that churches had played a major role in the downfall of Communism all over Eastern Europe, arguing in specific detail, with references to Rumania, Hungary, East Germany and Czechoslovakia, that this was not usually the case. He concluded,

> If we can learn anything from the events of Eastern Europe, it is not the loss of confidence in religious organizations or the strengthening of control over them . . . In dealing with larger religious circles the lesson to be learned is the earnest implementation of religious and ethnic policies. What is to be strengthened is the effort to educate and seek the support of the masses and religious leaders so that the various religions can be run better and our unity consolidated and expanded.[37]

Ting's views on the reform of religious policy and many of his speeches were published in the journal *Religion (Zongjiao)*, which he edited (see chap. 7). After 1989, this journal's essays on religion and religious policy, Christianity in China and religious studies made important contributions to the reformist views that Ting represented. By the early 1990s, *Religion* had a circulation of ten thousand copies distributed free of charge to RAB officials at all levels, placing it among the most widely distributed periodicals dealing with religion. Because it was a university publication, *Religion*'s contents were approved by the State Education Commission, not the RAB, and this gave it much more latitude on what it could print. Many contributions to the journal came from reformist RAB officials who published under pseudonyms.[38] *Religion* had a much more important impact than the theological publications of the church, for it was a significant voice in the broader debate on religious policy.

The contributions from K. H. Ting and others may have helped to modify and in places soften the new statement on religious policy, but they could not withstand government efforts to promote a more restrictive approach. The first National Religious Work Conference since June 4th was held in December 1990, and it featured major addresses by both Jiang Zemin and Li Peng.[39] Jiang Zemin affirmed the stabilizing role of religion in China, but both he and Li Peng also expressed fears about the growing number of believers and affirmed the need for stronger government control. At this conference, which was not attended by religious leaders, the all-but-finalized version of the new document on religious policy was introduced.

The following month, Jiang Zemin himself met with religious leaders for what had become an annual review of religious work preceding the Chinese Lunar New Year. Jiang introduced the new policy statement at this meeting and spoke about the meeting on religious work the month before.[40] This was Ting's first formal meeting with the new party leader, and he spoke to him forthrightly about continuing problems of government religious policy: too much "struggling against religion" and too much government control of religious organizations. Ting repeatedly stressed the need to adhere to Document 19, invoking the legacy of Zhou Enlai to reinforce his position.[41] Privately he was saying that although the continuing conservative drift in religious policy might not change, the gains of the previous decade could not easily be undone.

On 5 February 1991, Document No. 6 was finally released, at least six months later than intended. Entitled "Some Questions for the Further Improvement of Religious Work," this was the first major statement on religious policy since 1982, and it bears the conservative views of Jiang Zemin and Li Peng on the subject. A year in preparation, it was not as restrictive as it might have been without the contributions of K. H. Ting, Zhao Puchu and others. There is no mention of "reordering relationships" or "the reform of the administration of religious affairs," which were major concerns of K. H. Ting in the late 1980s; but it continues an emphasis on safeguarding religious freedom and strengthens the principle that religious freedom should be grounded in law.[42] It opens the door for the registration of venues of religious activity but does not speak of forbidding or disbanding unapproved meeting points. Like all policy statements, implementation depended on which sections of the document one chooses to emphasize and how the document as a whole is interpreted. This always varies from place to place and region to region, but in light of the continuing growth of Christianity and other religions, it is evident that Document No. 6 did not result in a curbing of religious activity.

Document No. 6 has been widely analyzed,[43] but scholars have tended to overlook the contributions of K. H. Ting and other religious and political leaders who negotiated changes in the drafting process. The reason for this omission is that the changes were not publicly available, and one is forced to rely on informal conversations or interviews to suggest the role religious leaders may have played.[44] The document was not changed as much as Ting and Zhao would have liked, but the consultative process did produce changes, particularly with regard to its treatment of unapproved meeting points. Ting made use of his political and church positions again and again to press for more open policies. Although he was pragmatic in negotiating for changes in policy, he could also be quite caustic in his criticism. In his 1994 speech to government officials at the annual Spring Festival Tea Party, he said,

> The leadership of the Communist Party rests mainly on maintaining correct policies and setting an example in implementing them, not on arrogantly and overbearingly forcing people to follow. Even less does it rely on interfering with or monopolizing or taking over the internal affairs of other political parties or organizations. It is because quite a few cadres are used to exceeding their functions and meddling in others' affairs under the pretext of fitting religion into socialism that the relations between the Party and the masses are strained. What they are really doing is making religion fit their own intentions and interests.[45]

Ting continued to argue that religion in China was a source for social stability, not subversion, infiltration or "peaceful evolution" toward capitalism. He pressed for more religious freedom and less government interference in the internal affairs of the churches. He dealt with specific cases of the infringement of religious rights as they were presented to him, but the sheer volume of requests made the effective resolution of church-state conflicts almost impossible. We shall see how he also spoke up for the Christian meeting points (or house churches) unrelated to the TSPM/CCC when the issue of registration came up.[46] Ting was not always successful in arguing for greater religious freedom, but in some cases he was able to make a difference. In his role as political and church leader he helped the churches in concrete ways and promoted the democratic reforms he had been working for all along.

Even as he was struggling for more religious freedom, K. H. Ting was respected by the government as a Chinese patriot, Christian leader and internationally renowned public figure. This accounted for his continuing influence. Ting was not a radical dissident, but a patriotic reformer. This meant that he often spoke in favor of government actions and policies, because he believed in them. Had he only been a critic, he would not have had the influence he did. During the severe flooding of the summer of 1991, for example, Ting lauded the role of the People's Liberation Army in responding to the crisis. The government's response to this crisis helped to win back some of the popular support it had lost on June 4th. In October 1992, K. H. Ting was one of the specially invited guests at the opening of the Fourteenth Communist Party Congress, as he had also been at the Twelfth and Thirteenth Party Congresses. The *Beijing Review* ran a cover story on Christianity in China in 1994, featuring a photograph of K. H. Ting in full episcopal regalia on the cover. It was in the interview with him in that issue that K. H. Ting observed that Bible distribution was so widespread that it had become second only to *The Selected Works of Mao Zedong* in terms of its circulation in China.[47] This interview could be dismissed as "government propaganda" for the benefit of foreigners, except that K. H. Ting was standing up for the church in this interview just as he did at official gatherings in China that were not open to the public.

On important national occasions, K. H. Ting made speeches to a broader public, as did many other prominent figures, and these were often carried on national television. Seeing K. H. Ting in public settings was a source of encouragement to many Chinese Christians. His presence on the national scene was both a sign and a symbol of greater respect for religious life in China. Chinese Christians often described Ting's role in terms of a Chinese proverb, which may be translated, "As long as there is a green mountain, we won't lack for firewood." In the 1990s, Ting was in some sense the green mountain of the church. Many Christians believed that the first order of business was to support him, so that he in turn could protect the church and work for religious freedom.

Up until Deng Xiaoping's "Southern Tour" in early 1992, the general political situation in China remained uncertain. Although officially retired, Deng's trip to the Special Economic Zones in southern China demonstrated his support for a bolder and a faster approach to economic reform. The major danger to modernization, he said, was from the conservative and hard-line officials on the left, not the reform policies of the right.[48] Deng's trip reassured business people as well as intellectuals and religious leaders, and it prefigured China's rapid economic growth over the next decade. Economic reform did not lead directly to political change, but it did encourage a shift in social values toward more competitiveness, individualism and pluralism. This would mean that there would be more space to press for freedom and openness in other areas.

The most important church–state issue Ting dealt with over the next few years was that of the registration of venues for religious activities. In chap. 8, we saw how he opposed the registration of churches and meeting points in Guangdong Province when it was begun in 1988.[49] It now appeared that these regulations may have been a test case for future national policy. Registration was particularly opposed by fundamentalist and evangelical

Protestants who were not affiliated with the TSPM/CCC. Overseas, anti–Communist China ministry groups used the registration issue to drum up support for their cause, drawing parallels with the unregistered Baptists who were now speaking up in the former Soviet Union. Registration would be another way of controlling the church and limiting the spread of Christianity, they argued.

But there was another way of looking at the issue. By the early nineties, the strengthening of China's legal system had become the order of the day and was needed to keep pace with the economic reforms. Legislation was passed on everything from the system of taxation to foreign currency law, from new protections in the civil code to intellectual-property rights. The Civil Affairs Bureau, where Yan Mingfu now served as vice-minister, was proposing registration for all social organizations, so as to regularize their organizational processes, safeguard their legal status and provide some form of accountability to state and society. There was widespread interest at home and abroad in China's legal reforms, and most of the outside analyses had a favorable review of the process. The TSPM/CCC argued that the registration of churches and meeting points as legal entities provided some measure of protection for these bodies.

It was no longer possible for K. H. Ting to oppose registration in principle, as he had in the late 1980s. TSPMs and Christian councils had already been registered under a law that went into effect in 1999.[50] Registration of churches would not be difficult for large rural and urban churches. But Ting was concerned about the process of registration, the role of TSPMs and Christian councils and the status of unaffiliated meeting points. He was also concerned about the criteria that would be used to register churches. There were reports from many places about the indiscriminate closure of meeting points and the high-handed actions of local officials seeking to control Christian growth and influence. As the government was drawing up religious legislation, he was once again consulted in the drafting process; and in the political settings that were open to him, he spoke about the issues that concerned him. In this way, he contributed to the revision of the laws that were eventually approved. Ting argued that religious bodies should be involved in the registration process; that unaffiliated meeting points should be allowed to register in their own right; that the criteria for registration should be well publicized ahead of time; and that there should be an appeal process for meeting points and churches that failed to meet the requirement. Unregistered or not-yet-registered meeting points were not illegal, and so the government should exercise restraint once registration procedures were in place. Ting went to great lengths to speak up on behalf of those meeting points that, for whatever reason, did not want to or were unable to meet government requirements.

The new decree on registration was published in January 1994, together with a separate decree regulating the activity of foreign nationals within China.[51] Both decrees had been suggested in Document No. 6, in the section dealing with the administration of religious affairs according to law. The two decrees were related because of government concerns about foreign "infiltration," but in his public comments, K. H. Ting focused on registration. Not everyone was pleased with the new legislation. Critics continued to say that registration would control the church, while supporters countered it would safeguard the church. Different provinces developed their own procedures for the registration of religious venues, and although these were meant to follow the national law, it was not always the case that they did.[52] Over the next months and years, churches and church organizations in many parts of the country wrote Ting about their own experiences with registration. Once again, the implementation of the law was uneven.

Ting urged churches to support the registration process now that it was law, and he spoke in detail in the pages of *Tian Feng* both about its safeguards and advantages, and its potential problems.[53] In some widely publicized cases—Henan (1993) and Anhui (1995)—he was able to help unaffiliated meeting points in the registration process. His major efforts were not publicized, but behind the scenes he worked patiently with government officials and churches to try to resolve contentious issues. Sometimes he was successful, but more often not. He hoped that registration would encourage dialogue and consultation between local churches and the government, so that a process of "mutual supervision," or oversight, would ensue.

In a situation in which the government saw the need to strengthen control over religious organizations under the terms of Document No. 6, many analysts believed that there was little possibility that supervision or oversight could be mutual. Nevertheless, Ting continued to urge church participation in the strengthening of supervision (or oversight) in order to work for improvement in the religious situation. Speaking to the TSPM/CCC Joint Committee in 1995, he summed up his views on the subject:

1. Oversight is a good thing in principle, and Christians should not oppose supervision or oversight of religious affairs in principle.
2. It is not only government officials who do the supervision; religious bodies and churches from the grassroots to the national level also must participate.
3. Government and religious bodies both need to strengthen supervision.
4. Those doing the supervision must also strengthen themselves, and disputes should be settled through a consultative process.
5. Government supervision is concerned with politics and law; it should not supervise church affairs but should respect the faith of the church and the good tradition and system of democratic supervision that the church has formed over time.
6. Supervision should be according to law, not arbitrary decisions of officials.
7. Church personnel should follow church regulations.

8. The national TSPM and CCC "should play a greater role in leading and guiding church affairs. This will be beneficial in strengthening supervision, but this is in no way to negate the principle of consultation.

9. Decree No. 145 contains clear regulations on the supervision of venues for religious activities. We should study and respect it.[54]

Ting's careful interpretation and advice on both strengthening supervision and registration was a combination of idealism and pragmatism. It was idealistic in the sense that it was close to impossible for most churches at the grassroots to stand up to local officials, even if they were willing to do so; and pragmatic, in the sense that government regulation and supervision were a *fait accompli*, so it was important to make the best of the situation. For the church to even begin to participate in mutual supervision, it had to become stronger as an institution, and we shall see below that K. H. Ting was working on this front as well. As a church leader, he realized the weaknesses of local Christian organizations and yet continued to urge churches to participate in the registration because he believed that this was in their best long-term interests.

From 1994 onward, China's legal system has been improved and strengthened in many ways, and religious communities in theory enjoy the same protections as other social organizations. Nevertheless, the scope for interpretation of religious laws remains very wide, and local officials have far more say in the implementation of the law than do religious leaders. Much more needs to be done to improve the legal standing of religious organizations in China, even though the situation is much better than before. There are still many meeting points opposed to the registration process, although the government maintains that the vast majority of Christians are duly registered. Ting's efforts in the years before and after Decree No. 145 was issued have helped churches whether or not they have chosen to register, even though his advice to the government and to unaffiliated meeting points has not often been accepted.

Ye Xiaowen became the new director of the RAB of the State Council in June 1995. A conservative CPC loyalist close to Jiang Zemin, Ye was much younger than previous RAB directors. He also had an academic background in the social sciences and experience in religious work at the UFWD.[55] Upon assuming office, Ye saw his tasks as completing the religious-registration process, educating a new generation of leadership in the church and the religious affairs bureaus, and improving the RAB's understanding of religion in local situations.[56] The week after his appointment, Ye flew to Nanjing to meet with K. H. Ting as a sign of his respect for a senior religious leader and as an expression of his willingness to listen. Ting spoke with Ye about his concerns over religious policy and registration as he had with previous RAB directors. Although the two men had different approaches, Ting was impressed that Ye came to see him so early in his tenure. Ye Xiaowen was a new voice in the state administration of religious affairs and one who would prove to be more open-minded than many of his predecessors.

The next year, Ye Xiaowen signaled a new emphasis in Chinese religious policy by drawing on the three summary sentences that Jiang Zemin had spoken at a UFWD conference three years earlier. According to Jiang, the "three sentences" (*san juhua*) for dealing with religious policy are (1) completely and correctly implement the party's policy of religious freedom; (2) strengthen supervision of religious affairs in accordance with the law; and (3) actively guide religion to adapt to socialist society.[57] The first two sentences had been part of the religious policy all along, with a continuing stress on strengthening control and the new religious laws of 1994. The third sentence follows from the other two. The adaptation of religion to socialist society had been suggested in Document No. 6, but Jiang Zemin gave it added importance. Guiding and encouraging Chinese religions to adapt (*shiying*) to socialist society meant for Jiang the reform of religious dogmas and beliefs to better serve socialism. It did not mean the abandonment of theism or of faith but a focus on the ethical import of religious beliefs, for ethics were a point of contact between believers and nonbelievers. Ye Xiaowen, in interpreting the three sentences in 1996, wrote that the purpose of religious policy and strengthening control in accordance with law "is to get religion and socialist society to adapt to each other." He goes on to say that religious believers "must continue to progress in the area of adapting to socialist society and must not regress."[58] In other words, the onus is on religious believers. It is clear that for Ye adaptation was by no means mutual, and that it was primarily the religions that had to change.

It was precisely this point that had been the subject of debate in the previous years, at least insofar as it affected religious policy and its implementation. K. H. Ting had not been criticizing socialist views on theoretical grounds but had been arguing for a more reform-oriented view of religious policy. This suggested, if only by implication, that the process of adaptation needed to be in some ways mutual. By the end of 1996, it seemed clear that the government's religious policy would remain more restrictive than had been hoped in the late 1980s. There was a firmer grounding in law, which meant that the churches had space to grow and develop, and there was still the possibility of working for limited change. In private, however, Ting would say that he did not want to paint a too optimistic picture of the overall situation.

Yet he responded positively to the idea that Christians also had to change and adapt. In contrast to more conservative theologians and church leaders, he increasingly wanted to emphasize the shared values between Christianity and socialism. In 1994, a friend had sent him a recent speech by Joe Slovo, the South African Communist leader, on the common ground of Christian-Communist cooperation. Ting was so moved by the speech that he spent all his spare time at one CPPCC meeting translating the essay into

Chinese for publication in the journal *Religion*.[59] Slovo was arguing for Christian and Communist cooperation in a new South Africa, and Ting wanted the same in China.

He also looked for other ways that the ethical dimension of religion could be strengthened. Together with his older friend Kuang Yaming, who had retired from his position as president of Nanjing University, Ting became a general advisor to the Mazu Association. Mazu may or may not have been an historical figure, but she has become known as the goddess of the sea and is worshipped in Fujian and Taiwan for her power in rescuing sailors and helping people in need.[60] The Mazu Association was established in Fuzhou in the mid-1990s to emphasize the ethical significance of Mazu, not her religious nature. Ting spoke highly of the humanistic and ethical qualities he saw in teachings about Mazu, and although his participation in the Mazu Association was only symbolic, it exemplified what he saw as the ethical importance in all religions.[61] Ting may have agreed to serve as an advisor because of his friendship with Kuang Yaming, and there is no record of any subsequent involvement that Ting had with the Mazu Association.

Ting's interest in religious ethics shows that in his efforts to promote changes in religious policy, he was attempting to work for more creative collaboration between church and society. He believed that Protestant Christianity in China had to break out of its narrow fundamentalism, which he viewed as an inheritance from the missionary movement and decades of isolation from the rest of the world. He hoped for a greater emphasis on the ethical dimensions of Christianity and the downplaying of the conflict between belief and unbelief that separated Christians from other Chinese. His own theology since the 1940s had moved in this direction, and he would come back to the task of theological reconstruction at the end of the 1990s. There were more immediate tasks after June 4th, however, for the church was in a very vulnerable and uncertain situation.

STRENGTHENING THE CHURCH

Government reform was part of the larger picture (*da qihou*) in which the church existed. But the church had its own context (*xiao qihou*) and internal problems. Churches had continued to grow since the early 1980s, as had other religious groups, but they were desperately short of pastors and trained leaders, despite the many new seminaries and lay training programs that had been organized. Rural areas had seen the greatest church growth, but they had the fewest number of trained leaders; and there were additional problems of heterodoxy owing to the low educational level of rural Christians.[62] June 4th had by no means stopped the growth of the church in urban areas, and it may even have contributed to the increasing interest in Christianity, especially on the part of young people and intellectuals.

The TSPM/CCC had internal structural problems that Ting and his supporters had begun to address in the late 1980s. The "reordering of relationships" between the TSPM and the CCC, the relationship of both bodies
to unaffiliated and disaffected Christian groups, the training of a new generation of leaders, and the development of a rationalized church order and
ecclesiology were foremost among these. If the church were to be run well
as "a school for the democratic spirit," as Ting hoped, then the process of
internal reform that had begun in the 1980s would have to be continued.
This was a noble ideal, but given the situation after 1989, it would be difficult to realize.

The TSPM/CCC Committee met in Shanghai at the end of 1989 and
reaffirmed the themes of "running the church well" and "reordering relationships" between the TSPM and the CCC.[63] At the end of the 1980s, K.
H. Ting was calling for a "change in function" of Three-Self organizations,
arguing that TSPM committees were merely "scaffolding" which would not
be necessary once the building of the church was complete. There were others in the national leadership who saw a more permanent role for the TSPM.
They did not like the idea of Three-Self as scaffolding, and they were not as
committed to building up the church. The government's response to the
"June 4th events" could be seen to strengthen their position in favor of a
more political orientation for the TSPM and the CCC, but this was not true.
The reaffirmation of "running the church well" and "reordering relationships" at the Shanghai meeting showed that a majority continued to support
Ting in the direction he had introduced in the 1980s.

The following summer (1990), a much larger meeting of the national
leadership was held a few days before the fortieth anniversary celebration of
the Three-Self Patriotic Movement. The TSPM/CCC work report at the plenary session touched on all the areas of work over the years since the Fourth
National Christian Conference, but in both tone and content, it clearly
reflects the conservative position of government hard-liners on recent events.
Near the beginning of the report, we read: "In the spring and summer of
last year, a tiny minority of supporters of bourgeois liberalization, with the
support of international hostile forces, stirred up political turmoil and
fomented a counter-revolutionary rebellion in Beijing, whose aim was the
overthrow of the Communist Party and socialism."[64] Even by the standards
of the time, this language was harsh and went beyond the formulaic statement made in the immediate aftermath of June 4th.

In contrast, K. H. Ting's address at the same meeting contained no such
language. He also made political references in his speech, but he chose his
quotations carefully, always emphasizing the need for reform. His emphasis throughout is not on the broader political context—for this was the summer he was proposing changes to what would become Document No.
6—but on the church. Ting's persistent themes are all included in this
address—running the church well, mutual respect in matters of faith, sup-

porting and relating to meeting points that are unaffiliated to the TSPM/ CCC, broadening unity and the need for a democratic spirit.

Ting wanted the TSPM and CCC to relate more closely to Christian meeting points that were alienated from it. He saw his role as a representative of all Protestant Christians in China, and not just those related to formally recognized church bodies. Just as he was willing to criticize the government over its implementation of religious policy, so too he was willing to criticize leadership in the church and the TSPM for the way it sometimes treated fellow Christians.

> Matters of faith, including ecclesiology, are extremely sensitive. For quite a number of people within the church, whether to use the term *shen* or *shangdi* when referring to God is no small matter, but rather a significant matter involving faith and people's sentiments. In some places, the church authorities are not terribly sensitive. It is not only that power over individual churches' budget and personnel is concentrated in their hands under the name of Three-Self or the two national bodies, even who will preach the sermon is not decided through seeking consensus of local Christians' expectations. This raises the spectre of conformity or uniformity of faith. I think it is worth considering whether things really need to be done in such a fashion. These things impinge on the question of running the church well in a democratic spirit.[65]

By a "democratic spirit" Ting did not mean that the minority follows the majority in elections, nor a respect of individual rights. Ting was a reform-oriented socialist who saw humanism as a way of moving toward a socialist democracy.[66] The churches could foster a democratic spirit in the interaction among Christians, implying a style of doing things through consultation, which was something he had learned at the CPPCC. The emphasis was on mutual supervision and mass participation, in the church as well as in government. As he told graduating seminary students some years later,

> I think the whole society, including us in the church, should do as follows: (1) everything must be done in consultation, one or two people must not have the power to decide things; (2) there must be oversight; where there is power there should be supervision; (3) people should have a voice in the discussion of important issues. Then the pastor will not be seen as a superman and the people as dummies. This is the path toward growth for everyone.[67]

Ting also hoped that seminary graduates would take this "democratic way of doing things" with them, so that their churches could become communities of equality, unity and love. He realized that this was far from the reality in most churches, TSPMs and Christian councils, but he wanted to encourage a democratic spirit in running the church well. This reflected his own deeply held beliefs about leadership and democracy in the church, as well as his way of relating to senior colleagues in the two national Christian organizations, even those who disagreed with him. It is consistent with his views on mutual supervision in the government registration process mentioned above.

In order to demonstrate his personal support for church building and running the church well, Ting made a well-publicized visit to Wenzhou in Zhejiang Province at the end of 1990. He had been invited to visit churches in many parts of the country, and he could not possibly go everywhere. The choice of Wenzhou was, therefore, significant. The city was known as "China's Jerusalem" because of its large number of Protestant Christians. Wenzhou Christians were fervent believers who continued to meet for worship even during the Cultural Revolution era. At the time of Ting's visit, the city and surrounding counties had at least 400,000 Christians, or half the number in the province, and the church was still growing very rapidly.[68] To put this another way, Wenzhou had a higher percentage of Christians than any other Chinese city in the world, including Hong Kong, Taipei and Singapore. It was also a flourishing economic center, and one of the first areas to experiment with market-oriented reforms. Independent researchers and some government officials observed that economic reform and the growth of churches went hand in hand. Churches were a very visible presence in every part of the city.

Wenzhou officials received Ting in a manner befitting his position as CPPCC vice-chair. But Ting had come to see the church and wanted to minimize government formalities, which were often designed to keep him away from grassroots Christians. In order get a true picture of the situation, Ting had gone to Wenzhou with Deng Fucun (whom he had ordained in the 1950s), a provincial church leader who knew the local leaders, and with two young seminary teachers, who knew their classmates who were working in the city.[69] Many meeting points were not related to the TSPM/CCC, but Ting wanted to see them as well. He met with Christians both inside and outside of the TSPM and with recent graduates of Nanjing Seminary. He heard about their problems, many of which had to do with relations with the local authorities. When he met with government officials, his position in the CPPCC gave him some leverage to resolve issues affecting the churches. He praised the RAB officials for their efforts to get back church property, but he also criticized their handling of some problems affecting the churches—making decisions on church leadership, for example—cautioning that he would be taking some of his concerns to be resolved at higher levels of government.

Ting saw the religious situation in Wenzhou in its complexity, and wherever he went he listened and spoke words of encouragement to the churches. The Christians of Longgang asked him to name their church. He chose the name Grace Church (*Zhu En Tang*), and the name now appears in his calligraphy on the building. Ting added the following words to the cornerstone: "Jesus Christ Is the Head of the Church and Its Cornerstone." Simple words, but they reflect what he had been saying about the need for strengthening the church during these years.

K. H. Ting made a few other well-publicized visits to churches, to Guangdong (1992) and Yunnan (1993), and he received a number of church delegations from other provinces in Nanjing. But the Wenzhou visit stands out for the in-depth way in which he was able to hear reports and respond to the needs of the local situation. Ting did not want to be a leader far away and isolated, but because of his workload, he was not usually able to develop a good picture of what was happening to churches at the grassroots.

One of the reasons that the churches in Wenzhou were flourishing was owing to the economic prosperity of the city as a whole, and the contributions of wealthy Christians to the building of the city's many churches.[70] For churches in most other parts of China, and particularly inland rural churches, the economic situation was very different. China's economic growth in the 1990s resulted in an increasing disparity between rich and poor parts of the country, and higher rates of inflation meant a decreasing purchasing power for accumulated institutional resources. The question of self-support that had surfaced in the 1980s became increasingly urgent in the 1990s. A great many church and seminary buildings were dilapidated and overcrowded. Some churches were unable to support their own pastors, whose salaries and benefits were already very low. Income from property rental was no longer what it once was, and contributions from church members could not keep pace with church growth or economic development. Younger pastors and seminary students often faced a life of economic hardship.

National and provincial TSPMs and Christian councils made efforts to help local churches, but the limited resources they had were needed for theological education, the production of Christian literature, and their own programs. Wealthier churches in coastal areas like Zhejiang, Jiangsu and Shanghai did contribute to churches in poorer areas, but interchurch aid was not systematic. Government bodies sometimes provided limited support for theological education and the work of provincial Christian organizations, but they could hardly be expected to finance the growing number of churches in China. Some donations had come from overseas, but the principle of "self-support" suggested to many Christians outside of China that larger contributions were not welcome.

At the beginning of the period of reform, Ting spoke of the need for maintaining a "protective tariff" on financial resources from overseas, so that Chinese churches could maintain and develop their principle of self-support. Self-support should be the principle, but in the 1990s, Ting had come to believe that the "tariff" could be lifted somewhat. In consultation with other church leaders, he had begun to see that they could relax the way in which the principle was interpreted, particularly to address the financial difficulties that churches were experiencing. After Deng Xiaoping's "Southern Tour" and in the spirit of "liberating the forces of production," many leaders felt that they should be able to accept international offers of financial assistance.

The experience of the Amity Foundation, whose programs had continued to grow and develop since the late 1980s, was very positive, but Amity support was not for the purpose of church building. In the "Fourteen Points" (1980), Ting had said there was no need to maintain a strict "closed-door policy" on receiving contributions from overseas,[71] but now he went even further. The churches not only needed to be self-supporting but also well-supported, and on this level, there was a great deal of work to do. He believed that many churches overseas who respected Three-Self had been too cautious about the ways they could help the Chinese church. The principle of self-support would not be abandoned, but the Chinese church was no longer dependent on foreign mission boards, and so there was a new willingness to accept contributions from "friendly" churches overseas without strings attached.

> We see that many Christians overseas want to share their resources with us. This sharing seems similar to what St. Paul spoke about in his correspondence with the Corinthians. We have seen this spirit of sharing in our work with the Amity Foundation . . . Insofar as the church is concerned, international Christian sharing can help to strengthen our oneness in Christ, because it arises from a spirit of love and mutual concern. We therefore want to broaden our understanding of sharing to embrace support for our churches, theological schools and other projects.[72]

Beyond the theological considerations, such sharing was a practical necessity and a great help to the development of the church. Ting would use his personal charisma to make requests to friends in overseas churches to contribute to the work of the church in China, but he did so quietly, and, it often seemed, reluctantly. He always seemed to be personally ambivalent about the idea of donations from overseas. He went back and forth about exactly what could be acceptable, and it is no wonder that churches overseas were sometimes confused. Ting did not want to see China or the Chinese church described as poor and miserable in order to get money. Many local churches were apparently willing to do away with self-support altogether. In 1994, he told the TSPM/CCC leadership that there had been "a partial breakdown in thinking" about self-support in Chinese churches, as reports came in about a variety of schemes to attract foreign donations.

> Some of our church leaders say that this is the age of the socialist market economy, where money is king and the church too can make

money. Christianity is an ethical religion, there are things we may do, and things we may not do, not everything is permitted. We may be poor, but we cannot abandon our principle; if we do, many of our own Christians and our international friends will be disappointed, and will not respect us. But some of our colleagues say: the important thing is money in the hand. When we do these things, we won't tell the national CCC and TSPM, they don't need to know. They pull the wool over our eyes, but we find out about it through foreigners . . . Independence is a serious matter. Let us all consider it well at this meeting.[73]

Ting urged Chinese churches to maintain their dignity and independence as they took new initiatives in international Christian sharing. They should not fall back on the colonial mentality of the past for the sake of money. At the meeting where he spoke these words, the TSPM/CCC approved a resolution that maintained a balance between the acceptance of foreign contributions and maintaining the principle of self-support.[74] In time, there would also be church directives and government regulations on the practical details. Document No. 6 also spoke about financial contributions from overseas, and church positions were within the framework set down there. But Ting wanted the church to have a policy of its own. As Chinese churches continued to grow, issues such as stewardship and church finance would continue to be at the forefront, as they were for churches all over the world.

If self-support was one important issue facing the church, self-government was another, especially as it related to the training of a new generation of leadership. Since the early 1980s, pastors all over China had been saying there were "too many sheep, but not enough shepherds," and that "a new harvest (of church leaders) would not come in time" to replace the generation that was passing away (*qing huang bu jie*). Ting believed that young people in positions of church leadership would be a democratizing influence, for they were not so rooted in the histories, politics and theologies of the past. In most local churches, however, the older generation was not willing to relinquish control. They had endured decades of repression, and now that the church was growing, they wanted to continue working so that they could see the fruit of their labors. The fact that the church had no retirement system meant that many retired church workers would have no place to go. Moreover, local officials were often more comfortable with elderly leaders and were concerned that a new generation of pastors would not be so compliant, especially after the democracy movement of 1989. Young seminary graduates were becoming impatient with the older church leadership. They were respectful, but a serious generation gap was evident in terms of opinions about what a well-run church would look like.

In the years leading up to the Fifth National Christian Conference at the end of 1991, Ting saw the promotion of young people to positions of leadership as one of the most important ways of strengthening the church. He was conscious of his own age, and of the aging leadership of the church overall, and this made the problem all the more urgent. In almost every issue of *Tian Feng,* there were reports of elderly pastors who had recently passed away. But churches at the grassroots were reluctant to make better use of young people, and so Ting decided to begin at the top. He urged the national leadership to adopt age requirements for delegates to the National Christian Conference, and despite objections from some provinces, it was agreed that 30 percent of the delegates would be under fifty years of age; no more than 40 percent above seventy; and none over eighty. This was an enormous improvement, for the average age of delegates at the Fifth NCC was seven years lower than the Fourth NCC, held five years earlier, a figure that Ting said was "better than he dared hope for."[75] The problem was that not many young people were given leadership positions.

In order to emphasize that more responsibility should be turned over to the younger generation, Ting organized an unprecedented ordination service for forty-two seminary graduates at the end of the conference in Beijing. Up until that point, it was estimated that since the early 1980s fewer than seventy-five of the more than one thousand seminary graduates had been ordained.[76] There was a deep reluctance on the part of some local pastors to face the inevitable transition. In his sermon at the ordination service, Ting expressed his hope that this service would have a twofold impact on the church:

> First, to encourage churches to ease up a bit, to open the gates wider and accept qualified candidates for ordination into the ministry of the church as soon as possible . . . Second, to encourage more young Christians, men and women, to heed Christ's call and dedicate their lives to the work of the church and the gospel . . .[77]

There were other ordinations of young seminary graduates over the next years, but the process of turning over leadership to a new generation was slow in both the provinces and at the national level.

Nanjing Seminary was itself an important force within the church for training and encouraging younger theologians and church leaders. As the only national seminary in China, there were Nanjing graduates in every part of the country, and Ting believed they had a strong belief in reform and democratization.[78] Nanjing graduates were the core faculty in the other twelve theological schools in China, and many were being groomed for positions of provincial leadership. In November 1992, Ting agreed to hold a reunion on the occasion of the fortieth anniversary of the seminary's founding, which in part emphasized the influence of seminary graduates on the churches. More than three hundred alumni/ae came from nineteen provinces for the reunion.[79] Relationships forged during university and seminary studies are particularly important in China, and the reunion in Nanjing became a time for renewal and the strengthening of old school ties. Ting hoped that these ties would encourage graduates to support one another in the future and to work for change in the church.

He continued to speak directly to Nanjing Seminary graduates in future years, both on and off campus,[80] and he sought out seminary graduates on his travels within China. Many seminary graduates went to see him at his home, or they wrote him letters about their work in the church. The perspective of former students was different from the views he heard through official channels. Ting worried about the low standard of living of young graduates, and he tried to help graduates when they were in difficulty. He was also concerned about the tensions between young graduates and older leaders in the churches, many of whom held rigid political and theological views. In one highly publicized incident, Ting worked with others to resolve a case involving a dispute between a seminary graduate and the elderly matriarch of the church in the northeastern city of Shenyang.[81] International publicity complicated the situation, but the problem was in time resolved, largely through the behind-the-scenes labors of Ting and other church leaders. The young graduate subsequently emerged as a respected leader in the province, where he continued to serve the church.

For each case that was successfully resolved, there were a great many more conflicts between young church leaders and government officials or senior pastors that were not. Despite the suppression of the 1989 democracy movement, educated young people in China were outspoken and impatient for a faster rate of change. They were not necessarily politically involved, but they were being shaped by new social values that emphasized democracy, individualism and openness more than "socialist" reform. In the church, some young people were extremely critical about the controlling function of the TSPM and its close cooperation with the government. Although Ting regularly urged patience and forbearance to seminary graduates in their dealing with government officials and older church leaders, many were no longer willing to listen to the advice of people from Ting's generation, and a few were willing to say so in public. At the Fifth NCC, several dissenting votes were cast by young people, something that had not happened before.[82] This was something that even Ting found surprising. Young people increasingly expressed their dissatisfaction with the older generation of church leaders, including K. H. Ting, as the gap between young and old widened. As we shall see, many who had been sent overseas for further study left the TSPM/CCC altogether.

In the late 1980s, the seminary sent several Nanjing graduates overseas for further theological studies. Buddhists in China were sending young people to Japan, Thailand and other countries in large numbers, and Roman Catholics also began sending many young priests and novices to Europe, North America and Asia for formative training. By the early 1990s, most of the Protestants had returned to China to teach at the seminary or work in the national offices. The TSPM/CCC did not continue to send young people overseas after June 4th, mostly because of increased government restrictions. But there were also hesitations among older church leaders about the kind of training Chinese students were receiving and the cultural values they were absorbing. Ting himself sometimes seemed to be of two minds on sending students overseas. He encouraged foreign language learning, international outreach and short periods of overseas theological study, but he questioned the desirability of sending students for several years of training to receive advanced degrees. This would alienate them from the Chinese context, he believed, and in any case, young seminary graduates were needed at home. Similar to his ambivalence about the receiving of foreign donations, Ting believed that the church should be independent (but not isolationist) in its theology and theological training. He did not want churches or theological seminaries overseas making decisions about Chinese students sent by the CCC.[83] He welcomed theologians from other parts of the world to lecture at the seminary, but he also insisted that Nanjing Seminary should stress theology in and for the Chinese church. Later in the 1990s, a few Protestants again went for further study in Hong Kong, Singapore, Europe and North America, but many went on their own, without the formal approval of the TSPM/CCC.

The 1990s were a time when some of China's foremost universities were developing religious studies programs, and many so-called "culture Christians" and secular university graduates were studying Christian theology in Europe and North America. It was K. H. Ting himself who coined the term culture Christians to refer to scholars in China outside the church who were studying Christianity.[84] In 1994, the first international consultation on Christianity was held, cosponsored by the Amity Foundation (whose president was K. H. Ting) and the Institute of World Religions of the Chinese Academy of Social Sciences.[85] It brought together Chinese and foreign scholars, both Christian and non-Christian, and helped to promote a dialogue in the academic world. Although there would be some tension between Ting and university-based religious scholars in the future, he believed that this kind of conference played an important bridge-building role, which was related to what he was trying to do in the TSPM/CCC.

The Fifth National Christian Conference had a larger number of young delegates than ever before, and they added to the focus on "running the church well," which was the general theme. The subject was discussed in committees focusing on a variety of issues, including the rural church, overseas relationships, church music, minority Christians and women's concerns.[86] Ting was reelected CCC president and TSPM chairperson at the Fifth NCC; this was to be his final term in both positions. He presided over a growing, complex and increasingly diverse Christian community. The conference report noted that the number of churches had risen from 4,000 in 1986, to more than 7,000 in 1991. There were more than 20,000 meeting points—government registration had not yet begun—and an estimated 6.5 million Protestant Christians. Other estimates double or triple these numbers.[87] Churches were very loosely related to one another, through provincial and municipal TSPMs and Christian councils, but there were also Christian communities unrelated to the TSPM/CCC with formal or informal networks of their own. They had different denominational backgrounds and traditions, but because there were a great number of new Christians, many believers had little sense of what it meant to be a church that was connected to other churches in the body of Christ.

In order to deal with this growing diversity in the churches, the previous NCC had appointed a committee to consider the question of church order and ecclesiology. Chaired by Peter Tsai (Cai Wenhao, 1913-1993), a former Presbyterian and an ally of Ting since the 1940s, the committee included respected representatives of many different denominational traditions. After years of careful work, it presented to the Fifth NCC a new "Church Order for Trial Use in Chinese Churches."[88] Although "reordering relationships" was not on the agenda at the conference, the "Church Order" was a way of getting at some of the same issues. Ting followed the progress of this committee closely, for he saw church order as an essential way of strengthening the CCC as an ecclesiastical organization and promoting greater unity in the churches. He took pride in the fact that the new order incorporated Episcopal, Presbyterian and Congregational elements, and commented that the church order marked "a high point on the road towards unity that the Chinese church had been following over the last forty years."[89] Because he hoped that the CCC would soon enter into a more formal relationship with the World Council of Churches, he believed that the new church order and the experience of postdenominational unity in China might also be seen as a Chinese contribution to the ecumenical movement internationally.

Separate sections in the "Church Order" dealt with the nature of the church, the sacraments, believers, ministry, and issues of organization and management. It reflected a practical and pragmatic approach to ecclesiology, and it did not attempt to define things too rigidly. The longest sections are about ministry and organizational concerns. It took into account some issues that were also addressed in the government regulations three years later. The spirit of the document reflects Ting's interest in a democratic spirit (i.e., consultation, supervision and people's participation). The "Church Order" was designed to be a model for provincial TSPMs and Christian councils, and it could be modified for local use. The committee recognized that local churches were preoccupied with pressing and immediate problems, but it hoped that the spirit of the new "Church Order" could be introduced to churches at provincial gatherings.

A key section of the "Church Order" defined the role of a postdenominational clergy, identifying the functions for bishops, pastors, teachers, elders, evangelists and deacons. Different terms were used in different places and traditions, and the section was meant to be loosely inclusive rather than narrowly definitive. Ting saw church order in terms of his own Anglican and Episcopal roots, and although he never tried to impose this on the church as a whole, he did see the Anglican tradition as worth preserving for the Chinese church. The episcopacy and the threefold order of ministry, with separate offices of deacon, priest and bishop, were part of his own faith and piety. He was not particularly "high church," but he did prefer Anglican liturgy to the more enthusiastic forms of worship favored by many, if not most, Chinese Protestants. For this reason, he had introduced more liturgically oriented worship in chapel services at Nanjing Seminary. Ting had a sacramental approach to the church and the world, and a preference for "decency and order" rather than spontaneity in religion. This was also in tune with his approach to Chinese and Christian culture and tradition.

K. H. Ting wanted the historic episcopacy to continue in the Chinese church. This was evident in his support for the consecration of the two Shanghai bishops, which we discussed in the last chapter. However, many Anglicans who were his friends, allies and supporters were passing from the scene. Bishop Zheng Jianye (1919-1991) died eight months before the Fifth NCC. Zheng was the first CCC general secretary but had been hospitalized for some years after a severe stroke. Zheng and Ting had been friends since the 1930s, and their approaches to the church and politics were similar. Like Ting, Zheng had run afoul of "leftists" in Shanghai beginning in the 1950s, even though he was a staunch supporter of socialism. After the end of the Cultural Revolution era, he played a key role in the formation of the CCC and was firmly committed to the church.

In his eulogy, Ting referred to Zheng as his friend and teacher. He particularly emphasized Zheng Jianye's contributions to unity in the church. Toward the end, he offers a moving reflection on his close friend's death.

> When we were young, we never thought of death, we knew only the joy of life which filled our hearts. It's different now. Our loved ones, those in the same generation, are dying one by one. Where do we find consolation? All that God has made is good, especially people. As Shakespeare said, "What a piece of work is man." God is love, therefore, it cannot be that it is the fate of all these good things to be obliterated. As on the day when Christ took up several loaves of bread and a fish, so he will accept them, give thanks to his father in heaven and break them. And in his hands they will be changed, they will be multiplied and offered up to God.[90]

It was not only those of his own generation who were dying. The most severe blow to the future church leadership was the untimely death of Bishop Shen Yifan in the summer of 1994. Shen had been elected vice-president and general secretary of the CCC, succeeding Zheng Jianye at the Fifth NCC.[91] An outstanding theologian and church leader, it was widely assumed that he would succeed Ting as CCC president. Like Ting and Zheng Jianye, Shen Yifan was from a respected Anglican family, and he had both a theological and a pastoral interest in building up the church. Shen's death shook the

CCC at a time when there were very few senior leaders with theological training.

Two of China's four remaining Anglican bishops died the next year. In February, the aged bishop Moses Xue Pingxi (1904-1995) passed away in Fuzhou. Xue had been consecrated in 1955, together with K. H. Ting and Liu Yucang (who had died some years earlier), at the last consecration service on the mainland of Anglican (Sheng Gong Hui) bishops.* In April, Bishop Sun Yanli (1907-1995) passed away in Shanghai. A former Methodist, he had been consecrated in 1988 with Shen Yifan. When Bishop Wang Shenyin (1915-1997) of Shandong died two years later, K. H. Ting became the last surviving Protestant bishop on the mainland.

In the spring of 1995, K. H. Ting made the opening speech to the joint standing committee of the TSPM/CCC when it was meeting in Nanjing. By the end of 1994, he had already indicated that he would not stand for CCC president and TSPM chair at the next NCC. The text of his 1995 speech was not published at the time, but Ting included it in his book of selected writings.[92] The speech is longer and more comprehensive than any other he gave at church meetings in China between the Fifth and Sixth National Christian Conferences, and it went through a long drafting process. This speech, entitled "A Look Back at the Way We Have Come," may be read as a summing up of some of what Ting was hoping to achieve in the eighteen months before he stepped down as head of the TSPM/CCC.

In this speech, Ting relates the accomplishments of the TSPM in the 1980s and 1990s to the continuing challenges facing the church. For example, the establishment of the China Christian Council and the emphasis on running the church well was related to the need for greater attention to church affairs and questions of ministry. This was his first point. His second point was that Chinese Christians had adjusted their view of Christians overseas, symbolized most importantly by the CCC becoming part of the WCC. Third, Chinese theological thinking had already been broadened somewhat, but theological renewal (or reconstruction) and a greater attention to ethics was still needed. Fourth, social concerns had begun to be raised in Chinese Christianity through the Amity Foundation and local social-service initiatives undertaken by the churches. This work, however, had only just begun. Fifth, Christian councils and TSPM organizations were changing their view of meeting points, or house churches, no longer wanting to exclude them. But Christian unity had to be broadened through a greater acceptance of theological diversity. The last part of his speech dealt with issues of registration and "strengthening oversight in religious affairs." His overall assessment of the church in China in this speech is cast in the best possible light, but he was

---

* There were no longer any Methodist bishops or bishops from the True Jesus church still living. As pointed out in the last chapter, they used a different Chinese term for bishop, *huidu* rather than *zhujiao*.

not delivering a self-congratulatory message, for the continuing challenges are there as well.

In public and in private, K. H. Ting could be as wise as a serpent and as innocent as a dove. "A Look Back at the Way We Have Come" shows something of both. More broadly, in his speeches and published writings for the church, he tended to speak of the accomplishments of Chinese Christianity, the possibilities in church-state relations and his hopes for the future. He was conscious of his role as church leader, and his pragmatic hopefulness was an aspect of his pastoral and priestly presence. In TSPM/CCC meetings, he could also be firm and unyielding, particularly in dealing with those whom he believed did not support his emphasis on running the church well. Ting often relied on trusted lieutenants in behind-the-scenes maneuvering when dealing with difficult matters or with people with whom he disagreed. As is true of all public figures, Ting functioned differently in different situations, but in style and approach, he has been remarkably consistent.

Throughout his last term as leader of the two national Christian organizations, Ting maintained a sense of perspective about what was and was not possible and what he himself as TSPM/CCC leader could and could not do. This did not make him sanguine about prospects for the future. There had been no reordering of relationships between the CCC and the TSPM, and in his final year as chair, the scaffolding that was the Three-Self Patriotic Movement looked as if it were there to stay.

In private conversations in China and overseas, he said again and again that he did not want to paint an optimistic picture of the political or the church situation in China. He sometimes expressed his own doubts about the future. "The best days are behind us *(da shi yi qu)*," he observed on more than one occasion in the mid-1990s, and now we are "treating a dead horse as if it were alive" *(si ma dang huo ma yi)*. He never gave into these sentiments, however, for he saw that there was always more that he could still do. China and the world were changing, and K. H. Ting believed that the church in China could contribute to the changes then in process and could itself still be changed.

CHINA AND THE WORLD

Political, ecclesiological, theological and ecumenical interests all intersected in the life and thought of K. H. Ting. If his role as a national political leader was a way of working to strengthen the Christian community, his international involvement contributed to the opening of China and the church. It was also important for the church ecumenical, for Christians overseas learned from the faith and witness of the Chinese church through K. H. Ting and other Chinese Christians. Ting's international outreach was at the same time a source of controversy, especially among persistent evangelical critics and human-rights activists. This created a complicated picture of China among Christians overseas, and Ting was seen to be at the center of it all.

After June 4th, Chinese educational, cultural and religious organizations hoped to maintain their opening to the outside world, which had been developing since the late 1970s. Despite warnings about "peaceful evolution" and "foreign infiltration," the Chinese government did not want to close itself off internationally either. The situation was uncertain, but there were many on all sides who told foreigners that the policy of reform and openness would continue. As noted above, the general atmosphere by late summer and early fall was to encourage foreign exchanges while at the same time demanding political conformity at home (*wai song, nei jin*).

Christians from around the world expressed their support for the China Christian Council after the violent suppression of the democracy movement. By the end of June 1989, more than ninety messages of solidarity and pastoral concern had been sent to K. H. Ting and the CCC. The Amity Foundation office in Hong Kong handled a large number of requests from the press for information about the situation of K. H. Ting and the church in China, as well as more discreet inquiries from friends and church leaders overseas. In a carefully worded message, the central committee of the World Council of Churches, meeting in Moscow in mid-July, wrote K. H. Ting, assuring the CCC of "our support as you continue in your prophetic and pastoral ministry, giving hope to people, calling them to repentance and affirming solidarity with the suffering."[93] Similarly worded messages had been coming from other churches and Christian leaders since early June.

Ting was unhappy about the way in which the government had dealt with the student movement, and he could understand the reaction of overseas churches that denounced in their public statements what had happened. At the same time, in conversations with foreign friends and visitors in the summer and fall of 1989, he expressed his hope that condemnation of the Chinese government would not result in the isolation of the Chinese church or the Amity Foundation. Moreover, he did not want foreigners considered to be close to the Chinese church to become, in his words, "marked persons" in China because of their criticisms. Ting and other leaders hoped that foreign-church visits would continue to strengthen ecumenical ties. Such exchanges also afforded a chance for mutual learning about what had really happened in Beijing, and how the church would continue.

Ting's first trip abroad after June 4th was as a representative of the CPPCC in January 1990 to attend a global conference on development and the environment in Moscow.[94] In his short speech he spoke on the common concern for the environment among religious believers in China and the world over.[95] In Moscow, he was invited to visit the headquarters of the Russian Orthodox Church and attended a worship service commemorating the Feast of the Presentation. There he met Metropolitan Kyrill, who came to China as head of a small Russian Orthodox delegation three years later. The Moscow trip demonstrated that K. H. Ting was not under a government cloud, as some had speculated, for he would not in that case have been allowed to travel overseas.

In April 1990, Ting went to North America to discuss ongoing cooperation with mainline church representatives in light of June 4th, including the sending of more teachers through the Amity Foundation and plans for future church visits to China. The trip also gave Ting the opportunity to assess the reaction to June 4th in the United States and put forth his own views on the subject. He was in the United States again in late November, where he delivered a lecture at the annual meeting of the American Academy of Religion and the Society of Biblical Literature.[96] Ting also delivered lectures at a number of North American seminaries at this time. Owing to his diplomatic efforts, international exchanges between North American churches and the CCC had already resumed, although the visits to and from China were still not at the level they had been eighteen months earlier.

The most important factor that would strengthen the international outreach of the CCC was its decision to become formally affiliated with the World Council of Churches at the Canberra Assembly in 1991. Ting had been an observer at the Vancouver Assembly in 1983, with several other Chinese church leaders, and he led an official delegation to Geneva the same year (see chap. 7), and again in 1988. Since that time, there had been regular contacts on both official and informal levels, and because of the growing interest in the church in China, many connected with the WCC hoped that the CCC would apply for membership. The WCC believed that China had much to contribute to ecumenical understanding.

K. H. Ting was the only church leader in China who had been deeply involved in the ecumenical movement as a young man and who continued to maintain relationships with friends in the ecumenical movement. He saw WCC membership as important for both China and the CCC. It would give both China and the CCC a voice in the most important international Christian body, and also greater visibility on the world stage. Membership would also help broaden the CCC's outlook on theology, the church and the world. In an unpublished lecture to students at Nanjing Seminary in 1987, Ting spoke about the "deepened understanding of Christian spirituality and an accompanying broadening of the scope of Christian concerns and commitments" that the WCC had made possible in the past forty years.

> We have no ground to assert that everything done in the name of ecumenism has been good. But in the last forty years, the ecumenical movement, with the World Council of Churches as one of its important embodiments, has proved itself to be providentially enriching and enabling. It has changed the face of world Christianity so greatly that we can only recognize in it the working of the Holy Spirit.[97]

K. H. Ting had been raising the issue of WCC membership with church leaders and government officials in China since the mid-1980s, but he needed to convince them of the benefits of a closer association with the ecumenical movement. After 1989, we have seen that some government officials believed that religious forces had been involved in the changes in Eastern Europe, but Ting countered that the picture was more complex, and that many in Eastern Europe were accusing the WCC of being too supportive of former Communist governments. The discussions continued throughout 1990, but in the end, the Foreign Ministry, whose permission was needed before any social organization could join an international body, agreed, providing that participation in the WCC would not violate the "One China" policy. In the church, some of the more conservative leaders questioned whether the WCC was a "friendly" organization. Ting responded that the CCC needed a voice in the world body precisely to put forth its own position and win over more churches to its understanding.

Four Chinese churches were founding members of the WCC in 1948, representing Anglican, Baptist, Methodist and Presbyterian traditions. Because they never formally withdrew, the China Christian Council as the successor body of these churches was in some sense still part of the World Council. This was the position of the WCC, but still some sort of application procedure was necessary. In 1990, Ting requested that WCC general secretary Emilio Castro write a letter to the CCC suggesting it become a formal member at the Canberra Assembly. Ting had already been invited to Canberra as a special guest, and Han Wenzao, Shen Yifan and Ms. Gao Ying were to be official observers. The CCC application for membership, written by K. H. Ting himself, was sent to the WCC just a week before they were preparing to leave. In it, Ting referred to the four founding members as "within the stream of the China Christian Council" which he described as "one united Church of Jesus Christ in the process of formation."[98] Application was made after a process of study and discussion and "reaching a common mind among the leaders of the China Christian Council."

> We have come to see that, important as it is for Chinese Christians to have a selfhood of our own, there cannot be a full selfhood of a church apart from its being a member of the Universal Church of Jesus Christ. The particularity of our church can be developed only within the universality embodied in such an organization as the World Council of Churches.[99]

Once Ting and the others had arrived in Canberra, there began a lengthy process of behind-the-scenes negotiation over how CCC membership would be possible within the context of the "One China" policy that the Foreign Ministry required. There had been some contact between the CCC and the Presbyterian Church in Taiwan (PCT) the previous decade, beginning with

K. H. Ting at the Canberra Assembly of the WCC, 1991. Reproduced with the permission of the WCC Archives. From left to right: K. H. Ting, Emilio Castro, Kao Chun-ming, general secretary of the Presbyterian Church in Taiwan.

a meeting in Bern facilitated by the World Alliance of Reformed Churches in 1988. In Canberra, the issue was what WCC membership would mean in light of PCT membership and its advocacy of Taiwan's independence. Castro had said that the WCC related to churches, not states, but Ting was concerned about how churches were listed and what names implied. These may be seen as small points, but they were politically important for China. In the end, the issue was resolved to the satisfaction of both sides, largely because of the efforts of Ninan Koshy of the Commission of the Churches on International Affairs (CCIA) office of the WCC who understood the political and diplomatic considerations that were involved. All churches would be listed under continents and not by country, and the name of a geographic entity in a church name did not imply a nation state.

The China Christian Council became the 317th member of the World Council of Churches in a unanimous vote (with one abstention) on 18 February. After the vote, Ting said, "our membership will in no way impair the independence and integrity of any church outside mainland China," a comment that was acceptable for Taiwanese Presbyterians and their supporters. PCT leader C. M. Kao went forward to embrace K. H. Ting after his speech, and they stood together with Emilio Castro during the applause by assembly delegates.[100] After returning to China, Ting said that joining the WCC would help fellow Chinese citizens see Christianity as part of a worldwide faith and "put us in a stronger position to gain their attention to what the church has to witness to."[101] This had been the motivation for Ting to push for WCC membership in the first place.

Despite mutual expressions of goodwill, there was, however, no reconciliation between the PCT and the CCC. Taiwanese Presbyterians claimed after the assembly that the CCC wanted them to change their name or be listed under China. In the PCT church magazine, Ting was depicted in a cartoon as a wolf in sheep's clothing, and representatives of the Taiwan church maintained that the CCC was trying to isolate Taiwan. Ting, reiterating what he said in his speech in Canberra, denied this.[102] The CCC had joined the WCC on the basis that it held to a "One China" stance, and Ting was reassured in this understanding in a subsequent letter from Emilio Castro, and he thanked Castro for taking the stance he did.[103] The relationship between the CCC and the PCT has continued to be a subject of discussion and debate in the ecumenical world in the years since the Canberra Assembly of the WCC.

The "One China" policy that rejects independence for Taiwan has been a nonnegotiable principle in the international and ecumenical relationships of the CCC. K. H. Ting has been as consistent in advocating this position as any religious or political leader in China.[104] In the 1990s, there were several attempts by churches and ecumenical bodies to somehow "reconcile" the PCT and the CCC despite their political differences, but none of these made any real progress. Ting never responded to initiatives for membership in the Christian Conference of Asia because of what he perceived to be the strong presence of the PCT in that body.

Although he has never been able to visit the island, Ting has encouraged visits to and from Taiwan on the part of Chinese Christians.[105] He has also met with many non-Presbyterian Christians from Taiwan, some of whom have developed close relations with the TSPM/CCC. Church projects in China in partnership with Christians from Taiwan began to develop in the early 1990s. Still, K. H. Ting has not refrained from making the strongest possible response to any suggestion of Taiwan independence. In his last international trip as TSPM/CCC leader, Ting led other Chinese delegates in walking out of the Fifth Assembly of the Asian Conference on Religion and Peace in protest over its position on Taiwan.[106] This was unrelated to the WCC, but it indicated the importance of the issue for the Chinese.

Membership in the World Council of Churches enhanced the visibility of the CCC internationally, and it generated renewed interest in China among many WCC member churches and Christian world communions. The Lutheran World Federation, the Baptist World Alliance and the World Alliance of Reformed Churches all hoped for increased involvement with the postdenominational China Christian Council, and their leaders met with K. H. Ting or invited him to speak at their world gatherings in the 1990s. The CCC has had to limit its ecumenical involvement, because of the heavy burden of work in China. Still, because of his belief in the importance of the ecumenical movement, Ting arranged for Gao Ying to serve on the staff of the WCC in Geneva in the mid-1990s, so that she could become more familiar with its work. He encouraged Chinese participation in WCC committees and events, sent students to the Ecumenical Institute at Bossey, and welcomed WCC staff to visit China or hold meetings there. All WCC general secretaries since Emilio Castro have visited China in order to encourage greater CCC participation, and others in the WCC have consciously tried to support the CCC in its programs.

This included dealing with sensitive political issues, such as human-rights abuses in China. In the 1990s, requests for clarification about alleged abuses of religious freedom often came to the CCC from churches overseas and international human-rights organizations. Given its small staff and heavy workload, it was not possible for the CCC to respond to most of these, nor did Chinese church leaders think it appropriate to do so. However, Ting did respond favorably to a request from the WCC to make an in-depth visit with a focus on church–state issues. In 1996, an ecumenical team organized by the WCC's Commission of the Churches on International Affairs visited three provinces, with arrangements made by the Nanjing office of the TSPM/CCC. They spent two weeks in China, at the end of which Ting and other leaders heard a report of the team's findings.[107] Ting welcomed the report, including its critical comments about the implementation of religious policy in China. The team's informal report was from an international body of which the CCC was a member, and so it helped to reinforce Ting's own efforts on behalf of Chinese churches.

Similarly, he always encouraged visiting church leaders to meet with government officials and voice their concerns about religious freedom in China. Billy Graham met with senior government officials on his second visit to China in 1994, and Archbishop of Canterbury Dr. George Carey did the same when he visited later in the same year.[108] Ting saw these meetings and the publicity they generated as helpful for the church in China on a political as well as religious level.

In contrast, Ting was not interested in the publications that came from groups such as Amnesty International and Human Rights Watch, and he refused to respond to their requests for information. He saw these organizations as being dominated by the West. He also discouraged churches overseas from supporting human-rights causes in China, including criticism of China's religious policy. Ting saw such criticism as unilateral, designed to put pressure on the Chinese government or play up criticism of China for an international audience. He believed it would not be helpful for the Chinese church. On one occasion in 1993, I was asked by a European ecumenical body to seek Ting's advice on whether it would be wise to issue a statement critical of governmental abuse of religious freedom. He was irked by the request, and replied, "Of course, I am not in the position to invite statements from overseas. And if I were in such a position, the statements would not be needed." Then he added, "I hope they realize that what we do in our efforts for religious freedom is a part of the struggle for human rights, done by Chinese in ways which will be useful for us." Ting was responding as a patriotic Christian leader who believed that human-rights issues in China should be dealt with by Chinese on their own terms, and who at the same time was working for reform.

Relationships with churches and councils in Europe and North America had been developing since the early 1980s, and concerns about religious freedom usually came from those quarters. But exchanges had only recently begun with churches in other Asian countries. In the 1990s, Ting led church delegations on visits to Korea, Indonesia and the Philippines—the CCC had visited India and Japan in the mid-1980s—as well as to Hong Kong and Singapore. He once observed that these churches never raised issues of human rights, for they knew what it was like to be under the pressure of the United States and other Western governments.

Ting received many invitations to speak at international church and ecumenical gatherings, more than he could possibly accept. In the summer of 1991, however, he accepted an invitation to visit Great Britain to speak at a conference organized by the Friends of the Church in China (FCC). He wanted to show his support for the FCC and its unique relationship with China. His close friend David M. Paton (1913-1992) had been an inspiration in starting the FCC, and that summer, Ting made a last visit to see Paton in the rest home where he was staying not long before his death.[109] Theirs was a friendship that lasted more than half a century, even though their times together had been infrequent. Ting spoke on the "cosmic Christ" at the FCC meeting,[110] and the speech brought together much of what Ting and Paton stood for theologically. It was a theme to which he returned again and again in his writings as he worked to get his theology more widely known in China and overseas.

On his way back from Britain that July, Ting passed through Hong Kong on a private visit, where he was hosted by his friend Bishop Peter K. K. Kwong, the first Chinese to serve as Anglican bishop of Hong Kong and Macao (Sheng Kung Hui). Ting had attended Kwong's consecration in Hong Kong in 1981, but so that he not be considered "too Anglican," he did not take part in the service. A few months later, Kwong visited Ting in Nanjing on his first trip since becoming bishop. Since then, Kwong had been helping K. H. Ting and Chinese churches in many ways, always quietly without publicity of any kind, and always responding to Ting's requests as best he could. The two became friends, and they have enjoyed a special relationship.

Kwong was viewed as a "pro-China" church leader as Hong Kong approached its return to China in 1997. He had been a member of the Basic Law Drafting Committee, and although he resigned after June 4th, he later became a delegate to the CPPCC. By the end of 1991, the Diocese of Hong Kong and Macao had voted to become a self-governing Anglican province. Kwong consulted with Ting about what this would mean for China, and although there was never the suggestion that the Sheng Kung Hui would be part of the CCC, Ting was pleased with the idea of having an independent Anglican Church in Hong Kong. In preparation for the establishment of the Hong Kong province, Bishop Kwong invited Ting and Wang Shenyin, the last remaining Anglican bishops on the mainland, to participate in the consecration of two new bishops at the end of 1995. This time, Ting did agree to take part in the service, and he asked the questions of the new bishops, which was a canonical requirement. In 1998, Ting spoke at the worship service inaugurating the province. His participation in both services did not mean that Ting wanted the CCC to become Anglican, but it did express his personal hope that something of the Anglican tradition would also continue in the Chinese church.

Ting met frequently with Hong Kong church leaders other than Peter Kwong as 1997 approached. In his visit that summer (1991), he hosted a dinner for Protestant leaders in the territory, in order to say that he hoped they would remain in the territory to work for the church there. Many Hong Kong Christians had demonstrated in support of the democracy movement in 1989, and they had been encouraged by the leadership of their churches, some of whom marched with them. Yet in the summer of 1991, churches in Hong Kong were also responding to appeals for help for victims of the flooding in central China, and this showed their love and concern for China. Ting could understand the sentiments behind both responses, and he hoped for closer relationships between churches in Hong Kong and the mainland. Although Hong Kong would continue to operate under a different political system after 1997, cooperation between churches was increasing.[111] Ting visited Hong Kong several times in the 1990s, and he sought out church leaders who wanted to improve relationships with the CCC.

Hong Kong was also a base for many "China Ministries" groups which regularly promoted Bible smuggling, underground evangelism and support for house churches that refused to relate to the TSPM/CCC. Critics, including Jonathan Chao T'ien-en (1938-2004), founder of the China Ministries International (CMI) and director of the Chinese Church Research Center, Tony Lambert of the Overseas Missionary Fellowship (OMF), and Paul Kaufman (1920-1997) of Asian Outreach, had a perspective on the church in China that was at odds with the image that K. H. Ting was trying to project in Hong Kong and overseas.[112] They supported Christians in China who refused registration and were often hostile to the government. Chao maintained there were two churches in China, the "official," or Three-Self, Church and the "underground" house churches. Chao, Lambert and others had a great deal of influence on evangelicals overseas, and on many Hong Kong Christians. The organizers of Lausanne II had relied on the counsel and advice of Jonathan Chao and other overseas Chinese evangelicals in trying to include Chinese Christians at their meeting in Manila in 1988, but the CCC refused to participate in an international conference organized under the terms they imposed.

Peter Kwong and K. H. Ting, ca. 1995. Peter Kwong was then the Anglican bishop of Hong Kong and Macao. Photograph taken by the author.

Not all evangelical groups were hostile to the CCC. Even in the 1980s, a growing number of evangelicals in Hong Kong, Southeast Asia and the West began changing their view of the Chinese church. They were able to visit churches in China and speak freely with Chinese Christians. They saw that many "Three-Self" pastors had deep evangelical commitments. The Bible was becoming more readily available; seminaries were training new leaders; and religious policy was not as rigid as it once had been. They also saw in K. H. Ting a church leader who, while not himself evangelical, was trying to work for the good of the whole church. Ting's defense of meeting points, or home churches, in the face of government pressure and his opposition to some of the more rigid elements in the TSPM were at times even praised by Chao and Lambert. By the early 1990s, some evangelicals had begun to see a way of working for the church in China in an open and public way.

Ting saw in these changes an opportunity to broaden support for the TSPM/CCC overseas and thereby lessen the hostility that still persisted toward China. Evangelicals were already contributing to the printing of Bibles at the Amity Printing Company, and the Southern Baptists were sending English teachers through the Amity teachers' project. Chinese evangelicals in Southeast Asia were looking toward cooperation in seminary education and the composition of Chinese hymns. Billy Graham, who had visited China in 1988, returned for a second visit in 1994. His son Ned Graham had started East Gate Ministries to supply Bibles printed at the

K. H. Ting and Zhao Puchu, Beijing, 1993. Photograph taken by the author.

Amity Press to groups that were not connected to the TSPM/CCC in China and to promote reconciliation. Other prominent evangelical leaders and groups visited China in the early 1990s, met publicly with K. H. Ting and drew closer to the CCC.

Yet there continued to be mixed reports in the evangelical press about the Chinese church. The differences in evangelical opinion were brought into the open in November 1993, when Ting was invited to bring greetings at the installation of Richard Mouw as the president of Fuller Theological Seminary. Ting had been invited to Fuller through the efforts of American evangelicals close to Ting in Southern California. As he began his speech, about thirty Chinese students, Fuller alumni and their supporters walked out to protest his inclusion in the service. They charged that the TSPM was dominated by Communists and was persecuting the "House Church." [113] There were unconfirmed reports that the walkout had been orchestrated or encouraged by Jonathan Chao.

Mouw and others stood by the invitation to K. H. Ting, and many evangelicals continued to work for improved relationships between North American evangelicals and the CCC. Ting was grateful for Mouw's support and for the efforts of all those who were working openly with Christians in China. Ting had gone out of his way to work with evangelicals in the 1990s, and he was willing to speak to their concerns when he met with them.[114] His work bore some fruit, at least in some evangelical circles overseas.

Still, Ting was clearly more at ease relating to mainline churches and seminaries associated with the ecumenical movement. In late 1994, he made what would be his last visit to North America, accompanied by Ting Yen-ren, his eldest son. He went to receive the Union Medal, which honored "individuals of religious faith whose lives and work reflect" the highest aspirations of Union Theological Seminary.[115] Previous recipients of the Union Medal included former Union president John Bennett, who had taught at Union when Ting was a student there, Allan Boesak from South Africa and Kim Dae-jung from Korea. There was also a protest against Ting at Union—from Taiwanese Presbyterians who objected to his "One China" stance—but these did not overshadow the occasion in the same way the Fuller protestors did.

Ting was deeply moved by the honor that Union had given him, and he spent a long time considering the speech he would give that night. He chose to begin with his own time at Union and in the ecumenical movement, and from there he turned to reflect on the importance of dialogue between Christians and Communists and Christians and Chinese intellectuals. The China of the 1990s, he observed, was an opportune place for dialogue, even though the broader climate did not make it easy for the church, and even though the church faced many difficulties. He concluded with these words:

> Paul says near the end of 1 Corinthians: "A wide door for effective work has opened to me, and there are many adversaries." It is interesting that the conjunction used is "and," not "but." This conveys the idea that opportunities and difficulties are often companions. We like to think that, in our own small way, we are doing an experiment on behalf of the church worldwide. As a Union alumnus and as the recipient of the Union Medal tonight, I like to think that we are doing this with the blessing of Union Seminary. [116]

Ting had one other thing that he wanted to do on his final visit to the United States, and that was to meet with former American missionaries who had served in China. On his initiative, separate reunions had been organized for Methodist and Presbyterian China missionaries, one before and one after the ceremony at Union. More than 250 missionaries and their friends and families attended the two gatherings. They had organized their own program, but the central event was K. H. Ting's speech. In the middle of his prepared remarks, Ting added the paragraph that stated his reason for coming. He apologized to the missionaries for the wrongs that they had suffered during the Denunciation Movement of the early 1950s.

> I want to apologize to former China missionaries and their families for all the suffering wrongly imposed on them forty years ago. I will be glad if you take my presence here as a token of healing and reconciliation in Christ . . .[117]

A distinction should be made, he continued, between missionary efforts and Western colonialism and imperialism. The Chinese church was not "antimissionary," but had discovered there was "a time for missionaries to come and a time for missionaries not to remain, not as a denial of their foundation, but as a fruition of their labours."[118] The elderly missionaries were deeply moved, not because they were looking for an apology, but because Ting had spoken from his heart about the injustices of the past.

This was a historic occasion. Ting had not taken part in the movement that accused and denounced the missionaries (chap. 4), yet he carried with him a sense of the wrong that had been done, not in opposing the continuing missionary presence or the association of the missionary movement with colonialism, but in the hurt that had been inflicted on men and women who gave a good part of their lives to China. His apology to the missionaries was an expression of reconciliation. In response, the Presbyterian missionaries made their own statement, including an apology for their own weaknesses, lack of sensitivity and judgmental attitudes.[119] Ting was criticized by some church leaders in China for making this apology, for they argued that the Denunciation Movement had been central to the history of the TSPM. Ting maintained that he did the right thing in making the apology. The early 1950s was a formative period for the TSPM, and the era remains an area of controversy within the Chinese Christian leadership to this day.

By the mid-1990s, a growing number of church tours and ecumenical delegations were visiting China, especially from North America and Europe, but also from Hong Kong, South Korea and other parts of Asia. As Ting often said, such visits helped the church by giving the China Christian Council prestige in the eyes of the government and at the same time curbing what he termed an overly "nationalistic strain" in the thinking of the TSPM. Ting welcomed these tours and tried to find time in his busy schedule to speak to as many groups as he could. Almost all Christian groups wanted to meet with him. He met with foreign visitors in Beijing or Shanghai when he was attending meetings there. In Nanjing, he would frequently invite smaller groups or delegation leaders to his home, so that they could discuss things in a relaxed setting. Ting had a presence and a charisma that impressed Christian visitors, and a pastoral side that allowed him to meet people where they were and respond to their questions in a way they could understand.

Ting traveled a great deal in the mid-1990s, and he had many responsibilities and visitors when he was at home in Nanjing. He still lived in the same house on Mo Chou Road that he had occupied with his family since the early 1950s. It was a modest home for one who was now CPPCC vice-chair and thus a national leader, but he described it as very large by Chinese standards and more than adequate for his family. He lived there with Siu-may, his eldest son and daughter-in-law and their son.

Siu-may's health was failing, but she always combined a cheerful spirit with an indomitable will, and never complained about her condition. She presided over family events from her wheel chair, and was thrilled to be able to go on a family trip through the Yangzi River gorges in the summer of 1989. In 1989 and 1990, her two books on the Bible as literature were published by Nanjing University Press.[120] They were intended for Chinese students of English and were used in the Foreign Languages and Literatures Department of the university where she had taught for decades. She still had advanced students of English meet with her in her home for seminars, and was always willing to meet with students who were just beginning their language work.

In the early 1990s, she seemed to be in decline, but always bounced back. While she was hospitalized for much of the late summer and fall of 1992, K. H. visited her twice each day. Though her stays in the hospital became longer and more frequent, Siu-may was well enough in January 1994 to go with her husband to Sanya (Hainan Island) for a meeting with religious leaders and their families. In May 1995, she was taken to the hospital in serious condition, but was then released in late July, only to be readmitted ten days later. K. H. continued to visit her daily in August and September.

Siu-may Kuo died with her family by her bedside on 24 September just after eight o'clock in the morning. She was seventy-nine years old. A private funeral took place a few days later, after which her body was cremated. On 22 October, a memorial service was held at the Mo Chou Road Church, just a few doors down from the Ting family residence. The church was packed with mourners, and the service was conducted by CCC leaders and the seminary faculty and choir. Han Wenzao, visibly moved, spoke about the significance of her life, and Chen Zemin delivered the eulogy entitled "Love Never Ends." Bishop Peter Kwong, who had flown up from Hong Kong for the service, pronounced the final benediction.

Public displays of grief and emotion are not common at funerals in China, and K. H. sat quietly through the service. He had lost his wife and companion of fifty-three years, one who had been his source of love and support in his private life, and one with whom he had shared his commitment to China, the church and the world. Ting's faith sustained him in his time of grief, and he was no stranger to death. In 1991 he observed that he had preached often on the subject of death and the afterlife.

> Just a few days ago I wrote a letter to the wife of a bishop in the Episcopal Church in the United States who passed away recently. And in the letter I said that I subscribe to the affirmation in the 1928 version of the liturgy of the Episcopal Church in the U.S.A. to the effect that a person after death will continue to grow in God's grace and in the presence of God and this gives Christians comfort; and how that comforted me when my mother died a few years ago at the age of 101.

And I think I preached about that at the memorial service for Zheng Jianye. I think it is an important source of comfort and encouragement to Christians to affirm an afterlife of growth.[121]

He deeply mourned the passing away of his wife, but Ting did not have time to step back from his continuing responsibilities as church leader and public figure. A month later, he spoke at the forty-fifth anniversary of the Three-Self Patriotic Movement, continuing his emphasis on running the church well and the need to pay greater attention to building up the church as a Christian community.[122] He would be stepping down from his positions as head of the TSPM and the CCC a year later, but this would not mean that his involvement in politics and governance (*zheng*), study and learning (*xue*) and ethical and religious life (*dao*) would be coming to an end.

10

Theological Reconstruction, 1997-2006

> Walking Ahead of the Times
> Requires bearing a greater burden of sorrow,
> Yet, to be able to love the world
> Through the eyes of those yet to be born—
> How great and beautiful a thing that is.
>
> Otto Rene Castillio[1]

By the mid-1990s, China's path toward continuing economic growth and political stability seemed to be on track. Jiang Zemin was firmly in control as head of the "third generation" of national leaders.[2] He had the support of aging Deng Xiaoping and party elders, but they were becoming less visible on the national scene. According to Joseph Fewsmith, the main problem of the Jiang Zemin era was to find a way of combining the centralization of state and party power (the legacy of Mao) with decentralized decision making (promoted by Deng) without stifling economic growth or encouraging political chaos.[3] All other issues were related to this basic problem, from fighting corruption and curbing inflation, to responding to the ultra-leftist critique of reform and developing China's position as a world power.

The year 1997 was an important time of political transition. The death of Deng Xiaoping on 19 February was followed by a short period of national mourning, but it did not lead to public demonstrations or leadership struggles as had happened in the past. On 1 July, Hong Kong was returned to China, and despite anxieties in Hong Kong about the transition, the end of more than a century of British colonial rule became a source of renewed national pride. Jiang Zemin consolidated his power at the Fifteenth Party Congress that September, by which time he had already begun to groom a new generation of leaders to succeed him.[4]

The phenomenal growth of the economy in the mid- and late 1990s was fueled by a tremendous increase in the private sector. In 1989, there were just over 90,000 private enterprises with 1.6 million employees and a capitalization of 8.4 billion yuan. By 1998, this had grown to 1.2 million private companies with more than 17 million employees and a capitalization of

333

almost 720 billion yuan.[5] Many smaller factories were in rural townships, but economic growth brought the most noticeable changes to larger cities along the coast. The "floating population" of migrant laborers from inland China numbered at least 150 million by 1998.[6] Many migrants went to factories in the Special Economic Zones in the southeast where they worked in foreign-operated joint ventures. Others became construction workers, factory employees and domestic helpers in Shanghai, Beijing and other coastal cities. An urban-based *nouveau riche* class was emerging, and university students were no longer interested in political protests but in finding good jobs and making money.

The growth of the economy and private enterprises led to an increasing gap between rich and poor and a decline in the public-welfare system that had been a hallmark of China's socialist society. The income differential between urban and rural areas and between coastal and inland China grew to levels higher than they were in Europe or the United States, and this had happened faster than in any country in history. Rural China was also reaping the benefits of economic development, but the growth rate could not compensate for educational, medical and welfare benefits that were being lost.[7] Voluntary associations, including religious and nongovernmental organizations, were encouraged to play a more active role in welfare and development, but there were limits to what they could do.

Economic growth encouraged the emergence of a more robust civil society, which had already become a hot topic of debate among Chinese intellectuals in the aftermath of June 4th.[8] Popular and unofficial expressions of civil society took many forms: religious and cultural, urban and rural, formal and informal, legal and illegal. The development of civil society was in one sense a natural outgrowth of the reforms, but it also produced unexpected results.

On 25 April 1999, the Chinese government was caught off guard when more than ten thousand followers of the eclectic religious sect Falun Gong assembled in Beijing outside Zhongnanhai, the compound near the Forbidden City where many national leaders live and work. The sect combines traditional Chinese religious beliefs, *qigong* exercises and the teachings of its charismatic leader, Li Hongzhi. Falun Gong had organized the largest demonstration in China since 1989, and the group had an estimated 30 million adherents nationwide and around the world.[9] The sect was quickly branded an "evil cult" by the government; thousands of followers were arrested and its activities banned in China. Chinese religious leaders, including K. H. Ting and Zhao Puchu, condemned Falun Gong as well, but the suppression of the sect affected all religious communities at the local level, at least in the first few months.

Still, people from all walks of life continued to flock to churches, temples and mosques. Chinese religions were growing, and many universities began to organize religion departments, partly in response to the increasing interest in religion among students. The growth of formal and informal religious communities was both a function of the reforms and a response to the changes taking place in society, culture and morals. Even before 1999, the government was aware of the moral vacuum developing in China as all energy was directed toward economic development, social stability and political control. In October 1996, the CPC passed several resolutions on strengthening "socialist spiritual civilization" in order to emphasize ethics, traditional virtues and patriotism, but this did not generate much popular enthusiasm.[10] Ideology had not kept pace with the reforms, and there was a search for other belief systems that addressed basic questions on the meaning of life.

In 2000, Jiang Zemin introduced the "three represents" as his contribution to Chinese Communist theory: the CPC was said to represent "the most advanced forces of production," "the most advanced culture," as well as "the broad masses of the Chinese people."[11] The CPC was no longer simply the party of workers, peasants and soldiers; it now embraced entrepreneurs, business people, intellectuals and everyone else interested in the modernization of China. Where Deng Xiaoping had stressed the "Four Cardinal Principles" to ensure party rule, Jiang Zemin downplayed Marxist-Leninist ideology, while still insisting on strong party control. Jiang's theory was endorsed at the Sixteenth Party Congress in November 2002, when he stepped down as CPC general secretary and was replaced by his protégé, Hu Jintao, thus initiating the "fourth generation" of leadership.[12] The page had turned.

By 2003, Hu Jintao was firmly in charge. He and Premier Wen Jiabao quickly assumed a different style of leadership, as China faced new problems and opportunities. They appeared to be more populist in orientation and more intent on addressing the growing social inequalities. At the same time, they gave priority to economic growth, which was further stimulated when China joined the World Trade Organization in April 2003. The SARS epidemic hit the country hard at the same time, and it preoccupied the leadership for much of that year.[13] After a slow initial response, the government quickly mobilized its collective resources to curb the spread of the disease.

With a confident leadership, new avenues in diplomacy and a booming economy, the country had fundamentally changed since the era of Deng Xiaoping. By the end of 2003, China was being described as an emerging global power.[14] Increasingly integrated into the global economic order, China was active in regional and global institutions of all kinds. A "strategic ally" in the U.S.-led war on terrorism, it was also the only power potentially able to challenge U.S. political and economic dominance on a global scale. At home, the country was connected through cell phones and the Internet, and the urban middle classes were embracing a culture of consumerism. Serious environmental and social problems with long-term implications were worrisome, as was the growing inequality, which often led to demonstrations and popular unrest. In October 2006, the CPC approved a resolution on building a "harmonious socialist society" in order to address the divisive issues confronting China. Religions were encouraged to play an active role in promoting social harmony.[15] Although there were continuing reports of human-rights abuses, including those affecting religious groups, progress was also evident in strengthening the rule of law. The "Taiwan question" was still to be resolved, but the "unity and stability" which had once been a political slogan now seemed self-evident in most parts of the country. In an era of globalization and rising nationalism, China had come of age.

In the first years of the new millennium, K. H. Ting said on many occasions that globalization was more of a challenge than an opportunity for the Chinese church. By this he meant that the challenges Christians faced in "running the church well" would not be resolved through greater international connectedness. The church had first to address its own internal problems and its relationship to society as a whole. Ting would continue to be involved in these areas even after he stepped down from his positions as national leader of the TSPM and the CCC.

"TO RETIRE BUT NOT TO TIRE"

K. H. Ting turned eighty in 1995, and he was presented with a special edition of the *Chinese Theological Review* that contained short tributes on his life and work from friends and associates in China and overseas.[16] Although beset with many of the ailments of old age, he continued to enjoy reasonably good health for the next decade, and his mind was as sharp as ever. His international travel came to an end, but he regularly attended meetings in Beijing and Shanghai and he made several trips to Hong Kong.[17]

Already in early 1989, K. H. Ting was telling friends that he wanted to "fade into the background," but that he did not yet think it was time. By his eightieth birthday, Ting had announced that he would be retiring from his positions in the CCC and the TSPM. He believed that he should help a younger generation of Christians grow into positions of leadership. There was the principle in the two national Christian bodies that leaders should not serve after they had reached the age of eighty, but this would probably not have applied to Ting as TSPM/CCC head, any more than it applied to vice-chairpersons of the CPPCC and other leaders in national religious organizations, including Zhao Puchu. Still, Ting was determined to step down, and at the end of 1994, he informed colleagues in the church and the government that he would not stand for office at the Sixth National Christian Conference.

All through 1996, Ting was as active as he had ever been in political and church affairs. In his speeches that year, he laid the groundwork for theological reconstruction, which we shall consider more fully below. Debates over the importance and relevance of "Three-Self" and "running the church well" continued in the TSPM/CCC in the lead-up to the Sixth NCC at the end of the year. Ting's position was that "running the church well" did not diminish "Three-Self," but was a further stage of its development.[18] The accent in the TSPM/CCC theme—"running the church well according to the Three-Self principle"—should be firmly on the first four characters (*ban hao jiaohui*), he said. These were not an ornamental addition to Three-Self, but its fulfillment, realization and means of implementation. To stress Three-Self alone was the position of the bureaucrat or Three-Self functionary alienated from Christians at the grassroots, not of the church leader trying to unite Chinese Christians, he argued. "During the Cultural Revolution, there were those who said grasping the revolution will inevitably promote production," Ting wrote. "In contrast, I cannot say that the church will be well run if only we act according to the Three-Self principle."[19] It was not enough to be politically correct. The issue was whether building up the church or stressing Three-Self patriotism should be the main emphasis in the work of the TSPM/CCC.

As Ting prepared to retire, a new element in the discussion was who would succeed him as national leader. The choices were limited, and there were a variety of factors in the selection process, but it is useful to see the issue in terms of the different emphases on "running the church well" among the candidates. It was widely assumed that Han Wenzao, Ting's associate in Nanjing, would succeed him as CCC president. Although a layman, he had become acting CCC general secretary after Shen Yifan's death. Han was identified with Ting's general position, and although he was not a theologian, he was known to be a good manager and administrator. He was respected overseas because of his work with the Amity Foundation and Bible printing.

Still, Han Wenzao would not become both CCC president and TSPM chair. By the time of the Sixth NCC, the national leadership had decided that Luo Guanzong would become chairperson of the TSPM, and he would share overall leadership with Han. Luo was a layman also and had been a close associate of Ting since the 1930s when they had worked together in the student movement and the YMCA. He took the position that "running the church well" and Three-Self patriotism were of equal importance. Luo published a small pamphlet of extracts from Ting's writings and church statements in September to help make this case.[20] Luo was from Shanghai, the base of many of those who emphasized a narrower definition of Three-Self, which meant the new leaders would embrace both sides of the debate. Luo (b. 1920) and Han (b. 1923) were a few years younger than Ting but were from the same generational cohort of Three-Self leaders.

The issue of the succession and shared leadership was decided late in the year. There were rumors at the time that the division of national leadership indicated a split between the TSPM and the CCC, but the separation of the two national organizations was never in doubt. Ting firmly denied any kind of split, but he stressed the continuing need to maintain unity in his opening address at the Sixth NCC.[21] Differences over the interpretation of "running the church well according to the Three-Self principle" were matters of emphasis in an internal debate, and an institutional division between the two national organizations was not a possibility.

The Sixth NCC opened in Beijing on 29 December 1996 and closed on 2 January 1997. The 299 delegates were once again considerably younger than those who attended the previous NCC, and they included a somewhat larger percentage of women than in the past. Han Wenzao delivered the work report, which reflected a careful balance between the life and work of the church (i.e., running the church well) and upholding the church's Three-Self stance and independence.[22] After five years of experimentation, a "Chinese Christian Church Order" was formally adopted at the conference—an indication that serious attention was given to "running the church well." It was similar in most respects to the church order approved for trial use in 1992, but was intended to be binding on churches throughout the country.[23] In addition to other business, the delegates affirmed their support for a CPC resolution on promoting "socialist ethical and cultural progress," an action that may be seen to foreshadow the subsequent development of theological reconstruction.[24]

K. H. Ting became honorary head of the TSPM and the CCC at the Sixth NCC, a position that was created especially for him. Four other older leaders, including Bishop Wang Shenyin, were named advisors, but they did not have the same national standing.[25] As honorary leader, Ting would not be involved in the day-to-day work of the two national organizations, but he would be consulted on matters of importance. He would no longer attend the annual Spring Festival meetings hosted by senior government officials, but Ting remained a leader to whom the government deferred, by virtue of his position as CPPCC vice-chair. This meant he was still the national leader with the most important voice on religious affairs.

After Siu-may retired as professor of Nanjing University, she liked to speak of "retiring but not tiring," a bilingual pun from the Chinese *tui er bu xiu,* meaning "to step back but not rest."[26] Initially, K. H. Ting seemed to be planning for a restful retirement, but he too was not tired. Shortly after the Sixth NCC, he told an interviewer from *Tian Feng* that he hoped to retire from his position as principal of Nanjing Seminary "as soon as that becomes possible" and that he would be putting together his papers, catching up on his reading, and enjoying life with his son and his family.[27] He sent a circular letter to friends and church leaders overseas that included a translation of this interview to underscore the fact that he had indeed retired.

In the same interview, Ting spoke very movingly of the prayers that had sustained him in his fifteen years as church leader.

> In the past fifteen years, I have become more and more aware of the fact that many Christians have been keeping me in their prayers. And that there are a growing number of colleagues and fellow Christians overseas who also pray for me. These prayers stem not only from their

love and concern for me personally, even more they represent a coalescence of everyone's care and concern for the Chinese church and the Three-Self spirit. I personally have no special talent, but God has heard these prayers. They have upheld me, almost like a swimmer who cannot drown in the Salt Sea. And so I can say that those prayers have been transformed into material strength. I want to thank all those who have prayed for me, whether in China or overseas, whether known to me or not. I hope they will continue in some way to support our new leaders with their prayers.[28]

This was more than a pro forma expression of thanks which might be expected of any Christian leader. Ting was a shy introvert who associated most public references to prayer with a kind of evangelical enthusiasm that he wanted no part of. He was thus very reticent in speaking in public about prayer and personal piety, even though he retained an attachment to the Anglican prayers he had learned from his mother.

The month after the closing of the Sixth NCC, Deng Xiaoping died in Beijing, and K. H. Ting was one of the large number of prominent people named to the funeral committee. He was again in the limelight, appearing prominently in the televised memorial service held at the Great Hall of the People. Ting admired Deng Xiaoping, although he never had the personal relationship with him that he had had with Zhou Enlai. Unlike Zhou or Mao or even Jiang Zemin, Deng had made no important statements on religion or religious policy, but he was the architect of reforms that made the restoration of religious policy possible.[29] In an interview after Deng's death, Ting said that Deng Xiaoping had contributed to a more open religious policy by righting the wrongs of the Cultural Revolution, including the rehabilitation of many religious people, through his emphasis on practice as the only criterion of truth, which was essential for united-front work, and in his belief that ultra-leftism was the greatest danger to China's reforms.[30] Since the late 1970s, Ting himself had seen the necessity of criticizing ultra-leftism, both outside and inside the TSPM; and this may be seen as part of Deng Xiaoping's legacy.

Over the next year, Ting continued to attend political meetings, meet friends and visitors from overseas and preside over the work of the seminary. He offered his advice to the new church leadership and also spoke out on matters that concerned him. That summer he issued a personal statement on U.S. policies in support of religious freedom for Chinese Christians, terming them a "present-day operation of the nineteenth-century American 'manifest destiny.'"[31] He continued working as before, but his focus shifted to putting together his papers for publication.

In March, the new joint committee of the TSPM/CCC met in Shanghai for the first time. The new leaders took the occasion to organize an international seminar and thanksgiving service to honor K. H. Ting in retirement.[32] At the seminar, Ting spoke of two large problems he had left his successors.

The first was maintaining the unity of the church. By this he meant the unity of *all* Chinese Christians, not simply those who were related to the TSPM/CCC. The number of Protestant Christians was estimated to be from ten to twenty million, and although the church was postdenominational, there were many splits and disagreements in local churches. The second problem was the need to challenge the "fundamentalist theology" that the majority of Chinese Christians had accepted uncritically. Ting noted with dismay that most faculty members at seminaries and Bible schools in China were extremely fundamentalist. They questioned the faith of those who did not agree with them. Many Christians concentrated on questions of justification and salvation to the exclusion of almost everything else, thus isolating them from the society of which they were a part. Because of their "low cultural level" (*wenhua suzhi di*), many new Christians oversimplified the Christian faith, and saw it only as a pathway to heaven. They did not pay attention to other Christian teachings or to Christian witness in society.[33] Ting wanted to address this second problem in particular in his retirement.

Maintaining church unity and criticizing the fundamentalist theology of Chinese Christians were in a sense conflicting goals. In his fifteen years as church leader, Ting had spoken and written very widely on theological issues, but for the sake of the unity of the church, he had avoided entering into theological debate or imposing his relatively "liberal" theological viewpoints on a very conservative Christian community. In the 1980s and 1990s, the church was in a process of rebuilding, and the fragile unity was grounded on the principle of "mutual respect" in matters of faith. By 1997, however, the situation had changed. The church was still growing and on a firmer footing, and K. H. Ting was no longer president of the China Christian Council. He now believed that he could address the theological issues facing the churches more directly.

In the early 1990s, many observers had begun speaking about a "Christianity fever" in China as many people flocked into newly opened churches and meeting points. Even the TSPM/CCC was now claiming that churches were opening or reopening at the rate of six or seven per day. More than fifteen million Bibles had been printed by the end of 1996, and the demand still outstripped the supply.[34] The vast majority of Christians were new believers who lived in rural areas. Protestant Christianity was growing in urban China and among intellectuals as well, but in terms of numbers, as many as 80 percent of Chinese Christians were then (as they are now, and as they have been since the nineteenth century) in the villages and towns in the countryside.[35] To say that their "cultural level" was low meant that many had only a rudimentary education. Some Christians could not read or write, and many did not have even a basic grasp of Christian beliefs. This was not to criticize the faith of unlettered believers but to observe that many new Christians had little understanding of the Bible, and no concept at all of theology. In the early 1980s, the TSPM/CCC had produced a simple catechism in large quantities, but there is no evidence about how widely it was used or studied.[36] Some rural Christians believed that faith and thought were contradictory categories. Clergy and lay training were the most urgent priorities for the church, but it was still common to hear that there were "many sheep, but not enough shepherds."

Most Chinese and foreign scholars have observed that the overwhelming majority of Chinese Christians are conservative and evangelical. Several explanations have been given to interpret this phenomenon. First, Protestant missionaries in rural China in the nineteenth and twentieth centuries tended to be fundamentalist or evangelical in outlook, and their influence has continued to shape the faith and beliefs of Chinese Christians.[37] In addition, well-known evangelists such as Wang Mingdao, Watchman Nee, and John Sung (Song Shangjie) had established Christian revivalism as an enduring religious tradition before 1949, and these evangelists were still held in high regard in Chinese churches.[38] It is often said that strong fundamentalist beliefs nurtured by revivalism helped to sustain Christians through the difficult years of the Cultural Revolution. Wang Mingdao in particular was cited as a model of steadfast faith, and the fact that he remained consistently opposed to the TSPM only added to his reputation in some parts of the church. Other evangelical leaders such as the late Allen Yuan Xiangcheng in Beijing, Moses Xie in Shanghai and Lin Xiangao (Samuel Lamb) in Guangzhou continued this tradition, and none of them related to the CCC or the TSPM. A new generation of evangelical personalities had emerged in the 1980s and 1990s to lead their own unofficial churches and networks.[39] The China Gospel Fellowship and the Fangcheng Mother Church, for example, were said to have extensive networks wielding enormous influence in rural China. Other communities advocated a return to Jerusalem to hasten the second coming of Christ.[40] All these communities prided themselves on their conservative beliefs and opposition to "liberal" Christian teachings. They maintained a strict sectarianism on matters of faith and church order, and promoted a version of Protestant Christianity that was often in defiance of the state. Many of these groups were supported by conservative Christians overseas—spiritually and financially—and the TSPM/CCC believed that their theology and political outlook were shaped by such relationships. The journalist David Aikman has gone so far as to suggest that most of these Christian groups were "pro-American" and opposed to the patriotic stance of the CCC and the TSPM.[41]

Christian fundamentalism in rural China is not simply an extension of its Western counterpart. It has also been influenced by syncretistic folk religious traditions, so much so that Chinese academics now speak of the "folk religionization" of Christianity in rural China.[42] Miraculous healings, "raising the dead," spirit possession, and exorcisms shaped by vivid images of heaven and hell drawn from the folk religious tradition have crept into the beliefs of rural Christians. Because many Christians are new believers and not well educated, they are easily led to interpretations of Christianity that cannot be described as orthodox but have roots in indigenous religious traditions. The TSPM/CCC has said that many sectarian rural Christian communities and house churches teach heretical doctrines. For example, "The Anointed King," "Eastern Lightning," "The Spirit-Spirit Sect," and the "Yellers" have been criticized for their unorthodox beliefs in the Chinese Christian media and even in Chinese evangelical publications overseas.[43] The heterodox aspects of rural Christianity also have important political implications for the government, especially in light of the long tradition of religiously inspired folk rebellion.

Evangelicalism, fundamentalism, sectarianism and folk religious traditions cannot be equated, but they have in different ways shaped the beliefs and forms of rural Chinese Christianity. The foregoing summary cannot do justice to the complexity and manifold nature of the Christianity that is emerging in rural China, but it does indicate why the TSPM/CCC and the Chinese government have been concerned about the rapid growth of Christianity in the countryside. The lack of trained leadership, rudimentary education in Christian teachings and decades of isolation from the rest of the world have contributed to a denigration of theology, ethics and social involvement. The Bible schools and seminaries have inadvertently helped to perpetuate the situation by their focus on the Bible alone, interpreted in a Chinese fundamentalist tradition.

This was the situation Ting contemplated as he prepared to retire. Both in public and in private, he had become increasingly critical of evangelicalism and fundamentalism. He believed that theology in China had not kept pace with the times and that it had been ignored by the TSPM/CCC during his tenure. He had been telling friends as early as 1994 that he would devote the rest of his life to broadening the theological and ethical base of the Chinese church once he was no longer TSPM/CCC leader. A colleague at NUTS, Chen Zemin, agreed with him, and they were determined to begin a process of reform by changing the way in which theology was taught at Nanjing Seminary. Ting wanted to encourage a more wide-ranging theological discussion and greater theological pluralism, for he believed that this would contribute theologically to "running the church well," which had been his aim as church leader. This, Ting believed, would also lead to more creative forms of Christian involvement in society.

THE COLLECTED WORKS

In late 1996, Ting began to select, edit and translate the sermons, speeches and papers he had written over the past eighteen years. He wanted to publish a volume of collected writings, not only to sum up his own position but also to stimulate theological discussion in the churches and promote an ethical Christian witness in society.

Even before this, Ting was indicating the direction in which he wanted to see the church move. We have argued that K. H. Ting's theology was written in response to contemporary issues of church and society and that his thinking had developed around a few central themes: the love of God in Christ, the work of the Holy Spirit inside and outside the church, the interrelatedness of creation and redemption, the importance of Christian ethics, the continuity between transcendence and immanence, human beings as "works in progress" (*ban chengpin*) who cooperate with God in historical movements for change and renewal. In the 1950s and again in the 1980s, these were the themes of what he then called "theological reorientation" (*shenxue zaisi*). In the late 1990s, these were key features for what would soon be termed "theological reconstruction" (*shenxue sixiang jianshe*). Long before the TSPM/CCC approved its resolution on the subject, K. H. Ting had made it very clear that he wanted to see Chinese theology develop in new and different directions.

In an important speech to the TSPM/CCC Joint Standing Committee in the spring of 1995, Ting spoke of his uneasiness about the emphasis on the doctrine of justification by faith, as he had in the 1950s. It is worth quoting at length because it predates other speeches on the theme that were given over the next year to secular audiences in China.

> When we study a doctrine, we should ask what it stands in opposition to as well as what it says. There are many doctrines in Christianity besides justification by faith: the never ending creation of God; the Incarnation, Christ's resurrection; the renewal of creation; the indwelling of the Holy Spirit which bestows wisdom; the beatitudes; the greatest commandment which is to love God and to love your neighbour as yourself; to do unto others as you would have them do unto you; not to be served, but to serve. Paul said that there are faith, hope and love, but the greatest of these is love—love is a higher virtue than faith. Why not stress these? If Chinese Christianity esteems only one doctrine, this doctrine could easily lead to the contradiction between belief and unbelief, which could lead to endless divisions, damaging the nation's stability. This cannot be God's will, can it?[44]

In the same speech, he went on to speak of a "theological renewal" (*shenxue de zaizao*) now needed in the churches. Ting was opposed to the way in which the doctrine of justification by faith separated believers from nonbelievers and divided religion and ethics. He was speaking about encouraging different theological viewpoints and the need to bring theology up to date. Protestant theology in China was in need of a paradigm shift, an *aggiornamento*. In his address to the Sixth NCC, he had expressed his hope for new developments in theology in order to recover a Christianity that stressed ethics and morality alongside religious faith.[45] This was similar to what he had said in his remarks at the international seminar after his retirement. He had been speaking on the same themes along the same lines since his early days as a student worker in the Shanghai YMCA, and so his overall direction was by no means new.

What was new was the added emphasis he believed should be given to theological issues in the TSPM/CCC. In 1996, Ting gave speeches on many of the same themes at national meetings of religious leaders and seminars organized by the CPPCC. He made it clear that he wanted to see changes in Chinese theology as he spoke about the need to "adjust" (*tiaozheng*) religious perspectives so that Christianity might better "adapt" (*shiying*) to socialism.[46] As we have seen, Ting responded positively to Jiang Zemin's statement that religion should accommodate itself to socialism.[47] Accommodation or adaptation to socialism required a stronger emphasis on the ethical dimension of Christian faith in order to create a common ground between believers and nonbelievers in church and society. When he spoke in a political context, Ting used a language that drew on a political or socialist rather than a religious or theological vocabulary, reflecting the difference between what he said as a Christian theologian (*dao*) and what he said as a political leader (*zheng*).

The *Collected Works of K. H. Ting* (*Ding Guangxun wenji*) was released by Yilin Press in Nanjing in September 1998. It contained speeches, sermons and essays on theological, political and social-scientific subjects; all but four of the texts were written between 1979 and 1998. Chen Zemin contributed a foreword to the volume which set the context for Ting's writings and theological perspective. The *Collected Works* represents a fairly complete picture of Ting's thinking in what might be called the Deng Xiaoping era of modern China. Ting observed in an afterword to the volume that his work should be interpreted in light of efforts to strengthen "socialist spiritual civilization."

> The "Resolution on Several Important Issues in Strengthening Socialist Spiritual Civilization" passed by the Party Central Committee of the Chinese Communist Party on 10 December 1996 states: "Socialism and communist thinking and morality should be conscientiously promoted throughout the whole of society. At the same time, advanced and wide-ranging ideas should be brought together to encourage support of all thinking and morality beneficial to liberating and developing the forces of socialist production, national unity, ethnic unity and social progress, and the pursuit of truth, goodness and beauty, while resisting falsehood and evil, and popularizing upright thinking and morality . . ." With this encouragement, I have selected and edited the contents of this book.[48]

In all the analyses of K. H. Ting's theology that I have seen thus far, no one has called attention to this important paragraph. It does not appear in either the English or Korean versions of the book.[49] Although Chinese Christians may simply take the context for granted, non-Chinese readers need to be reminded of the situation in which Ting was writing. The *Collected Works* were mostly written between 1979 and 1998. As such, they constitute the basis of what might be called a theology of "reform and openness" corresponding to the "reform and openness" of the Deng Xiaoping and Jiang Zemin periods in society as a whole. Ting's work is consistent with the theological views he had been developing since the 1940s, but they came to fruition in the period in which the church was rediscovering itself after the devastation of the Cultural Revolution.

The political and social context for Ting's theology is clear. However, it cannot be said that the essays in *The Collected Works* were "explicitly crafted to conform to a primordial commitment to Communist rule," as Jason Kindopp has argued.[50] One could only make such a claim if he or she were totally ignorant of the broader theological debates all over the world in the last century and of the ongoing debates over theology and Chinese government religious policy discussed in the last chapter. Ting works as a theologian (*dao*) and as a political leader (*zheng*), and his emphasis in both respects is contextualization. One may criticize his approach to accommodation, but he has not reduced theology to political ideology. The essays that appear in Ting's *Collected Works* represent a theology and a politics of "openness and reform" in a descriptive sense, insofar as they were written at a particular time in a particular place. But they also represent a theology focusing on the love of God, the cosmic Christ and the activity of the Holy Spirit in the broader world. Much of what Ting says in his *Collected Works* can be seen as a Chinese interpretation of some of the key theological themes in the ecumenical movement. His work is not at all "radical" when set alongside other liberationist, feminist and pluralistic voices from Asia, Africa and Latin America.

In publishing the volume when he did, and in light of the debate he elicited, K. H. Ting shifted emphasis away from "mutual respect" in matters of faith toward "theological reconstruction" as an extension of "running the church well." It was not that mutual respect was now forgotten, but that theology became central. The fundamentalists did not practice mutual respect in any case, and Ting now became determined to take them on. He hoped to offer a convincing theological alternative to fundamentalism that could broaden the base of Chinese theology for a new generation of Christians. In this way, the church would become more effectively involved in society, bearing witness to a faith that took engagement with the world very seriously.

In 1981, writing as the newly elected leader of the TSPM/CCC, Ting identified what he believed was needed for a theological reorientation in Chinese Christianity.[51] Many of the themes he introduced then were taken up in "theological reconstruction." More than 60 percent of the eighty-two papers in the *Collected Works* were written between 1979 and 1989. In the mid-1990s, he began to challenge fundamentalists in his critique of the doctrine of justification by faith, both in the essays we have already cited and in his publications after the release of the *Collected Works*. However, he had already questioned the centrality of this idea for Christians in essays he wrote in the 1950s, and which were later republished as *How to Study the Bible* (see chaps. 5 and 7). Ting's emphasis on ethics, on "downplaying" (*dan hua*) justification, on reducing the polarity between belief and nonbelief and on the adaptation of religion to socialism were given added emphasis in the late 1990s. But they were not new theological points of departure, for Ting had been saying many of the same things since the 1950s.

The *Collected Works* constitute the theological legacy that Ting has chosen to leave to the Chinese church. But the *Collected Works* are really selected works, for there are seminal essays missing from this volume. Only one of the essays he wrote when he was overseas appears here. Of the twenty essays he published in *Tian Feng* and *JL* in the 1950s, he has included only two in this volume. "On Christian Theism" (1957), his spirited apologetic for Christian faith first delivered as a speech on the eve of the Anti-Rightist movement, is not here (see chaps. 5 and 6).[52] Another important series of essays that are not included are those that comprise *How to Study the Bible*. Most of these were written in the 1950s, but they were revised and issued as a pamphlet in 1980 to appeal to evangelicals whose ideas Ting was now challenging.[53] They may not have been included because they lacked the depth and sophistication of other essays in the *Collected Works*. These omissions notwithstanding, the *Collected Works* includes almost all the important essays that Ting wrote between 1979 and mid-1998, and is a representative selection of his theological, political and social-scientific writing.

The *Collected Works* was published in September 1998 in a hardback edition of 2,000 copies and a paperback edition of 8,000 copies. The photograph on the dust jacket of the book is of K. H. Ting in full episcopal dress. On 25 November 1998, a symposium to discuss the book was organized in Beijing, attended by more than sixty representatives of the CPPCC, church leaders and senior government officials, including Ye Xiaowen, director of the newly reorganized State Administration of Religious Affairs (SARA).[54] Ting's close friend Zhao Puchu, who was seriously ill, left his hospital bed so that he could attend the symposium. Many senior officials and church leaders spoke of the significance of Ting's *Collected Works* on the occasion. Never before had a theological or religious work attracted such attention in the People's Republic of China. Earlier that same month, the TSPM/CCC approved a resolution on theological reconstruction, and over the next few years, the debate over Ting's theology would be at the center of this new initiative.

THEOLOGICAL RECONSTRUCTION

In the summer of 1998, there was serious flooding in central China. There had been such flooding before, and each time the government mobilized its resources to deal with rescue and relief operations. Donations poured in from around the country; the People's Liberation Army (PLA) was sent to severely stricken areas; and regularly televised bulletins covered progress in combating the floods.

In rural churches, some preachers saw the flooding as a sign of God's judgment on China, and an indication that the second coming was near. This was not new, but some students and faculty at NUTS were also interpreting the floods in the same way. In the seminary chapel, they preached that salvation was in God's hands, and in the prayers of fellow Christians, not in government relief efforts or the actions of the PLA.[55] K. H. Ting had spoken publicly in praise of the PLA relief efforts, and he was furious when it was reported to him what was happening at the seminary. This helped convince him that more decisive action against the entrenched fundamentalism that encouraged such thinking was now required.

Ting's first essay in *Tian Feng* after the publication of the *Collected Works* was inspired by the events of that summer. Entitled "Believing in What Kind of God?" it had been delivered as a talk at Nanjing Seminary in a response to those who said that the summer floods and other natural calamities were signs of God's judgment and the end of the world. Ting reiterated the biblical and theological themes he had been advocating all along: that God is a God of love; that a negative or pessimistic worldview is not the gospel; and that there is a need for Chinese Christians to update and transform their view of the Bible.[56] The essay is sharply critical of the way in which some Christians had distorted the meaning of the floods and the subsequent relief efforts, and it may be read as the opening salvo in what became the "theological reconstruction" initiative.*

In September of the same year, just prior to the publication of the *Collected Works*, Ting called a meeting of seminary teachers, students and pastors from Nanjing and neighboring provinces to a meeting to discuss theology and theological education. This too was in response to the events of the previous summer. During this meeting, which took place at the church-

---

* The term "theological reconstruction" or "the reconstruction of theological thought" is an English rendering of *shenxe sixiang jianshe*. A brief word should be said about this translation, for it has been the subject of much debate and speculation in the English-speaking world. Other terms that have been used in translation are "building theology," "theological construction," "theological renewal," and even *jianshe* theology. The translation of the term as "theological reconstruction" is in the same spirit as the translation of the name of the former Chinese periodical *Zhongguo Chongjian*, or *China Reconstructs*, a publication which K. H. Ting wrote for in the 1950s. "Theological reconstruction" has become the commonly accepted translation, and it follows this earlier usage. All of these renderings are questions of interpretation for a foreign audience. The term in Chinese is unambiguous. About the same time that Ting's *Selected Works* was published, political essays in China were using the term "ideological construction" (*sixiang zhengzhi jianshe*) to speak of the need to develop ideology and morality in the spirit of Jiang Zemin's vision of socialism. As Ting writes in the afterword to the *Collected Works*, he is offering a Christian theological contribution to this same overall effort.

related Xinde Guest House in Nanjing, he stressed the need for more theological pluralism and a more progressive orientation to theological education. He criticized the fundamentalist and evangelical views that were commonly taught at Chinese seminaries and challenged what he saw as the evangelical bias of *Tian Feng*. An informal report from this meeting was widely circulated in Nanjing, and Ting's views drew a strongly negative reaction from some senior students and teachers at the seminary.[57] Ting hoped to identify allies from the younger generation at the Xinde meeting, but apparently there were only a few younger teachers who agreed with him.

Ting was undeterred, for he was already advocating at the national level that more attention be given to theology. The TSPM/CCC held a meeting 11-18 November 1998 in Jinan, Shandong Province, where, in the opening speech, Ting presented his views on theological reconstruction.[58] Although church leaders were not unanimous in their views, most agreed that the TSPM/CCC needed to focus more attention on the development of a Chinese theology. The conference approved a "Resolution on Strengthening Theological Reconstruction" reflecting Ting's thinking. It reads in part:

> It is the opinion of this committee that in order to run the church well according to three-self principles, we must develop theological thought to function in guiding the church construction. Through their participation in the Three-Self Patriotic Movement, Chinese Christians have gained a great deal of valuable spiritual experience; a theological summing up of this experience is urgently needed. Even more, the deepening and opening up of self-propagation demands lively theological reflection and exploration of how to better spread the gospel; how to guide Christians in their spiritual and in their daily lives; how to promote Christian ethics and morality; how to glorify God and benefit the people.[59]

This was the formal beginning of theological reconstruction in the Chinese church. With this resolution, the theological debate that Ting had wanted to avoid during the time of renewal and rebuilding in the early 1980s now came to center stage. It should be noted that theological reconstruction was explicitly related to church construction in this resolution. The emphasis in both cases was on building up the church. Throughout the 1980s and 1990s, attention had been given to the return of church properties, the reestablishment of church institutions, the training of clergy, the printing of the Bible, and openness to the outside world, all in the context of the reimplementation of the policy of religious freedom. The most important thing at that time was maintaining the fragile unity of the church. At the Jinan meeting, attention was shifted to the kind of theology that should shape a self-governing, self-supporting and self-propagating Chinese church.

Over the next few years, theological reconstruction became a central concern for churches and Protestant seminaries. This was an initiative from above, not below. The government endorsed theological reconstruction, for it fitted with the broader agenda of the adaptation of Christianity to socialism. Symposia were organized by TSPMs and Christian councils in many cities and provinces, and training sessions were held for clergy, lay leaders and seminary teachers. Personnel changes were made in the TSPM/CCC publication department to fit with the new emphasis, and essays reflecting the new direction began to be published in *Tian Feng*. Ting advanced his own views on the need for a changed biblical and theological perspective, and his thinking was further developed in essays written by younger Chinese theologians. A national committee was set up to promote theological reconstruction under Ting's direction.[60] At all important TSPM/CCC gatherings, theological reconstruction was reaffirmed in speech after speech.

Other events underscored the need for the new initiative. The Falun Gong protests indicated the subversive potential of informal religious groups to the government and the church alike. Jiang Zemin's belief that Falun Gong represented the most serious threat to Communist rule in China since 1949 was hyperbole, but it illustrated the concern over organized religious efforts beyond the reach of the state. Falun Gong had nothing to do with Christianity, but, as we have seen, Christian leaders and representatives of all other Chinese religious organizations were quick to join in the denunciation of the sect.[61] Expressions of opposition to dangerous sects are formulaic in Chinese politics, but Christians did not want to see themselves associated with Falun Gong–type activity, either politically or theologically. Theological reconstruction would show that Christians could adapt to socialist society and not become a dissident or subversive force.

An important aspect of theological reconstruction in churches and seminaries was an emphasis on reading and interpreting the Bible in new ways. Ting was dissatisfied with the literalistic interpretation of the Bible in sermons and Chinese theological writing, and he wanted to introduce an updated and critical approach to biblical study. As an initial response, he reprinted the small book by Prof. Tang Zhongmo, who was principal of the Anglican Central Theological Seminary in Shanghai in the 1930s, entitled *A Modern View of the Bible.*[62] The book was long out of date in its approach to modern biblical scholarship, but it challenged the fundamentalist interpretation of the Bible that was still current in China. Ting had himself written essays on biblical interpretation, including *How to Study the Bible* and the speech he gave to the American Academy of Religion and the Society of Biblical Literature in 1990.[63] Now he wanted to tackle the problem more directly, and he called on Christians to develop a more critical view of the Bible. True to his Anglican heritage, he urged pastors to preach from the Gospels as well as from the Pauline letters, and to emphasize what he saw as the central biblical message of God's love.[64]

The most controversial element in theological reconstruction was Ting's idea that the doctrine of "justification by faith" needed to be downplayed or deemphasized (*dan hua*). The Reformation doctrine of justification had never been prominent in Anglican theology. It is there in the "Thirty-nine Articles," but it does not define the Anglican or Episcopal position on Christian faith. In Ting's speech at the symposium of religious leaders in 1996, he had raised questions about the doctrine of "justification by faith" as it was being interpreted by many in the Chinese church.[65] He had argued earlier that when St. Paul and Martin Luther spoke of justification, they were offering a progressive and liberating critique of ossified religion.[66] Ting maintained, however, that the Protestant missionaries who came to China in the nineteenth and twentieth centuries attached the idea of justification to a frightening picture of the hell that awaited nonbelievers in order to highlight the difference between Christians and non-Christians. This was interpreted by new Christians in light of the folk religious ideas they had left behind. Justification had in this way functioned to dilute the ethical element in Christianity, and it all but eliminated the Christian concept of social justice. Nineteenth-century Protestant theology still shaped Chinese Protestant views in the 1990s. Ting developed his ideas even further when he argued that many non-Christians, including Confucius and Laozi, Zhou Enlai and the worker-hero Lei Feng lived exemplary lives, and they should not be condemned to hell. In contrast, Adolf Hitler and Benito Mussolini were Christians, but it should not be assumed that they went to heaven.[67] It can be argued that Ting was reducing justification by faith to a polemic against the fundamentalist and evangelical view of salvation. But he was being deliberately provocative in order to stir up a debate. He wanted Christians to see justification alongside other Christian teachings, including God's continuing work of creation, the Incarnation, the resurrection, Pentecost and Jesus' teachings in the Sermon on the Mount.

His broader point was that theology required a social ethic, and that a simplistic interpretation of "justification by faith" by new Chinese Christians could lead to an antinomianism. Ting's theological position is similar to that of many other Third World theologians in its contention that justification by faith should not become a wedge to separate Christians from those of other religious traditions who were also struggling for justice and social change. The doctrine of justification should not be used to separate faith from works. When Ting spoke to non-Christian audiences, he was exploring ideas that could make common ground with those outside the church. When he spoke to Christian groups, he was arguing for openness and change. Ting repeated his ideas about justification again and again in his speeches over the next several years.[68] He wanted to emphasize the ethical dimension of Christian faith, and God as a God of love for all people.

The love of God became the primary category of Christian faith in Ting's theology. This was why he chose the title *Love Never Ends* for the English edition of his *Collected Works*. One of Ting's aims in promoting theological reconstruction was to oppose the teaching that God is a divine punisher, for this makes God "more like the King of Hell feared by so many in Chinese folk religion."[69] Ting has not written that "justification by love" (*yin ai cheng yi*) should be substituted for the traditional idea of "justification by faith" in Christian theology, but he has sometimes spoken of the idea in his speeches and informal conversations.[70] This has caused misunderstandings, because it removed a distinctive element in Christian faith. The idea of "justification by love" was for a time advanced by some of Ting's more ardent followers, which was unfortunate, for this served to alienate conservative Chinese Christians from the whole idea of theological reconstruction in the churches.

Ting had introduced most of his ideas on theological reconstruction in the 1980s, or even before, but in his speeches and writings after 1998, he gave some of these a new edge. As theological reconstruction was being promoted in the churches and seminaries, letters in response to some of the more controversial aspects of what he was saying began to pour in. Ting responded to many of these criticisms in an essay he wrote for *JL*.[71] For example, some critics attacked Ting for his use of the term "unfinished products" or "works-in-progress" (*ban chengpin*) as a way of speaking about human beings created in God's image and cooperating with God in the ongoing process of creation and redemption. In response to this criticism, Ting spoke of the importance of growth and change as part of creation and life. Referring to Old and New Testament sources (Psalm 8:4-5; 1 Corinthians 13:11-12; Philippians 3:12-14; Luke 2:52), he argued that Christian faith was not a once-and-for-all event, but a process in which learning and new discoveries took place enabling human beings to cooperate with God and work for the betterment of themselves and the world. In this respect, Ting was arguing for a doctrine of sanctification alongside the doctrine of justification.

In the same essay, he wrote that he had no intention of replacing faith and belief with ethics and morality. The core of Christianity was and remained its faith, beliefs and doctrine. "Basic Christian belief," however, needed to be distinguished from theology. Ting maintained that Chinese theology needed to put more emphasis on morality and ethics in order to recover the biblical teachings and reach out to others. An emphasis on ethics in no way undercuts the uniqueness of Christianity, but the Christian understanding of love and the human concept of love are not contradictory. This point was related to his earlier argument about the flooding of the Yangtze River. Ting praised the response of the PLA, which he saw as an example of God's love for the world, a love that was the impetus for all of God's actions in the world, whether inside or outside the church.

> During the television coverage of the floods, we saw a five or six year old child clinging to a branch, about to be swept away. Without a thought for his own safety, a PLA soldier guided his small boat over, grabbed the child and took her to safety. This act, braving death to

save another, is love. I cannot believe such love to be very small, hardly worth mentioning. I believe this is a great and holy love, and that the creator of this love is God. Seeing love like this, God is most certainly pleased, and we Christians, too, should be thankful for it and should not demean it. Can it be that we as Christians should criticize and demean even the good actions of others? Is this normal? Can our Christianity have no common language with the rest of our people? John 3:16 tells us "For God so loved the world . . ." May we know the will of God and see the world with [God's] loving heart.[72]

None of Ting's ideas were very radical when viewed from the perspective of contextual theological writing in other parts of the world over the last fifty years. They became controversial in China because Ting was challenging fundamentalism directly, and because many Chinese Christians saw his theology as part of a broader political initiative that was being imposed on them from above.

The theological changes Ting envisioned required institutional changes at Nanjing Union Theological Seminary. This was the only degree-granting theological institution in China, and many of its graduates assumed important positions of church leadership or joined the faculties of other seminaries. After Nanjing Seminary reopened in 1981, Ting spent a great deal of time with students, faculty and staff, giving careful attention to questions of reorganization, curriculum and student life, and often lecturing once or twice a week. In the 1980s, he regularly conducted worship services at the beginning and end of each semester. But as the pace of the reforms picked up and his duties as TSPM/CCC leader increased, he spent less and less time with students and faculty. He remained the seminary principal, but he left its administration in the hands of others. Young graduates who had returned from studies overseas were given an increasing share of responsibility for the running of the seminary on a day-to-day basis. This changed, beginning in 1996, as Ting became more concerned about the theology of the seminary graduates and the commitment of the new generation of students to Three-Self patriotism.

In 1998, there began a formal evaluation (*pinggu*) of the seminary by the national and provincial religious authorities and the TSPM/CCC. Educational institutions of other religious bodies were being evaluated around the same time, and so it was not unusual that Nanjing Seminary should also be assessed. According to an official involved in the evaluation, the authorities looked at the seminary's study plan, its theological direction, its leadership team, the quality of its teaching faculty and its work in political study.[73] All educational institutions in China had political study, and the government believed that this was an important part of the curriculum for religious institutions in particular. Other elements in the evaluation were integral to the education of ministers and church leaders and the work involved in running an educational institution. The evaluation process lasted six months, and it involved meetings between government officials and all faculty, staff and students.

In the spring and summer of 1999, there were a series of events at the seminary that cast the evaluation then in progress in a much more serious light. These events were widely reported from a variety of viewpoints, and here we can offer only a short summary of what actually happened. The controversy began when three postgraduate students announced that they would not sing "patriotic" Chinese songs at a concert to commemorate the seventieth anniversary of the May Fourth Movement. In a public statement, they stated that they stood on biblical and theological grounds in wanting to perform only Christian songs.[74] For K. H. Ting and other senior leaders, their statement appeared to cast their support for the stance of Three-Self patriotism in doubt. Seminary leaders negotiated with the three students for many weeks, but they failed to resolve the problem. In early May, the students were dismissed from the seminary, but they were told that if they retracted their position, they could return and receive their diplomas.

Other seminary students and some faculty saw this as an overly harsh action, for the students were due to graduate that summer. They sympathized with the three who had been dismissed, and questioned the seminary's decision. The following month, three other seminary students duplicated a statement and wrote a big character poster announcing their intention to withdraw from their studies in support of the three who had been dismissed. In a strongly worded statement, they attacked Ting personally, rejecting the TSPM and asserting that theirs was a prophetic stance in defense of Christian faith. They also denounced the theological-reconstruction initiative.[75] Seminary leaders called the student body together to refute the charges that had been made. Ting himself spoke to the entire faculty and student body to offer his perspective on the situation and to reassert his authority.[76] The whole situation has been widely—and often inaccurately—reported and discussed in the popular press and on the Internet, and there are very different perspectives and analyses of all that happened.[77] These need not concern us here, except to say that the events of that summer further reinforced K. H. Ting's belief that radical changes were needed at the seminary.

The changes involved personnel and the leadership of the seminary. Peng Cui'an, the vice-principal whom Ting had handpicked several years earlier, was forced to leave her position and pursue further studies overseas. Her husband, Li Yading, was already overseas, and he had been told that he would not be welcomed back at his former post. Wang Weifan, who had worked closely with Ting in the past, had reached retirement age and was asked to retire. All three were strongly identified with the evangelical wing of the church. In another widely publicized case, Ji Tai, a young seminary teacher who had studied in Germany, was suspended from his teaching duties, accused of violating "state laws and regulations" and carrying on "clandestine activities in conjunction with underground groups" in China.[78] Ji continued to live in his apartment at the seminary even after he had been dismissed, but he began to work with churches and meeting points unrelated to the TSPM/CCC. By the end of 2002, almost all the young faculty who had been sent overseas for advanced studies in the 1980s were no longer at the seminary. Some were serving the church in other places, but several had taken up residence overseas.

The student incidents and the faculty departures were unprecedented in Ting's long tenure at the seminary. It was highly unusual that young students would publicly attack a senior church leader then in his mid-eighties, and for some older Christians, this was reminiscent of the "Red Guard" activities during the Cultural Revolution era. Many pastors were sympathetic to Ting's response. However, the incidents showed that a wide gap had developed between Ting and a new generation of faculty and students whose theological and political convictions were different from his own. In Ting's view, Nanjing Seminary had not kept pace with the times, and the churches were not responding to new challenges coming from society. The theology taught at the seminary was too conservative, and there was little room for the discussion of new developments in biblical studies, ethics and theology. There were also students and seminary graduates who were more open-minded theologically, but they were drawn to what was happening in the universities and among intellectuals of their own generation. More than a few seminary students were dismissive of the TSPM/CCC and sharply critical of the Chinese government.

K. H. Ting again became directly involved in seminary affairs, despite his advanced years. He put an increased emphasis on political study, faculty leadership, student recruitment, and, of course, theological reconstruction.[79] In 2001, foreign teachers were invited to teach at the seminary, and Ting was particularly interested in having them introduce new approaches to biblical studies. He believed this would help update biblical interpretation and thereby contribute to theological reconstruction. Young seminary graduates were recruited as new teachers, and new leaders were brought in, including Wang Aiming, who had studied for some years in Switzerland, and his wife, Wang Peng. Wang Aiming became dean and vice-principal of the seminary, and he was subsequently ordained to the pastorate by K. H. Ting. He went overseas to continue his studies in 2003, and Wang Peng became acting dean. There were editorial changes at *JL*, and essays on theological reconstruction became more prominent. The essays for the journal written by younger teachers who remained at the seminary and by graduate students reflected an approach that was more open-minded than in the past, and many of these were of high quality.[80] By the time of its fiftieth anniversary in the fall of 2002, the seminary was on more solid footing.[81] However, many institutional issues had not been resolved, particularly future leadership and faculty development.

Ting was deeply involved in promoting theological reconstruction, particularly at Nanjing Seminary, but his continuing role in the church was much broader. He attended important meetings of the TSPM/CCC and offered advice to the leadership. He spoke out on issues of national concern, such as his support for the Catholic Patriotic Association in denouncing the Vatican's elevation of the martyrs of the Boxer Rebellion to sainthood.[82] Government officials continued to consult with him and seek his advice. He also liked to meet foreign Christian leaders visiting China, who always hoped they would be able to see him in Nanjing. Ting seemed to overshadow other TSPM/CCC leaders, and this led to inevitable tensions, especially with Han Wenzao, who had been his close associate in the previous decades.

Han was a different kind of church leader than Ting. A skillful administrator and keen negotiator, he had helped implement many of the ideas that Ting introduced in the TSPM/CCC. But Han was a lay person who lacked Ting's charisma and theological interests. He did not have the same diplomatic skills, nor did he command the same sense of authority in the churches. As CCC president, Han was sometimes criticized for making decisions on his own without consulting other leaders. Han had given a speech at the Jinan meeting, but he was not a theologian, and Ting may have seen him to be only a lukewarm supporter of theological reconstruction.[83] For all of these reasons, Han and Ting drifted apart, and they sometimes criticized each other indirectly in meetings with friends and foreign visitors. Toward the end of his term as CCC president, Han's health declined, and he stepped down at the Seventh National Christian Conference in 2002, as did TSPM chair Luo Guanzong.[84] Both Luo and Han continued to be involved in TSPM/CCC affairs in an honorary capacity.

K. H. Ting became increasingly critical of evangelicals in China, but he continued to relate to evangelicals from overseas. He found them more open and accessible than many of their Chinese counterparts. After his retirement, Ting was in touch with James Taylor, the grandson of James Hudson Taylor (1832-1905), the founder of the China Inland Mission. The younger Taylor was formerly director of the Overseas Missionary Fellowship (OMF), successor body to the China Inland Mission. Hudson Taylor had been a prominent target in the Denunciation Movement in the 1950s, when he was criticized by Y. T. Wu himself. As we have seen, Ting had disagreed with the Denunciation Movement. Taylor's grandson wanted to have a memorial to Taylor placed in a church in Jiangsu where his grandfather had been active. This would involve moving the memorial from Urumchi in the far west. Ting agreed that Hudson Taylor should be somehow rehabilitated, and he tried to have the memorial moved. He encountered considerable opposition, however, and he was not successful in his efforts.[85]

In China, K. H. Ting spoke of fundamentalists and evangelicals as more or less representing the same thing. Some of Ting's critics continued to refer to all Three-Self leaders as a "party of unbelief" (*buxin pai*) as they had in the 1950s. Ting liked to quote the words he had heard from an American visitor who told him that a fundamentalist was an evangelical who was angry about something.[86] Ting interpreted this to mean that the difference is more one of temperament than theology or basic stance. "I too am not inclined to elaborate on their 'differences,'" he observed.[87]

Still, Ting believed that many overseas evangelicals were open in their approach and willing to support his efforts at theological reconstruction. In the early years of the new century, Ting became particularly interested in relating to Richard Mouw of Fuller Theological Seminary, whose presidential-installation service he had attended in 1993. Mouw was received as an honored guest on several visits to Nanjing, and Ting went out of his way to welcome him.[88] Mouw also wrote an appreciative essay on some of K. H. Ting's views on theological reconstruction.[89] Despite their mutual appreciation, Ting did not agree to send Chinese seminary students for further studies to Pasadena, California, as Fuller Seminary had hoped. Ting's efforts to relate to overseas evangelicals were based on a recognition of their influence and potential for influencing anti-TSPM evangelicals in China and in North America, and a mutual commitment to building up the church in China.

When Zhao Puchu died at the age of ninety-three on 21 May 2000, Ting became the most senior religious figure in China. Zhao had been ill for a very long time, and he had been confined to the hospital for much of the two previous years.[90] Zhao Puchu and K. H. Ting had worked together on the reform of religious policy since the early 1980s. Zhao had not been a controversial figure among Buddhists in the same way that K. H. Ting was among Christians, a fact due more to the differences between international Buddhist and Christian religious communities than anything else. Zhao was as committed to the leadership of the CPC as K. H. Ting, and throughout his life, he advocated a "Buddha-in-society" (*renjian fojiao*) role for his community. This was a this-worldly ethic, a way for Buddhism to adapt to socialist society, and in some ways it paralleled Ting's emphasis on theological reconstruction. Ting mourned the passing of his close friend.

Ting succeeded in making theological reconstruction a subject of intense interest and debate within the churches, nationally and internationally. But the response to this new initiative—and to K. H. Ting's theology as a whole—varied greatly. It is still too early to assess the impact of theological reconstruction on the Chinese church, but it is possible to identify the broad range of opinion that has emerged about it.

DIFFERENCES WITHIN THE COMMON GROUND

In advocating theological reconstruction, K. H. Ting was not intending for his thought to become a new theological orthodoxy. What he did want was to challenge fundamentalism, which he saw as the de facto orthodoxy of Chinese Protestantism. It was never possible that his theology or any other theology might become a "hegemonic ideology" forced on grassroots Christians in China as some critics have maintained.[91] China had changed too much for the imposition of any religious or theological ideology, and the TSPM/CCC was not strong enough to force its will on a very diffuse constituency. Ting had more modest expectations. He was hoping to liberalize Chinese theology and advance the ideas he believed in, but he understood that conservative Christians could not or would not accept all of his views. That Christianity needed to adapt to socialism is only stating the obvious, in the same way that Christianity has adapted to capitalism and other social systems. In his speeches and writings, Ting was attempting to make space for a more positive acceptance of the context in which the church existed. In so doing, Ting's efforts may be compared to contextually oriented theologians in other times and places, both in terms of the content of what he was saying and on the need to challenge conservative Christian belief systems.

The difference was that Ting was speaking and writing from a position of power, and with the support of the CPC and the state. Because of who he was and how the new initiative was promoted, there was an implicitly coercive element in theological reconstruction, at least at the outset. This made many Christians uneasy, regardless of how they felt about the theological ideas themselves. Some seminary graduates and young pastors complained that they felt forced to "declare support" (*biaotai*) for the new initiative, for their future in the church was at stake. Although theological reconstruction was not in any way a "movement" like the campaigns of the 1950s or the Cultural Revolution—nowhere has the term "movement" or "campaign" (*yundong*) been used in Chinese—some people mistakenly compared the new initiative to these movements. The coercion from TSPMs and Christian councils was a far cry from the mobilizations of a previous time, but the pressure to conform to the spirit and direction of theological reconstruction was real.

Despite this pressure, there was both spoken and unspoken resistance to the new initiative. China is much freer than it was in the 1950s or even the 1980s and 1990s as far as religion is concerned. Young people who had come of age in the last twenty or thirty years could not easily be persuaded to follow a particular political or theological line, and in this sense they are different from the older generation. Many Chinese Christians have been generally supportive of the idea of theological reconstruction, but this does not mean they have accepted K. H. Ting's theological approach in every detail. Others in the churches have rejected, resisted, or ignored the new initiative.

As theological reconstruction gained momentum, the TSPM/CCC took the lead in promoting K. H. Ting's theology and ideas. As he approached his ninetieth birthday, he could not promote the initiative on his own. There is a difference, therefore, between what Ting has himself said and written about theological reconstruction and the way that his thought has been interpreted and promoted within TSPM/CCC. Pamphlets of Ting's writings were printed and distributed for popular use.[92] Essays in *Tian Feng*, TSPM/CCC statements and declarations by Christian leaders expressed support for theological reconstruction as the way to make Christian theology Chinese.[93] Meetings and seminars were organized in many provinces in order to generate support.

Even as the new initiative assumed a life of its own, no one could match the charisma and authority of K. H. Ting. He was invited to speak at provincial conferences, and his speeches on theological reconstruction were widely publicized.[94] He had a simple message, and, like other church speakers who are much in demand, he often became repetitive, making use of the same arguments and examples again and again. Ting was sometimes sharper and more direct in his speeches than in his writing, and some of his words were later softened or revised for publication. His writings in the early 2000s were not as nuanced or as carefully prepared as they once were, and they were sometimes edited for publication by others. This did not deter him from speaking out, however, for he was very clear about what he wanted to say.

Ting succeeded in introducing theological debate in the churches and seminaries, which was his original intent. In 2001, he observed that theological reconstruction had created divisions in the churches, and this meant a lively debate was underway.

> Over the past two or three years, the issue of theological reconstruction has created relatively large divisions among China's Christian intellectuals, and the effect of these divisions on other matters is growing. Some observers think that the existence of such differences indicates chaos. I do not agree. Since the idea of theological reconstruction was launched, theological discussion in China has grown livelier, and this is a quite different situation from chaos.

The divisions were even evident among students and faculty of Nanjing Seminary.

> At Nanjing Seminary, the staff and students are polarized. A great number of students work hard to participate in the reconstruction of Chinese theological thinking—they re-read the Bible, write papers, discuss and reflect. I think they will be the future pillars of the Chinese church. But there are also a number of indifferent students who exert a bad influence on their fellow students. Just as Nanjing Seminary is polarized at this point in time, so our whole church is divided into different groups. This diversification does not mean chaos but rather reflects a diversity of theological reflection and will help us to renew and deepen our theological thinking.[95]

Ting's strongest theological ally was Chen Zemin, who had spoken strongly in support of theological construction (*shenxue jianshe*) at the Jinan meeting.[96] Chen and Ting were from the same generation, and they had worked together for decades. Chen wrote the foreword to the *Collected Works,* and he has written several other important essays on theological reconstruction.[97] He is an important theologian in his own right, more of a systematician than Ting, and an unashamed theological liberal. Chen has exerted a strong influence on the younger generation at Nanjing Seminary, and many graduates revere him as a trusted teacher and mentor.

Chen Zemin's most important theological essay was originally written in 1956, but at the urging of friends and colleagues, he revised and republished this essay in 1991, many years before theological reconstruction had been introduced. In this essay, Chen surveyed the theological task, drawing extensively on classical Western theology, which he recasts in light of the new issues facing the Chinese church. This essay foreshadowed many of the ideas in Chen's own approach to theological reconstruction. He argued that "theological (re)construction will never be out of date," that "the road to theological (re) construction" had no end, for theology must always grow and develop. Because of the conservative missionary past, the present challenges to the church are very great.

> In our experience we lack maturity, our vision is narrow and shallow, and we do not dare pretend that our ignorance is wisdom, but we firmly believe that a road leading to higher truth lies before us. It will break through the impasse of western theology, cause people in the midst of new kinds of social relationships to better understand God's creative wisdom and saving love, and cause the gospel to truly become the good news for all humankind, just as the prophet announcing the coming of Christ proclaimed the good news that the human race would exist in harmony and peace, making God's glory shine over the whole earth. This is the theological task given to us by God. With a pious and humble attitude, without flinching or boasting, relying on the guidance of God's loving wisdom, and with hearts full of confidence, we should run the race set before us.[98]

One can see the influence of both Chen Zemin and K. H. Ting in the writings of some of the younger theologians in Chinese seminaries. Their voices have become much clearer, more nuanced and more confident over the last few years. For example, Chen Yilu, a Nanjing graduate and now the principal of Guandong Theological Seminary, has addressed problems in theological education as these relate to the church in China. Chen Yongtao, who teaches at NUTS, has written about the importance of developing an ethical Christology, drawing on resources from the Chinese classics and the Chinese theological tradition, as well as from the Bible and Western theology. Xiao Anping, the dean of Zhongnan Theological Seminary, writes in a more contemporary vein, analyzing the theological challenges of the church's attempt to adapt to socialist society. Wang Aiming, former dean of NUTS, has tried to link theological reconstruction to classical themes in Reformation theology. Gao Ying, who in 2006 became vice-principal of NUTS, Wang Peng, the seminary librarian, Kan Baoping, who works at the TSPM/CCC offices in Shanghai, and Zhang Keyun, who heads the Christian Council in Jiangsu Province have all approached theological reconstruction from the perspective of their respective positions and interests.[99] These younger scholars vary a great deal in their emphasis and approach. Some are deeply committed to evangelical theology, while others are more liberal and experimental. Their published work taken as a whole reflects a theological interpretation that seeks to relate Christianity to Chinese society and culture. What remains to be seen is whether they will be able to develop a more comprehensive approach to contextual theology that can provide a solid theological grounding for the churches in the future.

Fundamentalist and conservative evangelical Chinese Christians believe that they already have such grounding, and many have rejected theological reconstruction outright. Their attacks on K. H. Ting and theological reconstruction in some sense resemble the debates between Ting and Wang Mingdao in the 1950s (see chap. 4). The vehemence and anger of the rebuttals that have been directed at Ting personally recall the Fundamentalist-Modernist controversies in the first part of the last century.[100] Conservative Chinese thinkers, including the late Jonathan Chao (1938-2004), founder of the China Ministries International (CMI), was a persistent critic of the TSPM for three decades. He viewed Ting as an unreconstructed liberal who was promoting theological reconstruction as the agenda of the Chinese Communist Party. K. H. Ting "theologizes for politics," according to Chao. "He does not write what he believes; he writes for the Communist Party. The study of Ting's thought like the study of Chairman Mao's sayings," Chao continued, "is having an adverse effect for it serves to alienate him from TSPM pastors."[101] Jonathan Chao's analysis of Ting's politics and theology has always stressed the same themes. Although he was unfair in his judgments about Ting, it is true that theological reconstruction did alienate some TSPM pastors. Jonathan Chao had considerable influence in some quarters of the Chinese church, and, if contributions on the Internet are to be believed, similar criticisms are raised there.

The most well-documented and widely circulated essays criticizing theological reconstruction were written by Li Xinyuan, purportedly a theological writer and biblical scholar from mainland China.[102] Li writes as a fundamentalist steeped in classical Reformed theology, whose confident and uncompromising rhetoric is reminiscent of the late Carl McIntyre (1907-2002). Li's critique of Ting and theological reconstruction is based on what he terms "essential tenets of Christian faith," grounded in an interpretation of the thought of Luther and Calvin. His is exactly the kind of thinking that theological reconstruction was designed to refute, for his rigid adherence to Christian fundamentals and rejection of the Chinese political order stands against any possibility of creative interaction between Christianity and contemporary society, let alone the adaptation of the church to socialism. With a strong emphasis on God's judgment and human sin, Li criticizes Ting for his "lukewarm faith" and optimism about the world. Like Y. T. Wu before him, Ting is part of the "party of unbelief" steeped in the "social gospel," in Li's view. Li goes on to offer a point-by-point critique, focusing on Ting's view of God, Jesus Christ and human nature. There is no common ground at all between Li Xinyuan and K. H. Ting, and Li's categories of interpretation come from a different age. One can almost argue that Li Xinyuan provides a good counterpoint to Ting, for his arguments are so unreasonable as to be easily dismissed.

Not all opponents of theological reconstruction and the adaptation of Christianity to socialism can be written off as easily, however. The majority of Chinese Christians came of age after the end of the Cultural Revolution era. This includes many intellectuals who felt that they had been cheated or deceived by the high ideals of Communism. With a deep sense of their own personal sinfulness and the sinfulness of society, they became Christians in response to the message of forgiveness and grace in Jesus Christ. They tended to reject an ethical or humanistic interpretation of theology, or a one-sided theological adaptation of Christianity to socialism. Ethical humanism was what the Communist Party stressed in the 1950s, and it was a humanistic interpretation of Marxism that an older generation of intellectuals developed again in the 1980s (see chap. 7). However, a new generation of Christian intellectuals believe that this humanism failed in China, and they blamed the CPC for the "ideological vacuum" in society. Unlike K. H. Ting, younger intellectuals such as Liu Xiaofeng initially were drawn to the theology of Karl Barth, in part because of his rejection of the cultural and theological liberalism of his day.[103] They saw parallels between Barth and their own situation, and preferred to stress the differences rather than the common ground between Christian faith and socialist commitment. They were attracted by the Pauline message of "justification by faith" and its interpretation in modern European theology. Liu Xiaofeng has not, to my knowledge, written about theological reconstruction, but his writings suggest that he would be resistant to any theology too closely identified with the present social, cultural and political order. Other prominent Christian intellectuals outside the church would have a similar critique, and they have a following among a younger generation of church-based theologians.

Some of Ting's former seminary colleagues have also been critical of theological reconstruction, and particularly his belief on deemphasizing "justification by faith." Wang Weifan, whose relationship with Ting became severely strained after the changes at Nanjing Seminary in the late 1990s, has criticized some elements of Ting's new theological direction. Wang has always been a theological conservative and a fiery preacher, much in demand in the churches. Erratic at times, he is also an incisive and prolific writer, well versed in Marxist theory, Chinese classical literature and Christian theology. His criticism is not one-sided, however. Like Ting, he believes there is need for greater attention to theology in the Chinese church, and he is willing to acknowledge the achievements of theological reconstruction.

> Over the last four years, the accomplishments of theological recon-
> struction must be objectively affirmed. For example, it has helped
> Christians clearly understand several things: that patriotism and sup-
> port for the leadership of the Party and the government have a Bibli-
> cal basis; that "Three-Self" is the path for the Chinese church; that for
> Christians, there should be harmony with non-Christians, and that
> they should work together to build up a strong motherland; that from
> the perspective of faith, the relationship between belief and action, and
> this life and the next should be brought together so that we can have
> a positive attitude toward human life, social concerns, economic devel-
> opment and social welfare. All of these will help Chinese Christians
> play a positive role in building up material and spiritual civilization.

This is precisely what Ting himself had hoped to accomplish through theological reconstruction. However, Wang goes on to develop a Marxist critique of the relationship between ideology and consciousness, arguing that
theology and beliefs change slowly over time and cannot be rushed. He suggests that theological reconstruction is attempting to change Christian thinking too quickly, by the power of ideas imposed from above, and that this can
never succeed.

Moreover, Wang Weifan argues that the downplaying of "justification by
faith" is simply wrong, for it is a cornerstone of Protestant belief. Contrary
to Ting's view that it undercuts the ethical dimension of theology, justification by faith may actually help promote moral action.

> The moral function of "justification by faith" lies in the way it trans-
> forms the search for external righteousness and goodness into internal,
> spiritual, innate and self-regulating goodness and righteousness that
> are self-consciously revealed and expressed in concrete acts of goodness
> and righteousness. To distort or downplay (*dan hua*) "justification by
> faith" as "emphasizing the opposition between belief and unbelief" is
> to downplay basic Christian teachings and their moral function. This
> is something that no pious Christian can accept, and moreover con-
> tradicts the Marxist understanding of this teaching.[104]

Wang developed his critique of theological reconstruction in other writings,
most of which have not been published in China. His detailed essay on Luo
Zhufeng, a Communist who was a leading figure in developing in the 1980s
a more open approach to religious studies, urges tolerance in theological
debates and the need for a more nuanced understanding of Christian fundamentalism and conservative Christian beliefs.[105] It can be argued that the
fine points of Wang's historical discussion would be lost on the fundamen-

talists, but Wang could counter that the fine points have also been lost by supporters of theological reconstruction.

What is needed, Wang insists, is more attention to theological thinking, and on this point, he and Ting are in agreement. But they have very different assessments of the kind of theology that the Chinese church needs because their theological starting points are very different. So too is their relationship to the churches. Wang Weifan is closely associated with the local church. He has always written as a theological gadfly in the TSPM/CCC, but at the same time he believes that the national structures must be more attentive to churches at the grassroots. K. H. Ting writes from his position as a national church leader with a sense of responsibility for Christianity as a whole. Deeply aware of the fragile institutional existence of the church, Ting hoped the church could move in new directions so that it could be better grounded in Chinese society.

The debates over theological reconstruction have not been widely reported in either church or academic publications in China, for there is no publication that serves as a vehicle for theological debate. As is often the case in the discussion of controversial subjects in the church, legitimate differences in approach are deliberately avoided for the sake of unity and harmony. Because there has been little open debate or reporting about contrasting views on theological reconstruction, it is not possible to draw conclusions about the relative strengths of the different positions in the churches or seminaries. Much of the criticism has appeared on the Internet, but this may be an inaccurate reflection of the relative strengths of the different sides. Academic conferences in China and abroad, and informal discussions with Chinese Christians and intellectuals have provided some opportunities for discussing theological reconstruction in the early 2000s, but dialogue between theologians and intellectuals studying Christianity in China has only begun.

At least one Christian intellectual outside the church has openly called for more dialogue and cooperation. She is Rachel Zhu Xiaohong, a young instructor associated with the religious studies program at Shanghai's Fudan University. At a conference in Finland in 2003, she presented a paper entitled "A Call for Dialogue and Co-operation: On the Theological Reconstruction Movement in China." The conference involved university and church-based intellectuals from China and Europe, but there was little response to her call for dialogue from either side.[106] There have been appreciative reviews of the *Collected Works of K. H. Ting* from the Institute of World Religions of the Chinese Academy of Social Sciences.[107] The most thorough treatment of contextualization in Chinese Christianity was written by Duan Qi, a senior researcher at the Institute of World Religions at the Chinese Academy of Social Sciences.[108] She traces the history of Protestant thought in China from the nineteenth century to the present, and is generally sympathetic to what Chinese theologians, including Y. T. Wu and K. H. Ting, have been attempting. Duan writes from a historical perspective using categories of analysis different from those of the theological seminaries. Her work is not a study of theological reconstruction per se—it ends before the current initiative began—but it could enhance dialogue between academics and the church. However, some church leaders have voiced criticism of Duan's work, and her efforts to write about what they see as *their* history. Not wanting to enter into a debate with the TSPM/CCC, many intellectuals studying Christianity choose to avoid direct involvement in theological reconstruction, seeing it as an initiative for the churches rather than a subject for academic discussion.

Over the past ten years, the gap between Protestant church-based theology and the academic study of Christianity in China seems to have widened considerably. We have seen that K. H. Ting coined the term "culture Christians" (*wenhua jidutu*) as an appreciative reference to Chinese intellectuals studying Christianity whom he saw as breaking new ground in theology for an overly conservative church.[109] Since the mid-1990s, academic interest in Christian studies has grown tremendously in China, and there has been an outpouring of important books, periodicals and conference volumes from scholars at major universities and research institutes. In terms of intellectual rigor and publications, their research has overshadowed the work of younger theologians in the seminaries.[110] Seminary teachers and graduate students have not had sufficient opportunities for advanced theological study, and, like young theologians in other parts of Asia, their service to the church has taken time and energy away from writing, research and participation in academic conferences. In contrast, university-based scholars in Christian studies have developed cosmopolitan interests and are often more conversant with contemporary theological trends than their seminary counterparts.

The growing visibility and outspokenness of non-Christian intellectuals has led to tensions with the church leaders. Academics in Christian studies programs have become well known internationally, and they are invited to conferences and study programs that were once solely the province of the churches. Ting and other Protestant leaders have charged that they do not sufficiently understand the patriotic Three-Self stance of Chinese Christians, and that they should not presume to speak for Christianity in China. Ting has written that some intellectuals like to emphasize "cultural exchange," not imperialism, in their study of the missionary movement, and that they do not sufficiently appreciate the challenges facing Chinese churches today.[111] Because the new generation did not live through the experiences of the churches in the struggle for Liberation, and because they have had little contact with the churches in the years since, TSPM/CCC leaders have questioned the social commitment and church understanding of university-based intellectuals.

Some academics in Christian studies have countered that the TSPM/CCC is out of touch with the churches, and still steeped in the struggles of the 1950s. Their criticisms have generally been implicit and indirect, but the tension is very real. It reflects the difference between the relative importance given to cultural criticism over against patriotism or national pride. This is in part a generational issue that extends far beyond those who are involved in theology and religious studies, and it has been discussed in different ways in Chinese academic publications.[112] The increasing involvement of intellectuals from "Greater China" in academic debates on the mainland, greater access to the Internet, and the increased freedom of expression have spurred lively intellectual exchanges on many once-forbidden subjects in Chinese history and politics. This has only begun to influence the study of history and theology in Chinese seminaries, but it will no doubt play a more important role in the future.

Theological reconstruction has only begun to be discussed overseas, and there have been both appreciative and critical responses. Some Asian Christians have praised the attempts of K. H. Ting to transform the conservative face of the church in China. Kim Yong-bock, a Korean minjung theologian, has suggested that theological reconstruction is also needed in other Asian churches, for they too are beset by problems inherited from the missionary past.[113] Ecumenical interpreters from Europe and North America have also offered positive assessments of theological reconstruction and the importance of Ting's theology. An American interpreter speaks of K. H. Ting's "banyan tree theology," while others have offered more thoughtful and well-grounded reflections on the importance of Ting's theology for China and the wider world.[114] In general, they have seen theological construction as a way of promoting dialogue between Christianity and the world beyond the church.

Evangelical voices in North America have given mixed reviews, from the openly critical to the guardedly supportive.[115] Critical evangelical voices from North America emphasize the political and ideological dimensions of theological reconstruction and resistance by house churches.[116] They tend to be polemical rather than reflective, at least as they are reported on the Internet. Other evangelicals have defended Ting's theological work over against his critics, arguing that he stands well within the mainstream of Christian theology.[117] As noted earlier, an evangelical publisher from the United States has reprinted an edition of Ting's writings, and the TSPM/CCC celebrated the occasion with a book launch in December 2004.[118]

Theological reconstruction continues to be promoted in the Chinese church, but by 2006, the debates were not as intense as they once had been. The different responses in China and overseas represent different visions for the future of the church. This is the polarization that K. H. Ting himself spoke about in 2001. Senior church leaders with strong theological positions are seldom able to bring people together by the power of their ideas. Yet Ting has played a unique role in the Chinese church, and he stands among a handful of twentieth-century Christian leaders all over the world who have had a significant impact not only on their own church but on the worldwide ecumenical movement. The varied responses to his theology reflect different interpretations of his life and work as a whole. As he entered his tenth decade, K. H. Ting had become a great deal more than a religious leader promoting theological reconstruction.

THE PUBLIC PRESENCE

Deng Xiaoping was referred to as China's paramount leader after he had stepped down from all his positions, and even when he could no longer exercise all the functions of his office. Like Deng, Ting became a pragmatic reformer, held in high regard inside and outside the church, in China and overseas. Today, he no longer concerns himself with the details of governance (*zheng*) or church affairs (*dao*), but he is consulted by government and church leaders, and his opinions are respected, if not always adopted. He continues to be involved in decision making at Nanjing Seminary (*xue*), but in practical terms, seminary leadership has now passed to a new generation.

The prestige and respect that come with old age, the challenges facing the church, and his own interest in developing a Chinese contextual theology have made it all but impossible for K. H. Ting to "retire" in any traditional sense of the word. He still seems to enjoy the activity and public attention that would tire a much younger man. He turned ninety in 2005; he moved more slowly and was often forgetful, but he continued to meet Chinese and foreign visitors.[119] Even after he turned ninety, he was invited to speak on public occasions and at celebrations. No one in the church could afford to ignore him or to underestimate his considerable authority. When K. H. Ting stepped down from his positions of national leadership in the TSPM and the CCC, he became, in effect, an elder statesman and church patriarch.

Ting hoped to put his stamp on Chinese theology as his final contribution to the reconstruction and renewal of the church. But not all his efforts at reconstruction are theological in nature. In mid-2004, church leaders began discussing the possibility of consecrating new bishops, something that K. H. Ting had hoped for because he believed the episcopacy was an essential element in the nature of the church.[120] The proposal came as a surprise to many people, and the response was mixed. Considerable opposition to bishops would come from some of the same sections of the church that had distanced themselves from theological reconstruction. There were reports late in 2004 that several new bishops would be selected the following year, but thus far, nothing has happened. The subject seems to have been put aside, at least for the time being, which means there is still uncertainty over the future of the historic episcopacy in China.

After decades of negotiations, the Holy Trinity Pro-Cathedral in Shanghai and its adjacent school building were returned to the church several years ago. The building has now become the new national office of the TSPM/CCC. Holy Trinity was the cathedral where K. H. Ting was ordained deacon and priest more than sixty years earlier. The cathedral fell into disuse in the 1950s, and had been a theater until well after the end of the Cultural Revolution. The local district government later used the adjacent school as its headquarters. Because of this, when the offices on Jiu Jiang Road were returned, very little renovation was needed. At the dedication ceremony in June 2004, K. H. Ting related the opening of the new offices and anticipated renovation to the ongoing efforts for theological reconstruction.

At the center of this cathedral is a pulpit, that when renovated, will become a model for Chinese Christianity which will lead innumerable pulpits all over our country toward the message of loving China and loving the church. Our churches have been promoting theological reconstruction for six or seven years now, leading Chinese Christians to a faith that upholds rational doctrines, opposes fanaticism, and shakes off heretical teachings. Jesus Christ revealed a loving God, a God who wants his creation to become better and better, filled with more and more love, overcoming all darkness and suffering, and leading more and more people to become co-workers with God. We hope that a new and healthy Christianity with Chinese characteristics can be adapted to science and culture, and mutually adapted to socialism, will be salt and light to the world and the focus of all peoples' attention.[121]

That same summer, Ting traveled to Hong Kong with other church leaders for the opening of an exhibit that was organized by the TSPM/CCC on Bible Ministry in China. The exhibit included Christian art and Bibles produced in China since the eighteenth century but focused on contemporary Bible publication and distribution on the mainland. It attracted a great deal of attention among Christians in Hong Kong, whose churches had been supporting Bible printing at the Amity Press in Nanjing. This was Ting's first visit to the territory in six years, and perhaps his last. In remarks at the opening ceremony, he stressed the importance of the Bible for Chinese Christians. Without directly mentioning theological reconstruction, he also alluded to his critique of fundamentalism and some of the important themes he had been speaking on over the last few years.

Christians in China study the Bible carefully and try to understand the word of God regarding Himself and human life, so as to actively respond to the call of proclaiming in this new century the good news that God is love. To be able to encounter and listen attentively to God's word, we must try to get rid of the improper understanding that all human good comes from the devil and the beauties of the world trap or corrupt people. We are in need of a kind of Christianity that helps people exalt justice, enhance moral sense and distinguish right from wrong . . . The churches in China highly value all positive moral and ethical influences in society, are concerned about the global environment we live in, and care about the marginalized people.[122]

K. H. Ting and WCC general secretary Sam Kobia, November 2006. Reproduced
with the permission of the WCC Archives.

In January 2005, a plan was unveiled for a vast seminary complex in the
new university district on the outskirts of Nanjing. Situated in an area that
will have thirteen other institutions of higher learning, the new seminary
will have facilities for five hundred students. The establishment of this campus reflects how far China and the Chinese church have come in the last
twenty-five years. Church leaders, seminary faculty and government officials were joined by friends and dignitaries from around the world to take
part in the historic groundbreaking ceremony. In his remarks prepared for
the occasion, K. H. Ting said that the building of the new seminary would
be accompanied by the advance of theological reconstruction. The new academic complex would train students "in a well-rounded way" in the Bible,
theology, history, philosophy and the arts.[123] He also had ideas about future
faculty development and a graduate program at the seminary.

K. H. Ting no longer had the energy to do all that he hoped, however. He
still attended important government and church meetings in 2006 and 2007,
but not as many as in the past. In November 2005, Ting delivered a speech
at the celebration of the twentieth anniversary of the Amity Foundation, of
which he is still president, but many visitors commented that he appeared
more frail than he had been in the past. A few days later, he spoke at the
groundbreaking of the new buildings for the Amity Printing Company, eigh-

teen years to the day after the dedication of the original printing press. Amity had grown to become one of the most effective NGOs in China, pioneering in areas ranging from HIV/AIDS education to migrant schooling to integrated rural development. By the end of 2005, the production of Bibles and New Testaments at the Amity Printing Company had reached 46 million, and surpassed 50 million in 2007.[124] The accomplishments of the Amity Foundation and the Amity Printing Company must also be seen as part of Ting's legacy to church and society in China.

In 2006, he continued to be involved at the seminary and meet with visitors, but he was no longer as active as he had been even a year earlier. His health had declined, yet he enjoyed being with friends and colleagues. Ting attended the memorial service for Han Wenzao in February 2006. It was held at the Mo Chou Road Church in Nanjing, just a few doors down from Ting's home. Ting and Han had had their differences in recent years, and they were never fully reconciled, but Ting still valued the role Han Wenzao had played in the TSPM/CCC and the Amity Foundation when they worked together. In late 2006, he met with Rowan Williams, the archbishop of Canterbury, and with Sam Kobia, general secretary of the World Council of Churches.

K. H. Ting's agenda remains unfinished, and it will not be possible for him to complete all that he had set out to do. More than anyone, he has understood the enormity of the challenges facing the church in China over the last three decades and the challenges that the church continues to face. His time is now running out. Ting's work in promoting theological reconstruction has been welcomed but controversial, but his contributions as a church leader have been widely recognized. Both must be seen from the perspective of his life as a whole.

Conclusion

Shortly before he retired as leader of the TSPM and the CCC in 1996, K. H. Ting was asked how he would like to be remembered.

I don't know, really, how to deal with this question. It was in the last few years that the Chinese church has begun to talk about *ban hao jiaohui*, running the church well. I think I am related to those four characters, that is, to do a good job in building up the life of the church. I will be very happy if I am remembered as one who has had something to do with running the church well.[1]

Ting was responding in an interview with a Hong Kong–based church magazine, and he chose to focus on his work for the church. If he were asked the same question by a journalist in China, he might have answered differently. But his response is significant just the same, for most of what he has been involved in throughout his life is related to the reconstruction and renewal of the church and its mission. This is what we have termed reconstructing Christianity in China.

K. H. Ting believed in the church because he grew up in the church. He was formed in the Christian faith at St. Peter's Church in Shanghai and through the piety of his mother, with whom he had a close relationship throughout his life. St. Peter's was Anglican-Episcopal in the liberal broad-church tradition, but it was an unusual parish insofar as it was already independent by the time Ting was baptized. In other words, he grew up in a church that was self-governing, self-supporting and self-propagating, and this was what he expected the church to be. St. Peter's was led by strong Chinese priests, two of whom later joined the Communist Party. It was an urban middle-class church, but the parish was very active in relief efforts from the 1920s to the time of Liberation.

Ting was introduced to the National Salvation movement while still a university student in the 1930s. He later became involved with the Student Christian Movement (SCM) and the YMCA, and was part of the circle of young people who gathered around Y. T. Wu. Wu had a deep and lasting influence on K. H. Ting, and helped to awaken the social and political consciousness of a generation of Christian young people. Ting became a leader in the SCM, and during the Japanese occupation, he helped to organize the Student Church, which met in Shanghai Community Church, where Ting served as pastor. Other than his service as curate at Sheng Gong Hui parishes in Shanghai, this was Ting's only pastorate. He ministered to a very diverse ecumenical congregation, which helped him understand and relate to the international community. All during this time, he also maintained close relationships with the progressive underground movement in Shanghai and helped mobilize young people in the Student Church. Through this involvement, he met many CPC members, some of whom became government officials after 1949, many of whom became lifelong friends.

After the end of the war, K. H. and his wife, Siu-may, went overseas for service and further studies. They became part of a new generation in the ecumenical movement, which was then attracting some of the most socially committed men and women from churches all over the world. In Canada, at Union Seminary in New York, and in the World Students' Christian Federation in Geneva, Ting made many lifelong friendships. His ecumenical experience helped him develop a theological and political perspective on the international reality of the church that would be valuable for China in the 1950s, and once again in the 1980s and the decades since. He did this without ever losing his commitment to the movement for progressive social change in China or his determination to return to his country and serve his church.

When Ting and his family returned to Shanghai in 1951, they encountered the reality of the "New China." Y. T. Wu and many of Ting's colleagues from the student movement and the YMCA were working to give shape to the Chinese Christian Three-Self Patriotic Movement of the Protestant Churches of China (TSPM), and Ting became part of this project. He did not become a Three-Self "activist," however, and he did not participate in the Denunciation Movement. Within months of his return, Ting met Premier Zhou Enlai, who had an enormous influence on Ting's life and thought. More than Mao Zedong, Deng Xiaoping or any of his successors, Zhou Enlai was the CPC leader that Ting and many others from his generation admired most.

In 1952, Ting was named principal of Nanjing Union Theological Seminary, a position he still holds. He also became an important theological voice in China and an ecumenical spokesman for China in the West. Although he was not a TSPM insider in the 1950s, he was unwavering in his support for Y. T. Wu and the Three-Self principle, and he was critical of conservative Christians who attacked the TSPM. In the late 1950s, Ting embraced the ultra-leftist political line that was to shape every aspect of Chinese life until the end of the Cultural Revolution era. He took part in the Anti-Rightist movement, and continued to support the radical policies of Mao Zedong at the beginning of the Cultural Revolution. The more he learned about radical politics, however, the more skeptical he became. At least by the early 1970s, Ting had rejected the radicalism of the Cultural Revolution, and he subsequently became an unwavering critic of ultra-leftism. In the late 1970s, Ting emerged as China's most important Christian leader, and he soon began the task of rebuilding the church and reconstructing Christianity in China.

At the beginning of his tenure as Christian leader in the 1980s, Ting proposed the slogan *ban hao jiaohui,* or "running the church well." This was a development beyond the narrow and increasingly politicized emphasis of Three-Self patriotism in the 1950s. He suggested the formation of the China Christian Council (CCC) in 1980 as a body parallel to the TSPM that would be devoted to church matters. This was designed to appeal to the many Christians who had suffered during the Cultural Revolution and were alienated from the official structures. Three-Self patriotism had been the cornerstone of the TSPM since the 1950s, but it had often been interpreted in heavy-handed political terms. Ting consistently supported Three-Self patriotism, but he insisted that the church was the Body of Christ, and, as such, must be well run as well as self-run. The CCC was created to give attention to "the work that is the church's own."

This meant that the relationship between the TSPM and the churches would in some ways have to be changed or reordered. In the late 1980s, Ting said time and again that the TSPM was a scaffolding for building up the church. Once the church had been firmly established, the scaffolding would no longer be needed. Not all other national leaders agreed with him. Ecclesiologically, there was no way to explain the TSPM as anything but a temporary structure that came into being at a certain point in history; it helped to maintain a Christian presence during difficult times; and would one day fade out of existence. There had been an activist or ultra-leftist element in the TSPM from the beginning, but there had also been Three-Self leaders who continued to uphold the church and its Christian witness. It was this concern for the church that he sought to enhance and bring to the fore as TSPM/CCC leader, without in any way weakening the patriotic stance of Chinese Christians.

In the 1980s, the political movements of the past were being criticized all over China. The TSPM had begun in the early 1950s, but it was now institutionalized and no longer a movement in the original sense of the word. Still, some leaders continued to seek answers to new challenges by looking back to the struggles of the 1950s. In contrast, Ting and many other colleagues in the TSPM/CCC looked to the future as they worked for a broader Christian unity and envisioned the possibility that the China Christian Council would one day become the Christian Church of China. We see in retrospect that he was unable to do very much institutionally in reordering relationships between the TSPM and the churches, for there were entrenched interests at stake. The scaffolding is still there, but the TSPM/CCC has become somewhat more responsive to the needs of local churches in the ten years since Ting stepped down, and Protestant churches are growing all over China. This too reflects the vision of K. H. Ting and other leaders in building up the Body of Christ in a spirit of love and mutual respect.

The policy of "mutual respect" was also an expression of Ting's emphasis on running the church well. He developed this idea in the 1950s as principal of Nanjing Union Theological Seminary, when students, faculty and staff from diverse theological backgrounds had to learn to live and work together. Ting learned about mutual respect as a strategy for Christian unity in the ecumenical movement. A generation earlier, T. T. Lew (Liu Tingfang, 1891-1947) had made famous a similar idea in the Chinese National Christian Council, "We should agree to differ and resolve to love." In the 1980s, Ting reached out to conservative and sectarian Christians to persuade them that participation in the TSPM and the CCC would not compromise their beliefs. He spoke of the importance of mutual respect in matters of faith, and although he convinced some, many others stayed away. At the same time, he urged Three-Self veterans to practice mutual respect in their relationships with more conservative Christians, but here too he was only partially successful. Mutual respect was needed for "building up the body of Christ in love." This was what "running the church well is all about." Ting recognized that many Christians in the TSPM/CCC, like the Christians of Ephesus (Revelation 2:1-7), had abandoned the love they once had.

Mutual respect suggested that Christians could dwell in unity and work together despite their differences because they had a common belief in Jesus Christ. Ting wrote the inscription that appears on the cornerstone of a new church building that he dedicated in Wenzhou: "Jesus Christ Is the Head of the Church." This simple statement of faith has been the affirmation of Christians for over two millennia, and it implies the independence of the church from any form of outside control. If Jesus Christ is the head of the church, there can be no other head.

In China, there has never been a tradition of the separation of church and state or of religion from politics, but this has not meant that recognized religious structures are entirely subservient to the government. China's religious policy has changed enormously over the last thirty years, and there is today greater religious freedom in China than there has ever been. This is mostly due to the efforts of government officials themselves. As TSPM/CCC leader, Ting tried to create more space for the church by working for reform *within*, not *against*, established political structures. This sometimes meant that he came into conflict with government officials over the implementation of religious policy or the imposition of new regulations. He has always been a government loyalist and a patriot. He believes in the People's Republic of China, but this has not blinded him to the abuses of government power and policy that have continued to hamper the work of the church since the beginning of the period of openness and reform.

Even before he became TSPM/CCC leader, Ting challenged the view that it was the responsibility of the state to supervise religious activities. He pressed for the freedom to print Bibles, open seminaries, train new leaders and reclaim churches that had been occupied during the Cultural Revolution. He spoke out on behalf of Christian home-worship gatherings, arguing that they should be able to worship in their own way, provided they adhered to the Three-Self principle. He advocated for more openness in the wording of the constitutional provision on religious freedom. He addressed many specific instances of the abuse of religious policy that were brought to his attention by local churches. He worked to improve statements and regulations on religious policy. He criticized government officials' interference in the internal affairs of local TSPM committees, Christian councils and churches. He took the lead in establishing the Amity Foundation as a Christian initiative to serve society and make Christian presence more widely known. In countless ways, he tried to defend and protect the church, even as he regularly made public statements in support of Chinese government policies and China's right to go its own way.

In the 1980s and 1990s, Ting emphasized the importance of principled "legal struggle" for the rights of the church. In this struggle, he believed one should sacrifice neither one's principles nor oneself. It is of no use to strike eggs against a rock in an attempt to break it. It is always important to work with integrity for reform no matter how difficult the situation seems. China has changed enormously over the past three decades, and this is partly due to the efforts of religious and political leaders such as K. H. Ting who believe in working for what is possible. His principled pragmatism has meant negotiating for structural change while accepting the limitations of the existing political system, at least provisionally.

Not all Christians are willing to accept this position. Ting's support for the CPC and his approach to working for change within the existing system have been criticized by Chinese dissidents and some house-church leaders, and by Western human-rights activists and Christian advocates for religious freedom. This is one reason why the unfounded suspicions that he is a secret Communist Party member will not go away. There were secret CPC members who worked in the TSPM, but Ting has repeatedly asserted that he was not among them. Many other non-Communist intellectuals from his generation have taken a political stance similar to his. They have done so not for reasons of political expedience but in order to work for greater freedom and the betterment of society in a situation of limited possibilities. Ting has never hidden his political views, and he has chosen to work constructively within a Communist political system that he supports.

Unlike many others, Ting has been forthright about the mistakes he personally made in supporting extremist and ultra-leftist policies in the 1950s and 1960s, particularly during the Anti-Rightist movement and the early years of the Cultural Revolution. Since the late 1970s, he has been an unrelenting critic of ultra-leftism, and this has been reflected in all he tried to do as church leader.

Wolfgang Schmidt, former president of the Basel Mission in Switzerland, was deeply impressed by Ting after they first met in the 1980s. He later wrote,

> K. H. Ting is not a "red bishop." One of the greatest sins of Western Christianity is to accuse everyone, who still shows vital signs after a socialist take-over, of being a traitor. Christianity did not, does not,

and will not survive just because of its martyrs and rigid doctrine. Christianity had, and still has a chance only because of those who are able to bridge tense and wordless situations.[2]

Ting's influence in China has much to do with his approach to dialogue with the powers that be. This dialogue does not involve discussion and debate over political and religious beliefs; it is the much more difficult day-to-day dialogue over how to cooperate and work together despite genuine differences in faith and ideology.

To be effective politically and to bridge the "wordless situations," Ting has relied on the friendship and support of CPC leaders throughout his career. He came to know a number of Communists when he was working for the YMCA in the 1930s and early 1940s, and many became lifelong friends. Gong Peng was one of these, and she introduced Ting to Zhou Enlai shortly after he returned from Geneva. We have argued that Zhou helped to promote and protect Ting over the next two decades, something he no doubt did for other intellectuals as well, including Zhao Puchu. Ting counted other Communist leaders as good friends, including Feng Wenbin, Zhang Zhiyi, Luo Zhufeng, Kuang Yaming, and Yan Mingfu. They were all united-front-oriented Communists, and many suffered during the Cultural Revolution as they tried to maintain the courage of their convictions. Ting has been a patriotic supporter of the CPC and the united front, and throughout the years of openness and reform he has used the means available to him to pursue dialogue with government officials and friends in high places in order to create more space for the church and more openness in society.

Dialogue is important not only with government officials in China but also with Christians in the wider *oikoumene*. K. H. Ting has repeatedly said that "self-isolation" is not one of the Three-Self principles, and that a well-run church should not be cut off from the rest of the world. He believes that Chinese Christians can learn from and contribute to the broader ecumenical experience. Since his early work in the Shanghai Student Christian Movement, Ting has been a committed ecumenist. In his years overseas, in receiving visitors at home and in traveling abroad in the 1950s and 1960s, in his leadership of the TSPM/CCC in the 1980s and 1990s, and in retirement, Ting worked tirelessly for mutual understanding between Christians in China and other parts of the world. His wife, Siu-may, contributed to this outreach to the world until her death in 1995.

More than any other Chinese Christian, K. H. Ting has worked for mutual respect and improved relationships with churches in other countries. Without his concerted efforts, the China Christian Council would not have joined the World Council of Churches in 1991. He has also tried to promote mutual understanding with evangelical Christians overseas. Ting has had less interest in Roman Catholic–Protestant ecumenism or in interfaith dialogue, despite his cooperation with Zhao Puchu and Catholic bishops such as Jin Luxian on the implementation of religious policy. This may be one of the limitations of the church in China, where Catholic–Protestant as well as interreligious relations have not been as prominent as they have been in the ecumenical movement as a whole, or in countries as diverse as India, Japan or the United States.

K. H. Ting has been interested in theology since his studies at St. John's and Union Theological Seminary in New York, and his work in the SCM. We have argued that he has been remarkably consistent in his approach to theology. Although it is important to see his theology developmentally, he has continued to draw on the liberal, Anglican and ecumenical categories of understanding that he learned in the 1930s and 1940s. His theology has been in dialogue with his times: in the 1940s when he was WSCF secretary; in the 1950s, when he was principal of Nanjing Seminary; and since the late 1970s, when he became TSPM/CCC leader. He has not been interested in systematic, historical or philosophical theology, but in the political and religious issues of his context, and in the ethical witness that can help Christians play a more constructive role in society. As a political theologian, the traditional categories of church and country are more characteristic of Ting's writing than any radical understanding of faith and revolution. As a church theologian, he has attempted to respond to new challenges in the period of openness and reform. Since his retirement, he has promoted "theological reconstruction" in order to facilitate the adaptation of the church to Chinese society.

In Ting's understanding, theological reconstruction has been an extension of running the church well, for a well-run church should have its own theology, one that enables it to respond to the times. That theology should bear witness to God's love, confront Christian fundamentalism, play down the differences between believers and nonbelievers and give greater attention to social involvement. There is also a need for "mutual adaptation" between Christianity and Chinese society in order to facilitate the mission of the church and contribute to society. Ting's own theology has been a useful corrective to the narrow one-sidedness of Chinese evangelicalism, which has tended to close the church off from its social and cultural milieu.

The theological-reconstruction initiative has been important and necessary, but it may be one of the more controversial dimensions of K. H. Ting's legacy to the Chinese church, at least for some. In 1980, Zhang Zhiyi, who was then deputy head of the UFWD, said the TSPM should see itself as a locomotive pulling many carriages. It needed to move slowly forward and not leave grassroots Christians behind. Ting used to quote these words with approval. To race ahead as activist leaders had done in the past separated the TSPM from the masses of believers. However, theological reconstruction alienated some grassroots Christians, younger theologians and local pastors, at least when it first began. They saw it, rightly or wrongly, as an attempt to change theology too quickly, or to impose on the churches a theology that they were unable to accept. The government seems to have stressed not "mutual adaptation" but a one-sided adaptation of Christian theology to socialist society and government policy. This may not have been Ting's own intention, but it is the way that theological reconstruction has sometimes appeared to those who have withheld their support.

This is part of the reason why some younger theologians, trained at NUTS, have left the church or distanced themselves from the TSPM. It is also part of the reason why academics in religious studies have not embraced theological reconstruction. In 1990, the then–associate dean of Nanjing Seminary, preached a sermon entitled "Some Things Left Undone." In printed form and in translation, it is a careful and nuanced interpretation of Jethro's advice to Moses (Exodus 18:13-37) that even though Moses is leader of the people of Israel, he should not try to do everything himself. Some things need to be left undone and entrusted to God; in other things one must rely on one's colleagues, including those in the younger generation.[3] The sermon was suggesting in the gentlest and most indirect way possible that the older generation should not try to do everything on its own.

There is a generation gap in the church in China, as there is in many churches in the world today. In China, this disparity is widely felt but seldom spoken about or analyzed. As of this writing, the TSPM/CCC is still led by a cohort of women and men in their seventies who have given enormous time and energy to the work of the church, but who have in some ways, consciously or unconsciously, inhibited a new generation from assuming positions of leadership. The situation is changing, especially in provincial-level TSPMs and Christian councils, as capable younger leaders are given important positions and responsibilities. There will be even greater changes at the Eighth National Christian Conference, scheduled to be held in late 2007. Since the early 1980s, Ting has tried to nurture a new generation of leadership for the churches, especially at Nanjing Seminary. Yet the promotion of men and women of talent that is so vital for the future stands as a great task that still awaits completion.

K. H. Ting may one day be criticized in China in the same way that church leaders in Eastern Europe were criticized after the fall of the Berlin Wall. My hope in writing this book is that his critics will also remember all that he was able to accomplish and make possible for future generations. Under Ting's leadership, Christianity in China assumed a higher profile than at any time in its history.

A government official I know who is involved in religious affairs greatly admires K. H. Ting. But she has called him a tragic figure because he continues to hold onto ideals that he knows cannot be realized, at least in his lifetime. I would not call him a tragic figure, but a Christian and a patriot who holds onto a sense of idealism, despite the need to continually make adjustments.

There is a Confucian saying to this effect: "one knows it cannot be done, and yet one tries to do it anyway" (*zhi qi bu ke wei, er wei zhi*).[4] Ting's efforts to promote running the church well, the reordering of relationships, the separation of church and state, the critique of ultra-leftism and theological reconstruction are examples of these ideals. Because he is a "pragmatic idealist," he would say that even if his hopes cannot be realized, they are still worth fighting for, because something can be accomplished in the process. Talking about change is never enough. Pressing on toward the goal is important, for it helps to create the conditions for further changes.

Ting became China's most important Christian leader at a time when his country and his church were in need of radical change. The change had to be decisive, but not so disruptive as to result in political chaos or violent revolution. The political system itself was flawed, but it was all there was to work with. Ting shared in the hope and possibilities of the period of openness and reform, but also in its limitations and weaknesses. He has tried to put the church on more solid institutional footing, create space for its growth and renewal, and make possible greater public expression and mission outreach. He has also moved too quickly at times or has shown insufficient trust in younger people who hold different opinions.

Ting has made his share of mistakes, but he has never been troubled by self-doubt and he always sought to pick up where he left off and move forward. In the early 1980s, he discovered a poem by Bertolt Brecht which delighted him. He was particularly fond of quoting its last stanza.

> Alas, we
> Who wished to lay the foundation of kindness,
> Could not ourselves be kind.
> But you, when at last it comes to pass,
> That man can help his fellow man,
> Do not judge us too harshly.[5]

One cannot help but think that in reading this poem and commending it to others, he was also thinking about his own generation, the turbulent times in which they had lived and how they would be understood in the future.

Other international church leaders who risked new paths were also controversial in their lifetimes. Josef Hromádka has been mentioned in these pages as a theologian who attempted to bridge the gap between East and West in the ecumenical movement during the Cold War. Milan Opočenský, Hromádka's student and Ting's friend, is another example of such a theologian and ecumenical leader. Their work is today being debated in the Czech Republic, where they have been criticized because of their sympathy to Marxism.

A more fitting comparison to Ting might be V. S. Azariah (1874-1945), the first Anglican bishop of India.[6] Like Ting, Azariah was nurtured in the YMCA, and he was committed to Christian involvement in politics and society. He was an Indian patriot, who was at different times a supporter and a foe of Gandhi in the struggle for independence. Criticized by many in his own church, Azariah was an outstanding ecumenist who played a major role in the formation of the Church of South India. The YMCA of Azariah's youth was not the same as Ting's, nor was Azariah's separation from the missionaries as decisive. But V. S. Azariah and K. H. Ting were controversial leaders because they broke with the missionary Christianity that had nurtured them, and, in their own ways, tried to reconstruct a church that would be true to the mission of Jesus Christ in their own contexts.

In China, Ting's political stance was similar to that of other intellectuals in his generation. He shared his life and vision with his wife of fifty-three years, Siu-may Kuo, who was an intellectual in her own right. Zheng Jianye was closest to him in the church, but he never attained the same political stature, and he suffered greatly as he tried to remain true to his beliefs and convictions during the Cultural Revolution. Ting had many other friends in the TSPM and the churches who were close to him theologically, and he would always say that whatever he has been able to accomplish was part of a collective effort.

The Buddhist leader Zhao Puchu has been described in this book as a friend who worked closely with Ting during the period of reform and openness. Nearly a decade older than Ting, Zhao also became committed to the cause of liberation in the Shanghai of the 1930s, worked within the political system after 1949, and contributed to the reforms of the 1980s and 1990s. In the upstairs study of the Ting home on Mo Chou Road, there hangs a small piece of calligraphy that Zhao Puchu wrote in November 1997. It is inscribed, "To my brother Guangxun," and translated reads:

> Prudent reflection and even judgment,
>   Treating all with consideration,
> Neither excited nor overbearing,
>   The ancient ways and rules are with us still.[7]

This couplet was written by Sun Guoting (648-703), a Tang Dynasty poet and calligrapher. Sun was describing the virtues to which any Chinese leader concerned with governance (*zheng*), ethics or religion (*dao*) and scholarship (*xue*) should aspire, but which no one can fully live up to. Zhao Puchu's choice of this couplet for his friend was most appropriate. In his manner, his thought and his actions, K. H. Ting has sought to live by these ways and rules, and interpret them through the faith he believes in for the church and the country that he loves.

Notes

INTRODUCTION

1. See Philip L. Wickeri, "The Chinese Delegation at the Third World Conference on Religion and Peace, August 28-September 8, 1979: A Report," unpublished manuscript, 14 pp.

2. Jung Chang and Jon Halliday, *Mao: The Unknown Story* (New York: Knopf, 2005).

3. See, for example, the critical assessment by Joseph Esherick and comments from other scholars: http://orpheus.ucsd.edu/chinesehistory/mao/Mao.htm (accessed 9 September 2006).

4. Robert Lawrence Kuhn, *The Man Who Changed China: The Life and Legacy of Jiang Zemin* (New York: Crown Publishers, 2005).

5. Gao Wenqian, *Wannian Zhou Enlai (The Latter Years of Zhou Enlai)* (Hong Kong: Mirror Books, 2003).

6. Vera Schwarcz, *The Time for Telling Truth Is Running Out: Conversations with Zhang Shenfu* (New Haven and London: Yale University Press, 1992).

7. Biographical studies of Y. T. Wu have ranged from the official and hagiographic to the critical and academic. In Chinese, Shen Derong has written a highly sympathetic official biography, *Wu Yaozong xiao zhuan (A Short Biography of Wu Yaozong)* (Shanghai: TSPM, 1989). A more academic study, focusing on the development of Y. T. Wu's political and religious thought is Chen Chi-Rong, *Wu Yao-Tsung: Ein Theologe im sozialistischen China* (Munster and Hamburg: LiT Verlag, 1991). Leung Ka-lun has written a highly critical study of Wu's religious and political role, *Wu Yaozong san lun (Y. T. Wu's Understandings of Christianity and Its Relation to Chinese Communism)* (Hong Kong: Alliance Bible Seminary, 1996). In addition to the biographies of Y. T. Wu, there have also been studies of Wu's critics published in recent years, including Wang Mingdao, Watchman Nee, Chen Chonggui, Samuel Lam (Lin Xiangao), and Allen Yuan. Ng Lee-ming's comparative study of Y. T. Wu, T. C. Chao and Wang Mingdao, though dated, remains a reliable source, "Christianity and Social Change in China, 1920-1950," (Ph.D. diss., Princeton Theological Seminary, 1970).

8. There is a renewed interest in the theology of T. C. Chao in China today. Four volumes of his collected works are being published as *Zhao Zichen wenji* (Beijing: Commercial Press, 2003 and following). For a short biography of T. C. Chao in English, see Winfried Glüer, "T. C. Chao: Scholar, Teacher and Gentle Mystic," in *Mission Legacies: Biographical Studies of the Modern Missionary Movement*, ed. Gerald H. Anderson et al. (Maryknoll, N.Y.: Orbis Books, 1998), 225-31.

9. Ma Jia also draws on interviews with others who have been close to Ting,

including this author. See Ma Jia, *Ai shi zhenli* (*Discerning Truth through Love*) (Hong Kong: Chinese Christian Literature Council, 2006).

10. See, for example, Marites N. Sison, "The Last Anglican Bishop," *Anglican Journal* (October 2005) (accessed 13 October 2005 at http://anglicanjournal. com/131/08/world02.html). For a lengthy interview published just before his retirement in 1996, see "Running the Church Well: A Conversation with K. H. Ting," *Areopagus* 9, no. 4 (Winter/Spring 1997): 8-11, 33-35.

11. For an overview of the state-secrets law in China, see "Labor and State Secrets" http://hrichina.org/public/PDFs/labor-statesecrets.pdf (accessed 20 June 2007).

12. *Ding Guangxun wenji* (*The Collected Works of K. H. Ting*) (Nanjing: Yilin Press, 1998); and K. H. Ting, *Love Never Ends: Papers by K. H. Ting*, ed. Janice K. Wickeri (Nanjing: Yilin Press, 2000). I am thanked in both publications for my assistance in collecting some hard-to-find essays.

13. Perry Link, Richard Madsen and Paul G. Pickowicz, eds., *Unofficial China: Popular Culture and Thought in the People's Republic* (Boulder, Colo.: Westview Press, 1989), 9.

14. Barbara Tuchman, as quoted in Marc Pachter, *Telling Lives: The Biographer's Art* (Washington: New Republic Books, 1979), 133.

15. Timothy Cheek, "From Priests to Professionals: Intellectuals and the State Under the CCP," in *Popular Protest and Political Culture in Modern China: Learning from 1989*, ed. Jeffrey N. Wasserstrom and Elizabeth J. Perry (Boulder, Colo.: Westview Press, 1992), 128, 135 and passim. See chap. 7 for a further exploration of these ideas.

16. See my earlier discussion of the subject in Philip L. Wickeri, *Seeking the Common Ground: Protestant Christianity, the Three-Self Movement and China's United Front* (Maryknoll, N.Y.: Orbis Books, 1988), 177-79.

17. Marc Pachter, *Telling Lives*, 5, 20.

1. THE EARLY YEARS, 1915-1937

1. As quoted by K. H. Ting in "One Chinese Christian's View of God," unpublished lecture at Union Theological Seminary in the Philippines, October 1993, p. 10. Ting uses a longer version of this quotation in a post-Christmas circular letter dated February 1994 sent to friends overseas.

2. The figures are from F. L. Hawks Pott, *A Short History of Shanghai* (Shanghai: Kelly and Walsh, 1928), 211; Nicholas Clifford, *Spoilt Children of Empire: Westerners in Shanghai and the Chinese Revolution of the 1920s* (Hanover and London: University Press of New England, 1991), 9; and *All about Shanghai and Environs* (Shanghai: University Press, 1934-35), 33ff. Population figures from the International Settlement and the French Concession are more accurate than for Shanghai as a whole.

3. L. A. Lyall, writing of the British in 1934, as quoted in Clifford, *Spoilt Children of Empire*.

4. Clifford, *Spoilt Children of Empire*, 52.

5. Marie-Claire Bergere, *The Golden Age of the Chinese Bourgeoisie, 1911-1937* (Cambridge: Cambridge University Press, 1989).

6. Emily Honig, *Sisters and Strangers: Women in the Shanghai Cotton Mills, 1919-1949* (Stanford: Stanford University Press, 1986), 24-25.

7. K. H. Ting prefers to use the old romanization of his name rather than the *pinyin* form now in common usage. In this book, names are romanized in *pinyin*, except in cases where individuals are known to have another preference or where the older romanization is customary. Thus, Ting's father becomes Ding Chufan, his mother, Li Jinglan, etc.

8. Zhou Jiacai, *Zhao Puchu yu Jiangsu zongjiao (Zhao Puchu and Religion in Jiangsu)* (Beijing: Zongjiao wenhua chubanshe, 2003), 34.

9. Susan Mann Jones, "The Ningpo *Pang* and Financial Power in Shanghai," in *The Chinese City between Two Worlds,* ed. Mark Elvin and G. William Skinner (Stanford: Stanford University Press, 1974), 84. I am indebted to this article (pp. 74-96) for the information contained in the last two paragraphs.

10. *District of Shanghai Newsletter* 1, no. 1 (April 1915): 2.

11. K. H. Ting, interview with the author, Nanjing, China, 31 October 1990.

12. Siu-may Kuo (Guo Xiumei), interview with the author, Nanjing, China, 9 June 1991.

13. K. H. Ting, "The Cosmic Christ" (1991) in K. H. Ting, *Love Never Ends: Papers by K. H. Ting,* ed. Janice K. Wickeri (Nanjing: Yilin Press, 2000), 417.

14. See K. H. Ting, "That You Be Trustworthy," *CTR* (1991): 127.

15. For additional stories on Ting's family life and upbringing, see Ma Jia, *Ai shi zhenli (Discerning Truth through Love)* (Hong Kong: Chinese Christian Literature Council, 2006), passim.

16. Yao Minchuan, *Shanghai jidujiaoshi, 1843-1949 (A History of Christianity in Shanghai, 1843-1949)* (Shanghai: Shanghai Christian Council and TSPM Committee, 1993), 12-18.

17. Kenneth S. Latourette, *A History of Christian Missions in China* (London: S.P.C.K., 1929), 664.

18. *District of Shanghai Newsletter* 23, no. 5 (May 1937): 9-10.

19. *Shanghai Sheng Bide Tang ershi zhou zili jiniankan (Commemorative Volume on the Twentieth Anniversary of Independence of St. Peter's Church),* September 1933, p. 5.

20. Edgar Snow, *Red Star Over China* (London: Victor Gollancz, 1968), 47. Also see Thomas Kampen, "The Secret Life of Pastor Wang," *CCP Research Newsletter,* 2 (Spring 1989): 7-8.

21. Kampen, "Secret Life," 7. Other observations in this paragraph are from K. H. Ting, interview with the author, Nanjing, China, 16 December 1990. According to Chang and Halliday, Dong Jianwu and his former wife helped to raise two of Mao Zedong's children, Mao Anying and Mao Anqing; see Jung Chang and Jon Halliday, *Mao: The Unknown Story* (New York: Knopf, 2005), 184.

22. For a biographical sketch of Pu Huaren, see Edward Yihua Xu, "Religion and Education: St. John's University as an Evangelizing Agency" (Ph.D. diss., Princeton University, 1994), 173-78.

23. Rev. P. N.Tsu (Zhu Baoyuan), former deacon at St. Peter's, even spoke of "four selfs," adding "self-standing" *(zili),* a well-educated and qualified membership, to the other three. See *Shanghai Sheng Bide Tang ershi zhou zili jiniankan,* 38.

24. F. L. H. Pott as quoted in Mary Lamberton, *St. John's University, Shanghai, 1879-1951* (New York: United Board for Christian Colleges in China, 1955), 159.

25. Lamberton, *St. John's University, Shanghai, 1879-1951*, 158, 164.

26. K. H. Ting, interview with the author, Nanjing, China, 31 October 1990.

27. "The Chinese Bridge," *The Johannean 1934* (Shanghai), page unnumbered.

28. K. H. Ting, "The Cosmic Christ" (1991), in *Love Never Ends*, 417.

29. R. O. Hall, *T. Z. Koo: Chinese Christianity Speaks to the West* (London: SCM Press, 1950), 9.

30. *The St. John's Daily* 17, no. 7 (30 October 1936): 1.

31. *The St. John's Daily* 17, no. 7 (30 October 1936): 3.

32. K. H. Ting, interview with the author, Nanjing, China, 20 June 1982.

33. Charles Gore, "The Brotherhood of St. Andrew," in *St. Paul's Epistle to the Ephesians* (London: John Murray, 1898), 265.

34. K. H. Ting, "Youth and Religion," *Qingnian tuan kan (St. Peter's Youth Magazine)* (June 1936): 46-49. Translated in *CTR* 10 (1995): 7-9. Ting's theological essay reflects the social perspective of Pu Huaren in the same issue of *Qingnian tuan kan*, 42-44.

35. For an excellent study of Communist activity in Shanghai during this period, see Patricia Stranahan, *Underground: The Shanghai Communist Party and the Politics of Survival, 1927-1937* (Lanham, Md.: Rowman & Littlefield, 1998), 197 and passim.

36. K. H. Ting, interview with the author, Nanjing, China, 31 October 1990.

37. *The Johannean 1937* (Shanghai), page unnumbered.

2. LIFE AND WORK IN OCCUPIED SHANGHAI, 1937-1945

1. From Wen Yiduo's poem, "The Red Candle" (written in 1941), as quoted in K. H. Ting, *The Experience of the Church in China* (Cincinnati: Forward Movement Publications, 1984), 10.

2. *District of Shanghai Newsletter* 24, no. 3 (March 1938): 10; 24, no. 4 (April 1938): 7; 24, no. 9 (October 1938): 21; 24, no. 10 (November-December 1938): 7.

3. Poshek Fu, *Passivity, Resistance and Collaboration: Intellectual Choices in Occupied Shanghai, 1937-1995* (Stanford: Stanford University Press, 1993), xiv, 5-6. I am indebted to Fu Poshek for much of the analysis that follows.

4. Poshek Fu, *Passivity, Resistance and Collaboration*, 155.

5. For my earlier reflection on Y. T. Wu and the relationship between Communists and Christians in the 1930s and 1940s, see Philip L. Wickeri, *Seeking the Common Ground: Protestant Christianity, the Three-Self Movement and China's United Front* (Maryknoll, N.Y.: Orbis Books, 1988), 122-27. Also see Philip Wickeri, "The Christian Movement in Shanghai on the Eve of Liberation, 1946-1954"; and Chi-Rong Chen, *Wu Yao-Tsung: Ein Theologe im sozialistischen China* (Munster and Hamburg: LiT Verlag, 1991).

6. For an excellent overview, see Daniel H. Bays, "The Growth of Independent Christianity in China, 1900-1937," in Daniel Bays, ed., *Christianity in China: From the Eighteenth Century to the Present* (Stanford: Stanford University Press, 1996), 307-17.

7. K. H. Ting, "Forerunner Y. T. Wu," in *Huiyi Wu Yaozong xiansheng (In Memory of Y .T. Wu)* (Shanghai: TSPM Committee, 1982), 92, translated in K. H. Ting, *Love Never Ends: Papers by K. H. Ting,* ed. Janice K. Wickeri (Nanjing: Yilin Press, 2000), 72-85. Also by K. H. Ting, see "What Can We Learn from Y. T. Wu Today?"; and "The Ever-Renewing Mr. Y. T. Wu," in K. H. Ting, *Love Never Ends,* 328-38, 365-71. Of the three essays, "Forerunner Y. T. Wu" is the most personal reflection on Ting's relationship to Wu.

8. Hu Guotai, "The Struggle Between the Kuomintang and the Chinese Communist Party on Campus during the War of Resistance, 1937-1945," *China Quarterly* 118 (June 1989): 305 and passim. Hu's analysis is based on records from government universities and he does not treat the Christian colleges.

9. See Patricia Stranahan, *Underground: The Shanghai Communist Party and the Politics of Survival, 1927-1937,* passim.

10. See Patricia Stranahan, "Strange Bedfellows: The Communist Party and Shanghai's Elite in the National Salvation Movement," *China Quarterly* 129 (March 1992): 26-51. Also see Stranahan, *Underground: The Shanghai Communist Party and the Politics of Survival, 1927-1937,* passim.

11. The analysis in this paragraph is from Edward Yihua Xu, "Religion and Education: St. John's University as an Evangelizing Agency" (Ph.D. diss., Princeton University, 1994), 178-79.

12. The rumor about Ting's supposed membership in the CPC has been most recently repeated by David Aikman, *Jesus in Beijing: How Christianity Is Transforming China and Changing the Global Balance of Power* (Washington: Regnery Publishing, 2003), 145-46.

13. Stranahan, *Underground,* 218.

14. Stranahan, *Underground,* 225.

15. K. H. Ting, interview with the author, Nanjing, China, 16 December 1990.

16. K. H. Ting to Chris Woehr (News Network International), 17 April 1989; K. H. Ting to Chan Young Choi, 12 July 1989; K. H. Ting interview with the author, Nanjing, China, 16 December 1990.

17. K. H. Ting, interview with the author, Nanjing, China, 16 December 1990.

18. *St. John's Bulletin* 4 (December 29, 1937): 1. Ting's name appears as Ting Kwang-Hyuin in this and other St. John's publications.

19. Mary Lamberton, *St. John's University, Shanghai, 1879-1951* (New York: United Board for Christian Colleges in China, 1955), 186.

20. Wang Min, ed., *Shanghai xuesheng yundong dashi ji, 1919.5-1949.9 (Chronology of the Shanghai Student Movement, May 1919 to September 1949)* (Shanghai: Shanghai Communist Youth League/Youth Movement History Faculty, 1985), 205. On the role of Christian organizations in the resistance movement, see Ruan Renze and Gao Zhennong, eds., *Shanghai Zongjiao shi (A Religious History of Shanghai)* (Shanghai: Shanghai renmin chubanshe, 1992), 1016-17.

21. See Ruan Renze and Gao Zhennong, eds., *Shanghai Zongjiao shi (A Religious History of Shanghai),* 1017. On Huang Peiyong, see K. H. Ting, "Remembering a Friend: On the 30th Anniversary of the Death of Huang Peiyong," in *Love Never Ends,* 419-20. Zheng Jianye and Luo Guanzong are discussed in chaps. 4 and following.

22. K. H. Ting and Zhu Pei'en, "Xuesheng shiye" ("Student Work"), *Shanghai*

Qingnian (28 February 1939): 30-34. Zhu Pei'en was Ting's predecessor as the Shanghai YMCA student secretary.

23. K. H. Ting, *"Shanghai lian juban 'Cishan shichang,'" ("Shanghai Lian Holds a Charity Bazaar"), Xiaoxi* (March 1938): 28-29.

24. See Wang Min, *Shanghai xuesheng yundong dashi shi, 1919.5-1949.9 (A Chronology of the Shanghai Student Movement 1919.5-1949.9)*, 200-230; Ge Luoxi, "Ershi ge yue lai de Shanghai jidujiao xuesheng yundong," ("The Shanghai Christian Student Movement Over the Last Twenty Months"), *Xiaoxi* (June 1939): 44-50; K. H. Ting, "Xuesheng gongzuo" ("Student Work"), *Shanghai Qingnian* (20 January 1940): 16-17.

25. See "Serving Students in Wartime China, 1937-1940," Geneva, 1945.

26. David M. Paton, *"R. O.": The Life and Times of Bishop Hall of Hong Kong* (Hong Kong: Diocese of Hong Kong and Macao and the Hong Kong Diocesan Association, 1985), 103-5. The standard source on T. C. Chao is Winfried Glüer, *Christliche Theologie in China: T. C. Chao: 1918-1956* (Gütersloh: Gütersloher Verlagshaus Mohn, 1979). For a short biography of T. C. Chao, see Winfried Glüer, "T. C. Chao: Scholar, Teacher and Gentle Mystic," in *Mission Legacies: Biographical Studies of the Modern Missionary Movement*, ed. Gerald H. Anderson et al. (Maryknoll, N.Y.: Orbis Books, 1998), 225-31.

27. K. H. Ting, "Geng da de xinren, geng da de kuanrong: Zhao Zichen danchen yibai zhounian yougan" ("More Trust and More Tolerance: On the 100th Anniversary of the Birth of Dr. T.C.Chao"), *JL* (1988, no. 11): 99-100. The English translation is in *CTR* 19 (2005): 125-27.

28. "Quanguo jidujiao xuesheng daibiaohuiyi xuanyan" ("Manifesto of the National Christian Student Conference"), *Xiaoxi* (October 1939): 1-2.

29. "Duan Xun" ("News Briefs"), *Xiaoxi* (October 1939): 103.

30. Yao Minchuan, *Shanghai jidujiaoshi, 1843-1949 (A History of Christianity in Shanghai, 1843-1949)* (Shanghai: Shanghai Christian Council and TSPM Committee, 1993), 157; Wang Min, *A Chronology of the Shanghai Student Movement*, 228. In a somewhat different form, the Shanghai delegation presented these movements in their report to the Guandu Conference. See "Shanghai baogao" ("Report from Shanghai"), *Xiaoxi* (October 1939): 28-30.

31. Emily Honig, *Sisters and Strangers: Women in the Shanghai Cotton Mills, 1919-1949* (Stanford: Stanford University Press, 1986), 248.

32. *District of Shanghai Newsletter* 22, no. 10 (December 1937): 4.

33. Bishop Roberts's letter is quoted in Edward Xu, "Religion and Education," 218.

34. *The Johannean 1934*, page unnumbered.

35. Quoted in Edward Xu, "Religion and Education," 219.

36. *District of Shanghai Newsletter* 27, no. 7 (October 1941): 10; also Lamberton, *St. John's University*, 202.

37. A. M. Ramsey, *From Gore to Temple: The Development of Anglican Theology between Lux Mundi and the Second World War, 1889-1939* (London: Longmans, 1960), vii, 3, 89.

38. K. H. Ting, "'Wo . . . lai' shengdan dujing moxiang de zhaji," *Xiaoxi* (December 1940): 7-8. Translated as "Reading the Bible at Christmas," *CTR* 10 (1995): 12.

39. David M. Paton, *Christian Missions and the Judgment of God* (London: SCM Press, 1953). This classic interpretation of the Christian missionary experience in China was reissued by Eerdmann's in 1996, with a foreword by K. H. Ting.

David Paton's first thoughts about China were published in Chinese translation, "Gei zhongguo xueshengmen" ("To Chinese Students"), *Xiaoxi* (February 1940): 45-47. Also see David Paton, ed., *Reform of the Ministry: A Study in the World of Roland Allen* (London: Lutterworth Press, 1968).

40. See "Oxford Group," in *The Oxford Dictionary of the Christian Church*, ed. F. L. Cross and E. A. Livingstone, 3rd ed. (Oxford: Oxford University Press, 1997), 1204-05; E. R. Norman, *Church and Society in England, 1770-1970* (Oxford: Clarendon Press, 1976), 336-37.

41. Ge Luoxi, "Ershigeyue lai de Shanghai jidujiao xuesheng yundong" ("The Shanghai Student Christian Movement Over the Past Twenty Months"), *Xiaoxi* (June 1939): 46.

42. K. H. Ting, interview with the author, Nanjing, China, 16 December 1990.

43. K. H. Ting, "That You Be Trustworthy," *CTR* (1991): 131.

44. Transcript of K. H. Ting for Union Theological Seminary, 1947-48.

45. K. H. Ting, interview with the author, Nanjing, China, 16 December 1990.

46. K. H. Ting, interview with the author, Nanjing, China, 16 December 1990.

47. For a description of expatriate life during this period see Hugh Collar, *Captive in Shanghai: A Story of Internment in World War II* (Hong Kong: Oxford University Press, 1990).

48. K. H. Ting, interview with the author, Nanjing, China, 16 December 1990.

49. K. H. Ting, interview with the author, Nanjing, China, 16 December 1990.

50. Ruan Renze and Gao Zhennong, eds., *Shanghai Zongjiao shi (A Religious History of Shanghai)*, 1017.

51. Peter W. H. Tsai, interview with the author, Hangzhou, China, 6 April 1991.

52. Yao, *Shanghai jidujiao shi, 1839-1949 (A History of Christianity in Shanghai 1843-1949)*, 232.

53. Timothy Brook, "Toward Independence: Christianity in China Under Japanese Occupation, 1937-1956," unpublished manuscript prepared for the History of Christianity in China Project, 1990, pp. 27-28. The story is quoted from Brook's interview with Siu-may Kuo, Nanjing, 21 March 1989.

54. Siu-may Kuo, interview with the author, Nanjing, China, 9 June 1991.

55. Xiong Yuezhi and Zhou Wu, eds., *Sheng Yuehan daxue shi (History of St. John's University)* (Shanghai: Shanghai renmin chubanshe, 2007), p. 353.

3. SERVICE AND STUDIES OVERSEAS, 1946-1951

1. As quoted in K. H. Ting, "Sermon on Matthew 2: 1-13," unpublished manuscript, October 1984, p. 1. The translation is from *Li Sao and Other Poems of Chu Yuan (Qu Yuan)*, trans. Hsien-yi and Galdys Yang (Beijing: Foreign Languages Press, 1955).

2. Mao Zedong, "Opening Address at the First Plenary Session of the Chinese People's Political Consultative Conference," 21 September 1949, in *The Political Thought of Mao Tse-tung*, ed. Stuart R. Schram (New York: Praeger, 1972), 167.

3. Siu-may Kuo, interview with the author, Nanjing, China, 9 June 1991.

4. "Minutes of Personnel Committee, 16 May 1945"; and "Minutes of Personnel Committee, 16 October 1945" (84-58).

5. See Stephen Endicott, *James G. Endicott: Rebel Out of China* (Toronto: Uni-

versity of Toronto Press, 1980); Mary Rose Donnelly and Heather Dau, *Katherine: Katherine Boehner Hockin, a Biography* (Winfield, B.C.: Woodlate Books, 1992); and Katherine B. Hockin, "Canadian Openness to the Chinese Church," *International Review of Missions* 71, no. 283 (July 1982): 368-79. K. H. Ting wrote the foreword to *Rebel Out of China,* ix-x.

6. "Minutes of the Personnel Committee," 14 February 1946 (84-58); "Minutes of the Missionary Committee," 28 February 1946 (84-115-17).

7. *A Brief History of the Student Christian Movement in Canada, 1921-1974* (Toronto: SCM, 1975), 97-106.

8. See, for example, Dr. A. E. Armstrong's remarks in the "Report of the Meeting of Mission Board Executives with the Student Christian Movement, 18 June 1946" (84-115-17). He stated that he would like to say to the committee, "We have these fields and we need men [*sic*]. Here are the kinds of work, and here are the kinds of men needed. Can you help us find them?"

9. *The Messenger,* 24 October 1946.

10. "American Aid to China as Seen by a Chinese Student," *The Anglican Outlook* (April 1947), as quoted in Raymond L. Whitehead, ed., *No Longer Strangers: Selected Writings of K. H. Ting* (Maryknoll, N.Y.: Orbis Books, 1989), 112. Newspaper reports on K. H. Ting's speeches often muted his criticisms. The *Montreal Star* for 29 November 1946 quoted Ting as saying on another occasion: "The people of China are no longer resigning themselves to fate . . . They are pressing towards the goal of internal and world peace, and truly representative government"—with no mention of the criticisms he was making of American government policy.

11. "The Sociological Foundation of the Democratic Movement in China," *Bulletin of the Society of the Catholic Commonwealth* 3, no. 11 (4 January 1948): 3, 4. The author is described as "a Priest of the Holy Catholic Church in China, intimately familiar with the current Chinese scene." This could only have been K. H. Ting.

12. Tape transcript of "Conversations about K. H. Ting in Canada in the 1940s," Toronto, 3 February 1992. The people present for this conversation who got to know the Tings in the 1940s were Vince and Kathleen Goring, Jean (Ross) Wordsworth, Cyril and Marjorie Powles, Lois Wilson and Kay Hockin. Also present were Ray and Rhea Whitehead, who provided gracious hospitality, Cynthia McLean, then the director of the Canada China Programme, and myself.

13. The best source on the S.C.C. is Terry M. Brown, "Metacosmesis: The Christian Marxism of Frederic Hastings Smyth and the Society of the Catholic Commonwealth" (Ph.D. diss., University of Toronto, 1987). See also http://www.anglocatholicsocialism.org/smyth.html (accessed 10 January 2007).

14. Quoted in Brown, "Metacosmesis," 113.

15. Ting to Smyth, 14 May 1947.

16. "Report of the National Missionary Committee, 1946-1947" (84-5). This report, written in part by K. H. Ting, was presented at the meeting of the National Council of the SCM of Canada, 4-13 September 1947. A similar paragraph is found in his "Impressions and Thoughts about the Student Christian Movement of Canada," 1947 (84-86-21), 10.

17. K. H. Ting, "The Dilemma of the Sincere Student," *The Canadian Student* 25, no. 5 (May 1947): 92-93.

18. Quoted from "The Place of the Church in the Secular World," Work Camp

Logs, 1945-1953 (84-91). Also, "Conversations about K. H. Ting in Canada in the 1940s."

19. Tape transcript of "Conversations about K. H. Ting in Canada in the 1940s."

20. K. H. Ting, interview with the author, Nanjing, China, 16 December 1990.

21. Gregory Vlastos, *Christian Faith and Democracy* (New York: Association Press, 1939).

22. Lois Wilson, "An Intentional Life," *CTR* 10 (1995): 119. Also "Conversations about K. H. Ting in Canada in the 1940s."

23. Siu May (Siu-may) Ting, "The World Begins Now and Here," *The Canadian Student* 25, no. 3 (February 1947): 49.

24. Siu-may Kuo, interview with the author, Nanjing, China, 9 June 1991.

25. Siu-may Ting (Kuo), "Circular Letter," 7 January 1947.

26. K. H. Ting, "Impressions and Thoughts about the Student Christian Movement of Canada," 1947 (84-86-21). The quotations that follow are all from this report.

27. "Report of the National Missionary Committee, 1946-1947," p. 14 (84-5-8). The remarks were made by Dr. James S. Thompson.

28. "Chinese Students at Union Theological Seminary before 1950," compiled from the *Union Theological Seminary Alumni Directories*, 1837-1947 and 1837-1958, undated. Xu Yihua writes that thirty-nine Chinese scholars attended Union for a year or more; see "'Patriotic' Protestants: The Making of an Official Church," in *God and Caesar in China: Policy Implications of Church-State Tensions,* ed. Jason Kindopp and Carol Lee Hamrin (Washington: Brookings Institution Press, 2004), 114.

29. K. H. Ting, "The Simplicity of the Gospel," *The Canadian Student* 26, no. 2 (December 1947): 26-27 and 26, no. 3 (January 1948): 46-47.

30. K. H. Ting, "The Simplicity of the Gospel," *The Canadian Student* 26, no. 3 (1948): 47.

31. Robert T. Handy, *A History of Union Theological Seminary in New York* (New York: Columbia University Press, 1987), 214.

32. K. H. Ting, interview with the author, Nanjing, China, 9 March 1991.

33. H. S. Elliot, "Christian Education Can Preserve Democracy," unpublished paper dated 24 October 1947; "Harrison Sacket Elliot Papers, compiled by Ruth May Pollack, New York City, Spring, 1984.

34. Siu-may Ting, "A Grafted Growth," *Federation News Sheet* 11, no. 4 (May-June 1951): 10-11.

35. Siu-may Ting, "A Grafted Growth," 10.

36. Siu-may Kuo, interview with the author, Nanjing, China, 9 June 1991.

37. Mackie to Ting, 24 June 1947.

38. Mackie to Ting, 18 August 1947; WSCF U.S. Officers Meeting "Minutes," December 1947, p. 4.

39. Mackie to Kiang, 30 December 1947.

40. Kiang to Mackie, 16 January 1948.

41. See Mackie to Leung, 10 February 1948; Kiang to Mackie, 28 February 1948; Mackie to Kiang, 10 March 1948; and Mackie to Ting, 12 March 1948 and 30 March 1948.

42. Marie-Jeanne de Haller Coleman, "Coming Out of a Tunnel: 1944-1953,

Exciting Times for the Ecumenical Movement," in *Memoirs and Diaries: 1895-1990*, ed. Elizabeth Adler (Geneva: WSCF, 1994), 80.

43. K. H. Ting, "WSCF Circular," 13 October 1948.

44. Hans-Ruedi Weber, *Asia and the Ecumenical Movement, 1895-1961* (London: SCM Press, 1966), 221.

45. W. A. Visser 't Hooft, ed., *The First Assembly of the World Council of Churches—Held at Amsterdam August 22nd to September 47th, 1948* (New York: Harper Brothers, 1949), 230, 237 and passim.

46. K. H. Ting, interview with the author, Nanjing, China, 9 March 1991.

47. See Wickeri, *Seeking the Common Ground,* 170. The most complete report on Li Chuwen's relationship to the church and the CPC may be found in Xu Jiatun, *Xu Jiatun Xianggang huiyi lu (The Hong Kong Memoirs of Xu Jiatun)*, vol. 2 (Hong Kong: Xianggang lianhe bao, 1994), 475-76.

48. "Report of K. H. Ting on His Trip in the U.S.A., 1948."

49. K. H. Ting, "Forerunner Y. T. Wu," in K. H. Ting, *Love Never Ends: Papers by K. H. Ting,* ed. Janice K. Wickeri (Nanjing: Yilin Press, 2000), 76-77.

50. K. H. Ting, "The Task of the Church in Asia," *Student World* 42, no. 3 (1949): 240-41.

51. K. H. Ting, "A Report on the Church Situation in Czechoslovakia and Hungary, with Special Interest in the Light it Throws on China" *CB* 1, no. 69 (24 October 1949): 4. See also K. H. Ting, "Chinese Traveller in Eastern Europe," *Student World* 42, no. 4 (1949): 362-69.

52. Letter from Tung Biwu (Dong Biwu) and Li Fuqun, 13 January 1946. WSCF Archives Box 365.

53. John Coleman, "The Post-War Period," in *A Community of Memory and Hope* (Geneva, WSCF, 1992), 10.

54. John Coleman and K. H. Ting, "A Memorandum on Opening Christian Work in Universities in Communist China for Consideration at the Asian Leaders Conference," 9 December 1948.

55. K. H. Ting and John Coleman, "Memorandum on Proposed Visit to North China," 11 February 1949.

56. "Report K. H. Ting on His Trip to the USA, 1948."

57. K. H. Ting, "Report on South America" (January-March 1950), 1. The published version of his report is "A Latin American Travel Diary," *Student World* 43, no. 3 (1950): 258-65.

58. K. H. Ting, "The Task of the Student Christian Movement in South America," unpublished talk (1950), 2.

59. "Report on South America," p. 9. It is interesting to note that the same Carl McIntyre picketed Riverside Church when K. H. Ting was invited to preach there thirty years later.

60. "Report on South America," p. 11; "The S.C.M. in Latin America" (November 1950), 2.

61. "Report on South America," p. 11.

62. "Report on South America, p. 17. In an earlier version of the paper he had a sentence that made this thought even sharper: "In other words, if people must stumble let them stumble on account of that scandal in the content of the gospel alone, and not on account of the foreign form in which that gospel is put"; K. H. Ting, "My Latin American Travel Diary," unpublished manuscript, 2 April 1950, p. 2.

63. "Report on South America," p. 17.

64. See Wickeri, *Seeking the Common Ground*, 228-29.

65. Maury to Ting, 11 August 1950. See also Ting to Maury, 11 August 1950, which overlapped with the above. In this letter, K. H. indicates his own desire to "give more attention to the special fields of missions and evangelism," in part through more writing and reflection. The discussion of and action on Ting's reappointment is contained in "Minutes of the Meeting of the Executive Committee," 6-10 August 1950, pp. 15-16 and 30.

66. For a short survey of this period, see Timothy Yates, *Christian Mission in the Twentieth Century* (Cambridge: Cambridge University Press, 1994), 127-62.

67. Papers from the Rolle consultation as well as its mission statement were published in *Student World* 45, no. 1 (1952). The editorial for this issue was written by K. H. Ting as a WSCF circular for the 1951 executive committee. Almost none of his other missionary writings were published, but they are available in the WSCF archives. The discussion that follows is based on these largely unpublished reports and essays: "A Chinese Answers the Question," *Student World* 41, no. 4 (1948): 318-32; "Some Reflections on Students and Missions" (Spring, 1949?) 8 pp. typed manuscript used as the basis for "Can the Missionary Vocation Be Real to Students Today?"; "Christian Youth Looking at Missions Once More?" (Spring, 1949?) 4 pp.; "Can the Missionary Vocation Be Real to Students Today?" (June 1949) 7 pp.; WSCF circular in preparation for general committee, Whitby, August 1949, "The Commission on the SCM and the Growing Church"; "The S.C.M. in the Growing Church" 5 pp.; report from the Commission on the Growing Church, drafted by K. H. Ting and Philip Potter; "The Christian in a World of Many Religions" (April 1950?) 8 pp. typed manuscript. Written for WCYC, in preparation for 1952 conference?; "How Can They Claim Christianity Is Better?" (April 1950?) 8 pp. typed manuscript. Written for WCYC, in preparation for 1952 conference?; "Why Force My Religion on Others?" (April 1950?) 2 pp. typed manuscript. Written for World Christian Youth Commission, in preparation for 1952 conference?; "News-Letter," *Federation News Sheet* 10, no. 4 (May-June 1950): 75-78; "The W.S.C.F. and the Missionary Church" (June 1950) 19 pp. WSCF circular for 1950 Executive Committee, Bievres.; "Ecumenism, Missions and Evangelism" (October 1950) 9 pp. typed manuscript; "Can We See Sense in Evangelism and Missions Today?" (November 1950), 7 pp. WSCF circular to member SCMs; "Students and Missions—A Confrontation" (March 1951) 8 pp. WSCF circular in preparation for Rolle, April 1951; "The Missionary Concern of the W.S.C.F." (August 1951) 5 pp. WSCF circular for 1951 enlarged executive, Berlin, published as an editorial in *Student World* 45, no. 1 (1952): 1-7.

68. "A Chinese Answers the Question," 319.

69. "The S.C.M. in the Growing Church," 2-3.

70. "Evangelism, Missions and Ecumenism," 2.

71. "A Chinese Answers the Question," 319.

72. "The Christian in a World of Many Religions," 7.

73. "Some Reflections on Students and Missions," 2.

74. "Some Reflections on Students and Missions," 3.

75. "Can the Missionary Vocation Be Real to Students Today?" 4.

76 . This was especially evident in the WSCF meeting in Strasbourg in 1960. See Yates, *Christian Mission in the Twentieth Century*, 196-97.

77. "Christian Youth Looking at Missions Once More?" 4.

78. "The W.S.C.F. and the Missionary Church," 5.
79. "Can the Missionary Vocation Be Real to Students Today?" 5.
80. "News-Letter," *Federation News Sheet* 10, no. 4 (May-June 1950): 76.
81. He suggests this in "The Missionary Concern of the W.S.C.F.," 5.
82. "The Missionary Concern of the W.S.C.F.," 2.

4. RETURNING TO A "NEW CHINA," 1951-1956

1. Quoted in part in K. H. Ting, "The Church in China Today," *Student World* 50, no. 1 (1957): 45. These lines, often misquoted, are from the last part of Auden's lengthy "Commentary" to his sonnet sequence "In Time of War" (1938) and may be found in *The English Auden: Poems, Essays and Dramatic Writings, 1927-1939*, ed. Edward Mendelson (London: Faber & Faber, 1977).

2. Zhou Enlai, "Several Questions on China's Nationalities Policy," (4 August 1957) contained in *Zhou Enlai tongyizhanxian wenxuan (Selected Writings of Zhou Enlai on the United Front)* (Beijing: Renmin chubanshe, 1984), 383-84. My translation.

3. See Owen Chadwick, *The Christian Church in the Cold War* (London: Penguin Books, 1993), for an overview of the issues on churches in the East-West struggle.

4. Ting to Visser 't Hooft, 13 July 1951, Canada SCM Archives, Box 1508.

5. De Haller to Miss Edith Rawlings, 7 April 1952, Canada SCM Archives, Box 1508.

6. The previous year, Hall had written "China: Anno Domini 1950" (6 pp.), an unpublished manuscript widely circulated in churches overseas. It is a theological interpretation of the Chinese situation that expresses his general support for the new order.

7. Ting to de Haller, 28 August 1951; K. H. Ting, interview with the author, Nanjing, China, 9 March 1991.

8. See Suzanne Pepper, *Civil War in China: The Political Struggle, 1945-1949* (Berkeley and Los Angeles: University of California Press, 1978), 132ff.

9. Jonathan Spence, *The Search for Modern China* (New York: Norton, 1990), 518, 535 and passim.

10. This is the judgment of Frederick Teiwes, "Establishment and Consolidation of the New Regime," in *Cambridge History of China*, vol. 14, ed. R. MacFarquhar and John K. Fairbank, 89 (Cambridge: Cambridge University Press, 1987). He provides an excellent survey of the urban mass movements on pp. 88-92. For an in-depth study of one of these campaigns in Shanghai, see John Garner, "The *Wu Fan* ('Five Antis') Campaign in Shanghai: A Study of the Consolidation of Urban Control," in *Chinese Communist Politics in Action*, ed. A. Doak Barnett (Seattle: University of Washington Press, 1969), 477-539.

11. "Resolution on Certain Questions in the History of Our Party Since the Founding of the People's Republic of China," *Beijing Review* 27 (6 July 1981): 10-39.

12. The most recent study of Y. T. Wu is sharply critical of his theological and political perspective; see Leung Ka-lun, *Wu Yaozong san lun (Y. T. Wu's Under-*

standing of Christianity and Its Relationship to Chinese Communism) (Hong Kong: Alliance Biblical Seminary, 1996). Leung's views have been strongly criticized by the TSPM/CCC leadership. For a short biography representing the position of the TSPM, see Shen Derong, *Wu Yaozong xiao zhuan (A Short Biography of Y. T. Wu)* (Shanghai: TSPM Committee, 1989).

13. Philip L. Wickeri, "Zhou Enlai's Conversations with Chinese Christians: Introduction and Translation," *China Study Project Journal* 2, no. 1 (April 1987): 4-11.

14. On "the Christian Manifesto," see Philip L. Wickeri, *Seeking the Common Ground: Protestant Christianity, the Three-Self Movement and China's United Front* (Maryknoll, N.Y.: Orbis Books, 1988), 127-33. For a full translation, see Wallace C. Merwin and Francis P. Jones, eds., *Documents of the Three-Self Movement: Source Materials for the Study of the Protestant Church in Communist China* (New York: National Council of the Churches of Christ in the U.S.A., 1963), 19-20.

15. On the Denunciation Movement, see Wickeri, *Seeking the Common Ground,* 134-39. In some sources, it is also called the "Accusation Movement," but both terms are translations of the Chinese term *kongsu yundong.* Based on my own additional research, my interpretation of the Denunciation Movement has changed since the time of my earlier study. As will be seen in the discussion that is presented here, I now see the Denunciation Movement primarily as a government-inspired initiative of TSPM activists.

16. For the latter view, see Jung Chang and Jon Halliday, *Mao: The Unknown Story* (London: Jonathan Cape, 2004). Gao Wenqian has a more nuanced perspective. See his *Wannian Zhou Enlai (The Latter Years of Zhou Enlai)* (Hong Kong: Mirror Books, 2003).

17. Dick Wilson, *Zhou Enlai: A Biography* (New York: Viking, 1984), 295. Wilson attributes the quote on Zhou's years overseas to Professor Lucien Pye.

18. K. H. Ting, interview with the author, Nanjing, China, 1 May 1991.

19. K. H. Ting, interview with the author, Nanjing, China, 13 December 1991.

20. K. H. Ting, interview with the author, Nanjing, China, 1 May 1991.

21. K. H. Ting, interview with the author, Nanjing, China, 1 May 1991. He Chengxiang (1902-1967) was the first director of the Bureau of Religious Affairs of the State Council (now known as the State Administration of Religious Affairs) and served in that position from 1951 to 1961.

22. K. H. Ting, untitled and unpublished comment on Zhang Xiaofeng, "Qin Shang" ("Qin Elegy"), 2 pp., dated 9 April 1993. See also Ting's apology to American missionaries for the Denunciation Movement, which is discussed in chap. 9.

23. K. H. Ting, interview with the author, Nanjing, China, 1 May 1991.

24. Wickeri, *Seeking the Common Ground,* 311 n. 55. The statistics cited are from *Tian Feng.*

25. The letter is found in Merwin and Jones, *Documents of the Three-Self Movement,* 21. For a short discussion, see Wickeri, *Seeking the Common Ground,* 131.

26. K. H. Ting, "Ni zai nali?" ("Where are you?"), *Tian Feng* 301 (16 February 1952): 7. "The East is Red and the Sun is rising" is from the first line of what was then China's national anthem.

27. K. H. Ting, "Lun si yu huo" ("On Life and Death"), *Tian Feng* 308 (5 April 1952): 195-96.

28. K. H. Ting, *Kan na shangdi de gaoyang* (*Behold the Lamb of God*) (Shanghai: Christian Literature Society, 1952). A short excerpt from this pamphlet is translated as "The Lamb of God" in *CTR* 10 (1995): 22-23.

29. K. H. Ting, "The Lamb of God," 22.

30. Hu Zuyin, "Accusation Against the Christian Literature Society's Aggression Against China," *Tian Feng* 268-269 (21 June 1951): 304-6. Translated in full in *Documents of the Three-Self Movement*, 45-48.

31. K. H. Ting, interview with the author, Nanjing, China, 1 May 1991.

32. Kiang Wen-han has written his own account of the CLS, which shows the political influence of the times. See "Guang Xue Hui shi ze'yang de yige jigou" ("What Kind of Organization Was the Christian Literature Society?") *Wenshiziliao xuanji* (*Resources on Literature and History* 43 (Beijing: Wenshiziliao chubanshi, 1980), 1-42 (2nd printing).

33. "Kaizhan zhongguo shenxue jiaoyu xin de yiye" ("A New Page in Chinese Theological Education") *Tian Feng* 330 (6 September 1952): 506.

34. See Wickeri, *Seeking the Common Ground*, 223-24. The plan of union was published in *Tian Feng* 330 (6 September 1952): 507.

35. The seminaries were Trinity Theological Seminary (Ningbo); Central Theological Seminary (Shanghai); China Theological Seminary (Hangzhou); China Baptist Theological Seminary (Shanghai); Jiangsu Baptist Bible School (Zhenjiang); Ming Dao Bible Seminary (Jinan); Nanjing Theological Seminary; North China Theological Seminary (Wuxi); Minan Theological Seminary (Changzhou); Fujian Union Seminary (Fuzhou); and Cheloo Theological Seminary (Jinan). On the opening of the seminary, see *Tian Feng* 338-339 (15 November 1952): 641-49.

36. Information about the seminary's organization and curriculum may be found in the inaugural issue of *JL* (25 September 1953): 29-34 and passim.

37. See Suzanne Pepper, "Education Under the New Order," *Cambridge History of China*, 14:203-7.

38. K. H. Ting, interview with the author, Nanjing, China, 11 June 1991 (part 1).

39. K. H. Ting, "Ban nian lai de jinling xiehe shenxueyuan" ("The First Six Months of Nanjing Union Theological Seminary"), *Tian Feng* 358 (30 March 1953): 175.

40. K. H. Ting, interview with the author, Nanjing, China, 1 May 1991.

41. For my earlier interpretation of mutual respect at Nanjing Seminary, see *Seeking the Common Ground*, 223-26.

42. Wang Weifan, interview with the author, Nanjing, China, 19 April 1996.

43. The most important of these are "Zuo zhongxin de gongren" ("Be Loyal Workers"), *Tian Feng* 357 (23 March 1953): 154-55 (a sermon preached to the first graduating class at NUTS); "Chuanyang fuyin han jianli shenti" ("Spread the Gospel and Establish the Body") *JL* 1 (September 1953): 2-8 (this was also serialized in *Tian Feng*); "Ci ren zhihui he qishi de ling" ("The Spirit Who Grants Wisdom and Revelation to Humankind"), *Tian Feng* 398 (18 January 1954): 26-27 and 399 (25 January 1954): 42-43; "Wei shenma jintian hai yao zuo chuan daoren?" ("Why Must We Still Be Preachers?"), *JL* 2 (April 1954): 4-9; "Shenxue xuesheng yingdang ze'yang du shengjing" ("How Seminary Students Should Read the Bible"), *JL* 3 (February 1955): 12-19; "Shen yu ren zhi jian" ("Between God and Man"), *Sheng Gong* (February 1955): 6-8; "He Shangdi shuaijiao de ren"

("The Man Who Wrestled with God") *JL* 4 (November 1955): 1-4. This essay and "The Spirit Who Grants Wisdom and Revelation to Humankind"are the only essays from the period that he chose to include in his *Collected Works*. Translated excerpts from some of these essays may be found in Raymond L. Whitehead, ed., *No Longer Strangers: Selected Writings of K. H. Ting* (Maryknoll, N.Y.: Orbis Books, 1989). The essays from the *Nanjing Theological Review* vols. 3 and 4 are published in slightly different versions in *How to Study the Bible* (Hong Kong: Tao Fong Shan Ecumenical Centre, 1981).

44. K. H. Ting, "Why Must We Still Be Preachers?" 6.

45. K. H. Ting, "Spread the Gospel and Establish the Body," 6.

46. Ting, "Spread the Gospel and Establish the Body," 4-5.

47. Ting, "Spread the Gospel and Establish the Body," 6.

48. Ting, "Spread the Gospel and Establish the Body," 3.

49. The record of this trip is contained in Hewlett Johnson, *China's New Creative Age* (London: Lawrence & Wishart, 1953).

50. Bruce Cumings, *Korea's Place in the Sun: A Modern History* (New York and London: W. W. Norton, 1997), 289. On Chinese preparedness, see Zhang Shu Gang, *Mao's Military Romanticism: China and the Korean War, 1950-1953* (Lawrence: University Press of Kansas, 1995), which is cited by Cumings.

51. See Ruth Rogaski, "Nature, Annihilation, and Modernity: China's Korean War Germ-Warfare Experience Reconsidered," *Journal of Asian Studies* 61, no. 2 (May 2002): 408-10 and passim.

52. The "Appeal of Chinese Christian Leaders for Peace and Against the Use of Germ Warfare by American Forces in Korea" is dated 28 June 1952, and appears as an appendix in Johnson, *China's New Creative Age,* 190-91. The Chinese version is published in *Tian Feng* 320 (28 June 1952): 346-47.

53. See Cumings, *Korea's Place in the Sun,* 290. The Chinese figures are cited in Jonathan Spence, *The Search for Modern China,* 530-31.

54. Wickeri, *Seeking the Common Ground,* 140-46.

55. "Ding Guangxun mushi fayan zhaiyao" ("Excerpts from the Speech by Rev. K. H. Ting"), *Tian Feng* 425-427 (3 September 1954): 452-55.

56. See "Letter to the Churches" (5 August 1954), as translated in *Documents of the Three-Self Movement,* 98-99.

57. K. H. Ting, interview with the author, Nanjing, China, 1 May 1991.

58. K. H. Ting, interview with the author, Nanjing, China, 1 May 1991.

59. "Guanyu Zhongguo jidutu fandi aiguo da tuanjie de jueyi" ("Resolution on the Great Unity of Chinese Christians' Anti-Imperialist Patriotism"), *Tian Feng* 457 (28 March 1955): 212.

60. Article 2 states, "Its purpose shall be to unite the Christians of China and stimulate the Churches to achieve the Three-Self goals and work for world peace." The translation is from *Documents of the Three-Self Movement,* 97.

61. For general discussions of these conflicts from different perspectives, see Chao T'ien-en and Rosanna Chong, *Dangdai zhongguo jidujiao fazhanshi, 1949-1997 (A History of Christianity in Socialist China, 1949-1997)* (Taipei: CMI Publishing, 1997), 80-91; Francis Price Jones, *The Church in Communist China: A Protestant Appraisal* (New York: Friendship Press, 1962), 103-14; Bob Whyte, *Unfinished Encounter: China and Christianity* (Glasgow: Collins, 1988), 239-44 and passim; and Wickeri, *Seeking the Common Ground,* 154-70.

62. "Ding Guangxun changwei fayan zhaiyao" ("Excerpt from K. H. Ting's Speech to the Standing Committee"), *Tian Feng* 457 (28 March 1955): 214-15. The speech is translated in part in *Documents of the Three-Self Movement,* 106-8.

63. Cited in *Documents of the Three-Self Movement,* 107.

64. The most recent study of Wang Mingdao in English is also written along these lines; see Thomas Alan Harvey, *Acquainted with Grief: Wang Mingdao's Stand for the Persecuted Church in China* (Grand Rapids: Brazos Press, 2002).

65. Wang Mingdao, "We, Because of Faith!" (June 1955) 40 pp., partially translated in *Documents of the Three-Self Movement,* 99-114. See also Wickeri, *Seeking the Common Ground,* 164-70.

66. For a general discussion of the development of Chinese Protestant fundamentalism, see See Kevin Xiyi Yao, *The Fundamentalist Movement among Protestant Missionaries in China, 1920-1937* (Lanham, Md.: University Press of America, 2003).

67. K. H. Ting, "Zheng gao Wang Mingdao" ("A Stern Warning to Wang Mingdao"), *Tian Feng* 477-478 (15 August 1955): 604-8. This essay is excerpted under the title "Truth and Slander" in Raymond L. Whitehead, ed., *No Longer Strangers: Selected Writings of K. H. Ting* (Maryknoll, N.Y.: Orbis Books, 1989), 141-46.

68. K. H. Ting, "Truth and Slander," *No Longer Strangers,* p. 145.

69. See Joseph Tse-Hu Lee, "Watchman Nee and the Little Flock in Maoist China." *Church History* 74, no. 1 (March 2005): 68-96.

70. See, for example, Thomas Harvey, *Acquainted with Grief,* 7.

71. See the work of Martin Marty and R. Scott Appleby on religious fundamentalisms, especially *The Glory and the Power: The Fundamentalist Challenge to the Modern World* (Boston: Beacon Press, 1992).

72. Wickeri, *Seeking the Common Ground,* 151-53.

73. K. H. Ting, interview with the author, Nanjing, China, 1 May 1991.

74. Wickeri, *Seeking the Common Ground,* 66-68.

75. *Xinhua ribao,* 27 April 1955, p. 1.

76. *Xinhua ribao,* 27 April 1955, p. 6.

77. F. L. Hawks Pott, *A Short History of Shanghai,* 227. Pott adds that the only Chinese ever to serve as a bishop before this was the Roman Catholic Bishop Lo, who was consecrated in 1685.

78. For a brief historical overview, from which the above account is drawn, see G. F. S. Gray, with editorial revision by Martha Lund Smalley, *Anglicans in China: A History of the Zhonghua Shenggong Hui* (New Haven: Episcopal China Mission History Project, 1996), 27-28 and 53-54.

79. Francis James, *Reports on the Deputation of Australian Churchmen to Mainland China* (Sydney: Anglican News Service, 1956), 11.

80. Deng Fucun, interview with the author, Hangzhou, China, 3 December 1991. Deng adds that the other parishes included those in Tongfu (4); Yucan (4); Ningpo (3); Ningdong (4); Ningxi (4); Sanbei (5); Tianning and Tiantang (7); Huang Yan (4); Wenning (3); Zhuji (5); and Shaoxing (3).

81. K. H. Ting, interview with the author, Nanjing, China, 1 May 1991.

82. Report published in *Sheng Gong* 2 (May 1955): 32. *Sheng Gong* began in February of the same year as the official publication of the standing committee of the General Synod of the Sheng Gong Hui. Thirteen issues were published in all, and the last issue of *Sheng Gong* was issued in December 1957.

83. Shen Zigao (T.K. Shen), "Jieshou zhu de shiming" ("Accept the Lord's Commission"), *Sheng Gong* 3 (July 1955): 19-22. A report on the consecration service was published in the same issue (pp. 33-34).

84. K. H. Ting, "Chinese Christians: New Prospects, New Unity," *Student World* 49 (1956): 292. A somewhat different Chinese report from this same visit is found in Ting, "Ji yici nongcun jiaohui de fangwen" ("A Visit to a Rural Church"), *Tian Feng* 497 (23 January 1956): 10-12.

85. Deng Fucun, interview with the author, Hangzhou, China, 3 December 1991. The names of the priests Ting ordained are Deng Fucun, Sun Xipei, Yu Mingyue, Sun Jingwei and Cheng Nianbao, all of whom were serving as pastors or church workers in the early 1990s; Chen Enfu and Niu Zhifang, who were retired; and Zhu Tianming, Wang Jilan, Hua Yiming and Shou Zhongzhao, who were, by the time of our interview, deceased.

86. K. H. Ting, "Chinese Christians: New Prospects, New Unity," 292.

87. Yu Mingyue, interview with the author, Fuyang, China, 4 December 1991.

88. See *Sheng Gong* 7 (July 1956), especially "Zhonghua sheng gong hui zhujiao yuan zhi benhui quanguo shengpin xintu shu) ("Pastoral Letter from the House of Bishops to All Clergy and Laity in China"), 20 May 1956, pp. 4-7; Chen Jianzhen (Robin Chen), "Zhonghua sheng gong hui zong yihui zhujiao yuan ji changwu weiyuanhui lianxihui kaihui baogao" ("Report to the House of Bishops and the General Synod"), 14 May 1956, pp. 8-16; and Zheng Jianye's opening speech, "Yuan zhu de qi chui wo" ("May the Lord's Breath Blow on Me"), 18-19.

89. K. H. Ting, "Wo xin shenglin, wo xin sheng er gong zhi jiaohui" ("I Believe in the Holy Spirit, I Believe in the Holy Catholic Church"), *Sheng Gong* 7 (July 1956): 22.

90. *Tian Feng* 512 (3 September 1956): 7. A fuller interpretation of the reasons behind this decision may be found in Wickeri, *Seeking the Common Ground*, 230-32.

91. See *Quaker Mission to China: W. Grigor McLelland's Diary, 26 September-29 October, 1955*, p. 28.

92. K. H. Ting, "Hromádka as Reconciler," *From the Reformation to Tomorrow: Joseph L. Hromádka (1889-1969)*, ed. Milan Opočenský (Geneva: World Alliance of Reformed Churches, 1999), 93. See also J. L. Hromádka, *The Church and Theology in Today's Troubled Times* (Prague: Ecumenical Council of Churches, 1956), 64-65.

93. Rajah Manikam, "Interview with Chinese Church Leaders at Peking on Invitations from the IMC and the WCC," 17 March 1956. 5 pp.

94. This meeting is fully documented in George Hood, *Neither Bang Nor Whimper: The End of a Missionary Era in China* (Singapore: Presbyterian Church in Singapore, 1991), 228-30.

95. Tim Gorringe. *Alan Ecclestone: Priest as Revolutionary* (Sheffield: Cairns Publications, 1994), 167.

96. K. H. Ting, "In Memory of Alan Ecclestone," (13 January 1993), in K. H. Ting, *Love Never Ends: Papers by K. H. Ting*, ed. Janice K. Wickeri (Nanjing: Yilin Press, 2000), 428. Alan Ecclestone died on 14 December 1992.

97. "Bishop Ting Reports on Chinese Christians Today," *Ecumenical Press Service* 32 (10 August 1956).

98. "Minutes and Reports of the Ninth Meeting of the Central Committee of

the World Council of Churches," Galyateto, 28 July-5 August 1956, pp. 55-58. See also K. H. Ting, "On the Life of the Churches in China," *The Ecumenical Review* 9 (October 1956): 61-63.

99. K. H. Ting, "A Report on the Church Situation in Czechoslovakia and Hungary, with Special Interest in the Light it Throws on China," *CB* 1, no. 69 (24 October 1949), 80.

100. K. H. Ting to Eugene Smith, 2 January 1957. The letter was written from Nanjing (WCC Archives).

101. K. H. Ting's speech at Tutzing was published as "The Church in China Today," *Student World* 50, no. (1957): 45-59.

102. Fred Engel, "Reconciliation and Harsh Realities," *Memoirs and Diaries, 1895-1990*, ed. Elizabeth Adler (Geneva: WSCF, 1994), 114-17.

103. K. H. Ting, "Eluosi dongsheng jiaohui fangwen ji" ("A Visit to the Russian Orthodox Church"), *Sheng Gong* 11 (August 1957): 31-32.

5. TURNING WITH THE TIDE, 1956-1965

1. As quoted in Amanda Haight, *Anna Akhmatova: A Poetic Pilgrimage* (Oxford and New York: Oxford University Press, 1990), 138.

2. Mao Zedong, "Talk on Questions of Philosophy" (18 August 1964) in *Chairman Mao Talks to the People: Talks and Letters, 1956-1971*, ed. Stuart Schram (New York: Pantheon Books, 1974), 228.

3. For an overview of this period, see Frederick C. Teiwes, "The Establishment and Consolidation of the New Regime, 1949-1957," in *The Politics of China: The Eras of Mao and Deng*, ed. Roderick MacFarquhar, 2nd ed. (Cambridge: Cambridge University Press, 1997), 5-86.

4. See Roderick MacFarquhar, *The Origins of the Cultural Revolution: Contradictions among the People, 1956-1957*, (New York: Columbia University Press, 1974), 1:33-38; 1:75-85.

5. Hu Feng is discussed in Merle Goldman, *Literary Dissent in Communist China* (Cambridge: Harvard University Press, 1967), 129-157. The campaign against Hu Feng came just prior to the criticism of Wang Mingdao, discussed in the last chapter, and Hu was also denounced in *Tian Feng*. See *Tian Feng* 469-470 (24 June 1955).

6. The two speeches were not widely circulated at the time and remained subjects for internal debate. They were "On the Ten Great Relationships" (25 April 1956) and "Let a Hundred Flowers Bloom, Let a Hundred Schools of Thought Contend" (2 May 1956). See MacFarquhar, *The Origins of the Cultural Revolution*, 1:48-52.

7. See the chart on student enrollment for the fall semester 1956 and "Statistics on the Number of Students Enrolled at Nanjing Union Theological Seminary, 1952-1956," *JL* 6 (February 1957): 28, 39. On the denominational background of students enrolled in 1956, twenty-four came from the Church of Christ in China, seventeen from the Baptists, twelve from the Sheng Gong Hui, and twenty-five from the Methodists.

8. K. H. Ting, "Zhi er nian lai zou shang gong chang de xiaoyoumen" ("To Alumni/ae after Two Years in the Field"), *JL* 3 (February 1955): 35.

9. See K. H. Ting, "Wei shenma jintian hai yao zuo chuan daoren?" ("Why Must We Still be Preachers?)" *JL* 2 (April 1954): 4-9, translated in Philip L. Wickeri and Janice K. Wickeri, eds., *A Chinese Contribution to Ecumenical Theology: Selected Writings of K. H. Ting* (Geneva: World Council of Churches, 2002), 14-26.

10. He discussed these three decades later. See K. H. Ting, "Theological Mass Movement in China," *Christian Witness in China Today* (Kyoto: Doshisha University Press, 1985), 19-36; "Sanzi zai renshi" ("Another Look at Three-Self"), *Tian Feng* (February 1983): 2-9, translated in *CTR* (1985): 1-17. For a survey of this period of theological reorientation, see Philip L. Wickeri, *Seeking the Common Ground: Protestant Christianity, the Three-Self Movement and China's United Front* (Maryknoll, N.Y.: Orbis Books, 1988), 258-73.

11. See K. H. Ting, *How to Study the Bible* (Hong Kong: Tao Fong Shan Ecumenical Centre, 1981), edited by Philip L. Wickeri and translated from *Tian Feng* (20 October 1980): 45-63, a long selection of which was later issued as a pamphlet. *How to Study the Bible* is based on two essays published in 1955: "Shenxue xuesheng yingdang ze'yang du shengjing" ("How Seminary Students Should Read the Bible"), *JL* 3 (February 1955): 12-19; and "He Shangdi shuaijiao de ren" ("The Man Who Wrestled with God"), *JL* 4 (November 1955): 1-4. The earlier essays were revised for publication in 1980, and the English translation was itself revised by the author for overseas readers. In the discussion that follows, I will refer to the pamphlet as a whole.

12. Ting, *How to Study the Bible*, 2-3.

13. K. H. Ting, "Tan Jidujiao Youshenlun" ("On Christian Theism"), *JL* 7 (August 1957): 13-21. A translation appears in Wallace C. Merwin and Francis P. Jones, eds., *Documents of the Three-Self Movement: Source Materials for the Study of the Protestant Church in Communist China* (New York: National Council of the Churches of Christ in the U.S.A., 1963), 156-67. K. H. Ting was dissatisfied with this translation and did his own in 1985. This appears in *A Chinese Contribution to Ecumenical Theology*, 27-40. An excerpt is also found in Raymond L. Whitehead, ed., *No Longer Strangers: Selected Writings of K. H. Ting* (Maryknoll, N.Y.: Orbis Books, 1989), 42-49. A discussion of the translation problem of this essay is discussed in Janice Wickeri, "Filtered Out/Factored In: Text, Translation, Audience and Context," 1995, unpublished manuscript, pp. 5-9. The quotations cited here are from the translation in *A Chinese Contribution to Ecumenical Theology*.

14. M. M. Thomas, "K. H. Ting's Theology of Society," *Church and Society: Bulletin of the East Asia Christian Conference* (September 1960): 32-36; Francis Price Jones, *The Church in Communist China: A Protestant Appraisal* (New York: Friendship Press, 1962), 144.

15. He had used the same example earlier in "Lun si yu huo" ("On Life and Death") *Tian Feng* 308 (5 April 1952): 195-96.

16. See M. M. Thomas, "K. H. Ting's Theology of Society," 34-35, for further discussion of this point.

17. K. H. Ting, interview with the author, Nanjing, China, 1 May 1991.

18. Merle Goldman, "The Party and the Intellectuals," in *Cambridge History*

of China, vol. 14, ed. R. MacFarquhar and John K. Fairbank, 257 (Cambridge: Cambridge University Press, 1987).

19. Jonathan Spence, *The Search for Modern China* (New York: Norton, 1990), 574.

20. For a general discussion, see *Seeking the Common Ground*, 172-75; and Price, *The Church in Communist China*, 144-148. The seven were Marcus Cheng (Chen Chonggui), Liu Lingjiu, Fan Aishi, Zhou Qingze, Zhou Fuqing, Dong Hongwen and Sun Pengxi, all of whom were ordained pastors. The official report of the Tenth TSPM Plenum contains more that two hundred pages of criticism of these seven, almost 80 percent of the volume. Marcus Cheng was the most prominent to come under attack. Although not labeled a "rightist," he was never able to resume his work in the church, and he had still not been fully exonerated when he died in 1963. See *Tian Feng* 629-630 (31 March 1963): 18.

21. Frederick C. Teiwes, "The Establishment and Consolidation of the New Regime, 1949-1957," 82.

22. K. H. Ting, interview with the author, Nanjing, China, 11 June 1991 (part 1).

23. K. H. Ting, interview with the author, Nanjing, China, 11 June 1991 (part 1).

24. Wang Weifan, interview with the author, Nanjing, China, 19 April 1996.

25. K. H. Ting, interview with the author, Nanjing, China, 11 June 1991 (part 1).

26. K. H. Ting, interview with the author, Nanjing, China, 16 April 1996.

27. Wang Weifan, interview with the author, Nanjing, China, 19 April 1996.

28. Tens of thousands of "rightists" were rehabilitated after 1978, many posthumously. These included all those who were criticized at the Tenth Plenum, as well as those who had been identified at Nanjing Seminary. See *Seeking the Common Ground*, 174.

29. See J. Radvangi, "The Hungarian Revolt and the Hundred Flowers Campaign," *China Quarterly* 43 (July-September 1970): 121-29. The author was a senior diplomatic official in the Hungarian Foreign Ministry at the time.

30. Mao Zedong, "Speech at the Moscow Meeting of Communist and Workers' Parties" (November 18, 1957), *Quotations from Mao Tse-tung* (http://www.marxists.org/reference/archive/mao/works/red-book/ch06.htm, accessed 10 October 2005).

31. See Owen Chadwick, *The Christian Church in the Cold War* (London: Penguin Books, 1993), 3-18 and passim.

32. "Zhongguo jidutu gei xiongyali jidutu de xin" ("Letter from Chinese Christians to Hungarian Christians"), *Tian Feng* 531 (24 June 1957): 14. The letter is dated 24 May 1957, which was actually before the Anti-Rightist movement began. It is translated in *Documents of the Three-Self Movement*, 168-69.

33. "Cong Xiongyali shijian kan diguozhuyi jintian ruhe hai zai liyong jidujiao" ("How Imperialism Continues to Manipulate Christianity Today as Seen from the Hungarian Events"), *Tian Feng* 531 (24 June 1957): 13. W. A. Visser 't Hooft refutes these charges in his *Memoirs* (Geneva: WCC Publications, 1973). See also Ernest Payne, "Some Illusions and Errors," *Ecumenical Review* (April 1958).

34. K. H. Ting, interview with the author, Nanjing, China, 16 April 1996.

35. See Shen Derong, "Chu fang Xiongyali" ("A Visit to Hungary"), in *Zai sanzi gongzuo wushi nian* (*Fifty Years Working for Three-Self*) (Shanghai: TSPM/CCC, 1999), 31-40.

36. He did publish a short report on his vist to the Church of England; see K. H.

Ting, "Fangwen yingguo shenggonghui pianduan" ("Fragments of a Visit to the Church of England"), *Sheng Gong* (August 1956): 25-26.

37. K. H. Ting, "Xiongyali jiaohui fangwenji" ("Notes on a Visit to the Hungarian Church"), *Tian Feng* 546 (10 February 1958): 9.

38. K. H. Ting, "Xiongyali jiaohui fangwenji" ("Notes on a Visit to the Hungarian Church"), 10.

39. Spence, *The Search for Modern China*, 583-90.

40. K. H. Ting, interview with the author, Nanjing, China, 11 June 1991 (part 1).

41. Milan Opočenský, interview with the author, Geneva, Switzerland, 18 January 2003.

42. Margaret Flory, interview with the author, 10 July 1987, Stony Point, New York, U.S.A. K. H. Ting has admitted that he was part of the ultraleft line at the All-Christian Peace Assembly; K. H. Ting, interview with the author, 16 April 1996, Nanjing, China.

43. K. H. Ting, "The Defence of Peace as a Task for Christians," in . . . *And on Earth Peace: Documents of the First All-Christian Peace Assembly* (Prague, 1961), 100-107. The Chinese text of the speech is not available or has been lost.

44. K. H. Ting, interview with the author, Nanjing, China, 11 June 1991 (part 1).

45. K. H. Ting, "Sermon Preached at the Ecumenical Divine Service," in . . . *And on Earth Peace*, 160. A shortened and somewhat different version of the sermon was published in Chinese: "Fenbie shi fei" ("Discerning Right from Wrong"), *Tian Feng* (28 August 1961): 14-15. The sermon is the only piece of writing from the 1960s to be included in *Love Never Ends*, where it is entitled "Sermon in Bethlehem Chapel," 25-28. See also K. H. Ting, "Cong shijie jidujiao heping huiyi guilai" ("Thoughts after Returning from the Christian Peace Assembly"), *Tian Feng* (28 October 1961): 3-6. This was K. H. Ting's last published essay before the start of the Cultural Revolution.

46. For an overview of this period, see Frederick C. Teiwes, "The Establishment and Consolidation of the New Regime," in *The Politics of China*, 81-86.

47. There is a short discussion of this history in Chen Yongtao and Ji Fengwen, "Sishi nian zhu en shen, duan xiang jü tuan qimei; Jinling xiehe shenxueyuan sishi zhounian xiaoqing jishi" ("The Depth of God's Grace These Forty Years, a Beautiful Fellowship in a Short Time Together: A Record of the Fortieth Anniversary Celebration of Nanjing Union Theological Seminary"), *Tian Feng* 121, no. 1 (1993): 15-16. See also Xu Dingxin, "Zhuiyi Jinling 40 Zhounian, xi ying jinling xi da qing" ("Recollections of the 40th Anniversary and Greetings to the 50th Anniversary of Nanjing Seminary"), *JL* 53, no. 4 (2002): 69-71.

48. K. H. Ting, "Jinling xiehe shenxueyuan jinkuang" ("Nanjing Union Seminary Today"), *Tian Feng* 5 (27 May 1961): 10-11.

49. K. H. Ting, interview with the author, Nanjing, China, 16 April 1996.

50. K. H. Ting, interview with the author, Nanjing, China, 11 June 1991 (part 1).

51. K. H. Ting, interview with the author, Nanjing, China, 11 June 1991 (part 1).

52. See Jasper Becker, *Hungry Ghosts: Mao's Secret Famine* (New York: Free Press, 1996).

53. K. H. Ting, "Ji Xu Huai zhi xing" ("Notes from a Trip to Xuzhou and Huaiyin"), *Tian Feng* (22 October 1958): 16-17.

54. Wickeri, *Seeking the Common Ground*, 219-22. See also Shen Derong, "Wo guo jidujiao lianhe libai de xingcheng" ("The Formation of China's Unification of Worship"), in *Zai sanzi gongzuo wushi nian (Fifty Years Working for Three-Self)*, 40-44.

55. As I indicated in the introduction, the life of the churches and the work of the TSPM during this whole period is not well documented. Researchers at the Institute of World Religions of the Chinese Academy of Social Sciences are currently at work on oral histories of Christianity before the start of the Cultural Revolution.

56. K. H. Ting, interview with the author, Nanjing, China, 20 June 1982.

57. K. H. Ting, interview with the author, Nanjing, China, 11 June 1991 (part 1).

58. Gerda Buege, "Are We Trying to Understand the Christians in China?" *Ecumenical Review* 17 (January 1965): 54-61.

59. Hewlett Johnson, *The Upsurge of China* (Peking: New World Press, 1961), 362.

60. See K. H. Ting's letter to the editor of *The Church Times*, 5 August 1988, defending Hewlett Johnson against those who argued that he was a pawn of the Chinese government.

61. Individual Christians did continue to participate in peace delegations, however. Li Chuwen and Shi Ruzhang traveled to the United Kingdom in January 1963 to take part in an international peace meeting, and Shi went on from there to Tanganyika for the Afro-Asian Unity conference. See the report in *Tian Feng* 629-630 (31 March 2005): 15.

62. The meeting lasted from 12 November 1960 to 14 January 1961. See *Seeking the Common Ground*, 175-76. See also Shen Derong, "Ji zhongguo jidujiao di er jie quanguo huiyi" ("Remembering the Second National Christian Conference") in *Zai sanzi gongzuo wushi nian (Fifty Years Working for Three-Self)*, 45-50.

63. See *Documents of the Three-Self Movement*, 97 and 199, for a comparison of the two constitutions. Reports and speeches from the Second National Christian Conference are contained in *Tian Feng* 604-605 (27 February 1961).

64. K. H. Ting, interview with the author, Nanjing, China, 11 June 1991 (part 1).

65. K. H. Ting, "Ji jingti diguozhuyi liyong jidujiao de yinmou" ("Continue to Be Vigilant Against Imperialist Plots to Manipulate Christianity"), *Tian Feng* 604-605 (27 February 1961): 24.

66. Lazlo Ladany, *The Communist Party of China and Marxism, 1921-1985: A Self Portrait* (Hong Kong: Hong Kong University Press, 1992), 284-85. Li Weihan did not resurface until 1979, when he was given a public apology and was rehabilitated. See "Zhonggong zhongyang tongzhanbu guan yu jianyi wei quanguo tongzhan, minzu, zongjiao gongzuo bumen zhaidiao 'zhixing touxiang zhuyi luxian' mao zi de qingshi baogao" ("Instruction from the Party Central on the Request to Remove the Hat of 'going the capitulationist road' from the National Departments Concerned with United Front, Nationalities and Religious Work"), 3 February 1979, in *Xin shiqi zongjiao gongzuo wenxian xuanbian (Selected Documents on Religious Work in the New Period)* (Beijing: Zongjiao wenhua chubanshe, 1995), 1-4. A selected version of Li Weihan's speeches and writings was published in 1981, *Tongyi Zhanxian wenti yu minzu wenti (On Questions about the United Front and Nationalities)* (Beijing: Renmin chubanshe, 1981).

67. This, according to transcribed notes in a handwritten document purportedly written by a prominent official familiar with the subject. The document is an untitled informal history of Chinese governmental religious policy, and the discussion appears in the section "Guanyu yijiuliusi nian xiabannian zhi yijiuliuliu nian shang bannian guonei han minzu zongjiao gongzuo luxian shi fe wenti de ziliao" ("Materials on the Question of Right and Wrong in Religious Work among Han Chinese, from the Second Half of 1964 to the First Half of 1966"). The quotation in the sentence above is from page 3 of this document.

6. THE CULTURAL REVOLUTION ERA, 1966-1976

1. "Reply to Comrade Guo Mo Ruo (To the Tune of Man Jiang Hong)," *Chinese Literature* 5 (1966). Also quoted in Roderick MacFarquhar, *The Origins of the Cultural Revolution*, vol. 3, *The Coming of the Cataclysm, 1961-1966*. (New York: Oxford University Press and Columbia University Press, 1997), vi. Compare translation to that of Willis Barnstone, *The Poems of Mao Tse-tung* (New York: Bantam, 1972), 122-25.

2. Bei Dao (Zhao Zhenkai), "Tomorrow, No," trans. Bonnie McDougall, *Renditions* 19 and 20 (Spring and Autumn 1983): 195.

3. The best analysis of the origins of the Cultural Revolution in any language is Roderick MacFarquhar, *The Origins of the Cultural Revolution* (New York: Oxford University Press and Columbia University Press, 1974-1997) 3 vols.; and the best history is Roderick MacFarquhar and Michael Schoenhals, *Mao's Last Revolution* (Cambridge and London: Harvard University Press, 2006). For an insightful general history by two prominent Chinese intellectuals, see Yan Jiaqi and Gao Gao, *Turbulent Decade: A History of the Cultural Revolution*, trans. and ed. D. W. Y. Kwok (Honolulu: University of Hawaii Press, 1996). For a general overview, see Harry Harding, "The Chinese State in Crisis, 1966-1968," in Roderick MacFarquhar, ed., "The Succession to Mao and the End of Maoism, 1969-1982," in *The Politics of China: The Eras of Mao and Deng*, ed. Roderick MacFarquhar, 2nd ed. (Cambridge: Cambridge University Press, 1997), 148-340.

4. The most comprehensive biography of Mao is Philip Short, *Mao: A Life* (New York: Henry Holt, 1999). For an alternative view of Mao, drawing on many hitherto unknown sources see Jung Chang and Jon Halliday, *Mao: The Unknown Story* (London: Jonathan Cape, 2004).

5. MacFarquhar, *Origins of the Cultural Revolution*, 3:461.

6. For a description and analysis, see MacFarquhar and Schoenhals, *Mao's Last Revolution*.

7. The Gang of Four were Jiang Qing, Zhang Chunqiao, Yao Wenyuan and Wang Hongwen. Following their arrest, trial and conviction, they were blamed for all the errors and crimes of the Cultural Revolution era.

8. Lynn T. White III, *Policies of Chaos: The Organizational Causes of Violence in China's Cultural Revolution* (Princeton: Princeton University Press, 1989), 47. For an overview of the various explanations of the Cultural Revolution, see pp. 24-42.

9. "Nanking University Exposes K'uang Ya-ming as an Anti-Party, Anti-Socialist and Counter Revolutionary Element," *Renmin ribao* (16 June 1966), trans. *Survey of China Mainland Press* 3726 (27 June 1966): 1.

10. See "Religion and the Red Guard," *China Notes* 4, no. 4 (October 1966): 3-4; and Richard Bush, *Religion in Communist China* (Nashville and New York: Abingdon Press, 1970), 257.

11. This story of the division of the faculty into two (or more) groups is well known in Nanjing, and there are many different versions of the story. See also Jonathan Chao T'ien-en and Rosanna Chong, *Dangdai zhongguo jidujiao fazhan-shi, 1949-1997 (A History of Christianity in Socialist China, 1949-1997)* (Taipei: CMI Publishing, 1997), 192-93.

12. K. H. Ting, interview with the author, Nanjing, China, 11 June 1991 (part 1).

13. Gao Wenqian, *Wannian de Zhou Enlai (Zhou Enlai's Later Years)* (Hong Kong: Mirror Books, 2003), 85-133.

14. Despite these claims, MacFarquhar and Schoenhals note that Zhou Enlai reportedly sanctioned the destruction of property belonging to some religious groups; see *Mao's Last Revolution*, 120-21.

15. The story was related to me by two different people in Nanjing in the early 1990s. Neither wished to have their names revealed. For a somewhat different version of the events, see the section on the Cultural Revolution in Ma Jia, *Ai shi zhenli (Discerning Truth through Love)* (Hong Kong: Chinese Christian Literature Council, 2006).

16. K. H. Ting, interview with the author, Nanjing, China, 11 June 1991 (part 1).

17. K. H. Ting, "That You Be Trustworthy," *CTR* (1991): 126-27.

18. K. H. Ting, interview with the author, Nanjing, China, 11 June 1991 (part 1).

19. K. H. Ting, interview with the author, Nanjing, China, 22 March 1997.

20. K. H. Ting, interview with the author, Nanjing, China, 11 June 1991 (part 1).

21. K. H. Ting, interview with the author, Nanjing, China, 11 June 1991 (part 2).

22. Reinhold Niebuhr, *Moral Man and Immoral Society: A Study in Ethics and Politics* (New York: Scribner's, 1932), 277. Niebuhr later expressed the view that he wished he had never written this particular paragraph.

23. Jonathan Spence, *The Search for Modern China* (New York: Norton, 1990), 638.

24. See "There and Back Again: The Chinese 'Urban Youth' Generation," *Renditions* 50 (Autumn 1998). There was a nostalgic revival of this era among the generation sent down to the countryside beginning in the late 1990s, complete with specialized restaurants and revolutionary songs set to modern rhythms.

25. Ting Yenren, "Talk on the Cultural Revolution," 26 January 1997. He has retold this story several times in gatherings of Amity teachers.

26. See White, *Policies of Chaos*, 165.

27. E. H. Johnson, "K. H. Ting: Profile of a Chinese Christian," *One World* 16 (May 1976): 23.

28. Reported, *inter alia*, by E. H. Johnson, "K. H. Ting: Profile of a Chinese Christian," 24. Confirmed here and in the following paragraphs in K. H. Ting, interview with the author, Nanjing, China, 22 March 1997.

29. K. H. Ting, interview with the author, Nanjing, China, 11 June 1991 (part 1).

30. K. H. Ting, interview with the author, Nanjing, China, 22 March 1997.

31. "Westerner Reports Recent Visit," *China Notes* 2, no. 3 (Summer 1969): 37.

32. K. H. Ting, interview with the author, Nanjing, China, 11 June 1991 (part 1).

33. K. H. Ting, interview with the author, Nanjing, China, 1 May 1991.

34. K. H. Ting, "Remembering a Friend: On the 30th Anniversary of the Death of Huang Peiyong, September 1992," in K. H. Ting, *Love Never Ends: Papers by K. H. Ting,* ed. Janice K. Wickeri (Nanjing: Yilin Press, 2000), 418-20.

35. K. H. Ting, interview with the author, Nanjing, China, 1 May 1991. The Jiangsu UFWD was not operating at the time, so Ting was probably referring to the revolutionary committee made up of UFWD members.

36. K. H. Ting, "In Memory of Luo Zhufeng (1997)," in *Love Never Ends,* 538-39; and "Two Staunch Friends of Nanjing Union Theological Seminary: Y. T. Wu and Luo Zhufeng," *CTR* 17 (2003): 138. Ting does not name those who attacked him in his published essays, but the reference here seems obvious. He uses the term "secret group" in one of the formal interviews I had with him, where he does name Li Chuwen; K. H. Ting, interview with the author, Nanjing, China, 11 June 1991 (part 1).

37. K. H. Ting, interview with the author, Nanjing, China, 11 June 1991 (part 2).

38. K. H. Ting, interview with the author, Nanjing, China, 11 June 1991 (part 2).

39. Yan and Gao, *Turbulent Decade,* 335. For an overview of this period, see MacFarquhar and Schoenals, *Mao's Last Revolution,* 324ff.

40. See Bob Whyte, *Unfinished Encounter: China and Christianity* (Glasgow: Collins, 1988), 307-8; and Anthony Lambert, *The Resurrection of the Chinese Church* (London: Hodder & Stoughton, 1991), 23ff.

41. *Foreign Broadcast Information Service* 6 September 1972 (Peking NCNA English Press Report, FBIS, 7 September 1972 (175.1, B-1) #175.1 (7 September 1972); "Funeral Ceremony Held for NPC Vice Chairman Ho Hsiang-ning." See also Whyte, *Unfinished Encounter,* 308; *Church Times,* 16 November 1973.

42. K. H. Ting, interview with the author, Nanjing, China, 11 June 1991 (part 2).

43. K. H. Ting, interview with the author, Nanjing, China, 11 June 1991 (part 2).

44. E. H. Johnson, "Challenge of the New China, Report of a Visit to China, 23 March-14 April 1973," unpublished manuscript, 13 pp.; also "Notes on the Church in China," private paper, 1973; and *China Notes* (Summer 1973). On this first visit, the Tings met with the Johnsons in a hotel.

45. K. H. Ting, interview with the author, Nanjing, China, 25 August 1991.

46. "Zhao Puchu jushi shengping dashi nianbiao (zhengqiu yijian gao)" ("Chronology of Major Events in the Life of Zhao Puchu [Draft for the Solicitation of Opinions]"), undated, p. 14.

47. The poem is reproduced in Zhou Jiacai, *Zhao Puchu yu Jiangsu zongjiao (Zhao Puchu and Religion in Jiangsu)* (Beijing: Zongjiaowenhua chubanshe, 2003), 38-39.

48. K. H. Ting to Burgess Carr, 7 May 1974. WCC Archives.

49. He met with a visiting American congressional delegation in the summer of 1973 (Lambert, *The Resurrection of the Chinese Church*, 24); with Don MacInnis and others from a U.S.–China People's Friendship Association delegation in 1974 ("The Church in China Today: Report from a Recent Visit," in *Christianity and the New China* (South Pasadena, Ca.: Ecclesia Publications, 1976), 157-61; with John Fleming in 1975 (private report, 5 August 1975); with James Endicott; with Ted Johnson on a second extended visit ("Christian Voices from the Church in China, April 1975," *China Notes* 13, no. 3 (Summer 1975), to name only those who wrote reports. For a discussion of these visits, see Whyte, *Unfinished Encounter*, 312-13.

50. MacInnis, "The Church in China Today: Report from a Recent Visit," (1974), 160.

51. "Theologians See the Hand of God at Work," *SCMP* (17 December 1974). He continued to speak of himself as "Old Ting" into the late 1970s, including in early conversations with this writer.

52. See Philip L. Wickeri, *Seeking the Common Ground: Protestant Christianity, the Three-Self Movement and China's United Front* (Maryknoll, N.Y.: Orbis Books, 1988), 11-16; Whyte, *Unfinished Encounter*, 310-13; and Richard Madsen, *China and the American Dream: A Moral Inquiry*, (Berkeley: University of California Press, 1995), 106-15.

53. K. H. Ting, interview with the author, Nanjing, China, 11 June 1991 (part 2). Cora Deng (Deng Yuzhi) and George Wu (Wu Gaozi) were TSPM leaders. Deng was a prominent YWCA leader who was active in labor organizing in the 1930s, and Wu was a Methodist pastor. Both were in their seventies during the later years of the Cultural Revolution.

54. See Ann Thurston, *Enemies of the People: The Ordeal of Intellectuals in China's Great Cultural Revolution* (New York: Knopf, 1987); and Geremie Barmé and Bennett Lee, trans. and eds., *The Wounded: New Stories of the Cultural Revolution* (Hong Kong, 1979).

55. Roderick MacFarquhar, "The Sucession of Mao and the End of Maoism. 1969-1982," in *The Politics of China: The Eras of Mao and Deng*, 286-88. See also MacFarquhar and Schoenhals, *Mao's Last Revolution*, 358ff.

56. See Yan and Gao, *Turbulent Decade*, 457-60.

57. On the role of these groups, see Martin King Whyte, *Small Groups and Political Rituals in China* (Berkeley: University of California Press, 1974).

58. K. H. Ting, interview with the author, Nanjing, China, 11 June 1991 (part 2).

59. K. H. Ting, interview with the author, Nanjing, China, 25 August 1991.

60. Yan and Gao, *Turbulent Decade*, 459-60.

61. K. H. Ting, "Forerunner Y. T. Wu," in *Love Never Ends*, 83. The last sentence here may reflect the political situation in 1981 when people's experiences of hardship or suffering during the Cultural Revolution were being downplayed by the government.

62. Wickeri, *Seeking the Common Ground*, 102.

63. *A Practical Chinese-English Dictionary* (Nanjing: Jiangsu People's Publishing, 1983). Other seminary faculty who worked on the dictionary included Chen Zemin, Han Wenzao, Luo Zhenfang, Mo Ruxi and Xu Rulei. The dictionary was later published in Hong Kong and still later by the University of Washington Press in Seattle. These editions dropped the names of the three other editors, and list only

K. H. Ting, a fact that he has said he found embarrassing because of the substantial contributions made by the others.

64. K. H. Ting, interview with the author, Nanjing, China, 25 August 1991.

65. Philip L. and Janice K. Wickeri, "Portrait of a Chinese Buddhist Leader: An Interview with Zhao Puchu," *The Christian Century* (26 March 1980): 350-52.

66. Cited in Dick Wilson, *Zhou Enlai: A Biography* (New York: Viking, 1984), 293. On this period, see Roger Garside, *Coming Alive: China After Mao* (New York: New American Library, 1981).

67. On the first Tiananmen incident in 1976, see MacFarquhar and Schoenhals, *Mao's Last Revolution,* 422-30.

68. MacFarquhar and Schoenhals, *Mao's Last Revolution,* 435-36.

69. "Interview with Dr. and Mrs. K. H. Ting," reported by Eugene L. Stockwell, 22 October 1976 (8 pp.); "The Life of Christianity: Interview with Dr. and Mrs. K. H. Ting," *The Christian Century* (23 February 1977): 168-71, by the same author is a shortened version of this interview.

70. For a good overview of the more general critique, see William A. Joseph, *The Critique of Ultra-Leftism in China, 1958-1981* (Stanford: Stanford University Press, 1984), esp. 151-220.

71. "Interview with Dr. and Mrs. K. H. Ting," reported by Eugene L. Stockwell, 22 October 1976, p. 8.

72. K. H. Ting, interview with the author, Nanjing, China, 11 June 1991 (part 2).

73. Wang Weifan, *Lilies of the Field,* trans. and ed. Janice and Philip Wickeri; rev. ed. (Shatin: Foundation for Theological Education in Southeast Asia, 1989), 69.

74. K. H. Ting, "Bimu ci" ("Closing Address"), *Tian Feng* 1 (30 January 1983): 24-25. The translation is from *Religion in the People's Republic of China: Documentation* 11 (June 1983): 20-21. This address is not included in any of Ting's collected works.

75. His most significant statement to an overseas audience was his address in Lambeth Palace on 1 October 1982. It was originally cited in Whyte, *Unfinished Encounter,* 297-98. The full text was published as "Address in Lambeth Palace Chapel," *The Church in China* (London: British Council of Churches, 1983), and is reprinted in *Love Never Ends,* as "The Truth of the Resurrection," 86-89. A translation of this essay was also published in China, and may be found in *Wenji,* 8-11. The content of this address is similar to the one just quoted, which was delivered in China several months later.

76. K. H. Ting, interview with the author, Nanjing, China, 25 August 1991.

77. See *Seeking the Common Ground,* 184-85. For a theological interpretation on the Cultural Revolution by one of China's non-Christian intellectuals, see Leo Loeb, "Yang Huilin and His View of Christian Culture," *Interreligio* 38 (Winter 2000): 57-63.

78. "Open Letter to Brothers and Sisters in Christ in All of China from the Standing Committee of the Christian Movement for Self-Government, Self-Support and Self-Propagation," 1 March 1980, in *Religion in the People's Republic of China: Documentation* 2 and 3 (July 1980): 51-54.

79. K. H. Ting, "Inspirations from Liberation Theology, Process Theology and Teilhard de Chardin," in *Love Never Ends,* 199.

80. K. H. Ting, "Love That Loves to the End" (1988), in *Love Never Ends*, 314-15. See chap. 5 for Ting's self-criticism after the Anti-Rightist movement and chap. 7 for his continuing critique of ultra-leftism.

7. RESTORATION AND RENEWAL , 1977-1983

1. "In Memory of Zhao Dan," *Wen Hui Bao* (Shanghai), 15 October 1980. Cao Yu is a well-known Chinese playwright. The translation is mine.

2. Deng Xiaoping, "The United Front and the Tasks of the Chinese People's Political Consultative Conference in the New Period (15 June 1979)," *Selected Works of Deng Xiaoping* (People's Daily Online) http://english.peopledaily.com.cn/dengxp/vol2/text/b1300.html (accessed 21 October 2005).

3. Jung Chang, *Wild Swans: Three Daughters of China* (New York: Simon & Schuster, 1991), 499.

4. Roderick MacFarquhar, ed., *The Politics of China: The Eras of Mao and Deng*, 2nd ed. (Cambridge and New York: Cambridge University Press, 1997), 317.

5. The approach to "seeking truth from facts" was actually initiated by Deng's protégé, Hu Yaobang, but Deng promoted and helped popularize it. See Kenneth Lieberthal, *Governing China: From Revolution through Reform* (New York: Norton, 1995), 129. The *People's Daily* editorial "Practice Is the Only Criterion of Truth" (11 May 1978) was written by Nanjing University professor Hu Fuming.

6. The Cultural Revolution images here are from Lynn T. White III, *Policies of Chaos: The Organizational Causes of Violence in China's Cultural Revolution* (Princeton: Princeton University Press, 1989), 270.

7. See Richard Baum, ed., *China's Four Modernizations: The New Technological Revolution* (Boulder, Colo.: Westview Press, 1980); "Quarterly Documentation," *China Quarterly* 77 (March 1979); and Lynn White, *Unstately Power*, vol. 2, *Local Causes of China's Intellectual, Legal and Governmental Reforms* (Armonk, N.Y.: M. E. Sharpe, 1999).

8. Timothy Cheek, "From Priests to Professionals: Intellectuals and the State Under the CCP," in *Popular Protest and Political Culture in Modern China: Learning from 1989*, ed. Jeffrey N. Wasserstrom and Elizabeth J. Perry (Boulder, Colo.: Westview Press, 1992), 128, 135 and passim.

9. See "Discussions by Rev. Li Ch'u-wen with French Protestants," *China Notes* 2, no. 5 (October 1964): 7; and Ross Terrill, "Conversation in Peking," *The Christian Century* (11 January 1965): 47-50. The latter is a record of a conversation with Zhao Fusan.

10. See Philip L. Wickeri, *Seeking the Common Ground: Protestant Christianity, the Three-Self Movement and China's United Front* (Maryknoll, N.Y.: Orbis Books, 1988), 170. Li Chuwen's repudiation of the church came from reports widely circulated in Hong Kong and reportedly published in Hong Kong newspapers at the time.

11. Zhao Fusan was named vice-chair of the National TSPM Committee in 1980, and in 1985 became a board member of the Amity Foundation. He continued in these positions until his refusal to return to China after the suppression of the democracy movement in 1989.

12. See, for example, Edward Yihua Xu, "Religion and Education: St. John's

University as an Evangelizing Agency" (Ph.D. diss., Princeton University, 1994), 228.

13. Most of the relevant documents on national religious policy published between 1979 and 1992 may be found in *Xin shiqi zongjiao gongzuo wenxian xuanbian (Selected Documents on Religious Work in the New Period),* ed. Zhonggong zhongyang wenxianyanjiu shi zonghe yanjiu zu (CPC Central Committee Documentary Research Faculty of the Comprehensive Research Group) and Guowuyuan zongjiao zhiwujü zhengci fagui si (Policy, Law and Regulations Department of the State Council Religious Affairs Bureau) (Beijing: Religious Culture Publishers, 1995). Some translations of these are found in Don MacInnis, ed., *Religion in China Today: Policy and Practice* (Maryknoll, N.Y.: Orbis Books, 1989); and in the *China Study Project Documentation (CSPD),* 1979–.

14. See the bibliography to my earlier volume, *Seeking the Common Ground,* 331-148. Some of the more important book-length studies in English on different aspects of Chinese religious policy include Alan Hunter and Kim-Kwong Chan, *Protestantism in Contemporary China* (Cambridge: Cambridge University Press, 1993); Anthony S. K. Lam, *The Catholic Church in Present-Day China: Through Darkness and Light,* trans. Peter Barry and Norman Walling (Leuven and Hong Kong: Ferdinand Verbiest Foundation and the Holy Spirit Study Center, 1994); Anthony Lambert, *The Resurrection of the Chinese Church* (London: Hodder & Stoughton, 1991); Beatrice Leung, *Sino-Vatican Relationships: Problems in Conflicting Authority, 1976-1986* (Cambridge: Cambridge University Press, 1992); Luo Zhufeng, ed., *Religion under Socialism in China,* trans. Donald E. MacInnis and Zheng Xi'an (Armonk, N.Y.: M. E. Sharpe, 1991); Don MacInnis, *Religion in China Today: Policy and Practice* (Maryknoll, N.Y.: Orbis Books, 1989); Richard Madsen, *China's Catholics: Tragedy and Hope in an Emerging Civil Society* (Berkeley: University of California Press, 1998); James T. Myers, *Enemies without Guns: The Catholic Church in China* (New York: Paragon House, 1991); Julian Pas, ed., *The Turning of the Tide: Religion in China Today* (Hong Kong: Hong Kong Branch of the Royal Asiatic Society, 1989); Edmond Tang and Jean-Paul Wiest, eds., *The Catholic Church in Modern China* (Maryknoll, N.Y.: Orbis Books, 1993); Stephen Uhalley and Xiaoxin Wu, eds., *China and Christianity: Burdened Past, Hopeful Future* (Armonk, N.Y.: M. E. Sharpe, 2001). In Chinese, see Chao T'ien-en and Rosanna Chong, *Dangdai zhongguo jidujiao fazhanshi, 1949-1997 (A History of Christianity in Socialist China, 1949-1997)* (Taipei: CMI Publishing, 1997); Chao T'ien-en, *Zhonggong dui Jidujiao de zhengce (Chinese Communist Policy Towards Christianity)* (Hong Kong: CCRC, 1983); Deng Zhaoming, *Chengshou yu chishou: zhongguo dadi de fuyin huoju (The Torch of the Testimony in China)* (Hong Kong: Christian Study Center on Chinese Religion and Culture, 1998); Leung Ka-lun, *Gaige kaifang yilai de zhongguo nongcun jiaohui (The Rural Churches of Mainland China since 1978)* (Hong Kong: Alliance Bible Seminary, 1999); Ying Fuk-tsang, *Dangdai zhongguo zhengjiao guanxi (Church-State Relations in Contemporary China)* (Hong Kong: China Alliance Press, 1999); Yip Ching-wah (Francis), *Xun zhen qiu quan: zhongguo shenxue yu zhengjiao chujing chutan (Chinese Theology in a Church-State Context: A Preliminary Study)* (Hong Kong: Christian Study Center on Chinese Religion and Culture, 1997. A semi-official compendium of useful information on religion and religious policy in China is contained in Zhu Yueli, ed., *Jinri zhongguo zongjiao (Religion in Today's China)* (Beijing: Xinhua Publish-

ers, 1994). Important essays and translations on religion and religious policy in China are contained in the following specialized journals: *Bridge (1985-1997)*; *The China Study Bulletin*; *CTR*; *Ching Feng*; *Shijie zongjiao yanjiu (Research on World Religions)*; *Tripod*; *Zhongguo zongjiao (Chinese Religions)*; and *Zongjiao (Religion)*. See also Hon S. Chan, "Christianity in Post-Mao China," *Issues and Studies* 29, no. 3 (March 1993): 106-32; Lazlo Ladany, "The Church in China Seen in December 1980," unpub. manuscript distributed by *China News Analysis*; and Wang Hsueh-wen, "Tolerance and Control," *Issues and Studies* 27, no. 1 (January 1991): 126ff.; and *Religion in China Today, The China Quarterly* 174 (June 2003), esp. Pitman B. Potter, "Belief in Control: Regulation of Religion in China," 317-37.

15. On Zhao Puchu, see Tim Brook, "Travelling to the Trigram Mountains: Buddhism After the Gang of Four," *Contemporary China* 2, no. 4 (Winter 1978): 70-75; Holmes Welch, *Buddhism Under Mao* (Cambridge: Harvard University Press, 1972), 467 and passim; and Philip L. and Janice K. Wickeri "Portrait of a Chinese Buddhist Leader: An Interview with Zhao Puchu," *The Christian Century* (26 March 1980): 350-52. Zhao's writings regularly appeared in *Fayin*, the journal of the Chinese Buddhist Association, which has also published collections of his writings. A memorial to Zhao Puchu was published in *Zongjiao* 48, no. 2 (2000), on the inside front and back covers.

16. See, for example, K. H. Ting, *Love Never Ends: Papers by K. H. Ting,* ed. Janice K. Wickeri (Nanjing: Yilin Press, 2000), 113, 273 and passim.

17. For more on the role of these two bodies, see Lieberthal, *Governing China: From Revolution Through Reform*. The role of the CPPCC is described in Wickeri, *Seeking the Common Ground*, 66-68. K. H. Ting's explanation of the role of the CPPCC, the NPC and other government bodies to Christians overseas may be found in "Fourteen Points from Christians in the People's Republic of China to Christians Abroad," in Don MacInnis, *Religion in China Today: Policy and Practice*, 63-65.

18. For the relationship between the RAB, the UFWD and religious organizations in the united front see Wickeri, *Seeking the Common Ground*, 68-74.

19. Luo Guangwu, ed., *Xin zhongguo zongjiao gongzuo da shi gailan, 1949-1999 (An Overview of Major Events in Religious Work in New China, 1949-1999)* (Beijing: Huawen chubanshe, 2001), 254-55. See also "Guanyu fencui 'si ren bang' yihou zongjiao gongzuo zhuyao qingkuang de ziliao" ("Materials on the Major Situation of Religious Work after the Fall of the Gang of Four," handwritten manuscripts circa 1989, p. 1. This manuscript is part of a larger compendium of notes on religious work in China from 1956 to the end of the 1970s, purportedly written by a prominent official familiar with the subject. I obtained a copy of the manuscript in China in 1989.

20. Zhu Yueli, ed., *Jinri zhongguo zongjiao (Religion in Today's China)* (Beijing: Xinhua Publishers, 1994), 130, 152-53.

21. "Guanyu fencui 'si ren bang' yihou zongjiao gongzuo zhuyao qingkuang de ziliao" ("Materials on the Major Situation of Religious Work after the Fall of the Gang of Four"), 2-9. The summary document of this meeting was not approved until February of the following year, that is, after the Third Plenum. See "Instruction from the CPC-UFWD Proposing the Removal of the 'Capitulationist' Hat from the Nationalities and Religious Work Departments," in *Xinshiqi zongjiao gongzuo wenxian xuanbian (Selected Documents on Religious Work in the New*

Period), 1-4. The Eighth National Conference on Religious Work met 1-11 December 1978.

22. The first major article on religious questions was published in *People's Daily* as "Religion and Feudal Superstition," 15 March 1979. For a translation, see MacInnis, *Religion in China Today*, 32-34.

23. Excerpts of the speeches of Hua and Deng, as well as reports from the discussion called by the RAB, are found in *CSPD* 1 (November 1979): 1-3. The full text of Deng's keynote address (15 June 1979) is contained in *Xinshiqi zongjiao gongzuo wenxian xuanbian* (*Selected Documents on Religious Work in the New Period*), "The United Front in the New Period and the Role of the CPPCC," 5-8.

24. See MacInnis, *Religion in China Today*, 26-32 for a translation. See also "Freedom of Religious Belief Is a Basic Policy of the Party Towards Religions," *Guangming Daily*, 30 November 1980, translated in *CSPD* 4 (February 1981): 7-10.

25. Ulanfu, director of the UFWD, admitted as much in his report at the UFWD conference which met from 15 August-3 September 1979. See *CSPD* 2 and 3 (July 1980): 1.

26. See relevant documents in *Xinshiqi zongjiao gongzuo wenxian xuanbian* (*Selected Documents on Religious Work in the New Period*), 23-30.

27. "Guanyu fencui 'si ren bang' yihou zongjiao gongzuo zhuyao qingkuang de ziliao" ("Materials on the Major Situation of Religious Work after the Fall of the Gang of Four"), 3-5.

28. *Renmin ribao* (*People's Daily*), 9 September 1980, 1. Translation by Janice K. Wickeri. Zhao Puchu's comments on the problems with religious policy implementation among Buddhists appear here as well.

29. Xiao Xianfa, "Correctly Understand and Implement the Party's Policy on Freedom of Religious Belief," *People's Daily*, 14 June 1980. Translated in *CSPD* 4 (February 1981): 1-4.

30. K. H. Ting, interview with the author, Nanjing, 25 August 1991.

31. The published version of this document is contained in *Xinshiqi zongjiao gongzuo wenxian xuanbian* (*Selected Documents on Religious Work in the New Period*), 53-73, and a translation is found in MacInnis, *Religion in China Today*, 8-26. Bob Whyte has a point-by-point summary and analysis of this document in *Unfinished Encounter: China and Christianity* (Glasgow: Collins, 1988), 384-89. For different interpretations of Document 19, see Lambert, *The Resurrection of the Chinese Church*, 52-63; and Chao, *Dangdai zhongguo jidujiao fazhanshi, 1949-1997* (*A History of Christianity in Socialist China, 1949-1997*), 302-9.

32. "Resolution on Certain Questions in the History of Our Party since the Founding of the PRC (1949-81)," *Beijing Review* 27 (6 July 1981): 10-39. The resolution has a short paragraph on the policy of the freedom of religious belief, which explicitly says that upholding the "four fundamental principles does not mean that religious believers should renounce their faith, but that they must not engage in anti-party propaganda or interfere with politics or education." For a general comment on the resolution, see MacFarquhar, *The Politics of China*, 329-31.

33. Ru Wen (K. H. Ting), "Xuexi yige wenjian de xinde" ("What I Have Gained from Studying a Document"), *Zongjiao* (*Religion*) 6 (November 1984): 8-15. Ting published a revised version of this essay with some significant omissions, discussed below, under his own name in the Chinese and English edition of his

works. In English, see "Reading Document 19: A Talk to Government Cadres," in *Love Never Ends*, 166-79. The Chinese version is in *Wenji*, 386-97.

34. These are the so-called five characteristics of religion, originally formulated by Li Weihan. For a discussion, see *Seeking the Common Ground*, 83-89. Also "Reading Document 19," in *Love Never Ends*, 171.

35. For the paragraph in question, see MacInnis, *Religion in China Today*, 18.

36. See Ru Wen, "What I Have Gained from Studying a Document," 14-15. The omitted section would have followed the first full paragraph of "Reading Document 19: A Talk to Government Cadres," in *Love Never Ends*, 178; in *Wenji*, 396.

37. See MacInnis, *Religion in Today's China*, 34-35. A full discussion of the constitutional provisions for the freedom of religious belief is contained in *Seeking the Common Ground*, 101-6.

38. See K. H. Ting, "On the Thirty-Sixth Article of the Constitution," 114.

39. For a compilation of religious laws and regulations adopted on a national level adopted between 1982 and 1994, see *Jinri zhongguo zongjiao* (*Religion in Today's China*), 87-118.

40. This was the opinion of Francis Price Jones, *The Church in Communist China: A Protestant Appraisal* (New York: Friendship Press, 1962), 97-114.

41. For the term, see Andras Sajo as cited in Hon S. Chan, "Christianity in Post-Mao Mainland China," 131.

42. *Zhou Enlai tongyi zhanxian wenxuan* (*Selected Writings of Zhou Enlai on the United Front*) (Beijing: People's Publishing, 1984). The volume was given to me in February 1985.

43. See MacFarquhar, *The Politics of China*, 327-32; also Lambert, *The Resurrection of the Chinese Church*, 278-79.

44. See William A. Joseph, *The Critique of Ultra-Leftism in China, 1958-1981* (Stanford: Stanford University Press, 1984). This book contains a useful bibliography of Chinese sources published in the late 1970s and early 1980s. The number of books on the subject published in China since that time has been enormous.

45. Wang Ruoshui, *Wei rendaozhuyi bianhu* (*In Defense of Humanism*) (Beijing: San Lian Publishers, 1986), 217-33. In this essay, Wang was writing against Hu Qiaomu, who was then the chief CPC ideologue.

46. Letter from Ting to Wickeri, 30 December 1982. See also "A Chinese Christian's Appreciation of an Atheist," in *Love Never Ends*, 35-42.

47. See Wang Ruowang, "On '*wu wei er zhi*' in Literature and the Arts," *Red Flag* 1979 (9), 47-49. Ting may be referring to a section of this article in the letter just cited, where Wang quotes former Shanghai mayor Chen Yi as advocating "non-action" so that the masses could do things for themselves as reinforcing Mao's reliance on "the people" as a source of revolutionary change.

48. See Philip L. Wickeri, "Chinese Neo-Liberalism Has Lost Sight of Social Justice," *China Development Brief* 6, no. 1 (Spring 2004): 42-44. This is a review of Wang Hui, *China's New Order: Society, Politics and Economy in Transition* (Cambridge and London: Harvard University Press, 2003).

49. For the renewal of religious studies in China, see Philip Wickeri, "Reinterpreting Religion in China," *China News Analysis* 1485 (15 May 1993): 1-9. See also Ryan Dunch, "Protestants and the State in Post-Mao China" (M.A. thesis, University of British Columbia, 1991), 63-66; Whyte, *Unfinished Encounter*, 354-67; and Wickeri, *Seeking the Common Ground*, 89-92; Ying Fuk-tsang, *Church-State*

Relations in Contemporary China, 23-32; and David Yu, "Religious Studies in China at Crossroads," *Journal of Chinese Religions* 18 (Fall 1991): 167-72.

50. K. H. Ting, interview with the author, Nanjing, China, 25 August 1991.

51. K. H. Ting, interview with the author, Nanjing, China, 11 June 1991 (part 2); and K. H. Ting, interview with the author, Nanjing, China, 25 August 1991.

52. Kuang Yaming, "Thoughts on Religion," in *Qiusuji* (*Collected Writings*), ed. Kuang Yaming (Beijing: Renmin chubanshe, 1995), 75-82. This essay is based on a talk Kuang gave to students at Nanjing Theological Seminary in 1983.

53. K. H. Ting, "Remembering Kuang Yaming," in *Love Never Ends*, 534. Ting does not mention Ren Jiyu by name in this account.

54. "Ding Guangxun tan jidujiao" ("K. H. Ting on Christianity"), in *Daoyou zhishi* (*A Reference for Guides*) (Nanjing, 1979), 1-15.

55. See Whyte, *Unfinished Encounter*, 355; and *Guangming Daily*, 22 March 1979.

56. Wickeri, "Random Notes on Religion in China," unpublished manuscript, 1979, p. 5. The substance of this lecture, which I have not seen, is probably similar to the talk on liberation theology that he later presented to seminary students. See *Love Never Ends*, 192-220.

57. Ren Jiyu, "Remove Obstacles to the Realization of the Four Modernizations," *People's Daily*, 1 May 1979. Ren Jiyu also published the first essay on religious studies after the Cultural Revolution, "Investigate Religion and Criticize Theology," in *Guangming ribao*, 27 September 1977. For an early interpretation of Ren Jiyu, see Tim Brook, "Dying Gods in China," *Commonweal* 105, no. 15 (4 August 1978): 490-95.

58. "Ding Guangxun tan jidujiao" ("K. H. Ting on Christianity"), 12-15; K. H. Ting, "Science, Religion and Democracy in China," unpublished typescript (October 1979), from a speech delivered at McGill University; K. H. Ting, "Zhongguo shehuizhuyi shiqi de zongjiao wenti jieshao" ("A Review of Religious Issues in the Period of Socialism in China"), *Zongjiao* (*Religion*) 13 (June 1988): 28-32, translated in *Love Never Ends*, 295-304. Wickeri, "Random Notes on Religion in China," unpublished manuscript, 1979.

59. See Luo Zhufeng, ed., *Religion under Socialism in China*, trans. Donald E. MacInnis and Zheng Xi'an (Armonk, N.Y.: M. E. Sharpe, 1991); also K. H. Ting, "In Memory of Luo Zhufeng," in *Love Never Ends*, 537-39. See also Luo Zhufeng, ed., *Zongjiao* (*Religion*). *Zhongguo da baike quanshu* (*The Great Chinese Encyclopedia*) (Beijing and Shanghai: Zhongguo da baike quanshu chubanshe, 1988).

60. Philip L. Wickeri, "Reinterpreting Religion in China," *China News Analysis* 1485 (15 May 1993): 1-9.

61. K. H. Ting, "Religion as Opium," (23 October 1981) unpublished typescript from a speech in Saskatoon, Canada, 10 pp. Although this essay was delivered to an overseas audience, it represents a summary of K. H. Ting's thinking on the subject in 1981. See also K. H. Ting, "On Religion as Opiate," in *Love Never Ends*, 223-32.

62. "Geming daoshi you guan ruhe duidai zongjiao wenti de bufen lunshu" ("Revolutionary Leaders on the Question of How to Handle Religion," *Zongjiao* (*Religion*) 1 (1980): 1-7. The essay following this one, written under the pseudonym Jian Xue, provides an analysis of the whole issue of religion and opium, "Cong

zongjiao yu yapian tan qi" ("On Religion and Opium"), *Zongjiao (Religion)* 1 (1980): 8-14.

63. Gong Yu, "Lishi shang de yapian lun" ("Religion as Opium in Historical Perspective") *Zongjiao (Religion)* 5 (1984): 17-18.

64. "Marxist View of Religion Is Challenged," *SCMP*, 10 April 1985. See also Zhao Fusan, "Zongjiao, jingshen wenming, minzu tuanjie" ("Religion, Spiritual Civilization and Ethnic Unity," *Tian Feng* 7 (1985): 2-5; and "A Reconsideration of Religion," *Chinese Social Science (Zhongguo shehui kexue)*, 3 (1986), as translated in *CSPD* 2, no. 2 (1987): 4-16.

65. See especially Leung Ka-lun, *Gaige kaifang yilai de Zhongguo nongcun jiaohui (The Rural Churches of Mainland China since 1978)* (Hong Kong: Alliance Bible Seminary, 1999), 68ff.; also Raymond Fung, *Households of God on China's Soil* (Geneva: WCC, 1982).

66. See Wickeri, *Seeking the Common Ground*, 185-92.

67. Several of these testimonies are found in Fung, *Households of God on China's Soil*. For reports from foreign visitors, see *China Notes, China and Ourselves* and other Christian publications.

68. This was the perspective of Jonathan Chao, arguably the most influential evangelical "China watcher" of the time, who was then based in Hong Kong. See Jonathan Tian-en Chao and Rosanne Chong, *Dangdai zhongguo jidujiao fazhanshi, 1949-1997 (A History of Christianity in Socialist China, 1949-1997)* (Taipei: CMI Publishing, 1997) for a comprehensive statement of his views on the TSPM.

69. Luo Guangwu, ed., *Xin zhongguo zongjiao gongzuo da shi gailan, 1949-1999 (An Overview of Major Events in Religious Work in New China, 1949-1999)*, 264-65; Wang Bangzuo, ed., *Zhongguo gongchandang tongyi zhanxian shi (A History of the United Front in China)* (Shanghai: People's Publishers, 1991), 654.

70. Xing Wen, "Yi ci Yelusaleng huiyi" ("A Jerusalem Meeting"), *Tian Feng* 1 (20 October 1980): 4-6.

71. Shen Mingcui, "Yi ci you lishi yiyi de huiyi" ("A Meeting with Historical Significance"), *Tian Feng* 1, (20 October 1980): 10; on the opening address, see Xing Wen, "A Jerusalem Meeting", p. 5.

72. K. H. Ting, interview with the author, Nanjing, China, 25 August 1991.

73. Xing Wen, "A Jerusalem Meeting," 6. See also "Gei quanguo zhunei dixiong jiemei shu" ("Open Letter to Brothers and Sisters in Christ in China), *Tian Feng* 1 (20 October 1980): 2-3. In English, this letter from the standing committee of the Christian Movement for Self-Government, Self-Support and Self-Propagation," 1 March 1980 may be found in *CSPD* 2 and 3 (July 1980): 51-54.

74. K. H. Ting, "Retrospect and Prospect: Opening Address, the Third National Christian Conference," in *Love Never Ends*, 64ff.

75. K. H. Ting, interview with the author, Nanjing, China, 25 August 1991.

76. See Wang Weifan, "Shengjing yiben zai zhongguo" ("Bible Translation in China"), *Zongjiao yu wenhua (Religion and Culture)* (1992): 71-84; and Jost Oliver Zetzsche, *The Bible in China: The History of the Union Version, or, the Culmination of Protestant Missionary Bible Translation in China* (Sankt Augustin: Monumentica Serica Institute, 1999), 357-61. A translation committee was set up some time later and a new and slightly revised edition of the Union version was pro-

duced, but a thorough retranslation of the Bible from Hebrew and Greek texts has yet to be completed.

77. K. H. Ting, interview with the author, Nanjing, China, 25 August 1991.

78. Xing Wen, "A Jerusalem Meeting," 6.

79. K. H. Ting, interview with the author, Nanjing, China, 25 August 1991.

80. See Chao, *A History of Christianity in Socialist China, 1949-1997*, 313.

81. K. H. Ting, "Ze'yang du shengjing" ("How to Study the Bible") *Tian Feng* 1 (October 20, 1980): 45-63, later published as a 44-page pamphlet, *Ze'yang du shengjing* (Shanghai: China Christian Council, 1980). Not all of the essays in *How to Study the Bible* had been published in the 1950s, and previously published essays were slightly revised. The pamphlet was translated into English by myself and others at the Tao Fung Shan Ecumenical Centre in Hong Kong and published in January 1981. The page numbers cited below are from this English edition. The Chinese version has been reprinted many times, and as of this writing (2007) it is still in print.

82. On the popularity of allegorical interpretation in the Chinese Church, see Leung Ka-lun, "A Defense for Spiritual Interpretation in the Chinese Church," *The Role and Interpretation of the Bible in the Life of the Church in China, China Study Series*, vol. 3 (Hong Kong: Lutheran World Federation, 1997), 25-102.

83. Ever mindful of his audience, Ting published another essay on his approach to the Bible designed for an overseas audience; see "Chinese Christians' Approach to the Bible," in *Love Never Ends*, 378-91. Ting does not include *How to Study the Bible* in his selected writings.

84. See Y. T. Wu, *Meiyouren kanjianguo shangdi (No Man Hath Seen God)* (Shanghai: YMCA Bookstore, 1946). This story was related to me in 1988 by one of Ting's associates.

85. A full report on the Third NCC is contained in *Tian Feng* 1 (1981).

86. "Constitution of the China Christian Council," *Tian Feng* 1 (1981): 15. The translation is from *CSPD* 4 (February 1981): 40.

87. For Ting's reflection on Zheng Jianye, see "The Tree of Life Is Ever Green," in *Love Never Ends*, 405.

88. K. H. Ting, "Retrospect and Prospect: Opening Address, the Third National Christian Conference," in *Love Never Ends*, 54-71.

89. K. H. Ting, "Retrospect and Prospect," 68.

90. K. H. Ting, interview with the author, Nanjing, China, 25 August 1991.

91. For example, Ying Fuk-tsang, *Dangdai zhongguo zhengjiao guanxi (Church-State Relations in Contemporary China)*, 75-82.

92. Excerpts from the speeches by Zhang Zhiyi and Xiao Xianfa may be found in *Tian Feng* 1 (1981): 16-23 and 23-28 respectively.

93. K. H. Ting, interview with the author, Nanjing, China, 25 August 1991.

94. K. H. Ting, "Bimu ci" ("Closing Speech"), *Tian Feng* 1 (1981): 46.

95. See Han Wenzao, "Working Together in the Era of Openness and Reform," *CTR* 10 (1995): 52.

96. Yap Kim Hao, *Report on a Visit to China: October 1980* (Singapore: Christian Conference of Asia), 1.

97. For details on the number of Protestant churches and meeting points in China, see the Web site of the Amity News Service, http://www.amitynews service.org (accessed 23 November 2006).

98. K. H. Ting, "Another Look at Three-Self," in *Love Never Ends*, 105.

99. Both men are interviewed in the four-part DVD produced by Yuan Zhiming, "The Cross: Jesus in China," which may be accessed at http://www.china soul.com/e/cross-news.htm (accessed 5 October 2005). Short biographies are found in David Aikman, *Jesus in Beijing: How Christianity Is Transforming China and Changing the Global Balance of Power* (Washington: Regnery Publishing, 2003), 61-65 and 58-60.

100. K. H. Ting, "Tong huhanpai xintu tantan" ("A Few Words to the Yellers"), in *Jiangdao ji (Collected Sermons)* 5 (May 1983), 121-34. On Witness Lee (1905-1997), see http://www.witnesslee.org (accessed 24 November 2006).

101. K. H. Ting, "Statement on the Children of God," unpublished (1986); and K. H. Ting, "Jianjue yonghu he zhichi qudi 'Fa Lun Gong'" ("Resolutely Uphold and Support the Suppression of *'Falun Gong'*"), *Tian Feng* 9 (September 1999): 5. For short descriptions and polemical attacks on other sectarian groups, many of which began in the early 1980s, see Zhao Zhi'en, *Jianchi zhenli, dizhi yiduan (Uphold Truth and Resist Heterodoxy)* (Shanghai: TSPM/CCC, 1996).

102. K. H. Ting, "Love Never Ends," in *Love Never Ends*, 109. Ting here quotes St. Paul in support of his own position, "(love) does not rejoice in wrongdoing, but rejoices in the truth" (1 Corinthians 13:6).

103. See *Tian Feng* 2 (1981): 3. Much of this issue is concerned with the opening of the seminary, including moving testimonials by some of the new students.

104. K. H. Ting, "Guanyu woguo de shenxue jiaoyu" ("Theological Education in China"), *JL* 1, no. 9 (1984): 46-49, translated as "Concerning Theological Education in China," *Missiology: An International Review* 8, no. 3 (July 1985): 184-85.

105. See K. H. Ting, "Jinling xiehe shenxueyuan jinxun" ("Recent News from Jinling Theological Seminary"), *Tian Feng* 6 (1983): 3-5; and *CSPD* 14 (July 1984): 22-24.

106. K. H. Ting, "Theological Education in China," *CCA Consultation with Church Leaders from China* (Christian Conference of Asia: Singapore, 23-26 March 1981), 48-49. *Jiaocai (Curriculum)* continues to be published by the seminary.

107. K. H. Ting, "Jinling xiehe shenxueyuan jinxun" ("Recent News from Jinling Theological Seminary"), *Tian Feng* 6 (1983): 4. The translation here is from Janice K. Wickeri. Ting quotes this again in "Love Never Ends," in *Love Never Ends*, 110.

108. K. H. Ting, "Theological Education in China," 48.

109. K. H. Ting, "Another Look at Three Self," in *Love Never Ends*, 103.

110. "Bimu ci" ("Closing Speech"), *Tian Feng* 1 (1983): 23-24, translated in *CSPD* 11 (June 1983): 20.

111. "Carter Reveals Private Talk with Chinese Leader," *Kentucky Baptist Convention* 158, no. 26 (26 June 1984), 1. Carter retold this story on a TSPM/CCC promotional video produced for the 2006 "Bible Ministry in China Exhibition." See "Bible Ministry Exhibition of the Church in China Coming to the USA," ECF International, Monterey Park, Ca., 2006, available from http://www.ecfinter national.org (accessed 25 November 2006). Some sources say that Carter also asked Deng about Wang Mingdao; see Chao, *A History of Christianity in Socialist China, 1949-1997*, p. 284.

112. See *Xinshiqi zongjiao gongzuo wenxian xuanbian* (*Selected Documents on Religious Work in the New Period*), esp. 10-12 and 53-73.

113. Interview with K. H. Ting, 20 October 1995. See also "Taking a Softer Line on Religion," *SCMP*, 11 July 1978.

114. See, for example, Jonas Jonson, "A Documentation of My Encounters with Religious Life in the People's Republic of China, May 1978," unpublished manuscript, 9 pp. Also F. Thomas Trotter, "A Visit with Bishop Ting," *The Christian Century* (29 August-5 September 1979).

115. Vera Schwarcz, *Long Road Home: A China Journal* (New Haven and London: Yale University Press, 1984), 102-3. Her journal entry is from 31 May 1979.

116. K. H. Ting, interview with the author, Nanjing, China, 25 August 1991.

117. Philip L. Wickeri, "The Chinese Delegation at the Third World Conference on Religion and Peace, August 28-September 8, 1979: A Report," unpublished manuscript, 14 pp. It was as an interpreter for the Chinese delegation at WCRP III that I first came to know K. H. Ting (see Introduction). The other interpreter was Don MacInnis. See also Zhao Puchu, "Guanyu chuxi di sanjie shijie zongjiaozhe heping huiyi qingkuang de baogao" ("A Report on Participating in the Third World Conference on Religion and Peace"), *Zongjiao* (*Religion*) 2, no. 1 (1980): 23-27.

118. K. H. Ting, interview with the author, Nanjing, China, 25 August 1991.

119. K. H. Ting, "Human Collectives as Vehicles of God's Grace," in *Love Never Ends*, 43-48. Also, "China's Other Revolution," News Release of the NCCCUSA, 12 September 1979.

120. Stephen Endicott and Donald Willmott, "Canadian Missionaries and the Chinese Revolution of 1949: The Sympathetic Observers," unpublished manuscript, 1994, 27 pp. There were sympathetic observers among the Americans as well, such as Ran and Louise Sailor of Yenching, but their voices were drowned out by Walter Judd and the anti-China lobby of the 1950s.

121. Katherine B. Hockin, "Canadian Openness to the Chinese Church," *International Review of Mission* 71 (July 1982): 368-78.

122. "Conversations About K. H. Ting in Canada in the 1940s," 3 February 1992. Notes from the author's discussion with Vince Goring, Jean Wordsworth, Majorie and Cyril Powles, Lois Wilson and Katherine Hockin.

123. K. H. Ting, "Give Ye Them to Eat," in *Love Never Ends*, 29.

124. Joseph Spae, "Recent Theological Research on China and Future Church Policies," in *Western Christianity and the People's Republic of China: Exploring New Possibilities*, ed. James A. Scherer (Chicago, 1979).

125. K. H. Ting, "Facing the Future or Restoring the Past?" unpublished manuscript, November 1979, p. 5.

126. For example, see "Statement on the Jian Hua Foundation," typescript, 22 October 1982, 1 p.; "Interview with K. H. Ting on the Jian Hua Foundation," typescript, 28 April 1983, 2 pp.

127. "Fourteen Points from Christians in the People's Republic of China to Christians Abroad," in MacInnis, *Religion in China Today*, 61-70.

128. See the report in *Tian Feng* 2 (1981): 29.

129. See Homer Jack, "Some Notes on the Re-emergence Today of the Religions of China," 30 September 1980, typescript, 36 pp.; Yap Kim Hao, *Report on a Visit to China (October 1980)*. *Tian Feng* reported on both of these visits.

130. See Raymond Fung and Philip Lam, eds., *Zhu ai women daodi: zhongguo jidujiao daibiao tuan fang gang wenji (God Loves Us to the Very End: A Collection of Sermons and Speeches Delivered by Members of the Chinese Christian Delegation to Hong Kong, March 22-April 9, 1981)* (Hong Kong: HKCC, 1981).

131. *CCA Consultation with Church Leaders from China, Hong Kong (March 23-26, 1981)*.

132. See Theresa Chu and Christopher Lind, eds., *God's Call to a New Beginning: An International Dialogue with the Chinese Church* (Toronto: Canada China Programme, 1981). A listing of reports by conference participants appears at the end of this volume.

133. K. H. Ting, "On the Pope's Manila Message to China," unpublished typescript, September 1981, 2 pp.

134. K. H. Ting, "In China," in David L. Edwards, ed., *Robert Runcie: A Portrait by His Friends* (London: HarperCollins, 1990): 196-99.

135. For reports on these visits, see *CSPD* 7 (March 1982): 41-42 and 13 (March 1984): 17-23.

136. On the "spiritual pollution" campaign, see Richard Baum, "The Road to Tiananmen: Chinese Politics in the 1980s," in MacFarquhar, *The Politics of China*, 353-60 and passim.

137. "Visit of the Delegation from the British Council of Churches to the People's Republic of China," December 1983, p. 1. See also Ting, "In China," 198.

138. See Jonas Johnson, "A Documentation of My Encounters with Religious Life in the PRC, May 1978," pp. 4-5.

139. The Nam Tau Mariculture project was an ecumenical development initiative begun in 1981 in China's Guangdong Province. The project, led by Wolfgang Schmidt of the WCC, Harry Daniel, K. H. Ting's old friend, and Francis Yip, an Anglican priest in Hong Kong, attracted attention, support and questions from all over the world. Schmidt, Daniel and Yip sought, but did not receive, K. H. Ting's endorsement of the project. Despite their continuing efforts and the investment of more than three million dollars from churches all over the world, the project was a financial and developmental failure. In 1986, it was turned over to the Nam Tau commune, as mutually agreed in a signed contract. See Wolfgang Schmidt, *Memoirs in Dialogue, Asia*, vol. 1 (Hong Kong: Christian Conference of Asia, 2001). Chapter 4 deals with China and the mariculture project, and contains a response in dialogue written by this author.

140. Ninan Koshy, interview with the author, 15 November 2006, Beijing, China. Koshy was a close associate of Potter, and in 1975, a staff member of the WCC Commission of the Churches on International Affairs (CCIA).

141. This story was related to me by Bill Perkins, a former WCC staff member, in Geneva in July 1993.

142. K. H. Ting, "Address at Worship," in *Love Never Ends*, 119.

143. Potter to Ting, 16 November 1984. A copy of the letter is in my personal files.

8. THE VICISSITUDES OF OPENNESS AND REFORM, 1984-1989

1. Both epigrams were sources used by K. H. Ting in his writings in the 1980s. The famous lines from Qu Yuan's *Li Sao* (translation mine) is cited in "Fervor Seek-

ing Worship" (a sermon on Matthew 2: 1-13), 1984, unpublished manuscript, p. 1. The prayer of Anselm is cited in "Ultimate Questions," in K. H. Ting, *Love Never Ends,* 244.

2. Richard Baum, "The Road to Tiananmen: Chinese Politics in the 1980s," *The Politics of China: The Eras of Mao and Deng,* ed. Roderick MacFarquhar, 2nd ed. (Cambridge: Cambridge University Press, 1997), 341. See footnote 4 on the same page of Baum for other sources on *fang-shou cycles* in post-Mao China.

3. Baum, "The Road to Tiananmen," 341-471.

4. Zhao Ziyang, "Report" *Beijing Review* 30, no. 45 (9-15 November 1987): I-XXVII. Zhao's report is briefly summarized in Baum, "The Road to Tiananmen," 412.

5. See Wang Hui, *China's New Order: Society, Politics and Economy in Transition* (Cambridge and London: Harvard University Press, 2003); reviewed in Philip L. Wickeri, "Chinese Neo-Liberalism Has Lost Sight of Social Justice," *China Development Brief* 6, no. 1 (Spring 2004): 42-44.

6. Geremie Barmé, *In the Red: On Contemporary Chinese Culture* (New York: Columbia University Press, 1999), 23-24 and passim.

7. The doctorates came from the Theological Faculty in Budapest (1987); St. Olaf College in Northfield, Minnsesota (1988); the University of Kent in Canterbury, England (also 1988) and Emmanuel College, Victoria University in Toronto, Canada (1989), where both he and his wife Siu-may received honorary degrees. In 1992, he received an honorary doctorate from McMaster University in Canada and from Union Theological Seminary in the Philippines, and in 1993 from Yonsei University in Seoul. In 1957, he had been awarded an honorary doctorate from the Theological Faculty in Debrecen, Czechoslovakia.

8. In the 1980s, vituperative attacks against K. H. Ting were published almost weekly in both Chinese and English. Most of these came from the magazines and newsletters of Hong Kong–based China Ministries, such as Asian Outreach and Jonathan Chao's Chinese Church Research Centre. An Internet search of criticisms of K. H. Ting will reveal a number of articles and entries that raise longstanding questions about his personal integrity (whether he was a member of the Communist Party, discussed in chap. 2), his theological views and his relationship to the house churches, which is discussed below.

9. See Philip L. Wickeri, "An Ecumenical Theologian," *CTR* 10 (1995): 107-18; and the introduction to Philip L. Wickeri and Janice K. Wickeri, eds., *A Chinese Contribution to Ecumenical Theology: Selected Writings of K. H. Ting* (Geneva: World Council of Churches, 2002), vii-xii.

10. Other Protestant theologians writing in the 1980s were Shen Yifan from Shanghai, and Chen Zemin and Wang Weifan at Nanjing Union Theological Seminary.

11. K. H. Ting, "The Spirit and Us," in *Love Never Ends,* 155.

12. K. H. Ting, "Inspirations from Liberation Theology, Process Theology and Teilhard de Chardin," in *Love Never Ends,* 192-220. This is his longest theological essay from this period. I lived in Nanjing between 1981 and 1983, and from the regular meetings we had to discuss theology, I can personally attest to the broad and eclectic nature of his theological interests.

13. K. H. Ting, interview with the author, Nanjing, China, 13 December 1991.

14. K. H. Ting, "Another Look at Three-Self," in *Love Never Ends,* 102. On the theological fermentation at the grassroots in the 1950s, see K. H. Ting, "Theo-

logical Mass Movement in China," in *Love Never Ends*, 137-50; and Philip L. Wickeri, *Seeking the Common Ground: Protestant Christianity, the Three-Self Movement and China's United Front* (Maryknoll, N.Y.: Orbis Books, 1988), 258-61.

15. For a thorough introduction to the contextualization or indigenization of Protestant theology in China, see Duan Qi, *Fenjin de licheng: zhongguo jidujiao de bensehua* (*Struggling Forward: The Indigenization of Protestant Christianity in China*) (Beijing: Commercial Press, 2004).

16. K. H. Ting, "Inspirations from Liberation Theology, Process Theology and Teilhard de Chardin," in *Love Never Ends*, 209.

17. K. H. Ting, interview with the author, Nanjing, China, 13 December 1991.

18. K. H. Ting, "God Is Love," in *Love Never Ends*, 268.

19. K. H. Ting, "On Human Longing for Reconciliation," in *Love Never Ends*, 246ff. and "Love That Loves to the End," in *Love Never Ends*, 314ff.

20. K. H. Ting, "Love That Loves to the End," in *Love Never Ends*, 311.

21. K. H. Ting, "The Cosmic Christ," in *Love Never Ends*, 408-18. This essay was written in 1991, but it summarizes the ideas about Christ that Ting first began to articulate in the early 1980s.

22. K. H. Ting, "Life Should Have a Mission," in *Love Never Ends*, 182-84.

23. K. H. Ting, "The Experience of the Church in China," in *Papers on Evangelism and Mission* 8 (Cincinnati: Forward Movement Publications, 1984), 9.

24. K. H. Ting, "Inspirations from Liberation Theology, Process Theology and Teilhard de Chardin," 209; "Theological Mass Movement in China," 147.

25. K. H. Ting, "Life Should Have a Mission," in *Love Never Ends*, 185. See also Chen Zemin, "Foreword: Faith's Journey," in *Love Never Ends*, 7.

26. K. H. Ting, "The Spirit and Us," in *Love Never Ends*, 155.

27. "Preface to the *Chinese Theological Review*," in *Love Never Ends*, 236.

28. K. H. Ting, "Inspirations from Liberation Theology, Process Theology and Teilhard de Chardin," 199. See also "Theological Mass Movement in China," 147-48.

29. K. H. Ting, interview with the author, Nanjing, China, 13 December 1991.

30. K. H. Ting, "What Can We Learn from Y. T. Wu Today?" in *Love Never Ends*, 230.

31. K. H. Ting, "God Is Love," 267, 269. He repeated some of these same thoughts in a personal letter he wrote to me after my own mother died in 1987. In his 1957 essay "On Christian Theism," he observed that the evidence for God's existence that we see in nature may be compared to the evidence we see of our mothers in our homes when she is not there. "You know her and love her, and as you go in and look around, everything in the house reminds you of her" (see chap. 5).

32. Richard Baum, "The Road to Tiananmen," 413.

33. See Jonathan Spence, *The Search for Modern China* (New York: Norton, 1990), 727-29.

34. Lei Zhenchang, "Religious Issues in the Primary Stage of Socialism," *Guangming Daily*, 9 May 1988, translated in *CSPD* 3, no. 2 (August 1988): 35. I have slightly modified the translation.

35. See Kenneth Lieberthal, *Governing China: From Revolution through Reform* (New York: Norton, 1995), 302 and 458 n. 28; Timothy Brook and

B. Michael Frolic, eds., *Civil Society in China* (Armonk, N.Y.: M. E. Sharpe, 1997); and Richard Madsen, *China's Catholics: Tragedy and Hope in an Emerging Civil Society* (Berkeley: University of California Press, 1998).

36. K. H. Ting, "Retrospect and Prospect," 68.

37. See, for example, Jonathan Tian-en Chao and Rosanne Chong, *Dangdai zhongguo jidujiao fazhanshi, 1949-1997* (*A History of Christianity in Socialist China, 1949-1997*) (Taipei: CMI Publishing, 1997), 407-533.

38. Some of these visits were reported in *Tian Feng*. See, for example, the report on his visit to Tianjin with Han Wenzao and Cai Wenhao (Peter Tsai) in *Tian Feng* 5 (1984): 19. He also made a highly publicized visit to Wenzhou in 1991, which is discussed in the next chapter.

39. Letter of Li Yading to K. H. Ting, April 1984. I have a copy of this letter in my personal files.

40. K. H. Ting and Zhao Fusan, "Remarks on Further Implementing the Policy of Religious Freedom," *Zongjiao (Religion)* 6 (November 1984): 4-8; and K. H. Ting, "What I Have Learned from Studying a New Document: A Speech," *Zongjiao (Religion)* 6 (November 1984): 8-15.

41. K. H. Ting, "Zheng jiao yao fenkai" ("Religion and the State Should be Separate"), Speech to the CPPCC, March 1988.

42. The correspondence was published in an article entitled "Jidujiao pingmin yu guanfang de da bianlun" ("An Ordinary Christian's Debate with the Authorities"), *Baixing* 173 (1 August 1988). See also *Jindai Jiangsu Zongjiao*, 117-18. Ting's edited letter of response (dated 9 April 1988) is published as "Letter to a Believer," in *Love Never Ends*, 292-94; "Gei yiwei xintu de xin," in *Wenji*, 339-41. This version and translation of the letter has a different tone, and it conveys a message more sympathetic to the government regulations than the original to Zhang Shengcai.

43. See Ron MacMillan, "Bishop K. H. Ting: Ally or Adversary of the House Church Millions?" *Special Report of News Network International* (12 June 1989): 1-8.

44. See "Regulations for the Administrative Supervision of Places of Religious Activity in Guangdong Province," (December 1988) in Don MacInnis, ed., *Religion in China Today: Policy and Practice* (Maryknoll, N.Y.: Orbis Books, 1989), 45-49.

45. See "An Interview with Bishop K. H. Ting on the Growth of the Church in China," in MacInnis, *Religion in China Today*, 354. This interview took place on 16 October 1987. For other sources, see Ryan Dunch, "Protestants and the State in Post-Mao China" (M.A. thesis, University of British Columbia, 1991), 49 n. 87.

46. Ewing W. Carroll, Jr., "An Interview with K. H. Ting" (1 November 1988), in MacInnis, *Religion in China Today*, 357. See also Charles Kwok, "Bishop Ting's View of the Present Situation of Christianity in China," *Bridge* 33 (January-February 1989): 3-8. Kwok summarizes Ting's letter of 26 September to the RAB.

47. Letter from K. H. Ting to the Religious Affairs Bureau of the State Council, 26 September 1988.

48. On Lin Xiangao, see Bob Whyte, *Unfinished Encounter: China and Christianity* (Glasgow: Collins, 1988), 409-10; Dunch, "Protestants and the State in Post-Mao China," 46-51.

49. Letter from K. H. Ting to the Religious Affairs Bureau of the State Council, 26 September 1988. I have a copy of this letter in my personal files.

50. Luo Guangwu, ed., *Xin zhongguo zongjiao gongzuo dashi gailan, 1949-1999 (A Survey of Important Events in Religious Work in New China, 1949-1999)* (Beijing: Huawen Publishers, 2001), 391-93. The date of the circular is 18 October 1988.

51. K. H. Ting and Wang Weifan, "Recent Developments in the Study of Religion," in *Love Never Ends*, 348-64. This was a widely circulated and widely reprinted essay, originally written in October 1988 for a conference on UFWD theory. A summary entitled "New Advances in Religious Studies" appeared in *Beijing Review* 32, no. 12 (20-26 March 1989), though without the final section entitled "The Leadership and Administration of Religious Affairs Must Be Reformed" (pp. 361-64). In Chinese, the essay may be found in *Wenji*, 418-31. Its Chinese title is "Jin ji nian zongjiao yanjiu shang ruogan tupo."

52. K. H. Ting and Wang Weifan, "Recent Developments in the Study of Religion," 361.

53. K. H. Ting and Wang Weifan, "Recent Developments in the Study of Religion," 363.

54. K. H. Ting, "On Reordering Relationships," 13 December 1988, pp. 6-7; translated as "Three-Self and the Church: Reordering the Relationship," in *Love Never Ends*, 346.

55. "Some Opinions on China's Religious Work (Speech by K. H. Ting at the 2nd Session of the 7th CPPCC)," *Tian Feng* 5 (1989), supplementary pp. 1-2.

56. "We Need a Step Forward in the Implementation of Religious Policy" (Speech by Zhao Puchu at the 2nd Session of the 7th CPPCC), *Tian Feng* 5 (1989), supplementary pp. 2-4.

57. K. H. Ting, "Opening Address at the 30th Anniversary Celebration of the Three-Self Movement of Protestant Churches in China" (2 August 1984), in *Love Never Ends*, 181.

58. This and other estimates are from the Fourth NCC, which met in August 1986. For a summary of the figures, see "Changwu weiyuanhui gongzuo baogao," ("Work Report of the Standing Committee"), *Zhongguo jidujiao di si jie quanguo huiyi zhuanji (Records of the Fourth Chinese National Christian Conference)* (Shanghai: TSPM/CCC Committee, 1986), 13-36. See also "How Many Protestant Christians Are There in China," *Bridge* 25 (September-October 1987): 16.

59. K. H. Ting, "Retrospect and Prospect," in *Love Never Ends*, 64-71. See also K. H. Ting, "Building Up the Body in Love," *CTR* (1986): 103-6, which is discussed below.

60. See "A Report on Strengthening the Work of the Catholic Church in the New Situation," Circular of the Central Committee of the CPC and the State Council, transmitted through the Central Office of the United Front Department and the Religious Affairs Bureau, 17 February 1989, Section 2. This report is known as Document No. 3, according to the yearly numbering of Central Committee Circulars. I have a copy of the report in my personal files.

61. "Open Letter from the Fourth National Chinese Christian Conference," *CTR* (1986): 3.

62. K. H. Ting, "Building Up the Body in Love," 106. The version that appears in *Love Never Ends* has been altered. The *CTR* version is also in Wickeri and Wickeri, eds., *A Chinese Contribution to Ecumenical Theology*, 81-86. The Chinese original should be consulted (*Tian Feng* 11 [November 1986]: 35-37), but because

of the controversy surrounding this sermon (see below), even this has been changed from what was originally preached.

63. K. H. Ting, "Building Up the Body in Love," 107.

64. Wang Weifan, "A Church Leader of Vision," *CTR* 10 (1995): 90-91. I have in my files a copy of the original text of the sermon and changes, given to me in September 1986 by K. H. Ting. This is but one small example of such a document, and there are many more. It illustrates some of the tensions involved in the process of working for change in the TSPM and the CCC.

65. *Zhang gan ji* (*The Shepherd's Staff*), supplement to *Jiaocai* (*Curriculum*) (Nanjing: Nanjing Union Theological Seminary, July 1986), discussed in Wang Weifan, "A Church Leader of Vision," 90.

66. *Renmin ribao* (*People's Daily*), 28 March 1989; also *Tian Feng* 5 (May 1989), supplementary p. 4.

67. See "Zhongguo jidujiao gedi jiaohui shixing guizhang zhidu" ("Church Order for Trial Use in Chinese Churches"), *Tian Feng* (March 1992): 33-35, translated in *CTR* (1991): 21-30.

68. See "The Consecration of Two Bishops in Shanghai," *Bridge* 30 (August-September 1988): 3-4. The consecrations took place on 26 June 1988. Reports on the consecrations also appear in *Tian Feng* 9 (September 1988): 2-6.

69. K. H. Ting, "Taking a New Way," in *Love Never Ends*, 308. This was originally published as "Zouchu yitiao xin lu lai zhusheng zhujiao dianli shang de zhengdao" ("Entering a New Road: Sermon on the Consecration of New Bishops"), *Tian Feng* 9 (September 1988): 4-5.

70. K. H. Ting, "Taking a New Way," 307.

71. K. H. Ting, "On Reordering Relationships," 13 December 1988, pp. 2-3 (translation mine). This speech is another example of one that went through many drafts, and I am quoting from the manuscript eventually circulated for distribution. It was presented at the joint meeting of the TSPM and CCC Committee in December 1988. A slightly revised version of the speech was published as "Lishun sanzi zuzhi yu jiaohui de guanxi" in *JL* 10 (1989.6): 1-5. A revised version of the speech is translated as "Three-Self and the Church: Reordering the Relationship," in *Love Never Ends*, 339-47.

72. Here and in the preceding quote, K. H. Ting, "On Reordering Relationships," 2-3.

73. He spoke of the TSPM as "scaffolding" as early as 1982. See K. H. Ting, "Another Look at Three-Self," in *Love Never Ends*, 106.

74. *News Network International*, 20 March 1990, 3.

75. "Changing Role for the Three-Self Movement," *Amity Foundation Press Release*, 12 April 1989.

76. K. H. Ting to Philip L. Wickeri, conversation notes, Nanjing, China, 10 November 1988.

77. K. H. Ting, "Meiguo heiren jidutu gei wo de sanzi aiguo jiaoyu" ("Black American Christians Teach Me about Three-Self Patriotism") unpublished comment (in Chinese), June 1986, 3 pp. Ting wrote this after meeting with African Americans who attended the Nanjing '86 Conference discussed below.

78. See "The Chinese Welfare Fund for the Handicapped Set Up" (15 March 1984), *CSPD* 16 (April 1984): 3.

79. Deng Pufang, quoted in Geremie Barmé and John Minford, *Seeds of Fire: Chinese Voices of Conscience* (Hong Kong: Far Eastern Economic Review, 1986),

162. See also Deng Pufang, "Let Us Contribute All Our Strength to Welfare Work for the Handicapped," *Renmin ribao (People's Daily)*, 7 December 1984.

80. See "Prejudice against Humanitarianism," *China Daily*, 23 January 1985; and "Mother Teresa Visits the Disabled," *China Daily*, 25 January 1985.

81. Hu Qiaomu, "Yindao zongjiaojie ban shehui gongyi shiye" ("Leading Religious Circles to Run Enterprises for the Public Good"), 24 April 1984, *Xin shiqi zongjiao gongzuo wenxian xuanbian (Selected Documents on Religious Work in the New Period)* (Beijing: Zongjiao wenhua chubanshe, 1995), 105-6. Hu's proposal was not publicized at the time, but the fact that it was subsequently included in this collection of documents edited by the RAB and the CPC Central Committee testifies to its importance.

82. "Decision of the Central Committee of the CPC on the Reform of the Economic Structure," *Beijing Review* 27, no. 44 (29 October 1984): III-XVI. For a discussion of this decision, see Baum, "The Road to Tiananmen: Chinese Politics in the 1980s," 365.

83. The statement was informal, because Ting and Han did not want to appear to be directly encouraging such contributions. "On Contributions to China from Churches and Christians Overseas" is based on an interview with this author in Nanjing on 4 December 1984. It was initially published in *Bridge* 9 (January-February 1985): 3-5, together with my interpretation, and was widely reprinted overseas.

84. "On Contributions to China from Churches and Christians Overseas," 3.

85. K. H. Ting circular letter of 20 December 1984. For one reflection on this letter, see Rhea Whitehead, "Canadian Churches and Amity Foundation Partnership," *Growing in Partnership: The Amity Foundation, 1985-2005,* ed. Katrin Fielder and Liwei Zhang (Nanjing: Amity Foundation, 2005), 180ff.

86. A press conference announcing the forthcoming formation of Amity was held in Hong Kong the previous month (21 March 1985), taking advantage of Ting's and Han's presence in the territory on their return to China from India.

87. Arthur Waley, *The Way and Its Power: A Study of the Tao Te Ching and Its Place in Chinese Thought* (London: George Allen and Unwin, 1965). The idea of translating *aide* as "love and the power of love" came from the late John Fleming, a Scottish missionary in China before 1949.

88. K. H. Ting to Philip L. Wickeri, conversation notes, Nanjing, China, 28 March 1988.

89. For reflections on Amity's development, see the essays and articles in Katrin Fielder and Zhang Liwei, eds., *Growing in Partnership*.

90. "On the Amity Foundation," speech at the second orientation for Amity Teachers, 26 August 1986.

91. K. H. Ting circular letter of 24 June 1985. See also Philip L. Wickeri, "Development Service and China's Modernization: The Amity Foundation in Theological Perspective," *The Ecumenical Review* 41, no. 1 (January 1989): 78-87.

92. K. H. Ting circular letter of 20 December 1984.

93. See Moses Hsu, "The Rebuilding of the Church in China: Some Observations of a Traveller," unpublished report (June 1980), 10 pp. The report is in my personal files.

94. For Amity Bible production, see http://www.amityprinting.com/new/englishweb/efirst.htm (accessed 21 November 2005).

95. Raymond Fung, "On the Amity Foundation in the Context of Ecumenical Relationships: An Assessment," unpublished report (July 1985), 5. The report is in my personal files.

96. Letter of K. H. Ting to Eugene Stockwell, 18 May 1986. A copy of the letter is in my personal files.

97. K. H. Ting circular letter of 24 June 1985. See also Jim Endicott, Steve Endicott, Katherine Hockin, Cyril Powles, Majorie Powles, Ray Whitehead, Rhea Whitehead, Don Wilmott and Theresa Chu to K. H. Ting, letter of 22 October 1985, in which they expressed their qualified support for Ting's position.

98. See the Friends of the Church in China Web site: http://www.thefcc.org (accessed 21 November 2005).

99. For a personal perspective on the Ting's home life, see Siu-may Guo (Kuo), "Why I Don't Retire," *U.S.–China Review* 7, no. 6 (November-December 1983): 14-15, 29.

100. K. H. Ting, "Christian Sharing Across National Boundaries as a Chinese Christian Sees It," in *Nanjing'86: Ecumenical Sharing, A New Agenda (An Ecumenical Conference, May 14-20, Nanjing, China* (New York: NCCCUSA and Maryknoll, 1986), 76.

101. See Denton Lotz, ed., *Spring Has Returned . . . Listening to the Church in China* (McLean, Va.: Baptist World Alliance, 1986).

102. See Britt Towery, *Churches of China: Taking Root Downward, Bearing Fruit Upward*, 3rd ed. (Waco, Tex.: Baylor University Press, 1990). This book has been through many editions, beginning in the 1980s, and it has done much to influence Southern Baptist opinion on China.

103. See Han Wenzao, "Nan wang de yi zhou—ji nanfei tutu zhujiao zhongguo zhi hang" ("An Unforgettable Week—with Bishop Tutu on His Travels in China"), *Tian Feng* 12 (1986): 9-11. Bishop and Mrs. Tutu visited China 8-15 August 1986.

104. See Ed Plowman, *Billy Graham in China* (Minneapolis: The Billy Graham Evangelistic Association, 1988). A video was also made of this visit. See also reports on the Graham visit by various Chinese Christians in *Tian Feng* 7 (1988): 10-13; and Philip L. Wickeri, "Random Thoughts on Billy Graham's China Visit," unpublished (11 May 1988), 5 pp. Sidney Rittenberg, the only American ever to have joined the CPC, was instrumental in the Graham visit. See Rittenberg, *The Man Who Stayed Behind* (New York: Simon & Schuster, 1993). The Rev'd. and Mrs. Billy Graham visited China 13-28 April 1988.

105. See Stockwell's meticulous notes about the discussion in his "Report on Conversations with Bishop K. H. Ting in Nanjing, P. R. China, 19-20 November 1985," unpublished report, 11 pp. The report is in my personal files.

106. K. H. Ting, "Statement Against the Children of God," (1986). The statement is in my personal files.

107. K. H. Ting, "A Statement on Kairos Radio," 31 August 1987. The statement is in my personal files.

108. "Remarks by Chinese Christian Leaders on the Second Lausanne Conference," Shanghai, 18 May 1989 (in Chinese and English). The statement is in my personal files. For Jonathan Chao's version of events, see *A History of Christianity in Socialist China, 1949-1997*, 514-15.

9. REPRESSION AND RESURGENCE, 1989-1996

1. As quoted by K. H. Ting in "An Update on the Church in China (1994)," in K. H. Ting, *Love Never Ends,* ed. Janice K. Wickeri (Nanjing: Yilin Press, 2000), 453. Ting has slightly modified the translation of Arthur Waley; see *The Way and Its Power* (London: George Allen & Unwin, 1965), chap. 43, p. 197.

2. As quoted by K. H. Ting in "One Chinese Christian's View of God," in *Love Never Ends,* 440.

3. There are several English language sources on the 1989 democracy movement, including Han Minzhu, ed., *Cries for Democracy: Writings and Speeches from the 1989 Democracy Movement* (Princeton: Princeton University Press, 1990); Suzanne Ogden, Kathleen Hartford, Lawrence Sullivan and David Zweig, eds., *China's Search for Democracy: The Student Movement of 1989* (Armonk, N.Y.: M. E. Sharpe, 1992); and Michael Oksenberg, Lawrence R. Sullivan and Marc Lambert, eds., *Beijing Spring, 1989: Confrontation and Conflict: The Basic Documents* (Armonk, N.Y.: M. E. Sharpe, 1992).

4. *The Tiananmen Papers: The Chinese Leadership's Decision to Use Force against Their Own People—In Their Own Words* (New York: Public Affairs, 2001). Compiled by Zhang Liang, ed., with Andrew Nathan and Perry Link, and an afterword by Orville Schell. Although the papers cannot be taken at face value, they do indicate that there were serious differences of opinion among the top party leaders over how to handle the crisis in the spring of 1989.

5. Deng Xiaoping, "Zai jiejian shoudu jieyuan budui junyishang ganbu shi de jianghua" ("Talk on Reviewing Martial Law Cadres at the Army Level and Above in the Capital"), in *Deng Xiaoping wenxuan (Selected Works of Deng Xiaoping),* vol. 3 (Beijing: Renmin chubanshe, 1993), 302-8; also, "What Happened in Beijing?" *Beijing Review* 32, no. 6 (26 June-2 July 1989): 11-15.

6. On the "triumph of hope," see John Lewis Gaddis, *The Cold War: A New History* (New York: Penguin Press, 2005), 237-58.

7. Joseph Fewsmith, *China since Tiananmen: The Politics of Transition* (Cambridge: Cambridge University Press, 2001), 21ff.

8. For an overview of the religious resurgence, see the various essays in "Religion in China Today," a special issue of *The China Quarterly* 174 (June 2003).

9. On the intellectual debates, see Wang Hui, *China's New Order: Society, Politics and Economy in Transition* (Cambridge and London: Harvard University Press, 2003); also Geremie Barmé, *In the Red: On Contemporary Chinese Culture* (New York: Columbia University Press, 1999).

10. Timothy Cheek, "From Priests to Professionals: Intellectuals and the State Under the CCP," in *Popular Protest and Political Culture in Modern China: Learning from 1989,* ed. Jeffrey N. Wasserstrom and Elizabeth J. Perry (Boulder, Colo.: Westview Press, 1992), 128, 135 and passim. See chap. 7.

11. Wang Hui, *China's New Order,* 56.

12. Quoted in William Morris, "Between Sadness and Hope: A Reflection on Recent Events in China," *Bridge* 36 (July-August 1989): 6. William Morris was the pen name for this author.

13. Quoted in William Morris, "Between Sadness and Hope," 6. The second statement is dated 23 May. On 24 and 25 May, Christian members of the NPC and the CPPCC also sent two separate letters calling for emergency meetings. K. H. Ting

was the first of five names on the first letter sent to both bodies. See "Extremely Anxious—The Attitude of Church Leaders in China," *Bridge* 36 (July-August 1989): 6.

14. "Two Poems by Chinese Christians," *Bridge* 36 (July-August 1989): 19.

15. As overseas coordinator of the Amity Foundation in Hong Kong, I had to deal with questions coming from churches and families of Amity teachers all over the world, and I remained in daily contact with K. H. Ting, the Amity Foundation and CCC offices in Nanjing. Some of the observations that appear here are drawn from notes from those conversations.

16. Letter from K. H. Ting and Wenzao Han to Philip and Other Colleagues in the Amity Office, Hong Kong, Nanjing, 6 June 1989. The text of the letter was unfortunately changed in many publications. On 27 June, he sent a shorter circular letter to individuals and churches he had heard from overseas. This is discussed below.

17. K. H. Ting, interview with the author, Nanjing, China, 13 December 1991.

18. K. H. Ting, unpublished reflections, undated (1989).

19. "Quanguo lianghui fabiao shengming jianjue yonghu si zhong quanhui ge xiang jueding" ("The Two National Christian Organizations Issue a Statement Firmly Supporting the Resolutions of of the 4th CPC Plenum"), *Tian Feng* (September 1989): 29. The CPC plenum was held in Beijing 23-24 June 1989.

20. K. H. Ting circular letter, 27 June 1989. A copy of the letter is in my personal files.

21. NCNA, 1 July 1989; *Renmin ribao (People's Daily)* 2 July 1989.

22. For example, Anthony Lambert, "Bishop Ting and the Chinese Church Face Stormy Days Ahead," *World Perspective* 2, no. 9 (October 1989); also Anthony Lambert, *The Resurrection of the Chinese Church* (London: Hodder & Stoughton, 1991), 279.

23. He delivered a major speech at the NPC Standing Committee the following year. In 1993, the decision was made that persons could not serve on both the NPC and the CPPCC.

24. An enlarged meeting of the planning committee for Edinburgh '89 was held 21-24 September, but no Chinese were in attendance. The conference planned for Edinburgh has never been held.

25. I went to Seoul to carry a personal message from Ting to WARC general secretary Milan Opočenský.

26. K. H. Ting, "Tan shenxue jiaoyu" ("On Theological Education"), *Tian Feng* (November 1989), 4-5.

27. "Pastor Ignores Threat of Closure," *South China Morning Post*, 31 December 1991. See also "Lord, Have Mercy on These Ignorant Students!—Response of Home Meeting Groups Towards the Democratic Movement," *Bridge* 36 (July-August 1989): 15-16.

28. "Beijing, Shanghai deng di longzhong jinian Wu Yaozong xiansheng shishi shi zhounian" ("Solemn Services of Remembrance of the 10th Anniversary of the Death of Mr. Wu Yaozong Held in Beijing, Shanghai and Other Cities"), *Tian Feng* (November 1989): 2-3.

29. Cf. Shen Derong, "Wu Yaozong yu Weiaizhuyi" ("Wu Yaozong and Pacifism"), *Tian Feng* (September 1989): 8-11.

30. K. H. Ting, "What Can We Learn from Y. T. Wu Today? Speech at the

Memorial Meeting on the 10th Anniversary of the Death of Y. T. Wu," in *Love Never Ends*, 337. The second speech is "The Ever Renewing Mr. Y. T. Wu," in *Love Never Ends*, 365-71. Both speeches were originally published in *JL (The Nanjing Theological Review)* 11 (1990): 1-5 and 6-9.

31. Zhao Dingxi, *The Power of Tiananmen: State-Society Relations and the 1989 Beijing Student Movement* (Chicago: University of Chicago Press, 2001), 355.

32. K. H. Ting, "An Interview on the Present Day Church Situation," in *Love Never Ends*, 393-98.

33. Philip L. Wickeri "The Chinese Church After June 4th: An Interview with K. H. Ting," Press Release, The Amity Foundation Overseas Coordination Office, 15 November 1989. This interview appeared in Chinese as "Dui Ding Guangxun zhujiao de yi ci fangwen" ("An Interview with Bishop K. H. Ting"), *Tian Feng* (January 1990): 13-14. Zhao Ziyang's policies had been criticized for promoting "bourgeois liberalization"; see Fewsmith, *China since Tiananmen*, 30-32. See also "Policy of Respect for Religious Belief Unchanged," *CSPD* 5, no. 1 (April 1990): 48.

34. On the "unwritten social contract," see Timothy Cheek, "From Priests to Professionals," 128-29 and passim, discussed in chap. 7.

35. "Zhao Fusan Stays in Paris, Giving Up His Official Posts to Concentrate on Writing," *Ming Bao*, 13 August 1989. Zhao had been a member of the TSPM Standing Committee and a board member of the Amity Foundation; he was later removed from his positions in both organizations. He lived in Europe for a time, and then moved to the United States, where, as of this writing, he still resides.

36. Chen Yun, "Guanyu gao du zhongshi zongjiao shentou wenti de xin ("Letter on the High Level Importance of the Religious Infiltration Question"), 4 September 1990," in *Xin shiqi zongjiao gongzuo wenxian xuanbian (Selected Documents on Religious Work in the New Period)* (Beijing: Zongjiao wenhua chubanshe, 1995), 177. See also "The Present Situation of Religion in the USSR," *U.S.S.R.–Eastern Europe Situation* 57 (1990.9.3). This short report summarizes reporting on religion in the U.S.S.R. and describes the growth of religion outside the control of the state in an alarmist way. On "religious fever" and "Christianity fever," see the articles on these subjects in *Kaifang (Open Magazine)* (February 1994): 44-54 and *Ming Pao Monthly* 29, no. 12 (December 1994): 44-63.

37. "Speech by Bishop Ding Guangxun at the Standing Committee of the National People's Congress," 6 September 1990, translated in *CSPD* 6, no. 1 (April 1991): 55. Ting spoke again at the same forum on the same subject on 30 June 1992; see "Zhengque chuli zongjiao wenti" ("Correctly Resolve the Religious Question"), unpublished manuscript, 4 pp. On the Chinese Christian interpretation of the role of religion in the downfall of communism in Eastern Europe, see Xu Rulei, "Ruhe zhengque renshi zongjiao zai dong ou jibian zhong de zuoyong" ("A Correct Understanding of the Role of Religion in the Changes in Eastern Europe"), *Yanjiu dongtai (Research Trends)*, 10 December 1992 (4): 20-28.

38. Philip L. Wickeri, "Reinterpreting Religion in China," *China News Analysis* 1485 (15 May 1993): 1-9.

39. For a discussion of this conference, see Luo Guangwu, ed., *Xin zhongguo zongjiao gongzuo da shi gailan, 1949-1999 (An Overview of Major Events in Religious Work in New China, 1949-1999)* (Beijing: Huawen chubanshe, 2001), 428-30.

40. "Jiang Zemin Meets Religious Leaders," NCNA, 30 January 1991, in *CSPD* 6, no. 1 (April 1991): 25-26.

41. "Bishop Ting's Statement at the Meeting with Comrade Jiang Zemin," *Bridge* 46 (March-April 1991): 3-5.

42. The Chinese text is in *Xin shiqi zongjiao gongzuo wenxian xuanbian* (*Selected Documents on Religious Work in the New Period*), 213-22, translated as Document No. 6: "Some Questions for the Further Improvement of Religious Work," A Circular of the CPC Central Committee and the State Council, 5 February 1991, in *CSPD* 6, no. 3 (December 1991): 36-41.

43. See Chan Kim-kwong and Alan Hunter, "New Light on Religious Policy in the PRC," *Issues and Studies* 31, no. 2 (February 1995): 21-22; and Pitman B. Potter, "Belief in Control: Regulation of Religion in China," *The China Quarterly* 174 (June 2003): 317-37.

44. Here and in much of what follows I am drawing on my conversation notes with K. H. Ting, 1989-1995.

45. "Speech by Bishop K. H. Ting at Spring Festival Tea Party for Religious Leaders," *ANS* Special Release, 3 March 1994.

46. See, for example, "K. H. Ting Again Talks to Jiang Zemin," *Bridge* 53 (May-June 1992): 6-7; "The Religious Committee Symposium Discusses How to Go Further in Implementing the Policy of Religious Freedom (1)," *CPPCC Special Report* 64 (Third Issue on Religion), 12 September 1992, pp. 1-18; "CPPCC: Bishop Ting on Indiscriminate Attacks on Religion," *CSPD* 8, no. 1 (April 1993): 41-42; "Religious Work Should Reflect Reform and Openness," Bishop K. H. Ting's Speech to the CPPCC, 22 March 1993, *ANS*, March 1993; "*Tian Feng* Interviews Bishop K. H. Ting on the Registration Issue," *ANS*, June 1994.

47. "Bishop Ting on China's Christianity," *Beijing Review* 37, no. 15 (11-17 April 1994): 7.

48. Fewsmith, *China since Tiananmen*, 44ff.

49. See also Charles Kwok, "Bishop K. H. Ting's View of the Present Situation of Christianity in China," *Bridge* 33 (January-February 1989): 3.

50. "Zongjiao shehui tuanti dengji guanli shishi banfa" ("Implementation Procedures for the Registration and Management of Religious Social Organizations"), 6 May 1991, promulgated by the RAB of the State Council and the Civil Affairs Ministry, *Quangguo zongjiao xingzheng fagui guizhang huibian* (*Compilation of National Religious Administrative Rules and Regulations*), ed. Policy and Regulation Department of the RAB (Beijing: Zongjiao wenhua chubanshe, 1999), 8-9.

51. The text of the two decrees may be found in *Xin shiqi zongjiao gongzuo wenxian xuanbian* (*Selected Documents on Religious Work in the New Period*), 273-74 and 275-77. Translations of the two texts are available as "Regulation Governing Venues for Religious Activities, Decree No. 144 of the State Council," and "Regulation Governing the Religious Activities of Foreign Nationals within China, Decree No. 145 of the State Council," in *CSPD* 9, no. 1 (April 1994): 29-31.

52. On regional differences in religious policy, see Richard Madsen and James Tong, eds., "Local Religious Policy in China, 1980-1997," *Chinese Law and Government*, 33, no. 3 (May/June 2000).

53. "Jiu 'tangdian dengji wenti': Tian Feng jizhe fangwen Ding zhujiao" ("*Tian Feng* Interviews Bishop Ting on the Registration Issue"), *Tian Feng* (June 1994): 2-4. Translation in *ANS* (June 1994). See also "Jiu tangdian dengji wenti: Ding zhujiao zai ci tanhua" ("Another Talk with Bishop Ting on the Registration Issue"),

Tian Feng (March 1995): 28-29. This second interview clarifies many of the concerns that had arisen in the intervening months.

54. K. H. Ting, "A Look Back at the Way We Have Come," in *Love Never Ends*, 497-99.

55. See China Vitae: Ye Xiaowen, http://chinavitae.com/biography_display. phpp?id=2071 (accessed 31 March 2005).

56. Luo Guangwu, ed., *Xin zhongguo zongjiao gongzuo da shi gailan, 1949-1999 (An Overview of Major Events in Religious Work in New China, 1949-1999)*, 523-25.

57. Jiang's view of "adaptation" was introduced to religious leaders at an important conference at Sanya on Hainan Island which Ting attended in January 1994. Jiang Zemin's speech was originally carried in *Renmin ribao (People's Daily)*, 7 November 1993. I am quoting from "Jiang Zemin tongzhi you guan zongjiao gongzuo de san juhua" ("Comrade Jiang Zemin's 'Three Sentences' on Religious Work"), *Zongjiao (Religion)* 31-32, nos. 1-2 (1996): 1.

58. See Ye Xiaowen, "On the Importance of Sincerely Implementing the '3 Sentences' when Carrying Out Religious Work," *Renmin ribao (People's Daily)*, 14 March 1996, translated in *CSPD* 11, no. 2 (August 1996): 10-14.

59. Joe Slovo, "Shehui zhuyi he zongjiao zai jiazhiguan shang you gongtongdian" ("The Shared Values Between Socialism and Religion"), trans. K. H. Ting, *Zongjiao (Religion)* 25, no. 1 (1994): 19-22. The lecture by Slovo is dated 25 January 1994, and was originally entitled "The Right Not to Believe and the Shared Values Between Socialism and Religion."

60. Szan Tan, "The Cult and Festival of the Goddess of the Sea—A Maiden Encounter with Mazu," *The Heritage Journal* (Singapore) 1, no. 1 (2004): 13-20.

61. He wrote an unpublished essay entitled "Xiang Mazu xuexi" ("Learn from Mazu"), which I have not been able to obtain.

62. For one approach to the problem of the rural churches in China, see Liang Jialun (Leung Ka-lun), *Gaige kaifang yilai de zhongguo nongcun jiaohui (The Rural Churches of Mainland China Since 1978)* (Hong Kong: Alliance Bible Seminary, 1999).

63. "Yi ge gao jü sanzi mingque fangxiang de huiyi" ("A Meeting Reaffirming the Clear Direction of Three-Self"), *Tian Feng* (January 1990): 4-5.

64. "The Second (Enlarged) Plenary Session of the Joint Standing Committee of the National Three-Self Patriotic Movement and the China Christian Council: Work Report," translated in *CTR* (1991): esp. 1-2 and 10-11. The report was delivered to the meeting by CCC general secretary Shen Yifan on behalf of the joint standing committees.

65. K. H. Ting, "Address to the Plenary Session," translated in *CTR* (1990): 25.

66. On Chinese intellectuals and humanistic socialism, see Wang Hui, *China's New Order*, 153ff, and my discussion in chap. 7.

67. K. H. Ting, "On Being a Good Pastor," translated in *CTR* 11, no. 1 (1996): 111.

68. Philip L. Wickeri, "Christianity in Zhejiang: A Report from a Recent Visit to Protestant Churches in China," unpublished report, 31 May 1990. See also Zhi Huaxin, ed., *Wenzhou jidujiao (Wenzhou Christianity)* (Hangzhou: Zhejiang sheng jidujiao xiehui chuban, 1993); Ma Fayou, *Wenzhou jidujiaoshi (A History of Christianity in Wenzhou)* (Hong Kong: Alliance Bible Seminary, 1998).

69. See Zhang Xianyong and Li Yading, "Sui Ding Guangxun zhujiao fang Wen

xuyu" ("Notes on a Visit to Wenzhou with Bishop K. H. Ting"), *Tian Feng* (March 1991): 8-9.

70. See "Wenzhou: Open Port and Open Worship," and "Church Building Boom," *Bridge* 7 (September 1984): 3-6 and 6-9.

71. "Fourteen Points from Christians in the People's Republic of China to Christians Abroad," in Don MacInnis, ed., *Religion in China Today: Policy and Practice* (Maryknoll, N.Y.: Orbis Books, 1989), 70.

72. "Self-support and International Christian Sharing: An Interview with Bishop K. H. Ting," *ANS* (September 1992).

73. "With Independence and Initiative, Run the Church Well," *ANS* (December 1994).

74. "Resolution Passed by the Fourth Meetings of the Joint Standing Committee of the Fifth Session of the National TSPM and the Third Session of the CCC (summary)," translated in the *CSPD* 10, no. 1 (April 1995): 46-48. The meeting was held in Beijing, 22-26 November 1994.

75. K. H. Ting to Philip L. Wickeri, 10 January 1992.

76. "Forty-Five New Pastors Ordained," *ANS* (January 1992).

77. K. H. Ting, "That You Be Trustworthy," translated in *CTR* (1991): 127.

78. K. H. Ting, interview with the author, Nanjing, China, 13 December 1991.

79. "Nanjing Theological Seminary Holds 40th Anniversary Gathering," *ANS* (December 1992). Ting's welcoming speech is translated in *CTR* 9 (1994): 1-4.

80. See "Letter to Aumni/ae of Nanjing Seminary" (12 February 1995), translated in *Love Never Ends*, 500-505.

81. "The Dongguan Incident in Shenyang," *Bridge* 67 (September-October 1984): 3-9.

82. See "Some New Beginnings at the Fifth National Christian Conference," *Bridge* 52 (March-April 1992): 4-5.

83. K. H. Ting, "Statement on Theological Scholarships for Study Overseas," 5 January 1993, *ANS* 2.1 (February 1993).

84. Zhuo Xinping, "Discussion on 'Culture Christians' in China," in Stephen Uhalley and Xiaoxin Wu, eds., *China and Christianity: Burdened Past, Hopeful Future* (Armonk, N.Y.: M. E. Sharpe, 2001), 283-300.

85. Philip L. Wickeri and Lois Cole, eds., *Christianity and Modernization: A Chinese Debate* (Hong Kong: DAGA Press, 1995).

86. For reports, resolutions and other documents from the Fifth NCC, see *Zhongguo jidujiao di wu jie quanguo hui zhuanji (Records of the Fifth National Chinese Christian Conference)* (Shanghai: TSPM and CCC, 1992). The church order and other important documents are translated in *CTR* (1991).

87. For a discussion on reporting statistics from these years, see Alan Hunter and Kim-Kwong Chan, *Protestantism in Contemporary China* (Cambridge: Cambridge University Press, 1993), 66-71.

88. "Church Order for Trial Use in Chinese Churches," *CTR* (1991): 21-30.

89. "Bishop Ting Sums Up Conference, Talks about New Regulations," *ANS* (January 1992).

90. K. H. Ting, "The Tree of Life Is Ever Green," translated in *CTR* (1991): 119.

91. "Bishop Shen Yifan, 1928-1994," *ANS* (October 1994). For Shen Yifan's selected writings, see *Jiangtai shi feng: Shen Yifan zhujiao wenji (Service in the Pul-*

pit: Collected Writings of Bishop Shen Yifan, vol. 1) (Shanghai: China Christian Council, 1996); and *Luntan xinsheng: Shen Yifan zhujiao wenji (Forum of the Heart: Collected Writings of Bishop Shen Yifan,* vol. 2) (Shanghai: China Christian Council, 2000).

92. K. H. Ting, "Huigu zouguo de lu" ("A Look Back at the Way We Have Come"), in *Wenji,* 361-67; and in *Love Never Ends,* 491-99. As with many other essays in this book, the published version was revised. This speech was cited above in a summary of Ting's views on church-state relations and registration.

93. "Message to the China Christian Council," *The Ecumenical Review* 41, no. 4 (October 1989): 625.

94. "Ding zhujiao canjia Mosike quanqiu luntan" ("Bishop Ting Participates in Global Forum in Moscow"), *Tian Feng* (April 1990): 12.

95. K. H. Ting, "Caring for God's Creation," in *Love Never Ends,* 399-401.

96. K. H. Ting, "Chinese Christians' Approach to the Bible," in *Love Never Ends,* 391.

97. K. H. Ting, "Changes in Forty Years: A Talk to Chinese Students," unpublished manuscript, translated by the author, November 1987, 3 pp.

98. "Application for Membership," World Council of Churches, Seventh Assembly, Canberra, Australia, 7-20 February 1991, Document No. PL14.1, p. 1. See also Michael Kinnamon, ed., *Signs of the Spirit: Official Report of the Seventh Assembly* (Geneva: WCC Publications, 1991), 9-10.

99. "Application for Membership," p. 2.

100. "Chinese Church Resumes Membership in World Council of Churches," *Ecumenical Press Service,* 7-20 February 1991.

101. Amity Foundation circular letter, 26 February 1991.

102. Amity Foundation circular letter, 26 February 1991.

103. "Zhongguo jidujiao xiehui huizhang Ding Guangxun zhi Shijie jidujiao hui lianhe hui mishuzhang Aimiliou Kasiteluo de fuxin" ("CCC President Bishop Ding Guangxun's Return Letter to WCC General Secretary Emilio Castro"), *Tian Feng* (July 1991): 13. For one of a number of statements on the CCC's view of the Taiwan issue, see "Statement of the China Christian Council," 2 September 1994, *ANS* 3.4/5 (October 1994). See also "Interview with Mr. Han Wenzao, Vice-Chairman of the China Christian Council on the China Christian Council Becoming a Member of the World Council of Churches," translated in the *CSPD* 6, no. 3 (December 1991): 53-55. The interview originally appeared in *Tian Feng* (July 1991).

104. For example, see K. H. Ting, "Let Us Work for the Reunification of China," in *Love Never Ends,* 484-86. This statement was made at a meeting of religious leaders to study Jiang Zemin's speech on the peaceful reunification of China, 7 March 2005.

105. See "Chinese Church Leaders' Historic Visit to Taiwan Churches—Interview with Rev. Shen Cheng'en and Rev. Wang Weifan," *ANS* 2.5 (October 1992). Because the Taiwanese authorities do not allow senior political figures from the mainland to visit the island, Ting would not be allowed to go to Taiwan by virtue of his position as CPPCC vice-chair.

106. "Statement of the Chinese Participants of the Fifth Assembly of the Asian Conference on Religion and Peace," *ANS* 5.5/6 (1996).

107. *Ecumenical Team Visit to China, 5-18 May 1996.* Commission of the Churches on International Affairs, World Council of Churches, Geneva, Switzerland.

108. "Archbishop of Canterbury's Visit Most Helpful," *ANS* 3.4/5 (October 1994).

109. See Ting's preface to David M. Paton, *Christian Missions and the Judgment of God*, 2nd ed. (Grand Rapids: Eerdmans, 1996), ix-x.

110. K. H. Ting, "The Cosmic Christ," in *Love Never Ends*, 408-20.

111. The "Sino-British Joint Declaration on the Question of Hong Kong" (1984) stipulates that religious organizations in Hong Kong and the mainland shall relate to one another on the principles of "non-subordination, non-interference and mutual respect" (Annex 1, Section 13, Paragraph 3).

112. See Jonathan Chao and Rosanna Chong, *Dangdai zhongguo jidujiao fazhanshi, 1949-1997* (*A History of Christianity in Socialist China, 1949-1997*) (Taipei: CMI Publishing, 1997), passim; also Anthony Lambert, *The Resurrection of the Chinese Church* (London: Hodder & Stoughton, 1991); and *China's Christian Millions: The Costly Revival* (London: Monarch Books, 1999).

113. Shi Zhi, "Ambassador of Peace and Honored Chinese Guest: Reflections on K. H. Ting's Controversial Visit to Fuller Seminary," 1 December 1993, unpublished manuscript, 6 pp.

114. See K. H. Ting, "An Update on the Church in China," in *Love Never Ends*, 448-59. This was an address he gave at a retreat in Nanjing organized by the Baptist World Alliance in 1994. In form and content it is cast in a more evangelical style than other speeches he gave in the 1990s.

115. "Statement of Purpose," in Order of Service for the Presentation of the Union Medal to Bishop K. H. Ting, 13 October 1994. See also Susan Grant Rosen, "The Union Medal and the Union Plaque," *Union News* (Summer 1995): 14-16.

116. K. H. Ting, "Report to My Alma Mater," in *Love Never Ends*, 460-66.

117. "Two Missionary Reunions," *China News Update* (January 1995): 8. See also "Chinese More Open to Christianity, Bishop Reports," *Wesleyan Christian Advocate*, 21 October 1994; and "Presbyterian Legacy in China: Church Continues to Grow," *The News of the Presbyterian Church (U.S.A.)* (November/ December 1994), 5.

118. "Ex-'China Hands' Mark New Era for Chinese Church," *The United Methodist Reporter*, 21 October 1994. See also (in Chinese) Ting's untitled comment on Zhang Xiaofeng, "Qin Shang" ("Qin Elegy"), dated 9 April 1993, which is quoted in chap. 4.

119. "Message to Chinese Christians: A Response to Bishop K. H. Ting's Opening Address," *China News Update* (January 1995): 9.

120. Siu-may Kuo, *Journeying Through the Bible* (Nanjing: Nanjing University Press, 1990); and *Venturing into the Bible* (Nanjing: Nanjing University Press, 1989).

121. K. H. Ting, interview with the author, Nanjing, China, 13 December 1991.

122. K. H. Ting, "Congratulatory Remarks," in *Love Never Ends*, 467-72. This speech was delivered in Shanghai on 21 November 1995.

10. THEOLOGICAL RECONSTRUCTION, 1996 – 2006

1. K. H. Ting quoted this poem by the Guatemalan poet Otto Rene Castillo in his speech at the groundbreaking ceremony for the new campus at Nanjing Theo-

logical Seminary on 17 January 2005. See "Nanjing Seminary Breaks New Ground," *ANS* 2005.1/2 (http://www.amitynewsservice.org/page.php?page=1116 &pointer=, accessed 28 November 2005).

2. See Robert Lawrence Kuhn, *The Man Who Changed China: The Life and Legacy of Jiang Zemin* (New York: Crown Publishers, 2005), discussed in the introduction to this book.

3. Joseph Fewsmith, *China since Tiananmen: The Politics of Transition* (Cambridge: Cambridge University Press, 2001), 177.

4. Richard Baum, "The Fifteenth National Party Congress: Jiang Takes Command?" *The China Quarterly* 153 (March 1998): 141-56.

5. Fewsmith, *China since Tiananmen*, 173.

6. Most of these were women from inland provinces. For a recent study, see Pun Ngai, *Made in China: Women Factory Workers in a Global Marketplace* (Hong Kong: Duke University Press and Hong Kong University Press, 2005).

7. Sun Liping, "Tiaozheng liyi guanxi yu zhuanhuan zengzhang moshi" ("Adjust Profit Relationships and Transform the Pattern of Growth"), unpublished manuscript, presented as a speech at the Twentieth Anniversary Symposium of the Amity Foundation, Nanjing, 7 November 2005. Sun Liping is a well-known sociologist at Qing Hua University in Beijing.

8. Timothy Brook and B. Michael Frolic, eds., *Civil Society in China* (Armonk, N.Y.: M. E. Sharpe, 1997); also Wang Hui, *China's New Order: Society, Politics and Economy in Transition* (Cambridge and London: Harvard University Press, 2003).

9. Maria Hsia Chang, *Falun Gong: The End of Days* (New Haven: Yale University Press, 2004); Cheris Shun-ching Chan, "The *Falun Gong* in China: A Sociological Perspective," *The China Quarterly* 179 (September 2004): 665-83; and Ronald C. Keith and Zhiqiu Lin, "The '*Falun Gong* Problem': Politics and the Struggle for the Rule of Law in China," *The China Quarterly* 175 (September 2003): 623-42.

10. "Resolutions of the CPC Central Committee Regarding Important Questions on Promoting Socialist Ethical and Cultural Progress," *Beijing Review* 39 (4-10 November 1996): 20-31.

11. See "The 'Three Represents' Theory," http://news.xinhuanet.com/english/20010625/422678.htm (accessed 20 November 2005).

12. See Joseph Fewsmith, "The Sixteenth National Party Congress: The Succession that Didn't Happen," *China Quarterly* 173 (March 2003): 1-16.

13. See "Quarterly Chronicle and Documentation (April-June 2003)," *The China Quarterly* 175 (September 2003): 862-67.

14. See Evan S. Medeiros and M. Taylor Fravel, "China's New Diplomacy," and David Hale and Lyric Hughes Hale, "China Takes Off," *Foreign Affairs*, 82, no. 6 (November/December 2003): 22-35 and 36-53. Also, Todd C. Fishman, *China, Inc.: How the Rise of the Next Superpower Challenges America and the World* (New York: Scribner, 2005).

15. The "Resolution on Major Issues Regarding the Building of a Harmonious Socialist Society" was approved by the Sixth Plenum of the Sixteenth CPC central committee on 11 October 2006. For a short report on the resolution, see http://www.china.org.cn/english/2006/Oct/184810.htm (accessed 9 December 2006). A translation of the full text may be found at http://news.xinhuanet.com/

english/2006-10/11/content_5191071.htm (accessed 9 December 2006). On the role of religion in this process, see the interview with Ye Xiaowen, director of the State Administration of Religious Affairs, http://www.china.org.cn/english/government/175448.htm (accessed 9 December 2006).

16. *CTR* 10 (1995). This festschrift was edited by Janice K. Wickeri. Many of the essays were subsequently published in *JL*.

17. His last overseas trip was in October 1999 when he went to Seoul to receive an honorary degree from Yonsei University and take part in the launch of a book of his writings in Korean translation.

18. K. H. Ting, "Congratulatory Remarks," in K. H. Ting, *Love Never Ends,* ed. Janice K. Wickeri (Nanjing: Yilin Press, 2000), 467-72. This was his speech at the forty-fifth anniversary of the founding of the TSPM, Shanghai, 21 November 1995.

19. K. H. Ting, "Yixie fenxi he yijian" ("Some Analyses and Opinions"), unpublished typescript dated 26 August 1996.

20. Luo Guanzong, ed., *Lun Sanzi he jiaohui jianshe: Ding Guangxun zhujiao he zhongguo jidujiao lici huiyi wenjian you guan lunshu xuanbian, 1980-1995 (On Three-Self and Church Building: Selected Conference Documents Expounding the Subject by Bishop K. H. Ting and the Chinese Church, 1980-1995)* (Shanghai: TSPM/CCC, 1996).

21. K. H. Ting, "Greetings to the Sixth National Christian Conference," *CTR* 12 (1998): 3. The speech was delivered on 29 December 1996.

22. Han Wenzao, "Build Up the Body of Christ with One Heart and United Effort: Work Report," *CTR* 12 (1991): 6-45.

23. "Chinese Christian Church Order," *CTR* 12 (1991): 63-79.

24. "Endorsing the Resolution of the Central Committee on Important Issues in Strengthening Construction of Socialist Spiritual Civilization," *CTR* 12 (1991): 88.

25. The four were Ren Zhongxiang (from Shanghai), Ms. Shi Ruzhang (also from Shanghai), Bishop Wang Shenyin (from Shandong), and Yin Jizeng (from Beijing).

26. See Siu-may Guo (Kuo), "Why I Don't Retire," *U.S.–China Review* 7, no. 6 (November-December 1983): 14-15, 29.

27. "An Interview with K. H. Ting," in *Love Never Ends,* 530.

28. "An Interview with K. H. Ting," in *Love Never Ends,* 531. He also thanked Chinese Christians for their prayers at the end of his "Greetings to the Sixth National Christian Conference," *CTR* 12 (1998): 4. The Salt Sea is usually referred to as the Dead Sea in English.

29. Only two short texts are attributed to Deng in the selection of government statements on religious policy, *Xin shiqi zongjiao gongzuo wenxian xuanbian (Selected Documents on Religious Work in the New Period),* both of which are before the publication of Document No. 19. They are concerned with religion as part of united-front work; see "Xin shiqi de tongyi zhanxian he renmin zhengxie renwu" ("The United Front in the New Period and the Responsibility of People's Consultation," 15 June 1979), 5-9; and "Yi jian you shenyuan yiyi de shengshi" ("A Great Event with Long Lasting Significance," 19 April 1980), dealing with the monk Jian Zhen, who promoted exchanges between China and Japan in the ninth century (p. 22). (For more on Deng Xiaoping and China's religious policy, see chap. 8.)

30. Interview with K. H. Ting, Nanjing, China, 22 March 1997.

31. K. H. Ting, statement on "United States Policies in Support of Religious Freedom: Focus on Christians" *ANS* (August 1997). This statement was in response to a U.S. State Department report. See http://bahai-library.com/documents/97.07. 22.report.html (accessed 9 December 2006).

32. A short report on the meeting may be found in *Tian Feng* 4 (1997), inside cover; and "CCC/TSPM Committee Meets, Plans Work," *ANS* 6:3/4 (1997). Invitations to the international seminar and thanksgiving service were sent out well in advance, on 20 January.

33. For a report on Ting's speech, see He Ming, "March Song: A Sketch of the Thanksgiving Service of the Two National Christian Organizations," *Tian Feng* 4 (1997): 5; and "International Meeting Welcomes New CCC Leadership, Bids Farewell to Bishop Ting," *ANS* 6:3/4 (1997).

34. For detailed statistics on Bible and scripture production at the Amity Printing Company, Ltd. (Nanjing), see http://www.amityprinting.com/new/englishweb/ bibles.htm (accessed 21 November 2005).

35. See Liang Jialun (Leung Ka-lun), *Gaige kaifang yilai de zhongguo nongcun jiaohui (The Rural Churches of Mainland China since 1978)* (Hong Kong: Alliance Bible Seminary, 1999).

36. For an English translation, see "One Hundred Questions and Answers on the Christian Faith," *CTR* (1985): 211-42.

37. See Kevin Xiyi Yao, *The Fundamentalist Movement among Protestant Missionaries in China, 1920-1937* (Lanham, Md.: University Press of America, 2003).

38. See Daniel H. Bays, "Chinese Protestant Christianity Today," *China Quarterly* 174 (June 2003), 494-95 and passim. For an excellent summary of the historical background, see Daniel H. Bays, "The Growth of Independent Christianity in China, 1900-1937," in *Christianity in China: From the Eighteenth Century to the Present*, ed. Daniel Bays (Stanford: Stanford University Press, 1996), 307-17.

39. For a recent interpretation of China's "unregistered" evangelical leaders, see the four-part DVD series (in Chinese and English) entitled "The Cross: Jesus in China" (2003). It was produced by Yuan Zhiming, a convert to Christianity, who in 1988 produced the widely popular television series *He Shang (River Elegy)*. For information on the video see http://www.chinasoul.com/e/cross-news.htm (accessed 21 November 2005).

40. These are discussed in Jason Kindopp, "The Politics of Protestantism in Contemporary China: State Control, Civil Society and Social Movement in a Single Party State" (Ph.D. diss., George Washington University, 2004); and Paul Hattaway, *Back to Jerusalem: Three Chinese House Church Leaders Share Their Vision to Complete the Great Commission* (Carlisle: Gabriel Publishing, 2003).

41. David Aikman, *Jesus in Beijing: How Christianity Is Transforming China and Changing the Global Balance of Power* (Washington: Regnery Publishing, 2003).

42. Gao Shining, "Twenty-first Century Chinese Christianity and the Chinese Social Process," *CSPD* 15, nos. 2-3 (December 2000): 15. On popular religion more generally, see Hubert Seiwart, *Popular Religious Movements and Heterodox Sects in Chinese History*, in collaboration with Ma Xisha (Leiden and Boston: Brill, 2003).

43. Zhao Zhi'en, *Jianchi zhenli, dizhi yiduan (Uphold the Truth and Oppose Heresy)* (Shanghai: TSPM/CCC, 1996). Although written for polemical purposes,

this short pamphlet contains useful descriptions of some of the better-known heretical and sectarian groups. See also Edmund Tang, "Yellers and Healers—Pentecostalism and the Study of Grassroots Christianity in China," *CSPD* 17, no. 3 (December 2002): 19-29; and Liang Jialun (Leung Ka-lun), *Gaige kaifang yilai de zhongguo nongcun jiaohui (The Rural Churches of Mainland China since 1978)* (Hong Kong: Alliance Bible Seminary, 1999); Liang Jialun (Leung Ka-lun), "Rural Christianity and Chinese Folk Religions," *CSPD* 14, no. 2 (August 1999): 22-34. The latter article is a translation of the section of the author's longer work on rural churches in mainland China.

44. K. H. Ting, "A Look Back at the Way We Have Come," in *Love Never Ends,* 492. The speech was delivered in Nanjing on 24 April 1995.

45. K. H. Ting, "Greetings to the Sixth National Chinese Christian Conference," 3-4.

46. The most frequently cited of these is K. H. Ting, "Zai Sixiang shenchu shiying shehuizhuyi" ("On a Profound Ideological Level Adapt to Socialism"), unpublished manuscript, translated and revised in *Love Never Ends,* 506-10. The speech was first delivered in Dalian in May 1996. See also "Ding Guangxun zai quanguo zhengxie bajie sici huiyi xiaozu taolun de fayan" ("Speech by K. H. Ting in Small Group Discussion at the 4th Session of the 8th CPPCC"), *Zongjiao gongzuo tongbao* 3, no. 30 (8 March 1996).

47. K. H. Ting reiterated his support for Jiang Zemin's call for the adaptation of religion to socialist society in many subsequent speeches. See, for example, K. H. Ting, "Sanzi aiguo yundong de fazhan he chongshi" ("Development and Enrichment of the Three-Self Patriotic Movement"), *Tian Feng* (January 2000): 4-5; translated in *CTR* 17 (2003): 131-35.

48. *Collected Works of K. H. Ting (Ding Guangxun wenji),* 512. For full disclosure, I am among those thanked in the following paragraph of the afterword for helping to locate speeches and writings published abroad.

49. It should be noted here that the contents of *Love Never Ends (Collected Writings of K. H. Ting)* (Korean), ed. Kim Jong-goo (Seoul: Korean Christian Institute of Social Problems 1999), and *Love Never Ends: Papers by K. H. Ting,* ed. Janice K. Wickeri (Nanjing: Yilin Publishers, 2000) are not exactly the same as *The Collected Works,* due to the fact that the translation processes were going on as several new essays were added to the Chinese version. A slightly rearranged Hong Kong version in traditional Chinese characters was published as *Dangdai zhongguo jidujiao fayanren: Ding Guangxun wenji (The Spokesman of Contemporary Christianity in China: Collection of Bishop K. H. Ting's Essays),* ed. Frances Fang (Hong Kong: Chinese Christian Literature Council, 1999). In 2004, *God Is Love: Collected Writings of Bishop K. H. Ting* (Colorado Springs: Cook Communications, 2004) was published with new introductory notes, without Chen Zemin's preface or acknowledgment of translated sources, and with new titles assigned to previously published essays. Ting had been persuaded to have the volume issued by an American evangelical publisher in the belief that it would help introduce his ideas to evangelicals overseas.

50. Jason Kindopp, "The Politics of Protestantism in Contemporary China: State Control, Civil Society and Social Movement in a Single Party State," 306.

51. He outlined his priorities in a letter to colleagues prior to one of the first meetings to discuss theological questions in the TSPM/CCC. See K. H. Ting, "Tong

Gong" ("Letter to Colleagues"), mimeographed, 29 June 1981, 5 pp. This letter is briefly discussed in Philip L. Wickeri, *Seeking the Common Ground: Protestant Christianity, the Three-Self Movement and China's United Front,* 279-80. A copy of the letter is contained in my personal files.

52. K. H. Ting, "Tan Jidujiao Youshenlun" ("On Christian Theism"), *JL* 7, no. 8 (1957): 13-21; translated in *A Chinese Contribution to Ecumenical Theology: Selected Writings of K. H. Ting,* ed. Philip and Janice Wickeri (Geneva: WCC, 2002), 27-40.

53. K. H. Ting, "Ze'yang du shengjing" ("How to Study the Bible"), *Tian Feng* (20 October 1980): 45-63. This was the first issue of *Tian Feng* published after the end of the Cultural Revolution. A translation may be found in *How to Study the Bible,* ed. Philip L. Wickeri (Hong Kong: Tao Fong Shan Ecumenical Centre, 1981).

54. "Selected Writings of K. H. Ting Published," *ANS* (February 1999). Also, "Zhongguo shenxue shi shang zhongyao de lichengbei—*Ding Guangxun Wenji* chuban zuotanhui zai jing jü xing" ("An Important Milestone in the History of Chinese Theology—Symposium on the Publication of *The Collected Works of K. H. Ting* Held in Beijing"), *Tian Feng* (January 1999): 12. The State Administration of Religious Affairs (SARA) was the new name for Religious Affairs Bureau (RAB). SARA was established in the fall of 1998 as part of the institutional reforms of the State Council.

55. "Reporting and Observing the Theological Construction Movement in the Three-Self Church in China," unsigned, unpublished and undated paper circulated in late 2000. This report, purportedly written by a former staff member of the seminary, has been widely circulated and cited abroad, but it contains many factual errors and biased interpretations. There are conflicting reports on what actually happened at Nanjing Seminary during this period, and I have chosen to offer a minimalist interpretation based on sources that can be reasonably well documented. This report is cited only for events that can be confirmed by other sources.

56. K. H. Ting, "Xin zen'me yang yiwei Shangdi?" ("Believing in What Kind of God?" *Tian Feng* (October 1998): 16-17. A translation of the essay may be found in *ANS* 1998.11.2.

57. "Informal Memo of the Xinde Meeting, Nanjing, 10-11 September 1998" (in Chinese). This report was drawn up by seminary leaders. I have read the memo, but I do not have a copy. The narrative in the text is based on my notes.

58. K. H. Ting, "Shengjing zhong Shangdi de qishi he ren dui shangdi qishi de renshi" ("God's Self-Revelation in the Bible and Our Slowness in Grasping It"), *JL* (*Nanjing Theological Review*) 1 (1999): 3-4; and *Tian Feng* (February 1999): 17-18. An English translation may be found in *CTR* 14 (2000): 32-37.

59. "Guanyu jiaqiang shenxue sixiang jianshe de jueyi" ("Resolution on Strengthening Theological Reconstruction"), *Tian Feng* 1 (1999): 11.

60. "Zhongguo jidujiao shenxue sixiang jianshe xiaozu di yici huiyi zai ning jux-ing" ("The First Meeting of the Small Group on Theological Reconstruction Is Held in Nanjing"), *Tian Feng* 3 (2000), inside cover. The first meeting was held at the end of December 1999. See also "Zhongguo jidujiao shenxue sixiang jianshe tuijin xiaozu (kuoda) huiyi zai ning zhau kai" ("Small Group for the Promotion of Chinese Christian Theological Reconstruction Holds Expanded Meeting in Nanjing"), *Tian Feng* 10 (October 2001): 34; and "Lianxi shiji zhuzhong shixiao dali tuijin

shenxue sixiang jianshe" ("Connect to Reality, Emphasize Effectiveness, Exert Great Effort to Promote Theological Reconstruction"), *Tian Feng* 3 (March 2003): 10.

61. K. H. Ting, "Jianjue yonghu he zhichi qudi 'Fa Lun Gong'" ("Resolutely Uphold and Support the Suppression of *'Falun Gong'*"), *Tian Feng* (September 1999): 5. See also "Yiqie qingsheng de xingwei dou bushi shangdi suo yuanyi de" ("No Actions Which Devalue Life Are Willed By God"), *Tian Feng* (March 2001): 14.

62. Tang Zhongmo, *Xiandai shengjing guan (A Modern View of the Bible)*, special issue of *JL* (October 2000). Also published separately in Shanghai: China Christian Council, 2000 (July). Ting wrote a preface for the special issue of the book in *JL*. The book was first published in 1936.

63. See K. H. Ting, "Zhongguo jidutu zeyang kan shengjing" ("Chinese Christians' Approach to the Bible"), *Tian Feng* (July 2004): 25-32. This essay was also translated in the *Collected Works*, 77-89. It was reprinted in *Tian Feng* in connection with the "Exhibition of the Bible Work of the Chinese Church," Hong Kong, August 2004.

64. These views are summarized in K. H. Ting, "Shenxue sixiang jianshe jinru yige xin de jieduan" ("Theological Reconstruction Has Entered a New Period"), *Tian Feng* (September 2003): 4-7. This essay is summarized in *ANS* 2003.11/12.2.

65. "On a Profound Christian Question," in *Love Never Ends*, 506-10; and in *Wenji*, 285-89. He had already advanced this position the previous year in an unpublished essay, "Reviewing the Path We have Taken" (April 1995). See also K. H. Ting "Old Style Theological Thinking Needs Revision and Renewal," *Zongjiao* 1-2 (1999); originally in *Renmin zhengxiebao*, 5 March 1999; *CTR* 14 (2000): 30-31; and "A Call for the Adjustment of Religious Ideas," *Renmin Zhengxiebao* (4 September 1998).

66. He made this point as early as 1984. See K. H. Ting, "A Rationale for Three-Self," in *Love Never Ends*, 124. This speech was first delivered at Doshisha University in Japan; see K. H. Ting, *Christian Witness in China Today* (Kyoto: Doshisha University Press, 1985), 2. See also K. H. Ting, "Yige gei quan shijie dailai zhongyao xinxi de jidujiao" ("A Christianity with an Important Message for the Whole World"), *Tian Feng* 10 (October 2001): 30-33. This is translated as "Some Thoughts on the Subject of Theological Reconstruction," in *CTR* 17 (2003): 110-17.

67. K. H. Ting, "Zai zhongguo jidujiao sanzi aiguoyundong wushi zhounian jinianhui de jianghua" ("Speech at the 50th Anniversary of the Chinese Christian Three-Self Patriotic Movement"), *JL* 45, no. 4 (2000): 4, translated as "Theology in Context," *CTR* 17 (2003): 125.

68. For a selection of these in English translation, see the five speeches in the section "Recent Writings of K. H. Ting" in *CTR* 17 (2003): 110-38.

69. K. H. Ting, "God Is Love," in *Love Never Ends*, 508.

70. He mentioned this in a conversation with a study group from San Francisco Theological Seminary that met with Ting in his home in Nanjing, 26 May 2000.

71. K. H. Ting, "Da duzhe wen" ("In Response to My Readers"), *JL (Nanjing Theological Review)* 39, no. 2 (1999): 50-52, translated in *CTR* 14 (2000): 91-96.

72. K. H. Ting, "In Response to My Readers," *CTR* 14 (2000): 96. This translation has been slightly revised.

73. Zhou Jiacai, *Zhao Puchu yu Jiangsu zongjiao (Zhao Puchu and Religion in Jiangsu)* (Beijing: Zongjiaowenhua chubanshe, 2003), 55. Zhou Jiacai, former RAB head in Jiangsu Province, was a member of the evaluation team.

74. Cui Xiuji, Chen Shunfu and Chen Bing, "Women weishenma jujue zai wanhui shang chang shehui gequ?" ("Why We Refuse to Sing Social Songs at the Evening Performance?"), mimeographed circular dated 12 March 1999. I have a copy of this circular in my personal files.

75. The three students were Liu Yichun, Li Zhimin and Luo Yunfei. Their statement was "Women weishenma yao tuixue? Jinling xiehe shenxueyuan san wei tongxue de shengming" ("Why Are We Withdrawing from Our Studies? A Statement from Three Students at Nanjing Union Theological Seminary"), mimeographed circular dated 18 June 1999. I have a copy in my personal files.

76. "Ding Yuanzhang xiang Jinling xiehe shenxueyuan shi sheng jianghua (zhaiyao)" ("Principal Ting's Speech to the Faculty and Students of Nanjing Union Theological Seminary (Extracts)," mimeographed transcript dated 25 June 1999. I have a copy in my personal files.

77. For example, see Jason Kindopp, "The Politics of Protestantism in Contemporary China: State Control, Civil Society and Social Movement in a Single Party State," 337-57. Kindopp's analysis is based on unconfirmed, undocumented and unverifiable informal "interviews," which readers are asked to accept on his word alone. He consistently accepts his informants' testimony at face value and interprets "official" responses in the worst possible light. See also Mindy Belz, "Caesar's Seminary," *World* 16 (27 January 2001): 1-3. For other reporting, see Tetsunao Yamamori and Kim-Kwong Chan, *Witnesses to Power: Stories of God's Quiet Work in Changing China* (Carlisle: Paternoster Press, 2000), 87-95; and Daniel Kwon, "Rebel Trio Challenge Protestant Leader," *South China Morning Post,* 28 June 1999.

78. K. H. Ting, "Circular Letter," 27 June 2000. See also Gotthard Oblau, "Theology Needs Freedom: Personal Notes on a Questionable Campaign within China's Church," unpublished manuscript, 2001; and K. H. Ting to Gotthard Oblau, 29 May 2001; and Shen Mo, "Yi wei shenxueyuan jiangshi weihe bei kai chu?" ("Why Has a Seminary Lecturer Been Fired?"), *Shengming jikan (Christian Life Quarterly)* 4, no. 4 (2000): 22-26. Copies of the letters cited above are in my personal files.

79. Zhou Jiacai, *Zhao Puchu yu Jiangsu zongjiao (Zhao Puchu and Religion in Jiangsu)*, 55.

80. For example, see "Shenxuesheng lunwenxuan" ("Some Graduate Students' Papers"), *JL (Nanjing Theological Review)*, supplementary issue (March 2002).

81. See the special issue of *JL (Nanjing Theological Review)* 4 (December 2002) on the fiftieth anniversary of Nanjing Union Theological Seminary. The dates of the fiftieth anniversary observations were from 31 October to 1 November 2002.

82. K. H. Ting, "Zhichi zhongguo tianzhujiao hui de aiguo xingdong" ("In Support of the Patriotic Action of Chinese Catholics"), *Tian Feng* (November 2000): 9. Ting's statement came the day after the Vatican's action, 2 October 2005.

83. Han Wenzao's opening speech is quoted in "Quanguo jidujiao lianghui benjie di erci quanti weiyuanhui huiyi zai Jinan juxing" ("TSPM/CCC Committee Holds Second Plenary Meeting in Jinan"), *Tian Feng* 1 (1999): 8-9. Excerpts from the speech may be found in Han Wenzao, "Guanyu jiachang shenxue sixiang jian-

she wenti" ("On the Question of Strengthening Theological Reconstruction"), *JL* (*Nanjing Theological Review*), 39, no. 6 (1999): 4.

84. See *Zhongguo jidujiao di qi ci daibiao huiyi zhuanji* (*Proceedings of the Seventh National Christian Conference*) (Shanghai: TSPM/CCC, 2002). Han and Luo were named co-directors of the newly established TSPM/CCC advisory committee at this meeting, a committee made up of other older or retired leaders. Shortly after the Seventh NCC, Han also stepped down as Amity general secretary, and as chair of the board of the Amity Printing Company. Han Wenzao died in Nanjing in February 2006.

85. K. H. Ting to Philip L. Wickeri, 11 July 1997.

86. The words are from George Marsden, *Understanding Fundamentalism and Evangelicalism* (Grand Rapids: Eerdmans, 1991), 1. Marsden was quoting Jerry Falwell. He adds, "A more precise statement of the same point is that an American fundamentalist is an evangelical who is militant in opposition to liberal theology in the churches or to changes in cultural values or mores such as those associated with 'secular humanism.'"

87. K. H. Ting to Janice K. and Philip L. Wickeri, 25 November 1999.

88. Mouw was a guest of honor at the fiftieth anniversary celebrations of Nanjing Theological Seminary and at other recent ceremonial occasions. See also K. H. Ting, "Jianshe zhongguo tese de shenxue, ying lao gu shuli zhengque de shengjing'guan, shangdiguan, shirenguan" ("To Construct a Theology with Chinese Characteristics We Should Firmly Establish a Correct View of the Bible, God and People"), *Tian Feng* (May 2003): 4-5. In this essay he mentions Mouw's apology to him for the unfortunate protest demonstration at Fuller Theological Seminary. In 2003, Mouw led a delegation of Fuller faculty to Nanjing Theological Seminary, and their lectures at the seminary are published in *JL* (*Nanjing Theological Review*) 4 (2003).

89. Richard Mouw, "The Cosmic Mission of Christ," in *Seeking Truth in Love,* ed. Wang Peng (Beijing: Zongjiao wenhua chubanshe, 2006), 299-316.

90. *Renmin ribao* (*People's Daily*), 22 May 2000. K. H. Ting was named to the funeral committee; see http://www.people.com.cn/GB/paper464/697/83116.html (accessed on 25 June 2007).

91. These are the words of Jason Kindopp, "The Politics of Protestantism in Contemporary China: State Control, Civil Society and Social Movement in a Single Party State," 291-362.

92. K. H. Ting, *Lun Shenxue sixiang jianshe* (*On Theological Reconstruction*) (Shanghai: TSPM/CCC, 2000). In addition, a boxed set of five hardcover books with selected essays by K. H. Ting on theological reconstruction, the Bible, God, Jesus Christ, and Three-Self and church construction has been published. The set includes essays from *Wenji* as well as others written between 1998 and 2000, the year in which the set was released. See also K. H. Ting, *Shengjing, xinyang, jiaohui* (*The Bible, Faith and the Church*) (Shanghai: TSPM/CCC, 2001). *Tian Feng* had earlier produced a supplementary issue dedicated to the writings of K. H. Ting (1 March 2000).

93. See *Zhongguo jidujiao di qici daibiao huiyi zhuanji* (*Proceedings of the Seventh National Christian Conference*) (Shanghai: TSPM/CCC, 2002), passim. From 2000 onward, there were regular statements in support of theological reconstruction by Cao Shengjie, Ji Jianhong and other senior church leaders in *Tian*

Feng. In 2004, a regular column on theological reconstruction began in the same magazine.

94. See, for example, K. H. Ting, "Mantan shenxue sixiang jianshe" ("Informal Remarks on Theological Reconstruction"), *Beijing jiaohui zai sikao (The Church in Beijing Reflecting)* (Beijing: Beijing TSPM and Christian Council, 2002), 1-9; and K. H. Ting, "Yinxin yu shangdi jianli heyi de guanxi" ("Faith and the Reconciliation of Relationships with God"), *Tian Feng* 8 (August 2002): 34-36. The latter was a speech delivered at a conference on theological reconstruction in Wuhan.

95. K. H. Ting, "Some Thoughts on the Subject of Theological Reconstruction," *CTR* (2003): 110 and 117, a translation of K. H. Ting, "Yige gei quan shijie dailai zhongyao xinxi de jidujiao" ("A Christianity with an Important Message for the Whole World"), *Tian Feng* 10 (October 2001): 30-33.

96. Chen Zemin, "Jiaqiang zhongguo jiaohui de shenxue jianshe—Jinan huiyi de dahui fayan" ("Strengthen Theological Construction in the Chinese Church—Plenary Speech at the Jinan Meeting," *JL* (*Nanjing Theological Review*) 38, no. 1 (1999): 5-7.

97. Chen Zemin, "Qianyan" ("Preface"), in *Wenji*, 1-8, translated as "Foreword: Faith's Journey," in *Love Never Ends*, 1-8. Also, Chen Zemin, "Zhongguo jidujiao ying ze'yang mianmao jinru 21 shiji: guanyu *Ding Guangxun wenji*" ("How Should Chinese Christianity Face Entry into the 21st Century: Reflections on the Publication of *The Collected Works of K. H. Ting*"), *Tian Feng* (July 1999): 16-17. This essay was originally presented as a speech at the Jinan Meeting in 1998.

98. Chen Zemin, "Theological Construction in the Chinese Church," *CTR (1991)*: 74, and 74-76 (for quotations). The essay originally appeared in *JL* (*Nanjing Theological Review*) 5 and 6 (1957), and was revised and republished by the author in *JL* 14-15, nos. 1-2 (1991): 7-19.

99. Essays by these theologians regularly appear in the *JL* (*Nanjing Theological Review*) and other publications. Many have been translated in *CTR*. See, for example, Chen Yilu, "Some Concepts in Theological Education in China," *CTR* 17 (2003): 13-22; Chen Yongtao, "Toward a Tao Christology: Rethinking Christology in the Chinese Context," *CTR* 17 (2003): 23-50, and "Interpreting Christian Faith in Our Own Time and Context," *CTR* 19 (2005): 1-19; Xiao Anping, "Theological Change and the Adaptation of Christianity to Socialist Society," *CTR* 16 (2002): 96-103, and "The Church in the Modernization of China: A Theological Interpretation," *CTR* 18 (2004): 37-63; Wang Aiming, "Understanding Theological Reconstruction in the Chinese Church: A Hermeneutical Approach," *CTR* 16 (2002): 139-49; Wang Peng, "*Koinonia* and Ethical Thought in Paul's Epistles," *CTR* 19 (2005): 69-84; Kan Baoping, "'Jesus is Christ' as the Basis for Efforts at Indigenization and Contextualization in the Chinese Church," *CTR* 16 (2002): 72-95; Zhang Keyun, "Theological Reconstruction in Jiangsu," *CTR* 16 (2002): 131-38; and Gao Ying, "Tiaozheng shengjing guan shi shenxue sixiang jianshe renwu zhi yi" ("Adjusting Our View of the Bible Is a Responsibility for Theological Reconstruction"), in *Beijing jiaohui zai sikao*, 64-71.

100. Most of the debate has taken place on the Internet. See, for example, www.chinahousechurch.org (accessed 15 October 2005). English-language Web sites attacking K. H. Ting and theological reconstruction are largely based on Chinese sources. See, for example, www.wayoflife.org (accessed 27 October 2005).

101. Jonathan Chao, "Three-Self Theology Seminar: A Concluding Remark," *Anthology of Jonathan Chao*, http://www.cmi.org.tw (accessed 14 February 2005).

102. Li Xinyuan, *Theological Construction—or Deconstruction: An Analysis of the Theology of Bishop K. H. Ting (Ding Guangxun)* (Streamwood, Ill. and Mountain View, Ca.: Christian Life Press and Great Commission Center International, 2003). Li's book was originally published as a series of essays in Chinese as Li Xinyuan, "Yige 'buxinpai' de biaoben—*Ding Guangxun wenji* pingxi" ("A Classic Example of the 'Party of Unbelief'—A Critical Analysis of the Collected Works of Ding Guangxun"), *Shengming jikan (Christian Life Quarterly)* 4, nos. 2, 3 and 4 (2000): 23-29, 33-36 and 15-2. See also "A Cause for Controversy: *Love Never Ends,*" *ANS* 2000.7/8.2, http://www.amitynewsservice.org/page.php?page=774 (accessed 26 November 2005).

103. Liu Xiaofeng's book *Zhengjiu yu xiaoyao (Delivering and Dallying)*, rev. ed. (Shanghai: San Lian, 2001) was a bestseller among young intellectuals when it first came out in 1988. Liu has written very widely since then, and has modified his theological position He is now a professor at Zhong Shan University in Guangzhou. See also Liu Xiaofeng, *Zou xiang shizijiashang de zhenli (Walking Toward the Truth of the Cross)* (Shanghai: San Lian, 1990). In English, see Frederick Fällman, *Salvation and Modernity: Intellectuals and Faith in Contemporary China*, Chinese Culture Series 2 (Stockholm: Stockholm University, Department of Oriental Languages, 2004).

104. Wang Weifan, "Tan ban hao jiaohui yu shenxue sixiang jianshe" ("On Running the Church Well and Theological Reconstruction"), unpublished manuscript (third draft), dated 4 May 2002, pp. 4-5.

105. See the translation of this essay, originally published in China in 2003, in Wang Weifan, "A Heart as Magnanimous as the Sea: In Remembrance of the Seventh Anniversary of Mr. Luo Zhufeng's death," *CSPD* 19, no. 1 (April 2004): 5-16. This essay should be read alongside K. H. Ting, "In Memory of Luo Zhufeng," in *Love Never Ends,* 537-539. See also Wang Weifan, "Ye tan zhongguo Makesizhuyi zongjiaoguan de 'shiyinghua'" ("On the Adaptation of Religious Perspectives in Chinese Marxism"), unpublished manuscript dated 8 September 2004, 11 pp. Wang Weifan's writings need to be read carefully, for in Chinese literary style he skillfully uses indirect criticisms and allusions to make his point.

106. Zhu Xiaohong, "Huhan duihua he hezuo: guanyu zhongguo jidu-jiaoshenxue sixiang jianshe yundong" ("A Call for Dialogue and Co-operation: On the Theological Reconstruction Movement in China"). The paper was published in a substantially revised version in *Jidu zongjiao yu zhongguo wenhua: guanyu zhongguo chujing shenxue de zhong-beiou huiyi lunwenji (Christianity and Chinese Culture: Papers from a Sino-Nordic Conference on Chinese Contextual Theology)*, ed. Miikka Ruokanen and Paulos Huang (Beijing: Zhongguo shehui kexue chuban-she, 2004), 376-90.

107. Wang Xiaoyan, "*Ding Guangxun wenji* pingjia" ("Review of *The Collected Works of K. H. Ting)*, *Shijie zongjiao yanjiu* (1999, no. 1): 143-148. Also Zhuo Xinping's comment on *The Collected Works of K. H. Ting, Tian Feng* (July 1997), inside back cover. Zhuo is the director of the Institute of World Religions at the Chinese Academy of Social Sciences.

108. Duan Qi, *Fenjin de licheng: zhongguo jidujiao de bensehua (Struggling Forward: The Indigenization of Protestant Christianity in China)* (Beijing: Commercial Press, 2004).

109. Zhuo Xinping, "Discussion on 'Culture Christians' in China," *Christian-*

ity in China: Burdened Past, Hopeful Future, ed. Stephen Uhalley and Xiaoxin Wu (Armonk, N.Y.: M. E. Sharpe, 2001). See also Institute of Sino-Christian Studies, ed., *Wenhua jidutu: xianxiang yu lunzheng* (*Cultural Christians: Phenomenon and Argument*) (Hong Kong: Institute of Sino-Christian Studies, 1997). SMSC (Scholars in Mainland China Studying Christianity) is a somewhat cumbersome term in Chinese and English, but it is preferred to the term "culture Christians" by the scholars themselves.

110. See Frederick Fällman, *Salvation and Modernity: Intellectuals and Faith in Contemporary China,* 165-70. See also Yang Huilin, *Religious Studies in China* (Singapore: Times Academic Press, 2005).

111. See K. H. Ting, *"Qianshi bu wang, hou shi zhi shi* yi shu shoufa shishang de jianghua" ("Speech at the Launch of *Remembering the Past as a Lesson for the Future,* by Luo Guanzong"), *Tian Feng* (November 2003), unnumbered insert page.

112. For an overview see Geremie Barmé, *In the Red: On Contemporary Chinese Culture* (New York: Columbia University Press, 1999), 255-83 and 364-77.

113. Jin Rongfu (Kim Yong-bock), "Relie zhuhe *Ding Guangxun wenji* hanyuban yinxing" ("On the Publication of the Korean Version of the *Collected Works of Ding Guangxun*"), *JL* (*Nanjing Theological Review*) 43, no. 2 (2000): 11-14. See also Kim Yong-bock, "The Theology of K. H. Ting: From an Asian Perspective," 2006, unpublished manuscript, 9 pp. For Hong Kong church leaders' reflections, see "Theological Reconstruction and a Ministerial Order for the Chinese Church," *ANS* 2004.9/10.4, http://www.amitynewsservice.org/page.php?page=540&pointer (accessed 28 November 2005). The report is based on a longer essay by Pan Naizhao (Michael Poon), "Cong jiaohui tizhi de jianli kan zhongguo shenxue sixiang chongjian de zeren" ("Theological Reconstruction in Light of Establishing Ministerial Order"), *JL* (*Nanjing Theological Review),* 4 (2003), 151-64.

114. See Don Messer, "The Chinese Banyan Tree Theology of Bishop K. H. Ting," unpublished manuscript presented at the Ecumenical Forum on Ministry, Colorado Springs, Colorado, 23 February 2005 (http://d74249.u23.toughdomains.net/cms/user/3/docs/banyan_tree_theology.pdf, accessed 28 November 2005). See also John S. Peale, *The Love of God in China: Can One Be Both Chinese and Christian* (New York, Lincoln and Shanghai: iUniverse, 2005), 115-37; and Tobias Brandauer, *"Jianshe* Theology: Reflections about the Process of Theological Reconstruction in China," *International Review of Mission* 93, no. 369 (April 2004): 199-209. See also *Seeking Truth in Love,* ed. Wang Peng (Beijing: Zongjiao wenhua chubanshe, 2006). This is a bilingual volume of reflections on Ting's theology. The Chinese title is *Zai ai zhong xunqiu zhenli.*

115. "China's 'Theological Reconstruction' Campaign Intensifies," 17 July 2001 (http://www.worldevangelical.org/persec_china_17jul101.html, accessed 12 January 2005); Werner Burklin, "Theological Reconstruction—Necessity and Danger," in *Jesus Never Left China: The Rest of the Story* (Enumclaw, Wash.: Pleasant World, 2005), 159-78. See also the Web site "Christianity in China," http://christianityinchina.org/Common/Admin/showNews_auto.jsp?Nid=479&Charset=big5, accessed 28 November 2005, for several thoughtful essays on theological reconstruction.

116. See "Voices in the Dark: Quotes from the Suffering Church," *Compass Direct* (29 August 2005) http://www.compassdirect.org/en/newsheaden.php?idelement=3941, accessed on 19 December 2005.

117. Ralph Covell, "Reconstructing Theological Thinking," *China Partner News* 11, no. 2 (Spring 2004): 1-2. See also Danny Yu, "Understanding Theological Construction: A Missiological View," parts 1ff., http://www.christianity inchina.org/Common/Admin/showNews_auto.jsp?Nid=414&Charset=big5, accessed 19 December 2005.

118. *God Is Love: Collected Writings of Bishop K. H. Ting* (Colorado Springs: Cook Communications Ministries, 2004). "Ding Zhujiao zhuanzhu *Shangdi shi ai* zai meiguo chuban faxing" ("Bishop Ting's *God Is Love* is published in the United States"), *Tian Feng* 12 (2004): 14-15. The selections in *God Is Love* are mostly taken from *Love Never Ends*, but without acknowledgment. The contents have been rearranged, and Chen Zemin's original preface is not included.

119. By Chinese reckoning, his ninetieth birthday fell on 20 September 2004. See "A Devout Patriot: Bishop K. H. Ting Celebrates 90th Birthday," *ANS* 2004.11/12.1, http://www.amitynewsservice.org/page.php?page=526&pointer, accessed 28 February 2005. See also "Ding zhujiao zai Shanghai yukuai guole 90 sui shengri" ("Bishop Ting Celebrates 90th Birthday in Shanghai"), *Tian Feng* 10 (2004): 2.

120. See "Church Leadership Discusses Consecrating Bishops," *ANS* 2005. 1/2.1 http://www.amitynewsservice.org/page.php?page=1115&pointer, accessed 28 November 2005. See also "Zhongguo jidijiao you wang chansheng zhujiao" ("Chinese Christianity Hopes to Consecrate Bishops"), *Tian Feng* 11 (2004): 12-13.

121. K. H. Ting, "Songzan shangdi, fachu aiguo aijiao gan'en de xinsheng" ("Praise God and Let Our Hearts Pour Out Thanksgiving in Loving Our Country and Our Church"), *Tian Feng* 7 (2004): 12. The dedication of the new building is reported in this issue of the church magazine.

122. K. H. Ting, "To Share God's Love with More People" (5 August 2005), *ANS* 2004.9/10.7, http://www.amitynewsservice.org/page.php?page=543&pointer, accessed 28 November 2005. For more reports on the Bible ministry exhibition in Hong Kong, see *Tian Feng* 9 (2004).

123. K. H. Ting is quoted in "Nanjing Seminary Breaks New Ground," *ANS* 2005.1/2, http://www.amitynewsservice.org/page.php?page=1116&pointer, accessed 28 November 2005.

124. For reports on the Amity anniversary celebration and groundbreaking ceremony for the printing press, see the *Amity Newsletter* 77, no. 2 (April-June 2006): 1-15.

CONCLUSION

1. "Running the Church Well: A Conversation with K. H. Ting," *Areopagus* 9, no. 4 (Winter/Spring 1997): 35. These four characters appear on the cover of this book, and were written by my good friend Mr. Wong Siu-ling of Hong Kong.

2. Wolfgang Schmidt, *Memoirs in Dialogue,* vol. 1 (Hong Kong and Seoul: CCA and CLSK, 2002), 47.

3. Zhang Xianyong, "Some Things Left Undone," *CTR* (1991): 158-64. The author has since left the seminary and now teaches at Zhongshan University in Guangzhou.

4. See Confucius, *The Analects* (*Lün yü*). trans. D. C. Lau (Hong Kong: Chinese University Press, 1992), 144-45. In Lau's rendition (book XIV, chapter 8), this describes Confucius himself as one "who keeps working towards a goal the realization of which he knows to be hopeless."

5. Bertolt Brecht, *Selected Poems,* trans. H. R. Hays (New York: Reynal & Hitchcok, 1947), 177. The poem is also cited in K. H. Ting, "Hehao de xinxi" ("A Reconciling Faith"), *JL* 5 (December 1986): 6 and is quoted in Philip L. Wickeri, *Seeking the Common Ground: Protestant Christianity, the Three-Self Movement and China's United Front* (Maryknoll, N.Y.: Orbis Books, 1988), 194. This poem was popular in China among many intellectuals of Ting's generation.

6. See Susan Billington Harper, *In the Shadow of the Mahatma: Bishop V. S. Azariah and the Travails of Christianity in British India* (Grand Rapids: William B. Eerdmans, 2000).

7. Zhou Jiacai, *Zhao Puchu yu Jiangsu zongjiao (Zhao Puchu and Religion in Jiangsu)* (Beijing: Zongjiaowenhua chubanshe, 2003), 39.

Glossary of Chinese Terms

ai	爱
aiguo, aijiao	爱国爱教
ba luan fan zheng	拨乱反正
Bao Bao	宝宝
ban chengpin	半成品
ban hao jiaohui	办好教会
biaotai	表态
buxin pai	不信派
Cankao xiaoxi	参考消息
chukou zhuan neixiao	出口转内销
da qihou	大气候
dazi bao	大字报
dan hua	淡化
dangquan pai	当权派
dao	道
de	德
edu	恶毒
fang	放
gaibian zhineng	改变职能
guandao	官倒
guikou	归口
jiantao	检讨
jiating juhui	家庭聚会
Jinling kejing chu	金陵刻经处
Jinling shenxuezhi	金陵神学志
laosanjie	老三届
lao sanzi	老三自
liang hui	两会
lishun guanxi	理顺关系
nanqiang beidiao	南腔北调
neibu	内部

nei cha wai diao	内查外调
Ning Ban	宁办
niupeng	牛棚
pinggu	评估
qinghuang bu jie	青黄不接
renjian fo	人间佛
san juhua	三句话
san zi	三自
Sheng Gong Hui	圣公会
Shenxianhui	神仙会
shenxue sixiang jianshe	神学思想建设
shenxue zaisi	神学再思
shenxue zaizao	神学再造
shiying	适应
shou	收
tiba rencai	提拔人才
Tian Feng	天风
tiaozheng	调整
wai song nei jin	外松内紧
wenhua jidutu	文化基督徒
wenhua suzhi di	文化素质低
yingbian cuoshi	应变措施
xia hai	下海
xiao qihou	小气候
xie (as in xiehui)	协
xin you yu ji	心有余悸
xue	学
yundong	运动
zheng	政
zhi qi bu ke wei er wei zhi	知其不可为而为之
zhishi qingnian	知识青年
zhongguo jidujiao sanzi aiguo yundong weiyuanhui	中国基督教三自爱国运动委员会
zhongguo jidujiao xiehui	中国基督教协会
Zongjiao	宗教

Glossary of Chinese Names Mentioned in the Text

Ba Jin	巴金	prominent writer active from the late 1920s until his death in 2004
Bao Jiayuan	包佳源	TSPM/CCC leader in Nanjing and Shanghai
Bei Dao	北岛	pen name of "misty" poet Zhao Zhenkai, active from the 1980s onward
Bi Yongqin	毕咏琴	prominent woman evangelist from Zhejiang
Cao Shengjie	曹圣洁	TSPM/CCC leader and CCC president 2002–
Cao Yu	曹禺	renowned playwright, often regarded as China's most important dramatist of the twentieth century
Chao, Jonathan (Zhao Tian'en)	赵天恩	conservative evangelical critic of the TSPM/CCC and founder of the Chinese Church Research Center
Chao, T. C. (Zhao Zichen)	赵紫宸	China's most prominent theologian of the first half of the twentieth century and one of the first elected presidents of the WCC
Chiang Kai-shek (Jiang Jieshi)	蒋介石	Nationalist (GMD) general and political leader who came to international attention in the 1930s; defeated by the Communists and driven to Taiwan in 1949, where he served as president of the Republic of China
Chen, Julia		YWCA staff worker in the 1930s and 1940s
Chen, Jianzhen (Robin Chen)	陈见真	Sheng Gong Hui bishop of Anqing and later presiding bishop associated with the TSPM in the 1950s

449

Chen Shiyi	陈世义	faculty member at Nanjing Seminary, criticized during the Anti-Rightist movement in 1957-1958
Chen Yi	陈毅	Communist military commander and mayor of Shanghai after 1949
Chen Yilu	陈逸鲁	young theologian and vice-principal of Guangdong Theological Seminary
Chen Yongtao	陈永涛	young theologian on the faculty of Nanjing Seminary
Chen Zemin	陈泽民	dean of Nanjing Seminary from the 1980s to the late 1990s and prominent Chinese theologian
Chen Chonggui (Marcus Chen)	陈崇桂	president of Chunking Theological Seminary in the 1950s and widely known conservative evangelical leader.
Cheng Jingyi	诚静怡	prominent Chinese Christian leader and general secretary of the National Christian Council, 1922-1933
Cheng Zhiyi	诚执怡	vice-principal of Nanjing Seminary at its founding in 1952
Den, Kimber (Deng Shukun)	邓述坤	Sheng Gong Hui bishop of Zhejiang, 1950-1955
Deng Fucun	邓福村	TSPM/CCC leader from Zhejiang
Deng Pufang	邓朴方	director of Chinese Welfare Association for the Handicapped, and son of Deng Xiaoping
Deng Xiaoping	邓小平	China's paramount leader from the late 1970s to the early 1990s and architect of the policies of "reform and openness"
Deng Yuzhi (Cora Deng)	邓裕志	YWCA general secretary and prominent TSPM leader
Ding Baoxun	丁宝训	older brother of K. H. Ting and eldest son
Ding Baoli	丁宝理	older sister of K. H. Ting
Ding Chufan (Chu Van Ding)	丁楚范	father of K. H. Ting
Ding Guan'gen	丁关根	CPC official and director of the UFWD after 1989 (no relation to K. H. Ting)
Ding Shixun	丁式训	younger brother of K. H. Ting

Ding Yuzhang	丁玉章	theological conservative and vice-principal of Nanjing Seminary at its founding in 1952
Dong Jianwu	董健吾	Sheng Gong Hui priest at St. Peter's Church, Shanghai, who later joined the CPC; also known as "Pastor Wang"
Dong Biwu	董必武	CPC leader in the 1940s and later a prominent official in the People's Republic of China
Duan Qi	段琦	academic working on Christianity in China at the Institute of World Religions, Chinese Academy of Social Sciences, Beijing
Feng Wenbin	冯文彬	CPC organizer in Japanese-occupied Shanghai, and after 1949, a government official
Gao Ying	高英	graduate of Nanjing Seminary and currently its vice-principal
Ge Pilu (D. M. Koeh)	葛匹录	first Chinese rector of St. Peter's Church, Shanghai
Gong Peng (Kung Peng)	龚澎	CPC official and onetime secretary to Zhou Enlai
Gong Pusheng	龚普生	Onetime YWCA worker, elder sister of Gong Peng (Kung Pu-sheng) and later CPC official and diplomat; also known as Gong Weihang
Gu Ziren (T. Z. Koo)	顾子仁	prominent Chinese Christian leader active in the YMCA and the WSCF before 1949
Han Bide	韩彼得	pastor and faculty member of Nanjing Seminary
Han Wenzao	韩文藻	TSPM/CCC leader in Nanjing, first general secretary of the Amity Foundation and CCC president, 1997-2002
He Chengxiang	何成相	CPC official and director of RAB, 1951-1961
He Xiangning	何香凝	vice-chair of NPC who died in 1972; wife of Liao Zhongkai, a prominent Nationalist before 1949

Hong Guangliang	洪光良	student at Nanjing Seminary in the 1950s, later a pastor in Hong Kong and Canada
Hu Feng	胡风	left-wing literary critic targeted in a CPC campaign in 1955
Hu Jintao	胡锦涛	CPC official and, since 2003, China's paramount leader; currently president of the People's Republic of China and general secretary of the CPC
Hu Zuyin (T. H. Hu)	胡祖荫	general secretary of the Chinese Christian Literature Society, Shanghai, until 1952
Hu Qiaomu	胡乔木	CPC official and Communist theorist
Hu Yaobang	胡耀帮	CPC official and general secretary, whose death in 1989 triggered the protests at Tiananmen Square
Hua Guofeng	华国锋	Mao Zedong's designated successor as CPC leader after 1976
Huang Peiyong	黄培永	Methodist pastor and YMCA worker who became prominent in the TSPM in the 1950s
Ji Jianhong	季剑虹	TSPM/CCC leader and TSPM chair, 2002–
Ji Tai	季泰	young theologian and former teacher at Nanjing Seminary
Jia Yuming	贾玉铭	prominent evangelical associated with the TSPM in the 1950s
Jiang Peifen	将佩芬	prominent evangelical and faculty member of Nanjing Seminary in the 1980s
Jiang Qing	江青	wife of Mao Zedong and leader of the Gang of Four
Jiang Wenhan (Kiang Wenhan)	江文汉	YMCA leader and later TSPM leader in Shanghai
Jiang Zemin	将泽民	CPC official and China's paramount leader after the retirement of Deng Xiaoping, president of the People's Republic of China, 1993-2002
Jin Luxian (Aloysius)	金鲁贤	prominent Roman Catholic bishop and theologian in Shanghai

Kan Baoping	阚保平	young theologian on the TSPM/CCC staff in Shanghai
Kao, C. M. (Gao Junming)	高俊明	former general secretary of the Presbyterian Church in Taiwan
Kuang Yaming	邝亚明	CPC official and president of Nanjing University in the 1960s and 1980s
Kuo Siu-may (Guo Xiumei)	郭秀梅	wife of K. H. Ting and English professor at Nanjing University
Kwong, Peter K. K. (Kuang Guangjie)	邝广杰	bishop and archbishop of the Hong Kong Anglican Church (Sheng Gong Hui)
Laozi (Lao Tzu)	老子	Chinese philosopher active in the sixth-century B.C.E.
Lei Feng	雷锋	"model worker" promoted in the Cultural Revolution era
Li Changshou (Witness Lee)	李长寿	onetime follower of Watchman Nee and organizer of the offshoot "Yellers" sect
Li Chuwen (C. W. Lee)	李储文	TSPM leader in the 1950s and later CPC official
Li Hongzhi	李宏治	founder and leader of the *Falun Gong* sect
Li Jinglan (Li Lizi)	李静栏 (李力自)	mother of K. H. Ting
Li Jiaqing	李嘉青	Sheng Gong Hui priest and K. H. Ting's maternal grandfather
Li Peng	李鹏	CPC official and premier of the State Council from 1987-1998
Li Ruihuan	李瑞环	CPC official and Chair of the 9th CPPCC until 2003
Li Shoubao	李寿葆	YMCA president in the 1980s and TSPM/CCC leader
Li Xiannian	李先念	CPC official and president of the People's Republic of China, 1983-1988
Li Xinyuan	李信源	theological writer from China opposed to K. H. Ting and the TSPM/CCC
Li Yading	李亚丁	graduate and former teacher at Nanjing Seminary
Li Weihan	李维汉	CPC official and secretary general of the first CPPCC; head of the UFWD until he was purged in 1964

Liang Su' ning	梁素宁	YWCA worker; wife of Zheng Jianye
Lin Biao	林彪	CPC military commander killed in a plane crash in 1971 after a failed coup attempt
Lin, Paul (T. K.)	林达光	Canadian-Chinese academic who was on the staff of the Chinese Christian Students' Association in the 1940s
Lin Xiangao (Samuel Lamb)	林献羔	house-church leader from Guangzhou, imprisoned for many years and opposed to the TSPM
Liu Guojun	刘国俊	National Capitalist in Jiangsu and CPPCC member from the 1950s to the 1970s
Liu Liangmo	刘良模	TSPM leader in the 1950s and secretary of the National YMCA in Shanghai
Liu Tingfang	刘廷芳	prominent Christian educator and church leader before 1949
Liu Shaoqi	刘少奇	CPC official and president of the People's Republic of China, 1959-1968, imprisoned and killed during the Cultural Revolution
Liu Xiaofeng	刘小枫	prominent academic and Christian philosopher, now at Zhongshan University
Liu Yucang	刘玉苍	Sheng Gong Hui bishop, consecrated with K. H. Ting and Xue Pingxi in 1955
Lu Xun	鲁迅	May 4th-era writer and widely regarded as the "father" of modern Chinese literature
Luo Guanzong	罗冠宗	TSPM/CCC leader in Shanghai, and TSPM chair, 1997-2002
Luo Xunru	陆珣如	CPC official who headed Jiangsu RAB in the 1950s
Luo Zhenfang	骆振芳	biblical scholar and faculty member of Nanjing Seminary
Luo Zhufeng	罗竹风	CPC official in Shanghai involved in religious policy, and, after 1979, prominent in establishing the social-scientific study of religion
Mao Zedong	毛泽东	leader of the CPC and the Chinese

		Revolution, and chairman of the CPC until his death in 1976
Mo Ruxi	莫如喜	faculty member at Nanjing Seminary
Ni Tuosheng (Watchman Nee)	倪柝声	founder of the "Little Flock" and prominent spiritual writer, imprisoned in the 1950s
Niu Zhifang	纽志芳	YMCA worker ordained Sheng Gong Hui priest in the 1950s who assisted in the work of the Zhejiang Diocese
Peng Chong	彭冲	CPC official and vice-chair of the Fifth CPPCC
Peng Cui'an	彭萃安	graduate and former teacher and vice-principal of Nanjing Seminary
Pu Huaren (Paul H. J. Poo)	浦化人	Sheng Gong Hui priest at St. Peter's Church, Shanghai, who later joined the CPC, and, after 1949, served as China's minister of culture
Qiao Liansheng	乔连升	CPC official and director of RAB, 1981-1983
Qiu Zhonghui	丘忠惠	general secretary of the Amity Foundation
Qu Yuan	屈原	classical poet active in the fourth century B.C.E.
Ren Jiyu	任继愈	prominent religious scholar and upholder of orthodox Communist view of religion in the 1980s
Ren Wuzhi	任务之	CPC official and director of RAB, 1983-1992
Shao Jingshan (Luther Shao)	邵镜三	church leader and faculty member at Nanjing Seminary, criticized during the Anti-Rightist movement in 1957-1958, who later committed suicide
Shen Cheng'en	沈承恩	TSPM/CCC leader in Shanghai, editor of *Tian Feng*
Shen Derong	沈德溶	TSPM/CCC leader in Shanghai, editor of *Tian Feng* in the 1950s and TSPM secretary general in the 1980s
Shen Zaisheng (T. S. Sing)	沈再生	Sheng Gong Hui assistant bishop of Zhejiang in 1918; first Chinese Anglican bishop

Shen Zigao (T. K. Shen)	沈子高	Sheng Gong Hui bishop of Shaanxi, associated with TSPM in the 1950s; father of Shen Yifan
Shen Yifan	沈以藩	TSPM/CCC leader, elected bishop in Shanghai in 1988, who also served as CCC vice-president
Shi Ruzhang (Phoebe Shi)	施如璋	YWCA president in the 1980s and TSPM/CCC leader
Situ Tong	司徒桐	YMCA worker and faculty member at Nanjing Seminary
Song Shangjie (John Sung)	宋尚節	prominent Chinese evangelist, active in the 1930s and 1940s
Soong, T. V.	宋子文	prominent businessman and politician in Republican China
Sun Guoting	孙过庭	Tang dynasty poet and calligrapher
Sun Hanshu	孙汉书	conservative theologian and faculty member at Nanjing Seminary
Sun Xipei	孙锡培	TSPM/CCC leader from Zhejiang
Sun Yanli	孙彦理	TSPM/CCC leader, elected bishop in Shanghai in 1988
Tang Shoulin	唐守临	"Little Flock" leader associated with TSPM/CCC
Tang Zhongmo	汤忠谟	Sheng Gong Hui priest, scholar and theologian active in the 1930s and 1940s
Tao Yuanming	陶淵明	classical poet in the fourth and fifth centuries
Ting, K. H. (Ding Guangxun)	丁光训	China's most prominent Christian leader and Protestant theologian from the late 1980s to the present
Ting Heping (Ding Heping)	丁和平	younger son of K. H. Ting and Siu-may Kuo
Ting Yenren (Stephen) (Ding Yanren)	丁言仁	eldest son of K. H. Ting and Siu-may Kuo
Tsai, Peter W. H. (Cai Wenhao)	蔡文浩	TSPM/CCC leader from Zhejiang
Tzü Y. Y. (Zhu Youyu)	朱友渔	Sheng Gong Hui bishop in Hong Kong after 1940

Wang Aiming	王艾明	young theologian on the faculty of Nanjing Seminary, editor of the *Jinling shenxuezhi*
Wang Jingwei	汪精卫	leader of Japanese "puppet" government in the 1940s
Wang Mingdao	王明道	prominent fundamentalist from Beijing opposed to the TSPM, imprisoned for twenty-three years in 1955
Wang Peng	王芃	librarian on the faculty of Nanjing Seminary
Wang Shenyin	王神荫	Sheng Gong Hui bishop from Shandong and TSPM/CCC leader
Wang Weifan	王维蕃	teacher and theologian at Nanjing Seminary, criticized during the "Anti-Rightist" movement, but returned to Nanjing Seminary in the 1980s
Wang Yumin	王育民	historian and faculty member at Nanjing Seminary
Wang Zhen	王镇	evangelical leader associated with the TSPM/CCC in the 1980s
Wei Jingsheng	魏京生	prominent democracy rights advocate in the late 1970s, now in the United States
Wen Jiabao	温家宝	CPC official, premier of the State Council, 2003–
Wen Yiduo	闻一多	Chinese scholar and poet active before 1949
Wu Gaozi (George Wu)	吴高梓	TSPM/CCC leader from Shanghai
Wu Yaozong (Y. T. Wu)	吴耀宗	prominent Christian leader formerly with the YMCA; founder and leader of the TSPM in 1954
Wu Yifang	吴贻芳	TSPM leader and former president of Jinling Women's College
Xi Zhongxun	习仲勋	CPC revolutionary and high-ranking official
Xiao Anping	肖安平	vice-principal and dean of Zhongnan Seminary
Xiao Xianfa	肖贤法	CPC official and director of the RAB, 1961-1965 and 1972-1981

Xiao Zhitian	萧志恬	CPC official and religious scholar in Shanghai
Xu Baoqian (Hsü Pao-ch'ien)	徐宝谦	prominent theologian active in the 1920s and 1930s
Xu Dingxin	许鼎新	biblical scholar and faculty member of Nanjing Seminary
Xu Jiatun	许家屯	CPC official from Jiangsu, who later headed the Xinhua News Agency in Hong Kong; defected to the United States after 1989
Xu Rulei	徐如雷	TSPM/CCC leader and faculty member of Nanjing Seminary
Xue Pingxi (Moses Hsüeh)	薛平西	Sheng Gong Hui bishop from Fujian, consecrated with K. H. Ting and Liu Yucang in 1955
Yan Mingfu	阎明复	CPC official and ally of Zhao Ziyang in the late 1980s
Yang Liyi (Lanier)		Christian student worker in Shanghai in the 1930s and 1940s
Ye Xiaowen	叶小文	CPC official, director of RAB, now SARA, 1996–
Yin Xiang	尹襄	TSPM leader from Shanghai
Yuan Xiangcheng (Allen or Alan Yuan)	袁向诚	house-church leader in Beijing, imprisoned for many years; opposed to the TSPM
Yun Enci	俞恩嗣	Sheng Gong Hui bishop from Shanghai in the 1940s
Yu Mingyue	俞明悦	Sheng Gong Hui priest in Zhejiang, active in the 1980s
Yu Peiwen	俞沛文	YMCA worker in the 1930s and 1940s
Zang Antang	臧安堂	faculty member at Nanjing Seminary, criticized during the Anti-Rightist movement in 1957-1958
Zhang Boling	张伯苓	scholar and president of Nankai University in the 1930s and 1940s
Zhang Keyun	张克运	president of the Jiangsu Christian Council
Zhang Shengcai	张圣才	house-church leader in Xiamen
Zhang Shengzuo	张声作	CPC official director of the RAB, 1992-1996

Zhang Zhiyi	张执一	CPC official and deputy director of the UFWD in the 1980s
Zhao Fusan	赵复三	Sheng Gong Hui priest and TSPM/CCC leader in Beijing, prominent in the Chinese Academy of Social Sciences; left China in 1989
Zhao Puchu	赵朴初	president of the China Buddhist Association, and CPPCC vice-premier, active in religious reform in the 1980s and 1990s
Zhao Zhi'en	赵志恩	TSPM/CCC leader and teacher at Nanjing Seminary
Zhao Ziyang	赵紫阳	prominent CPC leader, who served as premier and CPC general secretary until 1989, when he fell from power
Zheng Jianye (C. Y. Tsen)	郑建业	Sheng Gong Hui bishop in Shanghai, and first general secretary of the CCC
Zhong Ketuo (K. T. Chung)	钟可托	Sheng Gong Hui priest at St. Peter's Church, Shanghai
Zhou Enlai	周恩来	prominent CPC leader and diplomat, premier of the People's Republic of China, 1949-1976
Zhu De	朱德	prominent CPC military leader and statesman, founder of the Red Army
Zhu Pei'en	诸培恩	YMCA student worker and church leader
Zhu Rongji	朱镕基	CPC official and premier of the People's Republic of China, 1998-2003
Zhu Xiaohong	朱小红	young religious scholar at Fudan University, Shanghai
Zhuo Xinping	卓新平	director of the Institute of World Religions, Chinese Academy of Social Sciences, Beijing

Bibliography

K. H. Ting was a prodigious writer, in both Chinese and English. His essays, papers, sermons, reports and other writings span a period of almost seventy years. Included here are his most important published works, as well as unpublished papers to which I have had access. Published and unpublished essays from the early period (1937-1941) are mostly from the TSPM/CCC archives in Shanghai. The writings from his years overseas (1946 -1951) are in the SCM and WSCF archives in Toronto and Geneva. The vast majority of his writings are from the 1980s and 1990s, including edited selections published in different editions of his collected works.

This listing is in chronological order, according to the first date on which an essay was published or a speech or sermon delivered. Many of Ting's papers were published in different versions, and in most cases, only the first instance of publication or original writing is listed here. A complete selection of his writings from *Tian Feng* and *Jinling shenxuezhi* (*The Nanjing Theological Review*) is given, because these two journals were the most important sources of his published work. With the exception of circular letters that were distributed quite widely, unpublished letters are not included. Important statements signed or authored by K. H. Ting are included here, but more general TSPM/CCC statements are not listed. English translations of most of the important essays not included in various editions of K. H. Ting's writings may be found in *CTR*.

The listing of unpublished or informally published materials from the 1980s and 1990s is inevitably selective, and the reports, essays and sermons that appear here are those that I was given in the course of my work in China. A few of these are from particular issues of TSPM/CCC bulletins, and one can assume that there are a great many more such publications that contain Ting's writings. In time, these may be open to scholars interested in more detailed study of Christianity during the period of "reform and openness" in China.

This bibliography is an "unfinished product." Readers who discover mistakes or omissions are encouraged to communicate with the author.

1. THE WRITINGS OF K. H. TING, 1937-2006

1937-1942

"Qingnian he zongjiao" ("Youth and Religion"). *Qingnian tuan kan* (*St. Peter's Church Youth Magazine*). June 1937. Pp. 46-49.

"Shanghai Lian juban 'Cishan shichang" ("Shanghai Christian Students' Union Runs a Welfare Market"). *Xiaoxi* (*News*) (March 1938): 28-29.

"Xuesheng shiye" ("Student Work"). *Shanghai qingnian* (*Shanghai Youth*), 28 February 1939. Pp. 30-34. Coauthored with Zhu Pei'en.

"Huadong ge daxue xialinghui" ("Summer Retreats in East China Universities"). *Xiaoxi* (October 1939): 99-102.

"Xuesheng gongzuo" ("Student Work"). *Shanghai qingnian* (20 January 1940). Pp. 16-17.

"Chedi de ai shi shenma?" ("What Is the Deepest Love?"). *Xiaoxi* (1940.2): 17-20. Written by Bei Si, a pseudonym, but attributed to K. H. Ting.

"'Wo . . . lai': shengdan du shengjing he moxiang de zaji" ("'I . . . come': Christmas Bible Study and Notes for Meditation"). *Xiaoxi* (December 1940): 7-8.

"Xuesheng shiye" ("Student Work"). *Xiaoxi* (*News*) (20 January 1941): 26-27.

(No entries between 1942 and 1947)

1947

"Passion Sunday, 1947: Letter from the East." *Bulletin of the Society of the Catholic Commonwealth* 11, no. 26 (1947): 1-4. Unsigned report, attributed to K. H. Ting and F. Hastings Smyth.

"Asia, China and the Chinese." 1949-1950? Typescript. 3 pp.

"American Aid to China as Seen by a Chinese Christian." *The Anglican Outlook* (April 1947). Unsigned report, attributed to K. H. Ting. 1 p.

"The Dilemma of the Sincere Student." *The Canadian Student* 25, no. 5 (May 1947): 81, 92-93.

"Impressions and Thoughts about the Student Christian Movement in Canada." Typescript. 1947. 10 pp.

"The Simplicity of the Gospel in the New Testament." *The Canadian Student* 26, no. 2 and 27, no. 1 (December 1947 and January 1948): 26-27 and 46-47.

1948

"A Chinese Answers the Question." *Student World* 41 (1948): 318-25.

"The Sociological Foundation of the Democratic Movement in China." *Bulletin of the Society of the Catholic Commonwealth* 3, no. 11 (4 January 1948): 1-4. Unsigned essay attributed to K. H. Ting.

"The Impact of the New Testament on the Non-Christian." *International Review of Mission* 37, no. 146 (April 1948): 129-37.

"Power and Its Denial on the Cross." *Student World* 41 (1948): 210-15.

"Report of K. H. Ting on His Trip to the USA." Diary, 29 November 1948 to 2 January 1949. Rough typescript. 17 pp.

1949

"A Creative Experience for Chinese Students." *Student World* 42 (1949): 22-32.

"The Task of the Church in Asia." *Student World* 42 (1949): 235-48.

"A Chinese Traveller in Eastern Europe." *Student World* 42 (1949): 363-69.

"The S.C.M. in the Growing Church." 1949. Typescript. 5 pp.

"Some Reflections on 'Students and Missions.'" Date uncertain. Rough typescript. 8 pp.

"Can the Missionary Vocation Be Real to Students Today?" Mimeographed WSCF circular. 14 June 1949. 7 pp.

"The Role of the Student in the West and in the Far East." Date uncertain. Typescript. 2 pp.

"Christian Youth Looking at Missions Once More?" Date uncertain, 1950? 4 pp.

"A Report on the Church Situation in Czechoslovakia and Hungary, with Special Interest in the Light It Throws on China." *CB* 1, no. 69 (24 October 1949). 4 pp.

"The Battle for China's Intelligentsia." (Review of Kiang Wenhan, *The Chinese Student Movement*). *International Review of Mission* 38, no. 152 (October 1949): 495-96.

"Memorandum on Proposed Visit to North China." 2 November 1949. 4 pp. Coauthored with John Coleman.

"A Memorandum on Opening Christian Work in Universities in Communist China for Consideration at Asian Leaders Conference." 9 December 1949. Coauthored with John Coleman.

1950

"A Latin American Travel Diary." *Student World* 43 (1950): 258-65.

"Report on South America (January-March 1950)." Mimeographed WSCF circular. 17 pp.

"The Uniqueness of Christ and Our Obligation to Proclaim Him." 1950. 8 pp.

"What Would You Do?" *Student World* 43 (1950): 278-81.

"Why Force My Religion on Others?" Date uncertain, 1950? Typescript. 2 pp.

"How Can They Claim Christianity is Better?" Date uncertain, 1950? Typescript. 2 pp.

"The Christian in a World of Many Religions. Date uncertain. Typescript. 8 pp.

"My Latin America Travel Diary." 2 April 1950. Rough typescript. 6 pp.

"K. H. Ting in South America." *Federation News Sheet* 10 (May-June 1950): 62-64.

"News Letter." *Federation News Sheet* 10 (May-June 1950): 75-78.

"The W.S.C.F. and the Missionary Church." June 1950. Mimeographed WSCF circular. 19 pp.

"The Work of the Student Christian Movement in South America." 2 June 1950. Rough notes for a speech. 6 pp.

"Evangelism, Missions and Ecumenism." October 1950. Typescript. 9 pp.

"Missions in Light of Ecumenism." October 1950. Typescript. 9 pp. (earlier version of above).

"Can We See Sense in Evangelism and Missions Today?" 20 November 1950. Typescript. 7 pp.

"The SCM in Latin America." November 1950. Typescript. 4 pp.

"Extracts of More Detailed Information from the Report of K. H. Ting on South America." November 1950. Typescript. 6 pp.

1951

"Review of *Missionary Education in Your Church.*" *Student World* 44 (1951): 89-90.

"Behold the Man." *Student World* 44 (1951): 148-55.

"Review of *The Gospel of God.*" *Student World* 44 (1951): 197-98.

"Review of *The Kingdom and the Power.*" *Student World* 44 (1951): 204.

"Students and Missions: A Confrontation." March 1951. Mimeographed WSCF circular. 8 pp.

"News Letter." *Federation News Sheet* 11 (May-June 1951): 55-59.

"Review of *A South India Diary.*" *Student World* 44 (1951): 302.

"The Missionary Concern of the W.S.C.F." Preparatory document for the meeting of the WSCF Executive Committee, Berlin, August 1951. 5 pp.

1952-1954

"Ni zai nali?" ("Where Are You?"). *Tian Feng* (16 February 1952): 7. K. H. Ting's first published essay after his return to China.

"Lun si yu huo" ("On Life and Death"). *Tian Feng* (5 April 1952): 195-96.

Kan na shangdi de gaoyang (*Behold the Lamb of God*). Shanghai: Guangxuehui (Christian Literature Society), 1952.

"Zuo zhongxin de gongren" ("Be Loyal Workers"). *Tian Feng* (23 March 1953): 154-55.

"Ban nian lai de jinling xiehe shenxueyuan." ("The First Six Months of Nanjing Union Seminary"). *Tian Feng* (30 March 1953): 174-76.

"Chuanyang fuyin he jianli shenti" ("Spread the Gospel and Establish the Body"). *Tian Feng* (16, 23, 30 November 1953): 644-45, 661-62, 674-75. Also in *JL* 1 (September 1953): 2-8.

"Ci ren zhihui he qishi de ling" ("The Spirit Who Grants Wisdom and Revelation to Humankind"). *Tian Feng* (18 and 25 January 1954): 26-27 and pp. 42-43. Also in *Jiangzhang xinji zhi er* (*New Collected Sermons*, no. 2). Shanghai: Guangxuehui (Christian Literature Society), 1955. Pp. 1-15.

"Wei shenma jintian hai yao zuo chuan daoren?" ("Why Must We Still Be Preachers?"). *JL* 2 (April 1954): 4-9.

"Ding Guangxun mushi fayan zhaiyao" ("Excerpts from the Speech by the Rev. K. H. Ting"). *Tian Feng* (3 September 1954): 452-55.

1955

"Shenxue xuesheng yingdang ze'yang du shengjing" ("How Seminary Students Should Read the Bible"). *JL* 3 (February 1955): 12-19.

"Zhi er nian lai zou shang gong chang de xiaoyoumen" ("To Alumni/ae after Two Years in the Field"). *JL* 3 (February 1955): 34-35.

"Shen yu ren zhi jian" ("Between God and Man"). *Sheng Gong* (1955.2): 6-8.

"Ding Guangxun changwei fayan zhaiyao" ("Excerpts from K. H. Ting's Speech to Standing Committee"). *Tian Feng* (28 March 1955): 214-15.

"Ding Guangxun weiyuan fayan" ("Speech from Delegate K. H. Ting"). *Xinhua ribao.* 27 April 1955. P. 6.

"Zheng gao Wang Mingdao" ("A Stern Warning to Wang Mingdao"). *Tian Feng* (15 August 1955): 604-8.

"He Shangdi shuaijiao de ren" ("The Man Who Wrestled with God"). *JL* 4 (November 1955): 1-4.

1956

"Ji yici nongcun jiaohui de fangwen" ("A Visit to a Rural Church"). *Tian Feng* (23 January 1956): 10-12.

"Chinese Christians: New Prospects, New Unity." *Student World* 49 (1956): 291-95. This essay was originally published in *China Reconstructs* (June 1956): 18-20.

"Meeting of Bishop R. B. Manikam with Chinese Church Leaders at Peking on Invitations from the IMC and the WCC." 17 March 1956. Typescript. 6 pp. An informal record of a conversation with twelve Chinese church leaders, including K. H. Ting.

"Wo xin shengling, wo xin sheng er gong zhi jiaohui" ("I Believe in the Holy Spirit, I Believe in the Holy Catholic Church"). *Sheng Gong* (1956.7): 20-23.

"Fangwen yingguo shenggonghui pianduan" ("Fragments from a Visit to the Church of England"). *Sheng Gong* (1956.8): 25-26.

"Bishop Ting Reports on Chinese Christians Today." 10 August 1956. Rough typescript. 6 pp.

"Visit of the Rt. Rev. K. H. Ting, Bishop of Chekiang to England for the Consultative Committee of the Lambeth Conference for 1958." 28 August 1956. Unpublished record of K. H. Ting's visit, with comments from his remarks. 4 pp.

"Notes on Speech of and Conversation with Bishop Ting of China." 27 September 1956. Mimeographed presentation of K. H. Ting's remarks in Europe to the general board of the N.C.C.C. U.S.A., by Eugene L. Smith, vice-president, Division of Foreign Missions.

"On the Life of the Churches in China." *The Ecumenical Review* 9 (October 1956): 61-63. Notes from a speech delivered to the WCC Central Committee.

"Christian Frontiers in China." *Newsletter*, 4 (October 1956): 23-29.

1957-1959

"The Church in China Today." *Student World* 50 (1957): 45-59.

"Tan Jidujiao Youshenlun" ("On Christian Theism"). *JL* 7 (August 1957): 13-21.

"Eluosi dongsheng jiaohui fangwen ji" ("A Visit to the Russian Orthodox Church"). *Sheng Gong*, 11, no. 8 (1957): 31-32.

"Xiongyali jiaohui fangwenji" ("Notes on a Visit to the Hungarian Church"). *Tian Feng* (10 February 1958): 9-12.

"Ji Xu Huai zhi xing" ("Notes from a Trip to Xuzhou and Huaiyin"). *Tian Feng* (22 October 1958): 16-17.

"Zai Shoudu huandu jianguo shi zhou nian" ("Celebrating China's Tenth Anniversary in Beijing"). *Tian Feng* (26 October, 9 November and 16 November 1959): 11-13, 23-24, and 19-20.

1961-1962

"Jixu jingti diguozhuyi liyong jidujiao de yinmou" ("Continue to Be Vigilant against Imperialist Plots to Manipulate Christianity"). *Tian Feng* (27 February 1961): 23-25.

"Jinling xiehe shenxueyuan jinkuang" ("Nanjing Union Seminary Today"). *Tian Feng* (27 May 1961): 10-11.

"Fenbie shi fei" ("Discerning Right from Wrong"). *Tian Feng* (28 August 1961): 14-15.

"The Defence of Peace as a Task for Christians.". . . *And on Earth Peace: Documents of the First All-Christian Peace Assembly, Prague, 13th-18th June 1961.* Pp. 100-107.

"Sermon Preached at the Ecumenical Divine Service, June 18th, 1961.". . . *And on Earth Peace: Documents of the First All-Christian Peace Assembly, Prague, 13th-18th June 1961.* Pp. 158-60. This is the English version of "Fenbie shi fei," cited above.

"Cong shijie jidujiao heping huiyi guilai" ("Thoughts after Returning from the Christian Peace Assembly"). *Tian Feng* (28 October 1961): 3-6.

"The Church's Mission in the Secular Movement of the People." *Church and Society* (March 1962): 56-58.

(No entries between 1962 and 1973)

1973-1976

"Christian Voices from the Church in China." *China Notes* 11, no. 3 (Summer 1973): 27-30. Interview notes by E. H. Johnson with Chinese Christians, including K. H. Ting.

"China: Conversations about Christianity with K. H. Ting." *Canadian Student* (Summer 1975). Interview with Ted Johnson.

"Interview with Dr. and Mrs. K. H. Ting." 22 October 1976. Typescript. 8 pp. Interview summary prepared by Eugene L. Stockwell.

1979

"Ding Guangxun tan jidujiao" ("K. H. Ting on Christianity"). *Daoyou zhishi (A Reference for Guides).* Nanjing, 1979. pp. 1-15.

"Is There Religion after Revolution?" *New China Magazine* (Summer 1979). An interview with Howard S. Hyman.

"A Visit with Bishop Ting." *The Christian Century*, 29 August-5 September 1979, 813-14. K. H. Ting quoted at length in a report by Thomas Trotter.

"Human Collectives as Vehicles of God's Grace." September 1979. Typescript. 4 pp. A widely reprinted sermon preached at Riverside Church, New York, on 9 September 1979.

"Vancouver, 1979 Speech." September 1979. Typescript. 12 pp.

"Science, Religion and Democracy in China." October 1979. Typescript. 5 pp. A lecture delivered at McGill University.

"Religious Policy and Theological Reorientation in China." October 1979. Typescript. 7 pp. A lecture delivered at Emmanuel College.

"Give Ye Them to Eat." 4 November 1979. Typescript. 5 pp. A widely reprinted sermon preached at Timothy Eaton Church, Toronto.

"Facing the Future or Restoring the Past?" November 1979. Typescript. 6 pp.

"Interview with K. H. Ting." *WSCF Journal* 1, no. 4 (1979): 39-41. Interview with Betsy Anderson.

1980

"A Chinese Christian's Appreciation of an Atheist." *China and Ourselves* (January 1980): 17-21.

"On Non-Religious Spirituality." *Ching Feng* 23 (January 1980): 48.

"Foreword." In Stephen Endicott, *James G. Endicott: Rebel Out of China*, ix-x. Toronto: University of Toronto Press, 1980.

"An Interview with Bishop K. H. Ting." *China and Ourselves* (May 1980): 4-10. Interview with John Gardner, the British Broadcasting Corporation, Toronto, November 1979.

"Tan luoshi zongjiao zhengci wenti" ("On the Implementation of Religious Policy"). *Renmin ribao (People's Daily)* 9 September 1980.

"Speaking as a Chinese Christian." *China Reconstructs* (September 1980).

"Ze'yang du shengjing" ("How to Study the Bible"). *Tian Feng* (20 October 1980): 45-63. This was the first issue of the new series of *Tian Feng*. Also published as *Ze'yang du shengjing*. Shanghai: China Christian Council, 1980 and 1989). 44 pp.

1981

"Remarks on the Policy of the United Board for Christian Higher Education in Asia as Regards China, Made by K. H. Ting and Zhao Fusan to the Representatives of the Board at Montreal, Canada, October 4th, 1981." Typescript. 3 pp.

How to Study the Bible. Edited by Philip L. Wickeri. Hong Kong: Tao Fong Shan Ecumenical Centre, 1981. An edited and revised translation. Also published by New York: Friendship Press, 1981.

"A Call for Clarity: Fourteen Points from Christians in the People's Republic of China to Christians Abroad." *Ching Feng* 24, no. 1 (March 1981): 37-48. Widely republished in English and other languages. Originally presented by K. H. Ting to Rev. Andrew Chiu and Rev. Arthur Wu, Nanjing, China, 2 December 1980.

"Huigu yu zhanwang" ("Retrospect and Prospect"). *Tian Feng* (20 March 1981): 4-11. Widely republished in English and other languages.

"Bimu ci." ("Closing Address"). *Tian Feng* (20 March 1981): 46-47.

"Theological Education in China." *CCA Consultation with Church Leaders from China*. Singapore. March 1981. Pp. 47-56.

"Zai Xianggang jiaohui lingxiu zuotanhui zhong de jianghua" ("Address at the Forum of Hong Kong Church Leaders"). *Zhu ai women daodi (God Loves Us to the Very End)*, 9-11. Edited by Raymond Fung and Philip Lam. Hong Kong: HKCC, 1981.

"Jinri zhongguo jiaohui" ("The Chinese Church Today"). *Zhu ai women daodi (God Loves Us to the Very End)*, 24-27. Edited by Raymond Fung and Philip Lam. Hong Kong: HKCC, 1981.

"Zai Jiangsu sheng jidujiao di san jie daibiao huiyi shang de fayan" ("Address at Third Jiangsu Christian Conference"). *Jiaocai (Curriculum)* 7-9 (May 1981): 23-27.

"Tong Gong" ("Letter to Colleagues"). 29 June 1981. Mimeographed typescript. 5 pp.

"Talk to Friends of the Federation." New York. 12 October 1981. Typescript. 2 pp.

"Religion as Opium?" 1981. Typescript. 10 pp. Lecture delivered in Saskatoon, Canada, 23 October 1981.

"Kunnan yu qianzhan" ("Difficulties and Prospects"). *Ching Feng* (Chinese edition) 68 (December 1981): 43-45.

1982

"Statements by the Archbishop of Canterbury, Dr. Robert Runcie, and Bishop K. H. Ting." *China Notes* (Winter 1981-1982): 199.

"Xianjin de Wu xiansheng" ("Forerunner Y. T. Wu"). In *Huiyi Wu Yaozong xiansheng (In Memory of Y. T. Wu)*, 87-102. Shanghai: TSPM Committee, 1982. Dated 22 December 1981.

"On the Pope's Manila Message to China." *China and Ourselves* 30 (May 1982).

"Jinian Jia Wensun Mushi" ("In Memory of Rev. Ted Johnson"). *Tian Feng* (30 July 1982): 26-27.

"Chinese Modernization in the Light of Her Cultural Heritage." 1982. Typescript. 10 pp. Lecture presented at McGill University, 1982.

"K. H. Ting Comments on the Constitution." *China Notes* 20, nos. 2 and 3 (Spring and Summer 1982): 212-13. An interview conducted by Jean Woo and Gail Coulson.

"Statement on the Jian Hua Foundation." 22 October 1982. Typescript. 1 p.

"The Church in China." 2 November 1982. Typescript. 9 pp. Later edited and published in different sources.

1983

"Jesus' Protest." 1983. Typescript. Sermon preached at Uppsala Cathedral, Sweden.

"Chinese Protestants Today." *Chinese Reconstructs* 5 (1983): 368.

"Bimu ci" ("Closing Address"). *Tian Feng* (30 January 1983): 24-25.

"Sanzi zai renshi" ("Another Look at Three-Self"). *Tian Feng* (February 1983): 2-9.

"Response to Andre Myre." *God's Call to a New Beginning: An International Dialogue with the Chinese Church*, 14-15. Edited by Theresa Chu and Christopher Lind. Toronto: Canada China Program, 1983.

"Difficulties and Prospects." *God's Call to a New Beginning: An International Dialogue with the Chinese Church*, 117-27. Edited by Theresa Chu and Christopher Lind. Toronto: Canada China Program, 1983.

Shiyong hanying cidian (A Practical Chinese-English Dictionary). Nanjing: Jiangsu People's Publishing, 1983. Edited by K. H. Ting et al.

"Interview with K. H. Ting on the Jian Hua Foundation." 28 April 1983. Typescript. 2 pp.

"Comment on *Human Rights: A Dialogue between the First and Third Worlds*." Edited by Robert A. Evans and Alice Frazer Evans. Maryknoll, N.Y.: Orbis Books, 1983. 1983 or 1984? Typescript. 3 pp.

"Tan xianfa di sanshiliu tiao" ("On the Thirty-Sixth Article of Our Constitution"). *Tian Feng* (30 May 1983): 10-12.

"Tong huhanpai xintu tantan" ("A Few Words to the Yellers"). *Jiangdao ji (Collected Sermons)*, 5 (May 1983): 121-34.

"Letter to the Editor." *China Daily*, 22 July 1983. The headline is "Religion Is Not Superstition."

"Fuhuo de zhenli" ("The Truth of the Resurrection"). *Tian Feng* (30 July 1983): 3-5. Originally a sermon delivered at Lambeth Palace on 1 October 1982. The English sermon is available in *The Church in China*. London: British Council of Churches, 1983. Pp. 2-6. "Evangelism as a Chinese Christian Sees It" may also be found in this pamphlet, pp. 7-20.

"Evangelism as a Chinese Christian Sees It." *China Notes* 21, no. 4 (Autumn 1983): 263-67. Originally delivered as a lecture in Uppsala, Sweden, in 1983.

"Jinling xiehe shenxueyuan jinxun" ("Recent News from Jinling Theological Seminary"). *Tian Feng* (November 1983): 3-5.

The Experience of the Church in China. Cincinnati: Forward Movement Publications, 1984.

1984

"Chinese Selfhood and the Church Universal." *China Notes* (Fall 1984): 313-14; and "A Sign for Something Beyond Itself." *One World* (January-February 1984): 16-17. A sermon delivered at the headquarters of the World Council of Churches, Geneva, 21 November 1983.

"Sermon in Sydney Cathedral." 1984. Typescript. 5 pp.

"'Suixiang' yinqi de suixiang" ("Random Thoughts on 'Random Thoughts'"). *Zongjiao (Religion)* 5 (March 1984): 47-49. Written under the pen name Guan Jiewen.

"An Interview with Bishop K. H. Ting." 6 May and 3 June 1984. Text of two radio interviews conducted by Tom Lung, Hong Kong.

"Christianity in China Today." *Beijing Review* (11 June 1984): 21-23.

"Shengling he women" ("The Holy Spirit and Us"). *Tian Feng* (30 September 1984): 4-8.

"Weiyan Wang Bide furen." ("Letter of Condolence to Mrs. Peter Wong"). *Tian Feng* (30 September 1984): 38. The letter was dated 30 May 1984.

Chinese Christians Speak Out. Beijing: New World Press, 1984. Contains several of K. H. Ting's essays published elsewhere.

"Guanyu wo guo de shenxue jiaoyu" ("Theological Education in China"). *JL* 1 (September 1984): 46-49. This was the first issue of *The Nanjing Theological Review* after the end of the Cultural Revolution era. This essay was reprinted in *JL* 2 (2002): 4-7.

"Ai yong bu zhixi" ("Love Never Ends"). *JL* 1 (September 1984): 70-72.

"Kai mu ci" ("Opening Address"). *Tian Feng* 23 (30 September 1984): 7.

"Fervour—Seeking—Worship." 1984? Typescript. 3 pp.

"Jin yibu guanche zongjiao xinyang ziyou zhengci chujian" ("Remarks on Further Implementing the Policy of Religious Freedom"). *Zongjiao (Religion)* 6 (November 1984): 4-8. Written with Zhao Fusan.

"Xuexi yige wenjian de xinde: yipian fayan" ("What I Have Learned from Studying a New Document: A Speech"). *Zongjiao (Religion)* 6 (November 1984): 8-15. Written under the pen name Ru Wen.

"Circular Letter." 20 December 1984. Circular on the possibility of setting up a foundation in China sent to several dozen friends overseas.

1985

"On Contributions to China from Churches and Christians Overseas." 30 December 1984. Typescript. 2 pp. Published in *Bridge* 9 (January-February 1985): 3. Interview notes with K. H. Ting and Han Wenzao by Philip Wickeri.

"Chuli zongjiao wenti yao jianchi tongzhan yuanze" ("Firmly Resolve Religious Questions According to United Front Principles"). *Zongjiao (Religion)* 9, no. 1 (1985): 16-22.

"Building a Chinese Church: An Interview with Bishop K. H. Ting." *China in Focus.* (Beijing, 1985). Pp. 3-9. Reprinted from *Beijing Review* (11 June 1984): 21-23.

Christian Witness in China Today. Kyoto: Doshisha University Press, 1985. 49 pp. The Sixth Neesima Lectures. 28 September 1984. Contains three essays: (1) "A Rationale for Three-Self"; (2) "Theological Mass Movement in China"; (3) "A Chinese Christian Selfhood." Also published in *JL* 4 (1986).

"This Your Brother." March 1985. Typescript. 4 pp. A sermon preached in India in March 1985.

"The Greater Christ." March 1985. Typescript. 4 pp. A sermon preached in India in March 1985.

"Zai Indu linbie zuotanhui shang Ding Gunaxun zhujiao de fayan" ("Bishop K. H. Ting's Farewell Speech in India"). *Tian Feng* (1 June 1985): 6.

"Shi zhu" ("It Is the Lord"). *JL* 2 (June 1985): 40.

"Shangdi bushi nanxing" ("God Is Not Male"). *JL* 2 (June 1985): 41-42.

"Huozhe gai you shengming" ("Life Needs a Mission"). *JL* 2 (June 1985): 43-44. Sermon preached on 9 September 1984 at the opening fall convocation of Nanjing Seminary.

"Circular Letter to Old Friends." 24 June 1985. 4 pp.

"Qianyan" ("Preface"). In *A Collection of Painting and Calligraphy Solicited for Charity in Aid of the Disabled.* Shanghai: TSPM/CCC, 1985. 2 pp. The preface in Chinese and English is dated 15 August 1985.

"Shangdi yuanwang heping" ("God Hopes for Peace"). *Tian Feng* (1 September 1985): 6-7. An address delivered in June 1985 in Beijing.

"Unity with Evangelicals: A Chinese Approach." 20 October 1985. Typescript. 2 pp.

"Preface." *CTR* (1985): v-viii. Translation published in *JL* 4 (1986).

"Report on Conversations with Bishop K. H. Ting in Nanjing." 19-20 November 1985. Typescript. 11 pp. Conversation notes recorded by Eugene Stockwell.

"Lai zi jiefang shenxue, Derijin shenxue han guocheng shenxue de qifa" ("Inspirations from Liberation Theology, Process Theology and Teilhard de Chardin"). *JL* 3 (September 1985): 15-28.

"Ni you yongsheng zhi dao" ("You Have the Words of Eternal Life"). *JL* 3 (September 1985): 63-66.

"Yige zhongguo jidutu dui jiefangshenxue han Derijin de renshi" ("A Chinese Christian's Understanding of Liberation Theology and Teilhard de Chardin"). 1985. Typescript. An earlier version of the essay from *JL* 3.

1986

"Statement on the Children of God." 1986. Typescript. 1 p.

"End der Konfessionen." *Deutsches Allgemeines Sonntagsblatt* 7 (16 February 1986): 14.

"Zai Wu Yifang xiansheng zhuisi libai de jianghua" ("Speech at the Memorial Service for Ms. Wu Yifang"). *Tian Feng* (1 April 1986): 3-6.

"Zai quanguo lianghui changwei huiyi jieshuqian de fayan" ("Closing Speech at the Meeting of the Standing Committees of the Two National Christian Organizations"). *Tongxun (Bulletin)* 12 (April 1986): 2-6. Informal publication of the Beijing CCC/TSPM.

"Christian Sharing Across National Boundaries as a Chinese Christian Sees It." *Ecumenical Sharing: A New Agenda. Report of an Ecumenical Conference, 14-20 May 1986.* Nanjing. Pp. 75-83.

"Meiguo heiren jidutu gei wo de sanzi aiguo jiaoyu" ("Black American Christians Teach Me about Three-Self Patriotism"). May 1986. Mimeograph. 3 pp.

"The Chinese Church since 1949." In *Spring Has Returned: Listening to the Chinese Church*, 15-28. Edited by Denton Lotz. McLean, Va.: Baptist World Alliance, 1986.

"The Future of the Church in China." In *Spring Has Returned: Listening to the Chinese Church*, 72-79. Edited by Denton Lotz. McLean, Va.: Baptist World Alliance, 1986.

"Zhongguo jidujiao zui gao lingxiu tan shen, ren, dang" ("China's Highest Christian Leader Discusses God, Humankind and the Party"). *Zhong Bao*, 10 September 1986. Interview with Tsui Siu-ming (Cui Shaoming).

"Zhongguo jidujiao di sijie quanguo huiyi kaimu ci" ("Speech at the Opening of the Fourth National Christian Conference"). *Tian Feng* (1 November 1986): 5.

"Yuan zhu jianli women shou suozuo de gong" ("May the Lord Build Up the Work of Our Hands," original title is "Building Up the Body in Love"). *Tian Feng* (1 November 1986): 35-37.

"Self Understanding of the Church in the People's Republic of China." *China Today: Report of a CCA-URM/WCC-URM Visit to the Church and People*. Hong Kong. November 1986. Pp. 67-82.

"Hehao de xinxi" ("A Reconciling Faith"). *JL* 5 (December 1986): 5-7.

"Shangdi shi ai" ("God Is Love"). *JL* 5 (December 1986): 80-81. A sermon preached in Hungary on 5 October 1986.

1987

"Psalm 23." 1987? Handwritten and typescript. 8 pp.

"An Interview with Bishop K. H. Ting on the Church in China and Hong Kong." *Bridge* 23 (May-June 1987): 3 An interview conducted by Ewing W. Carroll, Jr.

"A Few Words from Bishop Ting." *Amity Newsletter* 5 (Summer 1987): 1.

"Address to the Lutheran World Federation." *CTR* (1987): 19-25. The text of a lecture presented to the Executive Committee of the Lutheran World Federation, Viborg, Denmark, 12 July 1987.

"1987.6.6 Ding zhujiao zai Shanghai shenxue wenti yantaohui shang de fayan" ("Bishop Ting's Speech at Shanghai Symposium on Theological Education, 6 June 1987"). *Jiaoliu (Exchange)* 3 (20 August 1987). 23 pp. Mimeograph.

"Statement on Kairos Radio." 31 August 1987. typescript, later published in *Bridge* 25 (September-October 1987): 3.

"Guanyu zhongguo jiaohui he xianggang wenti dui Ding Guangxun zhujiao de yici fangwen" ("Interview with Bishop K. H. Ting on the Chinese Church and the Question of Hong Kong"). *Tian Feng* (1 September 1987): 12-13. Revised translation of interview on the same subject with Ewing W. Carroll, Jr.

"Xindeli guoji zongjiao ziyou huiyi shang de jianggao" ("Religious Liberty as a Chinese Christian Sees It"). *JL* 6-7 (September 1987): 80-85. A lecture presented at an International Symposium on Religious Liberty in New Delhi, India.

"Interview with K. H. Ting on the Growth of the Church in China." *Bridge* 26 (November-December 1987): 3.

"Changes in Forty Years." November 1987. Typescript. 3 pp. K. H. Ting's own translation of a lecture he gave at Nanjing Seminary.

1988

"Opening Speech by Bishop K. H. Ting at the Dedication of the Amity Printing Press." *Amity Newsletter* 6 (Winter 1987-1988): 2-3.

"Matthew 13:31-32." *CTR* (1988): 142-144. A sermon preached at a meeting of the Episcopal Church (U.S.A.) House of Bishops, Detroit, Michigan, U.S.A.

"John 18: 31-32." *CTR* (1988): 145-47.

"Gei yiwei xintu de xin" ("Letter to a Believer"). 1988. Typescript. 3 pp.

"Christians in China Today: A Growing and Independent Church." *One World* (March 1988): 13-19. An interview with Marlin VanElderen conducted in November 1987.

"Zheng jiao yao fenkai" ("Religion and the State Should Be Separate"). March 1988. Mimeograph. 1 p. Speech at the Chinese People's Political Consultative Conference.

"A Reconciling Church." *One World* (April 1988): 7-9. An interview with Marlin VanElderen conducted in November 1987.

"*Zhongguo shehuizhuyi shiqi de zongjiao wenti* jieshao" ("An Introduction to *Religious Issues in the Period of Socialism in China*"). *JL* 8 (June 1988): 4-8.

"Cong chuangzao kan jiangsheng" ("Creation and Incarnation"). *JL* 8 (June 1988): 65-66.

"Jing ai, zhu yuan" ("Respects and Best Wishes"). *JL* 8 (June 1988): 98-99. Speech presented at a meeting honoring sixty years of Prof. Huang Fakui's teaching.

"Ding Guangxun hui Zhang Shengcai de fuxin" ("Bishop K. H. Ting's Return Letter to Mr. Zhang Shengcai"). *Baixing* 173 (1 August 1988): 26. The letter is dated 9 April 1988.

"Response to the General Conference of the United Methodist Church (U.S.A.)." *China Talk* 8, no. 4 (October 1988): 11. The response is dated 3 May 1988, and was delivered at a meeting of the general conference in St. Louis, Missouri, U.S.A.

"The Theological Task in China." 16 May 1988. Typescript. 6 pp. A lecture presented at a meeting of the World Council of Churches.

"An Interview." *China and Ourselves* 54 (Summer 1988): 6-10. An interview with K. H. Ting conducted by Elizabeth Larsen, Midwest China Center.

"The Growing Vision." *The Ecumenical Review* 40, no. 3-4 (July-October 1988): 417-20. Based on an address given to students at Nanjing Seminary, January 1988.

"Letter to the Editor." *Church Times*, 5 August 1988. Headlined "Bias on Dean," a letter in defense of Hewlett Johnson.

"Zouchu yitiao xin lu lai zhusheng zhujiao dianli shang de zhengdao" ("An Untrodden Path: Sermon on the Consecration of New Bishops") *Tian Feng* (1 September 1988): 4-5. Sermon preached in Shanghai on 26 June 1988 at the consecration of Shen Yifan and Sun Yanli as bishops.

"Letter to the Religious Affairs Bureau on the Religious Regulations in Guangdong." 26 September 1988. 6 pp. K. H. Ting's own translation of the Chinese text.

"Jin ji nian zongjiao yanjiu shang ruogan tupo" ("Some Breakthroughs in Religious Research Over the Last Several Years"). October 1988. Mimeographed typescript. 12 pp. With Wang Weifan. A slightly different version was published in *Zongjiao (Religion)* 15 (June 1989): 1-8.

"Review of *The Myth of Christian Uniqueness: Towards a Pluralistic Understanding of Religions.*" *China Notes* (Autumn 1988): 498-99.

"Conversation with Bishop K. H. Ting." October 1988. Typescript from a video. Interview conducted by John Ankele.

"Interview with Bishop K. H. Ting." 1 November 1988. Typescript. 3 pp.

"Ai daodi de ai" ("The Love That Loves to the End"). *JL* 9 (November 1988): 60-62.

"Zongjiao yu daxue jiaoyu" ("Religion and University Education"). *JL* 9 (November 1988): 70. Speech on receiving an honorary doctorate from Kent University, U.K., on 3 July 1988.

"Geng da de xinren, geng da de kuanrong: Zhao Zichen danchen yibai zhounian yougan" ("More Trust and More Tolerance: On the 100th Anniversary of the Birth of Dr. T. C. Chao") *JL* 9 (November 1988): 99-100. Speech at a seminar held in Beijing, 3 April 1988.

"Jiaohui zai zhongguo yiran cunzai" ("The Church Survives in China"). *JL* 9 (November 1988): 1-4. Translation of 1987 address to the Lutheran World Federation.

"Interview with Bishop K. H. Ting." *Bridge* 32 (December 1988): 5-6.

"Jiangsheng yu chaoyue." ("Incarnation and Transcendence"). December 1988. Typescript. 4 pp.

Christianity with a Chinese Face. Cincinnati: Forward Movement Publications, 1989. 19 pp. Pamphlet with extracts of three sermons presented to the general convention of the Episcopal Church (U.S.A.) in Detroit, Michigan, in July 1988. Edited by C. H. Long.

1989

"Bishop K. H. Ting's View of the Present Situation of Christianity in China." *Bridge* 33 (January-February 1989): 3-8. Interview with *Bridge* conducted in Nanjing on 22 October 1988.

"Xuyan" ("Preface"). *Shengjing xinyu* (*New Thoughts on the Bible*). Typescript. 28 March 1989. 2 pp. Beijing.

"Breakthroughs in Religious Research." *Beijing Review* (20-26 March 1989): 18-23. With Wang Weifan. A popularization of the longer essay cited above.

"Presentation to Division of World Outreach Executive, United Church of Canada." 11-12 May 1989. Typescript. 8 pp.

"The Bible as Approached by Chinese Christians." 11 May 1989. Typescript. Toronto. 3 pp. The basis for other essays on the same subject.

"Minutes of Canada China Programme Board Meeting with K. H. Ting." 12 May 1989. 4 pp.

"Remarks by Chinese Christian Leaders on the Second Lausanne Conference." 18 May 1989. Typescript. 3 pp. Remarks by K. H. Ting and other Chinese Christian leaders on the Lausanne II Conference, planned for Manila, July 1989. Also published in *Bridge* 36 (July-August 1989): 22-23.

"Women jidujiao jie shengyuan xuesheng de aiguo xingdong" ("We Christians Support the Patriotic Actions of Chinese Students"). 18 May 1989. Typescript. 1 p. Signed by K. H. Ting as president/chair of the TSPM/CCC.

"Christians Support the Patriotic Actions of Chinese Students." 23 May 1989. Typescript. 1 p. Widely published statement, which includes the May 18th statement of the TSPM/CCC.

"Dui wo guo zongjiao gongzuo de jidian yijian" ("Some Opinions of China's Religious Policy"). *Tian Feng*, (1 May 1989): supplementary pp. 1-2. A speech delivered at the second session of the Seventh CPPCC, when K. H. Ting was elected vice-chairperson.

"Lishun sanzi zuzhi han jiaohui de guanxi" ("Reordering Relationships"). *JL* 10 (June 1989): 1-5. Address presented at the joint standing committees of TSPM/CCC, Shanghai, 13 December 1988.

"Letter to Philip and Other Colleagues in the Amity Office, Hong Kong." 6 June 1989. Typescript. 3 pp. With Han Wenzao. A widely published letter.

"Ding Guangxun weiyuan shuo" ("Delegate K. H. Ting Speaks on the Floor of the National People's Congress"). *NCNA* 1 July 1989; *RMRB* 2 July 1989.

"Bishop K. H. Ting Spoke at the CPPCC." *Bridge* 35 (May-June 1989): 3-4.

No Longer Strangers: Selected Writings of Bishop K. H. Ting. Ed. Raymond White-head. Maryknoll, N.Y.: Orbis Books, 1989. Also published by Philippine-China Development Resource Centre: New Manila, Philippines, 1991.

"Tan Shenxue jiaoyu" ("On Theological Education"). *Tian Feng* (1 November 1989): 4-5.

"The Church in China after June 4th: An Interview with Bishop K. H. Ting." 15 November 1989. *Amity News Release.* 3 pp. Interview conducted by Philip L. Wickeri.

1990

"In China." In *Robert Runcie: A Portrait by His Friends*, 196-99. Edited by David L. Edwards. London: HarperCollins, 1990. Originally entitled "Canterbury and Nanjing."

"Xu" ("Foreword"). In *Shengjing baike cidian* (*An Encyclopedic Dictionary of the Bible*), 1-3. Edited by Liang Gong. Shenyang: Liaoning People's Publishing, 1990.

"A Few Words from Our President." *Amity in Progress, 1985-1990*, p. 3. Chinese and English.

"Zai liang wei pengyou hunli shang de zhici" ("On the Occasion of the Wedding of Friends." 1990. Typescript. 2 pp.

"Jintian women xiang Wu Yaozong xiansheng xuexi shenma?" ("What Can We Learn from Y. T.Wu Today?"). *JL* 11 (February 1990): 1-5. Speech on the tenth anniversary of Y. T. Wu's death (1989).

"Sixiang bu duan de gengxin de Wu Yaozong xian sheng" ("The Ever Reforming Mr. Y. T. Wu"). *JL* 11 (February 1990): 6-9. Speech at CPPCC commemoration of the tenth anniversary of Y. T. Wu's death (1989).

"Ding Guangxun yuanzhang tan dangqian jiaohui ruogan wenti" ("Bishop K. H. Ting Discusses the Current Church Situation"). *JL* 11 (February 1990): 38-40; 19. A talk with seminary students around Christmas 1989.

"Baohu Shangdi de chuangzao" ("Protecting God's Creation"). *Tian Feng* (1 April 1990): 12-13. Speech at environmental meeting for world parliamentarians, Moscow, 15-19 January 1990.

"Eucharistic Homily." April 1990. Typescript. 2 pp. A sermon delivered at Stony Point, N.Y.

"A Conversation with K. H. Ting on Theological Opportunities in North America and Europe for Chinese Christian Leadership Development." *China Notes* (Spring and Summer 1990): 584-86.

"The Chinese Church as I See It." August 1990. Typescript. 6 pp. Presented at the Amity Teachers' Conference, Nanjing. Revised Chinese translation published in *JL* 18 (January 1993): 67-69.

"Zai Weiduoliya daxue biye dianli shang de yanjiang" ("Address at the Graduation Ceremony of Victoria University"). *JL* 12 (July 1990): 84-85. Speech on the occasion when K. H. Ting and Siu-may Kuo were given honorary doctorates by Emmanuel College, Victoria University, Montreal. 11 May 1989. English text available. 3 pp.

"Zhongguo jidujiao liang hui weiyuanhui Shanghai huiyi dahui fayan" ("Plenary Speech at the Shanghai Meeting of the TSPM/CCC Joint Committee"). 28 August 1990. Typescript. 7 pp.

"Ding Guangxun weiyuan fayan" ("Speech of Committee Member K. H. Ting"). 6 September 1990. Typescript. 5 pp. Speech at standing committee of the National People's Congress.

"Ding zhujiao de jianghua" ("Speech of Bishop Ting"). *Tian Feng* (1 November 1990): 3-4. Speech at the meeting marking the fortieth anniversary of the TSPM.

"Zai quanguo lianghui weiyuanhui huiyi shang de fayan" ("Address to the Plenary Session"). *Tian Feng* (1 November 1990): 20-23.

"Thanksgiving." November 1990. Typescript. 1 p. A meditation delivered in Dallas, Tex.

"Hear, You Who Have Ears to Hear . . ." November 1990. Typescript. 1 p.

"This Your Brother Was Dead, and Is Alive." November 1990. Typescript. 1 p.

1991

Conversation with Bishop K. H. Ting." *China Notes* (Winter/Spring 1991-1992): 667-70. A conversation with the National Council of Churches of Christ in the U.S.A. delegation visiting China, Nanjing, 25 February 1992.

"Yu Jiang Zemin tongzhi huijian de fayan" ("Speech on a Visit to Comrade Jiang Zemin"). 31 January 1991. Typescript. 2 pp. Beijing. Translation in *Bridge* 46 (March/April 1991): 3-5.

"Foreword." In *Religion under Socialism in China*, vii-xii. Edited by Luo Zhufeng. Translated by Donald MacInnis and Zheng Xi'an. Armonk, N.Y.: M. E. Sharpe, 1991.

"Understanding Religions in China." *Beijing Review* (11-17 February 1991): 31. A review of *Religion in China—100 Questions and Answers*.

"Speech on the Admission of the China Christian Council to the World Council of Churches." 18 February 1991. Typescript. 2 pp.

"Zhongguo jidutu ze'yang kandai shengjing" ("The Chinese Christians' Approach to the Bible"). *JL* 13 (March 1991): 1-7. Translation of a speech delivered at the Society of Biblical Literature, New Orleans, 18 November 1990.

"Dui Tian Feng de zhuyuan" ("Congratulations to *Tian Feng*"). *Tian Feng* (1 April 1991): 10-11. On the publication of the 100th issue of the magazine since its reissue.

"The Chinese Church as I See It." *The Christian Century* 108 (10 April 1991): 401-3.

"Church Unity and Ecumenicity." 21 April 1991. Nanjing. Typescript. 7 pp. An interview with Claudia and Gotthard Oblau.

"Shengming zhi shu chang qing" ("The Tree of Life Is Ever Green"). *Tian Feng* (1 July 1991): 2-3. Sermon preached at the memorial service of Zheng Jianye.

"Zhongguo jidujiao xiehui huizhang Ding Guangxun zhi shijie jidujiaohui lianhehui mishuzhang aimiliou.kasiteluo de fuxin" ("China Christian Council President

Ding Guangxun's Return Letter to WCC General Secretary Emilio Castro").
Tian Feng (1 July 1991): 13. The letter is dated 30 April 1991.
"Yuzhou de jidu" ("The Cosmic Christ"). *JL* 14-15 (September 1991): 1-6. Translation of a speech delivered at a meeting of the Friends of the Church in China, U.K., July 1991.
"Biyao de shuoming" ("A Necessary Clarification"). *Tian Feng* (1 September 1991): 18-20.

1992

"Zhongguo gudai jidujiao sixiang chutan" ("A Preliminary Investigation of Christianity in Ancient China"). *Selected Papers of the International Colloquium on Traditional Chinese Thought and Culture in the 21st Century*. Nanjing: Nanjing University Press, 1992. Pp. 168-73. Written with Wang Weifan.
"Bishop Ting Sums up the Conference, Talks About New Regulations." *ANS.* 1992.1.5. Summing up the Fifth National Christian Conference.
"Bi muci" ("Closing Address"). *Tian Feng* (1 March 1992): 23-25. Closing address at the Fifth National Christian Conference.
"Zai shiwu sheng lianhe anli mushi libai shang de jiangdao" ("Sermon at the Joint Service of Ordination"). *Tian Feng* (1 March 1992): 37-40. Sermon preached on 5 January 1992, Beijing.
"Continual Renewal of Self-Knowledge; Interview with Bishop Ding Guangxun Prior to the Fifth National Christian Conference." *Yi: China Message* 11, no. 3 (April 1992). The interview was conducted on 31 December 1991.
"A Report from China." *Amity Echo* (1 September 1992): 1-5. Convocation address at McMaster University, Hamilton, Ontario.
"Jianghua" ("Speech"). *Jiangsu jidujiao di wujie huiyi zhuan (Proceedings of the Fifth Jiangsu Provincial Christian Conference)*. Nanjing: Jiangsu TSPM and Christian Council, 1995. Pp. 41-43. A speech delivered on 28 May 1992.
"K. H. Ting Talks Again to Jiang Zemin, January 1992." *Bridge* 53 (May/ June 1992): 6.
"Zhengque chuli zongjiao wenti" ("Correctly Resolve the Religious Question"). 30 June 1990. Mimeographed. 4 pp. Dated 30 June 1990. Speech at the National People's Congress on problems with implementation of religious policy. Also published in *Zhongguo yu Jiaohui (China and the Church)* 94 (93:3-4): 11-12.
"Zongjiao gongzuo ye ying ju you zhongguo tese" ("Religious Work Should Also Have Chinese Characteristics"). *Zongjiao (Religion)* 21 (June 1992): 142-45.
"You guan juhuidian dengji de jige wenti" ("A Few Questions on the Registration of Meeting Points"). *Tian Feng* (1 August 1992): 20.
"Guanyu woguo jiaohui jianchi ziyang de ruogan yijian" ("Some Opinions about Upholding Self-Support in the Chinese Church"). 28 August 1992. Handwritten text. 3 pp.
"Self Support and International Christian Sharing." *ANS.* 1992.5.9. Interview with Philip L. Wickeri, Nanjing, 31 August 1992.
"Ding Guangxun fuzhuxi de jianghua" ("Speech by Vice-Chair Ding Guangxun"). *Zhongguo zhengxie xieshang huiyi jianbao (Chinese People's Political Consultative Conference Bulletin)*, 64, no. 3 (12 September 1992). Speech at the *Chinese People's Political Consultative Conference*, 3 September 1992.
"Yi gu you" ("In Memory of a Deceased Friend"). *Tian Feng* (1 December 1992): 18. Speech on the thirtieth anniversary of the death of Huang Peiyong.

"Qianyan" ("Foreword"). In *Jinling shenxue wenxuan xuyan (Theological Writings from Nanjing Seminary: Foreword)*, 1-6. Nanjing, 1992. Also published in *JL* 17 (December 1992): 45-47.

1993

"Tan banhao jiaohui" ("Running the Church Well"). *JL* 18 (January 1993): 29-31. Speech at the fortieth anniversary of Nanjing Union Theological Seminary.

"Ding Guangxun yuanzhang zai xiaoqing sishi zhounian kaimu dianli shang de jianghua" ("Principal K. H. Ting's Speech at the Opening Ceremony for the Fortieth Anniversary of Nanjing Union Seminary"). *JL* 18 (January 1993): 31-32.

"Zhongguo jiaohui zhi wo jian" ("The Chinese Church as I See It"). *JL* 18 (January 1993): 67-69. Translation of a speech from the Forum on "Christ and Culture," Columbia Theological Seminary, October 1992.

"Message at the Memorial Service for Alan Ecclestone." 13 January 1993. Typescript. 1 p.

"Remarks at Amity Teachers' Banquet." *Amity Newsletter* 24 (Spring 1993): 3. Speech at the closing banquet for the Amity teachers' orientation, August 1992.

"Qianyan" ("Foreword"). In *Zhongguo jidujiao sanzi aiguo yundong wenxuan: 1950-1992 (Selected Documents of the Chinese Christian Three-Self Patriotic Movement Committee: 1950-1992)*, 1-5. Edited by Luo Guanzong. Shanghai: TSPM/CCC, 1993.

"Statement on Theological Scholarships for Study Overseas." *ANS*. 1993.1.12. 1 p.

Untitled comment on Zhang Xiaofeng, "Qin Shang" ("Qin Elegy") with particular reference to the Denunciation Movement. 9 April 1993. Typescript. 2 pp.

"Ding Guangxun weiyuan de fayan" ("Delegate K. H. Ting's Speech"). *Tian Feng* (1 May 1993): 13 -15. Speech at the first session of Eighth Chinese People's Political Consultative Conference, 22 March 1993.

"Zai changwei shang de fayan" ("Speech at the Standing Committee"). May 1993. Typescript. 5 pp.

"Guanyu tigao woguo xintu de xinyang suzhi" ("On Raising the Cultural Level of China's Christians"). 18 June 1993. Typescript. 1 p.

"Chuangzao he jiushu" ("Creation and Redemption") July 1993. Typescript. 4 pp. Sermon preached at Nanjing Seminary commencement.

"Zhongguo jiaohui guanban daole shenme chengdu?" ("To What Extent Has the Chinese Church Become Officially Run?") 25 August 1993. Typescript. 1 p.

"Foreword." *Christian Art from China*. Catalogue of Amity Art Exhibit, Hong Kong, 30 September-19 October 1993.

"One Chinese Christian's View of God." October 1993. Typescript. 11 pp. Lecture given at Union Theological Seminary in the Philippines.

"The Church's Ministry in China." October 1993. Typescript. 9 pp. Lecture given in the Philippines.

1994

"Zai Zhongnanhai canjia Li Ruihuan tongzhi zhaokai de zongjiaojie chunjie zuotanhui shang de fayan" ("Speech at Teaparty for Religious Circles Hosted by Comrade Li Ruihuan at Zhongnanhai"). 29 January 1994. Typescript. 2 pp. Also published in *Zongjiao (Religion)* 25 (June 1994): 2-3.

"Bimu ci" ("Closing Address"). *Tian Feng* (1 February 1994): 12-13. Closing address at a meeting of the Joint TSPM/CCC Standing Committee, 12 December 1994.

"Difang dui zongjiao luan fan luan ya" ("Local Officials Suppress Religious Disturbances"). *Ming Bao*. 28 March 1994. Report quoting statement by K. H. Ting made at the Chinese People's Political Consultative Conference.

"Bishop Ting on China's Christianity." *Beijing Review* (11-17 April 1994): 7-12. Interview with Huang Wei.

"Jiu tangdian dengji wenti: Tian Feng jizhe fangwen Ding zhujiao" (*"Tian Feng* Interviews Bishop Ting on the Registration Issue"). *Tian Feng* (1 June 1994): 2-4.

"Taiwan Politics: Religion as a Pawn?" June 1994. Typescript. 1 p.

"Shehuizhuyi han zongjiao jiazhiguan you gongtongdian" ("There Are Common Values Between Socialism and Religion." *JL* 20 (June 1994): 22-25; and *Zongjiao (Religion)* 25 (June 1994): 19-20. K. H. Ting's translation of an essay written by Joe Slovo.

"Jianchi xinyang han liyi shang huxiang zunzhong de yuanze" ("Uphold the Principle of Mutual Respect in Faith and Worship"). *Tian Feng* (1 July 1994): 24.

"Dui yi nian lai *Tian Feng* neirong de yanjiu: 1993.7-1994.6" ("Research on the Contents of One Year of *Tian Feng*: 1993.7-1994.6"). 7 August 1994. 4 pp.

"An Update on the Church in China." October 1994. Typescript. 10 pp. Speech presented at gatherings for Presbyterian and Methodist missionaries and their families.

"A Report to My Alma Mater." October 1994. Typescript. 10 pp. Speech on receiving Union Theological Seminary Medal.

Untitled. October 1994. Handwritten manuscript. 1 p. K. H. Ting's statement on the Denunciation Movement. Note that it was to be inserted as the third paragraph on p. 4 of "An Update on the Church in China."

"Jiaohui zai zhongguo" ("The Church in China"). *JL* 21 (December 1994). Translation of speech at the Baptist World Alliance Retreat, Nanjing, April 1994. Pp. 1-4.

"Zai tan ban hao jiaohui" ("Another Talk on Running the Church Well"). *Qiao (Bridge)* 74 (December 1994): 12-15. Speech to provincial church leaders in Chengdu, August 1987.

"Duli zizhu banhao jiaohui" ("Independently Run the Church Well"). *Tian Feng* (1 January 1995): 2-4. Opening address to a meeting of the Joint TSPM/CCC Standing Committee, Beijing, December 1994.

1995

"Foreword." In *Christian Missions and the Judgment of God*, ix-x. Edited by David Paton. Second edition. Grand Rapids: Eerdmans, 1995.

"Gei xiaoyou de yi feng xin" ("Letter to Alumni/ae of Nanjing Union Seminary"). February 1995. Typescript. 2 pp.

"Jiu tangdian dengji wenti: Ding zhujiao zai ci tanhua" ("Another Talk with Bishop Ting on the Registration Issue"). *Tian Feng* (1 March 1995): 28-29.

"Yuan wei zuguo tongyi jin fen li" ("Let Us Work for the Reunification of China"). *Tian Feng* (1 April 1995): 2. Statement in a seminar to study Jiang Zemin's speech on peaceful reunification, Beijing, 7 March 1995.

"Huigu zouguo de lu" ("A Look Back at the Way We Have Come"). April 1995. Typescript. A speech presented at the Joint TSPM/CCC Standing Committee, 24 April 1995.

"Lijie Shangdi de xin" ("Understanding the Heart of God"). *JL* 22-23 (June 1995).

Sermon preached at All Saints Episcopal Church, Beverly Hills, Ca., September 1993.

"Wo hen zancheng ban zheige kanwu" ("I Support the Publication of This New Journal"). *Zhongguo zongjiao* (*Chinese Religions*) 1 (Summer 1995): 11.

"Informal Remarks at Closing Banquet for Amity Teachers." 29 August 1995. 1 p.

"Shouxian shuoming liangdian" ("An Explanation of Two Points"). 11 September 1995. Typescript. 3 pp.

"Qianyan" ("Preface"). 12 September 1995. Handwritten manuscript. 2 pp. Preface to a manuscript for a training manual for local churches in Wenzhou. Edited by Chen Dingtong.

"Quanguo liang hui bangong huiyi gewei tonggong" ("Letter to Colleagues in the TSPM/CCC Working Group"). 1 October 1995. 3 pp.

"Ding Guangxun zhujiao de fayan" ("Bishop K. H. Ting's Speech"). *Tian Feng* (1 October 1995): 7-8. Speech at a seminar of religious groups on the fiftieth anniversary of the victory in the war against fascism, August 1995.

1996

"Ding Guangxun fayan: shishi zaizai de ba jiaohui banhao: zai san zi 45 zhounian jinian hui shang de jianghua" ("K. H. Ting's Speech: Work Conscientiously to Run the Church Well: Speech on the 45th Anniversary of Three-Self"). *Tian Feng* (1 January 1996): 8-9. Speech dated 21 November 1994.

"Zuo hao de chuandao ren" ("On Being a Good Pastor"). *JL* 26 (January 1996): 73-74. Sermon preached at the 1995 commencement worship service of Nanjing Seminary.

"Ding Guangxun zai quanguo zhengxie bajie sici huiyi xiaozu taolunshi de fayan" ("Speech by K. H. Ting in Small Group Discussion at the Fourth Session of the Eighth Chinese People's Political Consultative Conference"). *Zongjiao gongzuo tongbao* (*Religious Work Bulletin*) 3, no. 30 (7 March 1996): 1-8.

"Zai sixiang shenchu shiying shehuizhuyi" ("On a Profound Ideological Level Adapt to Socialism"). Undated. Typescript. 4 pp. Speech at a meeting of Chinese religious leaders, Dalian, May 1996.

"Yixie fenxi he yijian" ("Some Analyses and Opinions"). 26 August 1996. Typescript. 2 pp.

Lun Sanzi he jiaohui jianshe: Ding Guangxun zhujiao he zhongguo jidujiao lici huiyi wenjian you guan lunshu xuanbian, 1980-1995 (*On Three-Self and Church Building: Selected Conference Documents Expounding the Subject by Bishop K. H. Ting and the Chinese Church, 1980-1995*). Edited by Luo Guanzong. TSPM/CCC: Shanghai, 1996. Short extracts from the writings of K. H. Ting and church statements on Three-Self.

"Yi qie dou chuyu shangdi ma?" ("Does Everything Come from God?") *Tian Feng* (1 October 1996): 24. Dated 18 August 1996.

"Running the Church Well: A Conversation with K. H. Ting." *Areopagus* 9, no. 4 (Winter/Spring 1997): 8-11 and 33-35. The interview was conducted in Nanjing, October 1996.

"Christianity and Chinese Intellectuals: History and the Present." *CTR* 11, no. 2 (1997): 71-75. Address at a consultation held in cooperation with Columbia Theological Seminary, 1994.

"Ding Guangxun zhujiao zhi Riben shenggonghui shouxi zhujiao de huixin" ("Bishop K. H. Ting's Return Letter to the Presiding Bishop of the Japanese

Anglican Church"). *Tian Feng* (1 January 1997): 27. A thank you for the expression of apology for Japanese aggression in World War II, dated 10 November 1996.

"Zai Zhongguo jidujiao di liu jie quanguo huiyi shang de jianghua" ("Greetings to the Sixth National Chinese Christian Conference"). *Tian Feng* (1 February 1997): 2-3. The speech was delivered on 29 December 1996.

1997

"Ding zhujiao fangwen ji" ("An Interview with Bishop K. H. Ting). *Tian Feng* (1 February 1997): 41-42. English translation by K. H. Ting is available.

"Statement on 'United States Policies in Support of Religious Freedom: Focus on Christians.'" *ANS* 1997.8.7.

"Buyao liyong zongjiao wenti ganshe wo guo" ("Do Not Use Religion to Interfere in China"). *Tian Feng* (1 September 1997): 4.

"Jintian women xiang Wu Yaozong xiansheng xuexi shenme" ("What Should We Learn from Wu Yaozong Today?"). *Tian Feng* (1 September 1997): 7-9.

1998

"Wei yifa zhiguo you biyao jiasu zhiding 'zongjiao fa'" ("To Run the Country According to Law We Should Quickly Formulate a 'Religious Law'"). *Zongjiao* (*Religion*) 1-2 (1998): 36-37. Written together with thirteen other delegates at a meeting of the Chinese People's Political Consultative Conference.

"Xin zenme yang yi wei Shangdi?" ("Believing in What Kind of God?"). *JL* 35, no. 2 (1998): 10-11.

"Xinren" ("A New Person"). *JL* 35, no. 2 (1998): 66. Sermon preached at Nanjing Seminary Christmas service.

"Jidujiao chuanjiao yundong he Shangdi de shenpan" ("Preface to *Christian Missions and the Judgment of God*"). *Tian Feng* (1 April 1998): 38. Translation.

"Zhi jinling tonggong" ("To Seminary Colleagues"). 11 May 1999. Typescript. 8 pp.

Ding Guangxun Wenji (*The Collected Works of K. H. Ting*). Nanjing: Yilin Press, 1998.

"Yu jinling tongxue tan ren de zhongyi xing wenti" ("On Ultimate Questions"). In *Ding Guangxun Wenji* (*The Collected Works of K. H. Ting*), 215-21. Nanjing: Yilin Press, 1998. Dated 1985.

"Zenme yang kandai jidu jiaohui yiwai de zhen shan mei?" ("How to View Truth, Goodness and Beauty Outside the Church"). In *Ding Guangxun Wenji* (*The Collected Works of K. H. Ting*), 240-53. Nanjing: Yilin Press, 1998. Dated 1997.

"Wei Wang Weifan tonggong zuopin suo xie de xuyan" ("Preface to *Chinese Theology and Its Cultural Sources* by Wang Weifan"). In *Ding Guangxun Wenji* (*The Collected Works of K. H. Ting*), 290-91. Nanjing: Yilin Press, 1998. Dated 1996.

"Qingzhu zhengxie sishizhou nian fayan" ("A Congratulatory Speech"). In *Ding Guangxun Wenji* (*The Collected Works of K. H. Ting*), 470-72. Nanjing: Yilin Press, 1998. Speech marking the 40th Anniversary of the Chinese People's Political Consultative Conference, 1989.

"Wei Chen Zemin xiansheng suozhu *Jidujiao changshi dawen* xie de xuyan" ("Preface to *Questions and Answers on Christianity* by Mr. Chen Zemin"). In *Ding*

Guangxun Wenji (*The Collected Works of K. H. Ting*), 488-89. Nanjing: Yilin Press, 1998. Dated 20 July 1993.

"*Shengjing wenxue cidian* qianyan" ("Preface to the *Dictionary of Biblical Literature*"). In *Ding Guangxun Wenji* (*The Collected Works of K. H. Ting*), 498-99. Nanjing: Yilin Press, 1998. Dated 1997.

"Huainian Kuang xiaozhang" ("In Memory of Principal Kuang Yaming"). In *Ding Guangxun Wenji* (*The Collected Works of K. H. Ting*), 500-501. Nanjing: Yilin Press, 1998. Dated 1997.

"Huainian Lu Xunru tongzhi" ("In Memory of Comrade Lu Xunru." In *Ding Guangxun Wenji* (*The Collected Works of K. H. Ting*), 502-3. Nanjing: Yilin Press, 1998. pp. 502-503. dated 1997.

"Huainian Luo Zhufeng tongzhi" ("In Memory of Comrade Luo Zhufeng"). In *Ding Guangxun Wenji* (*The Collected Works of K. H. Ting*), 504-6. Nanjing: Yilin Press, 1998. Dated 1997.

"Wei Deguo Gu Aihua boshi jieshao Zhao Zichen jiaoshou shenxue sixiang de zhuzuo suo xie de qianyan" ("Preface to the Theological Writings of Professor T. C. Chao as Introduced by Dr. Winfried Glüer"). In *Ding Guangxun Wenji* (*The Collected Works of K. H. Ting*), 509-22. Nanjing: Yilin Press, 1998. Dated 1998.

"Houji" ("Afterword"). In *Ding Guangxun Wenji* (*The Collected Works of K. H. Ting*), 512. Nanjing: Yilin Press, 1998. Dated 14 August 1998.

"Tiaozheng zongjiao guannian de huhuan" ("A Call for the Adjustment of Religious Ideas"). *Renmin zhengxie bao (CPPCC News)*. 4 September 1998. 1 p.

"Zhe yishi wo de shenxue sisuo" ("My Theological Ponderings at This Time"). *Tian Feng* (1 December 1998): 8-10. Dated 13 September 1998.

1999

"Hromádka as Reconciler." In *From the Reformation to Tomorrow: Joseph L. Hromádka (1889-1969)*, 93. Edited by Milan Opočenský. Geneva: World Alliance of Reformed Churches, 1999.

"Laode shenxue sixiang yao you suo tiaozheng you suo gengxin" ("Old Style Theological Thinking Needs Revision and Renewal"). *Zongjiao (Religion)* 43-44 (1999): 6. Dated 5 March 1999. Originally published in *Renmin Zhengxue bao (CPPCC News)*.

"Shengjing zhong Shangdi de qishi shi zhejin de, bushi yi ci wancheng de, er ren dui Shangdi de qishi de renshi, ye bushi yi ci wancheng de, ye shi zhejin de, zhubu tigao de" ("God's Self Revelation in the Bible and Our Slowness in Grasping it"). *Tian Feng* (1 February 1999): 17-18; and *JL* 38, no. 1 (1999): 3-5. Speech presented at a meeting of the TSPM/CCC in Jinan, 18 November 1998.

"Ren xin xiangwang hehao" ("Our Human Longing for Reconciliation"). *Tian Feng* (1 April 1999): 15-17. Sermon preached at the 1986 graduation ceremony of Nanjing Theological Seminary.

"Da duzhe wen" ("In Response to My Readers"). *Tian Feng* (1 June 1999): 15-16; and *JL* 39, no. 2 (1999): 50-51.

"Ding yuanzhang xiang Jinling xiehe shenxueyuan shisheng jianghua" ("Principal Ting Lectures the Students and Faculty of Nanjing Union Theological Seminary"). June 1999. Typescript. 5 pp.

Dangdai zhongguo jidujiao fayanren: Ding Guangxun wenji (The Spokesman of Contemporary Christianity in China: Collection of Bishop K. H. Ting's

Essays). Edited by Frances Fang. Hong Kong: Chinese Christian Literature Council, 1999.

"Jianjue yonghu he zhichi qudi 'Fa Lun Gong'" ("Resolutely Uphold and Support the Suppression of *'Falun Gong'"*). *Tian Feng* (1 September 1999): 5.

Love Never Ends (Collected Writings of K. H. Ting) (Korean). Edited by Kim Jong-goo. Seoul: Korean Christian Institute of Social Problems, 1999.

Preface to the Korean edition. In *Love Never Ends (Collected Writings of K. H. Ting),* 1. Edited by Kim Jong-goo. Seoul: Korean Christian Institute of Social Problems, 1999.

"Sanzi aiguo yundong de fazhan he chongshi" ("Development and Enrichment of the Three-Self Patriotic Movement"). *Tian Feng* (1 January 2000): 4-5. Speech given at a symposium on the TSPM, Shanghai, October 1999.

"Zongjiao duoyuanhua xianxiang de shenxue sikao" ("Theological Reflection on Religious Pluralism"). *JL* (2000:1): 5-11. Translated with Li Wanjun. The original is in *The Ecumenical Review* (1999.4).

2000

"Qishi de zhejin xing" ("The Progressive Nature of Revelation"). *Tian Feng.* 1999 special edition (1 March 2000): 2-3.

"Ding Guangxun zhujiao zai nanjing jiaohui di wu qi shenxue sixiang jianshe yigong peixun ban jieye dianli shang de jianghua" ("Bishop K. H. Ting's Talk at the Closing Ceremony for the Fifth Theological Reconstruction Volunteer Workers Training Program for the Church in Nanjing"). *Zongjiao (Religion)* 3, no. 49 (2000): 7, 19. Also published in *Nanjing Jiaohui,* 2000:3 (30 June 2000): 3-4.

"Tiaozheng shenxue sixiang de nanmian he biran" ("Adjustments in Theology Are Necessary and Unavoidable"). *Tian Feng* (1 March 2000): 4-5; and *JL* 43, no. 2 (2000): 9-10.

Love Never Ends: Papers by K. H. Ting. Edited by Janice Wickeri. Nanjing: Yilin Press, 2000.

Lun Shenxue sixiang jianshe (On Theological Reconstruction). Shanghai: TSPM/CCC, 2000.

"Yuanwei zuguo tongyi jinfenli" ("Strive Tirelessly for the Unity of the Nation"). *Tian Feng* (1 April 2000). Unnumbered page insert. Speech given on 19 March 2000.

"Shenxue sixiang jianshe zai san zi 50 lishi zhong de diwei" ("The Place of Theological Reconstruction in the 50 Year History of Three-Self"). *Shanghai Jidujiao jinian sanzi aiguo yundong 50 zhounian shenxue sixiang jianshe yantao hui zhuanji (Proceedings of the Shanghai Christian Three-Self Patriotic Movement 50th Anniversary Seminar on Theological Reconstruction).* Shanghai: Shanghai Municipal TSPM and Christian Council, 2000, pp. 123-28. Speech delivered to Shanghai pastoral workers on 7 April 2000 at the Shanghai Community Church.

"Wo zenme yang kan zhe wushi nian?" ("How I View These Fifty Years"). *Tian Feng* (1 August 2000): 4-5; and *JL* 44, no. 3 (2000): 3-4. Speech on the fiftieth anniversary of the TSPM.

Lun sanzi yu jiaohui jianshe (On Three-Self and Church Construction). Lun shenxue sixiang jianshe (On Theological Reconstruction). Lun Jidu (On Christ). Lun Shangdi (On God). Lun Shengjing (On the Bible). Shanghai: TSPM/CCC, 2000. A boxed set of five pamphlets containing previously published essays.

"Xie zai *Xiandai Shengjing guan* de qianmian" ("Written to Introduce *A Modern View of the Bible"). JL (The Nanjing Theological Review)* (October 2000): supplementary issue, p. 3.

"Zhichi zhongguo tianzhujiao hui de aiguo xingdong" ("In Support of the Patriotic Action of Chinese Catholics"). *Tian Feng* (1 November 2000): 9. Also published as "Wangji lishi jiu shi beipan" ("It Is a Betrayal to Forget History"). *JL* 45, no. 4 (2000): 12.

"Zai zhongguo jidujiao sanzi aiguo yundong wushi zhounian jinianhui de jianghua" ("Speech at the Fiftieth Anniversary of the Chinese Christian Three-Self Patriotic Movement"). *JL* 45, no. 4 (2000): 3-5.

"Our Belief." *Love in Action, 1985-2000* (On the Fifteenth Anniversary of the Amity Foundation). Nanjing: Amity Foundation, 2000. Pp. 1-2. In Chinese and English.

2001

"Yiqie qingsheng de xingwei dou bushi shangdi suo yuanyi de" ("No Actions Which Devalue Life Are Willed By God"). *Tian Feng* (1 March 2001): 14. Short comment on Falun Gong given at a TSPM/CCC meeting, 6 February 2001, Shanghai.

"Qingzhu Guoqing" ("Celebrate National Day"). *Tian Feng* (1 October 2001): 1.

"Yige gei quan shijie dailai zhongyao xinxi de jidujiao" ("A Christianity with an Important Message for the Whole World"). *Tian Feng* (1 October 2001): 30-33.

"Lijie Shangdi de xin" ("Understanding the Heart of God"). *Tian Feng* (1 November 2001): 19.

Shengjing, xinyang, jiaohui. (The Bible, Faith and the Church). Shanghai: TSPM/CCC, 2001.

2002

"Mantan shenxue sixiang jianshe" ("Informal Remarks on Theological Reconstruction"). In *Beijing jiaohui zai sikao (The Church in Beijing Reflecting)*, 1-9. Beijing: Beijing TSPM and Christian Council, 2002. Speech delivered on 21 November 2001.

"Yu shi ju jin" ("Moving Forward with the Times"). In *Sikao yu Xianshi (Thinking and Reality)*, 5-12. Edited by Luo Guanzong. Shanghai: TSPM/CCC, 2002. Number 2 in a series of pamphlets on theological reconstruction.

"Shenxue sixiang ye yao yushi ju jin" ("Theological Thinking Also Must Progress with the Times"). *Tian Feng* (1 June 2002): 22-23. Speech given at meeting on theological reconstruction in Hangzhou.

"Yinxin yu shangdi jianli heyi de guanxi" ("Faith and the Reconciliation of Relationships with God"). *Tian Feng* (1 August 2002): 34-36. Speech given at a meeting on theological reconstruction in Wuhan.

"Qianyan" ("Preface"). In *Jidu jiao sixiangshi (A History of Christian Thought)* by Justo L. Gonzales, 1-2. Translated by Chen Zemin et al. Nanjing: Nanjing Union Theological Seminary, 2002. Also published in *Tian Feng* (1 October 2002): 30; and *JL* 52, no. 3 (2002): 4.

"Huainian Wu Yaozong, Luo Zhufeng" ("In Memory of Wu Yaozong and Luo Zhufeng"). *Tian Feng* (1 December 2002): 32; and *JL* 53, no. 4 (2002): 23-24. Speech delivered at the fiftieth anniversary of Nanjing Seminary.

A Chinese Contribution to Ecumenical Theology: Selected Writings of K. H. Ting. Edited and introduced by Philip L. and Janice K. Wickeri. Geneva: World Council of Churches, 2002.

2003

"Jianshe zhongguo tese de shenxue, ying laogu shuli zhengque de shengjingguan, shangdiguan, shirenguan" ("To Construct a Theology with Chinese Characteristics We Should Firmly Establish a Correct View of the Bible, God and People"). *Tian Feng* (1 May 2003): 4-5. Speech delivered at a meeting of Theological Reconstruction Group, Nanjing, 1 April 2003.

"Sanzi jiaoyu zhi wo jian" ("How I See Three-Self Education"). *JL* 56, no. 3 (2003): 4-6. Closing speech delivered at a July 1999 seminar on *The Collected Works.*

"Shen'me shi shenxueyuan?" ("What Is a Theological Seminary?"). *JL* 56, no. 3 (2003): 7-16. Speech delivered at the opening of the fall term at Nanjing Seminary.

"Shenxue sixiang jianshe jinru yige xin de jieduan" ("Theological Reconstruction Has Entered a New Stage"). *Tian Feng* (1 September 2003): 4-7. Speech given at the East China Seminar on Theological Reconstruction.

"*Qianshi bu wang, hou shi zhi shi* yi shu shoufa shishang de jianghua" ("Speech at the Launch of *Remembering the Past as a Lesson for the Future*"). *Tian Feng* (1 November 2003)). Unnumbered insert page.

2004

"Songyang shangdi, fachu aiguo aijiao gan'en xinsheng" ("Praise God and Bring Forth Heartfelt Thanks of Loving God and Loving Our Country"). *Tian Feng* (1 July 2004): 12. Speech delivered at the unveiling of the plaque of the new TSPM/CCC headquarters on 219 Jiujiang Road, Shanghai, 6 June 2005.

"Zhongguo jidutu ze'yang kan shengjing" ("Chinese Christians' Approach to the Bible"). *Tian Feng* (1 July 2004): 25-32. The 1990 AAR/SBL speech, reprinted in connection with the "Exhibition of the Bible Work of the Chinese Church." Hong Kong, August 2004.

"To Share God's Love with More People." *ANS* 2004.9/10.7. Address at the opening of the "Exhibition of Bible Ministry of the Churches of China." Hong Kong, 5 August 2004.

"Glory to God." August 2004. Typescript. 2 pp. Address at a reception for ecumenical friends, Hong Kong.

God Is Love: Collected Writings of Bishop K. H. Ting. Colorado Springs: Cook Communications, 2004.

2005

"Zai Jinling xiehe shenxueyuan xin xiaoqu dianji dianli shang de jianghua" ("Address at the Groundbreaking Ceremony at the New Campus of Nanjing Union Theological Seminary"). *JL* 62, no. 1 (2005): 4.

"Zai Jinling luntan—shenxue jiaoyu yu shenxue sixiang jianshe yanjiu hui shang de jianghua" ("Speech at the Jinling Forum—Theological Education and Theological Reconstruction"). *JL* 62, no. 1 (2005): 28-30.

"Yu jiao wai you ren tan 'yapian wenti'" ("On Religion as Opiate"). *JL* 62, no. 1 (2005): 31-40. Republication of a 1985 essay included in *The Collected Works* and *Love Never Ends,* similar to 1981 essay on the same subject.

"Zhi ci" ("Congratulatory Message"). In *That All May Have Abundant Life, 1985-2005,* 3 (On the Twentieth Anniversary of the Amity Foundation). Nanjing: Amity Foundation, 2005. In Chinese and English.

2006
"Qianyan" ("Preface"). In *Zai ai zhong xunqiu zhenli (Seeking Truth in Love),* 1. Nanjing, 2006. In Chinese and English.

"Xianjin de Wu xiansheng" ("Forerunner Mr. Y. T. Wu"). *Tian Feng* 12, no. 1 (December 2006): 32-35. A republication of K. H. Ting's 1981 essay on Y. T. Wu.

2. INTERVIEWS WITH K. H. TING BY PHILIP WICKERI

K. H. Ting, interview with the author, Nanjing, China, 20 June 1982.
K. H. Ting, interview with the author, Nanjing, China, 31 October 1990.
K. H. Ting, interview with the author, Nanjing, China, 16 December 1990.
K. H. Ting, interview with the author, Nanjing, China, 9 March 1991.
K. H. Ting, interview with the author, Nanjing, China, 1 May 1991.
K. H. Ting, interview with the author, Nanjing, China, 11 June 1991. Part I.
K. H. Ting, interview with the author, Nanjing, China, 11 June 1991. Part II.
K. H. Ting, interview with the author, Nanjing, China, 25 August 1991.
K. H. Ting, interview with the author, Nanjing, China, 13 December 1991.
K. H. Ting, interview with the author, Nanjing, China, 16 April 1996.
K. H. Ting, interview with the author, Nanjing, China, 22 March 1997.

3. INTERVIEWS WITH OTHER PERSONS BY PHILIP WICKERI

Deng Fucun, interview with the author, Hangzhou, China, 3 December 1991.
Margaret Flory, interview with the author. Stony Point, New York, United States, 10 July 1987.
Ninan Koshy, interview with the author, Beijing, China, 15 November 2006,
Siu-may Kuo, interview with the author, Nanjing, China, 9 June 1991.
Milan Opočenský, interview with the author, Geneva, Switzerland, 18 January 2003.
Peter W. H. Tsai (Cai Wenhao), interview with the author, Hangzhou, China, 6 April 1991.
Wang Weifan, interview with the author, Nanjing, China, 19 April 1996.
Yu Mingyue, interview with the author, Fuyang, China, 4 December 1991.

4. LIST OF JOURNALS

Amity News Service, 1992-.
Bridge: Church Life in China Today, 1985-1997.
China Notes, 1962-1992.
The China Quarterly, 1960 -.

The China Study Bulletin, 1979-.

The Chinese Theological Review, 1985-.

Jinling shenxuezhi (*Nanjing Theological Review*), 1953-1957; 1984-.

Tian Feng, 1947-1963; 1980-.

Tripod, 1980-.

Yi: China Message, 1979-1997.

Zongjiao (Religion), 1979-2002.

5. BOOKS AND ESSAYS IN CHINESE

Beijing jiaohui zai sikao (*The Church in Beijing Reflecting*). Beijing: Beijing TSPM and Christian Council, 2002.

Chao T'ien-en (Zhao Tian'en). *Dong zhu xian ji: zhongguo zongjiao zhengci ji sanzihui lunping* (*Prophetic Penetration: Critique of Religious Policy and the TSPM*). Taibei: China Ministries International, 1993.

———. *Fu wo qian xing: Zhongguo fuyinhua yixiang* (*Leading Me to Go Forward: Vision of the Evangelization of China*). Taibei: China Ministries International, 1993.

———. *Ling huo cui lian: Zhongguo dalu jiaohui fuxing yu mijue* (*Purified by Fire: The Secrets of House Church Revivals in China.*) Taibei: China Ministries International, 1993.

———. *Zhonggong dui Jidujiao de zhengce* (*Chinese Communist Policy Towards Christianity*). Hong Kong: Chinese Church Research Centre, 1983.

———, and Rosanna Chong. *Dangdai zhongguo jidujiao fazhanshi, 1949-1997* (*A History of Christianity in Socialist China, 1949-1997*). Taipei: CMI Publishing, 1997.

Chen Tingxiang, ed. *Zhongguo xiandai shi* (*Modern History of China*). Chengdu: Sichuan Daxue Chubanshe, 2002.

Chen Zemin. *Jinling shenxue wenxuan: 1952-1992* (*Collection of Theological Essays of Nanjing Seminary: 1952-1992*). Nanjing: Nanjing Union Theological Seminary, 1992.

Deng Xiaoping wenxuan (*Selected Works of Deng Xiaoping*). Volume 3. Beijing: Renmin chubanshe, 1993.

Deng Zhaoming. *Cangsang yu jiongjing: sishinian lai de sanzi aiguoyundong* (*The Vicissitudes of the Three-Self Patriotic Movement in the 1950s and Its Predicament Today*). Hong Kong: Christian Study Center on Chinese Religion and Culture, 1997.

———. *Chengshou yu chishou: zhongguo dadi de fuyin huoju* (*The Torch of the Testimony in China*). Hong Kong: Christian Study Center on Chinese Religion and Culture, 1998.

Duan Qi. *Fenjin de licheng: zhongguo jidujiao de bensehua* (*Struggling Forward: The Indigenization of Protestant Christianity in China*). Beijing: Shangwu yinshuguan, 2004.

Fung, Raymond, and Philip Lam, eds. *Zhu ai women daodi: zhongguo jidujiao daibiao tuan fang gang wenji* (*God Loves Us to the Very End: A Collection of Sermons and Speeches Delivered by Members of the Chinese Christian Delegation to Hong Kong, March 22-April 9, 1981)*. Hong Kong: Hong Kong Christian Council, 1981.

"Gao quanguo zhunei dixiong jiemei shu" ("Open Letter to Brothers and Sisters in Christ in China). *Tian Feng* 1 (20 October 1980): 2-3.

Gao Wenqian. *Wannian Zhou Enlai (The Latter Years of Zhou Enlai)*. Hong Kong: Mirror Books, 2003.

Ge Luoxi. "Ershi ge yue lai de Shanghai jidujiao xuesheng yundong" ("The Shanghai Christian Student Movement Over the Last Twenty Months"). *Xiaoxi* (June 1939): 44-50.

"Guanyu fencui 'si ren bang' yihou zongjiao gongzuo zhuyao qingquang de ziliao." ("Materials on the Major Situation of Religious Work after the Fall of the Gang of Four"). Copy of handwritten manuscript, ca. 1989.

"Guanyu jiefang chuqi zhi yijiuwuliu nian guonei hanminzu zongjiao gongzuo luxian shi fe wenti de ziliao" ("Materials on the Question of Right and Wrong in Religious Work among Han Chinese, from the Early Years of Liberation to 1956"). Copy of handwritten manuscript, ca. 1989. 21 pp.

"Guanyu yijiuliusi nian xiabannian zhi yijiuliuliu nian shang bannian guonei han minzu zongjiao gongzuo luxian shi fe wenti de ziliao" ("Materials on the Question of Right and Wrong in Religious Work among Han Chinese, from the Second Half of 1964 to the First Half of 1966"). Copy of handwritten manuscript, ca. 1989. 98 pp.

"Guanyu yijiuwuqi nian zhi yijiuliusi nian shang bannian han minzu zongjiao gongzuo luxian shi fe wenti de ziliao" ("Materials on the Question of Right and Wrong in Religious Work among Han Chinese, from 1957 to the First Half of 1964"): "Liu Chun, Xiaoxianfa tongzhi yijiuliuwu nian ba yue zhaokai de quanguo zongjiao gongzuo zuotan huishang de jianghua" ("The Speeches of Liu Chun and Xiao Xianfa at the August 1965 Meeting of the National Seminar on Religious Work"). Copy of handwritten manuscript, ca. 1989. 28 pp.

Hou Futong, ed. *Jindai Jiangsu zongjiao (Religion in Contemporary Jiangsu). Jiangsu wenshi ziliao xuanji (Selected Materials on Jiangsu Literature and History)*. No. 38. Nanjing: Jiangsu wenshi ziliao bianji chubanshe, 1990.

Jiang Wenhan (Kiang Wen-han). "Guang Xue Hui shi ze'yang de yige jigou?" ("What Kind of Organization Was the Christian Literature Society?"). *Wenshiziliao xuanji (Resources on Literature and History)* 43. Beijing: Wenshiziliao chubanshi, 1980. Pp. 1-42.

Kuang Yaming. *Qiusuji (Collected Writings)*. Beijing: Renmin chubanshe, 1995.

Kuo Siu-may (Guo Xiumei). *Han-Ying chengyu shouci (A Chinese-English Handbook of Idioms)*. Nanjing: Jiangsu renmin chubanshe, 1980.

Lam, Wing-hung. *Jindai huaren shenxue wenxian (A Sourcebook of Modern Chinese Theology)*. Hong Kong: China Graduate School of Theology, 1986.

―――. *Qugaohegua―Zhao Zichen de shengping ji shenxue (The Life and Thought of Chao Tzu-ch'en)*. Hongkong: China Alliance Press, 1994.

―――. *Zhonghua shenxue wushi nian-1900-1949 (A Half Century of Chinese Theology: 1900-1949)*. Hong Kong: China Graduate School Theology, 1998.

Leung Ka-lun. *Gaige kaifang yilai de zhongguo nongcun jiaohui (The Rural Churches of Mainland China since 1978)*. Hong Kong: Alliance Bible Seminary, 1999.

———. *Wushi niandai sanzi yundong de yanjiu (The Three-Self Patriotic Movement in the 1950s)*. Hong Kong: Alliance Bible Seminary, 1996.

———. *Wu Yaozong san lun* (*Y. T. Wu's Understandings of Christianity and Its Relation to Chinese Communism*). Hong Kong: Alliance Bible Seminary, 1996.

Li Xinyuan. "Yige 'buxinpai' de biaoben—*Ding Guangxun wenji* pingxi" ("A Classic Example of the 'Party of Unbelief'—A Critical Analysis of the Collected Works of Ding Guangxun"). *Shengming jikan* (*Christian Life Quarterly*) 4, nos. 2, 3 and 4 (2000): 23-29, 33-36, 15-20.

Li Weihan. *Tongyi zhanxian wenti yu minzu wenti* (*On Questions about the United Front and Nationalities*). Beijing: Renmin chubanshe, 1981.

Li Zhigang. *Jidujiao yu jindai Zhongguo wenhua lunwenji* (*Collected Essays on Christianity and Modern Chinese Culture*). Volumes 1 and 2. Taibei: Yuzhou guang publishers, 1989 and 1993.

Liu Huajun, ed. *Tian Feng Gan Yu: Zhongguo jidujiao lingxiu Ding Guangxun* (*Heavenly Wind and Sweet Rain: China's Christian Leader Ding Guangxun*). Nanjing: Nanjing daxue chubanshe, 2001.

Liu Xiaofeng. *Zhengjiu yu xiaoyao* (*Delivering and Dallying*). Revised edition. Shanghai: San Lian, 2001.

———. *Zou xiang shizijiashang de zhenli* (*Walking toward the Truth of the Cross*). Shanghai: San Lian, 1990.

Luo Bingxiang, and Zhao Dunhua, eds. *Jidujiao yu jindai zhong-xi wenhua* (*Christianity and Modern Sino-Western Culture*). Beijing: Beijing daxue chubanshe, 2000.

Luo Guangwu, ed. *Xin zhongguo zongjiao gongzuo da shi gailan, 1949-1999* (*An Overview of Major Events in Religious Work in New China, 1949-1999*). Beijing: Huawen chubanshe, 2001.

Luo Guanzong, ed. *Lun sanzi he jiaohui jianshe: Ding Guangxun zhujiao he zhongguo jidujiao lici huiyi wenjian you guan lunshu xuanbian, 1980-1995* (*On Three-Self and Church Building: Selected Conference Documents Expounding the Subject by Bishop K. H. Ting and the Chinese Church, 1980-1995*). Shanghai: TSPM/CCC, 1996.

———. *Qian shi bu wang, hou shi zhi shi:diguozhuyi liyong jidujiao qinlue Zhongguo shishi shuping* (*Remembering the Past as a Lesson for the Future: A Commentary on the Historical Facts of How Imperialism Used Christianity in Its Aggression against China*). Beijing: Zhongguo wenhua chubanshi, 2003.

——— et al., eds. *Sikao yu Xianshi* (*Thinking and Reality*). Shanghai: TSPM/CCC, 2002.

———, ed. *Wu Yaozong xiansheng yu sixiang yanjiu: jinian Wu Yaozong xiansheng sheng danchen 100 zhounian* (*Mr. Y. T. Wu and Research into His Thought: In Commemoration of the 100th Birthday of Mr. Y. T. Wu*). Shanghai: Zhongguo jidujiao sanzi aiguo yundong weiyuanhui, 1995.

———, ed. *Zhongguo jidujiao sanzi aigo yundong wenxuan* (*Selected Works of the Three-Self Patriotic Movement of the Protestant Churches of China*). Shanghai: Zhongguo jidujiao sanzi aiguo yundong weiyuanhui, 1993.

Luo Zhufeng, ed. *Zongjiao* (*Religion*). *Zhongguo da baike quanshu* (*The Great Chinese Encyclopedia*). Beijing and Shanghai: Zhongguo da baike quanshu chubanshe, 1988.

———. *Zhongguo shehui zhuyi shiqi de zongjiao wenti* (*The Religious Question in China's Socialist Period*). Shanghai: Shanghai shehui kexue chubanshe, 1987.

Ma Fayou. *Wenzhou jidujiaoshi* (*A History of Christianity in Wenzhou*). Hong Kong: Alliance Bible Seminary, 1998.

Ma Jia. *Ai shi zhenli* (*Discerning Truth through Love*). Hong Kong: Chinese Christian Literature Council, 2006.

Quangguo zongjiao xingzheng fagui guizhang huibian (*Compilation of National Religious Administrative Rules and Regulations*). Edited by the Policy and Regulation Department of the Religious Affairs Bureau. Beijing: Zongjiao wenhua chubanshe, 1999.

Ruan Renze, and Gao Zhennong, eds. *Shanghai Zongjiao shi* (*A History of Religion in Shanghai*). Shanghai: Shanghai renmin chubanshe, 1992.

Ruokanen, Miikka, and Paulos Huang, eds. *Jidu zongjiao yu zhongguo wenhua: guanyu zhongguo chujing shenxue de zhong-beiou huiyi lunwenji* (*Christianity and Chinese Culture: Papers from a Sino-Nordic Conference on Chinese Contextual Theology*). Beijing: Zhongguo shehui kexue chubanshe, 2004.

Shen Cheng'en, ed. *Zhongguo jidujiao sanzi aiguo yundong 50 zhounian jinian yingji* (*Commemorative Photo Album of the 50th Anniversary of the Three-Self Patriotic Movement of the Protestant Churches in China*). Shanghai: TSPM/CCC, 2000.

Shen Derong. *Wu Yaozong xiao zhuan* (*A Short Biography of Wu Yaozong*). Shanghai: TSPM, 1989.

———. *Zai sanzi gongzuo wushi nian* (*Fifty Years Working for Three-Self*). Shanghai: TSPM/CCC, 1999.

Shen Mo. "Yi wei shenxueyuan jiangshi weihe bei kai chu?" ("Why has a Seminary Lecturer Been Fired?"). *Shengming jijan* (*Christian Life Quarterly*) 4, no. 4 (2000): 22-26.

Shen Mingcui. "Yi ci you lishi yiyi de huiyi" ("A Meeting with Historical Significance"). *Tian Feng* 1 (20 October 1980): 9-10.

Shen Yifan. *Jiangtai shi feng: Shen Yifan zhujiao wenji* (*Service in the Pulpit: Collected Writings of Bishop Shen Yifan*). Volume 1. Shanghai: China Christian Council, 1996.

———. *Luntan xinsheng: Shen Yifan zhujiao wenji* (*Forum of the Heart: Collected Writings of Bishop Shen Yifan*). Volume 2. Shanghai: China Christian Council, 2000.

Sun Liping. "Tiaozheng liyi guanxi yu zhuanhuan zengzhang moshi" ("Adjust Profit Relationships and Transform the Pattern of Growth"). Unpublished manuscript, presented as a speech at the Twentieth Anniversary Symposium of the Amity Foundation, Nanjing, 7 November 2005.

Tang Zhongmo. *Xiandai shengjing guan* (*A Modern View of the Bible*). Shanghai: China Christian Council, 2000.

Wang Bangzuo, ed. *Zhongguo gongchandang tongyi zhanxian shi* (*A History of the United Front in China*). Shanghai: People's Publishers, 1991.

Wang Min, ed. *Shanghai xuesheng yundong dashi ji, 1919.5-1949.9* (*Chronology of the Shanghai Student Movement, May 1919 to September 1949*), Shanghai: Shanghai Communist Youth League/Youth Movement History Faculty, 1985.

Wang Mingdao. *Wang Mingdao wenku: weidao* (*Treasures of Wang Mingdao: On Guard*). Touliu: Conservative Baptist Press, 1984.

———. *Women shi weile xinyang!* (*We Because of Faith!*). Undated. 39 pp.

Wang Ruoshui. *Wei rendaozhuyi bianhu* (*In Defense of Humanism*). Beijing: San Lian Publishers, 1986.

Wang Weifan. "Tan ban hao jiaohui yu shenxue sixiang jianshe" ("On Running the Church Well and Theological Reconstruction." Unpublished manuscript (third draft), 4 May 2002. 7 pp.

———. "Shengjing yiben zai zhongguo" ("Bible Translation in China") *Zongjiao yu wenhua (Religion and Culture)* (1992): 71-84.

———. "Ye tan Zhongguo Makesi zhuyi zongjiaoguan de 'shiyinglun'" ("Another Talk on 'Adaptation' in the Chinese Marxist View of Religion"). Unpublished manuscript, 8 September 2004. 11 pp.

Wang Xiaochao, ed. *Zhao Zichen xiansheng jinian wenji (Festschrift for Mr T. C. Chao)*. Beijing: Zongjiao wenhua chubanshe, 2005.

Wang Zhiyuan, ed. *Jinri zhongguo zongjiao (Religion in China Today)*. Beijing: Jinri Zhonguo chubanshe, 1994.

Wang Zuo'an. *Zhongguo de zongjiao wenti he zongjiao zhengce (China's Religious Question and Religious Policy)*. Beijing: Zongjiao wenhua chubanshe, 2003.

Wenhua jidutu: xianxiang yu lunzheng (Cultural Christians: Phenomenon and Argument). Hong Kong: Institute of Sino-Christian Studies, 1997.

Wu Yaozong (Y. T. Wu), ed. *Jidujiao yu xin zhongguo (Christianity and New China)*. Second edition. Shanghai: Association Press, 1948.

———, ed. *Jidujiao gexin yundong xuexi shouci (A Study Manual of the Christian Reform Movement)*. Shanghai: YMCA Bookstore, 1952.

———. *Jidujiao jianghua (Talks on Christianity)*. Shanghai: Qingnian Xiehui Shuju, 1950.

———. *Meiyou ren kanjianguo shangdi (No Man Hath Seen God)*. Shanghai: Qingnian Xiehui Shuju, 1946.

———. *Shehui fuyin (Social Gospel)*. Shanghai: Qingnian Xiehui Shuju, 1934.

Xin shiqi zongjiao gongzuo wenxian xuanbian (Selected Documents on Religious Work in the New Period). Edited by Zhonggong zhongyang wenxianyanjiu shi zonghe yanjiu zu (CPC Central Committee Documentary Research Faculty of the Comprehensive Research Group) and Guowuyuan zongjiao zhiwujü zhengce fagui si (Policy, Law and Regulations Department of the State Council Religious Affairs Bureau). Beijing: Zongjiao wenhua chubanshe, 1995.

Xu Jiatun. *Xu Jiatun Xianggang huiyi lu (The Hong Kong Memoirs of Xu Jiatun)*. Hong Kong: Xianggang lianhe bao, 1994. Vol. II.

Xu Rulei. "Ruhe zhengque renshi zongjiao zai dong ou jibian zhong de zuoyong" ("A Correct Understanding of the Role of Religion in the Changes in Eastern Europe." *Yanjiu dongtai (Research Trends)*. 10 December 1992 (4). Pp. 20-28.

Ying Fuk-tsang. *Dangdai zhongguo zhengjiao guanxi (Church-State Relations in Contemporary China)*. Hong Kong: China Alliance Press, 1999.

Yip Ching-wah (Francis). *Xun zhen qiu quan: zhongguo shenxue yu zhengjiao chujing chutan (Chinese Theology in a Church-State Context: A Preliminary Study)*. Hong Kong: Christian Study Center on Chinese Religion and Culture, 1997.

Yao Minchuan, *Shanghai jidujiaoshi,1843-1949 (A History of Christianity in Shanghai, 1843-1949)*. Shanghai: Shanghai Christian Council and TSPM Committee, 1993.

Ye Xiaowen. *Cong xin kaishi de jiao bu (Steps towards Harmony Begin in the Mind)*. Beijing: Zongjiao wenhua chubanshe, 2006.

Yi Yang. "Ding Guangxun tan 'shangdi zhi ai' yu 'aiguo zhuyi'" ("Ding Guangxun

Talks about the 'Love of God" and 'Patriotism'"). *Zhonghua ernü* 167, no. 4 (2001): 4-9.

Ying Yuandao. *Jidujiao de kongsu yundong* (*The Christian Denunciation Movement*). Shanghai: Qingnian hui, 1958.

Zhang gan ji (*The Shepherd's Staff*). Supplement to *Jiao Cai* (*Curriculum*). Nanjing: Nanjing Union Theological Seminary, July 1986.

Zhang Kaiyuan. *Chuanbo yu Zhigen: Jidujiao yu zhong-xi wenhua jiaoliu lunji* (*Mission and Rooting: Essays on Christianity and Sino-Western Cultural Exchange*). Guangzhou: Guangdong renmin chubanshe, 2005.

Zhang Xiping, and Zhuo Xinping, eds. *Bense zhi tan: 20 shiji zhongguo jidujiao wenhua lunwenji* (*Seeking Indigenization: A Collection of Essays on Chinese Christian Culture*). Beijing: Zhongguo guangbo dianshi chubanshe, 1999.

Zhang Zhiyi. *Shilun Zhongguo renmin minzhu tongyi zhanxian* (*On the Chinese People's Democratic United Front*). Beijing: Renmin chubanshe, 1958.

Zhao Puchu. "Guanyu chuxi di sanjie shijie zongjiaozhe heping huiyi qingquang de baogao" ("A Report on Participating in the Third World Conference on Religion and Peace"). *Zongjiao* 2, no. 1 (1980): 23-27.

"Zhao Puchu jushi shengping dashi nianbiao (zhengqiu yijian gao)" ("Chronology of Major Events in the Life of Zhao Puchu [Draft for Comment]"). Undated typescript, ca. 2003. Beijing.

Zhao Puchu. *Zhao Puchu yun wenji* (*Collected Poems of Zhao Puchu*). Edited by Chen Bangyan. 2 vols. Shanghai: Guji chubanshe, 2003.

Zhao Zhi'en. *Jianchi zhenli, dizhi yiduan* (*Uphold Truth and Resist Heterodoxy*). Shanghai: TSPM/CCC, 1996.

Zhao Zichen wenji. Volumes 1-3. Beijing: Commercial Press, 2003, and following.

Zhao Zichen zongjiao sixiang guoji xueshu yanjiuhui (*Symposium on Zhao Zichen's Religious Thought*). Beijing: Tsinghua University, 21-22 April 2004.

Zhi Huaxin, ed. *Wenzhou jidujiao* (*Wenzhou Christianity*). Hangzhou: Zhejiang sheng jidujiao xiehui chuban, 1993.

Zhongguo jidujiao di liu jie quanguo huiyi zhuanji (*Records of the Sixth National Chinese Christian Conference*). Shanghai: TSPM and CCC, 1997.

Zhongguo jidujiao di qi ci daibiao huiyi zhuanji (*Records of the Seventh National Chinese Christian Conference*). Shanghai: TSPM and CCC, 2002.

Zhongguo jidujiao di si jie quanguo huiyi zhuanji (*Records of the Fourth Chinese National Christian Conference*). Shanghai: TSPM/CCC Committee, 1986.

Zhongguo jidujiao di wu jie quanguo hui zhuanji (*Records of the Fifth National Chinese Christian Conference*). Shanghai: TSPM and CCC, 1992.

Zhongguo jidujiao sanzi aiguo yundong weiyuanhui (The Committee of the Chinese Christian Three-Self Patriotic Movement of the Protestant Churches of China), ed. *Huiyi Wu Yaozong xiansheng* (*In Memory of Mr. Wu Yaozong*). Shanghai: Zhongguo jidujiao sanzi aiguo yundong weiyuanhui, 1982.

———, ed. *Wu Yaozong xiansheng shishi shi zhounian jinian wenji* (*Commemorative Writings on the Tenth Anniversary of the Death of Mr. Y. T. Wu*). Shanghai: Zhongguo jidujiao sanzi aiguo yundong weiyuanhui, 1989.

Zhongguo jidujiao shengshi weiyuanhui (Chinese Christian Sacred Music Committee). *Zanmei shi: xinbian* (*New Hymns of Praise*). Shanghai: Zhongguo jidujiao xiehui, 1983.

Zhongguo jidujiao xiehui, ed. *Jidujiao yaodao wenda* (*A Christian Catechism*). Nanjing, 1983.

Zhou Enlai tongyizhanxian wenxuan (Selected Writings of Zhou Enlai on the United Front). Beijing: Renmin chubanshe, 1984.

Zhou Jiacai. *Zhao Puchu yu Jiangsu zongjiao (Zhao Puchu and Religion in Jiangsu)*. Beijing: Zongjiao wenhua chubanshe, 2003.

Zhu Yueli, ed. *Jinri zhongguo zongjiao (Religion in Today's China)*. Beijing: Xinhua Publishers, 1994.

6. BOOKS AND ESSAYS IN ENGLISH AND OTHER WESTERN LANGUAGES

A Brief History of the Student Christian Movement in Canada, 1921-1974. Toronto: SCM, 1975.

A Community of Memory and Hope. Geneva: WSCF, 1992.

Adeney, David H. *China: The Church's Long March*. Robesonia, Pa.: OMF Books, 1985.

Adler, Elizabeth, ed. *Memoirs and Diaries: 1895-1990*. Geneva: WSCF, 1994.

Aikman, David. *Jesus in Beijing: How Christianity Is Transforming China and Changing the Global Balance of Power*. Washington: Regnery Publishing, 2003.

All Around Shanghai and the Environs. Shanghai: University Press, 1934-1935.

. . . *And on Earth Peace: Documents of the First All-Christian Peace Assembly, Prague, 13th-18th June 1961*.

Auden, W. H. *The English Auden: Poems, Essays and Dramatic Writings, 1927-1939*. Edited by Edward Mendelson. London: Faber & Faber, 1977.

Anderson, Gerald H. et al. *Mission Legacies: Biographical Studies of the Modern Missionary Movement*. Maryknoll, N.Y.: Orbis Books, 1998.

Baker, Kevin. *A History of the Orthodox Church in China, Korea and Japan*. Lewiston, Queenston, Lampeter: Edwin Mellen Press, 2006.

Barmé, Geremie. *In the Red: On Contemporary Chinese Culture*. New York: Columbia University Press, 1999.

———, and Bennett Lee, trans. and ed. *The Wounded: New Stories of the Cultural Revolution*. Hong Kong: Joint Publishers, 1979.

———, and John Minford, trans. and ed. *Seeds of Fire: Chinese Voices of Conscience*. Hong Kong: Far Eastern Economic Review, 1986.

Barnett, A. Doak, ed. *Chinese Communist Politics in Action*. Seattle: University of Washington Press, 1969.

Baum, Gregory. *The Church for Others: Protestant Theology in Communist East Germany*. Grand Rapids: Eerdmans, 1996.

Baum, Richard. "The Fifteenth National Party Congress: Jiang Takes Command?" *The China Quarterly* 153 (March 1998): 141-56.

———. "The Road to Tiananmen: Chinese Politics in the 1980s." In *The Politics of China: The Eras of Mao and Deng*, 340-471. Edited by Roderick MacFarquhar. Second edition. Cambridge: Cambridge University Press, 1997.

Bays, Daniel H. "Chinese Protestant Christianity Today." *China Quarterly* 174 (June 2003): 488-504.

———, ed. *Christianity in China: From the Eighteenth Century to the Present*. Stanford: Stanford University Press, 1996.

———. "The Growth of Independent Christianity in China, 1900-1937." *Christianity in China: From the Eighteenth Century to the Present*, 307-17. Edited by Daniel Bays. Stanford: Stanford University Press, 1996.

Becker, Jasper. *Hungry Ghosts: Mao's Secret Famine.* New York: Free Press, 1996.

Bei Dao (Zhao Zhenkai). "Tomorrow, No." Translated by Bonnie McDougall. *Renditions* 19 and 20 (Spring and Autumn 1983): 195.

Bergere, Marie-Claire. *The Golden Age of the Chinese Bourgeoisie, 1911-1937.* Cambridge: Cambridge University Press, 1989.

Brook, Timothy. "Dying Gods in China." *Commonweal* 105, no. 15 (4 August 1978): 490-95.

———. "Toward Independence: Christianity in China Under Japanese Occupation, 1937-1956." Unpublished manuscript prepared for the History of Christianity in China Project, 1990.

———. "Travelling to the Trigram Mountains: Buddhism After the Gang of Four." *Contemporary China* 2, no. 4 (Winter 1978): 70-75

———, and B. Michael Frolic, eds. *Civil Society in China.* Armonk, N.Y.: M. E. Sharpe, 1997.

Brown, G. Thompson. *Christianity in the People's Republic of China.* Revised Edition. Atlanta: John Knox Press, 1986.

Brown, Terry M. "Metacosmesis: The Christian Marxism of Frederic Hastings Smyth and the Society of the Catholic Commonwealth." Ph.D. diss., University of Toronto, 1987.

Burklin, Werner. *Jesus Never Left China: The Rest of the Story.* Enumclaw, Wash.: Pleasant World, 2005.

Buege, Gerda. "Are We Trying to Understand the Christians in China?" *Ecumenical Review* 17 (January 1965): 54-61.

Bush, Richard. *Religion in Communist China.* Nashville and New York: Abingdon, 1970.

"Carter Reveals Private Talk with Chinese Leader." *Kentucky Baptist Convention* 158, no. 26 (26 June 1984): 1.

CCA Consultation with Church Leaders from China. Christian Conference of Asia: Hong Kong, 1981.

Chadwick, Owen. *The Christian Church in the Cold War.* London: Penguin Books, 1993.

Chan Cheris Shun-ching. "The *Falun Gong* in China: A Sociological Perspective." *The China Quarterly* 179 (September 2004): 665-83.

Chan Kim-kwong. *Struggling for Survival: The Catholic Church in China from 1949 to 1970.* Hong Kong: Christian Study Center on Chinese Religion and Culture, 1992.

———, and Eric R. Carlson. *Religious Freedom in China: Policy, Administration, And Regulation; a Research Handbook.* Santa Barbara: Institute for the Study of American Religion, 2005.

———, and Alan Hunter. "New Light on Religious Policy in the PRC." *Issues and Studies* 31, no. 2 (February 1995): 21-22.

Chan Hon S. "Christianity in Post-Mao China." *Issues and Studies* 29, no. 3 (March 1993): 106-32.

Chang Maria Hsia. *Falun Gong: The End of Days.* New Haven and London: Yale University Press, 2004.

Chang, Jung and Jon Halliday, *Mao: The Unknown Story.* New York: Knopf, 2005.

Chao, Jonathan. *Wise as Serpents, Innocent as Doves: Christians in China Tell Their Story.* Pasadena, Ca.: William Carey Library, 1988.

Cheek, Timothy. "From Priests to Professionals: Intellectuals and the State Under the CCP." In *Popular Protest and Political Culture in Modern China: Learning from 1989*, 124-45. Edited by Jeffrey N. Wasserstrom and Elizabeth J. Perry. Boulder, Colo.: Westview Press, 1992.

Chen Chi Rong. *Wu Yao-Tsung: Ein Theologe im Sozialistischen China*. Munster and Hamburg: LiT Verlag, 1991.

Chen Fu Tien. *The Current Religious Policy of the People's Republic of China (January 1, 1976-March 15, 1979): Part I: An Inquiry*. Norwalk, Conn., 1983.

Chinese Communist Party Central Committee, ed. *History of the Chinese Communist Party—A Chronology of Events (1919-1990)*. Beijing: Foreign Languages Press, 1991.

Christianity and the New China. Volume 1. *Theological Implications of the New China*. (Papers Presented at the Ecumenical Seminar Held in Båstad, Sweden, 29 January to 2 February 1974). Volume 2. *Christian Faith and the Chinese Experience*. (Papers and Reports from an Ecumenical Colloquium held in Louvain, Belgium, 9-14 September 1974). South Pasadena, Ca.: Ecclesia Publications, 1976.

Chu, Theresa and Christopher Lind, eds. *God's Call to a New Beginning: An International Dialogue with the Chinese Church*. Toronto: Canada China Programme, 1981.

The Church in China. London: British Council of Churches, 1983.

Ci Jiwei. *Dialectic of the Chinese Revolution: from Utopianism to Hedonism*. Stanford: Stanford University Press, 1994.

Clark, William H. *The Church in China: Its Vitality, Its Future*. New York: Council Press, 1970.

Clifford, Nicholas. *Spoilt Children of Empire: Westerners in Shanghai and the Chinese Revolution of the 1920s*. Hanover and London: University Press of New England, 1991.

Confucius. *The Analects* (*Lün yü*). Translated by D. C. Lau. Hong Kong: Chinese University Press, 1992.

Collar, Hugh. *Captive in Shanghai: A Story of Internment in World War II*. Hong Kong: Oxford University Press, 1990.

Commission of the Churches on International Affairs. *Ecumenical Team Visit to China, 5-18 May 1996*. Geneva: World Council of Churches, 1996.

Covell, Ralph. "Why I Don't Pray for China to Open." *Evangelical Missions Quarterly* 31, no. 1 (January 1995): 14-18.

Cross, F. L., and E. A. Livingstone, eds. *The Oxford Dictionary of the Christian Church*. Third edition. Oxford: Oxford University Press, 1997.

Cumings, Bruce. *Korea's Place in the Sun: A Modern History*. New York and London: W. W. Norton, 1997.

Deng Xiaoping. *Fundamental Issues in Present Day China*. Beijing: Foreign Languages Press, 1987.

———. *Selected Works of Deng Xiaoping (1975-1982)*. Beijing: Foreign Language Press, 1984.

Digan, Parig. *The Christian China Watchers: A Post-Mao Perspective*. Brussels: Pro Mundi Vita, 1978.

Donnelly, Mary Rose, and Heather Dau, *Katherine: Katherine Boehner Hockin, a Biography*. Winfield, B.C.: Woodlate Books, 1992.

Dunch, Ryan. "Protestants and the State in Post-Mao China." M.A. thesis, University of British Columbia, 1991.

EATWOT Visits China, May 2-13, 1986. Manila: Ecumenical Association of Third World Theologians, 1986.

Edwards, David L., ed. *Robert Runcie: A Portrait by His Friends.* London: Harper Collins, 1990.

Elvin, Mark, and G. William Skinner, eds. *The Chinese City Between Two Worlds.* Stanford: Stanford University Press, 1974.

Endicott, Mary Austin. *Five Stars Over China: The Story of Our Return to New China.* Toronto, 1953.

Endicott, Stephen. *James G. Endicott: Rebel Out of China.* Toronto: University of Toronto Press, 1980.

————, and Donald Willmott. "Canadian Missionaries and the Chinese Revolution of 1949: The Sympathetic Observers." Unpublished manuscript, 1994. 27 pp.

England, John, Jose Kuttianimattathil, sdb, John M. Pryor svd, Lily Quintos, rc, David Suh Kwang-sun and Janice K. Wickeri, eds. *Asian Christian Theologies: A Research Guide to Authors, Movements, Sources.* Volume 3. *Northeast Asia.* Maryknoll, N.Y.: Orbis Books, 2004.

Evans, Robert A., and Alice Frazer Evans. *Human Rights: A Dialogue Between the First and Third Worlds.* Maryknoll, N.Y.: Orbis Books, 1983.

Fällman, Frederick. *Salvation and Modernity: Intellectuals and Faith in Contemporary China,* Chinese Culture Series 2. Stockholm: Stockholm University, Department of Oriental Languages, 2004.

Fewsmith, Joseph. *China since Tiananmen: The Politics of Transition.* Cambridge: Cambridge University Press, 2001.

————. "The Sixteenth National Party Congress: The Succession That Didn't Happen." *China Quarterly* 173 (March 2003): 1-16.

Fielder, Katrin, and Liwei Zhang, eds. *Growing in Partnership: The Amity Foundation, 1985-2005.* Nanjing: The Amity Foundation, 2005.

Fishman, Todd C. *China, Inc.: How the Rise of the Next Superpower Challenges America and the World.* New York: Scribner, 2005.

Freytag, Walter. "Meeting Christians in China." *International Review of Mission* 46 (1957): 410-16.

Fung, Raymond. *Households of God on China's Soil.* Geneva: World Council of Churches, 1982.

Fu Poshek. *Passivity, Resistance and Collaboration: Intellectual Choices in Occupied Shanghai, 1937-1945.* Stanford: Stanford University Press, 1993.

Gaddis, John Lewis. *The Cold War: A New History.* New York: Penguin Press, 2005.

Garside, Roger. *Coming Alive: China after Mao.* New York: New American Library, 1981.

Glüer, Winfried. *Christliche Theologie in China: T. C. Chao: 1918-1956.* Gütersloh: Gütersloher Verlagshaus Mohn, 1979.

————. "T. C. Chao: Scholar, Teacher and Gentle Mystic." In *Mission Legacies: Biographical Studies of the Modern Missionary Movement,* 225-31. Edited by Gerald H. Anderson, et al. Maryknoll, N.Y.: Orbis Books, 1998.

Goldman, Merle. *Literary Dissent in Communist China.* Cambridge: Harvard University Press, 1967.

————, with Timothy Cheek and Carol Lee Hamrin, eds. *Chinese Intellectuals and the State: In Search of a New Relationship.* Cambridge: Harvard University Press, 1987.

————, and Leo Ou-Fan Lee, eds. *An Intellectual History of Modern China*. Cambridge: Cambridge University Press, 2002.

Gore, Charles. "The Brotherhood of St. Andrew." In *St. Paul's Epistle to the Ephesians*. London: John Murray, 1898.

Gorringe, Tim. *Alan Ecclestone: Priest as Revolutionary*. Sheffield: Cairns Publications, 1994.

Gray, Arthur R., and Arthur M. Sherman. *The Story of the Church in China*. New York: Domestic and Foreign Missionary Society, 1913.

Gray, G. F. S., with Martha Lund Smalley. *Anglicans in China: A History of the Zhonghua Shenggong Hui (Chung Hua Sheng Kung Hui)*. New Haven: Episcopal China Mission History Project, 1996.

Haight, Amanda. *Anna Akhmatova: A Poetic Pilgrimage*. Oxford and New York: Oxford University Press, 1990.

Hall, R. O. *T. Z. Koo: Chinese Christianity Speaks to the West*. London: SCM Press, 1950.

Han Minzhu, ed. *Cries for Democracy: Writings and Speeches from the 1989 Democracy Movement*. Princeton: Princeton University Press, 1990.

Han, Suyin. *Eldest Son: Zhou Enlai and the Making of Modern China, 1898-1976*. London: Jonathan Cape, 1994.

Handy, Robert T. *A History of Union Theological Seminary in New York*. New York: Columbia University Press, 1987.

Harvey, Thomas Alan. *Acquainted with Grief: Wang Mingdao's Stand for the Persecuted Church in China*. Grand Rapids: Brazos Press, 2003.

Hattaway, Paul. *Back to Jerusalem: Three Chinese House Church Leaders Share Their Vision to Complete the Great Commission*. Carlisle: Gabriel Publishing, 2003.

————. *The Heavenly Man: The Remarkable True Story of Chinese Christian Brother Yun*. Woodstock, GA: Monarch Publishing, 2003.

Henriot, Christian and Wen-hsin Yeh, eds. *In the Shadow of the Rising Sun: Shanghai under Japanese Occupation*. Cambridge: Cambridge University Press, 2004.

Henson, H. Hensley. *The Oxford Group Movement*. New York: Oxford University Press, 1933.

Hockin, Katherine. "Canadian Openness to the Chinese Church." *International Review of Mission* 71(July 1982): 368-78.

————. *Servants of God in People's China*. New York: Friendship Press, 1962.

Honig, Emily. *Sisters and Strangers: Women in the Shanghai Cotton Mills, 1919-1949*. Stanford: Stanford University Press, 1986.

Hood, George A. *Neither Bang Nor Whimper: The End of a Missionary Era in China*. Singapore: Presbyterian Church in Singapore, 1991.

Hromádka, Joseph L. *The Church and Theology in Today's Troubled Times*. Prague: Ecumenical Council of Churches, 1956.

Hu Guotai. "The Struggle Between the Kuomintang and the Chinese Communist Party on Campus During the War of Resistance, 1937-1945." *China Quarterly* 118 (June 1989): 300-323.

Hunter, Alan and Kim-Kwong Chan. *Protestantism in Contemporary China*. Cambridge: Cambridge University Press, 1993.

Jack, Homer. "Some Notes on the Re-emergence Today of the Religions of China." Unpublished typescript. 30 September 1980. 36 pp.

James, Francis, ed. *Reports on the Deputation of Australian Churchmen to Mainland China.* Sydney: Anglican News Service, 1956.

Jiang Wen-han (Jiang Wenhan). *The Chinese Student Movement.* New York: King's Crown Press, 1948.

The Johannean. Shanghai, 1934.

Johnson, E. H. "Challenge of the New China, Report of a Visit to China, 23 March-14 April 1973." Unpublished manuscript. 13 pp.

———. "K. H. Ting: Profile of a Chinese Christian." *One World* 16 (May 1976): 23-24.

———. "Notes on the Church in China." private paper, 1973. 12 pp.

Johnson, Hewlett. *China's New Creative Age.* London: Lawrence & Wishart, 1953.

———. *The Upsurge of China.* Peking: New World Press, 1961.

Jonson, Jonas. "A Documentation of My Encounters with Religious Life in the People's Republic of China, May 1978." Unpublished manuscript, 9 pp.

Jones, Francis Price. *The Church in Communist China: A Protestant Appraisal.* New York: Friendship Press, 1962.

———. "Theological Thinking in the Chinese Protestant Church under Communism." *Religion in Life* 32, no. 4 (Autumn 1963): 534-40.

Jones, Susan Mann. "The Ningpo *Pang* and Financial Power in Shanghai." In *The Chinese City Between Two Worlds,* 74-96. Edited by Mark Elvin and G. William Skinner. Stanford: Stanford University Press, 1974.

Joseph, William A. *The Critique of Ultra-Leftism in China, 1958-1981.* Stanford: Stanford University Press, 1984.

Kampen, Thomas. "The Secret Life of Pastor Wang," *CCP Research Newsletter* 2 (Spring 1989): 7-8.

Keith, Ronald C., and Zhiqiu Lin. "The '*Falun Gong* Problem': Politics and the Struggle for the Rule of Law in China." *The China Quarterly* 175 (September 2003): 623-42.

Kinnamon, Michael, ed. *Signs of the Spirit: Official Report of the Seventh Assembly.* Geneva: WCC Publications, 1991.

Kindopp, Jason. "The Politics of Protestantism in Contemporary China: State Control, Civil Society and Social Movement in a Single Party State." Ph.D. diss., George Washington University, 2004.

———, and Carol Lee Hamrin, eds. *God and Caesar in China: Policy Implications of Church-State Tensions.* Washington: Brookings Institutions Press, 2004.

Kirby, William C. *Realms of Freedom in Modern China.* Stanford: Stanford University Press, 2004.

Kuhn, Robert Lawrence. *The Man Who Changed China: The Life and Legacy of Jiang Zemin.* New York: Crown Publishers, 2005.

Kuo Siu-may. *Journeying through the Bible.* Nanjing: Nanjing University Press, 1990.

———. *Venturing into the Bible.* Nanjing: Nanjing University Press, 1989.

———. "Why I Don't Retire." *U.S.–China Review* 7, no. 6 (November-December 1983): 14-15, 29.

Ladany, Lazlo. "The Church in China Seen in December 1980." Unpublished manuscript distributed by *China News Analysis.*

———. *The Communist Party of China and Marxism, 1921-1985: A Self Portrait.* Hong Kong: Hong Kong University Press, 1992.

Lam, Anthony S. K. *The Catholic Church in Present-Day China: Through Darkness and Light.* Translated by Peter Barry and Norman Walling. Leuven and Hong Kong: Ferdinand Verbiest Foundation and the Holy Spirit Study Center, 1994.

Lambert, Anthony. *China's Christian Millions: The Costly Revival*. London: Monarch Books, 1999.

———. *The Resurrection of the Chinese Church*. London: Hodder & Stoughton, 1991.

Lamberton, Mary. *St. John's University, Shanghai, 1879-1951*. New York: United Board for Christian Colleges in China, 1955.

Lapwood, Ralph, and Nancy Lapwood. *Through the Chinese Revolution*. London: Spalding & Levy, 1954.

Latourette, K. S. *A History of Christian Missions in China*. London: S.P.C.K., 1929.

Lee, Joseph Tse-Hu. "Watchman Nee and the Little Flock in Maoist China." *Church History* 74, no. 1 (March 2005): 68-96.

Lee, Lydia. *A Living Sacrifice: The Life Story of Allen Yuan*. Kent: Sovereign Word, 2001.

Leung, Beatrice. "China's Religious Freedom Policy: The Art of Managing Religious Activity." *The China Quarterly* 184 (December 2005): 894-913.

———. *Sino-Vatican Relationships: Problems in Conflicting Authority, 1976-1986*. Cambridge: Cambridge University Press, 1992.

Li Sao and Other Poems of Ch'ü Yuan (Qu Yuan). Translated by Hsien-yi and Galdys Yang. Beijing: Foreign Languages Press, 1955.

Li Xinyuan *Theological Construction—or Deconstruction: An Analysis of the Theology of Bishop K. H. Ting (Ding Guangxun)*. Streamwood, Ill., and Mountain View, Ca.: Christian Life Press and Great Commission Center International, 2003.

Lieberthal, Kenneth. *Governing China: From Revolution Through Reform*. New York and London: Norton, 1995.

Lin, Manhong Melissa. "A Modern Chinese Journey of Inculturation." *International Review of Mission* (1998, no. 1): 9-24.

———. "Toward a Chinese Christian Ethic: Individual, Community and Society." Ph.D. diss., Graduate Theological Union, 2006.

Link, Perry, Richard Madsen and Paul G. Pickowicz, eds. *Unofficial China: Popular Culture and Thought in the People's Republic*. Boulder, Colo.: Westview Press, 1989.

Loeb, Leo. "Yang Huilin and His View of Christian Culture." *Interreligio* 38 (Winter 2000): 57-63.

Lotz, Denton, ed. *Spring Has Returned . . . Listening to the Church in China*. McLean, Va.: Baptist World Alliance, 1986.

Luo, Zhufeng, ed. *Religion under Socialism in China*. Translated by Donald E. MacInnis and Zheng Xi'an. Armonk, N.Y.: M. E. Sharpe, 1991.

Lutz, Jessie G. *China and the Christian Colleges, 1850-1950*. Ithaca: Cornell University Press, 1971.

MacFarquhar, Roderick, ed. *The Politics of China: The Eras of Mao and Deng*, Second edition. Cambridge: Cambridge University Press, 1997.

———. *The Origins of the Cultural Revolution*. 3 vols. New York: Columbia University, Press, 1974, 1983, 1997.

———, and John K. Fairbank, eds. *The Cambridge History of China*. Volume 14: *The People's Republic, Part I: The Emergence of Revolutionary China, 1949-1965*. Cambridge: Cambridge University Press, 1987.

———, and John K. Fairbank, eds. *The Cambridge History of China*. Volume 15: *The People's Republic, Part II: Revolutions within the Chinese Revolution, 1966-1982*. Cambridge: Cambridge University Press, 1991.

————, and Michael Schoenhals. *Mao's Last Revolution*. Cambridge and London: Harvard University Press, 2006.

MacInnis, Don. *Religion in China Today: Policy and Practice*. Maryknoll, N.Y.: Orbis Books, 1989.

————. *Religious Practice and Policy in Communist China*. New York: MacMillan, 1972.

Madsen, Richard. *China and the American Dream: A Moral Inquiry*. Berkeley: University of California Press, 1995.

————. *China's Catholics: Tragedy and Hope in an Emerging Civil Society*. Berkeley: University of California Press, 1998.

————, and James Tong, eds. "Local Religious Policy in China, 1980-1997." *Chinese Law and Government* 33, no. 3 (May/June 2000).

Mao Zedong. *Selected Works*. 4 vols. Beijing: Foreign Languages Press, 1967-1977.

Marsden, George. *Understanding Fundamentalism and Evangelicalism*. Grand Rapids: Eerdmans, 1991.

Merwin, Wallace C., and Francis P. Jones, eds. *Documents of the Three-Self Movement: Source Materials for the Study of the Protestant Church in Communist China*. New York: National Council of the Churches of Christ in the U.S.A., 1963.

Myers, James T. *Enemies without Guns: The Catholic Church in the People's Republic of China*. New York: Paragon House, 1991.

Nanjing '86: Ecumenical Sharing, A New Agenda: An Ecumenical Conference, May 14-20, Nanjing, China. New York: NCCCUSA and Maryknoll, 1986.

Niebuhr, Reinhold. *Moral Man and Immoral Society: A Study in Ethics and Politics*. New York: Scribner's, 1932.

Ng Lee-ming. "Christianity and Social Change in China, 1920-1950." Ph.D. diss., Princeton Theological Seminary, 1970.

————. "An Evaluation of T. C. Chao's Thought." *Ching Feng* 14, no. 1 (1971): 5-59.

————. "A Study of Y. T. Wu." *Ching Feng* 15, no. 1 (1972): 5-54.

Ngai Pun. *Made in China: Women Factory Workers in a Global Marketplace*. Hong Kong: Duke University Press and Hong Kong University Press, 2005.

Norman, E. R. *Church and Society in England, 1770-1970*. Oxford: Clarendon Press, 1976.

Ogden, Suzanne, Kathleen Hartford, Lawrence Sullivan and David Zweig, eds. *China's Search for Democracy: The Student Movement of 1989*. Armonk, N.Y.: M. E. Sharpe, 1992.

Oksenberg, Michael, Lawrence R. Sullivan and Marc Lambert, eds. *Beijing Spring, 1989: Confrontation and Conflict: The Basic Documents* (Armonk, N.Y.: M. E. Sharpe, 1992.

Opočenský, Milan. *From the Reformation to Tomorrow: Joseph L. Hromádka (1889-1969)*. Geneva: World Alliance of Reformed Churches, 1999.

Pachter, Marc. *Telling Lives: The Biographer's Art*. Washington: New Republic Books, 1979.

Pas, Julian, ed. *The Turning of the Tide: Religion in China Today*. Hong Kong: Hong Kong Branch of the Royal Asiatic Society, 1989.

Paton, David M. *Christian Missions and the Judgment of God*. Second Edition. Grand Rapids and Cambridge: William B. Eerdmans, 1996.

————. *"R. O.": The Life and Times of Bishop Hall of Hong Kong*. Hong Kong: The Diocese of Hong Kong and Macao and the Hong Kong Diocesan Association, 1985.

Patterson, George. *Christianity in Communist China.* Waco, Tex.: Word Books, 1969.

Paterson, Ross, and Elisabeth Farrell. *China: The Hidden Miracle.* Tonbridge, England: Sovereign World, 1993.

Peale, John S. *The Love of God in China: Can One Be Both Chinese and Christian?* New York, Lincoln and Shanghai: iUniverse, 2005.

Pepper, Suzanne. *Civil War in China: The Political Struggle, 1945-1949.* Berkeley and Los Angeles: University of California Press, 1978.

Plowman, Ed. *Billy Graham in China.* Minneapolis: Billy Graham Evangelistic Association, 1988.

Pott, F. L. Hawks. *A Short History of Shanghai.* Shanghai: Kelly & Walsh, 1928.

Potter, Pitman B. "Belief in Control: Regulation of Religion in China." *Religion in China Today, The China Quarterly* 174 (June 2003): 317-37.

Price, Frank W. "History of Nanking Theological Seminary, 1911 to 1961: A Tentative Draft." New York: Board of the Founders of Nanking Theological Seminary, 1961. Unpublished manuscript.

Quaker Mission to China: W. Grigor McLelland's Diary, 26 September-29 October, 1955.

Radvangi, J. "The Hungarian Revolt and the Hundred Flowers Campaign," *China Quarterly* 43 (July-September 1970): 121-29.

Ramsey, A. M. *From Gore to Temple: The Development of Anglican Theology between Lux Mundi and the Second World War, 1889-1939.* London: Longmans, 1960.

Rees, David. *Korea: The Limited War.* London: Macmillan, 1964.

Regulations on Religious Affairs (Zongjiao shiwu tiaoli). Bilingual edition. Beijing: zongjiao wenhua chubanshe, 2004.

Religion in China Today. Special issue of *The China Quarterly* 174 (June 2003).

"Resolution on Certain Questions in the History of Our Party since the Founding of the People's Republic of China (1949-81)." *Beijing Review* 27 (6 July 1981): 10-39.

Rittenberg, Sidney. *The Man Who Stayed Behind.* New York: Simon & Schuster, 1993.

Rogaski, Ruth. "Nature, Annihilation, and Modernity: China's Korean War Germ-Warfare Experience Reconsidered." *Journal of Asian Studies* 61, no. 2 (May 2002): 381-415.

"Running the Church Well: A Conversation with K. H. Ting." *Areopagus* 9, no. 4 (Winter/Spring 1997): 8-11, 33-35.

Schmidt, Wolfgang. *Memoirs in Dialogue, Asia.* Volume 1. Hong Kong: Christian Conference of Asia, 2002.

Schram, Stuart R., ed. *Chairman Mao Talks to the People: Talks and Letters, 1956-1971.* New York: Pantheon, 1974.

———, ed. *The Political Thought of Mao Tse-tung.* New York: Praeger, 1972.

Schwarcz, Vera. *The Chinese Enlightenment: Intellectuals and the Legacy of the May Fourth Movement of 1919.* Berkeley: University of California Press, 1986.

———. *Long Road Home: A China Journal.* New Haven and London: Yale University Press, 1984.

———. *Time for Telling Truth Is Running Out: Conversations with Zhang Shenfu.* New Haven and London: Yale University Press, 1992.

Seiwart, Hubert, in collaboration with Ma Xisha. *Popular Religious Movements and Heterodox Sects in Chinese History.* Leiden and Boston: Brill, 2003.

Short, Philip. *Mao: A Life*. New York: Henry Holt, 1999.

Sih, Paul K. T. *Decision for China: Communism or Christianity*. Chicago: Regnum, 1959.

Sison, Marites N. "The Last Anglican Bishop," *Anglican Journal* (October 2005). Accessed on 13 October 2005 at http://anglicanjournal.com/131/08/world02 .html.

Snow, Edgar. *Red Star Over China*. London: Victor Gollancz, 1968.

Spae, Joseph. "Recent Theological Research on China and Future Church Policies." In *Western Christianity and the People's Republic of China: Exploring New Possibilities*. Edited by James A. Scherer. Chicago, 1979.

Spence, Jonathan. *The Search for Modern China*. First edition. New York and London: Norton, 1990.

"Statement of the Central Committee on the Korean Situation and World Order, Toronto, Canada, July, 1950." In *The First Six Years, 1948-1954*, 119-20. Geneva: WCC, 1954.

Stranahan, Patricia. "Strange Bedfellows: The Communist Party and Shanghai's Elite in the National Salvation Movement." *China Quarterly* 129 (March 1992): 26-51.

———. *Underground: The Shanghai Communist Party and the Politics of Survival, 1927-1937*. Lanham, Md.: Rowman & Littlefield, 1998.

Tang, Edmond, and Jean-Paul Weist, eds. *The Catholic Church in Modern China: Perspectives*. Maryknoll, N.Y.: Orbis Books, 1993.

The Community Church of Shanghai: Annual Report. May 1932.

Thomas, M. M. "K. H. Ting's Theology of Society." *Church and Society: Bulletin of the East Asia Christian Conference* (September 1960): 32-36.

———. *My Ecumenical Journey, 1947-1975*. Tiruvalla: C.L.S. Bookshop, 1990.

Thurston, Ann. *Enemies of the People: The Ordeal of Intellectuals in China's Great Cultural Revolution*. New York: Knopf, 1987.

The Tiananmen Papers: The Chinese Leadership's Decision to Use Force against Their Own People—In Their Own Words. Compiled and edited by Zhang Liang, Andrew Nathan and Perry Link. New York: Public Affairs, 2001.

T'ien Ju-kang. *Peaks of Faith: Protestant Mission in Revolutionary China*. Leiden: E. J. Brill, 1993.

Towery, Britt. *Churches of China: Taking Root Downward, Bearing Fruit Upward*. Third edition. Waco, Tex.: Baylor University Press, 1990.

Uhalley, Stephen, and Xiaoxin Wu, eds., *China and Christianity: Burdened Past, Hopeful Future*. Armonk, N.Y.: M. E. Sharpe, 2001.

Van Slyke, Lyman P. *Enemies and Friends: The United Front in Chinese Communist History*. Stanford: Stanford University Press, 1967.

"Visit of the Delegation from the British Council of Churches to the People's Republic of China." Unpublished report. December 1983.

Visser 't Hooft, W. A., ed. *The First Assembly of the World Council of Churches— Held at Amsterdam August 22nd to September 7th, 1948*. New York: Harper Brothers, 1949.

———. *Memoirs*. Geneva: WCC Publications, 1973.

Vlastos, Gregory. *Christian Faith and Democracy*. New York: Association Press, 1939.

Waley, Arthur. *The Way and Its Power: A Study of the Tao Te Ching and Its Place in Chinese Thought*. Fifth impression. London: George Allen & Unwin, 1965.

Wang Hui. *China's New Order: Society, Politics and Economy in Transition*. Cambridge and London: Harvard University Press, 2003.

———. "Contemporary Chinese Thought and the Question of Modernity." In *Whither China? Intellectual Politics in Contemporary China*, 165-72. Edited by Xudong Zhang. Durham and London: Duke University Press, 2001.

Wang Peng, ed. *Seeking Truth in Love* (*Zai ai zhong xunqiu zhenli*). Bilingual edition. Beijing: Zongjiao wenhua chubanshe, 2006.

Wang Weifan. "A Heart as Magnanimous as the Sea: In Remembrance of the Seventh Anniversary of Mr. Luo Zhufeng's death." *CSPD* 19, no. 1 (April 2004): 5-16.

———. *Lilies of the Field*. Translated and edited by Janice and Philip Wickeri. Shatin: Foundation for Theological Education in Southeast Asia, 1989.

Wang Hsueh-wen. "Tolerance and Control." *Issues and Studies* 27, no. 1 (January 1991): 126ff.

Wasserstrom, Jeffrey N., and Elizabeth J. Perry, ed. *Popular Protest and Political Culture in Modern China: Learning from 1989*. Boulder, Colo.: Westview Press, 1992.

Weber, Hans-Ruedi. *Asia and the Ecumenical Movement, 1895-1961*. London: SCM Press, 1966.

Welch, Holmes. *Buddhism under Mao*. Cambridge: Harvard University Press, 1972.

White, Lynn T. III. *Policies of Chaos: The Organizational Causes of Violence in China's Cultural Revolution*. Princeton: Princeton University Press, 1989.

Whyte, Bob. *Unfinished Encounter: China and Christianity*. Glasgow: Collins, 1988.

Whyte, Martin King. *Small Groups and Political Rituals in China*. Berkeley: University of California Press, 1974.

Wickeri, Philip L. "The Abolition of Religion in Yunnan: Wang Zhiming." In *The Terrible Alternative: Christian Martyrdom in the Twentieth Century*, 128-43. Edited by Andrew Chandler. London: Cassell, 1998.

———. "The Chinese Delegation at the Third World Conference on Religion and Peace, August 28-September 8, 1979: A Report." Unpublished manuscript. 14 pp.

———. "Chinese Neo-liberalism Has Lost Sight of Social Justice." *China Development Brief* 6, no. 1 (Spring 2004): 42-44.

———. "The Christian Movement in Shanghai on the Eve of Liberation, 1946-1954." Unpublished manuscript prepared for the History of Christianity in China Project, 1990.

———. "Christianity in Zhejiang: A Report from a Recent Visit to Protestant Churches in China." Unpublished manuscript. 31 May 1990. 16 pp.

———. "Conversations about K. H. Ting in Canada in the 1940s." Notes from the author's discussion with Vince Goring, Jean Wordsworth, Majorie and Cyril Powles, Lois Wilson and Katherine Hockin. Toronto, Canada, 3 February 1992.

———. "Random Notes on Religion in China." Unpublished manuscript. October 1979. 12 pp.

———. "Reinterpreting Religion in China." *China News Analysis* 1485 (15 May 1993): 1-9

———. *Seeking the Common Ground: Protestant Christianity, the Three-Self Movement and China's United Front*. Maryknoll, N.Y.: Orbis Books, 1988.

———. "Zhou Enlai's Conversations with Chinese Christians: Introduction and Translation." *CSPD* 2, no. 1 (April 1987): 4-11.

———, and Lois Cole, eds. *Christianity and Modernization: A Chinese Debate.* Hong Kong: DAGA Press, 1995.

———, and Janice K. Wickeri. "Portrait of a Chinese Buddhist Leader: An Interview with Zhao Puchu." *The Christian Century* (26 March 1980): 350-52.

Wilson, Dick. *Zhou Enlai: A Biography.* New York: Viking, 1984.

Wire, Antoinette. "Chinese Biblical Interpretation since Mid-Century." *Biblical Interpretation* 4, no. 1 (1996): 101-23.

Wurth, Elmer, ed. *Papal Documents Related to the New China.* Maryknoll, N.Y.: Orbis Books, 1985.

Xu, Edward Yihua. "Religion and Education: St. John's University as an Evangelizing Agency." Ph.D. diss., Princeton University, 1994.

Yamamori, Tetsunao, and Kim-Kwon Chan. *Witnesses to Power: Stories of God's Quiet Work in a Changing China.* Carlisle: Paternoster Press, 2000.

Yamamoto, Sumiko. *History of Protestantism in China: The Indigenization of Christianity.* Tokyo: Toho Gakkai, 2000.

Yan Jiaqi, and Gao Gao. *Turbulent Decade: A History of the Cultural Revolution.* Translated by D. W. Y. Kwok. Honolulu: University of Hawaii Press, 1996.

Yang, C. K. *Religion in Chinese Society.* Berkeley: University of California Press, 1961.

Yang Fenggang, and Joseph B. Tamney, eds. *State, Market and Religions in Chinese Societies.* Leiden and Boston: Brill, 2005.

Yang Huilin, *Religious Studies in China.* Singapore: Times Academic Press, 2005.

Yao, Kevin Xiyi. *The Fundamentalist Movement among Protestant Missionaries in China, 1920-1937.* Lanham, Md.: University Press of America, 2003.

Yap Kim Hao. *Report on a Visit to China: October 1980.* Singapore: Christian Conference of Asia, 1980.

Yates, Timothy. *Christian Mission in the Twentieth Century.* Cambridge: Cambridge University Press, 1994.

Yeo, K. K. *Chairman Mao Meets the Apostle Paul: Christianity, Communism and the Hope of China.* Grand Rapids, Brazos Press, 2002.

Yu, Anthony C. *State and Religion in China: Historical and Textual Perspectives.* Chicago: Open Court, 2005.

Yu, David. "Religious Studies in China at Crossroads." *Journal of Chinese Religions* 18 (Fall 1991): 167-72.

Zetzsche, Jost Oliver. *The Bible in China: The History of the Union Version, or, the Culmination of Protestant Missionary Bible Translation in China.* Sankt Augustin: Monumentica Serica Institute, 1999.

Zhao Dingxi. *The Power of Tiananmen: State-Society Relations and the 1989 Beijing Student Movement.* Chicago: University of Chicago Press, 2001.

Zhao Fusan. *Christianity in China.* Edited by Theresa Carino. Manila: de La Salle University, 1986.

——— (Chao Fu-san). "The Penitence and Renewal of the Church in China." In *Essays in Anglican Self-Criticism,* 86-98. Edited by David M. Paton. London: SCM Press, 1958.

Zhou Enlai. *Selected Works.* Volume 1. Beijing: Foreign Languages Press, 1980.

Index

Ji Jianhong, 161
Ji Tai, 353
Jia Yuming, 108, 122, 151
Jiang Peifen, 229
Jiang Qing, 168, 187-90
Jiang Wenhan, 44, 204
Jiang Zemin, 5, 6, 286, 287, 303, 333, 335, 344, 345, 347, 349
  and religious policy, 304, 339
  on stabilizing role of religion, 298
  and "three represents," 335
Jiangsu People's Political Consultative Conference (JPPCC), 124-25, 150-51, 161-62, 173, 206, 216
Jiaotong University, 27, 56
Jin Luxian, 239, 275, 375
Jing Tianying, 119
Jinling Women's College, 42, 124, 173
John Paul II, 239
Johnson, Hewlett (Red Dean), 116, 132, 144, 163
Johnson, Ted, 60, 182
Jones, Susan Mann, 19

Kairos Radio, 282
Kan Baoping, 360
Kao Chun-ming (C. M. Kao), 322
Khrushchev, Nikita, 138
Kiang Wenhan (Kiang Wen-han), 44, 46, 60, 71, 75, 106
Kim Dae-jung, 329
Kim Yong-Bock, 365
Kindopp, Jason, 345
Kissinger, Henry, 181
Kobia, Sam, 368, 369
Koeh, D. M. *See* Ge Pilu
Koo, T. Z. *See* Gu Ziren
Korean War, 3, 46, 83, 93, 97, 98, 102, 108, 117, 125, 130
  and American use of bacteriological weapons, 104, 117
  effect on Ting, 83
Koshy, Ninan, 241, 277, 322
Kuang Yaming, 171, 215-17, 275, 276, 305, 375
Kuhn, Robert, 5
Kuo, Siu-may (Guo Xiumei). *See* Ting, Siu-may (Siu-may Kuo)
Kwong, Peter K. K., 238, 325-27, 331
Kyaw Than, 75

Ladany, Lazlo, 185
Lambert, Tony, 326
land reform, 96
lao sanzi (Old Three-Self), 11, 257, 264, 268
Laozi, 285, 350
Latin America: and harm done by conservative missionaries, 82, 83
Lee, C. W., 77
Lei Feng, 350
Lenin, Vladimir, 142
Levi, Primo, 35
Lew, T. T. (Liu Tingfang), 71, 373
Li Changshou (Witness Lee), 228
Li Chuwen (C. W. Lee), 77, 83, 164, 179, 204, 205, 221
  and the CPC, 40
  as TSPM activist, 11, 99, 102, 123, 148
Li Fuqun, 80
Li Hongzhi, 334
Li Jiaqing (K. C. Li), 19, 21, 24
Li Jinglan (Li Lizi), 19, 21, 22, 24
Li Peng, 280, 286, 290, 298
Li Rongxi, 207
Li Shoubao, 102, 157, 186, 207, 234
Li Weihan, 166, 210
Li Xiannian, 240
Li Xinyuan, 360, 361
Li Yading, 257, 353
Lian Sheng (student magazine), 43, 50
Liang Suning, 186
Liao Zhongkai, 181
Liberated Areas, 67, 79-81
liberation theology, 38, 217, 248, 252, 294
Lin Biao, 168, 169, 175, 180, 181, 185, 187, 197
Lin Xiangao (Samuel Lamb), 228, 259, 271, 280, 294, 341
Lin Xianyang, 127
Lin, Paul, 73
Little Flock, 119, 257
Little Red Book, 169, 174, 175
Liu Guojun, 173, 181, 187, 188
Liu Liangmo, 38, 182, 204, 206
Liu Shaoqi, 137, 167, 168, 172
Liu Tingfang. *See* Lew, T. T.
Liu Xiaofeng, 361
Liu Yaochang, 127
Liu Yucang, 127, 128, 317